Praise for *When Trumpets Call*

"*When Trumpets Call* is the best biography I have read in years. Patricia O'Toole has brilliantly recreated the final years of one of our greatest American presidents."

—David Herbert Donald, author of *Lincoln*

"O'Toole has written a fascinating book—just wonderful reading—about a wonderfully fascinating fellow.... As colorful and energetic as Teddy Roosevelt... O'Toole captures both sides of this binary man: one who loved his country and loved power, too.... She writes with grace and wit, with wonderful throwaway lines.... Read this book."

—Harry Levins, *St. Louis Post-Dispatch*

"Filled with surprises, stunning and vivid. Patricia O'Toole has contributed a powerful new addition to our understanding of Theodore Roosevelt's life and legacy."

—Blanche Wiesen Cook, author of *Eleanor Roosevelt*

"A fuller picture of the former president than existed before.... It breaks new ground even after acclaimed biographies by David McCullough and Edmund Morris.... O'Toole's research technique ought to serve as a model for biographers."

—Steve Weinberg, *The Baltimore Sun*

"With profound artistry and an empathy unclouded by sentiment, Patricia O'Toole recreates one of the most poignant chapters in presidential history—Theodore Roosevelt at twilight.... His public career is fascinating enough, but it is O'Toole's private Roosevelt that will haunt readers of this beautifully crafted book. Few will be able to put it down without a catch in the throat."

—Richard Norton Smith, Executive Director,
Abraham Lincoln Presidential Libraray & Museum

"Adds greatly to our understanding of Theodore Roosevelt's character, values, and his legacy.... O'Toole's graceful prose richly brings the aging Rough Rider to life.... [A] rich and complex portrait."

—Terry Hartle, *Christian Science Monitor*

"As president, Theodore Roosevelt set a new standard for activism, and he did so as an ex-president as well. This is a fascinating account of the impact he had during the tumultuous decade after he left office."

— Walter Isaacson, author of *Benjamin Franklin*

"Quoting previously unused records and letters, O'Toole captures the conflicted, complex character of a man struggling with the loss of relevance and power at the highest level of world affairs. Her book sets a high bar for future biographers of Roosevelt."

— David Hendricks, *San Antonio Express-News*

"*When Trumpets Call* is a bully biography. . . . Graced with Ms. O'Toole's gift for felicitous phrasing and her penchant for exploiting sources others have underutilized."

— Carl Rollyson, *The New York Sun*

"Roosevelt had an ex-presidency unlike any other in our history. And Patricia O'Toole manages just the right touch in chronicling it. . . . She knows Theodore Roosevelt very well. In fact, she probably knows him better than he knew himself. . . . A very fine book."

— John C. "Chuck" Chalberg, *The Washington Times*

"A thorough, affectionate and insightful look at a once-powerful man 'thrashing in the cage of his powerlessness' during the last decade of his life."

— John Pickering, Bloomberg

"Patricia O'Toole's *When Trumpets Call* is the wisest, most perceptive, best informed and most graceful study of Theodore Roosevelt ever published."

— John Morton Blum, author of *The Republican Roosevelt*

When

Patricia O'Toole

Trumpets Call

* THEODORE ROOSEVELT AFTER THE WHITE HOUSE

Simon & Schuster Paperbacks

New York   London   Toronto   Sydney

SIMON & SCHUSTER PAPERBACKS
Rockefeller Center
1230 Avenue of the Americas
New York, NY 10020

First Simon & Schuster paperback edition 2006

SIMON & SCHUSTER PAPERBACKS and colophon are registered trademarks
of Simon & Schuster, Inc.
For information about special discounts for bulk purchases,
please contact Simon & Schuster Special Sales at
1-800-456-6798 or business@simonandschuster.com

Designed by Karolina Harris
Maps © 2004 Jeffrey L. Ward

Manufactured in the United States of America

1   2   3   4   5   6   7   8   9   10

The Library of Congress has cataloged the hardcover edition as follows:
O'Toole, Patricia.
When trumpets call : Theodore Roosevelt after
the White House / Patricia O'Toole.
p.   cm.
Includes bibliographical references and index.
1. Roosevelt, Theodore, 1858–1919.   2. Presidents—United States—Biography.
3. United States—Politics and government—1909–1913.
4. United States—Politics and government—1913–1921.   I. Title.
E757.O77   2005
973.91'1'092—dc22   [B]   2004062590
ISBN-13: 978-0-684-86477-8
ISBN-10: 0-684-86477-0
ISBN-13: 978-0-684-86478-5 (Pbk)
ISBN-10: 0-684-86478-9 (Pbk)

PHOTO CREDITS
Theodore Roosevelt Collection, Harvard College Library: 1, 7, 8, 17, 18, 19, 21, 22, 25, 36, 37,
38, 39, 40, 42, 43. Library of Congress: 2, 3, 4, 9, 10, 11, 12, 13, 14, 15, 16, 20, 23, 24, 26, 29, 30,
31, 33, 34, 35, 41. Duke University, Rare Book, Manuscript, and Special Collections Library: 5.
Courtesy of Richard Derby Williams: 27, 28. Courtesy of the *Emporia Gazette*: 32.

To Thelma Jean Goodrich,
a power unto herself

CONTENTS

x CONTENTS

Precipice

How dull it is to pause, to make an end,
To rust unburnish'd, not to shine in use!
As tho' to breathe were life.

—Alfred, Lord Tennyson, "Ulysses"

When Trumpets Call

AUTHOR'S NOTE

THE IDEA of writing a book about Theodore Roosevelt's life after the White House was a gift from the gods of experience and synchronicity. While researching *The Five of Hearts*, a book about Henry Adams and his friends, I happened onto the fact that Roosevelt was only fifty when his presidency came to an end. Several years after finishing the book, as my own fiftieth birthday set off the usual reflections on things done and not done, I remembered Roosevelt. He had loved being president, and after nearly eight years of relishing the great power of his office, had been obliged by custom to give it up. What had that been like? I wondered. What had happened to this powerful man once his power was gone?

I recalled a safari, another run for the presidency, a trip down an uncharted river in Brazil, and hopes of taking soldiers to the front in World War I. Curious about the rest of the story, I read Joseph Gardner's *Departing Glory*, a graceful rendering of the events of what proved to be Roosevelt's last decade. He left office on March 4, 1909, and died on January 6, 1919. To find out more about how the loss of power shaped Roosevelt's life, I read several birth-to-death biographies and a number of memoirs by his contemporaries. Nearly all of them touched on his frustrations out of power, but I soon realized that what had not been said would fill a book.

The gaps were understandable. The years after a president leaves office tend to be anticlimactic, so biographers rarely treat them at length. (Kathleen Dalton's *Theodore Roosevelt: A Strenuous Life* is a splendid exception.) Also, Roosevelt's correspondence is so quotable and so voluminous (an estimated 150,000 outgoing letters and even more coming in) that it is possible to chronicle this phase of his life without going beyond the letters he exchanged with friends and family. I guessed that the letters Roosevelt's associates wrote to one another about him would be equally telling. Times had changed but humans had not, so it stood to reason that Roosevelt's friends, like the rest of us, would often share their concerns about a friend more freely among themselves than with the friend himself. My guess proved correct, and I benefited greatly from their thoughts—particularly their reactions to the wrenching events of 1912, when he persuaded himself that the trumpets of patriotic duty were calling him to run for president.

Roosevelt's sense of himself as a man summoned was intimately connected to his love of power. Power for him was not an end but an instrument for vanquishing the wicked and protecting the helpless, and the trumpets he heard rang in tones biblical as well as martial. From St. Paul's first letter to the Corinthians, Roosevelt had learned that no one would heed an uncertain trumpet, and while he was often faulted for blaring, it would never be said that his calls could not be heard. Asked during his last months in office to send a stirring word to a youth organization, he wrote, "The trumpet call is the most inspiring of all sounds, because it summons men to spurn ease and self-indulgence and timidity, and bids them forth to the field where they must dare and do and die at need." He lived by that creed and hoped that when Death caught up with him, it would be on a battlefield.

In the reminiscences of those who fell under his spell, the trumpet is a recurring image. "He sounded in my heart the first trumpet call of the new time that was to be," the journalist William Allen White wrote years after his first encounter with Roosevelt. ". . . He overcame me. And in the hour or two we spent that day . . . he poured into my heart such visions, such ideals, such hopes, such a new attitude toward life and patriotism and the meaning of things, as I had never dreamed men had."

Like many powerful men who give themselves to public service rather than the pursuit of wealth, Roosevelt often mistook the sirens of personal ambition for the trumpets of public duty. He could easily admit that he enjoyed power but could not admit, perhaps could not even see, how much he needed power in order to feel fully engaged. Unanalyzed, unaccepted, and unmet, the need gave this former president a decade filled with imagined trumpet calls.

THE LIBRARY OF CONGRESS card catalogue lists more than six hundred books about Theodore Roosevelt, and as I surveyed this well-worked mine, I wondered how much new ore I might turn up. I am happy to report that my investigations yielded a number of discoveries. The most historically significant came from an unexpected source, the letters of Archie

Butt. An army officer assigned to the White House from 1908 to 1912, Captain Butt was a constant companion of the president, and the letters he wrote about his experiences with Theodore Roosevelt and William Howard Taft have been a standard reference ever since their publication (one volume in 1924 and two more in 1930). After noticing the ellipses sprinkled across the pages of the first volume, I tracked down a microfilmed version of the originals and learned that Butt's editor had censored a great deal in all three volumes. Chief among the omissions was a conversation between Captain Butt and Dr. James Marsh Jackson, a Boston physician who examined Taft in the summer of 1910. Alarmed by the precariousness of Taft's health, Jackson urged Butt to discourage the president from seeking reelection in 1912. The story, told in Chapter 5, still lacks one crucial fact: a definitive diagnosis.

Other passages excised from Butt's letters make even sadder the sad facts of Taft's break with Roosevelt and of the Taft family's unhappy life in the White House. Helen Herron Taft, who had longed to be first lady since a girlhood visit to Washington, suffered a stroke two months after President Taft took office. Its effects circumscribed her activities for years.

I also discovered that Henry F. Pringle, Taft's most definitive biographer and author of one of the first feet-of-clay biographies of Roosevelt, had made only slight use of Taft's correspondence with a Washington journalist named Gus Karger. A correspondent for the Cincinnati Times-Star, which was owned by one of Taft's brothers, Karger often served as an informant for the Taft family, and Karger's loyalty to them appears to have freed William Howard Taft to write Karger with unusual candor. At the Cincinnati Historical Society I read the Taft-Karger correspondence as well as several memoranda Karger wrote after substantive conversations with Taft or Roosevelt. One of the memoranda gives Taft's version of events at a meeting with Roosevelt in New Haven on a September day in 1910, a crucial encounter that left each of them feeling betrayed.

Seeing that accounts of Theodore Roosevelt and his son Kermit on safari were based almost entirely on their say-so (in letters, diaries, and books), I wondered what the people they met might have had to say about them. I found much of interest in the papers of the naturalists who accompanied him and in the papers of Francis Warrington Dawson II, a Southerner who was the first Paris correspondent for the United Press. After refusing to take other reporters to Africa, Roosevelt gave in to Dawson's request to go and allowed him to spend several weeks with the safari. Dawson left photographs, memorabilia, and a curdling report of a monkey hunt with Kermit. Eventually Dawson befriended the rest of the Roosevelt family, and the notes he kept during World War I, when he served on the staff of the American embassy in Paris, add appreciably to existing accounts of the wartime experiences of two other Roosevelt sons, Archie and Ted. Dawson's notes also reveal that Roosevelt was mistaken in his belief that French military authorities were eager for him to bring soldiers to the front.

The Wilson administration's management of the American war effort had no more vitriolic critic than Theodore Roosevelt. His tone led many of his contemporaries and many biographers to dismiss his newspaper columns on the subject as the ravings of a jealous, vindictive has-been. In hopes of adjudicating the strong opinion on both sides, I read five volumes of testimony from hearings conducted in 1918 by the Senate Military Affairs Committee. Regrettable as Roosevelt's tone was, the transcripts of the hearings confirm his judgment: the war effort was a shambles. (Thomas Fleming's *Illusion of Victory* is an excellent and highly readable treatment of Woodrow Wilson's problems as commander-in-chief and peacemaker.)

No part of my detective work was more delightful than the search that led to Joseph Gurney Pease. From *African Game Trails*, Theodore Roosevelt's book about the safari, I knew that his first host in Africa had been a British settler named Sir Alfred Pease, but Roosevelt had written little about him. When I consulted the likely sources in search of more, I came away empty-handed, and at eleven-thirty one night, all but ready to consign Sir Alfred to my file of missing persons, I tried the last place I could think of, the Internet. Up came a family web site, with the information that Sir Alfred, born in 1857, belonged to an illustrious English clan, had served briefly in Parliament, and had moved to East Africa to take up farming after a financial panic obliterated the family fortune. The web site gave an e-mail address for Joseph Gurney Pease, so I wrote him at once, explaining my hope of making Sir Alfred into something more than a name on the page.

I awoke to an astounding e-mail from England. It seemed impossible, but I was communing with Sir Alfred's son! Gurney, as he is known, is the youngest of four children born to Sir Alfred and his third wife, whom he married in 1922, when he was in his late sixties. Thanks to Gurney's generosity, I soon had in hand Sir Alfred's diary entries for the seventeen days that the Roosevelts spent with him and his family, Lady Pease's thirty-page letter about the visit, photographs of the farm, and color copies of some of Sir Alfred's watercolor sketches, including one of Roosevelt shooting a lion.

The Pease papers were rich in detail and also enlightening on the subject of Roosevelt's reception in British East Africa. The colony's leading citizens went to extraordinary lengths to impress him and to ensure the success of his hunting. Aware before his arrival that he would visit England after the safari, the settlers hoped that his favorable reports to officials in London would translate into more local authority over East African affairs.

Theodore Roosevelt was a man who felt most at peace with himself when he was in a struggle with someone else, and the more powerful he deemed the adversary, the more worthwhile he seemed to feel. In the quieter moments of his last decade, he occasionally described himself as "a little ashamed" of the delight he took in the simple pleasures of family life. If delight is cause for shame, I ought to feel thoroughly disgraced, for I have enjoyed every day of writing this book. But I feel only the delight, and a hope that the gods will consider their gift put to good use.

PROLOGUE

Victory

ON NOVEMBER 3, 1908, Americans went to the polls to decide whether William Howard Taft or William Jennings Bryan would be the next president of the United States. The incumbent, Theodore Roosevelt, cast his ballot at 9:20 in the morning at Sleet's Hall, a room over a butcher shop in the village of Oyster Bay, New York. With him was his twenty-one-year-old son, Theodore, Jr., voting for the first time. Like his father, Ted was a Taft man.

By six-thirty in the evening, the president was back in Washington, sifting through telegrams and inquiring about the election bulletins on the tickers. He said little to the reporters who had been allowed into his office but seemed pleased when told that Taft had a wide lead in Oyster Bay. After dinner he and his wife, Edith Kermit Carow Roosevelt, proceeded to the Red Room for a party with cabinet members, their wives, and other members of the president's official family. Victory was imminent, and the victory, all knew, would be Roosevelt's as much as Taft's. It was Roosevelt who had persuaded Taft to run, Roosevelt who orchestrated Taft's nomination by the Republican Party, and Roosevelt who guided Taft, a political naïf, through the thickets of a presidential campaign.

The president slipped away from the Red Room as soon as he could. The first lady, gracious and practiced, had presided over scores of social gatherings and easily managed on her own, but when the administration's commissioner of labor came in, she asked an aide to look for the president. Aware of the commissioner's exertions in the campaign, she thought he might feel slighted if TR did not thank him in person.

"I found him, but he would not come for a long time," the aide would soon tell a confidante. "He was in his library comfortably ensconced and reading, the election already almost a thing of the past to him." No American president read more, or more broadly, than this one. Roosevelt could recite poetry by the yard and had near-total recall of hundreds of works of history and literature and natural science. Usually he read for the sheer joy of it, but he sometimes tunneled into a book for respite from the pressures of politics. Of late he had favored works on big-game hunting in Africa, homework for a safari set to begin as soon as he left office. When the president returned to the party, the aide watched him greet the commissioner and quickly disappear again.

Theodore Roosevelt, insatiably public man, choosing solitude when he might be feasting on admiration? The same Theodore Roosevelt whose children said that he longed to be the bride at every wedding and the corpse at every funeral? It was unnatural. Freakish. A phenomenon on the order of a sudden reverse in the course of Niagara Falls. What had happened?

As one who galloped away from introspection, Roosevelt did not, perhaps could not, explain. But clearly he had much to ponder that night. While the early returns gave the contest to Taft, two key states, Ohio and Indiana, had not yet been heard from. Neither should have been in doubt. Ohio was Taft's home, Indiana a Republican citadel. But Ohio Republicans were feuding, and it was just possible that Indiana had been knocked silly by its charismatic native son, Eugene V. Debs, the Socialist Party's candidate. Nine-fifteen, the moment appointed for Roosevelt to wire his congratulations to Taft in Cincinnati, passed with no word from the president.

There was another reason to wait. Voters seemed to like Taft as much as they liked Bryan, but the pundit class had fussed endlessly about Roosevelt's push to control the succession. His insistence was an affront to the sovereignty of the people, the critics said; crown princes were for monarchies. Whether the people minded as much as the pundits said they did had been hard to gauge, but if the affronted were voting in sufficient numbers—

The suspense of this election night made a strange climax to four months of listless campaigning. Taft and Bryan had argued mainly about which of them would be the better steward of Roosevelt's legacy. (Debs was a flamingo in a land of crows, an exotic without a chance.) "The voters refuse to be wrought up," the humorist George Ade complained in *The Saturday Evening Post*. They were still willing to fill auditoriums and mass at whistle-stops, but only to ogle. They wore campaign buttons if they liked the button and politely applauded all candidates. This, said Ade, was "Chautauqua politics—sterilized politics—imitation politics." Henry Adams, historian, descendant of two presidents, and Washington neighbor of nine more, concurred. "Everyone is so damnably kind and forbearing," he wrote an English friend. Americans had become "fairly decent, respectable, domestic, bourgeois, middle-class, and tiresome. There is absolutely nothing to revile except that it's a bore."

Roosevelt was certain that Taft would make a fine president. Incorruptible and demonstrably able, he had distinguished himself in public service as a federal judge, a diplomat, and cabinet secretary. But if the people, seeing no difference between Taft and Bryan, tilted toward Bryan, Roosevelt would take his party's stoning for the loss of the presidency. Having held the White House for forty of the last forty-eight years, the Republicans regarded it as theirs.

By ten o'clock the newsmen minding the tickers in the president's office knew that Taft had won, but it was nearly midnight before Roosevelt came down to wire his felicitations to Ohio. "I need hardly say how heartily I congratulate you, and the country even more," the telegram said. The reporter from the *New York Times* saw "a bland and satisfied smile" on the president's face, but when asked to comment, Roosevelt only shook his head. He passed through the party again and went back upstairs alone.

✳ *Labyrinth*

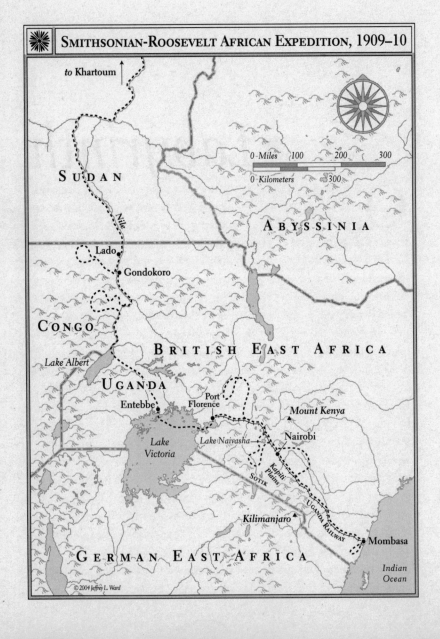

SMITHSONIAN-ROOSEVELT AFRICAN EXPEDITION, 1909–10

to Khartoum

SUDAN

Nile

ABYSSINIA

0 · Miles   100   200   300
0 · Kilometers   300

Lado

Gondokoro

CONGO

Lake Albert

BRITISH EAST AFRICA

UGANDA

Entebbe

Port Florence

Mount Kenya

Lake Naivasha

Nairobi

Lake Victoria

Kapiti Plains

SOTIK

UGANDA RAILWAY

Kilimanjaro

Mombasa

GERMAN EAST AFRICA

Indian Ocean

© 2004 Jeffrey L. Ward

ONE

Embarked

O F THE HUNDREDS OF WALKS Theodore and Edith Roosevelt took at Sagamore Hill, the one that began just after sunrise on March 23, 1909, surely ranked with the shortest. Breakfast, still ahead, had to be finished by seven-thirty, when Theodore and their son Kermit were leaving for a year on safari. By habit and temperament, husband and wife kept their intimate exchanges to themselves, so their conversation evanesced in the chilly spring air. But they would leave signs that the parting wrenched. Three days out to sea Theodore confessed his homesickness for Edith and supposed it would sharpen. Edith classed the leave-taking with the day when their son Archie nearly died of diphtheria.

The travelers left home on schedule, with Edith waving a handkerchief as their carriage descended the hill. Theodore waved back with his hat. Eleven-year-old Quentin, their youngest child, accompanied his father and brother to the Oyster Bay train station, where the travelers did combat with tearfulness. First they said farewell to the horse. Then Kermit, a boy-man of nineteen, boarded the train, slid into a window seat, and turned his wet face away from the other passengers. His father took cover in platitudes, reminding Quentin to be a good boy, a tactic that largely succeeded: the father's eyes filled but did not spill. When the train started to roll and Quentin yelled, "Take good care of yourself, Pop," Pop dammed another cascade by deploying a strategic cough and reaching for Kermit's shoulder.

The minutiae of the good-byes were preserved by journalists parched for news of Theodore Roosevelt. After almost eight years of conversation with

the newsmen who reported on the White House, he had cut them off on inauguration day, March 4, when the presidency passed to his friend William
Howard Taft. As soon as the new president uttered the last word of his address, Roosevelt tendered his felicities—"God bless you, old man. It is a
great state document"—gathered him up in a hug, then hurried to Union
Station for a train to Oyster Bay. Detained in Washington by a blizzard, he
avoided the newspapermen who came to the station in hopes of an interview. He wanted the day to be Taft's.

Next morning, when reporters and photographers climbed Sagamore
Hill to record Roosevelt's first day out of office, he sent them away. "Gentlemen," he said, "I do not wish you to think I am churlish. This seems like
giving you the marble heart, but I have nothing to say and am not going
to give interviews to anyone. Also I will not stand for any more photographs."

Never? they asked.

"Not while I am a private citizen."

Inquiring how long that might be, they were told, "As long as I can make
it."

However much Theodore Roosevelt might have wished that he wished
that, he did not set out for Africa in the garb of a private citizen. He wore a
gray-green military greatcoat trimmed with the black braid of his colonel's
rank, which he had earned as a Rough Rider in the Spanish-American War.
The war had made him what he most longed to be, a hero, and the hero's
coat selected for the departure must have elated reporters fearing that their
best story, one of the longest-running, most colorful serials in American history, had ended on March 4.

The story—by turns exhilarating, exasperating, amusing, and inspiring—had begun with an assassin's bullet. On September 6, 1901, Leon
Czolgosz, a neatly dressed young man with a snub-nosed revolver concealed in a handkerchief, shot President William McKinley in a receiving
line at the Pan-American Exposition in Buffalo. Asked to explain himself,
Czolgosz said he did not believe that one man should have so much and another man nothing. Eight days later, when McKinley died, Vice President
Roosevelt was President Roosevelt.

The press chronicled the new president's life in unprecedented detail for
reasons entirely without mystery. Whether one loved or despised Theodore
Roosevelt, he was electricity in the flesh. Forty-two when he took office, he

was the youngest of the nation's chief executives.* He brought with him to the White House an appealing, pretty wife, just turned forty, and six rollicking children: a daughter born to him and his first wife, who died in childbirth, and four sons and a daughter from his marriage to Edith. The young president had fun, his family had fun, and the public had fun reading about all the fun.

Photographed often and reported daily, the escapades of the Roosevelts gave Americans the pleasurable illusion that they knew the first family. No matter how far a citizen lived from Washington or the summer White House at Sagamore Hill, TR and Edith and Alice and Ted and Kermit and Ethel and Archie and Quentin seemed no more remote than the folks next door. The president, an extrovert's extrovert, invited a familiarity that was unimaginable with McKinley, a man once well described as a bronze in search of a pedestal. Called "Teddy" and "TR" in the headlines, Roosevelt naturally became "Teddy" and "TR" to the populace. "TR" he liked and used occasionally as a signature. To intimates he was "Theodore."

Alice Roosevelt, soon to be seen smoking cigarettes and roaring around the capital at the wheel of her runabout, seemed as newfangled and spunky as the century itself. When Archie carved his initials into a pew at Christ Episcopal Church in Oyster Bay, his parents learned about it from the newspapers. And the public was surely amused, as TR had been, by the news that the hammering and sawing of bleachers for Taft's inaugural parade inspired Quentin to sing, "Hurrah, hurrah, father's going to be hung."

Out of office, TR said he wanted to be out of the papers. By disappearing into the African interior for a year, he meant to leave the presidential stage to Taft alone. He also meant to disarm the snipers, who, if he stayed, would either say that Taft was acting on Roosevelt's orders or ignoring them. Wildly popular but not universally loved, TR knew that his departure caused jubilation among monopolists and stock market manipulators. Imagining their glee at his exit, he (along with J. P. Morgan) joked that "Wall Street expects every lion to do its duty." His more dyspeptic critics feared that the lions would fail. "Mr. Roosevelt is to leave us for a while, and certainly the manner of his going is appropriate," wrote one. "Shots will sound and blood will flow and his knife will find its living hilt. The scalps

*A distinction still his. John F. Kennedy was the youngest elected president (forty-three when he defeated Richard Nixon in 1960), but TR remains the youngest to have held the office.

and skins of the kings of the jungle will dry upon his tent pegs," and when he came home, he would resume his career as "the Dominant Note and the Big Noise."

THE TRAIN RIDE from Oyster Bay ended at Long Island City, on the East River. TR linked arms with Kermit and steered him through a cheering crowd to a Manhattan-bound ferry, which landed amid more cheers and blew a three-toot farewell to the hunters. They climbed into a waiting automobile and sped across Manhattan for a subway ride under the Hudson River to the piers of Hoboken, where they would board the SS *Hamburg*, a German liner headed for Naples. TR had never before traveled by subway (or airplane, although he had gone submarining for an afternoon), but the subway had figured in an inventive piece of patronage dispensed from his White House. In 1905, when Kermit gave his parents a copy of *The Children of the Night*, by Edwin Arlington Robinson, the president reviewed the book for *The Outlook*, a dignified journal of opinion. Robinson's poems showed "a curious simplicity," the critic thought, and "a little of the light that never was on land or sea."

After persistent lobbying by Kermit, the president rescued Robinson from a dreary job in subway construction, giving him a sinecure with a salary of $2,000 a year at the U.S. Customs House in New York. The poet so rarely appeared at the office that he had to be reminded—tartly, one imagines—to pick up his pay. Such dereliction ought to have pained a president proud of chopping cords of deadwood from the civil service, but Roosevelt considered Robinson a special case, an expenditure made more for the good of American letters than for the shovel work of the Republic. Anyone could be a clerk, but only a poet could perceive the "silver loneliness" of night. If the Roosevelts spoke of Robinson during their subway ride, the conversation went unrecorded. TR spent the trip peering into the tunnel.

On the pier by nine o'clock, TR and Kermit spent most of the next two hours in a mob of three thousand well-wishers—Rough Riders, Harvard men, friends, and strangers. Unruffled by souvenir hunters clawing at the gilt buttons on his coat or by the jostling that knocked off his hat, TR managed to shake some five hundred hands. He called for the Rough Riders to raise their hands and plowed toward the ones he could see. Over the human din, an indefatigable brass band of Italian immigrants blared "The Star-Spangled Banner" followed by the Italian national anthem followed by

"The Star-Spangled Banner" and so on. A lovely hubbub, and it might have continued for three thousand handshakes, but TR shut it off when a reporter asked if he would run for president again. "Good-bye," he growled. His jaw snapped shut, and he stalked up the gangway.

Strangers often saw ferocity in his large, white teeth, a feature made so famous by cartoonists that small children sometimes confused him with the wolf in "Little Red Riding Hood." Those who knew him understood that the bared teeth were benign. It was the snap of the jaw, startlingly loud, that signified his fury. The inquisitive reporter had insulted Roosevelt's honor. His presidency had lasted seven and a half years, a dram short of the traditional full measure. The two-term limit had not yet been written into law, but it was a sacred American precept, laid down by George Washington himself. Declining a third term, Washington had warned that a president too long in power could easily become a tyrant.

When Roosevelt ran for president in 1904, after filling out McKinley's term, he invited a crowd to the White House on election night to follow the returns coming in by telegraph. The moment he was certain he had won, he flabbergasted Edith and their guests by announcing that he would not use the technicality of the missing six months to justify a run for another term in 1908. "The wise custom which limits the president to two terms regards the substance and not the form," he said. "Under no circumstances will I be a candidate for or accept another nomination." Now, vacating the presidency just as he had said he would, Roosevelt wanted credit for voluntarily surrendering power he might well have kept.

But the reporter's question was pertinent as well as impertinent, for Theodore Roosevelt was an artist of power. It was the medium through which he most fully expressed himself, and without power, he was going to be a Mozart shorn of music. A man more introspective than Roosevelt might have wondered why he had not fielded the question with his usual ease, but this man possessed little insight into his personal relationship with power and none into how he would fare without it.

Aboard the *Hamburg*, TR headed for the starboard side of the upper promenade deck and Cabin 1, near the bow. There he visited with a handful of close friends and his sisters, Corinne Roosevelt Robinson and Anna Roosevelt Cowles, known in the family as Bamie. Taft had sent him a handsome gadget, a compact gold ruler with built-in pencil, inscribed with their names and Roosevelt's customary words of farewell, "Good-bye—Good luck." Taft had also sent a letter and a photograph of himself in the company

of portraits of Lincoln and Washington. Roosevelt replied with two telegrams sending thanks, love, and good wishes.

At eleven, the *Hamburg* sounded its backing-out whistle. Tugs nudged
the bow into position, and the liner, gaudy with bunting and signal flags, led
a bleating flotilla of a hundred vessels down the Hudson. Roosevelt was last
glimpsed standing on the bridge, hat waving, spectacles flashing in the sun.

AHEAD LAY AFRICA and a holiday—his first, he liked to say, since his
fighting in the Spanish-American War. He had turned fifty in October,
and a year on safari was his reward to himself for a lifetime of hard work,
most of it in public service. A conversation with Carl Akeley, a naturalist and
taxidermist who collected African specimens for American museums, had
given him the idea of going on safari, and at first he imagined a rather modest excursion. "I haven't the slightest desire to be a game butcher, but I
should like greatly to be in a land where I really saw multitudes of big game,"
he wrote Frederick Selous, an Englishman whose African hunting exploits
were widely admired in sporting circles. Roosevelt expected to content himself with a handful of rhinos, buffalo, antelopes, and, with luck, a lion. He
would hunt mainly in British East Africa, which promised immense herds
of wildlife and the hospitality of white settlers who knew his friends in England. From British East Africa, he would travel north through Uganda and
the eastern edge of the Belgian Congo, habitat of the rare white rhinoceros.
Then he would hunt his way north along the Nile into Sudan. Edith was to
meet him in Khartoum in March 1910.

The vision of a hunt with a small retinue of guides and porters gave way
to dreams of a scientific expedition under the aegis of the Smithsonian Institution. He wanted to take field taxidermists to prepare hides and skeletons
for shipment to Washington, where they could be studied and mounted.
"My house is small," he told Selous, "and I suppose it will be a good many
years before Kermit has any house at all, so that I should really not care for
many trophies for our own private glorification." On display in the Smithsonian, the animals they bagged would belong to all Americans.

The expedition quickly assumed biblical proportions. It would be one of
the largest safaris ever made, and TR hoped it would also be a paragon of
field study. He and Kermit would hunt, trailed by naturalists and 250 natives
toting food, guns, ammunition, scientific equipment, camping gear, and
tons of salt to preserve animal skins. He mentioned the idea to Selous in

May 1908, let it steep for six weeks, and then proposed it in a letter to the secretary of the Smithsonian, Charles D. Walcott. Carpe diem, Roosevelt urged. The safari offered a matchless opportunity to build a collection of African big game, small mammals, and birds. TR would underwrite his expenses and Kermit's but hoped the Smithsonian would pay for a taxidermist, a naturalist, and the care of the specimens. He closed with a flash of spur: if the Smithsonian had no interest, perhaps he would approach the American Museum of Natural History in New York. The suggestion that the Smithsonian might lose the expedition to a rival had the desired effect. Walcott, on vacation in Montana when he learned of the request, telegraphed his assent at once.

Roosevelt asked if the expedition could be funded without congressional approval, and Walcott obliged by creating a special fund to raise $30,000. Oscar S. Straus, Roosevelt's secretary of commerce and labor, put up $5,000, as did Jacob Schiff, the financier, and Robert Bacon, a diplomat and former J. P. Morgan banker who had known Roosevelt since their student days at Harvard. Walcott's appeal also drew a fistful of smaller contributions, including $2,750 from Andrew Carnegie.

On safari with Kermit, TR expected to spend $25,000, half the money he would receive for writing a dozen long dispatches for *Scribner's*, a magazine that published Edith Wharton and Henry James, among others. Fifty thousand dollars in 1909 had the heft of $830,000 in 2000, but ample as that was, Edith feared he would spend it all. Reared in a family whose fortunes had deteriorated year by year, she was perpetually anxious about money, and Theodore had neither aptitude nor appetite for pecuniary affairs. His grandfather, Cornelius Van Schaack Roosevelt, was one of the richest men in New York, with a thriving glass business and interests in banking and real estate, but TR's father, Theodore Sr., had felt more at home in philanthropy than business. He founded an orthopedic hospital and helped to start the American Museum of Natural History, the Metropolitan Museum of Art, the Children's Aid Society, and a lodging house for newspaper boys. As children, Theodore Jr. and his brother and sisters lived in splendor and learned about hardship by accompanying their father on errands in the poorer quarters of the city. The boy absorbed his father's love of fine things as well as his strong sense of public duty, but the acquisition of money seems to have figured incidentally if at all in the family's daily life.

On the death of his father, in 1878, TR, a nineteen-year-old sophomore at Harvard, inherited $125,000 ($2 million, adjusted for the passage of time). As a young man he wrote George Putnam a $20,000 check for a stake in Putnam's publishing house without understanding that $125,000 of invested capital was not the same as $125,000 in a checking account. TR's check had been drawn on an account with a balance of $10,000. "He never had any idea where his money went," Putnam said. Theodore himself would have agreed.

Financial worry was a constant of the Roosevelts' marriage. The travails began on their honeymoon, in January 1887, when they received word that the cattle on the ranch he owned in the Badlands had frozen to death, wiping out one-quarter of his capital. Until he reached the White House, his pay as governor of New York was the only salary he ever had that covered their expenses. Theodore and Edith destroyed most of their letters to each other, but in the handful that survive, Edith can be seen budgeting and scrimping, once telling Theodore that she was "serving more corned beef and stew than the children entirely approve of." A $100 bill for Theodore's stenographer collided with a $158 tax. Sagamore Hill needed a new furnace: $315. He overdrew his checking account. She couldn't pay the $365 they owed Groton for Ted's schooling. In 1900, when Theodore was elected vice president, he feared running aground in the political shallows, but Edith fretted about the family purse. At $8,000 the salary for his new job was $2,000 less than his gubernatorial pay, and the family lost the free housing it had enjoyed in the governor's mansion. Theodore's presidential pay was generous—$50,000 plus allowances for managing life in the White House—but he and Edith spent heavily to entertain with an elegance meant to convey that the president of the United States was the peer of any monarch.

As he planned for life after the presidency, TR understood that he had to earn a living. Only his two oldest children were launched in the world, Alice as the wife of Congressman Nicholas Longworth of Ohio, and Ted as an underling in a Connecticut carpet mill, where he sorted wool for $7 a week. The presidential pension had yet to be invented, and the income from his investments would not support Edith and the four children still in their care: Kermit, Ethel, Archie, and Quentin. "Until you boys all get to earning your own livelihood I am exceedingly anxious to save something each year," he wrote Ted just after Taft's election. "If things go well I ought to have at least ten years of some earning capacity before me."

A would-be impresario offered him $300,000 to star in a Wild West extravaganza, in which Roosevelt would thunder into view on a spirited mustang to reenact the battle of San Juan Hill, show off his marksmanship, and finish with his 1905 inaugural address. While such antics were out of the question, the most obviously suitable choices did not appeal to him. He declined suggestions to run for the Senate, the House, and the mayoralty of New York City. Some of his friends thought he should take the presidency of Harvard College, but he expressed little enthusiasm for the post, and at least two of the college's overseers blanched at the thought. William James, who had taught him at Harvard and watched his ascent, found him gratuitously contentious. Henry Lee Higginson, financier and philanthropist, wondered if such a lover of commotion could also possess good judgment. To be useful, Higginson thought, a man must understand "what a limited and damned fool he is."

When reporters came to see Roosevelt during his last weeks in office to ask for his thoughts on the proper role of ex-presidents, he replied that he had nothing to say about his predecessors, "but so far as it is concerned with this president, you can say that the United States need do nothing with the ex-president. I will do all the doing that is going to be done myself." Before his presidency he had written a dozen books, publishing the first of them, *The Naval War of 1812*, when he was twenty-three. He found the world of letters congenial, and in a time largely innocent of celebrity and the brand name, Theodore Roosevelt would be able to trade on both. He was the first American to arouse the frenzy and adulation that later generations gave to the Kennedys and the House of Windsor. Curious, confident, full of opinion, he would write thirty-eight books in all—biographies, histories, memoirs, and several collections of essays. While his prose lacked finesse, it abounded in force. A literary critic aptly characterized his style as "tinglingly alive . . . masculine and vascular." Whether the subject was politics, the past, nature, literature, or art, and whether one agreed with or boiled at the thoughts on the page, there was rarely a need to puzzle out his meaning.

Two magazines, *Collier's* and *McClure's*, dangled $100,000 for the safari articles he had promised to *Scribner's*. After accepting $12,000 a year to write regularly for *The Outlook*, which had published his essay on Edwin Arlington Robinson, he was offered three times as much by others. He turned them down. *The Outlook* shared his political philosophy, and its editors impressed him as deeply moral and "sincere, patriotic, painstaking men." He wanted to preach, and *The Outlook* gave him a pulpit. Still, he hoped he had not been financially reckless. To his closest friend, Senator Henry Cabot Lodge, he wrote, "It is very hard to strike the happy middle between being quixotic in such a matter, on the one hand, and, on the other, following a course which is not quite proper for an ex-president whose reputation is what I hope mine is."

Perhaps Edith could not slough her dread of the poorhouse, but the bargains struck by Theodore gave their household ledger a golden glow. *The Outlook* would pay a retainer while he was in Africa, and Scribner had promised to publish the African pieces in a book sure to yield additional income.

Roosevelt counted himself a most fortunate man. On his fiftieth birthday, a week before the election, he wrote an old friend that he could think of no one who had had a happier fifty years. "I have had about as good a run for my money as any human being possibly could have, and whatever happens now I am ahead of the game." Nor could he think of a president who had enjoyed the office as much as he had. He could admit that he would like another serving of presidential power ("any strong man would," he said), and he wondered fleetingly if he should feel melancholy at taking his hands off "the levers of the great machine." But he found "something rather attractive, something in the way of living up to a proper democratic ideal, in having a president go out of office just as I shall go, and become absolutely and without reservation a private man." He looked forward to his new life, he had a multitude of interests beyond politics, and, he told Lodge, "when I am through with anything I am through with it, and am under no temptation to snatch at the fringes of departing glory."

T HE GLORY SHIMMERING in his wake was a presidency that can be summed up in a word: enlargement. Theodore Roosevelt had enlarged the powers of the president, enlarged the government's control of the nation's economic life, and enlarged America's part in world affairs. "While president I have *been* president, emphatically," he said, emphatically. It was true. To him, the Constitution that divided power among legislative, judicial, and executive branches was "the greatest document ever devised by the wit of man to aid a people in exercising every power necessary for its own betterment." It was not "a straitjacket cunningly fashioned to strangle growth." Accused of trespassing on the territories of Congress and the courts, he would pause just long enough to fling a pejorative ("selfish" and "timid" were favorites), then hurtle off in search of more claims to stake.

Held accountable to the people, an emphatic president would pose no danger to democracy, he believed.

The fervor of Roosevelt's belief in himself as an instrument of noble purpose made him insufferable at times and in the last decade of his life would blind him to distinctions between the public interest and his own, but while he was president, his unconcealed relish of power and the daring that went with it mesmerized the country. There was no telling what Theodore Roosevelt would do, only the certainty that he *would* do.

The unabashed joy that TR took in power—acquiring it, exercising it, and contending against the powerful—was as complex as any large outcropping of the human psyche, but three layers of the bedrock beneath the joy are particularly suggestive: he had enormous self-confidence, a deep longing to be a hero, and an indomitable will. The self-confidence was a gift from his cherishing parents. The intense, almost sacred aspiration to heroism also started at home, with the idolization of his father—the finest man he ever knew, he would often say. The early death of the elder Roosevelt simultaneously transformed him into a mythic hero and deprived his son of the blessing he wanted most. Without it, TR could not be entirely certain that he measured up and would test himself constantly—against grizzly bears, on the battlefield, in politics. In a struggle, TR often cast himself as David against Goliath or St. George against the dragons, a habit his critics found self-aggrandizing. But it is also clear that Roosevelt's fear of falling short of his father's ideals tempered many of the excesses associated with the power-driven personality.

The powerful will seems to have originated largely in a childhood humiliation. As a spindly, asthmatic boy of thirteen, Theodore had found himself alone with two bullies who put him through a torment worse than a straight-out thrashing: they toyed with him. Forty years later, as he wrote his autobiography, he could still recall his shame: "when I finally tried to fight them, I discovered that either one singly could not only handle me with easy contempt, but handle me so as not to hurt me much and yet prevent my doing any damage whatever in return." Determined not to repeat the experience, he built up his body and invented the strenuous life, an ideal for himself and, in time, an ideal for the American male and the nation itself.

In 1880, the year he graduated from Harvard, he resolved to join the governing class and won election to the New York State Assembly the following year. He quickly fashioned a political identity as a knightly idealist, fighting corruption and righting the injustices of the world. In the legislature and later as a member of the U.S. Civil Service Commission and president of the Police Commission of New York City, he was on the attack against graft and bribery.

Slower to mature was the sense of social justice that would inform his presidential efforts to even the contest between the individual and the new Goliath of American life, the corporation. As a twenty-eight-year-old candidate (unsuccessful) for mayor of New York City, he confidently denied the existence of class in the United States. But by the time he became governor of New York in 1899, at the age of forty, he had befriended enough social reformers to understand the brutalities of poverty. Impelled by his own empathy, which was considerable, and by a large fear of socialism and anarchy, he began to search for a middle course between the injuries inflicted by laissez-faire and the crackpottery of overthrow and annihilation. He was no radical, he assured a fellow Republican. "All I want to do is cautiously to feel my way to see if we cannot make the general conditions of life a little easier, a little better."

Governor Roosevelt signed bills to improve working conditions, shorten working hours for women and children, and guarantee a minimum salary for schoolteachers. Seeing the ease with which a tycoon could diddle city hall, he began replacing local with state regulation—laws opening corporate ledgers to state inspection and higher corporate taxes to lighten the burden on farmers and owners of small businesses. He required insurance companies to increase their reserves and banned chancy investments by savings banks. For the first but not the last time, he took on the Zeus of American capitalism, J. P. Morgan, denying his request for an exemption from a new tax on railroads.

Wall Street and its Old Guard Republican allies had their revenge at the party's presidential convention in 1900. President McKinley needed a running mate, and when Governor Roosevelt's name appeared among the possibilities, the plutocrats rejoiced and ensured his nomination. Incarcerated in the vice presidency, he could do no more harm.

Roosevelt's vice presidential career was brief but telling. His one official duty was to preside over the Senate, and in his first address he sought to ingratiate himself by praising legislatures as the bodies in which democracy found its "loftiest expression." Translated into personal terms, the praise meant that if fate pitched Theodore Roosevelt into a legislature, then the legislature would be the seat of the political universe. Rather than shrink himself, he would enlarge the Senate. Sounding more like a president than the supernumerary he had become, he spoke grandly of the destiny of their "young nation, already of giant strength. . . . We stand supreme in a continent, in a hemisphere. East and west we look across the two great oceans toward the larger world in which, whether we will or not, we must take an ever-increasing share."

Roosevelt presided over the Senate for exactly four days. Then Congress adjourned for the summer, and when it reconvened after McKinley's assassination, the vice president had made his transit to the presidency. The planets of the Republic immediately ceased to revolve around the Senate. Wherever Roosevelt was, there did the center lie.

Although he had wished for the presidency, he had often said, with a sighing sort of boastfulness, that he did not expect to have it because of the power and money arrayed against him. For a man surprised, though, he had in his pocket a remarkably well-developed presidential agenda. In foreign policy he would, as he so often put it, "Speak softly and carry a big stick." He believed that the bully was as doomed in the community of nations as in a decent neighborhood, and he also believed that speaking softly would not avail "if back of the softness there does not lie strength, power."

If America was not yet the equal of England or Germany, it was certainly warden of the Western Hemisphere and, with the annexation of Hawaii and the acquisition of the Philippines, was a ponderable force in the Pacific. In Roosevelt's view, inaction and isolation were unthinkable: "If we stand idly by, if we seek merely swollen, slothful ease and ignoble peace, if we shrink from the hard contests where men must win at hazard of their lives and at the risk of all they hold dear, then the bolder and stronger peoples will pass us by, and will win for themselves the domination of the world." The twentieth century came to be called the American century, and it was Roosevelt's determination to enlarge his country's power that pointed the century on its way.

At home, he worked up a national version of the progressive economic reforms he had begun in New York. In the eternal struggle between haves and have-nots, the have-nots see redress of their grievances as a matter of common decency, while the haves tend to regard such an attitude as common theft—of property, of privilege, of power. Roosevelt proposed to put government between the combatants as referee. His Square Deal, as he called it, would not give everyone the same cards, he explained; it would merely prevent crookedness in the dealing. He meant to preserve opportunities for individual success but eliminate labor exploitation, price gouging, unfair competition, and other abuses of economic power. Tempered no doubt by the opposition he had met as governor, Roosevelt acknowledged that there was "mighty little good in a mere spasm of reform" and promised gradual, rational change.

But his first big offensive, in February 1902, registered as a spasm on Wall Street. Without preamble, the federal government sued the Northern Securities Company for restraint of trade and called for its dissolution. Northern Securities was a holding company that owned virtually all the railways from Chicago through the plains to the Pacific. Holding companies had come into vogue after an 1895 Supreme Court decision put them beyond the reach of the federal government's only law for preventing monopoly, the Sherman Antitrust Act.

J. P. Morgan, one of the founders and chief stockholders of Northern Securities, stormed the White House to inquire why he had not received advance notice of the suit. Roosevelt noted the unfairness of informing some investors before others. "If we have done anything wrong," Morgan snapped, "send your man to my man and they can fix it up." Roosevelt's man, Attorney General Philander C. Knox, let Morgan know that he had missed the point. "We don't want to fix it up," he said; "we want to stop it." When Morgan left, Roosevelt remarked that the financier seemed to see him as "a big rival operator." Certainly Roosevelt viewed Morgan as a big rival and enjoyed scrapping with him because of it. There was no sport in swinging a big stick at the puny.

In the spring of 1902, fifty thousand anthracite coal miners in Pennsylvania went on strike, demanding raises, an eight-hour day, and recognition of their union, the United Mine Workers. The mine owners retaliated with a shutout, putting another ninety thousand men out of work, and gambled that starvation would force the miners back to work without a union. The standoff continued into the autumn, the price of coal sextupled, and the possibility of a winter without fuel raised the specter of riots. When Roosevelt asked the owners and the union to settle their dispute for the good of the country, they declined.

Never had he faced a bigger perplexity, he wrote one of his sisters. The president had no constitutional authority to intervene, yet it was the president who would be blamed when the poor froze to death or were killed in riots. He decided to intervene, through his secretary of war, Elihu Root. A Wall Street lawyer before he entered government, Root cajoled J. P. Morgan into persuading the mine owners to cooperate, and after a few prickly sessions with the president, the warring parties agreed that the miners would go back to work while a panel of arbitrators worked out a settlement that would bind both sides.

Roosevelt is remembered as a soloist with little use for the choir, but his intervention showed a collaborative side well known to his associates. Having failed to bring the antagonists together, he readily acceded to Root (who called him the most "advisable" man he had ever known), bowed to Morgan's power with the mining companies, and consulted his cabinet secretaries. When they suggested change after change to a letter he wished to send the owners and the union, he joked, through his teeth, "I am much obliged to you gentlemen for leaving one sentence of my own."

As the coal bins filled up again, Roosevelt was relieved but not tranquil. What if his success encouraged a wave of strikes and set up the expectation that he would mediate all of them? The Old Guard complained of his high-handed disregard of the Constitution, and Wall Street called him a traitor to the propertied class. He wished that the rich understood that he was acting in their interests, for he felt sure that the moderate changes he sought would thwart the revolutionaries who wanted to overthrow capitalism.

The Square Deal included twenty-five antitrust indictments, stricter regulation of the railroads, industrial safety legislation, measures to promote fair competition, and a meat inspection law prompted by Upton Sinclair's novel *The Jungle*. As the inspection bill moved through Congress, the meatpackers declared that if the government would spell out the desired improvements, no law would be necessary. Roosevelt disagreed. Without a law, he said, the packers' "spasm of reform would not have outlived sixty days."

In the belief that enterprises affecting the well-being of millions of citizens needed a federal watchdog, TR persuaded Congress to create a Department of Commerce and Labor and endow it with broad investigative powers. To calm the capitalists—thankless, endless work—he said repeatedly that his administration was hostile not to great wealth but to the "malefactors" of great wealth. Those who dealt squarely with stockholders, competitors, and the public would have no reason to fear the government's scrutiny, he said. Only "the corporation that shrinks from the light" would have cause for dread, "and about the welfare of such corporations we need not be oversensitive."

Distilled, Roosevelt's philosophy of government was a secular version of the lessons of Sunday School. The good man and woman lived orderly lives, respected one another's rights, and abided by the Golden Rule. The good government enforced these principles, rewarding goodness with freedom and bringing malefactors to heel. The good country lived justly in the community of nations and held other countries to the same standard. In the winter of 1902–3, when Venezuela refused to honor its debts to English and German banks and the Europeans replied with bullets and a blockade, Roosevelt put a U.S. naval squadron on alert. Warning the Europeans that he would not tolerate further aggression, he invoked President James Monroe's 1823 edict banning new colonization of the Western Hemisphere. The Venezuelan crisis passed when the interested parties took Roosevelt's suggestion to submit their dispute to arbitration at The Hague.

The Venezuelan episode inspired the Roosevelt Corollary to the Monroe Doctrine: if the Latins defaulted on debts to other nations, the United States would intervene. It was only fair, he argued. Having told Europe and Asia that the Americas were off-limits, the United States had a duty to police the hemisphere and ensure that all its nations kept order and paid their bills. Critics who foresaw the ill will that such an arrangement would engender in Latin America he dismissed as myopic, ignorant, greedy, and "generally men who undervalue the great fighting qualities, without which no nation can ever rise to the first rank."

With tutelage from Captain Alfred Thayer Mahan, a naval strategist who believed that the United States could be master of its destiny by controlling a few key points on the globe, Roosevelt looked longingly at the Colombian province of Panama and the unfinished isthmian canal. Construction had started in 1881, stopped, sputtered on and off, and fizzled out altogether in a financial scandal. In 1903 Colombia agreed to cede control of the isthmus to the United States for $10 million in cash and a yearly rent of $250,000. After the Senate ratified the treaty, the Colombians dallied for months, then demanded more authority and raised their price. Roosevelt, incensed, told his secretary of state that he would have no further dealings with Bogotá. Either he would dig the canal in Nicaragua, or he would "interfere when it becomes necessary so as to secure the Panama route," he said. On November 3 the Panamanians rebelled against the Colombian government for the fifty-third time in as many years, the United States sent in the marines and refused to allow Colombian troops onto the isthmus, the rebels declared their independence, and within forty-eight hours the United States recognized the new republic.

"I took Panama," Roosevelt boasted. But he stiffened at any suggestion that he had incited the revolution. As he explained it, he had "simply ceased to stamp out the different revolutionary fuses that were already burning." By seizing a moment when he could act alone, he said, he "started the canal and then left Congress not to debate the canal, but to debate me." He counted the acquisition of the isthmus as his greatest presidential achievement, a gift to world commerce and a strategic boon to the United States.

As much as Theodore Roosevelt enjoyed a strut in the footlights, in 1905 he chose to work backstage in hopes of bringing an end to the Russo-Japanese War, climax of a decade-long struggle for dominance in East Asia. Two years of war had humiliated Russia and nearly bankrupted Japan, and more than 200,000 lives had been lost, but until Roosevelt interceded, neither side would quit. He worked out of sight for months, until the summer of 1905, when the Japanese and Russian envoys to the United States agreed to meet on the presidential yacht in Long Island Sound, near the village of Oyster Bay.

The president did not set out from Sagamore in a bright mood. The Japanese saw the wisdom of giving up before their economy collapsed but felt deprived of the glory they thought they deserved for beating Russia on land and sea. The Russians, bilious at being undone by an upstart, sent word to Roosevelt that they would not stand for a toast to the mikado before a toast to the czar. He handled the day with a finesse that was characteristic but would have surprised those accustomed to the bared teeth and snapping jaw. When it was time for lunch, he inserted himself between the two ambassadors and marched them together into the dining room. Both delegations were served from a buffet and seated side by side on a divan. He sat opposite, in a chair. For the toast he asked them to forgo the traditional round of responses, then drank to the "welfare and prosperity of the sovereigns and peoples of the two great nations."

The treaty, signed a month later in Portsmouth, New Hampshire, earned Roosevelt sheaves of accolades, which he accepted with "sardonic amusement," he said. The ovation was for his success, not for his sense of duty or his willingness to risk failure. Had the Japanese and Russians refused to negotiate, he wrote his daughter Alice, "I should have been laughed at and condemned."

ROOSEVELT WAS EXCEEDINGLY SENSITIVE to laughter and condemnation. He might have given himself a layer of insulation by keeping the press at a distance, but his great sensitivity collided with an even greater need for attention. His White House gave reporters unprecedented access, he spoke quite freely for publication, and in private he treated the newsmen to a highly seductive performance: the kimono came open for those who promised not to tell. The indiscreet were banished and publicly denounced as liars.

Roosevelt, more than any of his predecessors, used the press to speak to the people when Congress blocked his path. Whatever the issue, he framed his position as if any other were preposterous and morally defective. Out of self-respect and professional pride, most correspondents rounded out their stories with other views, and they often criticized him, but the dominant voice in their stories was his. The newspapers were Roosevelt's megaphone, enlarging him as he enlarged the presidency, the government, and the country.

He registered most of his complaints about the press in private, but in 1906, enraged by an attack on the Senate in a magazine owned by William Randolph Hearst, Roosevelt warned against the man with the muckrake, the character in *Pilgrim's Progress* who was offered a celestial crown for his rake but refused either to lay down the rake or look up from his work in the muck. To indulge in the character assassination of people in public life would deter "able men of normal sensitiveness" from entering public service, he said. And reporting only the bad in the world induced "moral color-blindness": when the whole picture was painted black, "there remains no hue whereby to single out the rascals for distinction from their fellows."

"Muckraking" instantly became the name for the investigative journalism of Lincoln Steffens, Ida Tarbell, Ray Stannard Baker, and many other fine reporters. For a dozen years, they had been exposing political corruption, financial chicanery, and deplorable social conditions—work that built public support for many of Roosevelt's reforms. Steffens tried to turn "muckraker" into a badge of honor, and Baker, who knew and liked Roosevelt, reminded him of democracy's need for "light and air." Roosevelt replied that he favored letting in light and air but not sewer gas.

Alarmed by the Japanese naval might on display in the Russo-Japanese War, Roosevelt decided in 1907 to send the U.S. Navy's battle fleet on a cruise around the world. It was a bold move, made without consulting the cabinet or the Congress. He had acted alone because he disapproved of councils of war, he said. They never got around to making war, "and in a crisis the duty of a leader is to lead and not to take refuge in the generally timid wisdom of a multitude of counsellors." Lacking a crisis, he justified the cruise by saying that he wanted "all failures, blunders and shortcomings to be made apparent in time of peace and not in time of war." When the Senate Naval Affairs Committee announced that it did not intend to seek funds for the voyage, Roosevelt said he had money enough to send the fleet to the West Coast. If Congress did not want the ships to return to the Atlantic, it could leave them there.

The fleet was politely received, and the president considered the voyage the apotheosis of speaking softly and carrying a big stick. "I want to make it evident to every foreign nation that I intend to do justice," he wrote his ambassador to England. He did not mean to threaten but to show the world that he was "entirely ready and entirely able to see that our rights are maintained." Roosevelt hoped that the sight of the gleaming white battleships, specially painted for the cruise, would squelch Japanese thoughts of expanding eastward across the Pacific, but he had his doubts. "No one dreads war as I do," he told his White House military aide, Captain Archie Butt, while the fleet was at sea. "The little that I have seen of it, and I have seen only a little, leaves a horrible picture on my mind. But the surest way to prevent this war with the East is to be thoroughly prepared for it."

Years later the long, rich letters that Butt wrote during his service to Roosevelt and Taft were discreetly edited for publication, and it appears that the originals were never again consulted by the biographers of either president. The published version of the letter in question ends with Roosevelt's thought on military preparedness, but he also told Captain Butt that Japan's leaders were unhappy with the terms of the Treaty of Portsmouth and felt that their prestige had suffered because Russia had not been smashed.

> [S]ooner or later they will try to bolster up their power by another war. Unfortunately for us, we have what they want most, the Philippines. . . . The security of the [Japanese] throne will depend upon some sensational war and the Japanese politician is not without the daring to try one later on. I regard the dispatch of the warships to the Pacific one of the greatest things which has been done during my administration. It has delayed this war five years at least. When it comes, we will win over Japan, but it will be one of the most disastrous conflicts the world has ever seen.

As president, Roosevelt built up the navy and the army, and despite the bellicosity of his rhetoric, he used them in the interest of defense, not aggression. He received a Nobel Peace Prize for his work in ending the war between Russia and Japan, he was the first head of state to send a dispute to The Hague for arbitration, and not a shot was fired at a foreign enemy during his seven and a half years in office.

Roosevelt's war with J. P. Morgan ended in a draw during the financial panic in 1907. When the stock market gave way, the president supposed it was only the inevitable bout of indigestion that follows a period of gluttony. Morgan, however, saw a country careening toward catastrophe. Speculators had piled loan upon loan, pledging stocks as collateral, and could not pay their bankers when stock prices plunged. Anxious bank depositors began withdrawing their funds, the lines lengthened, and when banks began running out of cash, panic set in.

With one more battered stock about to precipitate at least one more bank failure, Morgan thought he could stop the panic by acquiring the ailing corporation, the Tennessee Coal, Iron & Railroad Company (TCI), with shares of his largest trust, U.S. Steel. His steel men sped to the White House to explain the situation. They had no special desire for the company, which was unprofitable, but were willing to buy it to calm the stock market, they said. Before going ahead, they wanted to know if the government would prosecute the new enterprise under the antitrust laws. After consulting Root, Roosevelt said he saw no objection to the acquisition. The deal was done, the panic ended, and in the hurly-burly it was difficult to see whether Roosevelt had been a sage or a dupe. Although TCI's health was less than robust, U.S. Steel had acquired $1 billion worth of iron ore, coal, and limestone, the principal ingredients of steel, for $35 million.

Of all Roosevelt's crusades, the most original and far-reaching was the fight for conservation. Guided by his friend Gifford Pinchot, chief forester of the United States, he drew up a master plan for managing the nation's natural resources, replenishing forests that had been logged with no thought of the future, repairing thousands of square miles of erosion, and preserving endangered wildlife. "We are not building this country of ours for a day," the president declared. "It is to last through the ages."

He expanded the national forests, persuaded Congress to fund thirty massive irrigation projects, and added five national parks. On learning that plume hunters were depleting the bird population on Pelican Island, a four-acre dab of public land in Florida's Indian River, he asked if any law barred his declaring the island a bird sanctuary. No, said his counselors. "Very well, then I so declare it." Fifty more wildlife refuges followed. At Pinchot's suggestion Roosevelt also created presidential commissions on public lands, inland waterways, country life, and national conservation.

Roosevelt's steady accretion of power frayed his relationship with Congress, and the commissions were seen as one more device for enlarging the presidential domain. Well before the end of his presidency he became, as Henry Adams put it, "a severely dethroned king." His hold on the Republican Party also slipped because of growing animosity between the party's conservatives and its progressives. Both factions were marking time until the election of 1908, the Old Guard hoping that Taft would reinstate the torpor of the McKinley era, the progressives dreaming that Taft would euthanize the Old Guard and get on with the reordering.

As president, Roosevelt had overreached and overpreached, irritated, arrogated, and enervated. "He has 'got on the nerves' of the nation," the *Baltimore Sun* yipped as he left office. "The people need a rest."

Roosevelt had meant to preach, and he intended to continue. The world as he understood it was not fundamentally material. It was "a practical world of spiritual things," a world that "should feel the deepest scorn for those whose only virtue is their essential and efficient greed," he said. He left office knowing that his business was unfinished. The Panama Canal was not yet open. The tear in the Republican Party needed mending. Monopoly had not been extinguished. A tariff that enriched manufacturers but penalized nearly everyone else urgently needed reform. The army and navy would have to be kept up. He had made the public aware of the value of the country's natural resources, but the fiends of exploitation were still running ahead of the conserving angels. He had made mistakes, he knew. But throughout his presidency, he had endeavored to "secure and enlarge the opportunities of the men and women of the United States," he said, and he hoped that "the average American citizen, the man who works hard, who does not live too easily, but who is a decent and upright fellow, shall feel that I have tried to the very best of my ability to be his representative."

Summing up his presidency, the newspapers noted that its successes were almost entirely executive. Impatient with the Congress, he had defied it, a habit that worked against his legislative agenda but generally delighted the populace. As Alfred Henry Lewis, a newspaperman who had watched him closely, told Archie Butt, "He has not got as much respect for the Senate as a dog has for a marriage license, and every time he swats either House, it is so much popularity from the people." Lewis ventured a few predictions: Taft would hand the government over to the Old Guard, Roosevelt would be furious, and a cross-country speaking trip after his return from Africa would put him in the running for a presidential nomination in 1912.

But first there was a safari, an endeavor that fit Roosevelt's idea of suitable work for a man of action. A man of action he had always been, and a man of action he intended to remain.

A SEA VOYAGE can be a trial for such a man, and Roosevelt was not by nature a passenger. He preferred the rowboat to all other modes of locomotion, for reasons easily understood by us if not by him. In a rowboat he could be captain, crew, and engine. A transatlantic crossing also fretted him because he suffered from seasickness—"actively," according to Kermit. Writing home from the heaving Atlantic, however, the only queasiness TR mentioned was Kermit's. For the first few days father and son stayed mainly in their cabin and read.

Cabin 1, the largest and most luxurious on the *Hamburg,* was a suite with parlor, two bedrooms, and two baths. In honor of TR's voyage it had been damasked to a fare-thee-well, green and brown in his bedroom, blue and silver in Kermit's. The Hamburg-Amerika Line had offered them free passage, which TR declined, but he consented to a bargain fare of $600 for accommodations that ordinarily fetched $2,100. The choice of a German line had been a matter of practicality. Only the Germans would carry ammunition all the way to Mombasa.

Roosevelt is often described as the most natural of men, thoroughly Theodore wherever he went, but the difference between president and paterfamilias was pronounced. In public he showed his teeth and his fists, apparently in the belief that the appearance of weakness was as unmanly as weakness itself. At home he dropped the combativeness and operated from a tenderness that was oceanic. The most familiar images of the Sagamore Hill Roosevelts, preserved in photographs and early movies, present the family striding into the woods for the bliss they seemed to find in physical exhaustion. Togetherness the family had, but Theodore and Edith also nourished the individuality of their offspring. Edith's diary regularly notes outings with a single child.

Most of the letters Theodore wrote his children during his travels are adventure stories about their father, but when he was at home and they were away, he wrote them with particularity and understanding. To Archie's request for a good Spalding football or none at all, TR replied, "Blessed

Archie, I have directed that the very best Spalding football be sent to you at once." When Ted, at ten, began to suffer from debilitating headaches, TR was mortified to learn that he was the proximate cause. Impressed by the boy's intelligence, he had unwittingly pushed him beyond his emotional and physical capacities. Thereafter he was sympathetic with all his sons' travails in school and often warned them against overworking themselves. Kermit, a good student, hit a rough patch in school and was counseled not to worry. "I know you are studying hard," TR wrote him. "Don't get cast down. Sometimes in life, both at school and afterwards, fortune will go against anyone, but if he just keeps pegging away and doesn't lose his courage things always take a turn for the better in the end."

Theodore gave the children their first riding lessons and worried (proudly) when Ethel jumped a five-foot-six-inch hurdle on horseback. He feared that Quentin was "a little soft" but delighted in his intellectual precocity. At age ten, contemplating his sunburned legs, he had said, "They look like a Turner sunset, don't they?" Theodore and Edith had no idea how he had acquainted himself with the artist's work, but his tutor may have been their Washington neighbor Henry Adams, who owned a Turner or two and often entertained Quentin when he was a small boy. Quentin at four, said Adams, was "considerably older and less school-boy-like than his father."

Alice's wedding and Ethel's coming-out party were grand White House affairs, and throughout the family's years in Washington, the children brought friends home to play and spend the night. The president, who enjoyed a pillow fight as much as any other kind, wrestled with the boys and their company, joined them for hide-and-seek, and ran the obstacle courses they set up in the corridors.

Kermit was his third child, born in 1889—two years after Ted and five after Alice. Like his mother, Kermit was dreamy and interior. From his father he acquired a love of the outdoors and a bedeviling restlessness. The literary passions of both parents passed to all their progeny and in Kermit sank roots that spread wide. To the French, Latin, and Greek he learned at school, he would eventually add Italian, Portuguese, Spanish, Arabic, and Sanskrit for the pleasure of reading their literatures in the original. He would also become a collector of first editions and the author of a handful of books and magazine articles. The invitation to go on safari interrupted his studies at Harvard, and TR hoped that he would savor the holiday, then "buckle down." Kermit was a most agreeable traveling companion, TR wrote his sister Corinne. He disappeared for long periods to read Homer in Greek, but when he came back, TR said, he "solemnly kisses me, and then solemnly strums his mandolin or talks."

Kermit made friends easily, and chief among his new shipboard friends were the naturalists sent by the Smithsonian. Edmund Heller, a thirty-four-year-old zoologist on loan from the University of California, was making his third scientific expedition to Africa. Heller had the permanent tan of the field naturalist and parted his thick, dark hair in the middle, not bothering to use it to hide his large ears. He liked Kermit's straightforwardness and was impressed by TR's encyclopedic knowledge of American fauna. "He is well aware of the distinctions between the different genera of rodents and also with the characters of the northern species notwithstanding the extreme obscurity of many of them," Heller marveled to a colleague.

J. Alden Loring of Owego, New York, had sandy hair and a surprisingly boyish face for a man of thirty-eight. He had collected small mammals throughout the United States, Mexico, and Europe in the employ of the federal government and the Bronx Zoo. Said to be a man of "ardent temperament," Loring was available for the safari because he had just been sacked by the trustees of the Denver Zoo, who disapproved of his grand aspirations for their establishment. Loring felt immediately at ease with TR. "He wears old clothes and we do not fully dress unless there is something special doing," he wrote his family. TR had assigned Kermit to photograph the safari, and on the voyage to Africa, Loring helped him refine his darkroom skills.

The third naturalist, Edgar A. Mearns, was fifty-two, graying, and mustached in walrus fashion. A physician who had passed most of his career in the army, Mearns tramped the countryside in his off-hours and over his lifetime collected forty thousand faunal specimens and an unprecedented variety of flora for American museums. Benevolent and soft-spoken, Mearns shocked his safari companions one evening with a tale of collecting human skulls after a skirmish with a band of Moros in the Philippines.

All three men sang with Kermit and his mandolin, and Heller and Loring occasionally accepted a challenge to race him around the deck. Kermit was a hair shy of six feet tall and "imperially slim," like the title character of Edwin Arlington Robinson's "Richard Cory." All sinew, he was an indefatigable runner.

Raised in the orthodoxy of the strenuous life, Kermit fought his seasickness with walks on deck, and in the deep of one night valiantly tried by himself to tame a ferocious rash. He ran a bath, which woke his father, who looked at the rash and suspected bubonic plague. Mearns recognized it as hives, most likely a reaction to the quinine tablets they were taking for the fevers of Africa.

Soon after the Smithsonian agreed to sponsor the safari, Roosevelt had written the army from the White House to request that Mearns be furloughed to accompany him. "I fear that I shall have to coddle myself," TR explained. Thanks to the sedentary life he had led as president, he was "old and fat." As a Harvard freshman, standing five-feet-eight and weighing 124 pounds, he had been as slender as Kermit. The passage of three decades inflated his neck from fourteen and one-half inches to nineteen, his chest from thirty-six inches to forty-five, and his waist from twenty-six and one-half inches to forty-seven. He weighed 250 pounds, and the presidential thigh had a circumference only a shade smaller than the freshman's waist.

Now fifty, TR had a leg prone to abscesses, the result of an accident that had pitched him out of a carriage in 1902. The public knew of his boxing, wrestling, jujitsu, tennis, hiking, and riding, but not of his sclerotic arteries or of the blindness in his left eye, incurred while boxing with one of Edith's cousins. It was said that the blindness was never mentioned for fear of embarrassing the cousin. Such kindness was characteristic of TR, but he also would have been quick to see the inadvisability of letting political opponents know that the president, especially a president regularly accused of impetuosity, was half-blind.

THE AZORES pimpled onto the horizon on the *Hamburg's* seventh day at sea. The ship anchored off Horta, and Kermit scurried ashore for a "snoop," his mother's word for a shopping trip in search of treasures that were attractive, affordable, and distinctive. While Kermit stocked up on sweaters and jaunty bamboo cigarette holders, a busybody from the *Hamburg* told someone in the town that the former president had been attacked at sea by a deranged man from steerage. The story quickly appeared in newspapers in London and New York, where it chilled Edith, who had lived in fear of Theodore's assassination since his 1898 gubernatorial campaign, when he began plunging into crowds. In their lifetime, three presidents— Lincoln, Garfield, and McKinley—had been murdered in office. Writing

Kermit after reading of the incident on the *Hamburg*, she said, "I don't dare to think of such things for I must keep bright and well for the dearest children in the world."

At Gibraltar, the ship's next stop, Roosevelt explained to a reporter that a man from steerage had indeed come toward him, muttering in Italian, but was quickly apprehended by the crew. There had been no attack. Roosevelt had later gone down to steerage to shake hands with everyone and offer assurances of his high regard for the Italian people. He had done so, he said, as a courtesy to an Italian diplomat embarrassed by the incident, but there is a touch of grandiosity in the deliberate prolonging of the episode and the creation of a small drama in which he could play the hero. It is a familiar display of potency, with the strong man hastening to the aid of the weak. For those whose characters are organized around the exercise of power, the elation of carrying out a rescue lies not in a gain of dominion over the weaker party but in the rescue itself, which affirms the rescuer's power.

Except for the visit to steerage, Roosevelt's power was nearly invisible on the *Hamburg*. The passengers in first class found the man in Cabin 1 refreshingly modest. He drew little attention to himself and sought no special treatment. At dinner he was sociable but not overbearing. He spoke not a word about politics. A passenger who walked the deck with him one evening was given a lecture on the 2,500-year naval history of the Mediterranean. Out of Roosevelt's "vivid martial and romantic imagination" poured story after story of battles and burning cities and pirates and heroes, the listener recalled. Noticing that the narrator had said nothing of his Great White Fleet, the listener brought it up. TR stopped cold and said, "By George, that was me, wasn't it?" And then, fist uplifted and eyes bright in the setting sun, he spun a tale of what the fleet would have done if —

On April 4 the *Hamburg* glided into the Bay of Naples, where it was greeted with an Italian rendition of the festivities at Hoboken, a parade of yachts, fishing boats bearing musicians and fruit and flowers, larger vessels sporting signal flags and bunting by the bolt, and a racket of steam whistles. Crowds packed the pier and the streets and hung out windows for a look at Theodore Roosevelt. An international contingent of reporters had assembled in hopes of eliciting a political comment, but he would not answer their questions. "The only thing ahead of me now, the only thing I am thinking about, is my hunting trip in Africa," he said. "I am not worrying much about that. It is going to be a full-blooded picnic." The next day *Le Journal* of Paris published an interview that presented Roosevelt as an egotistical boor. He was livid. The effrontery lay not in the opinion but in the fact that he had given no interviews.

Months before the safari, Melville Stone, manager of the Associated Press, had warned Roosevelt that the demand for news of his adventures would drive the yellow press to fabrication and invasions of privacy. To head them off, Stone suggested taking a reporter or designating someone in the party to send regular messages to an AP bureau for dissemination to the newspapers. But Roosevelt had no intention of allowing the papers to scoop his articles for *Scribner's* and, failing to see the incongruity of orchestrating a spectacle and expecting it to proceed unnoticed, he insisted that as a private citizen he had a right to travel unmolested. He had instructed the American ambassador in London to notify the Foreign Office that he wanted the newspapermen kept out of his range in Africa, and he turned away the many reporters who asked to go with him.

F. Warrington Dawson of the United Press bureau in Paris, a young American journalist still hoping to inveigle his way into the safari party, had the good luck to turn up in Naples when Roosevelt was stewing about the faked interview in *Le Journal.* Introducing himself with a letter of recommendation from Henry White, the American ambassador to France and a Roosevelt favorite, Dawson persuaded Roosevelt that he had no wish to intrude; he wanted only to be on hand when Roosevelt wished to issue a statement. Together Dawson and Roosevelt crafted a denial of the interview and sent it clattering off to the rest of the world by telegraph. Stung twice by the press and still only halfway to British East Africa, Roosevelt agreed to take Dawson as far as Mombasa, and Dawson agreed not to file stories without Roosevelt's approval. It was an imperfect arrangement for a newsman, but going in hamstrings was better than not going at all.

As soon as the stevedores had transferred the safari impedimenta from the *Hamburg* to their new ship, the *Admiral,* the Roosevelts and the naturalists and the journalist headed south to Sicily for a look at the devastation of an earthquake and tidal wave that had struck in December 1908. Still one of the worst natural disasters on record, the quake took 100,000 lives, leveled the cities of Messina and Reggio, and gave the Sicilian coastline a raw, new face. President Roosevelt had immediately offered $500,000 in aid and ordered two of the navy's ships to head for the scene with food, clothing, and other relief.

In Messina the visitors picked their way through the rubble as ox-drawn carts stacked with corpses passed slowly by. "Ghastly," Kermit wrote in his diary. The Americans had hammered together 250 huts and would build 1,250 more. Windows lacked glass, and tar paper substituted for the traditional terra-cotta roofs, but the Sicilians were moving in and painting their names under the eaves in hopes of reconnecting with lost friends and relatives. TR fixed most of his attention on the assistance rendered by the navy, and after talking with the officers in charge asked Dawson to compose a statement that would give Americans an appreciation of the navy's contributions. In a book written years later Dawson tactfully claimed that he had suggested the statement, but in a letter posted just after the stop in Sicily, he said that the idea was Roosevelt's. TR, who had insisted on removing himself from the political stage for Taft's sake, was thousands of miles from Washington but still not in the wings.

The rest of the passage to Mombasa was notable only for its coziness. Frederick Selous, the celebrated English hunter, had joined TR's party in Naples and with coaxing would reenact his encounters with big game. Dawson walked the decks with TR and gushed in a letter to his mother, "He has completely conquered me, and I adore him." Kermit slept late, read *Alice in Wonderland*, and took all available shore leave as the *Admiral* threaded its way through the Suez Canal to the Red Sea and beyond. Mirages, strangely beautiful wailing music, and an Easter Sunday poker game reminded him that he and his father were a long way from home.

His mother and his sister Ethel felt their absence acutely. "It's horrid not having you and Father with us on Easter," Ethel wrote him. There had been no solace at church, where they and the rest of the congregation were browbeaten by a cleric convinced that humankind had "gone to the bow-wows." The day pushed Edith into a funk. She fared better at Sagamore than anywhere else, she wrote Alice, "but the prospect of not seeing Father until next March is insupportable."

Aboard the *Admiral* Father was becoming known as "Colonel," an honorific he liked and one that neatly solved the problem of what to call him now that he was no longer in the White House. He corrected anyone who called him "Mr. President," although many, including the new president, would find the habit hard to break. "Mr. Roosevelt" sounded plebeian after "President Roosevelt," but "Colonel Roosevelt" carried an echo of the Spanish-American War, the sublime moment of his life. Edith preferred "Mr. Roosevelt" and hoped that Theodore would be "the simplest American alive" when he left Washington. He seemed to share this wish, she told Archie Butt, "but the trouble is he has really forgotten how."

Theodore foresaw no difficulties. The duties of an ex-president were the same as those of any other good citizen, namely "to do his share of the work for the common good, in whatever position he may find himself." And for him, the good citizen was fused with the good soldier. In the last weeks of his presidency, imagining his future, he spoke of himself in military terms: "I step back in the ranks, and I shall certainly continue to fight for what I deem to be right." Colonel Roosevelt was a colonel without a regiment, but for the moment, steaming toward Mombasa, he was very much in charge.

TWO

A Full-Blooded Picnic

MOMBASA, "lovely and green and equatorial" to Kermit's eye, rose out of the sea on the afternoon of April 21. From the deck of the *Admiral* he and his companions could also see red roofs, white stucco, and a pink fortress until a curtain of rain closed over the scenery. That evening, in the downpour, he and his father wrapped themselves in cloaks and made for shore.

The landing levied two taxes on TR's patience, a pack of reporters and a fancy dinner at the Mombasa Club, where he and Selous were expected to make speeches. With the newsmen Roosevelt was civil but deliberately trite. He said he was happy to be ashore, excited about the hunt, and in splendid health, the last point undoubtedly a bulletin for Edith, who would get news of him from the papers weeks before his letters reached Sagamore.

The Mombasa Club, oasis of oligarchs and veritable zoo of hunting trophies, prided itself on its table and the originality of its cocktails. Roosevelt, who drank little and apart from an occasional mint julep shunned hard liquor, surely declined to sample the Waters of the Nile, a stunning mélange of distilled spirits laced with champagne.

In his speech Roosevelt praised England for bringing civilization to the barbarians. He would say more about imperialism during his travels, but his central conviction never wavered. Until the European march into Africa, the continent had indeed been dark, ruled by the law of the jungle. With other aristocrats Roosevelt maintained that imperialism had advanced the humanity of the world by protecting the weak from the savagery of the strong. Never parsimonious with advice, he declared that colonies were best governed locally rather than from distant imperial seats, and in this, he suggested, Britain might profitably follow the example of the United States in the Philippines. The notion must have amused diners whose heads were not swimming in the Waters of the Nile. The United States had practiced imperialism for a decade, practiced it reluctantly, and possessed only a few specks on the globe. Britain's empire was centuries old, and the Union Jack fluttered over a quarter of the earth's real estate.

Sixty miles south of Mombasa lay the border between the British and German sectors of East Africa. Germans often stopped at the Mombasa Club, and business-minded men in both colonies hoped their enterprises would not be disrupted by a war between England and Germany, which were building up their armies and navies at a disquieting pace. Roosevelt saw no danger. He cherished peace, he said, but no peace could last unless nations were strong enough to defend themselves.

With the courage of a lion hunter and the tact of a butler, Selous turned his moment before the crowd into a challenge for the illustrious American, voicing the hope that the former president would use his influence to bring about an entente between the English and the Germans.

The safari began at two-thirty the next afternoon, when Roosevelt's train chuffed out of Mombasa. TR rode alfresco, on a bench bolted to the cowcatcher, with Selous, Dr. Mearns, and the colony's lieutenant governor. Touchingly eager, the Colonel was already in sun helmet, khaki jacket with patch pockets, khaki trousers, and puttees. His companions still wore their suits.

They were headed for a lion hunt near Kapiti Plains Station, 275 miles to the northwest on the Uganda Railway. A ride on the railway, which spanned British East Africa from east to west, was 584 miles of exhilaration. The track shot across plains shimmering in the heat, climbed escarpments into the clouds, dropped vertiginously into flowered forests, and leapt swamp and gorge. A morning shave was an event, carried out with hot water drawn from the boiler of the locomotive. When the train paused for dinner, passengers caked in red dust and cinders were served by stewards in pristine white gloves. Even a delay was likely to be picturesque—a collision with a hippo, perhaps, or a rhino frozen in the beam of the headlamp. The telegraph poles lining the tracks were inordinately lanky in deference to the giraffe.

Honoring the Colonel's wishes, colonial officials promised to deport journalists who pursued the safari, but as soon as this protection was assured, he ignored it. Still finding it hard to bar his door after years of relying on newsmen to tell the world what he said and did, he invited Warrington Dawson and three other reporters to ride with him as far as Kapiti. After that the little press corps was to proceed on its own to Nairobi, the colony's capital, a few miles farther up the line.

Roosevelt was enchanted by his train ride. The animals delighted him, the flowers and trees delighted him, even the locomotive, a Baldwin made in the United States, delighted him. Amid majestic herds of giraffes, zebras, gazelles, and impalas, he imagined himself on a journey through the Pleistocene. The British had banned hunting along the railway, and other game laws had been in force for almost a decade. Endangered species were declared off-limits, as were calves and pregnant cows. Violators faced large fines and two months in jail. Roosevelt saw no contradiction between preserving game and killing it. He disclaimed all bloodlust, arguing—as did other enlightened conservationists of the era—that a game reserve enabled animals to breed in safety, while hunting ensured that they would not multiply unchecked and "crowd man off the planet." The humane society impulse to outlaw hunting for sport he dismissed as "mushy sentimentality."

British East Africa's hunting licenses gave each of the Roosevelts permission to kill more than fifty animals—elephants, rhinos, hippos, buffalo, elands, wildebeest, zebras, oryxes, cheetahs, and other species. The license cost £50, and another £17 secured the right to shoot one more bull elephant. Extra giraffes, rhinos, and elands went for £5 a head, various antelopes for £3, and additional pairs of wildebeest or waterbuck for £2. Lions and leopards, classed as vermin, could be shot in any number. The limits were devised to prevent unlimited slaughter, while the liberality of the bag incubated a profitable form of tourism.

Safari is a Swahili word meaning both the expedition itself and the personnel and paraphernalia that go with it. Ivory hunters had gone on safari for decades, but safari as sport burgeoned after 1885, when the European powers met in Berlin and divided Africa among themselves. Princes and dukes were soon trotting into the bush to shoot game and see the strange, dark peoples they knew only from the accounts of explorers and missionaries. Eccentrics, one in a balloon and another who hunted big game with a lasso, followed, as did anthropologists and naturalists. Roosevelt's safari was the Smithsonian's sixth foray into Africa. The Smithsonian would sponsor more safaris, but only Roosevelt's has lingered in the public imagination. It was immense and scientifically ambitious, and because of TR's popularity,

Americans followed it in *Scribner's* with the kind of intensity with which their descendants watched the first human voyage to the moon.

The expedition was organized like an army, with Colonel Roosevelt as commander-in-chief. Determined to reserve the big-game shooting for himself and Kermit, he initially balked at hiring a white hunter to manage the trip. "I shall not be more than half satisfied if there are bullets other than my own in the animals that I kill," he said. "I don't intend to go into this as a sham." He was equally resolved to prevent the power struggles that might arise if he took a deputy. His advisers disagreed and held firm until he retained one of the men they recommended, a Scot named R. J. Cuninghame, reputedly the greatest elephant hunter in Africa. And when Cuninghame persuaded the Colonel that no white hunter working alone could manage a 250-man safari for a year, he was given permission to hire an adjutant. He chose his friend Leslie J. Tarlton, a superb marksman and half of the firm of Newland and Tarlton, safari outfitters in Nairobi.

Below the white hunters was a small cadre of specialists. Every safari employed a cook conversant with curries and the arts of roasting, stewing, and grilling game, and each hunter was assigned other assistants in pairs. Askaris—armed sentries uniformed in red fez, blue shirt, and white knickerbockers—stood watch in camp and maintained order on the march. Tent boys waited table, tidied up, laundered, filled the master's tub, and oiled his boots. Syces managed the horses. Gun-bearers spotted game, reloaded firearms and, when necessary, flung themselves between a bwana and an oncoming lion.

In a country with few horses or roads, the feasibility of a safari rested, quite literally, on the shoulders of the porter. He was "the unit of locomotion and the limit of possibility," Winston Churchill wrote after his safari in 1907. "How much can he carry? How far can he carry it? These are the questions which govern alike your calculations and your fate." A day's march of fifteen miles was considered humane, and by law a porter carried no more than sixty pounds.

Newland and Tarlton recommended thirty porters per hunter, but the Smithsonian expedition needed forty to support the scientific work as well as the hunting. Three porters were needed to carry Roosevelt's tent, and an elephant skull or a rhino skin made a load for four. The naturalists traveled with hunting gear and a bulky armamentarium: pliers and knives, measuring instruments, soldering iron, formaldehyde by the gallon, plaster of Paris, thousands of specimen tags, Higgins Eternal Ink, arsenic, axes, botany press and blotting paper, hundreds of traps, ton upon ton of salt for preserving an-imal skins, packing materials (excelsior, cheesecloth, burlap, twine), and numberless boxes and barrels for shipping specimens to the Smithsonian. Mearns traveled with an army medical field kit, a hefty canvas-covered chest bound in brass.

Along with a pittance of a wage, porters received blankets and other gear, a daily ration of one and a half pounds of rice or corn flour, and a uniform—boots, khaki shorts, and dark blue jerseys with the red Newland and Tarlton monogram. Like most safaris, this one employed porters from several tribes in the belief that language barriers would thwart any mutiny. Food was boxed in porter-sized loads, and the padlock on each box was either a com-ment on the character of porters or a pragmatic judgment of the relation-ship between poverty and theft.

THE COLONEL'S ARMY met him at Kapiti Plains Station. Cuning-hame had marched them down from Nairobi, and Sir Alfred Pease, the Roosevelts' first host, had rehearsed them to ear-splitting perfection in the hip-hip-hurrahs of the hero's welcome. TR and Kermit said their hellos as well as a few good-byes, to Dawson and the other reporters and to Selous, who was heading upcountry to hunt with friends.

The safari pitched its first camp on lion-colored stubble a few miles from the station. Thirteen large tents fronted their canvas village, and the Colonel's was easily identified by the Stars and Stripes floating overhead. After considering two tents from Abercrombie and Fitch, one waterproofed with paraffin and another of lightweight balloon silk, he selected an English model of green waterproof canvas, twelve feet wide and nine feet high at the roofline. A fly provided a modicum of insulation. And when the flap above the door was unfurled, it made a passable porch roof, under which Roo-sevelt dined and wrote. Mosquito netting, canvas carpet, and cot minimized fraternization with insects. Laced to the back of the tent was a small com-partment outfitted as a bathroom, complete with tub. For a man accus-tomed to camping in the American West, where he had slept in the open on a tarp, the tent was "almost too comfortable," he told the readers of *Scrib-ner's*. With Selous he was more candid: the tent made him feel "a little ef-feminate." Of the dozen other large tents, one served as a dining hall, another as laboratory. The rest housed the naturalists and the white hunters or sheltered horses. Staked in neat rows behind the big tents stood sixty smaller ones for the natives.

The army's meat would be shot in the field, and other food would come out from Nairobi as needed. To these stores Roosevelt had added a long list of comestibles from London: coffee and tea, sixty-five pounds of tinned sausage, beef, brawn, lamb's tongue, pâté, sardines, and cod roe. There were canned vegetables (corn, butter beans, baked beans, canned tomatoes), pickles from H. J. Heinz, chutney, seasonings (salt, white pepper, curry powder, and dried onion), and seventy-two cans of pea soup. Safari memoirs of the period mention the lust for sweets that overtook a hunter in the bush, where fresh fruit was scarce. The Colonel came prepared, with eighteen pounds of chocolate, fifty-six pounds of dried fruit (apricots, pears, apples, plums), three dozen puddings (apple as well as the traditional plum), and ninety-two pounds of jam.

TR carried dental floss and nine pairs of eyeglasses, and he and Kermit were armored head to toe: helmets against the sun, slickers against the rain, mackinaws and greatcoats against the cold, leather gloves and leather-patched trouser knees against knives of grass, close-fitting trousers against the ubiquitous tick. A safari hunter needed boots with soles that would not slip (rubber or rope, not leather), and TR required footwear with a precisely calibrated fit. The strenuous life was lived on surprisingly delicate feet; his skin, said Kermit, was "as tender as a baby's."

Expecting six weeks of spring rains and wanting to ease into the physical arduousness of hunting, Roosevelt had arranged to do his early shooting in relative comfort, at farms owned by friends of his English friends. He went first to Sir Alfred Pease's Kitanga, seven thousand acres draped over the Mua Hills outside Nairobi. A former member of Parliament and an excellent hunter, Pease and his wife, Helen, and their daughter, Lavender, raised ostriches. A flock could be started with a few eggs pilfered from a nest, the birds fed on wild sweetpeas, and as long as plumes stayed in fashion, the farmer could turn a profit.

Kitanga's chief attraction to Roosevelt was its inexhaustible supply of lions, which favored the locale because it swarmed with easy prey. His desire to shoot a lion verged on obsession, and he rarely spoke of it without adding that he did not expect to succeed, as if he felt a need to curb his passion and ease an inevitable disappointment. In the hunting world's unending debate over the relative dangers of pursuing lions, rhinos, elephants, and African buffalo, Roosevelt sided with those who cast their votes for the lion. He wrote of killings and maulings by lions, encounters with the mauled, and a visit to a Nairobi churchyard where seven victims of lions lay in their graves. A cold reading provokes the ungenerous thought that TR exaggerated the peril to puff up his valor, a suspicion that deepens a few pages later, when the reader finds the author in the confines of a ravine, trying to rouse a lion, any lion, napping in the brush. But in with the swagger was a sharp fear for Kermit, whose boyhood hunting excursions had not tested him against any creature more vicious than a duck.

The lion-stalking at Pease's got off to an unpromising start, undoubtedly a surprise to both host and guest, who occupied a broad swath of common ground. Pease loved the outdoors, was a fine shot, and had written a classic of hunting literature, *The Book of the Lion*. The two men were virtually the same age and products of the same kind of family, aristocrats with a deep sense of civic duty. Pease had served in Parliament, and he shared Roosevelt's wariness of the power of the privileged few and his concern about man's destruction of nature. Growing up in northern England, Pease had worried about "the spoiling industrial hand" of his family, whose holdings included mines and factories. While most of the Peases took pride in the employment they created, young Alfred fretted that "the more they did this, the more families of boys would be produced for whom more and more mines and pits and factories would have to be made, till our lovely world would be ash heaps and chimneys and hideous houses under smoke clouds."

Before Roosevelt's arrival, Pease had been bombarded with unsolicited advice from all quarters, specious offers of help from locals angling to meet Roosevelt, and interference from colonial officials anxious to impress a former president of the United States. Nairobi dispatched the district game commissioner to suggest game-spotters on every hilltop so that no lion would go unseen. Pease, understandably piqued, replied that he planned to leave the hilltops free for lions and predicted that he would "find the big man lions enough to keep him busy for as long as he liked."

Roosevelt's uneasiness in his first days at Kitanga was a mix of doubt and impatience. Promised a lion, he expected one, and after two days of shooting gazelles, he announced that his schedule allowed only three more days for lions. Pease reassured him, but the absence of lions on the next day must have hardened the Colonel's skepticism. Much of the following day was drained away in waiting for the exuberant Kermit, who had thundered ten miles off in pursuit of a hyena, which was no one's idea of a trophy. On the last day, after a lionless morning and a lunch in the field, Sir Alfred led the party into a dry creek bed scattered with tawny bushes. Two obliging lions sprang from a tuft of brush, someone yelled "Shoot!" and TR killed them in two shots. The marksmanship proved more impressive than the lions, which were cubs, not the large, full-maned beasts he had envisioned for the floors at Sagamore.

At three o'clock, with waning hopes, they started back to the farm. The Colonel professed to be pleased with his lions, but Lady Pease could see that he was not. Sir Alfred cantered off to another creek bed, where he spotted the fresh tracks of two large lions. The hunters crept toward one bush and then another, shouting and throwing stones until they were rewarded with leonine growls. For a thrilling moment, TR did not know whether the beasts crashing through the brush would pounce or flee. They fled. Kermit fired at one of them and missed. TR felled the other on the first shot, he told his readers. "Crack! the Winchester spoke; and as the soft-nosed bullet ploughed forward through his flank the lion swerved so that I missed him with the second shot; but my third bullet went through the spine and forward into his chest. Down he came, sixty yards off, his hind quarters dragging, his head up, his ears back, his jaws open and lips drawn up in a prodigious snarl." Fearing a charge, TR, Kermit, and Sir Alfred all fired into its chest. "His head sank, and he died."

One big lion bagged, TR hastened to help Kermit with the second. To Sir Alfred's dismay the Roosevelts continued firing after it was out of range, delaying the pursuit. As soon as their fusillade ended, Pease ordered Kermit into the saddle, and they set off—at "a wonderful gallop," Kermit thought— after his lion. A lion can outrun a horse, but only for a time, and within two miles Kermit was close enough to fire again. Shot after shot missed. TR, who had followed with Lady Pease, tried a few rounds from his horse, then dismounted and killed the lion in two shots. The Colonel was "perfectly delighted," Lady Pease reported. "We got home to dinner at nine, and all went to bed very happy."

All, it seems, but Sir Alfred. Kermit had spent three dozen bullets and ten minutes killing his lion, a worrisomely long engagement with a wounded beast. The Colonel's bear hunts had refined his appreciation of risk, but his nineteen-year-old boy seemed almost driven to endanger himself. On another day, when TR went hunting elsewhere and left Kermit in Pease's care, Kermit capered off alone after an oryx and disappeared, setting off a panic.

Sir Alfred sent several men to look for him, and toward evening, just as Pease was rounding up lanterns and preparing beacons for the hilltops, Kermit turned up, surprised and a bit annoyed to find that anyone was worried about him. He had had a glorious day, pursuing the oryx till he lost it, then chasing a roan, and finally ending up at the Kapiti Plains train station, where he watered his horse and headed back to Kitanga. Kermit, Sir Alfred confided to his diary, was "a very keen nice boy, but a handful in the field."

In the evenings, when the visitors' Winchesters were safely stowed and the lions were off prowling the plains for dinner, Sir Alfred could relax, which he customarily did with Egyptian cigarettes and a few glasses of wine. He found Roosevelt a rewarding guest, "simple in his habits & wants— always kind, genial, courteous & tactful." Roosevelt's "great love of distinc- tion" and preoccupation with the world's opinion of him were also on dis- play, and he volunteered that he enjoyed his eminence. "Everyone likes to be important and to have power and influence," he told his host. Pease was startled by the vehemence of some of Roosevelt's views but took the frank- ness as a compliment after observing that Roosevelt had reserved his strong opinions until he felt comfortable with his host. Pease found him "most amusing about the German Emperor, whom he regards as half mad with conceit and though mainly theatrical, capable of being very dangerous."

The Peases had hoped to finish their house before Roosevelt's visit, but only the dining room had been fully plastered and painted. The Colonel en- deared himself to Lady Pease by assuring her that he liked the place be- cause it reminded him of homes in his beloved American West. Sometimes, from elsewhere in the house, she heard him calling Kermit to admire a de- tail that charmed him, like the rhino skull on the veranda. "Now isn't this just grand, Kermit!" she would hear him say. "I want you to come and look at this."

African Game Trails, the compilation of Roosevelt's pieces for *Scribner's,* is as much nature walk as hunting journal, and his description of the view from the Peases' veranda shows his joy in the natural world and his desire to bring it to life for his readers. He wrote about the ostriches and told of flat- topped acacias and the prickly, aromatic mimosa, source of the mythic thorn in the lion's paw. There were lilies in orange and red, tall bushes of pink flowers that looked like jasmine and smelled like narcissus, and blos- soms reminiscent of morning glories and lilacs. Late in the day, gazing across 120 miles of plains and hills, he could watch the white peak of Mount Kilimanjaro flare red in the sunset before the sky darkened to violet and gave him the magic of a night filled with constellations of both hemi-spheres, the Southern Cross and the Great Bear "upside down and pointing to a North Star so low behind a hill that we could not see it."

In their seventeen days with the Peases, the Roosevelts hunted, TR wrote his first articles for *Scribner's*, and Kermit plunged into his photographic du-ties, occasionally staying up till one-thirty in the morning to develop pic-tures in his tent, a special model lined in red for service as a darkroom. On a single day at Pease's, TR killed two giraffes, an eland, and a rhino. Kermit bagged a cheetah and gamboled on horseback in a pack of giraffes until he found his target, a big bull, while Sir Alfred tested his horsemanship by rid-ing along under the midriff of another. "[N]othing makes you realize the immensity of giraffes more than galloping under them," he wrote; "it is a most curious sensation of littleness." Unlike his guests, who would shoot nine giraffes on their safari, Pease could not make himself take aim at them.

Lady Pease saw in the Colonel a "sympathetic heart united to courage, good sense, and intelligence," a combination that amounted to "a streak of genius," she thought. "I do not wonder the American people love him." Sir Alfred viewed him as a great man who knew how to "be a boy and enjoy things like a boy." But it was exhausting to care for such a boy. To plan and lead the hunts, Sir Alfred had stayed up late and risen early, constantly "fix-ing up things, sending notes and arranging for horses, meals and all de-tails—so that with Nellie and Lavender's splendid help, our guest has never had to worry about a single thing but his sport." Pease was too gentlemanly to show even a hint of strain, and TR departed in bliss—"devoted" to the Peases and convinced that whatever came next, he would have no happier weeks in Africa.

WHILE THE ROOSEVELTS HUNTED, the naturalists gathered. Lor-ing and Mearns were bivouacked nearby, collecting birds and small mammals. Loring combed a valley, Mearns worked his way up the sur-rounding hills. Heller was suffering the first of many bouts of "rhinoceritis," his name for the breakneck job of keeping up with the hunters, who to-gether killed nearly seventy big-game animals at Kitanga. "The preservation of large mammals under men who lead the strenuous life in their pursuit is a terrifically absorbing occupation," he noted dryly.

Racing predators and decay, Heller and his native crew skinned the beasts, rubbed salt into the hides, rolled them up, and packed them in bar-

rels of brine for shipment to Washington. "Six Wakambas, with their inci-
sors filed to sharp points, are the men who have come to my relief, and saved
all the skins for science and the U.S.A.," he informed the Smithsonian. "At
the pace we are going I am sure you will be able to fill every nook of the new
museum with large animals."

From Sir Alfred's the hunters moved on to Juja, a farm owned by
W. Northrup McMillan, heir to an American industrial fortune, and his
wife, Florence, daughter of an English diplomat. The McMillans also
owned one of the few grand houses in Nairobi and kept a home in London,
where the foyer was guarded by a terrifying stuffed lion, teeth bared, tail
aloft, and powerful legs poised in a run. Florence had blasted it into eternity
with two shots from her Mauser. Northrup, tall and bulky, was an enthusiastic animal breeder whose experiments were increasing the hardihood of the
mule. He also removed the hump from native cattle by crossing them with
English bulls, and the hybrids yielded notably tastier meat. But as there is
no pleasing all the people all the time, settlers who had acquired a taste for
hump grumbled about its disappearance.

Nor did the settlers entirely approve of Juja, which was large and luxe—
twenty thousand acres with vast cornfields and its own electric power plant.
The farmhouse was plain-faced, but inside were amenities rarely seen at the
time in the heart of Africa—telephones, magazines, and vase upon vase of
cut flowers—and the majordomo had instructions to offer refreshments to
all passersby. In the eyes of colonial officials the McMillans' openhanded-
ness made Juja an attractive nuisance, a haven for the class of whites they described as "work-shy."

At Kitanga the Roosevelts had shot twenty-two species of big game; Juja
added the hippopotamus and the leopard. TR hoped to kill the first of every
species bagged on safari and assumed that when the animals went on display, the ones tagged "Shot by Theodore Roosevelt" would have special
value. The first hippo was his, but chance gave the first leopard to Kermit in
a dangerous encounter that ended with the mauling of one of the porters.
Out hunting lions with McMillan when the leopard charged out of
nowhere, Kermit fired quickly enough to stop it, although not straight
enough to kill it, and it attacked the porter. No more shots could be fired
until the porter had worked himself free.

For TR the surprise of safari life was its ease. In the provisioning he had
vetoed white tablecloths and china as effete, but he had not been roughing
it with the Peases and the McMillans. He hunted comfortably, spending

most of the day on horseback, while his retinue spared him the tasks that were tedious and enervating. The hunting had been unexpectedly success-ful—so successful that he and Kermit occasionally stayed out of the field to allow Heller and the skinners to catch up.

The Colonel devoted many of his days off to writing for *Scribner's*. He worked on a folding camp table, composing with indelible pencil on custom-made tablets with two carbon sets beneath each sheet. Copies of each completed article went into blue canvas envelopes carried by native runners to the post office in Nairobi. At Kitanga and Juja he wrote six arti-cles in as many weeks, a pace that put him well ahead of his deadlines.

Except for being fiercely homesick for Edith, "I am absolutely con-tented," he wrote his sister Bamie. Contented he was, tan and healthy, and free of all cares but Kermit, who was "a very big load of responsibility, and keeps me worrying all the time," he wrote Corinne. Edith, certain that Theodore was exaggerating the risks, wrote Kermit that the family referred to Father as "the hen with one chicken."

Quartered in a cottage near Juja, the naturalists were trapping small ani-mals and shooting birds for the museum. "We are having the times of our lives," Mearns wrote his family. He was doing triple duty as physician, natu-ralist, and bookkeeper, so it was his lot to inform the Colonel that the expe-dition's treasury would be empty by the end of July, seven months too soon. The problem was not profligacy or Roosevelt's habitual inattention to money, it was simple miscalculation. The last of their outfitting, done in Nairobi, had been unexpectedly expensive, and the battalion of porters would be a continuing drain. By Mearns's estimate, carrying the fieldwork to its planned conclusion in March 1910 would take $25,000 beyond the $30,000 already raised.

Roosevelt asked Mearns to deliver the news to the Smithsonian, and after giving Mearns's report a ten-day head start, he sent his own letter. It was a masterpiece of Rooseveltian cajolery, brimming with appreciation and self-congratulation, hinting at the dire, and proposing alternatives in a manner calculated to make his choice seem the only sane course. "Three better trav-eling companions, or more energetic and efficient zoological collectors, I don't believe you would find on the broad earth," he wrote Charles Walcott, the head of the Smithsonian. "We are making, I think I can say, a great trip; but one cannot make a proper trip of this kind . . . without paying for it." Grateful as he was for the Smithsonian's backing, he stressed that he too was doing his utmost. He had advanced $7,000 to cover unforeseen expenses, and he and Kermit were donating all but a few of their trophies to the Smithsonian. His very presence on the safari was an asset, he said, as many doors were opened to the naturalists "because of the desire that people have to be courteous to me." In his judgment it would be a pity to halt the naturalists in the middle of their admirable work. If that proved necessary, he intended to carry on with the hunt but would not be able to afford to send specimens to Washington.

Roosevelt suggested soliciting Andrew Carnegie and took aim, as he had once before, at Walcott's institutional pride. If Walcott could not raise the money, perhaps the American Museum of Natural History would split the cost in exchange for half the specimens. Roosevelt was confident that there would be plenty of stuffable hides to go around, and "each museum could have a series of groups of mammals shot by me."

So began a tense three-way chess match, with Roosevelt pitting Walcott against the Smithsonian's archrival, Walcott maneuvering delicately to avoid displeasing a former president, and Carnegie gambling that if he underwrote the rest of the expedition, Roosevelt would do him a favor. Disturbed by the arms race between Germany and England, Carnegie, now in his seventies, was devoting himself and $25 million of his fortune to pursue his dream of a world court where nations would routinely submit their disputes to arbitration. The courthouse and library at The Hague were built largely with his money, and he wanted Roosevelt to promote arbitration and disarmament with the kaiser and the other European leaders he would see on his way home from Africa.

By the time Walcott's letter reached Carnegie, Carnegie had already heard from Roosevelt, who had upped the request from $25,000 to $30,000. Carnegie offered to add $5,000 to the $2,750 he had given before the expedition and told Walcott to seek the rest elsewhere. Others would give again to the Roosevelt safari, Carnegie said, "if they know he wishes it. . . . We must not fail. . . . We must not let our greatest man suffer, remember."

Walcott followed Carnegie's advice—slowly. Much of the original $30,000 had been pledged rather than given outright, and he had just sent a round of letters asking the donors to make good. Wanting a seemly interval between appeals, he approached only three contributors. With their money and Carnegie's he could forward $10,000 to Nairobi and would collect the rest in the fall. "I will do all in my power to sustain the expedition to the end," he promised Roosevelt. But he would not ask the American Museum of Natural History to share the expense. He wanted the Smithsonian to have sole credit for the expedition and to be unencumbered in distributing any surplus specimens.

Toward the end of May, TR and Kermit and Heller went into Nairobi to stock up for the bush and ship the first sixty-eight skins to the Smithsonian. At TR's request Heller also dispatched a scientific description of an apparently new species of burrowing mole. The Colonel wanted the discovery published. The love of distinction Pease had noticed included a drive to be first in everything, even moles.

DRUMS BEATING, flag flying, flutes and whistles piping, the Colonel's party and a half-mile-long string of two hundred porters headed west in early June. A trio of rifle-carrying askaris at the rear ensured that no one fell behind or deserted. Also in the procession was Warrington Dawson, who had been invited back as secretary and journalist. Roosevelt told himself that Dawson and his typewriter would speed the writing for *Scribner's*, and with Roosevelt's permission, Dawson would send an occasional news bulletin. Years later Dawson claimed that when other members of the safari objected to the presence of a reporter, Roosevelt had cut them off, saying, "Dawson's in trouble in a new country and has no friends except Kermit and myself." Dawson's unnamed trouble was undoubtedly the recent death of his mother. Roosevelt was keenly sensitive to the grief of others, and his invitation may have been prompted by memories of his own early losses—the death of his father and, a few years later, the deaths of his wife and his mother on the same day, February 14, 1884.

In the wild at last, with the comforts of Juja and Kitanga behind them, the safari trekked for five days across a terrestrial frying pan, sleeping when the sun was high and marching by night to the shrieking of jackals. Beyond lay the Sotik and Lake Naivasha, rich hunting grounds that would add a thousand birds and small mammals to the Smithsonian's collection. TR had the glandular frisson of killing a charging lion, and in a small wooden boat on Lake Naivasha he and Kermit found themselves looking into the jaws of a furious hippo. Kermit, arms braced on the gunwale, snapped photographs while his father fired from behind. The dead hippo was lashed to the boat and hauled back to camp.

Until their long interlude in the Sotik and at Lake Naivasha, the eight white men in the party—the Roosevelts, Dawson, the naturalists, and the white hunters—had rarely camped ensemble for more than a day or two.

Settled in for a few weeks, they had time for Kermit to bring out his mandolin and for Cuninghame and Tarlton to tell stories of their African hunts.

Cuninghame was lean and tan, and to judge by photographs, a manly man at home in his body. He had a dark, bushy beard, and the pipe smoke that issued steadily from the center of it gave him a faintly volcanic air. Cuninghame's leadership of the safari won favorable notice in *African Game Trails*, although the author did not pause to explain a white hunter's responsibilities. He was expected to be a superb shot, speak Swahili, and possess a minute understanding of the habits of the game—knowledge that virtually guaranteed his clients the quarry they desired.

Tarlton was a red-haired, blue-eyed Australian with a deeply cleft chin and a droll sense of humor. Remembering a fierce craving for sweets on one safari, he told of nearly killing a companion who ate their last jar of jam. He regretted his loss of nerve, he said, for it had cost him a chance to write a safari memoir called *The Jam That Jerked Him to Jesus*.

Roosevelt believed that life in the wild peeled a man to his essence. Exhausted and aching, famished, afire with insect bites, a man lost his power to pretend. If a safari with cooks and tent boys did not impose the same tests of character as a hunt alone in the Badlands, a year of African camping undoubtedly showed Theodore Roosevelt as he was. And he was, it seems, an ideal companion—"always jolly, not in the least domineering" and "positively the finest man to be in camp with that I have ever met," Loring wrote his family.

Roosevelt observed the natives with the same keen eye he cast on birds and beasts, which is to say that he took in physical detail and assumed a low degree of intelligence. His concern for the porters' fatigue and thirst is the only hint of an effort to enter into native ways of thinking. The words "naked" and "savage" appear even more often in *African Game Trails* than in his books on the American West, and his repertoire of ideas about the natives was small. Africans, he thought, were like children—wild, pagan, heedless of the morrow. When water was scarce, they drank their allotments in one draft, and pastoral tribes who measured wealth by the size of the herd often chose starvation over the sale or slaughter of their livestock. Watching the Kikuyu gardeners at Juja, he had been amused to see that the blankets they were given to conceal their privates were worn instead as capes and veils, a choice he interpreted as foible rather than protest. He would express unqualified admiration for only one tribe, the Nandi, who hunted lions armed with nothing but spears.

Native opinion of the whites on the Roosevelt safari survives in a handful of nicknames. The Colonel was Bwana Tumbo (Master with a Big Stomach) and Bwana Makuba (Great Master). Knowing of kings but not presidents, the natives were puzzled by Bwana Makuba's standing. *Americani* was their word for the loincloths the missionaries made of New England calico, so "President Americani"—king of the loincloths—he became.

Kermit was sometimes Junior Bwana, and sometimes Bwana Merodadi, the Dandy, which in Swahili means intelligent as well as fashionable. He was deserving on both counts. The natives could see his aptitude for languages, and his cork sun helmet, lined with green silk, was "a gorgeous affair," according to Dawson. At Harvard he once ordered four dozen monogrammed silk shirts from a tailor in China. On the voyage to Mombasa, he had bought his father some dress shirts after noticing that a family servant had packed the oldest, sorriest-looking specimens in his wardrobe, the ones evidently considered most suitable for a year among the savages.

Cuninghame's impressive whiskers earned him the title of Bearded Master. Certain that Loring's preoccupation with rodents and other small creatures was a testament to his cowardice, his first native helper ran away to escape the shame of working for such a man. "I lived for several months, despised, jeered at, and known only as Bwana Panya [Mouse Master]," Loring reported. Mearns answered to Moustache Man and Man Who Never Sleeps, in honor of his nocturnal specimen gathering. Heller was the Skin Bwana, and Dawson was christened Bwana Mazarowe (Master with the Trumpet Voice) after an unthinking outburst that scared away the game.

The diaries kept by father and son give no clue to the evolution of their relationship on safari. Kermit's contains an occasional paragraph about the day, but his diary and TR's are, in the main, terse notes to help them remember their kills. TR sometimes drew outlines of the animals he shot, adding dots to show where the bullets entered. The information was given at greater length in letters home, causing Archie Roosevelt, age fourteen, to complain that the hunters sent nothing but catalogues of death.

Together and separately father and son passed many hours reading the books in a collection TR had carefully assembled with money Corinne had sent for his last birthday. He began with a given of safari life, the sixty-pound limit on a porter's load. From the classics he selected fifty-odd volumes to be taken apart, trimmed at the margins, and bound anew in pigskin, the material he thought most likely to withstand the beating of a year on safari. The library's bookcase, fashioned of lightweight aluminum, was twenty-seven inches tall, ten inches wide, and five inches deep. In its oilcloth slipcase the Pigskin Library, as he called it, weighed a trig fifty-eight pounds.

TR read with the intensity he gave to everything else, all his wattage focused on the book. He read before going to sleep at night, on rainy afternoons, aboard trains and ships, and whenever he needed a few minutes' escape. The Pigskin Library was stocked with reading matter that took time to ingest—the Bible, Homer, Dante, Shakespeare and Milton, a dash of Euripides, medieval classics such as *La Chanson de Roland* and the *Nibelungenlied*, and a serving of English poets (Shelley, Keats, Browning, and Tennyson). He did not care for dramatic poetry but regarded Shakespeare's oeuvre, which fit into three small volumes, as the literary equivalent of a soldier's emergency ration—"the largest amount of sustenance in the smallest possible space." He took history too, which he enjoyed for narrative and ideas and the comfort of seeing that "our great-grandfathers were no less foolish than we are."

The frothiest selections were the poems and tales of Bret Harte, five novels by Sir Walter Scott, and samplings of Cooper, Twain, Thackeray, and Dickens. He disliked novels with unhappy endings, seeing no point to vicarious suffering unless it was instructive. Once attached to a hero and heroine, he was crestfallen if they did not marry in the end. He had already read, more than once, most of the books that went with him to Africa.

The Pigskin Library gave him "the utmost possible comfort and pleasure," he wrote Corinne. "Fond though I am of hunting and of wilderness life I could not thoroughly enjoy either if I were not able from time to time to turn to my books." He always carried a book into the field, reading under a tree during the noonday halt or next to a fresh kill as he waited for Heller and the skinners. To show his readers that pigskin had been the right choice for the bindings, he told them about slitting the throat of a deadly adder and tossing it into his saddlebag. He forgot about the snake, and when he found it days later, he discovered that it had bled on his *Nibelungenlied*. Blood, gun oil, dirt, sweat—the pigskin absorbed them all.

CONCEALED FROM EVERYONE ELSE at Lake Naivasha was the Colonel's homesickness. By the middle of July, he had killed every big-game species he wanted except an elephant and a white rhinoceros. "[H]ow glad I shall be to get home!" he wrote Bamie. He longed for Edith, and the

articles for *Scribner's* had become a chore. His prose flagged with his enthusiasm. The aquatic battle with the hippo was narrated with gusto, and Lake
Naivasha's bird life inspired lyric bursts, but the article about the region was
dark and defensive. He estimated that the dozen lions he and Kermit had
killed would save as many as eight hundred harmless animals such as zebra
and bushbuck. "Death by violence, death by cold, death by starvation—
these are the normal endings of the stately and beautiful creatures of the
wilderness," he wrote, as if he felt a need to justify the extent of the killing.
An ancient thorn tree set him to wondering about the tragedies it had witnessed.

Edith, unfortunately, had no sense of his loneliness, and his year on safari was a severe trial. "I really do believe that if it were not for the children
here I would not have the nervous strength to live through these endless
months of separation from Father," she wrote Kermit. Alone, she often felt
"done for," and constantly reminded herself that self-control was a "moral
muscle," strengthened by exercise. After months of struggling to radiate the
pleasantness the world expected of Mrs. Theodore Roosevelt, she decided
that for Christmas she wanted only the privilege of losing her temper.

In spite of Theodore's princely arrangements with *Scribner's* and *The
Outlook*, Edith was anxious about money. In 1908 the family had run
through $46,000, and she wrote Kermit that she feared she would not be
able to meet them in Khartoum at the end of the safari. "Don't say this to Father," she added. Theodore, guessing that the sheer size of his African expenses would corrode Edith's faith in their new financial security, asked
Ethel to loosen the family purse strings. "Don't let Mother economize in
foolish ways," he instructed. He saw no point in small savings that caused
big inconveniences.

With reassurances from Corinne's husband, Douglas Robinson, who
managed the Roosevelts' money, Edith decided to take Ethel and Archie
and Quentin to Europe for the summer and planned to minimize expenses
by spending a month with her sister, Emily Carow, who lived in Porto Maurizio, on the Italian Riviera. The trip began badly, with an offhand remark
from Theodore's dear friend Henry Cabot Lodge. Cabot chivalrously came
to New York to see them off but rather unchivalrously mentioned a letter in
which Theodore had said the excitement of a safari left no time for homesickness. Theodore had said the same to Edith, who took it to mean that she
was not missed, and she was furious with him for singing such a joy to Cabot.

Two weeks at sea restored Edith's equanimity, and as the holiday progressed she noticed a growing confidence in her ability to manage life without Theodore. She allowed Quentin to dispense with his thick knee socks and wander about in socks with garters, a look she named "knickerbockers à l'italienne." Her letters express no annoyance with the pack of reporters and photographers who came to Porto Maurizio to watch the Roosevelt children ride bicycles and splash in the sea. Edith ventured into the water herself and was seen moving gingerly across the stony shore, her feet evidently as tender as Theodore's.

From Italy she took the children to Paris, happily abandoning plans for touring Holland when they asked to stay in France. They went sightseeing with Henry Adams, charming explicator of the Gothic. Adams spent most of his time in Washington but summered in Paris and had taught himself medieval French history in the course of writing a book on Mont-Saint-Michel and Chartres. As curmudgeonly as Theodore was eupeptic, Adams complained about playing "dancing bear to Mrs. Roosevelt," but in truth he admired her and was fond of the children, Quentin in particular. For Ethel's eighteenth birthday, on August 13, he gave a party in a little palace on the Left Bank.

Paris also dispelled Edith's irritation with Theodore. From Dawson, who had just returned from Africa, she learned that Theodore was bored. He would not have a shot at the grand prize of safaris, the rare white rhinoceros, until January, when he reached the Congo. In the meantime he sought relief from ennui with visits to Nairobi every few weeks, a palliative Edith found "pathetic in the extreme." The news from Dawson gave her a fresh hypothesis for the maddening silences in Theodore's letters: he missed her but dared not say so for fear of losing his battle with the demon of homesickness. It was only a guess, but it was a sunnier guess than the one she had taken to Europe.

THREE

One White Man's Burdens

HOWEVER primitive Edith imagined Nairobi to be, it offered Theodore a degree of luxury unattainable on safari. When a man tired of eating bushbuck, he said, it was a joy to have "an interlude of thoroughly civilized life." In from the bush, TR and Kermit stayed at Chiromo, the grand villa owned by Florence and Northrup McMillan, and lived like pashas. Chiromo, set in a shaded park with a brook, was Eden with servants.

But Edith's intimations of Nairobi were not groundless. Even the authors of a frankly promotional travel guide confessed that the capital was, in a word, hideous. The vernacular architecture did not venture far beyond the tin shanty, and most public buildings were unhappy marriages of European form and African function. At Government House, hipped roof and veranda cohabited with Romanesque arches, medieval turrets, Tudor half-timbering, and Palladian windows.

On the map Nairobi seemed an ideal spot for a colonial capital—midway between Mombasa and Lake Victoria on the Uganda Railway and a mile above sea level, with a climate cool enough for Englishmen dreaming of what they called "a white man's country" in equatorial Africa. But maps did not reveal the interminable muck of the rainy season or summer's desiccation, cause of a chronic annoyance the settlers named "Nairobi throat."

Five years old in 1909, Nairobi was an anglicized version of the cow towns Roosevelt had known in the American West. The butcher doubled as cattle dealer, the accountant took in typing, and an establishment called the

Exchange trafficked in stocks, bonds, and firearms. Esthetes seldom roost in the wild, and in the absence of art, Nairobi entertained itself with pranks and midnight shooting matches. On one memorable evening, bets were laid to settle the question of whether a man could or could not jump a horse over a barbershop housed in a large tent. A man could not. Prostitution had spread across British East Africa along the railway, the fleshpots following the construction crews. In Nairobi, police shuttered all the local bordellos but one, an orderly house with an Asian madam and a clientele who referred to the place as the Japanese legation.

The capital was a contentious little cauldron of six hundred whites, eleven thousand blacks, and three thousand East Indians who had come to build the railway and stayed on as tradesmen. Blacks clashed with whites, Indians fought with blacks and whites, and whites, despite their slender ranks, battled one another. Winston Churchill's experience of the free-for-all may have inspired his later jest that democracy is the worst form of government except for all the others. During a visit in 1907, soon after his appointment as Britain's undersecretary of colonial affairs, he quickly discerned the problem: "Every white man in Nairobi is a politician." Apart from a shared determination to prevail over blacks and browns, East African whites seemed bound only by an unrequited love of king and country. Even as they protested the decision-making done on their behalf in England, it was England they longed to reproduce in Africa. Cricket and foxhunting were early imports, and Nairobi's railway station would have looked at home in Stoke-on-Trent.

TR and Kermit came into the capital from Lake Naivasha at the end of July for race week, an orgy of Englishness—polo matches, tennis tourneys, horse racing, luncheons, and parties. The familiar sight of whites in their summer finery elicited little comment from TR, but he was charmed by the crowds of Indian women in bright saris, Somalis on horseback, Kikuyu girls with faces painted to announce their marriageability, and a huddle of spear-carrying Masai.

Kermit gamely accepted an invitation to ride in the races, which were conducted by a turf club struggling valiantly with complications unknown at Ascot or Saratoga. On occasion a lion strayed onto the course, terrifying the horses, which reared and threw their riders. The climate disagreed with the horses, so no reward or punishment would induce them to speed. Nor did the grandstand quiver with suspense, for the settlers knew one another's mounts and easily guessed whether Wee Woman would nose out Gladys or vice versa. Kermit finished his half-dozen races to cheers and applause but near the back of the pack. He blamed the horses. His father concurred, writing the family that Kermit had raced with pluck and courage.

The week climaxed with a banquet in Roosevelt's honor. He had hoped that Africa would spare him such affairs, but having accepted innumerable favors from colonial officials, he could not graciously demur. On August 3, turned out in cutaway, TR rose before a crowd of two hundred to deliver a speech that might well have been made in the robes of a bishop. His experiences in the American West and the White House had convinced him that if "the government official does not understand that it is his duty to promote the welfare of the people, the sooner he gets out of the country, the better for all concerned," he said. "If the settler thinks he can sit quietly and abuse the Government officials, he will find that the country can spare him too." They were indispensable to one another, he said, and "failure to work together, [each] recognizing the difficulties of the other's task, means not only waste of effort but the possibility of far-reaching trouble."

It was an old hymn, but Roosevelt sang it from so deep in his heart that the banalities ascended to the plane of eternal truth. His listeners were thrilled. Years before, after sitting through just such a homily, his friend Thomas B. Reed, Speaker of the House, had archly congratulated him on his discovery of the Ten Commandments. Reed had many sympathizers, and their complaints always irritated Roosevelt. I *live* those platitudes, he would protest. Few of his critics understood the power of the spell cast by his conviction. The people—ordinary people, not politicians or intellectuals or financiers—liked Theodore Roosevelt for his rough-riding and trust-busting, but they loved him for knowing the best that was in them and making them feel they could reach it.

RACE WEEK OVER, the settlers scattered to their farms, and the safari left for Lake Naivasha and Mount Kenya. The expedition's finances had improved but were hardly secure. Walcott had wired $10,000 (half of it from Carnegie), enough to fund the scientific work through October. The Colonel pressed for a commitment and set a deadline: unless the naturalists received another $20,000 by October 1, they would not have time to outfit themselves for the last phase of their work. But whether the money materialized or not, the safari was already a scientific coup, Roosevelt assured Walcott. Mearns and Loring had gathered thousands of specimens, and with

Heller's first two shipments of skins and skulls, the Smithsonian would possess "a collection of large mammals such as has never been obtained for any other museum in the world on a single trip."

Twenty barrels and nine crates, each embellished with "T.R." in large white letters, reached Washington in mid-August. The monogram was the handiwork of newspaper photographers who had watched the cargo come ashore in New York and found it unphotogenic. Museum officials peevishly reminded the public that the safari was a Smithsonian expedition, not a Roosevelt expedition. Next came an apocalyptic rumor, untrue but widespread, that eggs of the deadly tsetse fly had been found in the skins and would be hatched for scientific experiments. Such bothers were easily disposed of, but unknown to the Colonel, the Smithsonian had deeper troubles. A tide of specimens sweeping in from three expeditions in Asia and from field studies in the United States had overwhelmed the staff. The museum also lacked the money and the room to mount the specimens.

The African expedition had become Walcott's bête noire. Except for Carnegie, who hoped to use Roosevelt to further his peace plans, most of the original donors declined to give again. And while Walcott probably knew nothing of the wish to enlist Roosevelt in the peace crusade, he was skittish about accepting Carnegie's new offer to put up the rest of the money. It was bad policy, he told Roosevelt. When an expedition was funded largely by one person, there was a risk that he would regard it as his rather than the Smithsonian's. For want of an immediate alternative, however, Walcott accepted $20,000 from Carnegie, and planned to repay at least a portion of it with funds to be raised elsewhere. Forwarding the money to Nairobi in October, Walcott asked Roosevelt to warn the naturalists that there would be no more. "They must distinctly understand that they are to keep within the $20,000." That was as close as Walcott dared come to giving a former president an ultimatum.

MOUNT KENYA, seventeen thousand feet high and permanently crowned with snow, is one of nature's grand impossibilities, a glacier on the equator. Commanding even when viewed from Nairobi, ninety miles south, the mountain promised elephants for the hunters and a rich assortment of specimens for the naturalists. Roosevelt was awed by the mental and physical powers of elephants and enthralled by the thought of killing one. The notion that elephants should be spared because of the wonder they inspired was "worse than silly," he thought. "The unchecked increase of any big and formidable wild beast, even though not a flesh-eater, is incompatible with the existence of man when he has emerged from the stage of lowest savagery." Wherever an East African game warden had banned the hunting of hippos, rhinos, buffalo, or elephants, they destroyed crops and menaced human life, he wrote.

As the killing went on, Roosevelt's defense of hunting grew more and more strident. After a phase of asserting that the hunter was essential to population control, he presented hunting as mercy killing, a humane alternative to a cruel death in the jaw of a predator or the prolonged agony of starvation. By the time he reached Mount Kenya he had decided that elephants and other large game animals were suitable targets because they obstructed the advance of civilization and because they might rampage at any moment. But the natives of the region, farmers of considerable sophistication, hunted elephants only occasionally, using pits and spears. And although they sometimes asked a passing bwana to shoot a rogue, their general contentment with primitive weapons suggests that the elephant was not the clear and present danger that the white man liked to suppose.

Still, the elephant was a formidable foe. It lived in jungles where the trees were close and tangled in vines and creepers. On his first elephant hunt, Roosevelt, with Cuninghame, Tarlton, and Heller, inched through the forest, crawling over logs and pushing past wet boughs and ferns. Native trackers studied spoor with Cuninghame and shinnied up the trees to look for swaying treetops, evidence of elephants moving below. Elephants see poorly but can pick up a scent two miles off, forcing hunters to stay downwind. A slight shift in the breeze could give them away, warning the elephants to move on.

The first day turned up no elephants, but the next morning Roosevelt's party picked up the trail of a herd. By noon hunters and hunted were separated only by a scrim of vegetation, and Roosevelt could hear the rumble of the elephants' stomachs. Minds cocked, the hunters stole along next to the herd for a half-hour. "It made our veins thrill," Roosevelt would tell his readers. When at last he caught sight of an elephant's head, thirty yards off, he studied it long enough to confirm that the tusks weighed more than the required minimum, then fired. The elephant stumbled, and Roosevelt fired again. "This time the bullet sped true, and as I lowered the rifle from my shoulder, I saw the great lord of the forest come crashing to the ground." Seconds later he and his empty shotgun faced a big bull ripping through the trees. Cuninghame fired twice, and the elephant wheeled, quickly disappearing in the jungle.

"I felt proud indeed as I stood by the immense bulk of the slain monster and put my hand on the ivory," TR would write of his first dead elephant. Together the tusks weighed a respectable 130 pounds. The skinners were soon whooping and dancing on the elephant's body, but when they set to work, they skinned assiduously. One squatted naked inside the carcass. Soon all were bloody, and red ribbons of elephant flesh dangled from the trees. After sundown, as the natives feasted and sang in the firelight, Roosevelt gazed at a young moon in a glittering sky and cooked his dinner. "I toasted slices of elephant's heart on a pronged stick before the fire, and found it delicious; for I was hungry, and the night was cold."

In the five hundred pages of *African Game Trails*, there is no more ecstatic passage. The adrenaline of the hunt, the gutting of the slain giant, and the blood-soaked natives seemed to throw Roosevelt's senses wide open and sweep him into the state called joy. By killing a lord of the forest, he showed himself a lord of creation, and for dinner he devoured the universe— elephant heart, song, stars, moon, the night itself.

THE ROOSEVELTS WOULD SHOOT eleven elephants in Africa. Without explanation they had abandoned their original plan to create a kind of ark of the dead, filled with pairs of big-game animals, and in the end their bag of 512 African animals included fifty-five species of large mammals, forty-five of them represented by at least three members.

Protests were few and quickly rebutted: "it is well to remember that he has never been a game butcher, and is not likely to have become one now," said the *New York Times* after TR's critics seized on a report that the Colonel had shot twenty big-game animals in a single day. The *Times* speculated that either the count had been exaggerated or the porters needed meat, and it chided the reporters in Nairobi for their prose. Instead of writing that Roosevelt had been out "shooting monkeys," why not say that he had "secured specimens of the colobus species"? Such a report would have been accurate and "not such unpleasant reading."

Unpleasant as the *Times* found the phrase, it proved to be a mild description of what could happen when a man secured monkey specimens with a gun. On one such errand Kermit and Warrington Dawson, with two Kikuyus and a Swahili, scrambled up hill and down, battled thorns and vines, and traipsed through acres of muck before Kermit got a shot at the rare green-faced monkey they had set out to find. He fired at two of them. One disappeared from sight. The other, wounded in midair, leapt from tree to tree, "quivering visibly," Dawson wrote in the log he kept on safari. Kermit chased after it and fired at the fur visible in the branches. "A husky half-groan, half-rattle reverberated with chilling horror through the trees; another scream of death, and a rustling of leaves." Twigs snapped, and then came "the dull thud of an inert body striking a great branch; and we saw our monkey, his white plume-like tail stained crimson with blood, caught in a fork."

The Kikuyus scampered sixty feet up the trunk. When one got within a few yards of the monkey but could go no farther, his partner handed him a long stick. "A moan more fearful than either of the others told us that the poor thing was not quite dead as the stick touched the bundle of fur in the fork," Dawson wrote. "The Kikuyu now had no choice but to climb cautiously out on the limb . . . and grasping the monkey by the tail, he dropped it to the ground." Kermit raced off in search of the other monkey, and Dawson followed, arriving in time to see it trembling in a tree until Kermit finished it off.

TR saw no need for euphemism or apology. The mounting pile of skins and skulls was easily defended in the name of science: a single specimen might be anomalous, but with eight or ten a zoologist could begin generalizing about the species. "I can be condemned only if the existence of the National Museum, the American Museum of Natural History, and all similar zoological collections are to be condemned," he said.

His wish to serve science was genuine but is not entirely satisfying as an explanation of his new hunting ambitions. After two months in Africa, TR was longing for Sagamore, and after three he and Kermit had herded all but a few of the desired animals aboard the Smithsonian's ark. Seven more months yawned ahead. He could not go home. Colonels did not desert, and he believed that his long absence from the United States was essential to Taft's success in the White House. Nor could he give in to his elephantine loneliness for Edith. Melancholy, like other bad feelings, was a beast to be met and slain. Africa was his fate, and hunting big game was Africa's readiest antidote to his ennui.

A century after Roosevelt's safari the death toll of 512 has the unmistakable look of slaughter. Fairness obliges the critic to exclude vermin and animals killed in self-defense or for the table, an adjustment that cuts the toll to about 250. The number is still hard to reconcile with his intentions before the safari and with the line he had chosen from the *Anglo-Saxon Chronicle* as an epigraph for *African Game Trails*: "He loved the great game as if he were their father." The dissonance between the profession of love and the killing lies not in the dissonance between the values of one era and another, or between the hunter and the foe of hunting, but in Roosevelt himself. Seeing himself as a lover of nature, he could not see himself as a butcher.

As a young man Roosevelt had allied himself with the hunter-naturalists, a new movement of men eager to distance themselves from the thrill-killers then exterminating the buffalo of the Great Plains and, in the process, turning public sentiment against hunting. In 1887 he and his friends founded the first American organization of hunter-naturalists, the Boone and Crockett Club. Members pledged themselves to "manly sport" with the rifle, exploration of the wild, the study and preservation of wildlife, and the exchange of ideas on hunting and natural history. By their restraint, the hunter-naturalists drew a line between kill and overkill, suggesting that as long as one hunted like a gentleman, hunting itself was beyond reproach.

In times past, Roosevelt observed, hunters knew hunting, zoologists knew laboratory specimens, and the casual wanderer of the woodlands loved nature without understanding it or getting close to its "wilder and more imposing forms." The hunter-naturalist was an outdoor Renaissance man: intimate with nature, self-sufficient in the wilderness, protective as a father, and able to write about hunting and nature with "interest and charm." In the field and on the page Roosevelt lived up to his ideal, and as president he gave the country its environmental conscience.

But the ideal of the hunter-naturalist and the manly sport advocated by the Boone and Crockett Club hinged entirely on one's definition of manliness. If manliness meant indifference to suffering, then hunting was indeed manly, one critic argued; if, however, it signified sympathy with all creatures and protection of the weak, hunting for sport was indefensible. The manly sportsman disdained traps and bait, and he held his fire when he thought he might wound an animal without killing it, but the argument that such sportsmanship put man and beast on an equal footing was absurd. The odds overwhelmingly favored the party with the rifle.

Even the soundest rationale for hunting, the need to keep animal populations in check once humans have altered the balance of nature, does not always hold. By TR's reckoning the seventeen lions he and Kermit shot had saved the lives of hundreds of herbivores. At least one English settler reckoned otherwise. "[H]e has done us an injury," the man told Loring, because farmers needed lions to thin the herds of zebra and hartebeest, which barged through fences and demolished crops. And the notion that delivering a swift death by bullet was more humane than leaving an animal to the haphazard cruelties of nature camouflages the darkest attraction of hunting, the power over life and death.

Theodore Roosevelt's intimacy with the wild, and his long acquaintance with the works of Charles Darwin, had led him to believe that nature gave humankind a stark choice: conquer or be conquered. As a boy he had read *On the Origin of Species*, and he knew the works of Herbert Spencer, whose phrase "survival of the fittest" allowed powerful men and powerful nations to believe that their might was proof of their superiority, and their superiority was proof of their fitness to rule the world.

Roosevelt's enthusiasm for conquest and imperializing dated from his ranching days in the 1880s. In *The Winning of the West*, one of his earliest works, he argued that whether the unsettled interior of the United States was won by force or negotiation, it must be won. "All men of sane and wholesome thought must dismiss with impatient contempt the plea that these continents should be reserved for the use of scattered savage tribes," he wrote. Although he counted himself an expansionist rather than an imperialist—interested only in fortifying the Americas against the territorial designs of Europe and Asia—he had gloried in the excursions that raised the American flag over Cuba and other points in the Caribbean, the Pacific outposts of Hawaii and Guam, and the Philippines.

Throughout his safari Roosevelt was sizing up the British Empire's management of its colonies in Africa, and at the end of November he settled in for a fortnight with Lord Hugh Delamere, one of the first Englishmen to see the possibilities for a white civilization in the temperate highlands of East Africa. Near forty, Delamere was a daredevil in the spirit of Kermit Roosevelt. As a boy his lordship had delighted in riding a bicycle full tilt downhill toward a brick wall, jumping off at the last second. He often appeared in Nairobi in bandages or a cast, and if he happened to be without, he was still easy to spot. He wore an outsized pith helmet beneath which hung a shoulder-length fringe of carrot-colored hair.

Equator Ranch, Delamere's spread a hundred miles northwest of Nairobi, had nearly bankrupted him in the beginning, but by the time Roosevelt arrived, its grain fields and livestock herds were thriving. It was famed for its butter (which liberated the colonists from tinned ghee), for Lady Florence Delamere's library, and for Lord Delamere's habit of inviting his Masai neighbors into his living room each evening for a chat. He disapproved of British efforts to create tribal reserves, believing that they consigned the natives to a sort of zoo and retarded the colony's growth. Delamere shared Roosevelt's convictions that the earth's resources were to be developed to the full, for the good of humankind, and that humankind would fare best by adopting the ways of the white man. To Roosevelt, the Delameres embodied "the high courage that one likes to think of as distinctive of the race," and he admired their decision to shoulder their share of what Rudyard Kipling called the "white man's burden"—the work of civilizing the savages.

But where Roosevelt and Delamere saw an imperative and a noble work in progress, Winston Churchill saw a "herd of rhinoceros questions—awkward, thick-skinned, and horned." Britain's desires were irrelevant, Churchill thought. "In the end Africa belonged to the Africans. The question was what they would do for it and what it would do for them." The settlers needed native labor to build up their enterprises, but the native wanted only to subsist. "Is the native idle? Does he not keep himself and pay his taxes? Or does he loll at his ease while his three or four wives till the soil, bear the burden, and earn his living? And if idle, has he a right to remain idle—a naked and unconscious philosopher, living 'the simple life' without cares or wants—a gentleman of leisure in a panting world?"

Often at odds with Churchill and the empire's other policymakers in London, Delamere was eager to impress Roosevelt in the hope that he would speak favorably of the settlers when he visited London after the safari. For months Delamere had been planning a hunt intended to give Roosevelt the honor of being the first white man to shoot a bongo, a large antelope that rarely emerged from the depths of the forest. The ground was thoroughly "rested," and elkhounds were imported from England to aid in the chase. After several luckless days in the field with Roosevelt, Delamere selected a set of ridges cut by three passes and took him out again. Delamere posted himself at the mouth of one pass, his guest at another, and a native archer at the third. Two bongos bolted down the archer's pass, crossing within a yard of him, apparently too close for the shot that was supposed to send them bounding toward Roosevelt. TR resigned himself to shooting monkeys, but Kermit kept after the bongo for days, doggedly following every trail his trackers could find. He came back with a cow and a calf and whatever laurels crowned the first white man to bag the bongo.

A WEEK BEFORE CHRISTMAS, under a bright moon, the Colonel sailed west across Lake Victoria to Uganda for a long march north toward the white rhinoceros, on the Belgian side of the Nile. On Christmas Eve, Kermit tried to kindle a celebratory flame by strumming carols on his mandolin and breaking out a tin of cigars, but he felt strange and a bit sad to find himself camped on the equator, with no snow and no stockings to open.

TR was as homesick as Kermit, and although he had kept his resolution to ignore American politics while he was on safari, politics had not ignored him. In July he had learned that Taft intended to replace Henry White, ambassador to France and the American diplomat Roosevelt admired most. The news came as a shock. Taft had assured Roosevelt that he wanted White to stay on. "It was, of course, not a promise any more than my statement that I would not run for president was a promise," Roosevelt wrote White. "But it was an expression of intention." Trusting that White would hold the letter in confidence, Roosevelt hinted that his sense of duty might oblige him to run for president in 1912. The chances of his return to politics were "infinitesimal," he wrote Lodge a few days after hearing from White. But infinitesimal, however small, was a species wholly different from "never."

A few weeks later, while Roosevelt was in pursuit of the white rhino, a native runner brought the dumbfounding news that Gifford Pinchot, chief of the U.S. Forest Service and principal architect of Roosevelt's conservation policies, had been dismissed. The runner had been sent by reporters hoping that TR would comment for publication, but the only message he sent back was a private note asking Pinchot to write him in care of the American embassy in Paris.

With three giant elands and nine specimens of the white rhinoceros, the big-game hunting came to an end. White rhinos were disappearing, he knew. After learning that Churchill had been reproved for shooting them in a reserve on the English side of the Nile, TR had quietly asked the Belgian government for permission to hunt the white rhino on their side of the river. He justified his bag of nine with the argument that museums needed "good groups" of them. And without explanation he broadened his mandate from one museum to three: the Smithsonian, the American Museum of Natural History, and the collection of heads and horns at the Bronx Zoo.

Roosevelt judged the expedition a landmark. Heller had preserved more than a thousand specimens of mammals, most of them large, while Loring and Mearns had added nearly four thousand small mammals, as many birds, two thousand reptiles and amphibians, and five hundred fishes. The director of the Smithsonian sent his congratulations, but the museum's enthusiasm never matched the Colonel's. Expenses had been high, and only a handful of the 11,397 creatures were new to science.

In Africa, Roosevelt had proved that he could eat cakes and have them too. He stayed off the political stage, but his *Scribner's* articles kept him in the spotlight. He spent a huge sum on his holiday, but his magazine work paid for all of it and, despite Edith's doubts, stabilized the family's finances. The power of the presidency was gone, but so far he had not missed it. The year with Kermit had been a joy. The boy's marksmanship was still mediocre ("rank," in Loring's opinion), but his daring and indifference to bat-filled swamps and gauntlets of thorn had made him "tougher than whipcord," TR boasted to Corinne. TR too was in excellent physical shape, and he had hunted to the limits of his desire. "I don't care if I do not fire off my rifle again," he told her.

On the morning of March 11, three days from Khartoum, Roosevelt was summoned from breakfast to watch a little navy coming at him full speed. It was the press. Wire service correspondents and newspaper reporters had chartered several steamers and organized a race for the first interview with the Colonel. The *Chicago Daily Tribune* man spotted him first, standing on deck, his bathrobe and pajama legs flapping in the wind. The reporters, coming for his pronouncements on American politics, would leave empty-handed. He grilled them one by one in his cabin and warned that any report of an interview with him would be denied. For publication they were allowed to say only that Colonel Roosevelt had no comment on political matters.

Lodge and Root had persuaded him not to say or do anything political until he came home and was fully briefed. Though disturbed by Pinchot's dismissal, he assumed he would campaign for Republican candidates in the fall elections in the hope of aiding Taft's reelection in 1912. "At present it does not seem to me that it would be wise, from any side, for me to be a candidate," he mused to Lodge. "But all this can wait."

FOUR

Into the Thick of Things

To travel with Theodore Roosevelt was to travel in a carnival led by a conjurer and trailed by an idolatrous throng. People were drawn by his energy and joy, qualities he possessed in quantities rarely found in persons over the age of eight. They wished for his courage, and if they did not always admire his pugnacity, they forgave it, for what was pugnacity but courage overspilling its banks? A conjurer beguiles by seeming guileless, and over the next three months Roosevelt would present himself as a former statesman on a grand tour, peregrinating from palace to palace, orating, collecting honors. Although few in Washington were deceived, the conjurer kept up the illusion, hoping, perhaps, to beguile himself.

TR and Kermit had planned to dress up for their reunion with Edith and Ethel in Khartoum on March 14, but a mix-up with luggage forced TR into a stained shirt of gray flannel and a khaki suit impervious to beautification after a year in the bush. Junior Bwana, the dandy, hid his dishevelment under a duster.

To Edith they looked splendid. Theodore had shed "that look of worry and care," she thought, and Kermit, although still "of the hatpin type," had gained muscle. He had also sprouted a wispy mustache.

Would she like him to shave it off? he asked.

She said it was lovely.

In a hail of kisses from Theodore, Edith announced that their son Ted, twenty-two, was engaged. When Ethel told her father that Ted's fiancée,

Eleanor Butler Alexander, would remind him of Edith, TR wrote her a welcoming letter and sent his congratulations to Ted.*

Pledged to silence on American politics, Roosevelt uncaged his political
energies on behalf of British imperialism. The petty warlords who long tyr-
annized Egypt and Sudan had been subdued by the English, but the natives
were calling for independence, and an extremist in their number had just
assassinated Egypt's prime minister for supporting new censorship rules imposed by the British. After only a day with his official hosts in Khartoum, the
Colonel agreed to lecture the native officers on their duty to uphold British
law. The Sudanese immediately protested, and the Colonel immediately returned their fire. Britain's successes in the region resembled his own struggle to build the Panama Canal, he said. Victory had come from standing fast
in a barrage. In blood and pounds sterling, the price of pacifying the region
had been immense, and Britain should resist the pressure to set a date for independence: "you are really ruling the country now and ruling it for its
good, using Egyptians and Sudanese as your instrumentalities. You must indeed have a genius for government when you can so well manage a strange
people like these."

The speeches in Sudan pleased his English friends, angered the natives,
and signaled his return to the political stage. By lecturing other governments, the conjurer pulled off the neat trick of keeping himself in the news
while honoring his promise not to comment on American affairs. On
March 20 he announced that the speech he planned to make when he
landed in New York in June would neither praise nor criticize the administration of William Howard Taft. There was no need for TR to announce the
speech, much less to characterize it, and the promise of neutrality was a
veiled insult: withholding support from his chosen successor was tanta-
mount to attacking him. Roosevelt was drawing a line between Taft and
himself, drawing it publicly, and drawing it less than a week after emerging
from his safari.

The Colonel's utterances in Khartoum preceded him to Cairo, where
they were received as an affront to the aspirations of the Egyptian people.
Anxious British officials put Roosevelt in a cocoon of bodyguards and asked
him not to mention the assassination when he spoke at Cairo University. He
refused. Everyone was thinking about the slaying, and if he did not speak of

---

* The Eleanor who married Ted is not to be confused with the one who married Franklin Delano
Roosevelt. Ted's wife became Eleanor Alexander Roosevelt. FDR's wife was Eleanor Roosevelt Roosevelt. Her father was Theodore Roosevelt's brother Elliott. FDR and Theodore were fifth cousins.

it, he would be branded a coward, he said. This Theodore Roosevelt, an English newspaper declared, had "a propensity to put himself into the thick of things."

The speech proved to be little more than a compendium of bland preachments on goodness until the end, when he condemned the assassination and declared that preparation for successful self-government was the work "not of a decade or two but of generations." He shot his point home with an Arab proverb: "God is with the patient, *if they know how to wait.*"

For two days students shouting "Down with autocracy!" marched in the streets near Shepheard's Hotel, where the Roosevelts were lodged. The protesters resented his assumption that everyone who favored independence approved of the assassination, and they were appalled by his suggestion that Egypt, progenitor of Western civilization, was unprepared to govern itself. Colonel Roosevelt, said one of his Egyptian critics, knew no more about the region than a tourist and had been "deceived by bad company, such as is always the curse of great men."

The second most interesting American at Shepheard's Hotel was Oscar Straus, ambassador to Turkey. The first Jew to hold a cabinet post, Straus had been appointed by Roosevelt to serve as secretary of commerce and labor. He had come to Cairo to talk politics and to show Roosevelt a sober, unsettling editorial in the *North American Review.* The voters of the United States had been hoodwinked, the *Review* said. They had "accepted Mr. Taft at Mr. Roosevelt's word" and expected him to stay the progressive course, but Mr. Taft's first year showed that Mr. Roosevelt's word had been broken, his judgment misplaced.

To progressives, it seemed that the new president had tacked hard to the political right. He had fired Gifford Pinchot, replaced Henry White, and gutted the cabinet after telling Roosevelt that he hoped Straus and several others would stay on. Taft had asked Roosevelt to let the cabinet members know of his wishes, and when Roosevelt asked why he did not tell them himself, Taft said he wanted them to know of his wishes but thought it best not to make promises.

That was Roosevelt's version of events, recounted several years after the fact. Taft left two versions, and in the one that found its way to biographers and historians—a letter written just before the inauguration to William Rockhill Nelson, publisher of the *Kansas City Star*—Taft said he had decided to fill his cabinet with lawyers. Roosevelt's administration had created a public demand for reform on several fronts, and Taft proposed to meet it by amending the relevant statutes. "The people who are fitted to do this, without injury to the business interests of the country, are those lawyers who understand corporate wealth, the present combination, its evils, and the methods by which they can be properly restrained," he told Nelson. Most of the new cabinet secretaries were honorable men, but they were also laissez-faire men, men from the grand duchies of American capitalism. Although Taft sensed that his choices would be sharply criticized, he believed he could accomplish more with the help of "conservative men who know what they are talking about" than with progressives clamoring for greater reform. "With more radical men I should split the party and do nothing," he said.

A year later, aware that Roosevelt felt betrayed by the cabinet purge, Taft angrily defended himself in a private talk with two reporters. He was the one who had been betrayed, he said. "Mr. Roosevelt told me that he would make absolutely no suggestion to me, but I told him that I did not want to be deprived of the privilege of consulting him. Notwithstanding his dec-laration of neutrality, Mr. Roosevelt did take great interest in the selec-tions, and, although, perhaps, he made no out-and-out request of me, I didn't have to be hit with a club ten times a day to understand the workings of his mind."

Watching the new cabinet take shape and hearing about it from the Roo-sevelt loyalists who gathered at his home, Henry Adams had reported to a friend that Taft was starting out with "a series of what the French call *bêtises*, stupidities which have thrown me into consternation." Adams said he might be wrong about Taft, but if so, "I am mistaken in company with everyone else. I am only an echo of underground society. . . . I have no candidates to offer, and no scheme to suggest; but if the new president is so bent on mak-ing a clean sweep of Roosevelt's men, why did we elect him expressly to carry on the Roosevelt regime?"

While Roosevelt was on safari, Taft had bungled his chance to lead Con-gress through a sorely needed economic reform. The Dingley Tariff, en-acted in 1897 to protect American manufacturers from competition with foreign producers who could undersell them, created big profits for industry but high prices for consumers. The tariff had passed when the Northeast's senators and congressmen, captives of the factory owners, persuaded their fellow lawmakers that it would also protect the high wages of American workers. It did, but only momentarily: between 1897 and 1909, prices rose 50 percent faster than wages.

After expeditiously making good on a campaign pledge to call a special session of Congress for tariff reform, Taft stood by while the high-tariff men merrily reshuffled their stacked deck. He did not want to antagonize either the progressive or the conservative wing of the Republican Party, he explained. Early on, Taft suspected that the conservative legislators' promise of substantive tariff reform might be insincere, but he did nothing to hold them to their word, and rather than veto the bill, he settled for a few trivial alterations, then pronounced it "the best bill that the Republican Party ever passed."

Taft loathed conflict of all sorts and frequently absented himself from the White House for long periods, crisscrossing the country and setting a presidential record for railroad travel—28,000 miles during his first year in office. He wanted to be the president of all the people and learn their views firsthand, he said, but the public began wondering if he was doing his job. Republicans in Congress complained about his inaccessibility, and when Democrats saw that he had overspent his travel allowance, they threatened to eliminate it from the next budget. Taft ignored the complaints. The trips were relaxing, and away from his wife, who fretted about his ever-increasing weight, he could eat without restraint. He now weighed 330 pounds.

Singularly deaf to the voice of the people, Taft pouted at their angry reaction to the revised tariff, while they in turn gaped at the changeling they had put in the White House. Before his nomination, "Taft always insisted he had no qualifications for the job," William Rockhill Nelson wrote TR in the spring of 1910. "We thought differently. But he was right and we were wrong. . . . The president must carry a big stick and be ready to fight. But when you come to think of it, you never saw Taft fighting with his nose all bloody and one eye hanging down on his cheek, and his front teeth knocked out."

The White House press corps, which Roosevelt had charmed and used to great effect, was a nuisance to Taft. "Must I see those men again?" he once whined to his secretary. "Didn't I just see them the other day?" Cut off from Taft, the newsmen cultivated other sources, many of them critical of his administration. The newspapers had treated Taft "with the greatest gentleness," Nelson told TR. "But he thinks he has been very badly treated and goes about sobbing over it publicly. A crybaby won't do."

Failed presidents attract few biographers, and the handful who have dissected Taft in search of explanations for his dismal presidential performance have wondered in exasperation how Roosevelt ever could have considered him fit for the presidency. Taft was indolent, irresolute, dependent, and undone by opposition and criticism—a dooming combination. But the Taft that Roosevelt knew had distinguished himself as governor-general of the Philippines, problem-solver in Cuba and Panama, and secretary of war. Under Roosevelt's energetic leadership, Taft kept his lassitude in check, and his other shortcomings easily could have manifested themselves as virtues. A dependent man makes an excellent lieutenant, for he is happiest when carrying out the orders of others. And a man who shies away from conflict can be an exceptionally agreeable colleague. TR thought his friend Will had "the most loveable personality" of anyone he had ever known.

Transfixed by Taft's deficiencies and Roosevelt's misjudgment, biographers have not probed the deeper question of what happened to Taft between his decades of success and his sudden, total failure. Taft was a man who thrived by anchoring himself to intimates and striving to please them by doing what they thought best, and in the standard telling of the tale, Taft's course had been set by a voracious, controlling wife who pushed him toward the presidency to gratify her own ambitions. Helen Herron Taft ("Nellie" among family and friends) had yearned to be first lady since a girlhood stay in the White House of President Rutherford B. Hayes. She had grown up in comfortable circumstances in Cincinnati, studied chemistry and German at Miami University in Ohio, and taught school after graduating from college. Born a century too soon for a career of her own, she put her energy and intelligence into the rise of William Howard Taft.

Nellie's efforts were fully supported by his mother and his three brothers. Will's only ambition was to be chief justice of the Supreme Court, but the family often discussed their presidential aspirations for him. When Roosevelt offered him a seat on the court in 1902, his brother Charles encouraged him to take it but not to feel obliged to honor the custom of staying for life. His mother urged him to hold out for chief justice. Associate justices were poorly paid, and at forty-six he was too young for such an inactive life, she wrote him. "I would rather see you fighting corruption in the Senate, or winning prizes in the open arena at the Bar."

As early as 1903 Roosevelt began encouraging Taft to consider the presidency, and three years later, when they had their first serious talk about it, the possibility seemed so fantastical to Taft that he reported the conversation to Nellie as if he were awaiting orders from her or TR: "He wants to talk to you and me together. He thinks I am the one to take his mantle and that now I could be nominated."

Taft was not Roosevelt's first choice. TR considered Elihu Root more qualified, but Root was too closely identified with Wall Street to appeal to the country as a whole, and the asperity of his wit intimidated all but a hardy few. On one occasion, as the Big Stick wondered aloud if the American diplomatic corps should follow the European tradition of dressing in uniform, Root swiftly killed the idea by musing that the American version would have to include coattails embroidered with a sprig of mistletoe. TR also considered Charles Evans Hughes, whose reforms and straight-as-string governorship of New York had won him a national following among progressives, but Hughes seemed to radiate cold. Taft was the sun itself and had excelled as judge, executive, and diplomatic troubleshooter.

But in the fall of 1907 TR began to wonder if he had chosen the right man. Roosevelt often had a private chat with a reporter while the White House barber gave him his midday shave, and on October 30 he summoned Gus Karger, Washington correspondent of the *Cincinnati Times-Star*. The conversation was obviously meant to find its way back to Will and surely did, as the *Times-Star* was owned by his brother Charles. When Roosevelt said he was puzzled by the Republicans' lack of excitement for Taft's candidacy, Karger explained that the party's chieftains were waiting until they were certain that the Rough Rider would keep his promise not to run again. TR said he had no wish to run but would do it if the party seemed likely to choose a conservative candidate. If Taft were nominated, he would honor his pledge, but he considered it a sacrifice, he said, and "I do not wish to have made it in vain, by paving the way to the selection of a successor not in sympathy with the politics of my administration."

In January 1908 TR's advisers warned him that if he did not settle on a candidate and start promoting him, the electorate would conclude that he meant to run again himself. Taft still longed to be chief justice, but with no sign that the presiding chief planned to retire, he allowed Roosevelt to talk him into running for president.

Two months into the Taft administration, the first lady had a stroke. She collapsed on May 17, 1909, a few hours after watching their son Charlie, age eleven, have an operation on his adenoids. The surgery was a success, but Nellie saw a great deal of blood, and Charlie emerged from anesthesia in hysterics. Her speech was seriously impaired, she was subject to fainting spells, and she was unable to function as first lady for more than a year.

The stroke was Will's third major blow in eighteen months. His mother died in December 1907. Roosevelt disappeared into Africa. Now Nellie was powerless to help him, and there was little he could do to help her. The stroke paralyzed them both.

The fullest picture of the Tafts' unhappy life in the White House comes from the letters of Archie Butt, who stayed on as military aide when Roosevelt left office. A career soldier and twice a gentleman (officer and Southerner), Captain Archibald Willingham Butt was assigned to the White House in the spring of 1908 and stayed for four years. As a physical being, Archie Butt resembled nothing so much as a tropical bird—a ginger-crowned, broad-breasted popinjay—readily identified by the gaudy blue and gold plumage of his dress uniform. With piping, epaulets, two columns of brass buttons, and a lasso's worth of gold braid slung over one shoulder, the Captain had no need for accessories, but he sometimes added a sword. Fearing that a diary might fall into other hands in Washington, he recorded his experiences in long letters to his family. "No one knows how [he] suffers over his wife's illness," he wrote his sister-in-law, Clara Butt, in the spring of 1910. "He bears up beautifully under it, but as the weeks go by and there does not seem to be any permanent improvement, his hope sinks pretty low at times."

Roosevelt would soon be home, but plainly not in his old role of anchor. Gifford Pinchot was on his way to Italy to see him, and Taft believed the rumor that Pinchot was making the trip at Roosevelt's request. "It would seem strange to me for Roosevelt to do that," Taft said to Butt, "but he may want to hear from him, first hand, Pinchot's side of the case."

Roosevelt, with his usual scrupulous daring, had stopped half a hairsbreadth short of issuing an invitation: "I do wish I could see you," he wrote Pinchot. "Is there any chance of you meeting me in Europe?"

Taft might have sent a note asking Roosevelt to reserve judgment until they could talk about the dispute, a tangle of claims and counterclaims involving coalfields in Alaska. Instead Taft declared himself helpless. "Of course, I can say nothing until he asks me," he sighed to Butt. It was a curious assumption, given his affection for TR and the prerogatives of the president of the United States.

THE ROOSEVELTS' ITALIAN TRAVEL PLANS called for quiet—a bit of sightseeing in Rome, a reprise of a few honeymoon days in Liguria, and the seclusion of Porto Maurizio, with Edith's sister. Nothing went as planned. A few weeks before their arrival in Rome, Charles W. Fairbanks, vice president of the United States during Roosevelt's last four years in the White House, unwittingly offended the pope by calling first on another vicar of Christ. The faux pas might have been overlooked had the cleric been a friend of the Vatican, but he was the Reverend Doctor B. M. Tipple, an American Methodist Episcopal divine who had settled in Rome to proselytize and preferred insulting the papacy to spreading the joyous creed of John Wesley. Vatican officials canceled the pope's audience with Fairbanks and insisted that Roosevelt see the pope before he saw Tipple. Negotiating privately with the Vatican's secretary of state, Roosevelt's aides asked that the condition be dropped. The Vatican refused. Roosevelt extricated himself as decorously as he could, saying that he recognized the pope's right to receive whomever he chose but not his right to dictate the itinerary of an American citizen.

After a day or two of unsuccessfully eluding crowds of the curious, Theodore and Edith gave up their second honeymoon and fled to Porto Maurizio, where they were not allowed to retire until the Colonel had been given a parade and made an honorary citizen of Italy. Taft, still unable to bring himself to write to Roosevelt, sent a telegram thanking the village for its homage to an illustrious American. As an attempt to close a breach, the gesture was tardy, wan, and symptomatic of Taft's aversion to conflict.

Sequestered at last in a villa near Emily's, the Colonel burrowed into his correspondence and awaited Pinchot. Roosevelt and his secretaries worked on the terrace in the warm spring sun, composing replies to hundreds of supplicants in search of autographs, blessings, advice, and money.

Pinchot arrived in Porto Maurizio late on April 10 and set off at nine the next morning for his meeting.

How did he feel? asked the newsmen.

"Like a fighting cock," he said.

In fact he was suffering from a whanging toothache.

Tall, fit, elegant, Gifford Pinchot had a face with features so fine he could have modeled for coinage. Like TR, he was a patrician moralist with a strong ethic of service. A great-grandfather had been speaker of the House, and Gifford's father, James Pinchot, was a public-spirited New Yorker in the mold of the elder Theodore Roosevelt, whom he had known. Both men had raised money for the Statue of Liberty's pedestal and were founding patrons of the American Museum of Natural History.

Seven years younger than TR, Pinchot was one of the first Americans to study forestry, a new discipline dedicated to the proposition that a forest would last forever if the pace of logging and planting were properly regulated. He became chief forester of the United States in 1898, at the age of thirty-three. Pinchot had entered the Boone and Crockett Club under Roosevelt's auspices, and when Roosevelt was elected governor of New York he asked Pinchot to help him modernize the management of the state's natural resources. In those days Pinchot had no more political cunning than an astronomer, TR said, but once TR reached the White House and the two of them sketched their grand design for conserving the nation's natural resources, the forester proved as inventive as the president in the accumulation and exercise of power. The number of national forests grew from 32 to 149, and Pinchot's annual budget swelled from a mere $28,000 to more than $5 million.

With the spread of electricity, demand for waterpower grew apace, and to prevent the ills of monopoly Roosevelt and Pinchot won federal control over the development of waterpower sites on public lands. Pinchot helped Roosevelt create the federal Inland Waterways Commission, which they charged with devising a plan to coordinate management of navigation, flood control, and electric power generation on American rivers. Roosevelt also summoned the governors of all the states to Washington to discuss conservation. Held during his last year in the White House, the conference outlined his administration's progress in conservation and the work still to be done. The governors left feeling like ordained sheriffs, eager to preach conservation and hell-bent on stopping crimes against Mother Nature. All but a handful of states soon started conservation programs of their own.

The drive toward a new Eden ended with Roosevelt's departure from Washington, and a year later, the baggage that Gifford Pinchot carried to Porto Maurizio was heavy with grievances against Taft. Pinchot and Roosevelt spent their day together walking in the olive groves and vineyards above the village, and although neither of them left a record of the conversation, Pinchot undoubtedly gave him an account of the contretemps that led to his dismissal. Roosevelt's secretary of the interior, James R. Garfield, had been succeeded by Richard Achilles Ballinger, a lawyer and former mayor of Seattle. Like many a booster of the West, Ballinger believed that if the region's natural resources were developed, prosperity would follow. To speed the process, Ballinger aimed to give railroads, mining interests, cattle barons, and logging companies a freer hand on public lands. As an opening move, he surrendered federal control of 1.5 million acres that Roosevelt had set aside as potential waterpower sites. Pinchot complained to Taft, Taft overruled Ballinger, and Ballinger retaliated by curtailing his department's cooperation with Pinchot and the Forest Service.

Next a Department of the Interior underling who shared the Roosevelt-Pinchot philosophy accused Ballinger of expediting a questionable sale of claims to a rich coalfield on public lands in Alaska. The claims had been disputed for years, Ballinger's past business ties to some of the participants in the transaction created at least the appearance of a conflict of interest, and the low price negotiated by the buyers, the House of Morgan and the Guggenheim family, suggested a land grab.

Ballinger insisted that the sale was a public boon, because only a well-capitalized syndicate like the one the newspapers called "Morganheim" could afford to mine the coal and build the railroad needed to move it to market. Cities along the Pacific coast would gain a new source of cheap fuel. From Pinchot's point of view, Ballinger was about to help Morgan-heim swindle the people of the United States.

Taft wanted the quarrel settled quietly, but Pinchot decided that the national welfare called for public exposure. He mentioned it in a speech and shared official documents with the press. Taft asked Ballinger for a report on the handling of the claims, concluded that no wrong had been done, and called for the firing of the informant. Two more informants came forward, and Pinchot began talking about the case with conservation's friends in Congress. Taft countered with an executive order aimed directly at Pinchot: henceforth no one in the executive branch was to ask any action of Congress or answer any question from Capitol Hill without the consent of his ultimate superior, the cabinet secretary in charge of the department.

Pinchot spent his New Year's Eve taking stock of political affairs in a letter to TR. "We have fallen back down the hill you led us up," he said, choosing an image certain to stir the Rough Rider. Taft was a man of integrity, but he temporized, cowered, and evaded, Pinchot said. Instead of seizing the lead and casting himself as the people's chief advocate, as Roosevelt had done, Taft waited, like a judge, for issues to be brought before him. Progress had ceased.

Like others who are excessively eager to please, Taft was easily exploited, and he seemed unaware that the conservatives who controlled Congress were working for a return to the days of the figurehead presidents who preceded Roosevelt. They encouraged Taft's inaction by criticizing Roosevelt for roaming far beyond the constitutional limits of his authority, and so far as can be told, Taft rarely questioned their motives or wondered how they might benefit from a weak president.

By the time Pinchot wrote his letter, a chill and a calm had settled over the president. He and the forester were finished, he told his brother Charles.

Why not fire him? Charles asked.

"I am going to give Pinchot as much rope as he wants," Will said, "and I think you will find that he will hang himself."

Pinchot reeled out the rope on January 5, 1910, when he wrote a friendly Republican senator, Jonathan Dolliver of Iowa, to protest the banishment of the informants. They had spoken out to head off "a raid on public property," Pinchot said, and for risking their jobs, they deserved praise, not the ignominy of being fired. With Pinchot's permission, Dolliver read the letter on the floor of the Senate.

Two days later came the notice of the hanging. In place of Taft's customary "My dear Gifford" stood a lone, icy "Sir." The letter to Dolliver was an "improper appeal to Congress" in defiance of the executive order, Taft said. "By your conduct you have destroyed your usefulness as a helpful subordinate of the government, and it therefore becomes my duty to direct the secretary of agriculture to remove you from your office as the forester."

A long congressional investigation ensued, and the controversy became a cause célèbre of the new conservation movement. When Pinchot testified, he was blunt: Ballinger was an unfaithful steward, the informants had been unjustly punished, and the despoilers were again on the loose.

At the end of his day with the Colonel in Porto Maurizio, Pinchot returned to his hotel, and the reporters lurking about were given only a smile. He was almost as guarded in his diary. "One of the best and most satisfactory talks with TR I ever had," he wrote. The morass in Washington left Roosevelt "in a very embarrassing position, but that could not be helped."

Roosevelt offered the reporters a piece of fluff—details of the route he and Pinchot had taken in the hills—and a stick of dynamite. He would make a speech in Colorado on August 27, he said, and the subject would be conservation.

Pinchot seems to have left Italy with the impression that TR might be persuaded to run for president in 1912. The Colonel's attitude toward the political situation was ideal, Pinchot wrote his brother. "If you and I had made it to order it couldn't be better from our point of view." Gifford was certain there would be "great developments after TR announces his platform, which he will do in Kansas in August, and I want to be getting things in line as much as I can." The word "platform" suggested much.

L EAVING EDITH AND ETHEL in Porto Maurizio, TR and Kermit spent a few days in Vienna and Budapest, two of many destinations TR had not intended to visit when he planned his European sojourn. But after accepting invitations from Oxford and Cambridge, he could not easily refuse other great universities or the heads of state who asked to see him. For three months he would be perpetually in motion, his days gorged with personages and performances and state occasions. Demanding as the schedule was, he had enough energy left for a study of the two most significant European developments of the time: the rise of militarism and the disintegration of monarchy. Each sovereign he met was "obviously conscious that he was looking a possible republic in the face," TR would write a friend.

On April 21 the Orient Express deposited TR and Kermit in Paris, where they joined Edith and Ethel at the home of the new American ambassador, TR's college friend Robert Bacon. All hope of spending time as a simple tourist was abandoned when he saw the arrangements his hosts had made: a visit to the Louvre (where he boycotted the voluptuous nudes of Rubens), teas with Edith Wharton and Rodin, visits to Notre Dame and the Bibliothèque Nationale, a round of formal dinners, evenings of theater and opera, and induction into the Académie des Sciences Morales et Politiques. The Colonel also made a closely watched excursion to the tomb of Napoleon, whose return from Elba inspired a ream of editorial cartoons showing TR in Napoleonic hat and breeches. Several of the cartoonists hung a dark cloud labeled "Waterloo" in the distance.

Roosevelt had come to Paris to speak at the Sorbonne on the duties of a citizen in a republic, a subject on which he had one hour and forty-five minutes' worth of definite opinion. A democratic republic like France or the United States represented "the most gigantic of all possible social experiments, the one fraught with greatest possibilities alike for good and for evil," he said. A monarchy's fate reposed in a handful of leaders, but a democracy's hinged upon the quality of its people. "The average citizen must be a good citizen if our republics are to succeed," he said; a democracy needed leaders of the highest caliber in order to hold the average citizen to a high standard.

TR held his notes in his left hand and axed the air with his right. His right shirt cuff came unmoored and shot out over his hand, but he went on flapping and slashing his way through his convictions on the duties of the press, the need to back ideals with the will to defend them, and the wrongheadedness of birth control. Husbands and wives who chose not to reproduce were guilty of "crimes of ease and self-indulgence, of shrinking from pain and effort and risk." The audience tittered, but Roosevelt earnestly plodded on. A high civilization had a fundamental duty to perpetuate itself, or its achievements would vanish, he said. He had long viewed a woman's willingness to risk her life in childbirth as an obligation akin to a man's willingness to risk his life in war, a revealing analogy in light of the death of his first wife in childbirth and his combat in the Spanish-American War. Roosevelt's thoughts about "race suicide," as he termed it elsewhere, have been forgotten, and much of the address did not rise above the level of cliché. But it contained, almost as an aside, his most eloquent expression of the standard by which he judged himself and every other man in public life.

It is not the critic who counts; not the man who points out how the strong man stumbles, or where the doer of deeds could have done them better. The credit belongs to the man who is actually in the arena, whose face is marred by dust and sweat and blood; who strives valiantly; who errs, and comes short again and again, because there is no effort without error and shortcoming; but who does actually strive to do the deeds; who knows the great enthusiasms, the great devotions; who spends himself in a worthy cause; who at the best knows in the end the triumph of high achievement, and who at the worst, if he fails, at least fails while daring greatly, so that his place shall never be with those cold and timid souls who know neither victory nor defeat.

France was about to hold a general election, and candidates across the spectrum rushed to claim the man in the arena as political kin. The French press was less enthusiastic, calling Roosevelt a charlatan and a self-promoting Caesar eager to return to America and install himself as dictator.

In Belgium, where socialism had gained a toehold, Roosevelt inveighed against class warfare. "Never trust a man who says he will benefit you by pulling down your neighbor," he said. Fresh from *Samson and Delilah* at the Paris Opera, he reminded his audience that when Samson pulled down the pillars of the temple, he was crushed beneath them. In the Netherlands he mounted a church pulpit and crooned a Dutch lullaby he remembered from childhood, then urged the rich to do right by the poor. In Denmark his walk on the ramparts of Elsinore inspired a cartoonist to draw him as Hamlet, bearing a scroll marked "1912" and shadowed by an anxious-looking specter tagged "Third Term Taboo."

In Norway, accepting the Nobel Peace Prize he had been given four years earlier for his role in ending the Russo-Japanese War, Roosevelt called upon the leaders of the world to curb "unhealthy" militarism as they worked to curb the excesses of capitalism. But the noblest of human goals was peace with righteousness, not peace for the sake of peace, he said. A peace that masked cowardice or appeased a despot was an execration. A man must be willing to fight for his ideals: "No nation deserves to exist if it permits itself to lose the stern and virile virtues," whether through a love of ease or "deification of a warped and twisted sentimentality." He encouraged the great nations to agree to arbitrate their disputes at The Hague and to draw up an agreement limiting the growth of armaments, but the lawlessness of frontier life had taught him that it was "both foolish and wicked to persuade [a man] to surrender his arms while the men who are dangerous to the community retain theirs." Lasting peace required a police power to enforce the decrees of the court.

The speech proved a brilliant overture to his encounter with Wilhelm II, emperor of Germany. It sounded the notes that his safari patron, Andrew Carnegie, wanted the kaiser to hear, and now that the kaiser had heard them, Roosevelt would have no need to mention arbitration or disarmament in Germany. The chess match that had begun in Africa ended with the checkmate of Andrew Carnegie.

Edward VII, king of England and uncle of the kaiser, died while Roosevelt was in Scandinavia, and Roosevelt, knowing that the German imperial household would be in mourning, offered to forgo his visit to Berlin. But the kaiser, who had long suspected Edward of leading a European conspiracy to encircle Germany, was not immobilized by grief. He elected to cancel only part of his plans with Roosevelt.

On the marble steps of the palace of Frederick the Great, the emperor and the Colonel pumped hands for a full minute. The kaiser, gleaming in white uniform and silver helmet, looked "every inch the War Lord," one witness thought. Later the two could be seen but not heard in conversation.

Fists shook. Arms waved. Heads bobbed. Several observers, including Edith Roosevelt, remarked upon Theodore's physical resemblance to Wilhelm — the stockiness, the mustache, the body language spoken fortissimo.

The kaiser and the Colonel spent the next day on horseback, watching twelve thousand Prussian soldiers wage a mock battle. Locked in mutual fascination, TR and Wilhelm talked almost continuously throughout the five-hour display of German military strength. The kaiser brought up disarmament, but only to say that he had no control over it. "[T]he German people, or at least that section of the German people upon whom he relied and in whom he believed, would never consent to Germany's failing to keep herself able to enforce her rights either on land or at sea," Roosevelt later wrote a friend. When the talk turned to relations between England and Germany, Roosevelt ventured the opinion that a war between them would be "an unspeakable calamity."

The kaiser, son of a German emperor and an English princess, pointed out that he had spent much of his youth in England. "Next to Germany, I care more for England than for any other country," he said. Then, with such force that Roosevelt would render the sentence in capital letters, Wilhelm exclaimed, "I ADORE ENGLAND!"

Roosevelt averred that he himself would not go quite so far.

The kaiser surprised the Colonel by agreeing that Britain, as an island nation, needed the world's strongest navy. But he resented the English habit of citing Germany as the reason for building up the Royal Navy. The assertion aroused the "worst feelings" of both peoples, the kaiser said, and he wanted Roosevelt to pass the word when he met with England's leaders.

As the troops passed in review after the military exercises, the kaiser introduced TR as *Mein Freund*, a claim meant to flatter him and impress the army. When the review ended, the kaiser turned to TR and said, "Well, my dear Roosevelt, you are the first private citizen that has ever reviewed the Prussian troops!"

Roosevelt may have been the only person who observed four powerful European armies on the eve of the world war. His royal hosts in Italy and Austria had showed him their cavalry, and he had spent a day on maneuvers with the French army.

The Colonel found the kaiser a "curious combination of power, energy, egotism, and restless desire to do" — a curious combination also found in Theodore Roosevelt, although he seemed unconscious of the similarity. The growing power of parliaments was steadily undermining old notions of divine right and absolute sovereignty, and Roosevelt deduced that Wilhelm, like his fellow monarchs, kept his throne by following the lead of his people: "whenever Germany made up its mind to go in a given direction he could only stay at the head of affairs by scampering to take the lead in going in that direction." Having noticed that the kaiser always did his bullying outside Germany, Roosevelt guessed that the belligerence was a rebellion against limited power at home. So far, the other great powers had succeeded in compelling the bully to retreat. Roosevelt left Germany convinced that Kaiser Wilhelm II was an unpleasant neighbor but only a minor threat to world peace.

President Taft invited Roosevelt to serve as special ambassador to the funeral of Edward VII, Roosevelt accepted, and Archie Butt mused that with the Colonel and the kaiser on the scene, "it will be a wonder if the poor corpse gets a passing thought." Before going abroad, as he thought about his attire for the courts of Europe, TR considered taking his U.S. Cavalry dress uniform. The 1898 edition he was entitled to wear was positively operatic, gaudy with plumes and gold lace, and he thought he might complete the ensemble with patent leather boots. Edith, fearing ridicule, exercised her veto power, and he made his court appearances in black evening dress. He wished he could wear his uniform for Edward's funeral, but as the gods had it, his black suit made him a conspicuous figure among the silver helmets, sashes, medals, and flashing scabbards in the cortege.

Roosevelt's triumphal march through Europe ended with a speech in London on the duties of empire. At the behest of his new friends in Africa and with the approval of Sir Edward Grey, the foreign secretary, the Colonel urged England to take a hard line in Egypt. "It is not worthwhile belonging to a big nation unless the big nation is willing when the necessity arises to undertake a big task," he told an audience assembled at the Guildhall. In Cairo, speaking to the nationalists, he had counseled patience. In London he called for resolve. "You have tried to do too much in the interests of the Egyptians themselves," he said. "Those who have to do with uncivilized peoples, especially fanatical peoples, must remember that . . . weakness, timidity, and sentimentality may cause infinitely more harm than violence and injustice." If England felt it had no right to be in Egypt, it should get out.

The champions of empire heard the speech as "a trumpet call to imperial duty that chimes magically with the national mood." Others noted that the British had tried Roosevelt's hard line in Ireland with tragic results. Roo-

sevelt, said the *National Review*, knew no more than the "tourist who im-
bibes a casual prejudice in the smoking room at Shepheard's Hotel and
vents it in a letter to a provincial newspaper."

Between public engagements TR visited old friends, dined with England's hunter-naturalists, and saw three of his safari companions. With Kermit he called on Rowland Ward Ltd. in Piccadilly to arrange for the
mounting of some African trophies—rhinoceros feet to be fashioned into
boxes and inkstands, cigar boxes of elephant hide, elephant's foot wastebas-
kets, and assorted whips, bowls, and walking sticks. The Roosevelts paid
£129.8s.6p for their curios, the animals considerably more.

TR spent a day bird-watching with Sir Edward Grey, and each time Grey
identified a bird by its song, Roosevelt rattled off a detailed description. He
had never before gone birding in England. He knew the birds from his reading. He recognized each song on the second hearing and astonished Grey
with his ability to distinguish one song from another when the birds sang in
chorus.

In London, Theodore and Edith made another excursion into their early
life together, and Theodore, hoping not to be recognized, went without
spectacles. At St. George's Church in Hanover Square, where they were
married on December 2, 1886, they asked the verger for a look at the register. The register was locked away, but the verger volunteered that it contained three entries of special value: two pairs of royal signatures and the
signature of Theodore Roosevelt.

You don't say, one of the visitors remarked.

"Many Americans come here solely to see the entry," the verger went on.
"We keep a sheet of paper inserted at the page, with a cutting from a newspaper of that day, which describes how Mr. Roosevelt came here from
Long's Hotel wearing a bowler hat, how he entered by the back door, and
was married in the simplest manner possible."

The Roosevelts thanked the verger and departed undiscovered.

TWO DAYS BEFORE SAILING, Roosevelt received a letter from the
White House, the first since his departure for Africa. "It is now near a
year and three months since I assumed office and I have had a hard time,"
Taft wrote. "I do not know that I have had harder luck than other presidents
but I do know that thus far I have succeeded far less than have others. I have

been conscientiously trying to carry out your policies but my method of doing so has not worked smoothly." The economy was flourishing, but the press was hostile, an attitude he blamed on their anger over the tariff reform, which had failed to lower the duties on newsprint. The war between Ballinger and Pinchot had given him "a great deal of personal pain and suffering," he said, "but I am not going to say a word to you on that subject. You will have to look into that wholly for yourself without influence of the parties if you would find the truth." The first lady's paralysis had quickly receded, but her aphasia had not. She had recently begun taking part in receptions where her only task was to utter a word of greeting, but conversation was still beyond her, Taft reported. She was "not an easy patient and any attempt to control her only increased the nervous strain." He invited TR to the White House and in a postscript told him of the grand homecoming awaiting him in New York. It would be nonpartisan, he said—"a sincere expression of all the people of their joy at your return. You will be fairly overcome at the warmth of feeling that your return will evoke."

Roosevelt answered at once in a tone that was courteous but nowhere in the realm of genial. "I do not know the situation at home," he wrote. "I am of course much concerned about some of the things I see and am told; but what I have felt it best to do was to say absolutely nothing—and indeed to keep my mind as open as I kept my mouth shut!" He sent his and Edith's warmest regards to the first lady and asked to defer his response to the invitation until he reached Oyster Bay and sized up the work awaiting him.

As Roosevelt's arrival approached, Taft grew increasingly irritable. He had been invited to the reception—and advised not to go. At a celebration of Theodore Roosevelt, Archie Butt explained, everyone else, even a president of the United States, would be invisible. Taft would spend the day receiving an honorary degree in Pennsylvania, and Butt would represent him in New York. Taft complained again that Roosevelt had not written from Africa or thanked him for the gold pencil-and-ruler thingamajig he had sent as a farewell present. The president had either forgotten or did not count the telegrams Roosevelt had managed to send him in the pandemonium of leaving New York. Nor did the president seem to remember that there would have been no present if Butt had not suggested it. Reviewing Butt's draft of the orders he was to carry out as the president's emissary at the reception, Taft demoted Roosevelt from "Colonel" to "Mr." and then, perhaps aware that he was transgressing, asked Butt's opinion of the change.

Butt said he thought that Roosevelt would prefer "Colonel." "The President thought otherwise," Butt wrote his sister-in-law, "and so ordered the change."

A thick fog threatening to delay the Roosevelts' arrival lifted on his last night at sea and gave him a honeyed summer morning for his return. "Roosevelt weather," the papers called it. Welcomed by the mayor, TR spoke for two minutes. As promised, his message was devoid of politics, although its last sentence read like a memo from his conscience to his ambition: forever in the debt of the people, a former president was obliged to conduct himself in a manner that never made them "regret that once they had placed him at their head."

New York was wrapped in red, white, and blue, a hundred Rough Riders had come to town, and 500,000 people were out to see their former president. Or was it a million? The newspapers' estimates varied with the depth of their love for Theodore Roosevelt. The parade up Broadway and Fifth Avenue was "one continuous heartfelt ovation," said Archie Butt. "I have never witnessed anything like it." Minutes after it dispersed, near the Plaza Hotel, the heavens delivered thunder, lightning, hail, and a deluge. Seventeen people were killed. Roosevelt's luck held. When the sky opened, he was only steps away from his destination, the home where Ted and Eleanor's wedding presents were on display. The wedding was two days off, and at the couple's request, TR had come to see their gifts, one of which was a silver pitcher from President and Mrs. Taft.

During the parade Butt had asked Lodge and others who knew Roosevelt what they thought when they saw him, and all agreed that he had changed. Butt thought he glimpsed "an enlarged personality. To me he had ceased to be an American, but had become a world citizen. His horizon seemed to be greater, his mental scope more encompassing. I don't think this was in our imaginations alone. . . . He is bigger, broader, capable of greater good or greater evil, I don't know which, than when he left; and he is in splendid health and has a long time to live. What a horoscope to cast if one could cast it!" Butt had apparently forgotten the predictions he had heard from a White House correspondent on TR's last day in office: Taft would hand the government over to the Old Guard, Roosevelt would be furious, and a cross-country speaking trip after his return from Africa would put him in the running for a presidential nomination in 1912.

FIVE

Prairie Fire

A s Captain Butt and the rest of Washington waited for Theodore Roosevelt to discover his future, Roosevelt was spinning in the whirlpool of the present. He was a private citizen with no privacy, an opinion-maker who had promised not to opine—at least for a while—and an ex-president who had entrusted his legacy to the wrong heir. For the first time since his exit from the White House, Roosevelt was eye to eye with his powerlessness. It was not a condition he cared to contemplate, so he hurled himself into action.

On June 20, Ted and Eleanor's wedding day, he started his work at *The Outlook*, where the editors had set him up in a dignified, manly suite of three rooms with parquet floors, walls clad in bronze burlap, and a desk that was a replica of George Washington's. Fresh gold leaf on the front door advertised his presence, and a rear door allowed him to escape without passing through his anteroom or the corridor. A single foray from *The Outlook* demonstrated the need for such protections. Mobbed as soon as he appeared on the sidewalk, he finally sought sanctuary in a hat shop. A few minutes later, sporting a broad-brimmed straw number, he sprang out and sprinted back to *The Outlook*.

Later in the day, at the Fifth Avenue Presbyterian Church, the police held back the crowd that collected during the wedding, but there was no restraining the cheers that greeted TR's emergence. If his children were right when they teased that he wanted to be the bride at every wedding and the corpse at every funeral, he got half his wish at Ted and Eleanor's wedding.

Their exit from the church drew only mild applause. Asked to comment on the ceremony, the Colonel said only that he wished to live "as other people do, and say nothing, absolutely nothing, for the newspapers."

He deceived himself. While serving his two-month sentence of silence, he was preparing for a speaking tour of fifteen states, hardly the strategy of a man pining for solitude. It was not attention he hoped to escape, it was unwanted attention. Every day brought a bale of correspondence—as much as he had received at the White House. In Washington a half-dozen men had tended to the mail, at Sagamore he had only one. Strangers wrote asking for money, oculists offered spectacles, insurance agents longed for his custom, land salesmen fabricating his endorsement had to be reprimanded, and A. J. Krank, president of the A. J. Krank Manufacturing Company, makers of Pink Blush massage cream and other fine goop, needed thanks for his gift of a tube of Lather-Kreem. TR dictated at a gallop, and the secretary matched his pace, but their finish line steadily receded. "I am almost driven mad by work," TR wrote a friend.

Again he was invited to the White House, and again he demurred, this time saying that he considered it bad form for an ex-president to visit Washington "except when he cannot help it." Sometime he would have to go to the Smithsonian about the safari, he added, but he hoped to do it during a congressional recess, when most of Washington was away.

Taft vowed not to extend another welcome, and with mounting agitation eyed the smoke signals from Sagamore, where the Colonel was receiving dozens of political callers, few of them admirers of the Taft administration. But before the month was out, president and ex-president were chatting on the veranda of Taft's summer home in Beverly, Massachusetts, north of Boston. The meeting, requested by neither of them, had been arranged by Henry Cabot Lodge. After learning that Roosevelt would be in Cambridge for Harvard's commencement, Cabot suggested an overnight stay at his home in Nahant, a few miles from Beverly. Once in the vicinity, Lodge reasoned, Roosevelt would have a natural opportunity to pay his respects to the president.

Taft and Archie Butt were waiting when Lodge's automobile rolled up the drive, and Roosevelt greeted his old friend with a chipper "How are you, Mr. President? This is simply bully."

Taft clapped him on the back and asked him to drop the "Mr. President."

Roosevelt resisted. "You are Mr. President and I am Theodore. It must be that way."

Taft persisted in addressing TR as "Mr. President," TR continued to object, and Taft repeatedly overruled him, declaring that he always thought of Roosevelt as president.

After sixteen months in office, Taft still had trouble conceiving of himself as the chief executive of the United States. The chief justice of the Supreme Court had finally resigned that summer, and as Taft sought a replacement, he was suffused with regret. Had he not allowed himself to be seduced into running for president, he would have been appointed to the court during Roosevelt's presidency, and the post of chief justice, the only prize he had ever wanted, would now be his.

Taft slipped his arm through Roosevelt's, steered him to the veranda, and kept up the "Mr. President." Roosevelt was so ill at ease that he asked the butler for a scotch and soda, a drink far more potent than the Madeira he occasionally drank with Edith.

Flummoxed by the awkwardness in the air, Butt wondered whether he should remain in attendance or leave Taft and Roosevelt alone. When Lodge stepped around a corner of the house to light a cigar out of the wind, Butt leapt after him for guidance. Stay, said Lodge; Roosevelt did not want to be alone with Taft. The trust between them had frayed, and with others present, Roosevelt had an excuse not to speak frankly.

Mr. President and Mr. President talked superficially of Republican politics in New York, where Governor Charles Evans Hughes was jousting with the bosses over a bill to institute primary elections, which would shift the power to choose political candidates from the bosses to the voters. At Harvard's commencement, Hughes and Roosevelt had had a conversation about the bill, and Roosevelt offered to say a public word in favor of it—out of a sense of civic duty, he told Taft.

To Lodge's relief, the first lady and the Tafts' nineteen-year-old daughter, Helen, joined the party, and there ended the discussion of New York. Certain that the primary bill would fail, Lodge wanted Taft and Roosevelt to steer wide of it.

The Colonel greeted the first lady warmly and in deference to her speech difficulties asked her no questions. When the president inquired about Europe, Roosevelt obliged with more than an hour's worth of anecdotes about kings and queens. Taft asked about the tension between Germany and England and wondered if TR would head a new peace commission established to study the feasibility of creating an international peacekeeping navy. Roosevelt professed to be flattered but declined. His participation would trouble the European leaders who had shared state secrets with him, he said, and he considered such commissions pointless as long as Germany and England kept up their arms race.

As the Colonel prepared to leave, Lodge, still choreographing, asked what the two hundred newspapermen at the gates should be told. Roosevelt proposed that he say only that he had passed a delightful afternoon. Taft approved and remarked that the visit had transported him back to the "dear old afternoons when I was Will and you were Mr. President." After the visitors departed, Taft gave Captain Butt a smile and said, "Well, Archie, that is another corner turned." Toward what, away from what, he did not say.

N EW YORK'S PRIMARY BILL died the next day, and the bosses were certain that Roosevelt's political future had died with it. "Teddy is licked to a frazzle," gloated William Barnes, the Republican boss of Albany. "We no longer worship the gods, we laugh at them."

The defeat was a minor symptom of a major disorder in the body politic. "Democrat" and "Republican" had not yet evolved into synonyms for "liberal" and "conservative," and both parties were top-heavy with devotees of the status quo. Congress had been ruled for a decade by a handful of Republican reactionaries. In the Senate, Nelson W. Aldrich, proud, handsome plutocrat who toiled unceasingly to mold government to the desires of business, reigned by controlling assignments to the Senate's committees.

Speaker Joseph Gurney Cannon, who cussed with originality and was seldom seen without a well-masticated cigar in his lips, had entered Congress in 1873. Known to all as Uncle Joe, Cannon dominated the House of Representatives simply by controlling its rules. A congressman who wished to address the House needed Uncle Joe's permission before the day's proceedings, a catch that effectively stifled debate. Like Aldrich in the Senate, Cannon had made himself the sole supplier of House committee seats. During Roosevelt's presidency, Cannon and Aldrich used their committees to strangle most progressive legislation and adulterate the rest. Roosevelt was not wholly wrong in claiming that the split between his White House and their Capitol—"I pushing forward and they hanging back"—had forced him to take issues directly to the people.

From his perch in Roosevelt's cabinet, Taft had observed that TR's bombast did not faze Cannon or Aldrich and wondered if honey would prove more efficacious. Roosevelt, watching President-elect Taft's obsequiousness in their presence, glimpsed the future. Taft meant well and would do his best, but he was weak. "They'll lean on him," TR predicted.

Embittered by Pinchot's dismissal and the phony tariff reform, constantly thwarted by Cannon and Aldrich, and abandoned by the White House, Republican progressives in the House and Senate began thinking of themselves as Insurgents, in open rebellion against the Regulars of the party. Most of the Insurgents represented states in the Middle and Far West, which resented the power of Eastern capital. The East bought Western meat and grain at market prices but sold the West clothing and other manufactured necessities at prices inflated by the tariff. As one critic complained, "from the nipple on the baby's milk bottle to the spade that dug the old man's grave there was not one object in all the industrial round of life that did not rise in cost to the consumer, while none or very little of the increase went into the hands of the laborers who produced it." Another wondered why champagne coming through the custom house carried a duty of 54 percent while the duty on clothing ran upward of 80 percent.

The Insurgents' claim that the tariff enriched a handful of industrialists at the expense of millions of consumers drew scoffs from the elected retainers of the manufacturing class. "Where is this separate and isolated public of consumers?" demanded Senator Lodge of Massachusetts. His America was "a nation of producers." But the vast majority of producers—farmers and factory hands—did not earn enough to savor the fruits of the tariff.

By 1910 the chasm between East and West was political as well as economic. In Wisconsin, Oregon, and elsewhere, states and cities were governing themselves with more democracy than the boss-ridden East could bear, choosing candidates in primaries, enacting laws through ballot initiatives, repealing them by referendum. Through the recall, they were also overturning judicial decisions and ousting corrupt officials.

When Taft took office only fourteen senators and thirty congressmen thought of themselves as Insurgents, but the ranks of the reactionaries were shrinking. More than half the members of the Senate were in their first terms, and while Roosevelt was in Africa, the House contingent managed against all odds to overthrow Uncle Joe. In a contest that went on for weeks and ended with a fight on the floor that lasted for thirty-six hours straight, the House voted to triple the size of the House Rules Committee, elect its members, and exclude the speaker. Cannon gallantly offered to resign as speaker, but the rebels, satisfied that he was now harmless, voted to let him stay.

In ecstasy over Cannon's demise, the Insurgents saw an opportunity to jettison Taft in 1912 and bestow the nomination on a true progressive. But the Regulars, including Lodge and Congressman Nicholas Longworth, TR's son-in-law, were certain that the long-term survival of the Republican Party required unity behind Taft even though he would lose. A splintered party might prove impossible to reconstitute.

One of TR's first visitors was Senator Robert M. La Follette of Wisconsin, personification of the Insurgency and leader of the revolt against the sham tariff reform. Three years older than Roosevelt, La Follette had been born in a log cabin in Primrose, Wisconsin, grew up without a father, and at fourteen became the family's breadwinner. With a soulful face and magnificent voice, he dreamed of a career on the stage but turned to law and politics when he learned that his small stature ruled him out as a leading man. As Wisconsin's governor, "Fighting Bob" La Follette led a triumphant battle for primaries, and his exposure of the financial chicanery of the railroads forced them to submit to state regulation.

The squire of Sagamore was out haying when the senator arrived but soon strode in, wearing linen knickerbockers and, La Follette noted, "a rather liberal quantity of timothy." La Follette had come in hopes of winning TR's support for the Insurgency, but TR would not go beyond confessing his dismay with Taft. La Follette, who left Oyster Bay with the sense that Roosevelt did not yet apprehend the magnitude of the fissure in the Republican Party, apparently missed the real significance of his audience with the Colonel. TR had long considered Fighting Bob intransigent and extreme, so the mere fact of their meeting bespoke the depths of Roosevelt's displeasure with Taft, who despised the Insurgents. He wanted them "cut out like you would cut out a cancer," he told Captain Butt. A more engaged leader would have feigned interest in the enemy if only to gather intelligence.

Roosevelt was sympathetic to the revolt against Taft but not comfortable with the Insurgents in Congress or their followers, a perfervid band that included his close friends Gifford Pinchot and former Secretary of the Interior James Garfield, one of the casualties of the cabinet purge. TR believed the Insurgents were headed in the proper direction but traveling faster than the people would follow. An Insurgent, in his view, was a progressive who was "exceeding the speed limit."

Although Roosevelt promised nothing to Insurgents or Regulars, the rumors wafting to Beverly deeply distressed the Tafts. Nellie did not care who won the election of 1912, she told Will, but "you must not allow [Roosevelt] to defeat you for the renomination." Captain Butt, anxiously watching over his chief, observed that nothing upset him more than the "constant reports that Colonel Roosevelt has a dagger out for him."

The dagger was still in its sheath. Flashing it would have called attention to Roosevelt's blunder in selecting Taft to succeed him and would raise (from its shallow grave) the suspicion that Roosevelt coveted another term. After a published report that the councils at Sagamore were discussing 1912, Roosevelt issued a denial and said that if he decided to comment on the subject, he would do so over his own signature.

Roosevelt's thoughts about the tales brought by his visitors crystallized into a conviction that party unity was imperative and could be achieved if the Regulars in the House and Senate joined with the Insurgents to work for some common goal. "The truth is that we have had no national leadership of any real kind since election day in 1908," he wrote Lodge. Taft was a puppet of the reactionaries, and the Insurgents were led by "narrow fanatics, wild visionaries and self-seeking demagogues, with the result that a great many sober and honest men are growing to hate the word 'Reform' and all reformers, including myself."

As Lodge and other Regulars constantly reinforced Roosevelt's belief in the need for party unity, the Insurgents and their sympathizers tugged from the opposite direction. "You are the leader to whom all look," Pinchot wrote him after an early visit to Sagamore. "I understand and respect your desire not to run again. It may or may not be necessary. But I think with you that this is not a question of personal wishes. Rather it is a question of a marvelous opportunity and a great national need. You alone meet the situation. . . . Taft has deceived us all once. That was his fault. If he does it again it will be our fault. And if he should be renominated and reelected, what else could we expect?"

Roosevelt did not say so publicly, but he expected to support Taft in 1912. The president was a disappointment but not a disgrace, he wrote Garfield, and as their beloved Lincoln had said, when it is impossible to do the best, one must do the best possible.

Restless at Sagamore, Roosevelt hired a large touring car with chauffeur at the beginning of August to make what he hoped would be an anonymous investigation of social conditions in the anthracite coal country of Pennsylvania. To his annoyance, reporters and photographers, tipped off by the agency that rented him the car, were waiting when the chauffeur called for him at *The Outlook*. TR refused to disclose his destination and said he would consider any notice of his trip distasteful.

TR had engaged a car in order to avoid the train, where he was sure to be recognized, and had persuaded himself that the miners would speak candidly about their lives only if they did not know who he was. But his anonymity perished almost instantly, on a walk through the hot, gritty streets of Dickson City, Pennsylvania, a hamlet near Scranton. Although his face was shaded by a Panama hat, an old man spotted the spectacles and mustache beneath and scurried off to broadcast his discovery. TR soon had the whole of Dickson City trailing after him. When the informant rejoined the procession, he inquired about 1912. TR indulged him with a smile.

In the towns of the Lackawanna and Susquehanna and Wyoming valleys, Roosevelt was saluted with bouquets and blasts of dynamite. A mother of twelve children and another woman with seventeen and dreams of twenty were brought to meet him. He praised their fecundity. Villagers took him into their homes and showed him his portrait, which had hung on local walls since 1902, when he settled their strike. Covered with soot after inspecting a coal breaker, he was taken to wash up as the miners did, at a kitchen sink. He would soon call for washrooms in the coalfields. Most of the villagers told him that the region was more prosperous than it had been a generation ago, and the urgent social problem seemed to be the dearth of suitable entertainment for young people. For lack of an alternative, they were congregating at saloon dancehalls, veritable academies of sin.

TR motored home by his usual route, the middle of the road. In Pennsylvania as in the rest of the country, he said, reformers too often tended toward "hysterical" overstatement, while the ruling class was too often content with small progress. "There has been progress," he wrote in *The Outlook*; "there is great need of further progress; and if there is not continuous improvement, there is almost certain to be retrogression." Retrogression—that was the consequence of Taft's failure to lead, and to a man of action, the failure to lead was more reprehensible than anything that might transpire in a dancehall.

Roosevelt left the coalfields with a raw throat and none of the euphoria he usually carried home from a round of flesh-pressing. He passed August 6, Edith's forty-ninth birthday, in silence, on doctor's orders, and dreading his speaking tour. Hoping to bring the Insurgents and Regulars together for the fall elections, he had set himself the impossible task of expounding his progressive political philosophy without praising or criticizing his successor.

Taft, suffering from gout and limping through his golf games at a North Shore country club called Myopia, was annoyed by TR's excursion to Pennsylvania and furious about the speaking tour. As Taft saw it, Roosevelt had paraded himself before the miners in hopes of nudging the proletariat to demand that he run again. The president half-wished for the showdown. "I should like for nothing better . . . than to have the issue drawn between us, if one is to be drawn, between conservatism and socialism, for that is how such a campaign would develop," he told Archie Butt. The president's golf deteriorated with his temper. "The other day he swore a terrific oath and threw his club twenty-five yards," Archie wrote Clara. The caddies were dumbstruck, and the Captain confessed to a twinge of disapproval. It seemed to him that the president was "losing just a little bit of command of himself."

A S ROOSEVELT was about to head west, the bosses who had bragged about licking him to a frazzle inflicted another insult. At the invitation of Lloyd Griscom, leader of the New York County Republicans, Roosevelt had agreed to serve as temporary chairman of the party's state convention, to be held at Saratoga in the fall. A temporary chairman was no potentate, but he made the address that laid out the party's direction for the campaign. The bosses overrode Griscom and selected another prominent New York Republican, James S. Sherman, vice president of the United States. Griscom telephoned Sagamore, where the news was received with thunderous rage.

Although Roosevelt blamed Taft, the perpetrator was Taft's secretary, C. D. Norton, a Midwestern businessman who presented himself as a progressive but carried water for the reactionaries. Norton seems to have been unpopular with everyone but the president. In the opinion of the normally chivalrous Archie Butt, Norton had "a thoroughly Chicago business view of things." Butt particularly disliked him for his habit of seeking out an unfair advantage and ruthlessly exploiting it. However useful elsewhere, such tactics were useless in Taft's White House, Butt thought. "All the President has gained in life has been by contrary methods and it is too late for him to scheme for petty advantage here and there."

For a few days after Griscom's call TR seemed to be of two minds—relieved to be out of an election the Republicans were sure to lose yet willing to entertain Griscom's notion of taking the contest to the floor of the convention, where the delegates would decide.

The president was "worried sick" by the episode, Butt said, and Butt worried with him. The Captain no longer understood his place. His loyalty to Taft was complete, but his affection for the Roosevelts had put Taft on guard, and that, he wrote his family, left a presidential aide in "a rather uncomfortable position."

Shortly before Taft took office, a pundit exerting himself to explain the differences between him and his predecessor declared that by temperament Taft was a locomotive, Roosevelt a volcano. Taft would not step on a man while he was down, Roosevelt refused to get off until certain the man could not get up. Taft was a steam heater, Roosevelt a prairie fire. On August 23, five days after the expiration of the two-month gag order that Lodge and Root had issued before he came home, Roosevelt boarded a train at Grand Central Terminal. The prairie fire would blaze for eighteen days, sweeping through fifteen states and leaving his friend Will Taft feeling "seared to the very soul."

A railroad car filled with seventeen reporters was going with Roosevelt, five more reporters would join the caravan in Utica, another carload would be added in Chicago, a third in Denver. Still a master of press agentry, Roosevelt issued a bulletin even before the train left the station: he would challenge Sherman at the state convention for the post of temporary chairman. To see Theodore Roosevelt scrap for so minuscule a prize is to see both his impotence and his inability to accept it.

TR reminded the newsmen that he would be speaking for himself, not the Republican Party. He also told them that no matter what he or Taft did in the fall campaign, the Republicans would be drubbed in Congress, in statehouses, and in local government. Asked why he had volunteered for the flogging, he answered, "I couldn't live with myself if I didn't go in. These men who are asking me for support now were always ready to do all they could whenever I, as president or governor of this state, called on them for support." If he stayed safely in the rear, they would feel that he had forsaken his principles only because he had nothing to gain from the election.

Explaining his involvement to Lodge, he said he had been called by "a very stern sense of duty." As unhappy as he was with Taft's performance, he did not feel he could stand by while the Insurgents destroyed him. Roosevelt's sense of patriotic duty was as large as his love of power, and through his habit of rationalizing the liberties he took with power, he had convinced himself that he valued it only as an instrument for good, as the big stick enabling him to fulfill his duty. He seems never to have grasped the immensity of his need for power, and after his years in the White House would often mistake the call of personal ambition for a call to serve his country.

He had no desire to return to the White House, he assured O. K. Davis of the *New York Times:* "I've had all the work and all the fun, all the honor and all the glory of it," and he guessed that a third term would detract from his reputation. Africa had awakened a desire for more scientific expeditions, in South America perhaps, or Asia, and he hoped to distinguish himself as an ornithologist or explorer. Nothing would incline him toward a presidential run, he said—except, of course, a demand from the people.

By one estimate more than a million people came out to see Roosevelt on his speaking tour, and if they were not ready to demand his candidacy, they were thrilled to see him. "My papa is a Roosevelt man, so is my mama and so am I," a small boy from Kansas wrote TR. An English member of the press corps felt "an almost revivalist intensity" in the crowds that massed at railway stations and packed opera houses to the roof. In St. Paul, where 100,000 people came to the fairgrounds to see him, he had to work all four corners of the rostrum to make himself heard.

On a rainy afternoon in a barren stretch of Kansas, Davis called his attention to a woman standing by the tracks with a baby in her arms. TR dashed to the rear of the train to wave, and when she saw him, she raised the baby in his direction and held it aloft. "A thing like that gives you a lump in the throat," he told Davis. "It makes me feel like a great calf. These people have such trust and confidence, and so often they think a man can do all sorts of things that no one can do." The lump in the throat was the mark of a man who yearned not to temper the hopes of the people but to deserve their faith.

The prairie fire reached white heat in Colorado. Speaking in Denver on August 29, Roosevelt attacked the Supreme Court for decisions that put corporations in a shadowy world where they were ungoverned by state or federal law. Here "the lawless man of great wealth," aided by clever lawyers, could stay "equally distant from the uncertain frontiers of both state and national power." He ridiculed the court's 1905 decision in *Lochner v. New York,* which nullified a state law passed to safeguard the health of bakers and the quality of their bread. After Joseph Lochner had been found guilty of allowing an employee to work longer than the statute permitted, the court overturned the conviction and struck down the law. In this instance, the court said, the right of employee and employer to strike their own bargain outweighed the state's regulatory authority, because there was no compelling evidence that long hours harmed a baker's health or his bread. TR scoffed that the court had acted because "men must not be deprived of their right to work under unhygienic conditions." While the ruling purported to be about limiting the power of the state, it was "really against popular rights," he said

When the speech set off alarms among the princes of capital, Elihu Root speedily assured them that the former president was not out to dynamite the temple of law. If a litigant disliked a decision, it was his privilege to go down to the tavern and swear at the court, Root told an audience of Republicans. As far as he knew, such grumbling had never done any harm. Cabot wrote his dear Theodore that encouraging hostility to court decisions tended to encourage hostility to the law itself. Bad practices should be changed, he said, "but we ought to preserve, I think, public respect not only for the law but the declarations of the courts as to what the law is."

Roosevelt was irritated by Root's trivialization and mystified by the uproar in other quarters. The speech was his own, but many of the ideas had been suggested by William H. Moody, a former Supreme Court justice, and a former district attorney had reviewed it, he wrote Cabot. To be branded as an incendiary struck him as "curious," which in his lexicon often meant "asinine."

WHILE ROOSEVELT was in Denver, the town of Osawatomie, Kansas (pop. 3,000), weeded, pruned, and gussied up for his arrival, a local newspaper proudly reported. "We put on our biled shirts, brought the galluses out of their hiding place, had our better halves darn our socks, put on a smile, and thank you, we are ready for plutocrat and peasant." A deluge the day before his arrival had turned the streets into fens, but thirty thousand people came out to see the Colonel.

The ostensible reason for Roosevelt's visit was the dedication of a park in memory of John Brown, the abolitionist who had conducted bloody raids on pro-slavery settlements in Kansas and seized the U.S. arsenal at Harpers Ferry, Virginia. Captured and hanged for treason, Brown became the martyr of the anti-slavery cause.

Standing on a kitchen table, Roosevelt said little about John Brown, whom he did not admire, and much about Lincoln, praising him for not yielding to radicals or reactionaries. In a ninety-minute address that Gifford

Pinchot and others had labored over for weeks, Roosevelt told the crowd that Americans had fought one war to win their independence and another to preserve the Union. Now they faced a new war, "between the men who possess more than they have earned and the men who have earned more than they possess." To disarm his conservative critics, he took his gospel from Lincoln. Capital was the fruit of labor, Lincoln had said, and in his judgment, that made labor the superior of capital, deserving of "much the higher consideration."

Roosevelt summoned the country to a New Nationalism, with the federal government as arbiter of the common good, curbing abuses of economic power and improving the lot of the ordinary citizen. His quarrel was not with men who amassed their fortunes honorably but with those whose riches were gained at the expense of the people. Those who put property rights ahead of human rights now had to "give way to the advocate of human welfare, who rightly maintains that every man holds his property subject to the general right of the community to regulate its use to whatever degree the public welfare may require it." The regulatory powers he advocated would require "a far more active governmental interference with social and economic conditions in this country than we have yet had," he acknowledged, "but I think we have got to face the fact that such an increase in governmental control is now necessary."

Before the federal government could serve the needs of all the people, the special interests had to be driven out of politics, Roosevelt said, and to that end he recommended disclosure of campaign contributions and a ban on the use of corporate money for political purposes. He also wanted managers and directors held personally responsible when their companies broke the law. A man in charge of a corporation means to do well, he said, "but I want to have enough supervision to help him realize that desire to do well."

Into the mix Roosevelt stirred demands for laws to protect the health and security of the laboring class, a graduated income tax, an inheritance tax on large fortunes, a strong navy and army, farsighted management of the nation's natural resources, and individual character. His ideal government would remove obstacles to equal opportunity, but it would not tolerate the man who sought to build himself up by attacking the property of others, nor would it help the man unwilling to help himself.

The idea that social and economic problems were national in scope and required national solutions was an old one with Roosevelt, as was the notion that without the federal government to broker a Square Deal for all, capitalism would destroy itself. The Osawatomie speech was a summa of his presidency and a repudiation of Taft's.

The speech struck many as old wine in old bottles. Root wondered what was new about the New Nationalism, and one of the correspondents on the tour noted that apart from the Colonel's oratorical hammering, the doctrine was "for the most part mild and wholesome." The phrase "New Nationalism" came from *The Promise of American Life*, a book by the journalist Herbert Croly. TR had read it on his way home from Africa and was impressed by its argument that only a strong central government could check the excesses of capitalism and ensure that the benefits of economic growth would flow to more than a favored few. The idea gave Roosevelt a way to update and codify the Square Deal, and in an admiring letter to Croly he had announced his intention to borrow liberally from the book.

The available evidence indicates that Roosevelt meant it when he told O. K. Davis that he had no wish to return to the White House, but the New Nationalism speech was a fair approximation of a presidential platform, and William Howard Taft understood it as such. To his brother Charles he wrote, "I am bound to say that his speeches are fuller of the ego now than they ever were, and he allows himself to fall into a style that makes one think he considers himself still the President of the United States." It was a peculiar complaint after Taft's "Mr. President" curtsies during Roosevelt's visit to Beverly. Where Root and others saw bromides, Taft saw a wildness "going quite beyond anything that [Roosevelt] had advocated in the White House." Short of overhauling the Constitution, Taft said, there was no way for the federal government to carry out Roosevelt's ideas.

As the newspapers debated whether Roosevelt was barnstorming the country in aid of Taft or himself, Taft worried that Roosevelt was making the trip to settle an old grudge. In thanking TR for his help in the election of 1908, Taft had put his contributions on a par with those of his brother Charles, the campaign's most generous donor. The parallel had irritated TR, and when word of his pique reached Taft, Taft considered it the ultimate in "swelled-headedness." The question of who put Will Taft in the White House annoyed Will as much as it annoyed TR, and it annoyed Charles as well. Archie Butt, who walked in on one of the brothers' heated discussions of the subject, heard Will promise not to minimize Charles's part if Charles would stop deprecating Roosevelt's. "Possibly I had nothing to do with it at all," Will added. He said it with a smile, but the words had an edge.

Hurt by the outbreak of Roosevelt worship, Taft began abusing him and seemed not to care who heard the tirades. "He launches forth whenever he feels like it, and of course a great deal of it finds its way back to Mr. Roosevelt," Captain Butt wrote his sister-in-law. "It is a very trying position for him, but when he reflects that Mr. Roosevelt put him in the cabinet, then brought about his nomination, it ought not to be so hard for him to remain silent at least. As long as people don't talk, they can make up; but after they have admitted others to their animosities it is difficult to get together again."

A T THE SUGGESTION OF C. D. NORTON, Taft's mischief-making secretary, the Republican leader Lloyd Griscom asked Roosevelt if he would meet Taft on September 19 to discuss the fall canvass in New York. Taft's train would pass through New Haven en route from Beverly to Cincinnati, and New Haven lay just across Long Island Sound from Oyster Bay. Roosevelt agreed in the interest of party harmony. By clouding the details of who had asked for the meeting, Norton led Taft to think that Griscom had requested it at Roosevelt's behest and that Roosevelt was coming to seek the president's help in uniting New York's fractious Republicans. Among friends the question of who called the meeting would not have mattered, but in the limbo between a dead friendship and a feud still taking shape, it assumed enormous proportions. Taft dreaded seeing TR again, Roosevelt was wary, and an anxious Captain Butt wondered, "Comes he in peace or comes he in war?"

He came in a speedboat, through a gale that blew up after he set out from Oyster Bay. Late, soaked, and undoubtedly seasick, TR sped to New Haven in a police escort, and after an amiable lunch with Taft and a few others, he and the president were alone. Both men were apprehensive. "For a time we sat in silence," Taft confided a few days later to Gus Karger of the *Cincinnati Times-Star*. "I felt like a man playing checkers. It shot through my mind that Mr. Roosevelt wanted to be able to say that I had broached the subject" — the subject being a president's use of federal patronage to persuade party members to do as he wished in New York and elsewhere. For some reason, and in spite of feeling that it would be undignified to dicker with Roosevelt about patronage, Taft went "deliberately and joyfully into the trap," he told Karger. " 'I suppose it is the New York situation you want to discuss,' I began. 'If that is the case I am willing to help you to the extent of reasserting what I have written to Griscom.' " Taft hoped that the bosses would not dictate the party's platform or its candidate for governor, but he had told Griscom that he would not pull the lever of patronage to influence the results. "Further than that I cannot go," he told Roosevelt.

"Nor would I ask," said the Colonel. "That would not help."

When they finished their conversation, Taft invited Roosevelt to ride with him to the train station. Roosevelt accepted, and during the ride they spoke of the tariff, the cost of living, and other issues likely to figure in the campaign. Roosevelt expatiated in his usual body English, and Taft's expressions alternated between wooden smiles and fretfulness. Newspapermen peering into the two faces reported that they had seen the storm clouds of 1912.

The press was overinterpreting, Taft told Karger. "We both looked grave, but it wasn't on account of anything [Roosevelt] had said. My anxiety was on account of the train," which was being delayed for him, and Roosevelt's hyperkinetics were not signs of anger, Taft said. The newsmen had forgotten that "Roosevelt can't talk at all without gesticulating."

Roosevelt went home certain that he had asked no favors, and Taft headed for Cincinnati certain that Roosevelt had come to him for the prestige of the president's support in the New York election. "I was glad to give it, and that is all there is about it," he wrote Nellie.

Reading the papers the next morning, Griscom was startled to find that the account of the meeting given to the press by C. D. Norton claimed that Roosevelt had gone to New Haven to patch up his relationship with Taft and to enlist his aid in the fight against bossism in New York. Griscom's phone rang. "What did I tell you?" the Colonel shouted. Norton had accomplished his purpose: Roosevelt had been made to look as if he could not stay afloat in the small pond of state politics without Taft's help.

Norton was also spreading rumors of a quid pro quo: Taft had given his support in New York, and Roosevelt had agreed to back him in 1912. Roosevelt deduced that Norton's rumors were meant to discredit him with progressives and, he told Lodge, "unless I am mistaken it has been circulated in the interest of one or two insurgent leaders who themselves want to be nominated for president, and who think it would be good to break me down."

Taft was equally furious. If Roosevelt had had no favors to ask, why had he come to New Haven? Taft asked Karger. Casting wide for an explanation of Roosevelt's hostility, the president blamed TR's egotism. The safari had allowed him to forget his loss of power, and when Europe received him "like a monarch returning to his own," he overestimated his importance, Taft said. "It made him lose all his powers of self-restraint. He is a changed man. At banquets he manifests the keenest pleasure at the terms of adulation that are heaped upon him. He is unhappy without the power he wielded as president. I have been made to feel it. His treatment of me has left scars that will never heal."

Taft's latest analysis of the black mood at Sagamore explained even less than his belief that Roosevelt had been permanently offended by the cabinet purge and by the gaucherie of equating Roosevelt's help with Charles's money in the election of 1908. The source of TR's wrath was simpler and deeper. After promising the country that he would "complete and perfect the machinery" built by Roosevelt, Taft had allowed it to be dismantled. Roosevelt had not foreseen the dangers of leaving his progressivism to a maintenance man. Progress requires motion, change, momentum. Taft was a creature of stasis.

Baffled by Roosevelt's animosity, Taft said more than once in the summer of 1910 that if he knew what Roosevelt wanted, he would do it. "I am absolutely in the dark," he told Butt. The Captain understood the nature of TR's rage, but beyond that he too was in the dark. "The game has passed out of the ken of most of us, and there is nothing to do but wait and hope for the fall elections to teach them all a lesson," he wrote his sister-in-law. "The situation is interesting, most interesting. I would like to get away from it all, but I presume the man who puts his hand to his pen is like the man who puts it to the plow; he should not turn back merely because he strikes rocks and stones and heavy earth."

In Cincinnati the president faced another unpleasant fact of the break with Roosevelt. Nick Longworth represented Taft's congressional district, the Taft and Longworth families were old friends, and Nick was married to Alice Roosevelt. Will had known Alice since her adolescence and found her a delight, but Nellie distrusted her. Will sometimes invited Alice to the White House without telling Nellie in advance, for fear that she would refuse to come to the table. Nellie had her way when she could, declining to ask Alice to be part of the receiving line at the president's annual reception for the diplomatic corps and neglecting to invite her to the first White House garden party of the spring of 1910. Alice had fumed to Archie Butt that she had a mind to put up a tent nearby and open a saloon.

After spending a summer evening in Cincinnati with Alice and Nick, Will wrote Nellie, "I am afraid she is gradually drawing away from me on account of the present situation between her father and me, though she professes to be very affectionate still." The evening had been tense and sad. Nick's mother and his sisters deeply disliked the Roosevelts, and Alice loathed her mother-in-law and "Cincin-nasty," as she called it.

Caught in the middle, Nick at first bore his misfortune gracefully. A Republican Regular who had been in Congress since 1903, Nick was a fiscal conservative and a skilled debater. He charmed his confreres with his natural wit and an encyclopedic repertoire of bawdy jokes and songs. Alice shared Nick's pleasure in shocking polite company, and they once treated Taft to their parody of a suggestive dance, with Alice in the role of *danseuse* and Nick on violin. Taft ordered them to stop and never do it again in his presence. On occasion Alice gave him a wiggle to tease him about his prudery. Congressman and Mrs. Longworth may not have known it, but Taft rather enjoyed tangy stories. Out riding with Archie Butt one afternoon, he laughed so hard he nearly fell off his horse as he told of a letter from a Washington socialite who begged him to prevent the installation of public urinals near her home in Dupont Circle. With no apparent humor she had asked why they could not be installed a few blocks away, on P Street.

Sympathetic to the conflicting pulls on Nick's loyalties, TR encouraged him to "stand straight by Taft and the administration. He is your constituent." But TR warned Nick against getting so entrenched that he would have trouble working with the progressives when the tide swept their way: "you must not be left behind."

NEW YORK'S REPUBLICANS convened in Saratoga a week after the president and the ex-president met in New Haven. Roosevelt took the train upstate with his friend and neighbor Henry L. Stimson, an upstanding U.S. attorney and onetime law partner of Elihu Root. Stimson, a Rooseveltian progressive, was about to be nominated for governor and run a race he was sure to lose simply because the country had decided to switch parties. "It is like a man in bed," Root explained. "He wants to roll over. He doesn't know why he wants to roll over, but he just does; and he'll do it."

Stimson, forty-three, had no dreams of elective office but was allowing himself to be sacrificed for Roosevelt's idea of a nobler good—obstructing the bosses' plan to nominate reactionaries to run on a reactionary platform. (For a time the most cynical bosses had harbored an even more daring ambition. With the Democrats certain to win, they hoped to run Roosevelt for governor and turn him into a political corpse.) Stimson worried that his defeat would diminish TR's political influence, but TR claimed not to care, because he had no intention of taking part in politics after the election of 1910. "Bet you a dollar," said Root.

In Saratoga, the Colonel descended from the train in a warring mood, announcing that he would lick Vice President Sherman to a frazzle in the fight for the temporary chairmanship of the convention. It was the same idiom Barnes had used after the battle over the primary bill. When Roosevelt and Sherman were nominated, Roosevelt asked to address the convention, and O. K. Davis of the *Times*, who knew him well, saw a face he did not recognize. "Cave man" crossed Davis's mind. The jaw thrust forward, the fists clenched, the restless pacing—these were familiar, but the sentences were uncharacteristically choppy, and the eyes narrowed to flashing slits. Reading a transcript of the speech the next day, Davis was surprised by its mildness. The fire had been in the man.

The delegates chose Roosevelt by a wide margin, allowed him to name several committees, and left him to pick the slate of candidates. In short, they elected him boss. In his keynote address Roosevelt took a softer tone and even managed to describe Taft as "able, upright and distinguished." Roosevelt also endorsed the convention's platform. While less progressive than he would have liked, it declared the Republican Party in favor of primaries, the plank he wanted most. He left Saratoga claiming victory. "We have beaten the reactionary machine," he said, "and the progressives are in charge of the party."

The president and the ex-president managed to avoid a public confrontation before election day, but rivers of venom flowed in private. Whenever the Taft family convened, "they wanted to flay the Roosevelts alive," Butt said. Taft heard that Roosevelt was calling him lazy, and there were reports that Roosevelt now believed that he had been the engine of Taft's diligence in the cabinet. Roosevelt began to be haunted by memories of events that he had misinterpreted. As secretary of war, Taft had constantly consulted him before making decisions, and Roosevelt, awed by Taft's ability to argue both sides of a case, had failed to see Taft's dependence.

On October 27, Roosevelt's fifty-second birthday, he was midway through the fifty speeches made on behalf of Republican candidates, mostly in New York state. He ventured briefly up to Boston to campaign for Lodge and out to Indiana to help his friend Albert J. Beveridge, who was also up for reelection in the Senate. The president, as was the custom, did not campaign, but in a talk he gave at a boys' home in Cincinnati, his unhappiness in the White House was plain. "It is enough for you to grow up to be good men, to be always honest, kindly, and to do right," he said. "The satisfaction that you can get from that life is much greater than you would get by being president."

On election day the heavens were as divided as the Republican Party, unsure whether to snow or to rain. Kermit, newly turned twenty-one, sloshed forth to vote in Oyster Bay. It was a disheartening initiation. Nationally the election gave the Democrats control of the House for the first time since 1894. Nick managed to hang on to his seat, although his victory was appreciably smaller than in 1908. In the Senate, Republicans kept a slim majority, but new alliances between Insurgents and Democrats ended the dictatorship of Senator Nelson Aldrich. He decided to retire with the expiration of his term, March 4, 1911. In New Jersey a Democrat named Woodrow Wilson, a political scientist and former president of Princeton College, was elected governor. Jacob Riis, whose books on tenement life had greatly influenced Roosevelt's thinking on poverty, wrote him that the Democratic victory was probably a good thing: "There is nothing like wiping the slate clean and it *was* dirty."

Expecting the rout, Taft jauntily summed it up as "not only a landslide, but a tidal wave and holocaust all rolled into a general cataclysm." When friends came to console him and damn the Colonel, Taft suggested that the results might have been the same even if Roosevelt had stayed in the jungle. The visitors praised his "beautiful, unselfish" disposition. The president seemed to enjoy the flattery, but Archie Butt found it grotesque.

Lodge won by a hair, but Stimson, Beveridge, and nearly all of Roosevelt's other candidates were beaten. So was his own congressman—a sign to some that Roosevelt's political career was over. "The verdict of the vicinage always has been held to be conclusive," said the *North American Review*. The debacle might have occurred in any case, "but the present point is that he could not prevent it."

Roosevelt admitted no regrets and accepted no blame. "From my personal standpoint," he told Lodge, "the bright spot in the business is that I think it will put a stop to the talk about my being nominated in 1912, which was beginning to make me very uneasy. I am not really responsible for the present situation, and I don't want to have to take responsibility."

Gifford Pinchot sent his condolences and expressed confidence that TR would be ready "when the next call comes," but he thought the Colonel's moderate stance ill suited to a moment when the public longed for the demise of the bosses and the plutocrats they served. Gifford had scolded him for praising Taft at Saratoga, and Amos Pinchot, Gifford's brother, saw TR's centrism as a strategy for self-advancement. "It makes me feel tired that he is trying to get himself in a position where he can shift to the leadership of the insurgents or the reactionaries," Amos said. He saw no point in "shouting about driving out the crooks when he remains silent about the thing that makes the crooks, that is to say, the tariff."

Roosevelt shared the Pinchots' desire to improve the lives of the masses, but he refused to join in their categorical condemnation of the rich and of corporations. Certain that his was the "right attitude," he nevertheless understood that it was "not an attitude which can possibly evoke much enthusiasm among the people at large." He was also certain that his overzealous friends had "no conception of the difference in difficulty between tearing down and building up."

T HE MOST IMPORTANT STORY of the election went unreported until the publication of *Taft and Roosevelt: The Intimate Letters of Archie Butt* in 1930, and that version was heavily censored. It mentioned Taft's gout and his weight, which in the autumn of 1910 stood at 330 pounds. It also reported some of Butt's conversation with Dr. James Marsh Jackson in Boston, who had told him that the running, rolling, bending, and medicine-ball-throwing prescribed by another physician, Dr. Charles Barker, had weakened the president's heart. But the published account omits Jackson's startling opinion that Barker's regimen had "very materially" shortened the president's life. Nor is there any mention of two urine specimens with several worrisome irregularities, including high levels of albumin and sugar. When Butt asked whether the specimens indicated Bright's disease, the kidney disorder now called nephritis, Jackson said he could not be certain, as the symptoms often occurred in large men. But if the symptoms were not controlled, they would rapidly become serious, and because the condition had been overlooked for so long, Jackson said, "I fear you will soon have an invalid on your hands."

When told that the president often fell asleep in the middle of writing or playing cards, the doctor "shook his head in such a way as to cause chills to run up and down my spinal column," Archie wrote his sister-in-law. Jackson doubted that Taft would survive another presidential campaign and urged that he be dissuaded from running. The Captain, who considered a withdrawal "fraught with impossibilities," told Jackson that he would rather see the president "die in active work than linger on in a state of semi-invalidism." Butt took Jackson's diagnosis to Dr. Matthew A. Delaney, an army surgeon assigned to the White House, and Delaney ordered Taft to limit his exercise to gentle rides on horseback. The doctors "don't dare to let the president know his own condition and they will not tell anyone but myself, leaving me to communicate to the family what I think it best to tell them," Butt continued. "I shall not tell them anything for now for I feel that he may get well and strong again and there is no need to frighten any of them unless absolutely necessary."

No president has ever left office on account of his health, and it is unlikely that Taft's family would have encouraged a resignation. But with his life in jeopardy and the first lady in fragile condition, he could have made an honorable departure. Had he done so, Roosevelt would have had no serious rival for the Republican presidential nomination in 1912. Archie Butt undoubtedly understood all the ramifications. A good soldier, he set aside his love of Theodore Roosevelt and did what he judged his commander-in-chief would have him do.

Jackson's diagnosis is not specified in Butt's letters, but a study published in the medical journal *Chest* in 2003 shows that whatever it was, Taft also had the classic symptoms of obstructive sleep apnea, a complication of obesity. The fat in the patient's tongue blocks his throat, causing him to wake repeatedly in the night, gasping for breath. Chronically short of sleep, obstructive sleep apnea patients have difficulty staying awake during the day and are at high risk for hypertension and coronary artery disease.

Soon after the election TR went to Washington at the invitation of the National Geographic Society to lecture on "Wild Man and Wild Beast in Africa." Taft was in Panama, checking on the progress of the canal, a trip that Dr. Jackson had begged Captain Butt to cancel. Butt ignored him, reasoning that if the president was about to expire, "he had better do so in the active pursuit of his duties." Knowing that TR was expected in Washington, the president asked the first lady to invite him to the White House for lunch or dinner, but she fled to New York two hours before the Colonel reached town. Archie Butt thought it "a great pity that she could not have nerved herself to do it."

Earlier in this melancholy autumn, Will had joshed that he dared not go to Panama or anywhere else, because Nellie feared that Theodore would swoop down and repossess the White House. For a moment he did. He stopped by to leave his card—it would have been discourteous not to—and when the servants seemed glad to see him, he lingered. He inquired about the kitchen's cornbread, which he remembered fondly, and the staff brought him a piece. He ate it as he followed the chief usher on a tour, which included an inspection of the new tennis court and a stop in the executive office, where he sat at the president's desk and said how natural it felt to be there.

Forgive him his trespass. It was as hard for Theodore Roosevelt to organize himself around the fact that he was an ex-president as it was for Taft to grasp that he, not Roosevelt, was the real Mr. President.

✻ *Rift*

SIX

Duels

TAFT returned from Panama laden with olive branches. One went to the Senate Insurgents, who were invited to the White House to discuss candidates for two vacancies on the Supreme Court. Another, in the form of a cigarette holder, went to Alice Longworth, an amusing nod to her racy streak. To Edith Roosevelt he sent a mahogany settee, one she had purchased with her own money when she was first lady and expected to take to Sagamore until an overzealous red-tapist pronounced it government property. Bemoaning the cloddishness of bureaucrats, Taft explained that he was righting the wrong by returning her settee and ordering a copy of it for the White House.

For Theodore there was an armload of peace offerings. The president apologized for the first lady's absence, ascribing it to the lingering effects of her stroke. He proffered another invitation, forwarded a copy of his forthcoming annual message to Congress, and telephoned Sagamore at least twice. Archie Butt overheard the president's end of one conversation about an election fraud and another about financial legislation. Writing Roosevelt about the progress of the canal, Taft first praised TR's decisiveness in gaining control of the isthmus, then noted that the great shortcut between the Atlantic and the Pacific would probably open in the summer of 1913, "a date at which both you and I will be private citizens and then we can visit the canal together."

The remark could be taken as jest or jab. TR ignored it in his reply but told Ted that he found the letter "helpless and pathetic." Taft's overtures were even more pathetic than Roosevelt knew; Archie Butt had suggested both the invitation (graciously declined) and the return of the settee. The olive branches did not put TR in a pacific mood. He felt alienated from Taft and the Regular Republicans, exasperated by the spite and impracticality of the Insurgents. The antipathies were mutual. To the Regulars, Roosevelt was Judas times two, a traitor to his party and to his friend Will Taft, while the Insurgents saw him circling, raptorlike, above the party's struggle until he could swoop in and snatch the presidential nomination for himself.

The Insurgents, perhaps hoping to broaden their appeal, went back to calling themselves Progressive Republicans soon after the election of 1910. In January 1911, intent on derailing Taft in 1912, they founded the National Progressive Republican League, claiming that they were coming together to recruit citizens for a campaign to make government more democratic through the direct election of senators and through primaries, initiatives, referenda, and the recall of public officials who strayed outside the law. The league also promised to push for legislation to limit campaign contributions, require disclosure of donors and recipients, and disqualify candidates who did not comply. With these changes, the league asserted, politics would be purged of "special privilege and selfish interest."

The progressive fires still burned hottest on the prairie. Most of the names on the league's letterhead belonged to men from the Midwest and West: Bob La Follette of Wisconsin, former Secretary of the Interior James Garfield of Ohio, the newspaper editor William Allen White of Emporia, Kansas, and a dozen more. Gifford Pinchot was one of only two Easterners. They invited the Colonel to join, but he demurred. Aligning himself with the enemies of the president would be the same as declaring war, something he still hoped to avoid. He also thought that his membership would stir talk that the National Progressive Republican League was a front for a Roosevelt presidential campaign. Rather than join, he would support the league's goals in *The Outlook*, he wrote the organization's president, Senator Jonathan Bourne of Oregon. Saying nothing of his ragged relations with Taft, he attributed his decision to his reservations about the initiative, referendum, and recall. At best, the initiative supplemented legislative action, and it was legislation, thoughtfully crafted, that created lasting progress. Unless sparingly employed, the new ballot measures would merely enable the cranks and the self-interested to subvert the work of the democratically elected representatives of the people.

Always of two minds about the masses, ready to champion Lincoln's "plain people" when battling a man of property but skeptical of their sagacity when they pressed agendas more radical than his own, Roosevelt wondered if Americans were ready for the large dose of change prescribed by the league. "I think that we wish to be careful not to seem to be dictating to good people who may not be quite as far advanced as we are," he wrote La Follette. "I am often held up to obloquy as a would-be dictator; and when tired of this accusation my enemies turn cheerfully round and say that I am a trimmer and an opportunist—regardless of the fact that the accusations are not mutually compatible. But as a matter of fact I am not a dictator at all; I want to try to lead the people and not drive them."

La Follette, who was acutely sensitive to language, could not have missed Roosevelt's use of the present tense in describing himself as a leader. Fighting Bob and the Rough Rider, temperamentally too much alike to be anything but rivals, were headed for a collision. Both were passionate and cocksure, generously endowed with self-esteem, and experienced the ego's drive to power as a deep desire to serve others. Each considered himself the one true progressive. La Follette was the purist, a self-appointed martyr with a closetful of hair shirts. As a freshman senator, he had been assigned a dank subterranean office by the Old Guard, and he insisted on staying there long after his seniority and committee memberships entitled him to finer quarters. A journalist who watched La Follette for decades remembered his "strong instinct for self-drama" and his sense that "if he was not being persecuted he must be guilty of some lapse of worthiness."

La Follette disapproved of Roosevelt for excoriating Wall Street when he spoke to radicals and damning radicals when he courted Wall Street. "This cannonading, first in one direction, then in another, filled the air with noise and smoke, which confused and obscured the line of action," La Follette would write; "but when the battle cloud drifted by and quiet was restored, it was always a matter of surprise that so little had been accomplished." Roosevelt was a centrist and a compromiser, and his pantry was indeed stacked high with half-loaves. La Follette flaunted his defeats as necessary steps on the road to moral triumph and liked to say that no bread was often better than half a loaf, because compromise weakened a cause and destroyed a reformer's constancy.

Roosevelt's belittlers supposed that he spurned La Follette and the league because he wanted the presidential nomination for himself, and eventually he would want it, but as the league was forming early in 1911, he believed that his involvement would injure the Republican Party. The party might heal its wounds before its next convention, he wrote Will White, but "I am not the man under whom the recovery should take place. There is too bitter antagonism toward me from every side."

Roosevelt consistently said that he did not wish to run and consistently refused to promise that he would not, a bit of straddling that convinced La Follette that TR was holding himself aloof only because he believed that Taft was certain to win the nomination. La Follette also suspected that the Colonel would be keen to run as soon as he realized the depth of the public's progressive yearnings. But with Roosevelt refusing to rule himself out, La Follette hesitated to advance his own candidacy. As he would tell it in his autobiography, progressivism had been his life's work, and he refused to be Roosevelt's stalking horse. "I estimated my own worth to the progressive cause too highly to consent to being used as a candidate for a time, and then, to serve some ulterior purpose, conveniently broken and cast upon the political scrap heap."

THE COLONEL TRIED TO CONTENT HIMSELF with his work at *The Outlook* and his life at Sagamore. "Home, wife, children—they are what really count in life," he wrote Ted and Eleanor in January 1911, when he learned that they were expecting their first baby. "I have heartily enjoyed many things; the presidency, my success as a soldier, a writer, a big game hunter and explorer; but all of them put together are not for one moment to be weighed in the balance when compared with the joy I have known with your mother and all of you; and, as a merely secondary thing, this house and the life here yield me constant pleasure."

In fact, Theodore was depressed, as was Edith, whose mood often mirrored his. One winter night as Butt was escorting Taft back to the White House, he told the president that both Roosevelts were "blue as indigo." Taft marched directly into the Red Room and sat down without stopping to shed his overcoat. "Archie, I don't see what I could have done to make things different," he said. He was deeply distressed—"more deeply than anyone can know, to think of him sitting there at Oyster Bay alone and feeling himself deserted. I know just what he feels."

There was a long silence, then Taft wiped his eye. The Captain, a model of masculine tact, rose to leave. He was waved back to his seat. Taft composed himself, blamed Roosevelt for causing his own unhappiness by meddling in the 1910 election, and wondered aloud if a bit of soul-searching might restore TR's sense of proportion. "To feel everything slipping away from him, all the popularity, the power which he loved, and above all the ability to do what he thought was of real benefit to his country, to feel it all going and then to be alone!" Taft said. "I hope the old boy has enough philosophy to see him through. . . . If he could only fight! That is what he delights in." But the newspapers were ignoring him—"with a view of driving home the iron," Taft had heard—and their silence deprived him of the opportunity to strike back. "It is all sad!"

The old boy could not be philosophical about his need for power, for he understood it no better than fish understand water. Theodore Roosevelt had been born to a privileged, influential family and had risen from there. As he ascended, he developed a profound understanding of power in politics and world affairs, but the higher he climbed, the more he seemed to regard power as something outside himself—an instrument for action rather than an organizing force of his character. As his friend William Allen White put it, Roosevelt's rise had left him with an "unconsciousness of power."

Now Roosevelt was the proverbial fish out of water, flailing but unable to comprehend his trouble. Relegated to the margins of politics, he began to pick quarrels in other spheres. He grew impatient with the safari's zoologist, Edmund Heller, who had not finished writing scientific papers on the giant eland and the white rhinoceros. If he continued to tarry, TR warned him, English or German zoologists might beat him into print. TR was also annoyed by the rhinocerene pace of the Smithsonian's work and its decision to mount only fifty of the safari's thousands of specimens. When his complaints appeared in the newspapers, the Smithsonian issued a testy statement noting that only about fifty of the specimens were new to the museum.

Beyond the swats at Heller and the Smithsonian, Roosevelt indulged in a shrill fight with Abbott Thayer, a New England painter whose observations of light and color had led him to a theory of animal camouflage. Thayer's Law held that all animals were colored for concealment and that nature achieved its aim through countershading, assigning dark colors to the body parts most brightly lit by the sun and light shades to the nether parts. Roosevelt first raised his cudgel in an appendix to *African Game Trails*, saying that Thayer had pushed his idea to "preposterous extremes." If the coloring of a blue jay was protective in the blue shadows cast by snow, then how could it provide camouflage in the greenery of summer? TR asked.

Roosevelt (driven, he claimed, by Thayer's "tone and temper") wrote a 112-page monograph on the subject for the *Bulletin of the American Mu-*

seum of Natural History, and when the controversy continued in an ornithological journal, friends squirmed at the spectacle of their great man
battering so small an adversary.

Thayer's Law was too broad by half. Some animals were colored for display, some for concealment. But camouflage, as it happened, was one of
Roosevelt's grievances against Taft: "he takes his color so completely from
his immediate surroundings that he is continually finding himself in situa-
tions where he really has broken his word, or betrayed some former associate," and then, "very naturally, he himself feels irritated against the man to
whom he has not behaved very nicely." Made by one who preferred display
to concealment, the observation left no doubt about the identity of the former associate.

In early March, trying once more to bluff himself into contentment, TR
professed that when a man reached his fifties, he wanted to stay home unless there was "a very real call. I should go away for a war, of course, but
nothing but real need of some kind or other would force me to go for anything else." With Mexico lurching toward revolution, war was a possibility,
and twenty thousand U.S. soldiers had been moved to the border. Roosevelt
had no interest in patrolling the border, he wrote Taft, but if Japan or another of the great powers decided to back the rebels, "I would wish immediately to apply for permission to raise a division of cavalry, such as the
regiment I commanded in Cuba." He had already drawn up a list of officers—every one a good horseman and rifleman, self-sufficient and able to
live in the open, easily trained for war. "I ask, Sir, that instead of treating this
as a boast, you will remember that in the war with Spain our regiment was
raised, armed, equipped, mounted, dismounted, drilled, kept two weeks on
transports, and put through two victorious aggressive fights . . . and all this
within sixty days."

Six months earlier Roosevelt had been infuriated by the rumor that he
had sought Taft's help with New York's feuding Republicans. Now he was
willing to supplicate. Powerless in politics, he longed for military glory and
the ecstasy he had known under fire in Cuba. Escaping from the war with
only a nick in the wrist, he said he genuinely envied those who were given
"the supreme good fortune of dying honorably on a well-fought field for
their country's flag." Hard as he had found it to see his men lying dead, the
sight of one wounded soldier about to die had moved him to offer his congratulations. "Well, old man," he said, "isn't this splendid!"

Taft answered that he did not expect a war but would honor Roosevelt's request if the occasion arose and if Congress would authorize a division of volunteers.

M UCH OF THE SPRING TR spent in the West on a speaking tour— his last, he said. The Eastern press largely ignored his travels, but it appears that Colonel Roosevelt was as warmly received by the people as President Roosevelt had been. Crowds waited at railroad stations, parents held out their children to be touched, and, Edith reported to a friend, countless men "begged to follow him to fight Japan or Mexico or anyone!" The greatest satisfactions of the trip were personal—several days with Ted and Eleanor, who were living in San Francisco; a descent of the Grand Canyon; and the dedication of the Roosevelt Dam in Arizona, the colossus of the irrigation projects begun during his presidency.

The age of such marvels demanded a new language of appreciation, a rhetoric of gee-whiz, and found it in statistics. The New York Times rhapsodized that the Roosevelt Dam was the world's second largest (after the Aswan, in Egypt), rising 284 feet and spanning a 1,070-foot gorge. Atop the dam ran a road twenty feet wide, broad enough for two Model Ts. One hundred seventy feet thick at the base, the Roosevelt was the sum of 336,000 cubic yards of sandstone masonry and 340,000 barrels of cement. Behind it, in a reservoir twenty-five miles long, lay 66,628,000 cubic feet of water, enough to put Delaware in a shin-deep puddle or (the vital point) to irrigate hundreds of thousands of acres of previously worthless land.

At 5:48 P.M. on March 18, 1911, Roosevelt pressed an electric switch, three massive iron gates ascended, and three cataracts plumed forth. In his remarks, which the Times did not see fit to print, Roosevelt said he was "pleased and touched" that the dam bore his name. Undoubtedly he was. The Reclamation Act of 1902, which brought the dam into being, was the first major legislative victory of his presidency and an example of Rooseveltian big government at its best, funding and supervising public works too large for individual states to manage and too easily turned into monopolies if left to private enterprise.

It seemed to Senator La Follette that Roosevelt came home from the West "quite another man," his confidence restored by the cheering throngs. Roosevelt continued to say he had no White House desires, but his relations with La Follette and with Taft took an aggressive turn. In The Outlook, TR praised La Follette's accomplishments as Wisconsin's governor and privately spread his opinion that there was no popular demand for a La Follette candidacy. He also began to say that the progressives had produced leaders who were "first-rate on a state scale, but no one who is big enough to size up to the nation scale."

With Taft there was less subterfuge. Roosevelt did not pitch into him personally, but the target he chose was one so dear to Taft that he might as well have. Taft belonged to the class of optimists working toward a day when nations would renounce war and settle their differences in a world court. Roosevelt was both a friend and skeptic of arbitration. In 1902, as president, he had persuaded Mexico to join the United States in giving the international tribunal at The Hague its first case, a small but interminable spat over charitable contributions. Taft revered the law for its power to resolve disputes without force, while Roosevelt believed that the slow grind of the law's machinery would hamper a president coping with an international crisis. Far wiser, he thought, to rely on the judgment of a strong, principled leader and his advisers. Arbitration was a tool for occasional minor repairs.

Roosevelt's first secretary of state, John Hay, negotiated several bilateral arbitration agreements, but when the Senate crippled them with an amendment requiring a two-thirds majority on every arbitration, Roosevelt saw no point in signing them. Hay's successor, Elihu Root, fared better, securing ratification of twenty-five treaties to arbitrate all disagreements save those related to "the vital interests, the independence, or the honor of the two contracting states" — exceptions wide enough to march an army through.

Taft aspired to arbitrate the questions Root had excluded. To omit them was "to arbitrate everything that is highly unimportant," he said. "We leave out the questions which when they arise are likely to lead to war." Anticipating objections to the wide sweep of the treaties, Taft and his secretary of state, Philander Knox, specified that only "justiciable" differences would be arbitrated. By their definition, a justiciable difference arose when one nation believed that another had infringed upon its rights. If nations disagreed on justiciability, they would turn to a joint commission of inquiry with three representatives from each country, and the issue would not go to arbitration unless at least five of the six agreed that it was justiciable.

To Taft a war was as senseless as a duel. "If we go to battle and win, we come home and say the Lord is on our side, and that our honor has been avenged, but if . . . we are driven off the field, we will have to reason a long time to understand how that satisfies our honor." In his view, the United States, as the only great nation without entangling alliances, was the nation best situated to take the lead in realizing the dream of international arbitration.

Roosevelt strenuously disagreed and felt he had a duty to say so. "I am a perfectly practical man," he wrote Lodge, "and if there was a greater good to be obtained by keeping silent or even acquiescing in this matter, I should be willing to do it." Silence was cowardice. He fired from *The Outlook*'s parapets in May, while the treaties were still being negotiated. Honor was no more arbitrable in world affairs than in private life, he argued. A good citizen obeyed the law but also had a right to defend himself. If a ruffian slapped a man's wife, the husband would be an object of scorn if he chose to sue rather than punish the assailant on the spot, he said. An agreement to arbitrate similar affronts to a nation's honor was sure to be broken.

The silence that felt like cowardice to Roosevelt was Taft's idea of stoic, dignified statesmanship, and he met the Colonel's first fusillade with outward calm. But he resented the meddling, as did Butt, who was sufficiently provoked to break his rule against speaking ill of his old chief in front of the president. The article exposed Roosevelt's "petty malice" and his jealousy, Butt told Taft, and the wife-slapping analogy was "undignified and unworthy of the colonel."

Roosevelt's timing rankled as much as the attack itself. The diplomats were nowhere near the end of their negotiations, and Taft, in one more attempt to please Roosevelt, had just appointed his friend Stimson as secretary of war. At a White House garden party just after the *Outlook* article appeared, Stimson's predecessor, J. M. Dickinson, confided to Archie Butt that most of the cabinet disapproved of the appointment because of Stimson's closeness to Roosevelt. They were also "very sore" at Taft for springing it on them as a fait accompli. "And what good has it done?" Dickinson asked. "The first chance the Colonel has to attack the administration after the appointment is announced, he does it."

Although Butt had just been promoted to Major, life with the Tafts was growing sadder and sadder. The president was floundering, and the first lady's illness had flared up again. During the party, when Butt chanced to look up at the house from the garden, he saw her watching alone from a window.

Taft feared that Roosevelt's bellowing about the treaties would prejudice the Senate and prayed that other voices would drown him out. The prospect of comprehensive arbitration agreements was well received in England and France, and Americans seemed more pleased with the treaties than with any other measure Taft had proposed. The new Carnegie Endowment for International Peace was proselytizing for the treaties by subsidizing pamphlets, mass meetings, and peace societies. Pacifists long in despair over the European arms race were infused with new hope, the clergy lauded the president's proposals, and business also cheered, believing that the stability fostered by arbitration portended a golden age for American commerce. If the Senate approved, the agreements would be the "great jewel" of his administration, the president told Butt.

THE COLONEL SPENT THE SUMMER at Sagamore, imagining that he was a satisfied man and, it would appear, not imagining that most of the challenges of adjusting to life without power lay in his own character. By his analysis, the problems inhered in the role assigned to him by American political tradition. "An ex-president has only a small field of possible work open to him," he explained to an English friend. As a younger man, he would have chafed, he said, "but I don't mind it in the least now, and if anything I am rather glad of it for I am devoted to my home. I have my books and all the things with which I have association around me, plenty of interests without and within, and Mrs. Roosevelt and I ride together and row together, and my life is very full and happy."

Ted and Eleanor's baby girl, first of a new generation of Roosevelts, arrived safely in August. Edith marked the event by planting a grove of pine seedlings—"a splendid place for wee Grace to play when she comes on to visit her grandparents," TR wrote Ted. Kermit, who had returned uncomplainingly to Harvard after the safari, was allowed to spend part of the summer hunting mountain sheep in the deserts of northern Mexico. TR prophesied that he would have a glorious time, given the scorching heat and "a reasonable chance of being killed or kidnaped by Mexican *insurrectos*." Ethel, now twenty, was widening her circle of friends and developing serious interests, and thirteen-year-old Quentin was "an affectionate, softhearted, overgrown-puppy kind of a boy, absorbed in his wireless and in anything mechanical."

Archie, sixteen, devoted the summer to his studies and was working "very hard, really almost too hard," his father thought. Edith tutored him in French, and he and TR spent an hour at history and civics each evening. By summer's end Archie had passed some of the examinations required for his admission to Harvard in two years' time, but he had failed civics. The former president, regarding the failure as his, investigated with admirable humility. Allowed to review the examination questions, he saw that he had not drilled Archie sufficiently in state government (an understandable lapse in a fervent nationalist) or the Constitution (a fact that would not have surprised critics of his broad construction of presidential power).

At Groton, Quentin often stood first in his class, and Kermit and Ted had acquitted if not distinguished themselves, but Groton for Archie was academic, social, and physical hell. He repeated a grade and decades later still smarted at the memory of himself as the dunce who finished last in all subjects but English and history. His body permanently weakened by a bout with diphtheria, he often fell sick in the school's cold, spartan quarters and was too fragile for athletics—a serious deficiency at a school where football was a form of worship. Archie slogged on, and apart from once grinding his heel into a plate of liver, rarely rebelled. His poor health won him a respite at the Evans School in Mesa, Arizona, and permanent deliverance followed when the rector of Groton, the Reverend Endicott Peabody, was handed a letter from Archie to a school chum. On the envelope Archie had inquired, "How is the old Christ Factory?" Theodore Roosevelt was informed that Archie was no longer welcome at Groton.

At the Evans School each boy had a hut of his own and a horse to care for. Weekends were spent riding and camping in the mountains. The climate agreed with Archie, his scholarship improved a bit, and rules were few. "Mr. Evans is a peach," he wrote the family's friend Warrington Dawson in Paris. "He jollies fellows along or curses them out at just the right time."

Tender and fiercely loyal, Archie had often nursed his mother through headaches, and he had a well-deserved reputation for knightliness. As a small boy he had once braved stiff winds to sail his pocket-sized craft to the aid of a much larger boat in trouble. At the end of Archie's studious summer TR wrote Ted, "He is sometimes a little short on pure intellect, but he is long on character, which is a mighty sight more important."

TR's summer idyll had few political interruptions, all of them brief. In June, as guests at the silver jubilee of James Cardinal Gibbons of Baltimore, Taft and Roosevelt exchanged closely watched handshakes, laughter, and a few words. They "played the game beautifully," in Major Butt's opinion. An Associated Press reporter in attendance wired the country that Roosevelt had promised to support Taft in 1912, a rumor quickly scotched by Roosevelt. Taft too was unhappy about the AP story but had done nothing, rationalizing that the less said about an error, the faster it would fade.

In July, after receiving assurances of support from Gifford Pinchot and other Roosevelt friends, La Follette announced his intention to challenge Taft for the Republican presidential nomination. Roosevelt offered no public comment and in private said only that he thought La Follette and the more radical progressives had lost ground.

In August, TR was summoned to testify before a congressional committee investigating the U.S. Steel Corporation's purchase of the Tennessee Coal, Iron & Railroad Company during the Panic of 1907. He was certain that he had taken the right course in giving his word that the government would not oppose the acquisition, he told the committee. It would have been "well nigh criminal" to do otherwise, and he had not been under any illusions about the altruism of the steel men. Furthermore, no monopoly had ensued. Before the transaction, U.S. Steel controlled 58 percent of the nation's steel production, and by 1910 its share had fallen to 54 percent.

Politics at last seemed on the periphery of TR's life, but his old friend Cecil Spring Rice, an English diplomat who had been best man at his wedding to Edith, guessed that Theodore would be sorely tempted to leap into the Republicans' breach. Hoping to prevent the catastrophe, Springy tried a tactic that often succeeds with a small boy who is both headstrong and eager to do right: complimenting him on the hoped-for behavior. How honorable to let others have their turn in politics, Springy wrote him. "It must require immense courage—greater to step out of the fight than step into it. . . . My ideal for you always was to be great in practical life first and then when you had done your job to be great as a quiet, unselfish influence for good with a great past behind you and a great present power." If Theodore Roosevelt could live in repose, the world would see that "at least to one man—and that the most considerable man of his age and country—those things are the things that really matter and give real happiness."

Be a sage, sharing your wisdom and setting an example by living gracefully without power, Springy advised. "No doubt Taft's people egg him on against his predecessor and tell him to forget you laid him and give a different sort of crow to show his independence. And I daresay there are lots of nice people who egg you on to remind you of some recent facts in his history. I hope you will leave each other alone."

The role of sage was several sizes too small for Roosevelt and demanded a serenity at odds with his nature. He was, as Will White said, "over-engined"—a man with outsized physical and emotional needs for action. As a contributor to *The Outlook*, he was a sage of sorts, but with no power to enact his ideas, he found the work unfulfilling. Although he claimed not to mind, in an unguarded moment he wondered if his writings were as ineffectual as the earnest, soporific tracts that arrived daily in his mail. Bucking up another discouraged social preacher, he said, "We must not permit ourselves to become soured by our experiences, for being gloomy does not in the least help a man to reach others, and merely makes him less attractive to himself and to all around him."

P RESIDENT TAFT and the ambassadors of France and England signed the arbitration agreements at the White House on a rainy afternoon early in August. The ubiquitous Major Butt, sure that he was witnessing a great moment in history, furtively pocketed the pen the president used to sign the letter transmitting the treaties to the Senate for ratification.

Roosevelt struck at the treaties in September, after Lodge and Root presented the first senatorial criticisms of the agreement with Britain. Seeking peace was a noble pursuit, Roosevelt said, but it was "an even higher duty to seek righteousness." The fatal feature, in his view, was the joint commission's power to decide that any question might be justiciable. Ceding such authority was worse than silly, he wrote. "If a president, after consulting with his constitutional advisers, the Senate, could not make up his own mind about such a vital question . . . it would be proof positive that he was not fit to hold the exalted position to which he had been elected."

Lodge recommended that the treaty's offending clause be excised, while Root suggested supplementing it with a statement that the treaty exclude "all purely governmental policies." TR noted that Root's change "quite properly leaves the clause meaningless and ineffective, as 'governmental policies' may include anything and everything. . . . Uncle Sam does not intend to wrong any one, but neither does he intend to bind himself, if his pocket is picked, his house is burglarized, or his face slapped, to 'arbitrate' with the wrong-doer. . . . Our chief usefulness to humanity rests on our combining power with high purpose. Power undirected by high purpose spells calamity; and high purpose by itself is utterly useless if the power to put it into effect is lacking."

The power Roosevelt had in mind was of the cannon-and-battleship variety, but his observation on the consequences of severing power and purpose was an uncannily accurate — and seemingly unconscious — depiction of the turbulence that dominated his inner life after the presidency. Blind to his longing for power, he would repeatedly deceive himself about the loftiness of his purpose.

For once Taft stood fast, out of principle certainly and perhaps also from a hope that the popularity of the treaties might salvage his presidency. The agreements would be toothless without the justiciability clause, he insisted, for if a nation could decide on its own whether to arbitrate or not, it would be inclined to go to The Hague only when it thought it could win. "To make a treaty that shall always work our way, to play the game of 'Heads I win, tails you lose,' is to accomplish nothing," he said. He wrote a friend that he saw Roosevelt's new attack as the raving of a berserker. "The truth is he believes in war and wishes to be a Napoleon and to die on the battlefield. . . . It is curious how unfitted he is for courteous debate. I don't wonder he prefers the battle-ax." Taft vowed to carry on and ignore the Colonel.

Harder to dismiss was the criticism of Senator Lodge and most of the Foreign Relations Committee, which quickly recommended against ratification. In their judgment, the latitude given the joint commission was excessive. If the commission decided that an issue arising from the Monroe Doctrine or immigration policy was justiciable, the United States would either have to arbitrate or abrogate, Cabot wrote Theodore. "I will not put my hand to a treaty that promises to do things which we know we would not do. That is not advancing peace but promoting war and trouble." The senators also saw the commission's broad authority as usurpation of their own constitutional prerogatives in making foreign policy.

The Colonel and the Senate were formidable antagonists, but the great phalanxes of the public and the press, including *The Outlook*, were arrayed on Taft's side. In the same September number with Roosevelt's vitriol was the first of three editorials praising the treaties. Several proponents of arbitration pointed out that Roosevelt's argument for "righteousness" was easily shredded: one nation's sense of right often conflicted with another's. The president asked that the treaties not be debated until December, and when the Senate agreed, Taft took his brief to the people. Beaten down by his life in the White House, he no longer looked forward to the long railroad jaunts he had once used to refresh himself. He sometimes felt like resigning, he confessed to Butt, "but damn it, what is a man to do when they get him in a corner and crowd him as they are crowding me now? I have got to go through with it. I would not be a man if I did not fight it out." Back and forth across fifteen thousand miles and twenty-eight states, Taft fought it out for fifty-eight days, promoting the treaties and defending his administration in nearly four hundred speeches to more than four million citizens.

But his despair showed itself almost daily. Barely launched on the trip, he met a shout of "Three cheers for the next president of the United States!" with a defeatist "My friend, I fear you are not a prophet." He praised TR for awakening the country to the cause of conservation but blamed his own administration's poor record in that sphere on a paralysis created by "extremists" (one of whom was surely Gifford Pinchot). In Minnesota, scene of his disastrous 1909 speech on the best of all possible tariffs, he scolded a boisterous audience of college students and veered off on a strange tangent about the Northern races and their unbecoming pride in forthrightness. "Heaven save me from a candid friend," he said, inadvertently exposing one of his most serious defects as a leader. In Cheyenne, Wyoming, he fervently promised to reduce the tariff on wool—unwelcome news in sheep country.

Writing about Taft long after his presidency, William Allen White observed that he always spoke without "remotely realizing the import of the spoken words of a president to a multitude" and had "no sense of the importance of a speech as a speech." Nor did Taft ever acquire the knack of pleasing an audience. The speeches without gaffes were arid and stiff. His aides tried in vain to nudge him away from legalisms and statistics, toward broad themes and simple, heartfelt truths. Watching Taft's bored audiences and seeing them flicker to life at any mention of his predecessor, Archie Butt wrote his sister-in-law, "I feel so sorry for him sometimes I could almost cry."

Taft's visit to San Francisco squeezed Theodore Roosevelt, Jr., between his need to show the respect due a president and his wish not to enthuse. He decided to attend the banquet welcoming Taft to the city but declined a place at the head table. Ted was thinking of voting Democratic in 1912 if New Jersey's progressive governor, Woodrow Wilson, was the nominee. TR urged him to wait and to keep the thought to himself, as such a defection would undoubtedly be attributed to his father's influence.

Taft came home from his travels thinking that he would win the nomination but not the election, a judgment shared by the first lady. He seemed content with his prospects. "If we lose the election I shall feel that the party is rejected, whereas if I fail to secure the renomination it will be a personal defeat," he told her.

A FTER TOURING CALIFORNIA with Taft, Hiram Johnson, the state's progressive new governor, wrote Oyster Bay that he had not heard in the president's speeches "a single syllable of sympathy with human beings, except, possibly, the apostrophe in his speech on peace, when it said that 'the poor are the food for powder.' There was never in his attitude any indication that he was governing for any but one class and for one purpose: business." Johnson asked Roosevelt what California's progressives should do. If they supported Taft, they would hand the state back to the reactionaries, but as laudable as they found La Follette, they did not believe he could wrest the nomination from Taft. "I do not believe this would be the case as against you," he told Roosevelt. "I think you underestimate entirely the feeling of the people toward you."

In reply Johnson received one of Roosevelt's last stout professions that he did not wish to run and one of the first definite hints that he might. "My honest opinion is that the East would resent my nomination, would feel that in some way I had intrigued to bring it about, and would experience a revulsion of feeling about Taft and think that I had treated him badly," he wrote. "Now I would not feel that I had a right to object to being sacrificed if it were necessary to sacrifice me, if we had to lead a forlorn hope and that I was the best person to lead it. But I do very strongly feel that I ought not to be asked to have my throat cut when the throat-cutting would damage me and in addition, what is infinitely more important, would damage the progressive cause we have at heart."

While Taft was in California, three hundred progressive Republicans from twenty-five states convened at the La Salle Hotel in Chicago to endorse La Follette and organize their campaign against Taft. Jim Garfield rose early and watched a beautiful autumn sunrise over Lake Michigan before putting in a long, arduous day of trying to persuade the convention to think of its support of La Follette as a recommendation rather than a pledge. La Follette was not well liked in the East, he told them, and they should leave a door open in case they needed to back another candidate. Garfield argued all day but was outvoted by progressives who believed that La Follette deserved their support. No Republican but Fighting Bob had been brave enough to challenge Taft openly, and the cause of the progressive Republicans needed an identifiable leader.

A week later, when an *Outlook* editorial characterized the endorsement as "a recommendation rather than a committal of the movement to any one man," La Follette deduced that it had "suddenly dawned upon Roosevelt that Taft could be beaten." Gilson Gardner, a Washington correspondent for the Scripps newspapers, confirmed La Follette's hunch and his fears. "Roosevelt wants to be president again," Gardner told him after a visit with the Colonel. TR finally understood the popular momentum behind the progressives, saw that La Follette had a chance at the nomination, and grasped that even if La Follette did not get it, he would emerge from the 1912 fight as the leader of the progressive wing of the Republican Party. Gardner was blunt with the senator: as the Colonel saw it, "you would be in the way in 1916."

ROOSEVELT WAS EDGING toward the presidential race, but for much of the autumn, his chief concern was Edith's health. On September 30 she was pitched from her horse, landing hard on macadam. She was knocked out, suffered a concussion, dislocated three vertebrae, and lost her senses of taste and smell. By October 27, Theodore's fifty-third birthday, she was recovering but still weak and plagued by headaches. "Mrs. Roosevelt had a very narrow escape," TR wrote a friend. Colonel Roosevelt also had a narrow escape, although he did not say so in his letters, perhaps because the possibility of losing her was too terrifying to contemplate. But his anxiety fairly bounded off the page. He described Edith as "shattered" and "wasted," and he seemed unable to retain even the simplest facts about her fall. Some of his letters say her unconsciousness lasted twenty-four hours, others say forty-eight, still others seventy-two. Needing a villain, he came close to accusing the horse of malice aforethought, declaring that it had made a "deliberate and vicious swerve."

The newspapers delivered on his birthday landed another blow. Taft's attorney general had filed suit against the U.S. Steel Corporation, charging that its purchase of Tennessee Coal and Iron was intended to reduce competition in the steel industry. The suit did not accuse Roosevelt of any illegality, but it mentioned him by name and said that the Morgan men who had sped to the White House to confer with him during the panic were less than frank about their motives. The suggestion was that Roosevelt had been hoodwinked.

TR was livid. Taft himself, as a member of Roosevelt's cabinet at the time, had praised his handling of the incident. TR assumed—correctly— that Taft had not read the charges before they were filed, but in Roosevelt's view, that excused nothing, as a president was ultimately responsible for the official actions of his cabinet. The documents had been drawn up in secret, allegedly to prevent speculation in the stocks and bonds of steel companies, but there would have been no reason to conceal them from the president. Perhaps the attorney general, like the rest of the cabinet of this disengaged president, was so accustomed to operating on his own that it did not occur to him to involve Taft. Or perhaps he saw no reason to intrude on the president's speaking tour. The principal author of the indictment was J. M. Dickinson, the former secretary of war who had collared Archie Butt at the garden party to vituperate about Stimson's appointment and Roosevelt's assault on the arbitration treaties.

TR retaliated in *The Outlook*, defending his honor and offering a pointed brief for the Roosevelt way of running the country. The Taft administration, although mostly warmhearted toward big business, was committed to trust-busting, but its strategy of filing one lawsuit after another was chaotic and economically unsound, Roosevelt declared. It left corporations in a fog of uncertainty. Big was not intrinsically bad, he argued, and nothing would be gained by breaking up a colossus *"which has not offended otherwise than by its size."* Well-behaved giants needed regulation, not prosecution—"constructive legislation" rather than "destructive litigation." He proposed a federal corporations commission with broad regulatory powers.

Taft read the article and concluded that Roosevelt had blundered. The commission idea was one long favored by Wall Street, which believed that a small regulatory body would prove even more malleable than Congress and the courts. Roosevelt would now be regarded as the tool of the trusts, Taft told Butt on an afternoon walk a few weeks after the suit was filed. Taft wished Dickinson had not mentioned Roosevelt in the indictment, and he blamed the attorney general for not asking him to review the documents. A lame excuse, thought Butt, who understood that the suit destroyed any hope of a reconciliation between Taft and Roosevelt. The long-dreaded duel was about to begin.

Back at the White House, Butt asked if he could do anything else before leaving for the night. "I really feel so blue and depressed that I shall spend the evening alone," Taft replied. "I simply don't feel like talking to anybody." The next day, pleading a cold, he canceled all his engagements.

SEVEN

Off the Pedestal

Q UIETLY AND ALONE, Theodore and Edith Roosevelt celebrated
their twenty-fifth wedding anniversary on December 2. With
century-old Madeira carried to New York in a sailing ship owned
by Edith's grandfather, Theodore toasted her health. She was at last hale
enough to take walks, although the doctors could not say when she might
reach full strength or whether her senses of taste and smell would return.

As Edith made her slow climb, Theodore was scrambling down the barren alp reserved for ex-presidents, and by the time the Madeira was poured
he had made up his mind to challenge Taft for the nomination. The day before, he had instructed Alice to warn Archie Butt that he should leave the
White House staff soon, "before the crash came." TR also had written Jim
Garfield that he would no longer object to tub-thumping on his behalf.
Garfield's friend Walter Brown, chief of Ohio's Republicans, immediately
declared Roosevelt the party's choice, a stinging humiliation for Ohio's favorite son, William Howard Taft.

Roosevelt, whose self-knowledge was spotty, had a sheaf of high-minded
rationales for entering the fight but not a single credible insight into his motives. The border between self-restraint and self-gratification is porous, and
Roosevelt easily slipped across, giving himself permission to do the thing he
had been telling himself he must not do. Had the next presidential election
been two or three years out, his fury with Taft and his jealousy of La Follette
might have burned away, but given the circumstances, Roosevelt was, as the
awed Irishman said of Niagara, unable ta kape himself back.

The enthusiasm for his proposal to regulate trusts through a strong federal commission allowed him to imagine that he had hit upon "the one really practical platform put forth by any leader." Taft means well, he wrote a fellow progressive, "but he means well feebly," and La Follette was too radical for the East. Depicting himself as a leader with a platform exposed his desire, but he went on as if the idea of running for the White House in 1912 had not occurred to him before the *Outlook* piece "caused what evidently had been a very strong undercurrent to come to the surface in the shape of talk about my nomination for the presidency."

In early December, when emissaries from Taft and La Follette asked Roosevelt to state his intentions, they received a dodgy reply selected from his favorite impeccable source, Abraham Lincoln: no one had a right to ask a man whether he would cross a bridge until he came to it. In the letters he wrote as the calendar marched inexorably toward 1912, TR recited reasons for avoiding the contest—the morass awaiting any president who succeeded Taft, Wall Street's Roosevelt allergy, and the likelihood of alienating voters who would feel that he had betrayed his protégé.

But privately TR began telling his associates that he would accept the nomination if it came to him properly—not through intrigue and not to fulfill his own ambitions "but simply and solely because the bulk of the people wanted a given job done, and for their own sakes, and not mine, wanted me to do that job." Such a demand probably would not develop, he said, but if it did, "I should feel that there was a duty to the people which I could not shirk." Unable or unwilling to acknowledge the frustrations of powerlessness and his hunger for action, TR seemed to believe that duty had compelled him to attack Taft's arbitration treaties and the administration's antitrust policy, duty required him to withhold support from La Follette, and duty would force him to respond to a call from the people.

When word of Roosevelt's willingness to accept the nomination reached La Follette's advisers, they understood at once that their candidate was finished, but La Follette, scorning surrender, summoned his war council to compose a letter to Roosevelt, a demand that he declare himself. The effort quickly foundered on the senator's refusal to offer the obvious quid pro quo, a pledge to support Roosevelt if he emerged as the party's candidate. La Follette rejected the proposition on principle: Roosevelt was not a true progressive and would compromise the movement into oblivion. A few hours after the council dispersed, Gifford Pinchot returned to report that he and a few others had decided to switch their allegiance to the Colonel in the event of a split between him and La Follette. "You must know that he has this thing in his own hands and can do whatever he likes," Pinchot told him. La Follette was granitic, vowing to remain in the race until the convention's gavel fell for the last time.

La Follette refused to meet with Roosevelt for fear of creating the impression that they might join forces, but the senator's emissaries soon met with the Colonel at Amos Pinchot's home in New York. Roosevelt had no plans to announce his availability, he told the gathering, although he might allow his name to be put forward if it appeared that La Follette could not capture the nomination. But he would do so reluctantly unless he thought he could win the election, he said. The optimists went home convinced that Roosevelt would not be a candidate, the pessimists that he might step in at any time. The cynics believed that he was already running.

During this half-in, half-out phase, Roosevelt insisted that he was not a candidate and bridled at any accusation of duplicity, but his construction of "I am not a candidate" was easily misunderstood. To him, not being a candidate meant only that he was not actively in pursuit of the nomination. It did not necessarily mean that he would decline the nomination if it were tendered or that he *never* would be a candidate.

The Colonel finished the year with another blast at the arbitration treaties, timing it to coincide with Taft's appearance at a banquet of peace activists in New York. (Asked why he would not attend, Roosevelt had snapped, "I'm not hungry.") The pretext for his new onslaught in *The Outlook* was the administration's desire to abrogate an old commercial treaty with Russia, which was harassing Russian-born American Jews who returned as visitors. Roosevelt favored the abrogation but thought it proved his point that the United States would break a treaty before agreeing to arbitrate a dispute over the rights of American citizens. To Taft, abrogating the Russian treaty demonstrated the opposite: if the Senate ratified his arbitration treaties, only justiciable quarrels would go to The Hague, and a nation's right to protect its citizens was clearly not justiciable.

"It is very hard to take all the slaps Roosevelt is handing me," Taft told Archie Butt on the night of the banquet. "Everyone wants me to answer his last attack, in which he practically calls me a hypocrite." Roosevelt had gone as far as he dared, using the word "hypocrisy" in the title and working it into each of his last three sentences. If the critic were anyone else, Taft said, he would respond, but he still hoped to avoid a public clash with his old friend. "He knows that, and he has me at a disadvantage."

As always Taft gravitated toward inertia, but for once Butt thought inertia a wise choice, because any duel with Roosevelt was bound to end in disaster for Taft. Too agitated to sit as they waited for their signal to enter the banquet hall, Taft paced and for the umpteenth time confessed his bafflement. "I don't know what he is driving at except to make my way more difficult. I could not ask his advice on all questions. I could not subordinate my administration to him and retain my self-respect, but it is hard, very hard, Archie, to see a devoted friendship going to pieces like a rope of sand."

The Major volunteered no consolation, although he thought Roosevelt was wrong about the treaties and wrong to urge him to flee the White House. After Alice's warning, Butt had quickly resolved to stay on until the next inauguration. Only a coward would abandon a sinking president, he decided. But while the Major's loyalties tugged him toward Taft, his affections tossed him toward Roosevelt, and he did not know where to lay the blame for the rift. On this bleak winter evening, Butt was inclined to fault Taft. The president often spoke scathingly of Roosevelt in front of gossips and had waited too long to pay Roosevelt the compliment of soliciting his advice. A few such gestures soon after Roosevelt's return from Africa would have won his loyalty, Butt thought. And it seemed to the Major that whatever regret the president felt, he had deliberately forced the break in an effort to draw a line between Roosevelt's White House and his own.

By January 1912 the White House had become a torture to the Tafts. As if to demonstrate his affection for TR, the president continued to invite Alice and Nick Longworth for dinner, and they accepted, but Alice flaunted her displeasure by ignoring the first lady. Mrs. Taft, hoping perhaps to minimize the possibility of encounters with people she did not care to see, asked Archie Butt to instruct the chauffeur to meander in unpopulated directions when she and the president went out for a ride. On New Year's Day, Taft announced that he would stay in the running for the nomination, grimly adding that nothing but death would stop him. Soon laid up with a piercing case of gout, he begged his aides to conceal the illness for fear that Roosevelt would use it against him.

The arbitration treaties died in March, victims of asphyxiation by amendment. A resolution added by Henry Cabot Lodge empowered the Senate to override any decision by the joint commission. Forwarding a draft to Sagamore, Lodge said it was "easy to say that the adoption of this resolution makes the treaties of little value, but that I am prepared to admit." TR was elated. "It seems to me that you have covered everything, that is, that you have taken the guts entirely out of the treaty, which was just what was needed. More power to your elbow!"

When the amended treaties went to the White House for the president's signature, "their own father could not recognize them," Taft wrote long after the fact. "So I put them on the shelf and let the dust accumulate on them in the hope that the senators might change their minds, or that the people might change the Senate, instead of which they changed me."

The failed treaties exposed the chasm between those who believe that humankind fundamentally aspires to goodness and those who believe that human nature is a beast in need of a short leash. Taft hoped the United States could start the world on a glorious path away from war. But for Lodge and Root and Roosevelt, peace was an ideal, conflict was the inevitable reality, and the nation unable to hold its own in a dispute had no hope of winning. Taft cared less for victory than for justice. In his vision, military might would count for nothing at The Hague, where all nations would be equal before the law. To Roosevelt, the law was insufficient—cumbersome, violable, inconsistently administered. More important were the character of the man behind the law and the arsenal behind the man. Roosevelt was not wholly wrong, but his bludgeoning of the treaties was disingenuous and unnecessary. He had no patriotic duty to speak out. As he knew from his own presidential experiences in treaty-making, the Senate would defeat the new arbitration agreements with or without his advice and consent. His lash had been directed at Taft, and his refusal to admit it had a tinge of the cowardice he despised.

FOR THE PASSIONATE, believing is seeing, and once Roosevelt believed that the nomination could be his, he could see no other acceptable course, no other sensible candidate. No one in the running would do the country as much good as he would, he told a longtime friend in December. The mail arriving at Sagamore affirmed his belief. "You would be astounded at the feeling for you in the [Republican] National Committee," a friendly journalist wrote from Washington. "Men who have opposed you now favor your nomination." La Follette could not carry the convention, Taft could not win the election, therefore Roosevelt was the Republicans' best hope. Lodge laid out another syllogism making the rounds: Roosevelt had selected Taft to succeed him, Taft had failed, therefore Roosevelt had a duty to undo the damage. Even William Allen White, who wanted Roosevelt to avoid the complications of 1912 and wait for 1916, had begun thinking that Roosevelt would be forced to run. Thousands of Republican postmasters and small-town mayors and dogcatchers stood to lose their jobs when Taft lost his, White pointed out. "This large illuminated fact is before their eyes now every moment of the day. I think you might just as well prepare for the fireworks because it is coming."

To his friends' reasons, Roosevelt added his own. The Republican Party, Lincoln's party, was in danger of losing its soul to reactionaries. Governor Woodrow Wilson of New Jersey, the Democratic star rising in the East, struck Roosevelt as "pretty thin material for a president," and the Democrats were likely to return the country to a kind of rural toryism, with a weak federal government. Roosevelt either did not discern or would not own his wish to annihilate Taft, his need to depose La Follette, or his longing for a return to power. In the pages of *The Outlook* he could opine and propose, criticize and analyze, but he could not make anything happen. And as he had told his audience at the Sorbonne, the man in the arena mattered infinitely more than the critic in the stands. Opinions were wind. The essence of politics was action, and effective action required power.

Taft's and La Follette's adjutants continued to press Roosevelt to declare himself in or out of the contest, while his friends steered him in the direction of silence. As William Rockhill Nelson of the *Kansas City Star* told him, "You have your opponents bottled up. Why pull out the stopper?" Bottled up they were. Legions of middle-of-the-road Republicans, tepid about Taft and fearful of La Follette, were not reaching into their pockets for either of them as long as there was a chance that Roosevelt might run.

In the middle of January, Governor Herbert S. Hadley of Missouri presented the first compelling practical argument for ending the silence. Unless Roosevelt announced soon, the nomination would go to Taft because the bosses who controlled Republican organizations around the country were calling early state conventions to elect delegates pledged to vote for Taft at the national convention. A half-dozen other progressive Republican governors, perhaps with encouragement from Roosevelt's coterie, sent similar messages to Oyster Bay.

It occurred to Roosevelt that the governors could ease his entry into the campaign by writing him that the people of their states wished he would run and asking if he would accept the nomination. In a letter sketching the idea for one of the governors, Roosevelt claimed that speaking out had come to seem the lesser of two evils. But his new sense of urgency undoubtedly came from the danger flagged by Hadley: if he did not act soon, the possibility of the nomination would vanish.

Despite the crisis inside the La Follette campaign, Fighting Bob was at the apex of his popularity in January. Toward the end of the month he spoke at Carnegie Hall to a crowd that overflowed into the streets. He was welcomed with warm applause and a radiant introduction by Gifford Pinchot. TR was soliloquizing at a dinner table elsewhere in the city.

The newspapers found La Follette's brand of progressivism a bit severe, and the *New York World*, piecing together hints of the disintegration of his campaign, concluded that he had been set up. "The plan is working well," said the *World*. "Mr. Roosevelt is playing fast and loose. Roosevelt headquarters have been opened in Chicago. . . . Roosevelt clubs are being organized throughout the West. . . . With Taft out of the way the road is clear for Roosevelt and a stampeded convention. That is the real work that La Follette is doing. Consciously or unconsciously, he is the Roosevelt decoy duck."

La Follette too would soon believe that he had been set up, but the men funding his campaign were in agony over the coming split. Amos Pinchot, recognizing that La Follette's appeal would never match Roosevelt's, saw that if Roosevelt decided to run and they stood by La Follette, the two factions would be "at each other's throats and practically work for the nomination of Taft." Certain that La Follette's cause was lost, the Pinchots and others asked at the end of January to be released from their pledge of support. La Follette reminded them of his promise to fight till the end of the convention and theirs to do the same. He could not hold them to their vow but would not give them the satisfaction of consenting to their departure.

Both the decoy and the real duck were now racing downstream. Years later, reflecting on his friend Roosevelt's return to politics, the novelist Owen Wister would recall the June day in 1910 when Governor Charles Evans Hughes of New York bore down on Roosevelt at Harvard's commencement exercises and solicited his support of the primary bill then pending in the state legislature. Roosevelt agreed to help for "the same reason that a duck takes to water," Wister wrote. "In the appeals made to him before he met Hughes, the water had not come quite so close to the duck. Hughes had dragged him to the edge of a definite pond, and into the pond he plumped. What a small pond after all—one bill in one State—for an ex-President to notice! And then the pond flowed speedily into a brook, and the brook speedily into a river, and down the river he went toward a sea that neither he nor friend nor enemy dreamed of."

On February 2, a few days after the defections, La Follette's candidacy imploded, and by another of those contingencies that neither friend nor enemy dreamed of, Wister saw it happen. Curious about Senator La Follette and Governor Wilson, one of whom might be the next president, the Periodical Publishers Association invited them to Philadelphia to address its annual banquet. Wister, who lived in the city, attended as a guest of *The Saturday Evening Post*. Wilson spoke first—with "flawless art," Wister thought—making an eloquent case for a progressivism rooted in American traditions and ideals.

La Follette began by saying that if a Democrat were elected president, he hoped it would be Woodrow Wilson, then spoiled the compliment with a histrionic bow. From there he launched a barrage at the press, and as a few editors and publishers made for the door, he accused them of cowardice. He ranted on, repeating great chunks of his speech (many of them more than once), and ignoring a chorus of catcalls. Wister surmised that "a lifetime of fighting against the odds had trained him to face the music to the finish." Seeing no end to the spectacle, Wister left after ninety minutes. La Follette raged for another forty minutes, took his seat, and slumped to the table.

The speech as written was a bold, reasoned warning of the perils of a press dependent on advertising revenue. Unless publishers were vigilant, he argued, they would find themselves publishing only what their advertisers deemed acceptable. In top form, Fighting Bob could have presented his brief with sparkle and wit. But the crumbling of his campaign had backed him to the brink, he had been ill since eating tainted oysters a week before, and one of his children was in the hospital awaiting a difficult, risky surgery.

The day after the debacle, La Follette met with reporters at his home in Washington and was surprised to learn of his endless repetition. Before the banquet he had clocked the speech at forty minutes and assumed that he had spent the other ninety minutes extemporizing. He admitted to being worn out but offered no excuses, and, perhaps because he did not understand that the damage was fatal, was not particularly upset. Philadelphia was a setback, he said, "but I have grown fat on that sort of thing all my life."

W ITH LA FOLLETTE'S COLLAPSE, the question hanging over Sagamore was not "if" but "when." Theodore judged it unseemly to make an announcement until the shock of Philadelphia subsided, and he had not yet heard from the governors. Edith, wanting no part of the bedlam, absented herself in early February for a long stay in Manhattan followed by a three-week excursion to the Caribbean. "Politics are hateful," she wrote Kermit. She could foresee "no possible result which could give me aught but keen regret."

Three days after La Follette's breakdown, Cabot wrote Theodore of an awkward encounter at the White House, where an aide had ambushed him in Taft's presence, requesting a statement in support of the president's nomination. The ploy was in "execrable taste," Cabot thought, and showed "a kind of sharp smartness, as if he thought that by asking that question in the presence of the president he could get me to commit myself to him." Cabot had met the lunge squarely, telling the aide that the president understood his situation perfectly. "He knows that if in any way I should declare against or oppose Mr. Roosevelt I should be the veriest dog that ever walked the earth." With a good-natured chuckle Taft mused that Lodge's position was almost as ticklish as his own. When the aide suggested that TR's desire for a third term might offend the citizenry, Lodge said he saw no hazard to the Republic and bade the president good morning.

On the same day Taft cornered another of Roosevelt's friends, Secretary of the Navy George von Lengerke Meyer, one of the few survivors of the cabinet purge, and asked him to make some campaign speeches. After three years in Taft's administration Meyer could not honorably refuse, but as a friend of the Colonel, he found the request unnerving. "I have never felt more distressed over a situation in my life," he wrote his wife.

Meyer and Lodge hoped that Roosevelt would remain silent, as did Elihu Root, although Root understood Roosevelt's weaknesses in this line. Silence would be "very difficult, especially difficult because of your temperament," he had written TR. The need for action induced a state of "unstable equilibrium," Root told him; "your whole nature will frequently cry out and urge you to end it. No thirsty sinner ever took a pledge which was harder for him to keep than it will be for you to maintain this position."

Nick Longworth, one more voice for silence, mustered arguments aimed at Roosevelt's preoccupation with posterity. If TR merely waited for the convention to choose a candidate, he would win the nomination and the election, Nick predicted. If he announced his availability, the public would think he was acting to spite Taft. And if he pursued the nomination and lost, his prestige would suffer, but if he stood by and the nomination went to Taft, the result could not be construed as a Roosevelt defeat.

Months before, TR had encouraged Nick to support Taft and still believed that as a Republican congressman representing a Republican president's home district, Nick had no alternative. Nick had publicly put himself in the Taft camp but emphasized that he was a progressive, an effort to separate himself from the Old Guard. "[M]y political bed will not be by any means a bed of roses," he wrote TR in early February. Whenever possible, Nick turned away speaking engagements so that he would not have to laud the president, but there was no escape from a forthcoming conclave of the Republican clubs in his district. Taft and Root were also scheduled to appear, Nick said. "Under the circumstances I cannot avoid some reference to the presidency. Alice thinks I ought not again to say that I am for Taft. I don't see how I can help it, with the president there. Would you mind giving me your judgment as to which of us is right?"

The Colonel was violently sympathetic. "You let me know how matters are in your district and I will try to smash up any Roosevelt creature who antagonizes you. . . . Of course you must be for Taft." He declined to arbitrate the dispute between Nick and Alice but alerted them that he had finally decided to declare himself. "If I were longer doubtful, I would telegraph you to come on and talk with me, but it would not be any use now, Nick. I have got to come out."

Roosevelt told some of his associates that he had to show himself to rebut charges of double-dealing, but the deeper consideration was practical. Primaries were about to play their first significant role in a presidential election. In twelve states, ordinary voters, not party bosses, would be allowed to express their preference among the candidates or elect delegates to the national convention or both. If Roosevelt made a good showing in the primaries, he could present himself as the choice of the people and would go to the Republican presidential convention with hundreds of delegates committed to vote for his nomination.

On February 10, as Nick was going through his charade with Taft and Root in Cincinnati, eight progressive Republican governors sounded the trumpets calling Roosevelt to duty. After careful investigation, they said, they had concluded that most Republican voters favored his nomination and most Americans favored his election. "We believe that your candidacy will insure success in the next campaign. We believe that you represent, as no other man represents, those principles and policies upon which we must appeal for a majority of the votes of the American people, and which, in our opinion, are necessary for the happiness and prosperity of the country." They requested that he declare soon whether he would accept the nomination if it came to him "unsolicited and unsought" and told him that if it came, he had a "plain public duty" to accept.

Asked to comment when the letter was released to the press, the Colonel promised to respond in a fortnight.

ROOSEVELT'S FORTNIGHT gave Taft a year's worth of misery. Archie Butt could see it in his face—thin-lipped, waxen, hollow-eyed—and implored him to summon his doctors. Taft implored him to go to hell. The president was living in a Roosevelt delirium, babbling that Roosevelt would win the nomination, Roosevelt would disgrace himself, Roosevelt had to be fought to the death. The tragedy had begun, Butt wrote his family. "It is moving now from day to day with the irresistible force of the Greek drama, and I see no way for anything save divine Providence to interpose to save the reputation of either should they hurl themselves at each other."

Providence neglected to appear, and into the vacuum pranced the imps of the perverse. On February 20 Roosevelt left home to address a state constitutional convention in Columbus, Ohio. He had planned to declare himself after the trip, but the opportunity to transgress on Taft's native soil proved irresistible. Asked by a newspaperman if he planned to run, he told all: "My hat is in the ring; the fight is on and I am stripped to the buff."

TR's speech was wholesomely entitled "A Charter of Democracy," but stripped to the buff, it was an indictment of the American judicial system. Too often, he asserted, judges rested their decisions on technicalities, ignoring "the great immutable principles of justice." And too often, by abusing their power to declare a law unconstitutional, they subverted the will of the people, whose elected representatives were charged with making the law.

This power of the judiciary had troubled Roosevelt since his days as a young state assemblyman, when he visited New York City tenements where cigars were made and saw the diseases caused by the presence of large quantities of tobacco. Eye and lung ailments were rampant, and sores covered the bodies of many young children. Back in Albany, Roosevelt championed a ban on cigar-making at home, got it passed, then saw it struck down by a judge who ruled that it violated an individual's right to do as he chose in his own home. "It was this case which first waked me to a dim and partial understanding of the fact that the courts were not necessarily the best judges of what should be done to better social and industrial conditions," he would write in his autobiography. Too many judges "knew legalism, but not life."

Throughout the 1890s, judges (including William Howard Taft) regularly blocked the path to decent wages and working conditions with injunctions against strikes and boycotts. Without irony they invoked the Sherman Antitrust Act, the law passed to curb abuses by large corporations, to rule that a strike was a conspiracy to deprive an employer of the use of his property. Over time, Roosevelt wrote, "the courts had been twisted into the exaltation of property rights over human rights." The Square Deal had addressed some of the wrongs, but judges continued to find that health and safety legislation, workmen's compensation laws, and other public welfare measures infringed upon individual liberties.

Beneath the conflict between individual rights and the collective well-being lay another great struggle, between the power of the legislature and the power of the courts. On the one side was the legislature's so-called police power—its constitutional authority to pass laws protecting the general welfare—and on the other was the power of the courts to interpret the law. Observing that the power to interpret the law was in effect the power to establish the law, Roosevelt said there was little point in enacting a progressive agenda only to have it whittled away by the courts. When a state's legislators and its judges disagreed on the constitutionality of a law, Roosevelt thought the dispute should be settled by popular vote. And through the mechanism of the recall, the electorate could vote to uphold or overturn a judicial decision and vote a judge out of office if necessary.

Oregon and California had instituted the recall of public officials, but the issue drew no lightning until 1911, when Taft vetoed the bill granting statehood to Arizona because the state's constitution included a provision for recalling judges. In Taft's opinion the average voter was not equipped to interpret the law, and justice in Arizona would degenerate into "legalized terrorism."

In Columbus, Roosevelt took issue with the power of the courts. Judges should be as accountable to the people as legislators were, he said. "If the American people are not fit for popular government, and if they should of right be the servants and not the masters of the men whom they themselves put in office, then Lincoln's work was wasted and the whole system of government upon which this great democratic Republic rests is a failure."

The speech was received as a desecration. Every educated American had been taught that the rights of a minority were secured by a judiciary fully insulated from the roiling passions of the majority. And Western civilization for centuries had operated on the assumption that the law could be fairly applied only if it was a settled thing—predictable, understood, and accepted.

Taft declared that Roosevelt was "sowing the seeds of confusion and tyranny." Judicial recall "lays the axe at the root of the tree of well-ordered freedom and subjects the guarantees of life, liberty, and property without remedy to the fitful impulse of a temporary majority of the electorate." Overflowing with contempt for the "extremists" who favored the recall of judges or judicial decisions, he said they were not progressives but "political emotionalists or neurotics." Freud's ideas being new and not entirely respectable in the United States, Roosevelt's allies read "neurotic" as a synonym for "crazy."

Cabot was "pained and depressed" by the Columbus speech. He had known that he and Theodore disagreed about the courts, but he had not realized that they occupied the antipodes. "I have had my share of mishaps in politics, but I never thought that any situation could arise which would have made me so miserably unhappy as I have been during the past week," he wrote Sagamore. He had promised to give an address on the Constitution at Princeton, after which he would remain silent, he said. "I cannot tell you how much I have suffered from these harsh necessities and so I shall say no more."

Theodore did not know whether to be touched or amused. "My dear fellow, you could not do anything that would make me lose my warm personal affection for you. . . . I shan't try to justify my viewpoint because it would seem as if I were attacking yours. . . . Of course, you will stand by your convictions. Now, don't you ever think of this matter again."

FROM OHIO TR went buoyantly to Massachusetts for a meeting of Harvard's board of overseers and a dinner with Kermit and Ted and Nick at the Porcellian Club, the choicest of Harvard's eating clubs and an institution that ranked close behind the Rough Riders in TR's affections. He had belonged, as had Ted and Nick, and Kermit's membership, just gained, called for a feast.

Next afternoon Roosevelt went to the home of his friend Robert Grant, a Boston judge and fellow overseer. Grasping the full significance of the moment, Grant recorded Roosevelt's visit in a remarkably detailed letter to a man likely to preserve it, the historian James Ford Rhodes. It was Sunday,

February 25, twenty past three, when Roosevelt arrived, and the house was already "the storm center of the country, not altogether to my relish, fond as I am of Theodore," Grant wrote.

The fortnight had ended, and Theodore had composed his reply to the governors, a brief statement of his willingness to accept the nomination should it be offered. He was acting "purely from the standpoint of the interests of the people as a whole," he said. He promised to remain available until the convention cast its final ballot and voiced his hope that voters would "be given the chance, through direct primaries, to express their preference as to who shall be the nominee of the Republican presidential convention." At six o'clock TR met briefly with reporters.

Dinner lasted until eleven-thirty, and the conversation — "an absorbing monologue punctuated by questions and suggestions — was mainly on the burning topic," Grant wrote. He and TR were joined by Mrs. Grant and two of the Grants' sons; William Allen White; Arthur Hill, a Boston attorney who had influenced Roosevelt's thinking on the judicial system; and William Roscoe Thayer, a future Roosevelt biographer. Judge Grant handled the interrogation, and his questions left no doubt about his concerns. Hadn't Roosevelt's friends advised him against entering the race? Hadn't Taft been improving as president? Wouldn't the public be offended by Roosevelt's turn against Taft? Would any Republican leaders support Roosevelt? At bottom, wasn't he acting because he wanted to be president again?

Roosevelt submitted to the examination with a composure that impressed both Grant and Thayer. "Vehement he was — because he could not describe even a butterfly without vividness which easily passed into vehemence," Thayer would recall. But he thought that Roosevelt spoke throughout the evening with "the underlying gravity of one who knows that he is about to make a very important decision."

Yes, Roosevelt told his companions, his friends opposed the run. He himself had been uncertain but in the end concluded that it would be cowardly to turn away from the call sounded by the governors. TR agreed that Taft was improving but said that his wishy-washy presidency had reduced the Republican Party to the party of "respectable inactivity." He owed Taft nothing, he said, and when Grant pressed the point, Roosevelt insisted that the debts were on Taft's side of the ledger. ("Taft never did anything for me," he had just written a friend. "I made him president.") No, he could not count on support from Republicans, not even from Lodge. Yes, the odds were long, but he saw a chance to win the nomination if he fared well in the primaries. To the question about his longings for the White House, he said simply, "I like power, but I care nothing to be president as president. I am interested in these ideas of mine and I want to carry them through, and feel that I am the one to carry them through."

White left the dinner in a state of "bewildered zeal," and Grant's feelings had no more clarity than White's. Grant suspected that Roosevelt was making a futile, possibly fatal error. "He might so easily have waited," he told Rhodes. "To have declared that he would not on any account accept a nomination this year . . . would have kept him on the pedestal . . . and shown him also more magnanimous." And yet, said Grant, "I am so in sympathy with his desire to right humanitarian wrongs, and such a true admirer of his, that I am generally classed as one of his supporters, though I disapprove of what he has done, and feel a little as if a baby had been left on my doorsteps."

At midnight, done in by the strenuous day, Grant escorted his guest upstairs to his room. TR paused at the threshold, treated his body to a grand stretch, and made one last announcement: "I feel fine as silk."

EIGHT

Another Cup of Coffee

ROOSEVELT'S emergence raised few ripples at the White House, where the president had been expecting it for weeks. The first lady, grimly triumphant, said, "I told you so four years ago," and recalled his skepticism. With a laugh he conceded her prescience and returned cut with thrust: "I think you are perfectly happy now. You would have preferred the Colonel to come out against me than to have been wrong yourself."

Archie Butt was no more surprised than his wards, although the timing pitched him into a quandary. About to depart for a month's rest, prescribed by his physician, he felt he should stay as a comfort to the Tafts yet feared that without a holiday he would crack. "I drive myself like a steam engine and feel tired all the time," he wrote his family. He decided to go, took a moment to tell his sister-in-law where his papers were stored ("in case the old ship goes down"), and within a week was sailing for Italy on the SS *Berlin*, an almost-new ship of the North German Lloyd line.

One of the last to hear TR's news was Archie Roosevelt, who had been camping with his schoolmates in the mountains of Arizona. Startled and a bit apprehensive, he wrote home for an explanation. "I got into the fight with the utmost reluctance simply because I did not see that any other man was leading it now," TR told him.

Reaction beyond Roosevelt's circle was censorious. The Colonel had behaved with "indecent eagerness," one Boston worthy wrote another. Aware that their kind was vastly outnumbered at the polls, the Brahmin took heart from the tut-tutting he overheard on the streetcars and among his servants.

H. H. Kohlsaat, a newspaper publisher who admired Roosevelt, tried flattery. "You are the most courageous man I ever met in reversing your opinion or position if you were convinced you were doing right by doing so," Kohlsaat wrote him. He urged immediate withdrawal. Andrew Carnegie told the Colonel that he had "ignominiously diminished" Taft by seeking to deprive him of a second term. Have a frank talk with the president, Carnegie urged. "You are big enough to discard mean, petty trifles and renew your idyllic relations before history records you as fools, or worse."

In Henry Adams's vivid judgment, Roosevelt had, "deliberately and effectively, cut the throats of Cabot, George Meyer, Stimson, Gussy Gardner, and Nick Longworth, with a butcher's knife." Augustus P. Gardner, Cabot's son-in-law and a congressman from Massachusetts, retaliated by publicly challenging TR to a debate. Roosevelt dismissed the challenge with a scoff but was deeply hurt. Secretary of War Stimson and Secretary of the Navy Meyer would campaign for Taft and do their writhing in private. As the unpalatable work began, Stimson wrote TR, "I feel very much as if the horizon of my little world was swimming a good deal, and it is hard to look forward to a time when I am not working and thinking with you."

Adams, claiming that he always expected the worst and always found things worse than he'd expected, concluded that Roosevelt was insane. Adams's dark wit relied heavily on exaggeration, but in this instance his fear was earnest. Rumors of Roosevelt's insanity and of alcoholic excesses abounded—understandably, as there was no rational motive for his conduct. Had a lion devoured him on safari, the script for the presidential election of 1912 would scarcely have differed. Taft would have staggered through as the lost and wounded king, La Follette would have played Roosevelt's part as the bright prince of what might be, and in the *guerre à mort* their palace would have fallen to the enemy. As the public wondered why Roosevelt would humiliate his old friend, break his 1904 pledge not to run again, defy the unwritten law limiting a president to two terms, squander his prestige, and risk his high standing in history, "crazy" and "drunk" seemed plausible hypotheses.

Rumors of drunkenness would trail him throughout the campaign, and alienists would speculate on the stability of his mind. Dr. S. Weir Mitchell of Philadelphia wrote Taft that he and his fellow neurologists saw "something abnormal" in Roosevelt's compulsion to gratify his "lust for power." Allan McLane Hamilton of New York, specialist in nervous diseases and student of madness in high places, warned the public of "the perils of an insane administration." Hamilton did not mention Roosevelt by name but pointedly declared that until the death of President McKinley, there had been no question about the mental soundness of the nation's presidents. Then came "meddlesome reforms" and muckrakers and socialists spreading "the poison of discontent." He urged the country not to elect a "self-interested and shrewd paranoid" who would arouse the passions of the ignorant, "implanting dissension and dissatisfaction, and possibly overthrowing the long-established laws made by other minds."

Morton Prince, a Boston psychiatrist, used Roosevelt's behavior to introduce the readers of the *New York Times Magazine* to the workings of the subconscious. "When we put something that we do not wish to think about out of our minds, the real thing that we do is to put it into our minds; that is, it becomes subconscious," Prince explained. An unacceptable wish was stowed in the subconscious, often emerging in dreams and sometimes breaking through to consciousness but only in a form "so veiled that we shall not consciously recognize it."

Son of a former mayor of Boston and obviously well briefed on the strains between Taft and Roosevelt, Prince argued that Roosevelt's sadness at leaving the presidency, Taft's ingratitude, and the cabinet purge disappeared into Roosevelt's subconscious during the safari. Afterward, through the talks in Italy with Pinchot, the adulation in Europe, and the hero's parade in New York, Roosevelt was reconnected to his buried melancholy and resentment. But the forbidden wish to depose Taft and recapture the presidency could present itself only in disguise. "This it does," Prince wrote; "it makes him believe, without knowing his real reason for the belief, that the grievances of the Insurgents are the grievances of the people."

The coldness that hurt and puzzled Taft in the months after Roosevelt's return was readily understood by Prince: "If [Roosevelt] goes to the president he is lost! If once more he puts his arms around Mr. Taft, if he advises him, becomes more or less responsible for his actions, he cannot as a man of honor oppose him. . . . So his subconscious wish takes advantage of the situation, converts itself into specious reasons which appear in consciousness and keep him distant from the president."

Guessing that Roosevelt would dispute his interpretation, Prince noted that the fiercer the resistance, "the greater the probability of the truth of the analysis. So it is always." Roosevelt had no comment on the article, fierce or otherwise.

For the first time since leaving the White House, the conscious TR was fully alive—exhilarated to find dragons to the left of him, dragons to the right. "The amusing thing is that in the Dakotas I am being opposed on the ground that I am being a conservative and in the East on the ground that I am a radical," he wrote one of the governors who had sounded the summons. He had nailed his colors to the mast, he informed another correspondent, and win or lose, intended to "make it a fight worth fighting." In professing that he was "as happy as possible" and that not even his political work shadowed his bliss, Roosevelt revealed that his self-deception was total, for the political work was the very mainspring of his joy. But if self-deception were proof of insanity, few humans would escape the asylum. That Theodore Roosevelt was not St. George is a trifle next to the life made possible by the illusion that if he tried hard enough, he might be.

ELIHU ROOT, who had watched morosely as Roosevelt took up judicial recall, primaries, and other causes more radical than any he had espoused as president, was as dubious as La Follette of the depths of TR's new convictions. Roosevelt was "essentially a fighter and when he gets into a fight he is completely dominated by the desire to destroy his adversary," Root told one of their mutual friends. "He instinctively lays hold of every weapon which can be used for that end. Accordingly he is saying a lot of things and taking a lot of positions which are inspired by the desire to win. I have no doubt he thinks he believes what he says, but he doesn't. He has merely picked up certain popular ideas which were at hand as one might pick up a poker or chair with which to strike."

If there is a distinction between believing and merely thinking that one believes, it would have meant little to Roosevelt, whose beliefs were both wholehearted and subject to constant revision. Entering public life with a sense of noblesse oblige and the expected social prejudices of the nineteenth-century aristocrat, he had shed them willingly when he could see that they did not square with the facts. Sometimes his shifting stances were opportunistic, but just as often they were graceful concessions to superior arguments or new information. Root himself had called TR the most "advisable" man he ever knew. Roosevelt had begun his investigation of cigarmaking in the tenements with the assumption that he would support the practice, because the people he respected were in favor of it. His inspections persuaded him the miseries must be stopped.

In 1912 Roosevelt believed, or thought he believed, that the United

States faced its gravest crisis since the Civil War, and it seemed to him that no election since the earliest days of the Republic had appealed so strongly to citizens committed to democracy and "the root ideas of public right." Such assertions wrapped his personal wishes in a noble cloak and furnished comforting evidence for the fantasy that he was answering a call to duty. The comparisons also elevated him to the heroic plane of Lincoln and Washington, whom he would invoke constantly during the campaign. No doubt Roosevelt magnified the crisis to justify his involvement, but it is also true that the election of 1912 was no ordinary election. It was a moment of transfiguration in American politics, with the Democrats fashioning themselves into the party of liberal ideals and the Republicans pointing their craft toward the far shores of conservatism.

For Roosevelt as for La Follette, democracy itself was at stake. Both were persuaded that the election would determine whether the country was to be governed by the few or the many. Taft had no sympathy with the progressives' desire to transfer political power to the people by extending the suffrage to women and allowing voters to change their laws through initiatives and referenda. "Popular government we all believe in," Taft had said in a speech as 1912 began. "There are those of us, however, who believe that not all the people are fitted for popular self-government. Some of us don't dare to say so. But I do."

Taft's wariness of popular rule handed Roosevelt another poker, which he wielded in his first campaign speech, on March 20 at Carnegie Hall. "Mr. Taft fairly defines the issue when he says that our government is and should be a government of all the people by a representative part of the people," he said. "This is an excellent and moderate description of an oligarchy. It defines our government as a government of all the people by a few of the people." In Columbus Roosevelt had declared, "I believe in pure democracy," and at Carnegie Hall he said he believed in the Columbus speech. Where there was tyranny of the majority, he would fight it, but the tyranny of the age was "the tyranny of minorities," he said. A small minority monopolized, and a small minority stood behind "the whole calendar of social and industrial injustice. . . . No sane man who has been familiar with the government of this country for the last twenty years will complain that we have had too much of the rule of the majority."

The word "sane," certainly meant to signal his own stability, became a staple of his campaign rhetoric. He would also speak often of the necessity of "self-control on the part of the people," an old theme with him and now a message of assurance to those wondering about his lust for power.

Roosevelt devoted much of the address to his judicial ideas, hoping to dispel the widespread impression that he wanted every court decision subject to recall. He was aiming only at state supreme court rulings that declared laws unconstitutional, he explained with a professorial calm that surprised his listeners. He also muted his demand for the recall of judges, saying that it was merely one possible means of ridding the bench of scoundrels and obstructionists.

Though their voices were lost in the roar from Roosevelt's critics, Judge Grant and many other cool-headed members of the legal profession agreed that the courts were often guilty of legislative trespass. In Grant's opinion, Roosevelt had erred only in making his case when it was still an *indigestaque moles*, an idea not yet properly worked out. Henry Adams's brother Brooks concurred with Grant. Instinct had taken Roosevelt to the crux of the problem, but as a layman, he was "trying to solve problems in celestial mechanics without the calculus," Adams wrote Lodge.

Roosevelt's efforts to clarify loosed another hail of opprobrium, giving Taft's campaign managers one more opportunity to present their man as the dam against the anarchy sure to flow from pure democracy. Taft advised America not to listen to those who would tamper with its institutions. "Agitation that creates a lack of confidence among those who have capital invested is not good for the people," he said. Better to strive for "the quiet confidence that makes everybody look after his own business and put as much money in it as he can, and then jobs will be many, wages will go up, we will all have money to buy shoes for our children, and those that like comfort can enjoy it."

William Howard Taft did not see his country in crisis, and that, to Roosevelt, was a grave defect. America needed inspiration from "leaders to whom are granted great visions, who dream greatly and strive to make their dreams come true; who can kindle the people with the fire from their own burning souls," Roosevelt said. "We, here in America, hold in our hands the hope of the world, the fate of the coming years; and shame and disgrace will be ours if in our eyes the light of high resolve is dimmed, if we trail in the dust the golden hopes of men. If on this new continent we merely build another country of great but unjustly divided material prosperity, we shall have done nothing; and we shall do as little if we merely set the greed of envy against the greed of arrogance." He stood against all tyranny, he said, whether by the few or the many, and he stood for the rule of the many "in a spirit of courage, of common sense, of high purpose, above all in a spirit of kindly justice toward every man and every woman."

The speech touched a note octaves higher than any Taft could reach. Repeatedly Taft insisted that Roosevelt was a menace, but never made a persuasive case. Nor did Taft present a cogent brief for the respectable conservative conviction that a nation needs the anchor of tradition. Instead of meeting Roosevelt's cry of "oligarchy versus democracy" with "chaos versus order," the president spoke of "socialism and an unlimited control of the majority of the electorate on the one hand, or our present government on the other." To an electorate deeply dissatisfied with the present government, it was a dispiriting thought.

The "we" of Roosevelt's campaign speeches was the familiar, all-embracing "we" of "we the people" and also the "we" of "we and not they." President Taft called himself a progressive, but a progressive was one who actively fought against privilege, Roosevelt reminded an audience in Philadelphia. Those who upheld it, whether from selfishness or indifference, were the reactionary, reprehensible "they."

By definition a progressive was discontented with the status quo and impatient for change. Progressive women, many of them reformers in education or health or social work, wanted the vote in the forty-two states where they did not yet have it. The progressive Republicans drawn to La Follette and to Roosevelt closely resembled the Regulars they hoped to displace— white, male, Protestant, urban, educated, and relatively prosperous. Across the country the leaders of both groups were lawyers and other professionals, businessmen, and members of the clergy and the press. The biggest divides were age and political experience. The Regulars' leaders were fifty-four years old on average, and more than a third were politicians by profession— mayors, governors, legislators. Their progressive counterparts were younger by a decade, sometimes two. Few were practicing politicians.

By rules set at earlier Republican conventions, the party's 1912 gathering would seat 1,078 delegates—two from each of the 435 congressional districts plus 208 delegates-at-large. To win the Republican presidential nomination, a candidate needed a majority of the national convention—540 votes. Each state elected its own delegation, and until the advent of presidential primaries, in 1912, the electing took place in state conventions and caucuses tightly controlled by party bosses. In 1912 the bosses would dominate in the selection of 706 delegates representing thirty-six states, but the other 362 would be elected by voters in a dozen statewide primaries.

As the primary battles opened, it sometimes seemed that the Colonel would be done in by his own green troops. In their eagerness, the neophytes made financial promises the campaign could not keep, committed Roosevelt to more speeches than any human could make, and volunteered opinions without the remotest thought of the likely repercussions.

The central command of this bumptious army was the Roosevelt National Executive Committee, headed by Joseph M. Dixon of Montana, an energetic senator with an angelic grin and a tiger's affinity for the jugular. Dixon, forty-five, was a lapsed Quaker whose politics were infused with the Quaker concern for social well-being. When he met Roosevelt in 1902, it was veneration at first sight. O. K. Davis, Washington correspondent for the *New York Times*, left the paper to serve as the campaign's secretary and chief publicist. A trinity of Republican bosses (none of whom fit Roosevelt's definition of a progressive) also served on the committee, along with a handful of Midwesterners. The money was raised by Frank A. Munsey, a publisher, and George W. Perkins, a former partner of J. P. Morgan.

Product of a struggling farm in Maine, Munsey as a young man had started a children's magazine with $40 of his own and a loan of $260. Patterning himself on the conglomerateurs he saw in other industries, he built an empire of newspapers and magazines that had made him $9 million by 1907. He amassed millions more in the stock market. A self-confessed trial-and-error man ("creating and killing till I happen to hit the public's taste"), he killed at the first scent of red ink, throwing hundreds out of work, a habit that offended even the genial William Allen White. Years later, White would immortalize Munsey in an obituary, saying that he had contributed to journalism "the great talent of a meat packer, the morals of a money changer, and the manners of an undertaker."

Fifty-eight in 1912, Munsey liked Roosevelt and was annoyed with Taft, whose interminable procession of antitrust suits had unsettled the stock market. A political operative dispatched early in Roosevelt's campaign to ask Munsey for a check found him in a gargantuan office, at the far end of seventy-five feet of carpeting, behind a desk on a platform. He was a "crabbed" fellow who looked as if he had been "weaned on a pickle," the visitor said.

George Perkins was charming, tall, lithe, and "exquisitely undertailored," White noticed. White considered him a man of "good habits"—soft-spoken, pleasant, and "as careful of the punctilios as a preacher at the front door of a church." Perkins's father, a socially progressive Midwesterner, thought his son slow and kept him at home until he was ten. George finished grammar school at fifteen, decided that he had had enough education, and went to work as an office boy. In his thirties he became president of the New York Life Insurance Company and was soon taken up by J. P. Morgan, reportedly for $250,000 a year and a share of the firm's profits. A master of organizational order, Perkins assisted in the formation of two of the largest industrial corporations of the day, U.S. Steel and International Harvester. It is alleged that he once stood with Theodore Roosevelt beneath a starry sky and marveled, "Look at that, Mr. President! Someone has organized all that."

Troubled by the malefactors of great wealth, Perkins persuaded several large corporations to disclose their finances to investors and to improve their relations with labor through pensions and profit-sharing. Certain that large-scale business enterprises were a necessity of modern life, he maintained that the trusts needed less busting and more federal supervision. Rather than dissolve corporations that violated antitrust laws, he would hold the offenders personally responsible, punishing them with fines and jail sentences. The mere threat of such humiliation would keep corporate officers on their best behavior, Perkins thought. He also advocated the creation of a national commission to examine the affairs of large corporations and, if all was in order, to give them a stamp of approval. Perkins envisioned a body composed of experienced business leaders and took it on faith that they would put statesmanship ahead of self-interest.

Perkins retired a rich man at forty-eight, explaining to a friend that he wanted to be "more broadly useful for a few years" and "do this free from restraint and restriction. . . . It was simply a question of taking the course I have or going on grinding away to make a few more dollars which, I am told on reliable authority, I could not take with me when I finally depart." He intended to seek converts to his business creed and to complete a task begun years before at the request of Theodore Roosevelt, the creation of a fifty-square-mile public park on the Palisades of the Hudson River. After his retirement, in 1910, Perkins remained on the boards of directors of U.S. Steel, International Harvester, and sixteen other corporations.

Always welcome in Roosevelt's White House, Perkins had quietly provided guidance on business matters by sending along the speeches he gave and the articles he wrote for newspapers and magazines. Most of Perkins's ideas on the place of the corporation in modern society appealed to Roosevelt, and in 1912 Perkins was obviously hoping that his philosophy would shape policy if Roosevelt returned to the White House. In George Perkins, Roosevelt saw a public-spirited pragmatist who understood the workings of economic power. La Follette and the Pinchot brothers suspected that Perkins viewed Roosevelt as an investment and would use him to adulterate if not destroy the progressive movement.

The work Perkins and Munsey undertook for Roosevelt began at least two months before he announced his candidacy. They started in the South, where the Republican Party was, as White put it, "a corrupt alliance between the rich and the purchasable." The Southern states in 1912 had ninety-eight representatives in Congress, ninety-five of them Democrats. Of the votes cast by Southerners in the 1908 election, only one in three went to Taft. Roosevelt, who won by an unprecedented margin in 1904, had fared no better than Taft in the South. But under the Republican Party's rules, each Southern congressional district was entitled to two seats at the national convention, with the result that the South had a disproportionately large say in the presidential nomination.

Southern delegates were often willing to sell their votes, and it was said that the currency for these transactions was cut diagonally in half, one piece being given to the delegate in advance, the other payable upon delivery of the vote. Many Southerners active in the Republican Party were minor officeholders by virtue of presidential patronage, and Perkins retained Ormsby McHarg, a New York lawyer who had managed Southern affairs for the Republicans in 1904, to encourage defections.

By the time Roosevelt announced himself, Taft had 100 of the 540 delegates needed for the nomination. Some had been secured in state conventions held early for the purpose of thwarting Roosevelt. Taft's men also rolled through the South and threatened to withdraw his patronage. At least one small-town postmaster received word that his post office was not run as well as it might be, but he would be reappointed if the problems were fixed and a Taft delegation was delivered to the national convention.

Unable to overtake the president's brigade, McHarg decided to challenge the Southern results and instruct Roosevelt's Southern supporters to devise evidence of unfair play. McHarg contested the votes purely for "psychological effect," a reporter for one of Munsey's newspapers later admitted. "In the game, a table showing Taft 150, Roosevelt 19, contested none, would not be very much calculated to inspire confidence, whereas one showing Taft 23, Roosevelt 19, contested 127, looked very different." Sophisticates understood McHarg's strategy, but the public was left with the impression that Taft's Southern delegates were somehow illegitimate.

SENATOR DIXON made his first sortie for the Colonel in early March, proposing in a letter to the Taft campaign that all delegates be chosen in a national primary. Six states had already passed primary laws, six states were about to follow suit, and Dixon knew that Taft's agents were quietly working to chloroform the pending bills. Orthodox Republicans fanned out to say that primaries were wickedness itself—bad for party unity because they forced candidates to argue. Bad for the farmer, who might not be able to reach his polling place on a snowy day. Bad because they would attract a herd of contenders, splintering the vote and giving the victory to a candidate who did not represent the sentiments of the majority. But argument was the forge of democracy, the farmer needed no coddling and, as would soon be apparent, the ruinous expense of running in the primaries would thin the herd with Darwinian efficiency.

Taft's campaign manager, Congressman William B. McKinley of Illinois, had a reputation for shrewdness, but when he replied to Dixon that he did "not favor changes in the rules of the game while the game is in progress," he unwittingly handed Roosevelt another poker. Only "professional politicians" treated politics as a game, Roosevelt declared. To progressives, politics was a serious endeavor, a means of "ascertaining and putting into effect the will of the people," who deserved more than an opportunity to "sit on the bleachers as spectators." Taft, politicking in Boston, had little choice but to praise the primary bill then before the Massachusetts legislature.

The New York World noted astringently that Roosevelt had shown no fervor for primaries before he had a personal need for them, and indeed he would be their chief beneficiary in 1912. He could not compete with Taft in the state and local conclaves controlled by the Regulars, but in the primaries, he and Taft would meet on equal ground.

Some of the primary states would permit voters to select convention delegates pledged to a particular candidate, in others they could voice a preference for president, and in others they could do both. New York did not yet have a statewide primary, but New York City would hold closed primaries, restricting a voter to the slate presented by his own party. The Taft campaign objected to open primaries because the winner was the choice of the general public, not of party members, and because the contest was vulnerable to sabotage by the opposition. Democrats voting in a Republican primary might throw their weight to La Follette, for example, in the belief that he would be the easiest Republican to defeat in the general election.

On March 19, 68,925 citizens of North Dakota braved a blizzard for the privilege of voting in the nation's first statewide presidential primary. La Follette, who had recovered his vim in the six weeks since his collapse in Philadelphia, was heavily favored, and Dixon had hesitated to enter Roosevelt, fearing that a loss would be seized upon as evidence that he had no following. But the Roosevelt recruits were impatient for action, so Dixon turned them loose with bales of campaign literature about the man who had once lived in North Dakota as a cattle rancher.

The candidate himself was at home with an unassailable excuse — jury duty. He campaigned a bit from his desk, telling a friendly Minnesota congressman in a confidential letter that Midwesterners should be made to realize that La Follette had no chance to win the presidential nomination, so a vote for him in the primaries was a vote for Taft. "Can't you just say this to them?" Roosevelt asked.

North Dakota gave La Follette a landslide — 57 percent of the vote and all ten of its delegates. When a Roosevelt novice tried to dismiss the victory by saying that thousands of Democrats had voted for La Follette, the boomerang came back at decapitating speed. "I told you so," said the president's forces, sounding much like Mrs. Taft on the evening of Roosevelt's announcement. The Roosevelt council of elders rushed to control the damage, claiming that La Follette had been subsidized by Taft for the sole purpose of embarrassing Roosevelt. Dixon scrubbed Roosevelt's name from the ballot in Wisconsin, where La Follette was certain to win.

The next week, Taft whipped Roosevelt 67 to 33 percent in the local primary held in New York City. In Colorado and Indiana, where Republicans were selecting delegates in a series of conventions and caucuses, the first returns were solidly anti-Roosevelt. The *Brooklyn Eagle* bared its talons, pointing out that "The Call of the People was almost inaudible."

Roosevelt condemned the Indiana and Colorado results as sordid machine politics and the New York City primary as "a criminal farce." In scores of New York precincts where he was expected to win, his election inspectors had been dismissed, and ballots were delivered late or not at all. Charging fraud and theft, Roosevelt insisted that the vote was "in no shape or way representative of the Republican Party" and had "no binding force whatever."

Garfield was allowed to hint that Roosevelt might have to form a new party if the old crowd continued to dominate. An investigation of the irregularities in New York City found that they were real but not extensive enough to have cost Roosevelt the election. The North Dakota loss was purely symbolic, but the defeat in New York suggested that Roosevelt had little hope of capturing the nomination. A week later Wisconsin gave La Follette its 26 delegates, and the Republican National Committee released the results of a straw poll of its members: 40 votes for Taft, 8 for Roosevelt, and 5 undecided. Neither the people nor the party wanted Roosevelt.

"The plain fact is that little is left of his campaign but anger, wrath, malice, and all uncharitableness," said the *New York Evening Post*. For posterity's sake "and in order that his brilliant career may not go out like a lamp with a bad smell, his true friends ought from this moment to make every effort to induce him to withdraw." But the losses did not signal Roosevelt's demise. Together with his cries of foul play and McHarg's strategy of disputatiousness, they were transforming an indecently eager candidate into a sympathetic underdog.

The primaries of 1912, which might have occasioned a grand debate on the nature of modern democracy, became instead the first American presidential battle waged by the masters of spin. Taft's lieutenants said the North Dakota vote proved that the people did not want Roosevelt, while the Roosevelt managers used it as evidence that Taft money had been used to thwart the people's will. A spinner could insist that New York was a repudiation of Roosevelt or proof of the degeneracy of the Republican Party.

And with the introduction of primaries, would-be presidential nominees had to take their case directly to the people, an undertaking vastly more expensive than wooing a handful of party bosses. Perkins and Munsey raised and spent more than $600,000 on Roosevelt's primary campaign—20 percent more than Taft and considerably more than the three leading Democratic hopefuls combined.

Roosevelt outspent Taft in part because the president's campaign managers had difficulty persuading men of means to invest in a forlorn hope, and some of the disenchanted felt that if the Taft family wanted Will to run, his brother Charles could pick up the check, as he had in 1908. The Roosevelt campaign also spent heavily to offset its disadvantage with the country's eighteen thousand newspapers, which overwhelmingly opposed his decision to run. He had the support of only a dozen metropolitan dailies. Except in the South, most small newspapers had been Republican Party organs since the Civil War. Hundreds were published by men who also served as postmasters, courtesy of presidential patronage. And the newspaper publisher who augmented his revenues with commercial printing was more often than not the supplier of choice to state and local governments controlled by Republicans.

Joseph Medill McCormick put his family's paper, the *Chicago Daily Tribune,* behind Roosevelt and by postcard invited 7,500 newspapers to receive dispatches from the Roosevelt campaign's news service. More than five thousand accepted. At the Roosevelt publicity bureau in Washington, O. K. Davis prepared daily campaign bulletins for the 250 members of the capital's press corps and weekly dispatches for the smaller dailies. To some two thousand country papers went weekly shipments of a half-page of well-spun news, interviews, attacks, and rebuttals, delivered in plates ready for the printing press. Publishers ran the boilerplate because it saved money on typesetting, but it cost Roosevelt's campaign $1,500 a week. George Kibbe Turner, a *McClure's* magazine reporter assigned to write about the manufacture of public opinion in that first primary season, noted that the "machinery of reaching the voter direct was growing to tremendous proportions—both in documents and cost."

On April 8, the day before the Illinois primary, the progress of Roosevelt's campaign could be measured in inches. He had lost three out of three primaries. Taft's lead continued to lengthen in states electing delegates at conventions and caucuses. But Roosevelt's raw recruits were beginning to march in step, and with assistance from the *Chicago Daily Tribune,* Medill McCormick's money, and the governor of Illinois, TR won 61 percent of the vote and 56 of the state's 58 delegates. He was in Pittsburgh, giving a speech, and both arms shot into the air when someone handed him news of the victory in Illinois. "The people are with us," he exulted, "and if the leaders pay no heed to the voice of the people, their day of reckoning is bound to be swift and certain." Four days later he carried Pennsylvania with 60 percent of the vote.

La Follette sourly declared that neither election was a progressive triumph, because Roosevelt had won Illinois by spending heavily on publicity, and Pennsylvania was only a revolt against the machine that backed Taft. Illinois may have voted for Roosevelt, but its legislature had just rejected the initiative, referendum, and recall, La Follette noted. Pennsylvania had been a battle of bosses, with the odious Boies Penrose supporting Taft and $144,000 from the slightly less odious William Flinn behind Roosevelt.

Unnerved by the losses, Taft's campaign manager branded TR a demagogue and charged him with leading the party to "rank socialism" and conducting a campaign of "vilification and assault."

THE VILIFICATION and assault were suspended for a few days in mid-
April, with the sinking of the *Titanic*. One of the disaster's 1,500 victims, Archie Butt, was last seen tucking blankets around the passengers in a
lifeboat and watching it descend into the dark, still sea. A recipient of his
ministrations remembered him tipping his hat and saying good-bye with a
smile. "Luck is with you," he told her. "Will you remember me to all the
folks at home?"

Taft and Roosevelt grieved, and Henry Adams, who had reserved a cabin
on the *Titanic's* return voyage, wrote a friend, "The strain gets on my nervous system and gives me dyspepsia. Only in history as a fairy tale does one
like to see civilizations founder, and to hear the cries of the drowning. . . .
The sum and triumph of civilization, guaranteed to be safe and perfect, our
greatest achievement, sinks at a touch, and drowns us, while nature jeers at
our folly." In the preoccupation with the *Titanic*, the foundering of the Republican Party had been forgotten, Adams said. "Politically we are drifting
at sea, in the ice, and can't get ashore. No one can guess what is ahead, but
it can hardly be anything good. Our dear Theodore is not a bird of happy
omen. He loves to destroy."

Adams suffered a stroke a few days later, and the destruction of William
Howard Taft continued with losses in Nebraska and Oregon, where he finished third, behind La Follette. The defeats jolted Taft from his lethargy and
put him on the offensive, a position unsupported by anything in his temperament. "This wrenches my soul!" he told a crowd at a whistle-stop in
Massachusetts. He had come, he said, to reply to "an old and true friend of
mine, Theodore Roosevelt, who has made many charges against me. . . . I
do not want to fight Theodore Roosevelt, but sometimes a man in a corner
fights. I am going to fight." To crowds of thousands in the Boston Arena and
at Symphony Hall, Taft recited the charges against him: disloyalty, the
shameless use of patronage, fraud in the primaries and state conventions,
abandonment of progressive principles, and a failure of vision and purpose.

Taft swore that he had not been advocating oligarchy when he spoke of a
government of all the people by a representative part of the people. He was

merely calling attention to the fact that only about one-quarter of Americans were entitled to vote, he said. Roosevelt had taken the remark out of context and distorted it.

The president accused the Square Dealer of hypocrisy, making his case with quotations from letters Roosevelt had written him. After privately supporting the president's pending trade agreement with Canada, Roosevelt had ridiculed it in public. Roosevelt the hypocrite had scorned Taft for consorting with bosses while omitting mention of his own long history with political machines. He had charged fraud in New York but had not taken his grievance to court, evidence to Taft that the allegations had little substance. President Roosevelt had filed numerous antitrust suits but lacerated the Taft administration for doing likewise. And the same Roosevelt who had promised in 1904 not to seek a third term was now running for the presidency. "Not because he wishes it for himself," Taft said with bitter sarcasm. "He has disclaimed any such desire. He is convinced that the American people think that he is the only one to do the job . . . and for this he is ready to sacrifice his personal comfort."

Wrung out by the speeches, Taft returned to his railroad car to await the journey back to Washington. A newspaperman with a question found him alone, head in hands. Taft looked up and spoke from his wrenched soul. "Roosevelt was my closest friend," he said. Then he wept.

Roosevelt counterattacked the next day, in Worcester, Massachusetts. Fists clenched, voice high and piercing, he accused Taft of violating "every canon of ordinary decency and fair dealing." TR said he had changed his mind on the trade agreement when it was debated in Congress and had refrained from criticizing Taft's position until the bill was defeated. Yes, he had cooperated with bosses, he said, "when they chose to go my way" (an assertion that was open to debate). "The trouble with Mr. Taft is that he gets their assistance at the price of going their way."

Revealing the contents of a personal letter was "an unpardonable sin," Roosevelt said, just before committing it himself. After winning the election of 1908, Taft had written him, "I can never forget that the power I now exercise was voluntarily transferred from you to me, and that I am under obligation to you to see that your judgment in selecting me as your successor and bringing about the succession shall be vindicated according to the standards which you and I . . . have always formulated." Not wanting the audience to miss his point, Roosevelt added, "It is a bad trait to bite the hand that feeds you." As for oligarchy, Roosevelt claimed that he had not misrepresented the president's speech, which had in fact suggested the dangers of "direct action by the people."

When the mud-slinging in Massachusetts ended, Roosevelt and Taft had won 18 delegates apiece, but Taft edged past Roosevelt (50.4 to 48.3 percent) on the presidential preference part of the ballot. A statement from TR's headquarters said that as Roosevelt had "steadily contended for a free expression of the will of the voters themselves," and notwithstanding his rival's chicanery in other states, he would respect the will of the people of Massachusetts. He urged his delegates to throw their support to Taft. It was a shrewd move, communicating great confidence and allowing TR to ride out of the wallow on a spotless white horse.

After Massachusetts, Taft sized up the five remaining contests and unthinkingly announced that the victor in Ohio would be the victor at the national convention. The statement seemed to imply that he should not be nominated if he lost Ohio, and it suggested to the citizens of the other four states—Maryland, California, New Jersey, and South Dakota—that their primaries mattered little.

Also without thinking Taft asked Elihu Root to make a campaign speech in Ohio. Root heartily disapproved of Roosevelt's candidacy but could not bear the thought of working against him. "I have no question that you are justified in attacking him in your defense, because he has attacked you," Root wrote the president, "but he has not attacked me." Taft was understanding about Lodge's friendship with Roosevelt but refused to show Root the same mercy. "Root has failed me," he wrote one of his brothers.

Panicked by the prospect of more losses, the Taft forces tried the smear. The Justice Department filed suit in late April to break up International Harvester and disclosed a letter insinuating that President Roosevelt had asked his attorney general to drop a similar suit in 1907, after a visit from George Perkins. Perkins, then chairman of Harvester's finance committee and partner of J. P. Morgan, Harvester's investment bank, had indeed gone to Washington, where Harvester was under investigation by Herbert Knox Smith, the government's commissioner of corporations. The Justice Department was contemplating a lawsuit, and Perkins proposed that Smith be allowed to complete his investigation first and give Harvester an opportunity to set matters right if it was in violation of the antitrust laws. The commissioner volunteered that he had not yet found substantive reasons for a suit. Perkins, not entirely reassured, promised that if the government prosecuted

Harvester on purely technical grounds, the House of Morgan would fight back with full force.

In a memo summing up the conversation, Smith wrote that while the Roosevelt White House had "never hesitated to grapple with any financial interest, no matter how great, when it believed that a substantial wrong is being committed, nevertheless, it is a very great practical question whether it is well to throw away now the great influence of the so-called Morgan interests, which up to this time have supported the advanced policy of the administration." Taft stopped short of charging corruption but asked the public to consider Roosevelt's duplicity. Roosevelt quickly pointed out that he had merely asked the Justice Department to wait, not to table the suit, and that Perkins had neither sought nor received special treatment.

Incensed by the suggestion that he had behaved improperly, Perkins reminded Taft headquarters (and the rest of the world, in a widely published open letter) that he had contributed to Taft's 1908 campaign, the 1909 New York mayoral run of one of Taft's friends, and Stimson's 1910 campaign for governor. All the contributions were made while he was a "corporation man," Perkins said, and if it was "a heinous crime for a great political cause to accept support from me now, it must have been far more heinous to accept it in the above-named three instances."

The nation refused to be scandalized by the Harvester revelations. Nor did it blaze with moral outrage when Republican leaders revived an old charge that TR had personally asked E. H. Harriman, one of the tycoons prosecuted in the Roosevelt administration's first antitrust suit, for $260,000 for his 1904 campaign. Roosevelt released their correspondence, which supported his claims that the talks took place at Harriman's request, that Harriman raised the money on his own initiative, and that the funds went not to the president's election effort but to the flagging campaign of the Republican candidate for governor in New York.

Nor were the voters roused to indignation at Roosevelt's break with the two-term tradition. The newspapers fulminated, but it appears that most voters were no more exercised than *The Outlook*, which dismissed the issue in a breezy metaphor: "When a man says at breakfast in the morning, 'No, thank you, I will not take any more coffee,' it does not mean that he will not take any more coffee tomorrow morning, or next week, or next month, or next year."

When Roosevelt's 1904 renunciation of a third term was cited in 1912 as evidence of his hypocrisy, he professed surprise. "I thought I had guarded myself explicitly," he wrote a friend in London. "If I had said that I did not believe in a third consecutive term, it would have been accepted by all my enemies and a large number of my friends as an actual announcement of candidacy after one term had expired. . . . Of course, the objection to a third term is merely that a president can perpetuate himself in office. When he is out of office, it is simply preposterous to suppose that the fact that he has been in office is of any consequence, for the whole, immense machinery of patronage is in the hands of someone else." Hankering now for another cup of coffee, TR felt perfectly entitled to it.

"THE BITTERNESS of this campaign will leave scars for life," Jim Garfield had written in his diary after the Massachusetts primary. Ohio would prove even more scarring than Massachusetts, and the list of the scarred would include Nick and Alice Longworth. Nick went to Cincinnati early in May, two weeks before the primary, to speak for Taft and shore up his own reelection campaign. As TR's son-in-law, he was constantly suspect in the Taft camp, and for the first time since entering Congress, he faced a Republican challenger. "I have no idea that he can beat me," Nick wrote TR, "but I am going home . . . to take hold a little bit." Alice was supposed to join him, but Nick warned her away because of the Longworth clan's fanatical hostility to TR. Nick also asked her to cancel a plan to attend one of TR's speeches in Cleveland, fearing questions about why she was at her father's side and not her husband's. Alice would remember the spring of 1912 as a long and variegated illness—full of colds, indigestion, colitis, anemia, low blood pressure, and, she said, "quite marked schizophrenia."

Taft crisscrossed the state for nine days, stopping in every congressional district and giving more than seventy-five speeches blasting Roosevelt as a demagogue and an egotist. In Steubenville, where their trains were parked side by side, Taft said that Roosevelt spoke of nothing but "I, I, I. If you feed that vanity and egotism by giving him something Washington did not get, Jefferson did not get, and Grant could not get, you are going to put him in office with a sense of his power that will be dangerous to this country." No man was indispensable to the life of the nation, Taft said; "ask him when he comes here if he is going to have a third term, why not a fourth term, and why not for life. That is not exactly popular government."

Roosevelt spoke even more often and in even blacker tones, calling Taft a "puzzlewit" and a "fathead." On May 21, the voters of Ohio, deciding that they preferred Roosevelt's fury to Taft's, gave their native son only 40 percent of the vote.

When the primaries ended, on June 4, George Kibbe Turner of *McClure's* went away aghast. Taft and Roosevelt together had spent an unprecedented sum, more than $1 million. At Roosevelt headquarters, Turner learned that contributions from ordinary citizens totaled no more than $50 a day, perhaps $5,000 in all. Virtually all the money in both campaigns had come from a handful of very rich men. Perkins alone contributed $123,000 (more than $2 million when extrapolated into the twenty-first century). "Now, everybody who reads understands what this means," Turner wrote. "It means simply the underwriting of presidential candidates for hundreds of thousands of dollars—exactly as a bond issue is underwritten before it is offered to the general public. This has been done, in many cases, with excellent motives. . . . But, no matter how good individual motives may have been, it is not a practice that can be continued."

Money helped TR win nine victories and 278 of the 362 delegates elected in primaries. Taft lagged far behind with 48, only 12 more than La Follette. Fighting Bob, who was still fighting, was confident that when the national committee dismissed Ormsby McHarg's trumped-up claims, the president and the Colonel would be so evenly matched that he, with his 36 delegates, would hold their fates in his hands.

The president's campaign managers calculated that despite his poor showing in the primaries, his control of the state caucuses and conventions had given him 557 delegates, 17 more than he needed for the nomination. Roosevelt was talking like a conqueror and issuing a warning. The people had spoken in the primaries, he said. They wanted him to lead the Republicans, and he would not allow "the discredited bosses, the discredited politicians, the representatives of special privilege in politics and business to offset the verdict that the people have come to."

NINE

Saturnalia

S TRANGE, the dissonance between the conqueror's certitude and the
doubt implicit in his warning. Even stranger that the dissonance has
been ignored, for it resolves in a chord of explanation more satisfying
than any heard in either of the standard tellings of the Republican convention of 1912. In the party's version, Roosevelt was simply a sore loser, defeated in a fight governed by rules he knew well and had used to his
advantage in 1904 and Taft's in 1908. In Roosevelt's rendition, he had
earned the right to the nomination in the primaries, battled fiercely for it at
the convention, and was beaten in a saturnalia of fraud. But the truth clanging through the dissonance is that Roosevelt had no chance to win and had
concluded as much before the convention.

The insuperables were party leaders craving his ruin, and stark arith-
metic. Two-thirds of the convention's delegates came from states without
primaries, states where the Regulars had brought in bountiful harvests for
Taft. Unable to win but unwilling to lose, Roosevelt would descend into his
own saturnalia of untruth, discrediting the convention in order to give himself a pretext for bolting the party. Only a bolt could spare him the humiliation of being defeated by Taft, and only a bolt would allow him to continue
his run for the presidency.

The Republican National Committee assembled in Chicago on June 6,
two days after the last primary and twelve before the opening thwack of the
convention gavel. By the party's long-standing rules, the committee's fifty-
three members (one from each state and territory) were charged with or-

ganizing the convention, which was a matter of drawing up a temporary roll of delegates. The delegates on the temporary roll elected a temporary chairman, who presided over the creation of a permanent roll and the election of a permanent chairman, and with these parliamentary formalities concluded, the convention took up the business of adopting a platform and selecting a nominee.

The claimants for delegate seats typically outnumbered the seats, and in 1912, due largely to the exploits of Ormsby McHarg, 254 of the convention's 1,078 seats were in dispute. It fell to the national committee to decide which of the claimants to register on the temporary roll. George Perkins, not yet ready to surrender the nomination to Taft, watched in distress as McHarg presented one risible challenge after another. It was impossible to overestimate the damage McHarg was doing, Perkins wrote Sagamore. Among McHarg's flimsiest cases were four involving Roosevelt delegates chosen in rump sessions held weeks after the party's official caucuses and state conventions had elected delegates for Taft. In 164 of the disputes, even the pro-Roosevelt members of the national committee felt obliged to reject McHarg's claims.

McHarg's strategy, rooted in the cynical assumption that the more one claims, the more one gets, meshed perfectly with the Colonel's needs. The rejection of 164 challenges still left 90 seats in dispute. If nearly all of them went to Taft, as seemed likely, there would be at least the appearance of fraud, and if the party could be convicted of fraud in the court of public opinion, Roosevelt could bolt as a hero, presenting his exit as an act of moral courage.

At the Roosevelt campaign's convention headquarters in the Congress Hotel, Perkins and Dixon were overseeing a clandestine scramble for delegates while promoting the Colonel as the people's choice and boasting that he would carry the convention. Some of the scrambling took the form of combing rules and precedents in search of loopholes. Much of the rest was baldly practical. At least two members of the national committee were offered $5,000 to lean toward Roosevelt in voting on the contested seats, and smaller but not inconsiderable blandishments were laid before delegates thought to be suasible. Taft's agents were making similar overtures.

By a quaint and tender custom, such transactions were concealed from the candidates. Taft was safely distant in Washington, Roosevelt in Oyster Bay. The president had no thought of going to the convention—presidents of the day rarely attended—and Roosevelt was following the proceedings from Sagamore, which was connected to the campaign's hotel suite by a private telegraph line. William Allen White, acting on a brotherly impulse to shield Roosevelt from his surging passions, encouraged him to stay home, but Dixon and Perkins soon began pressing him to come. They needed him as a peacemaker at headquarters, where idealists of the Pinchot type were colliding with the likes of William Flinn, the free-spending boss behind Roosevelt's primary victory in "Flinnsylvania."

Nor were the idealists happy about Perkins's prominence in the campaign. He was a superb executive with a gift for political showmanship but no appetite for collaboration, a failing that irritated his colleagues. They also resented his closeness to Roosevelt and the power that flowed from his checkbook. After contributing more than $100,000 to the primaries, he was putting up much of the $50,000 the campaign would spend in Chicago, and with his thousands came a certain imperiousness. But the greatest objection to Perkins was political. Still a director of International Harvester and U.S. Steel, both embroiled in antitrust suits, he was constantly under attack in Republican newspapers. The attacks were filled with falsehoods and innuendo, and they were unceasing—all of which blurred the image of Roosevelt as an unfettered advocate of the people. Only those who remembered E. H. Harriman's 1904 gift of $260,000, which Roosevelt repaid by calling Harriman one of the malefactors of great wealth, understood that Roosevelt was entirely capable of taking Perkins's money without feeling a whit of obligation.

At breakfast on Friday, June 14, Roosevelt announced to the family that he had to go to Chicago. Edith was "dreadfully upset," said a cousin who had dropped by, and Theodore seemed uncharacteristically subdued. They packed, gathered up Kermit and a few friends, and left New York by train at five-thirty that evening. An hour later, the train crashed into a boulder. Apart from the cowcatcher, nothing was spoiled but the pleasure a biographer might take in devising a subtler portent.

Next afternoon, hired marching bands blared a welcome at La Salle Street Station, and a merry bunch distributed handbills promising that Theodore Roosevelt would walk upon the waters of Lake Michigan. His automobile inched through roaring crowds to the Congress Hotel, where he needed a police cordon to make his way inside. When he disappeared from view, the crowd bellowed in the direction of his campaign headquarters, a suite on the second floor, and would not stop until he stepped onto the balcony to greet them. How did he feel? someone yelled. "Like a Bull Moose," he yelled back. The people had not called Roosevelt to duty, but once he volunteered, they seemed raring to go with him.

The family, if not raring, was steadfast and energetic. Edith hosted a tea for the women of the press and went to the convention nearly every day, sometimes in the company of Ethel and Quentin. When Theodore's meetings ran late, Edith often entertained the caller he would see next. In the eyes of William Allen White, who was often in waiting, she exuded the calm of an Olympian goddess. Kermit, who had just completed his studies at Harvard, was trying to decide whether to accept an offer to join a chemical company or go to South America to work as an engineer on the construction of the Brazil Railway. He and Ted served as campaign lieutenants, meeting delegates and attending dinners when their father could not. "No smokes or drinks," Kermit noted in his diary after one affair. The rumors of TR's drinking had not gone away.

Roosevelt headquarters had the feel of a town square on market day, all bustle and hum. A town crier in the form of a mimeograph machine kept things stirred up elsewhere in the hotel. "The whole nation is watching the attempted assassination of the Republican Party in order that certain politicians may pick its pockets when [it is] dead," read a bulletin from Gifford Pinchot. "The situation is perfectly clear. A majority of the National Committee represents the bad old order of politics for spoils." One room featured a huge photograph of TR on safari, standing over a dead lion. Between denunciations there were pep talks, and a hired piano player stood by to instigate a sing-a-long whenever quiet threatened.

In a banquet room down the corridor, Roosevelt's deacons carried on a dawn-to-midnight revival meeting, promising victory for the righteous and an overheated eternity for cheats and thieves. "As soon as one speaker wore out, another took his place," O. K. Davis would recall. "Chairmen served in relays. There was always a crowd. . . . Everybody in Chicago had opportunity repeatedly to hear just exactly what [TR's men] thought of the National Committee and its action."

The functionaries of William Howard Taft declaimed in a ballroom cheery as a mausoleum. Nineteen-year-old Nicholas Roosevelt, who idolized his cousin Theodore, gaped in disbelief as William Barnes, boss of Albany ("a regular caricature of a boss," Nicholas thought—fat, with beady eyes buried in a fleshy face), droned on about the need to save the Republic from would-be kings. The listeners applauded, Nicholas reported, but faintly and only on cue from a "very ancient colored gentleman" who had been retained to stand behind Barnes and start the clapping.

Away from these public exhibitions, in the penetralia of the Taft and Roosevelt campaigns, the mood was savage. The Taft majority on the national committee had indeed deprived Roosevelt of delegates legitimately his and in its wrath had awarded every debatable seat to Taft. But the extent of the fraud would remain a matter of dispute even in the Colonel's camp. Soon after TR's arrival, Herbert Hadley of Missouri, one of the governors who had supplied the summons Roosevelt felt he needed to run for president again, informed him that he had undoubtedly been defrauded of 24 delegates.

"Twenty-four seats!" Roosevelt shouted. "Twenty-four! What is the use of contesting twenty-four? You must contest seventy-four if you expect to get anywhere."

Seventy-odd contests were essential even for a bolt. With only 24 delegates at issue, Roosevelt would be vulnerable to the accusation that he had bolted because he could not carry the convention, but with 70 or so he and Taft would be evenly matched. Hadley so admired Roosevelt that he had once asked a portrait painter to show him in a blue tie with white polka dots, an echo of the Rough Rider bandanna. Suffering from tuberculosis, he ran a temperature of 102 degrees during the convention, but in hopes of pleasing his hero he set forth in pursuit of 50 more delegates.

O N S UNDAY the subject of a bolt arose in a curious conversation between TR and William Jennings Bryan, who was covering the Republican and Democratic conventions for a newspaper syndicate. After losing three presidential elections for the Democrats, Bryan was unlikely to be asked to carry their standard again, but he had a sizable following. He sketched an intriguing scenario: *if* the Republicans nominated Taft, and *if* Roosevelt bolted, and *if* the Democrats chose a candidate as reactionary as Taft, then Bryan would bolt too—and support Roosevelt. Roosevelt's reaction went unrecorded.

Between meetings and strategy sessions Roosevelt reworked an address to be delivered on Monday night, the eve of the convention. By speaking before a word was uttered in the official Republican forum, he could upstage the party, and by planting the idea that the convention was about to perpetrate a swindle, he could pave the first mile of road for his bolt. He showed a draft to Edith and Alice and trimmed it to their specifications. As a performance the evening would far surpass the advertised walk on the water. The crowd, nearly six thousand in Chicago's Auditorium and thousands more in the streets, was whipped into a froth by patriotic songs and the eloquence of Senator William E. Borah of Idaho, a Republican who spoke rousingly of stolen delegates and reminded his listeners that they, the people, were the court of last resort.

After a long, thundering avalanche of cheers, TR delivered an indictment, once again casting himself as David against a gang of Goliaths. The fight in Chicago was no ordinary party quarrel, he said, it was "a naked issue of right and wróng." To ignore the choices made in the primaries was to usurp the sovereignty of the people. George Perkins, not one to settle for less than he thought he deserved, would privately estimate that Roosevelt had been robbed of 40 delegates, but Roosevelt insisted at the Auditorium that between 60 and 90 of his delegates had been placed on the temporary roll as Taft's. The bosses and their representatives on the national committee had practiced "political theft in every form, from highway robbery to petty larceny," stealing not from him but from "the plain men and women who make up the bulk of the Republican Party." But he saw an equitable solution, he said: as the contested cases of 72 Taft delegates on the temporary roll had not yet been reviewed by the credentials committee, they could simply be excluded from voting for the temporary chairman.

The proposal sounded fair, but as Roosevelt knew from a lifetime in politics, it was hokum, because it would allow any minority to bid for control merely by challenging as many seats as it needed for a majority. The party's rules followed a tradition of the U.S. House of Representatives and the British House of Commons and were standard practice in bringing large assemblies into being. Once convened, a body could replace one contested member with another, but everyone on the temporary roll had a vote in the matter (except in his own case) until he was voted out.

The parliamentary fine point eluded the plain men and women, of course, and they would be left with the impression that Roosevelt was willing to cooperate, but the national committee was bent on thievery. He told the crowd that he looked at America and saw a nation embattled, with the champions of human rights arrayed against the army of privilege. "The parting of the ways has come," he said. "The Republican Party must definitely stand on one side or the other."

Roosevelt too was embattled, with his unrecognized rage at his powerlessness squared off against a conscience keenly sensitive to accusations of megalomania. But in the wondrous realm of the human mind, it is possible to stand without a wobble on both sides of a conflict, and through his love of country—a trait as deep and true as his love of power—Roosevelt could simultaneously pacify the sterner gods of his character and gratify his ego. So it was that he could end his blatantly self-serving speech by declaring, with total conviction, that he was not fighting for himself.

> What happens to me is not of the slightest consequence; I am to be used, as in a doubtful battle any man is used, to his hurt or not, so long as he is useful, and is then cast aside or left to die. I wish you to feel this. I mean it, and I shall need no sympathy when you are through with me, for this fight is far too great. . . . We fight in honorable fashion for the good of mankind; fearless of the future, unheeding of our individual fates, with unflinching hearts and undimmed eyes, we stand at Armageddon, and we battle for the Lord.

Reading the speech in the morning papers, Elihu Root would have had reason to recall his opinion that Theodore Roosevelt merely believed that he believed what he was saying. Now Roosevelt had to believe himself. He was standing at Armageddon and battling for his political survival.

IN A SURPRISINGLY WILY MOVE, the president sent Root to Chicago to chair the convention. Root had presided over the 1904 convention, which nominated Roosevelt, and Roosevelt had once called Root "the ablest man that has appeared in the public life of any country" in their time. Candidate Roosevelt publicly attacked Taft's choice when it was announced, but only with a peashooter. Root had "ranged himself against the men who stand for progressive principles," and he represented "the men and policies of reaction," Roosevelt said. Proudly conservative all his life, Root could scarcely have winced. But he had been sorrowing for months over the rampage of the rogue elephant, and when he arrived in Chicago, he was suffering from a cold and dysentery. Taft had put him in the position of the man on the gallows who used his last words to say that were it not for the honor of the thing, he would have preferred to skip it.

The convention—"sullen, ugly, ill-tempered," in the opinion of the *Times*—came to order at noon on Tuesday, June 18, in Chicago's Coliseum. By all accounts, the order was fleeting. A twenty-five-year-old author named Edna Ferber, hired to pen colorful sidelights to the serious dispatches of William Allen White, would despair. The Coliseum was in perpetual pandemonium—"never for one minute anything but a mass of screaming, shouting, stamping, hooting maniacs," she wrote years later. The straight news stories, "too bizarre, too incredible," made her feel superfluous. Chicago's police chief, fearing general mayhem and a riot led by the Flinnsylvanians, assigned nearly a thousand bluecoats to the convention hall, where the precautions also included barbed wire concealed under the bunting on the railings along the stairs to the rostrum.

Governor Hadley, flushed with fever but relaxed and smiling, made a motion to submit a new temporary roll, one with 72 Roosevelt delegates in the disputed seats. Forty and darkly handsome, Hadley spoke for twenty minutes, long enough for many on the convention floor to begin wondering if they could bind the party's wounds by nominating him instead of Taft or Roosevelt.

Hadley's motion was denied on parliamentary grounds: the delegates on the temporary roll had no power to transact business until they elected a temporary chairman. The Taft forces nominated Root, and Roosevelt's men submitted the name of Francis E. McGovern, governor of Wisconsin, La Follette's home state. The crowd was stunned. When a La Follette man sprinted to center stage to say that McGovern's candidacy did not mean that Fighting Bob had released his 36 delegates to Roosevelt, the Taft legion ascended into thrilled ruckamuction. The voting began at 3:21 P.M., and when it ended, three hours later, Root had won, 558 to 502.

That night Roosevelt's followers talked seriously and openly of a bolt. Borah moved forcefully to squelch the idea, arguing that a third-party run would be futile, while Dixon insisted that the closeness of the vote for temporary chairman foretold a Roosevelt victory. "We have them whipped," he assured reporters, as if he felt not a twitch of uncertainty. By his analysis, 70-odd delegates who had voted for Root for temporary chairman were pledged to Roosevelt, not Taft.

The Colonel, waiting for a better moment to make his move, declared that he would not bolt until every possibility for a square deal had been exhausted. He was more candid with a newspaperman who dared to inquire why he would stay in Chicago after Root's victory, which more or less guaranteed Taft's. Because, said Roosevelt, "I intend to see that Mr. Taft is nominated." Perkins had concluded before the convention that the next best thing to a square deal would be "the rawest kind of deal," but it is not clear how long it took Perkins to grasp that Roosevelt actually needed a raw deal, and a bolt, in order to keep his candidacy alive. After months of abusing the party's leaders, Roosevelt was a most implausible applicant for the job of chief Republican.

O N WEDNESDAY MORNING, after four hours of sleep, TR breakfasted with Edith, Ethel, and Quentin, stoking himself with two whole grapefruits, four soft-boiled eggs, four lamb chops, and two wheat cakes. At the Coliseum, a blue wall of policemen stood between the delegates and the rostrum. Hundreds of other policemen roamed the aisles and ringed the convention floor, moving swiftly to break up the fistfights, which were too numerous to count. Root presided—with "basilisk imperturbability," it seemed to White. Lean and elegant in morning coat and striped trousers, with close-cropped gray hair and chiseled face, Root struck him as "the perfect symbol of a propertied class struggling for its privileges which it honestly deems to be its rights." When Hadley came to the stage to make his motion again, White thought of the morality plays of the Middle Ages, with Root in the role of "aggrandized enterprise" and Hadley the personification of "pity for the exploited . . . and the inner urge for justice which has been the motor of human progress as man has struggled for the thing called liberty through the ages. They were old, old forces . . . Root and Hadley, not villain and hero, not the dragon and St. George, but Samson blind in Gaza and Laocoön and his struggle with his snakes."

Hadley's following gave him a twenty-minute ovation. From the front row, Alice and Nick Longworth, closely watched by the press, wore poker faces but suspected that the Regulars would willingly abandon Taft for Hadley if the move definitely eliminated Roosevelt. Dixon stopped the cheering for Hadley by signaling the Roosevelt delegations to parade through the aisles. They marched, hollered, stood on chairs, and waved banners, and when chaos reigned, an attractive young woman in a white suit dangled a poster of TR over the lip of the spectators' gallery. To mad applause she was escorted down to the convention floor and up an aisle to the press gallery, where she stood on a table and led another ovation.

When the Roosevelt faction had cheered itself out, the convention defeated Hadley's motion. Perkins, no more willing than Roosevelt to concede the reasonableness of the established rules, left in a rage and hailed a cab.

With no destination in mind, he asked to be driven south and eventually found himself in the neighborhood where he had been born. Suddenly remembering a night when his father hitched up the family horse and took him to a torchlight parade for Ulysses S. Grant, Perkins felt clear and calm and decided. As he would put it later, "I had enlisted for the war."

A T TWO O'CLOCK on Thursday morning, after hours with his advisers, Roosevelt appeared before his followers and urged them to bolt. "So far as I am concerned, I am through," he told them. The credentials committee was reviewing the national committee's decisions on the 72 contested delegates, but it seemed unlikely that any rulings would be reversed. "I went before the people and I won," he said, ignoring Taft's successes in the states without primaries. "Now the national committee and a portion of the convention, which is made a majority only by the aid of delegates not elected but chosen by the national committee, are trying to cheat me out of the nomination. They can't do it." Insisting that the convention had lost all claim to moral authority, he exhorted his delegates "not to lie down again."

Awaiting the decisions of the credentials committee, the convention did little business on Thursday, which may have been the day when White took Ferber to meet TR. With a charm she found overpowering, he inquired about her plans for one of her fictional heroines, Emma McChesney, who had slipped the bonds of domesticity and gone into the business of manufacturing ladies' undergarments. Abashed, Ferber stood mute, leaving the Colonel alone with his question. "Well now, I'll tell you," he said. "What became of her first husband? Die? Or did she divorce him? You never said." TR wanted Emma to take T. A. Buck, another of Ferber's characters, as her second husband. Emma could hold her own, Roosevelt said. "She could manage business and marriage all right."

The independent woman was an object of intense interest to Roosevelt in 1912. Until then he had been largely indifferent to women's voices calling for political equality and described himself as only "tepidly" in favor of suffrage for women. He did not think women needed the vote, although he supposed it would do them no harm. He became an ardent suffragist as soon as he grasped what women could do for him. They now voted in six states, and even where they were not enfranchised, they had been working enthusiastically on state and local political campaigns.

Sometime on Thursday, Hadley came by to say that the opposition had offered him the presidential nomination. When TR asked if the offer had been authorized by Taft's closest advisers, Hadley said he did not know; he thought he might have been recruited merely to signal that the Regulars were willing to consider a compromise candidate. TR feigned interest but laid down a condition unlikely to be met: the 72 allegedly fraudulent delegates must be stricken from the roll. It seemed to Alice that the governor had "a large and obvious bee . . . buzzing in his bonnet," and in fact Hadley's thoughts were bounding ahead to the question of what to do if the offer took more definite shape. The presidency might kill him, he told Roosevelt. A small sacrifice, replied the Colonel. If the presidency came to a man, it was his patriotic duty to take it, whatever the personal consequences.

Borah, fresh from a talk with Taft's managers, was waiting for Roosevelt when Hadley left. The Taft side was willing to set aside the 72 contested delegates and draft a platform acceptable to Roosevelt, Borah reported, but only if Roosevelt and Taft withdrew in favor of Hadley.

Roosevelt flew out of his chair, raised his fist so high it hit the chandelier, and pounded a table. "By God, I will never do it," he yelled. "Let them purge the roll and then come to me, and I'll tell them what I will do."

Shocked to realize that Roosevelt had no intention of cooperating with the Regulars, Borah needed a moment to compose his thoughts, which were not sympathetic. "Well, Colonel," he said, "in the future you and your friends can do as you please, but you can't make a jackass out of me any longer."

Toward the midnight of that aimless, grueling Thursday, twenty of Roosevelt's closest allies gathered at his headquarters, where he was pacing in silence. As William Jennings Bryan explained to his readers, the convention's rulebook had trapped Roosevelt in a cage of "regularity, formality, and orderly procedure," and he could not, despite his formidable strength, "bend a single bar." As Roosevelt paced, Perkins and Munsey whispered in a corner. The subject was money, and Amos Pinchot would recall the group's tense wait and its effort not to stare. At last the millionaires finished their caucus, took TR by the shoulders, and made their vow: "Colonel, we will see you through."

WHEN THE CONVENTION came to order on Friday, the credentials committee had finished its work, upholding the national committee's decisions in all 72 contests. The task now was to call the roll state by state and ask the delegates to ratify or reject the results. It was a noxious day,

full of recrimination and fisticuffs. The California delegation was particularly incensed by the credentials committee's refusal to overturn a decision
that assigned two of its delegates to Taft. The dispute arose from a conflict
between a new state election law and the party's rules, and the party, following a practice routinely upheld by the courts, decided the case in its own
favor. Governor Hiram Johnson delivered a philippic in the "Shall the people rule?" vein, and when the convention voted with the credentials committee in the California case, Edith Roosevelt made a widely noticed exit
from the gallery.

Friday night brought one last attempt to prevent a bolt. A Taft delegate
from Michigan told O. K. Davis that he and thirty others unhappy with the
steamroller tactics of the national committee had figured out how to tip the
convention to Roosevelt. The roll call votes of the day had gone against Roosevelt, but only by narrow margins. If the voting on the nomination appeared to be heading in the same direction, the Michigan delegates were
willing to support a compromise candidate, but they needed some of the
Roosevelt men to join them in order to create the appearance of a shift to another nominee while they carried out their real work—blocking a Taft win
on the first ballot. "I guess I don't need to tell you any more," the man said.

"He certainly did not need to say any more," Davis would write in his
memoir, "for everybody . . . knew that if Taft were not nominated on the
first ballot, he never would be nominated." Davis raced off in search of Roosevelt and was astonished when Roosevelt cut him off. "No! No! No!" he
roared. "I won't hear it! I won't have it! You needn't talk to me at all! You go
back and tell your man that I won't have anything to do with it. You tell him
that this is a crooked convention, and I won't touch it with a forty-rod pole.
. . . You tell him that if they will purge the roll, I will support any man they
want to nominate except Taft. . . . But, until they purge the roll, neither I
nor any other honest man can touch this convention. Now, you go tell him
what I say."

Davis tried to explain that once Roosevelt's forces controlled the convention, they could purge the roll, revise the platform, and capture the nomination. Roosevelt wanted none of it. "You go tell him what I say!" he
shouted.

Davis gloomily returned to the man from Michigan and delivered the
news. Certain that he had misunderstood, the visitor asked Davis to repeat
TR's reply and sat stock-still as he took it in. He rose to leave, sighed heavily,
and muttered, "Say! Don't that beat hell!"

For Davis, the episode showed unequivocally that TR was not driven by personal ambition in 1912. The delegate had offered victory, and Roosevelt had refused it on the ground that the convention had been corrupted. But TR's rejection can also be taken as one more sign that he did not want the nomination as much as he wanted to bolt. Had he wanted the nomination, he could have pursued the Michigan delegation's plan, and had it worked, he easily could have revised his story, transforming the tale of a scandalous fraud into proof that a lone hero armed only with justice had nothing to fear from the armies of evil.

O N SATURDAY, the last day of the convention, with all 1,078 delegates finally seated, Root was elected permanent chairman and cheered to the roof for five minutes. "Over Mr. Root's wintry face there came a smile, and the weary look he had worn since he came here disappeared," one of the newspapermen noticed. The impish glint was back in Root's eyes, his face pinked, and he was clearly enjoying himself. The newsman guessed that after four bruising days at the podium, it must be "a pleasant sort of thing to feel that you have made 1,078 persons reverse their opinion of you and that you have done it just by being on the level."

Root delivered a few warm words of thanks and bravely plunged into the chill of unfinished business. First on the agenda was Henry J. Allen of Kansas, who had come as a spokesman for his fellow Roosevelt delegates and for the Colonel himself. The Roosevelt men, Allen said, would no longer be bound by any act contrary to the wishes of the majority who rejected Mr. Taft in New Jersey, the majority who rejected him in Wisconsin—and so on through a long list of other states. Allen was not announcing a bolt, he said. "We merely insist that you, not we, are making the record. . . . We shall sit in protest and the people who sent us here shall judge us." Allen also read a carefully worded statement from Roosevelt, who reiterated the case he had been making all week: "A clear majority of the delegates honestly elected to this convention were chosen by the people to nominate me," but the Taft men on the national committee had behaved with "scandalous disregard of every principle of honesty and decency," stealing 80 or 90 delegates to defeat the will of the people.

Stealing there had been, but on the scale of 40 delegates, not 80, and TR was still refusing to acknowledge the dichotomy between the people's choice and the party's choice. The party had rejected him in the states without primaries, in the national committee's decisions on the contested seats, in the credentials committee's review of the contests, and finally in the convention itself, beginning with the vote for temporary chairman. In short, he had been beaten by the same rules (and many of the same players) he had used to dominate the conventions of 1904 and 1908.

Reading on, Allen voiced Roosevelt's hope that his delegates would refuse to cast any more votes at the convention. The convention was a fraud, Roosevelt said. It would be "deeply discreditable" for any man to accept the convention's nomination, and the man who did had "no claim to the support of any Republican on party grounds, and would have forfeited the right to ask the support of any honest man of any party on moral grounds."

Their morals impugned, the Taft delegates reacted with physical fury, starting fistfights across the convention floor. "Montana man clawed up a Florida delegate," Kermit wrote in his diary. "I helped separate them." He was sitting with the Maine delegation and serving as a sergeant-at-arms. Root and his gavel eventually imposed peace, and Charles Fairbanks, vice president in Roosevelt's second term, read the party's platform, which was solidly conservative. La Follette's platform was also read, but no one would second the motion to bring it to a vote.

At five o'clock the clerk of the convention, audible only through a megaphone, began the roll call of the states, asking for "ayes" and "nays" on the platform. Alabama, Arizona, and Arkansas voted in favor, but at the call for California, a delegate announced the group's intention to abstain. The crowd exploded in cheers, jeers, hisses, and catcalls. When he could be heard again, the clerk polled the California delegation, but only the two Taft men answered. The voting ended just before six o'clock, with 666 in favor, 53 nays from La Follette's contingent, a scattering of absences, and, from the Roosevelt ranks, 343 abstentions.

All that remained was the nomination. The clerk started through the alphabet of the states, getting no response until the call for Ohio, which was answered in a ringing voice by a burly man who nominated his fellow Ohioan William Howard Taft. The speaker was Warren G. Harding, small-town newspaper editor, former lieutenant governor, failed gubernatorial candidate, and future president.

As Harding spoke, lauding Taft as "the greatest progressive of his time" and making a pointed reference to Washington's refusal of a third term, Roosevelt was dining alone in his and Edith's rooms on the top floor of the Congress Hotel. Borah went to see him to say good-bye. TR took his hand

and asked him to stay for the evening to chair a convention of sorts at Orchestra Hall. He had decided to call for a new party.

Borah declined. "I have gone about as far as I can go," he said. In his judgment, a new party was a folly. With Hadley and many other progressive Republicans, Borah chose to stand by the Grand Old Party, flawed though it was, in the belief that elected Republicans could accomplish more than unelected Don Quixotes.

Visibly annoyed, TR asked what he was supposed to do. "Those men are in earnest. If they do not nominate me they will nominate La Follette. The movement cannot be stopped."

Borah pointed out that Roosevelt's followers would do whatever he asked and suggested that the third-party idea be mulled for a few days in the tranquility of Sagamore.

Roosevelt, turning to steel, began boasting that he would break the Democrats' hold on the South, but he was soon interrupted by an invasion of whooping Roosevelt fanatics. Borah slipped away in the chaos.

THE VOTING at the Coliseum was still under way when Theodore and Edith and their children reached Orchestra Hall. By 9:26 P.M., when Taft was declared the winner, with 561 votes, Roosevelt had divorced himself from the Republican Party and moved on. At ten o'clock, as Root was leading the Republicans to adjournment, Roosevelt's delegates and thousands of the curious were listening to battle cries at Orchestra Hall. "To any man with red blood in his veins, it's always a pleasure to fight a fraud," said Hiram Johnson, still flaming over his two lost delegates. The national committee had destroyed the Republican Party, but on its ruins honest citizens could build another party to ensure that the people would rule.

In a cart-before-the-horse maneuver as unorthodox as the ones Roosevelt had demanded of the Republican convention, he was nominated to lead a party that did not yet exist. The *Times* reporter present, his fund of adjectives depleted by five days of tumult, was as tongue-tied as Edna Ferber. The crowd went wild, he wrote. The cheers were deafening. It took some time before order was restored. When Roosevelt stood at the podium and agreed to accept the nomination, there was another frenzy, undescribed.

Roosevelt was brief and blunt. The word "fraud" was used more than a dozen times, and the national committee was denounced as unscrupulous, crooked, and vicious. He was accepting the new party's nomination on one condition, he said. He wanted those who favored a new party to determine the sentiment of the people in their states, then hold a convention that would nominate a progressive candidate and approve a progressive platform. He promised to support anyone they chose. "If you wish me to make the fight I will make it," he said, as if his wish—or theirs—were in doubt.

Roosevelt called for a party that would appeal to progressive-minded citizens, Democrats and Republicans alike, in every section of the country. Such a party would live by two simple principles, he said: "the people have the right to rule themselves," and duty obliged them to "rule in a spirit of justice toward every man and every woman within our borders and to use the government so far as possible as an instrument for obtaining not merely political but industrial justice." For those hesitant to abandon the party of Abraham Lincoln, he offered the assurance that they were Lincoln's rightful heirs, breaking the shackles of the past as Lincoln had done and facing "new issues in the new spirit that the times demanded."

Alice found the moment exhilarating, and although the family had no illusions of a victory in November, she wrote, "We all behaved as if we had suddenly been presented with the one gift we had always longed to have." Certainly it was the one gift her father had longed to have, and his saturnalia of distortion, brilliantly staged, gave it to him. He had pretended he wanted the nomination, insisted he was entitled to it, falsely professed a willingness to compromise, grossly inflated the number of stolen delegates, railed against rules he had once embraced, and arrived at the audacious conclusion that under such circumstances, an honorable man had no choice but to bolt. Errand accomplished, Theodore Roosevelt left Orchestra Hall still in the running for president, with one more chance to bury Taft.

TEN

A Barn-Raising

T AFT was ecstatic. "Nothing has occurred in my life that has given more gratification," he wrote Dr. S. Weir Mitchell, one of the alienists who had questioned Roosevelt's sanity. Sure that Roosevelt could not win in November, Taft faced his own doom with equanimity. "The dangerous menace" of a third-term president had been forestalled, and a defeat might remind discontented Republicans that without unity, a political party could accomplish nothing. To Nick Longworth's sister Nannie, an old friend, Taft wrote that the new National Progressive Party had no raison d'être apart from Roosevelt's "insatiate ambition." The picture of the Bull Moose foraging for issues to justify his candidacy struck Taft as "humorous and grotesque." The new party would cut into the Republican vote, he knew, but he dared to hope that Roosevelt would finish last.

In a lifetime in politics, William Jennings Bryan said, he had witnessed nothing to equal the spectacle of Roosevelt's desertion, which was almost certain to end with the election of the first Democratic president in twenty years. "Surely the ways of Providence are mysterious!" Bryan marveled. Until the bolt Bryan and his fellow Democrats had assumed that they could eject Taft from the White House by running a candidate from the progressive wing of their party, and their primaries had produced two: Governor Woodrow Wilson and House Speaker Champ Clark. Bryan was more progressive than either of them but had no reason to think he could win. In Chicago, when a reporter asked Bryan why he would not press for his own nomination, he had answered, "Young man, do you think I'm going to run for president just to pull the Republican Party out of a hole?"

Wilson was the darkest of dark horses, a man of fifty-five whose political career spanned all of two years. He came to the governorship from twenty years at Princeton University, first as a professor of law and political economy, then as president. His understanding of government was theoretical, acquired at a desk as he prepared his lectures and wrote studies of American political institutions. Before running for governor he had shown little concern for the social and industrial problems that touched the sympathies of Theodore Roosevelt, but in office he quickly grasped the larger possibilities open to a progressive Democrat with a successful record. "The question of my nomination for the governorship is the mere preliminary of a plan to nominate me in 1912 for the presidency," he wrote a friend in the summer of 1910. During his first year as governor he persuaded the legislature to institute primaries, pass workmen's compensation and corrupt practices laws, create a public utilities commission, and authorize municipalities to include initiatives, referenda, and recall measures on their ballots.

The only son of a Presbyterian clergyman and a pious, reserved mother, Thomas Woodrow Wilson was born in Virginia and raised in Georgia and the Carolinas. "As a boy who grew up in three towns, he had no lifelong friend," William Allen White wrote in a perceptive sketch published after Wilson's death. The adored younger brother of two much older sisters, he was coddled "when he should have run wild . . . trying his fists, his arms, his feet, and his brain in a thousand contests with his fellows." He matured into a man less at ease with peers than in the lecture hall, where his verbal athleticism thrilled students and nearly everyone else who heard him.

In the summer of 1911, traveling the country with Taft as he promoted his arbitration treaties, Archie Butt had taken Governor Wilson's measure precisely: "handsome in a cold, intellectual kind of way, yet magnetic too," and alert in the manner of foxes in search of dinner. Watching Wilson in Ocean Grove, New Jersey, during one of the president's speeches, Butt noticed the governor's extra applause when Taft declared that whether the White House or the Senate was right, the treaties must eventually be referred to the people. Butt saw that Wilson would seize the point to make a case for the referendum and the recall, measures the president despised.

Taft, who perennially underestimated his opposition, reported to the first lady that Wilson was "a good deal of a 'butter in.' They call him 'Dr. Syntax,'

'the Open Mouth,' and 'Wouldrun Wilson.' " To the president's amusement, one of the clergymen on the rostrum had rushed forward to deliver a
benediction as soon as Taft finished his address. Governor Wilson was popular, Taft's hosts explained, and they did not want to increase his flock by
giving him an opportunity to speak. Taft seemed oblivious to the possibility
that the benediction had spared him the embarrassment of being upstaged.

Champ Clark was an affable country lawyer from Pike County, Missouri,
who entered Congress in 1893 and rose to speaker in 1911. He regularly
voted with progressives of both parties but followed more than he led, never
authoring a bill and rarely voicing an original thought. When someone inquired about Oyster Bay's wishes for the Democratic ticket, Kermit stated
the obvious: "Pop's been praying for Clark."

At the outset of the Democrats' convention, which opened in Baltimore
on June 25, it looked as if Roosevelt's prayer would be answered. Clark had
arrived with 436 delegates, Wilson with 248. Although Wilson had matched
him in the primaries, the Democrats elected most of their delegates at state
party caucuses, where Wilson had not yet built a following. But an ocean lay
between Clark's 436 votes and the 729 needed for the nomination. No one
would win on the first ballot. Alice and Nick went to watch, as did Nellie
Taft and Fighting Bob La Follette, who was seen doodling a face with spectacles, blunt nose, and a fierce set of teeth.

Clark's momentum built for ten ballots, slowed for a few rounds, and
then the convention, unofficially steered by Bryan, began a slow turn toward Wilson. More than one reporter portrayed Bryan as a has-been and
commented on his wrinkled suit and generally frowsy appearance. White
would remember him as "a curious figure in that convention," a kind of
"adorable old rag baby" with a core of steel. None of the correspondents
seemed to know that Bryan immured himself in the convention hall for
days, subsisting on sandwiches supplied by his brother as he pleaded, whee-
dled, and negotiated. "My one thought was to save the Democratic party
from defeat at the polls," he wrote years later.

The voting dragged on for eight days and forty-six ballots. News of
Wilson's victory was telephoned immediately to Sagamore Hill. TR, conferring on the veranda with two longtime political associates, excused himself
to take the call in his office. After a lengthy absence he returned with the
verdict, which he delivered from the doorway. One of the visitors would remember him rooted there, "his face betraying no emotion of any kind."

In the evening, standing hand in hand with Edith, TR outlined his choices to the children. He could drop out and wait for the next presidential election, when the Republican nomination would be his if he wanted it, or he could stand and fight as a Progressive for all who shared his beliefs. The odds of victory were long, friendships would end, and men who disapproved of his campaign might hold it against his sons, he said. The children offered no dissent, and a houseguest who witnessed the scene remembered that Edith was "radiant with trust and affection." Whatever she felt, she "expressed her faith that the path through honor to defeat was the one to take."

A few of Roosevelt's friends suggested that he withdraw. Chase Osborn of Michigan, one of the governors who had encouraged the challenge to Taft, urged him to support Wilson. Wilson was a good, clean progressive, Osborn argued; if he failed, TR could form a new party in 1916. But Roosevelt was determined to run and certain that his course was selfless and brave. Stepping aside would be seen by friends and enemies as "an avowal of weakness on my part," he wrote Osborn. "They would think that I was flinching from the contest, that I was not game enough to stand punishment and face the possibility of disaster."

He would not be a Hadley or a Borah, slinking back to the Republicans. "What a miserable showing some of the so-called progressive leaders have made!" he fumed. "They represent nothing but mere sound and fury. A year or two ago, when it was merely a question of loud words, they were claiming to be much farther advanced than I was, but they have not the heart for a fight, and the minute they were put against deeds instead of words, they quit forthwith." When trumpets call, only a coward retreats.

B EFORE GRAPPLING with Wilson, Roosevelt sent *The Outlook* not one but three articles on the Republicans' misdeeds in Chicago. His case rested on a simple point: Taft had received the nomination with 561 votes, only 21 more than the bare majority; therefore, if more than 21 votes had been stolen, so had the nomination.

In search of a more dispassionate analysis La Follette retained his friend and former law partner Gilbert Roe, a man of impeccable integrity, to examine all the evidence in the national committee's records. Roe found that by mutual agreement, 6 of the 254 original disputes had been thrown out, leaving 248. Nineteen of the contests went to Roosevelt, and in the 229 cases remaining, the Roosevelt and Taft factions agreed to award 164 seats to Taft. That left 65 seats in contention (a number that had been pushed up to the oft-mentioned 72 by the scurrying and scrapping of Hadley and Borah). Giving Roosevelt the benefit of the doubt wherever possible, Roe concluded that the Colonel had plausible claims to 49 more delegates. As La Follette's friend, Roe might not have been free of bias, but 49 was 9 more than George Perkins, Roosevelt's right-hand man, thought he deserved.

Moving the 49 to Roosevelt's column trimmed Taft's vote to 512, taking away his first-ballot majority. Roosevelt's tally rose to 515, putting him an eyelash ahead of Taft but still 25 away from a majority. What might have transpired after a 515 to 512 vote is unknowable, but it can be said that Roosevelt's story of his indisputable claim to the Republican nomination is a fairly tall tale.

Amos Pinchot wished that Roosevelt would drop the subject. "We cannot ask the people to vote against Wilson because Taft stole Roosevelt's nomination," he wrote one Progressive, and he told another that unless the Progressive candidates made their fight purely on principle, they would be "wiped off the map, and deservedly so. If anyone can claim with any show of justice that we are simply the outs trying to become the ins, the whole people will certainly hand us a full portion of lemon salad."

With the *Outlook* pieces completed, Roosevelt worked on his speech for the Progressive convention and tried once more to stop the gossip about his drinking. Friends understood that his physicality—the flailing arms, rising voice, and reddening face—was merely an overflow of his ebullience and energy. As Henry Adams explained the phenomenon, Theodore Roosevelt was drunk on himself, but strangers naturally associated such behavior with the barroom and drew the likely conclusion. As the rumors spread, more and more supporters wrote to ask for reassurance. Though he found the task humiliating, Roosevelt responded with admirable calm and occasionally enclosed an affidavit of sobriety from the Reverend Lyman Abbott, editor of *The Outlook* and a Gibraltar of rectitude. Beyond posing an obvious danger to a presidential campaign, the rumors must have stirred up painful memories. His beloved only brother, Elliott Roosevelt, was an alcoholic who had died at thirty-four.

THE MEN WHO DEFECTED with Roosevelt spent the weeks between the Republican and Progressive conventions setting up state party organizations to support the national ticket and recruiting Progressive candidates to run for the House, the Senate, and state and local offices. Roosevelt wanted Progressives on the ballot for every elective post—from president to school superintendent, he said. It was a rare voter who chose candidates from more than one party, so a full ticket was both a practical necessity and a convincing riposte to cynics who charged that the Progressives were a party of one.

On August 3, at the Congress Hotel in Chicago, Chairman Joseph Dixon of Montana opened the new party's Provisional National Committee meetings with a rhapsody. "I doubt if in the history of the Anglo-Saxon race there has ever been such a development, such an evolution politically among ninety millions of people as you have witnessed during the past twenty-nine days," he said. The hyperbole was forgivable. All but one state (South Carolina) had built some semblance of an organization and sent a delegation to the convention. Utah, bastion of Republican conservatism, created its Progressive Party organization by "pure spontaneous combustion," Dixon reported—"not a telegram sent or letter written." Roosevelt's friends in New York had organized nearly every county, and William Rockhill Nelson was putting out his *Kansas City Star* with a skeleton crew while the rest of the staff fanned out to organize Missouri.

"I sometimes have to stop and translate myself when I think that I used to be a Republican," Dixon went on. Just returned from Washington, where he had spoken with some of his colleagues in the Senate, he reported that the reactionaries finally understood they were finished. "Positively it was like an old-time country funeral," he said.

Privately, though, Dixon was awash in doubt. "Some hours it really looks as if we were real Crusaders writing history," he wrote his wife, "and then again I get so tired of the whole worry and strain and responsibility that I want to run away from it all and rest and sleep and to go home to you and the children and let the processions pass by." With no time to go home and tend to his own campaign, for reelection to the Senate, he was anxious about losing. But as chairman of the Bull Moose Party he worked day and night to stiffen the weak-kneed, educate the fledglings, and, he said, "smile and assure all men that there was nothing to it but a joy ride in November."

The elation of the committee's first meeting evaporated within the hour, and Dixon spent the next three days mediating a bitter quarrel over the new party's position on "the Negro question." In 1912, the fiftieth anniversary of the Emancipation Proclamation, Americans of African descent numbered 9.8 million, including 2.5 million men of voting age. Heavily concentrated in the South, they were legally entitled to vote, but onerous property ownership requirements and literacy standards selectively applied kept all but a small fraction of blacks from the polls.

For blacks, the Negro question of 1912 was, which candidate will do right by us? North and South, many African-Americans believed they would gain more from Theodore Roosevelt than from Woodrow Wilson, a native Southerner at the head of a party filled with senators and congressmen devoted to white supremacy. Certainly Roosevelt would do more than Taft, who had made and kept a promise to appoint no federal officials for the South unless white Southerners approved.

President Roosevelt's treatment of blacks had not been without blemish. Quick to invoke the principle of national necessity when he took Panama and sent the Great White Fleet around the world, he had not used the power of the federal government to protect voting rights or to suppress lynching, which ended more than six hundred lives while he was in the White House. He also had dismissed 167 black soldiers after a shootout in Brownsville, Texas, an incident that left one man dead and wounded two others. No suspects were arrested, but the townspeople believed (wrongly, as it turned out) that the raiders were from a nearby army camp, and all were dishonorably discharged, denied pensions, and barred from the civil service.

Still, Roosevelt had invited Booker T. Washington to dine at the White House and occasionally braved white opposition to bestow minor presidential appointments on Southern blacks. Less publicized but more significant were the gains registered in the civil service, which hired African-Americans in unprecedented numbers during his administration. In the summer of 1912 W. E. B. Du Bois of the National Association for the Advancement of Colored People and other black leaders were looking past their disappointments in Roosevelt and hoping that because he was no longer beholden to a political machine, he could work toward an ideal they knew he espoused: all men up and not some men down.

For the Progressive Party the Negro question was a question of how white the party was going to be. The ranks of Northern Progressives included many blacks, but Southern white Progressives were immovable in their insistence that without lily-white leadership, the new party would never rival the Democrats in the South. Enfranchised by two constitutional amendments passed after the Civil War, Southern blacks had gravitated toward the Republican Party, the party of the Great Emancipator, making it anathema to whites. Below the Mason-Dixon line, a Republican was almost certain to be black, a Democrat white.

Black Southerners drawn to Roosevelt's Progressive Party came to Chicago and offered to deliver black votes in exchange for a voice in the party's affairs, a trade that white Southerners resolutely refused to make. H. L. Anderson, head of the Progressive Party in Florida, told the committee that he did "not want to exclude anybody in the world, but . . . the salvation of this movement so far as the state of Florida is concerned depends upon one proposition and one proposition alone, and that is this, whether or not the organization . . . is to be led by a colored man or a white man, that is all."

Florida had come to the convention with two delegations, whites elected at one meeting and blacks chosen at another. Anderson claimed to have suggested that the blacks meet separately, for the purpose of organizing the black vote, but the blacks had understood his suggestion as a call to elect black delegates. A Mr. Groves, the leader of the black delegation, said his group appreciated the delicacy of the situation and the need for a white leader but told the committee that they wanted at least a small gesture in return: "Give these delegates half a vote in your convention, the colored folks will stand to [Anderson's] back and do everything he says for them to do."

Anderson was allowed to keep his committee seat, but the committee refused to accredit either of the Florida delegations. While the refusal appeared to chastise Anderson for misleading the blacks, it was in fact a concession to the whites of the Deep South, who insisted that a single Southern black on the convention floor would make it impossible to recruit their white neighbors to the Progressive cause.

Mississippi's white Progressives, not content to monopolize party leadership in their state, wanted to exclude blacks altogether. Perry W. Howard, a black lawyer from Jackson, appeared before the committee to protest and to suggest that the blacks of Mississippi might not vote Progressive. "[I]t is entirely up to you to force us and drive us away from you," he said. The committee decided to seat Mississippi's white delegates but publicly censure their leader for calling an all-white convention. The censure was short-lived and hollow, for the committee soon agreed that each state could set its own rules for electing delegates to the party's future presidential conventions.

On the last day of the discussion, Julian Harris, the national committee's member from Georgia and son of Joel Chandler Harris, author of the "Uncle Remus" tales, said it seemed to him that the answer to the Negro question did not matter. Only 12,000 of Georgia's 200,000 black men voted—a fact he attributed not to impediments thrown up by whites but to a desire peculiar to the Negro: "I have lived in the South all my life, and the

Negro has made no political purpose; his purpose has been agricultural and industrial, by the side of the white man, and at the side of the white man is his only chance for advancement."

Northerners on the committee protested that its decisions on the Negro question would matter greatly to progressive-minded voters outside the South. If the party treated the Negro badly, one Northern committeeman said, "we are damned to defeat in the North, where the electoral votes will have to come from."

In the end the committee decided to follow in the tracks of Br'er Roosevelt, who was circling roun' an' roun' de briar-patch. In a long letter just published in *Uncle Remus's*, a magazine edited by Julian Harris, Roosevelt had said that the Progressive Party would address the Negro question by pursuing separate strategies in the North and the South: "In the South the Democratic machine has sought to keep itself paramount by encouraging the hatred of the white man for the black; the Republican machine has sought to perpetuate itself by stirring up the black man against the white; and surely the time has come when we should understand the mischief in both courses, and should abandon both." Black and white Progressives were participating on equal terms in many Northern states, Roosevelt said, but conditions differed in the South. By appealing to "the best white men in the South, the men of justice and of vision as well as of strength and leadership, and by frankly putting the movement in their hands from the outset we shall create a situation by which the colored men of the South will ultimately get justice." With Booker T. Washington, Roosevelt maintained that "the only white man who in the long run can effectively help the colored man is that colored man's neighbor."

Matthew Hale, the committee member from Massachusetts, observed that Roosevelt's letter, "plucked of its verbiage, is merely saying, 'Get out of here, we don't want you.' " Dixon disagreed and wanted recognition of the party's racial harmony outside the Deep South. Delegations from thirteen states—Tennessee, Arkansas, and Kentucky among them—included blacks. "[T]his does not make a white man's party," Dixon said. In its final act before the convention, the committee adopted Roosevelt's double standard as its own, without a nay from Hale or anyone else.

Dixon and Perkins had planned a tranquil convention, fearing that the "Barnum feature" of Roosevelt's campaign was wearing thin and that the public, put off by the acrimony of the Republican gathering, might ignore the Progressive proceedings. Four thousand seats were removed from the

Coliseum. Roosevelt's staff, usually at ease with the press, was asking re-porters to save their questions for the Colonel, and it was rumored that the Colonel was unduly short-tempered even with the men in his ranks. If they wished him to lead, he had said, they must get in line and follow. His mood jangled the *Times* correspondent, as did the absence of familiar faces. "In-stead of forcing your way through a crowd of tobacco-stained political veter-ans," he wrote, "you raise your hat politely and say, 'Pardon me, Madam.' " He was struck by the abundance of Progressives in petticoats and noticed that everyone in trousers seemed to be an "ex"—ex-senator or ex–cabinet secretary or ex–lieutenant governor.

A few days before the convention, Taft tried to ignite the Barnum feature by filling a minor civil service post with one of the dishonorably discharged Brownsville soldiers, Sergeant Mingo Sanders. Roosevelt, asked to com-ment as he boarded the train for Chicago, noted that the soldiers had been dismissed on the recommendation of his secretary of war at the time, William Howard Taft. "If Mr. Taft did not tell the truth about Mingo Sanders and his colleagues in his report . . . then his conduct needs no characterization by me; if he did tell the truth, then his reinstatement of Mingo Sanders in the public service stands still less in need of any charac-terization by me." In other words Taft had either lied then or was lying now.

Roosevelt had deflected the blow, but the appointment of Mingo Sanders added to the Progressives' discomfort over the Negro question. Finding himself in a rain of queries about it when he reached Chicago, TR ducked under an umbrella: he would discuss the subject only with reporters whose papers printed his letter to *Uncle Remus's* magazine. At three thou-sand words, the letter was of course too long for all but the most indulgent editors. That evening Roosevelt received a group of black delegates, who warned him that if he stood by the letter, he would lose the black vote in the North. Roosevelt did not yield. He had acted with the Negro's interests at heart, he said, and they must make the best of it.

T HE CONVENTION PROVED to be a communion of the sacred and the civic, an ordination of a high priest with an old-fashioned barn-raising thrown in. "Suddenly, as if by magic, the city of Chicago became filled with men and women from every state in the Union who were evidently haunted by the same social compunctions and animated by like hopes," wrote Jane Addams, founder of Hull House and champion of woman suffrage, world peace, racial justice, and a dozen other causes. Politics and social reform had converged, with the reformers finally grasping that their dreams could be realized only through political action and the politicians seeing that the reformers' concerns were widely shared by voters. In their exuberance many states had sent two or three times their allotted share of delegates and divided up their votes accordingly.

The galleries of the Coliseum were packed on August 6, the first day of the convention, but only after a last-minute distribution of free passes. The list of very important absentees included all of the governors who had helped Roosevelt into the running. "They have sought the tall grass," said the *New York Herald*. Also missing were the Roosevelt children. Ted was settling into a new job, and Kermit was en route to Brazil to start his career as an engineer. Ethel and Quentin had gone off separately to visit friends. Archie, who lived as eventfully as his father, spent his time in parts unknown except for a trip to the doctor's office, where he had a large sand spider removed from his ear.

Alice had longed to attend but was overruled in a conference on the veranda at Sagamore — "Father and I in rocking chairs, rocking violently," she would recall. TR and Nick concluded that her gambol with the Progressives in Chicago would be held against Nick, whose reelection campaign was foundering. Republicans distrusted him because of his father-in-law, and thanks to his father-in-law's new party, he was battling a Progressive opponent along with the Democratic challenger. TR and Nick were angelic in their sympathy, Alice said, but decided that political necessity trumped personal desire. Edith doubted that Alice's sacrifice would help. "Nick still sits upon the fence with both legs on the Republican side, nicely precluding all help and support for his candidacy from either party," she wrote Kermit.

Escorted by one of Theodore's young cousins, Edith sat above the convention floor in a box near the rostrum, a perch that gave her a good view of the delegates' faces. So young, she thought. White, surveying the scene from the press gallery, was struck by the similarities of the people on the convention floor. They were "successful middle-class country-town citizens, the farmer whose barn was painted, the well-paid railroad engineer, and the country editor," he wrote, and the thirty-four women delegates were "our own kind, too" — doctors, lawyers, teachers, reformers, and civic leaders. "If the Progressives were a party of protest, they were not in the least proletarian." This was the petite bourgeoisie, equally wary of organized labor and organized capital. From the delegates' clothing, White reckoned that incomes ranged from $2,000 to $10,000 a year, and as a man who thought to wear pale gray kid shoes with his pale gray suit, he was eminently qualified to make the call. Only Amos Pinchot was unhappy with the look of the crowd on the convention floor. To his eye, it seemed that the large-minded men and women he admired were greatly outnumbered by "people bent chiefly on riding to power or prestige on Roosevelt's broad back."

TR reached the Coliseum at one o'clock in the afternoon and beamed and waved from the rostrum for nearly an hour as delegates stood on their chairs and yelled themselves hoarse. The din reminded Addams of the "psychic uproar which accompanies a great religious conference when the sword of the spirit bursts through its scabbard." Thousands waved flags, thousands more pumped red bandannas. TR found Edith's eye, shook his bandanna in her direction, and as she fluttered hers in return, the din grew even louder.

When the crowd was ready to listen, the Roosevelt they heard was the Roosevelt of the bully pulpit, the old preacher of civic virtue daring his congregation to bring the noblest American ideals to life. For two hours he stood before them and delivered his confession of faith. He began by congratulating them for taking a bold and much needed step. The old parties had become "husks, with no real soul," controlled by the minions of privilege and reaction, he said. The Progressives had come together to make "a contract with the people," putting citizens in charge of governing themselves and putting the government at the service of the citizenry.

More litany than credo, Roosevelt's speech reiterated his demands for popular rule, including the recall of court decisions, and defined the great challenge of the age as economic. He called for a national commission to regulate large industrial corporations and a permanent, nonpartisan tariff commission to furnish the Congress with expert, disinterested advice. The most heartfelt articles addressed the injustices of industrialization. He proposed to give financial aid to workers injured on the job, abolish child labor and the seven-day workweek, create a broad program of social insurance for those unable to work, and institute a living wage, a concept even more radical than judicial recall. In his vision of a just society, a worker's pay would provide for a family, allow for recreation, and permit savings for sickness and old age. Woman suffrage, federal management of conservation and of public health, a government body to improve the conditions of rural life—there was scarcely a progressive tenet he did not confess to.

Toward the end of the recitation, someone on the Coliseum floor called out for Roosevelt's thoughts on the Negro question. A few hands applauded, and over the applause came a few shouts of "Don't answer him."

Roosevelt was unruffled. "Nobody can ask me a question I am afraid of," he said. The number of blacks in the delegations from the North and from the border states was unprecedented at a presidential convention, and it was the result of "simply encouraging the best men in the North to act as squarely by the colored man as they would by the white man. We have not done it by trying to dragoon the white man into such action." He said he believed that the Progressive Party in the South would one day follow the same course, but only if the South were allowed to transform itself from within.

In the last two minutes of his address, Roosevelt approached the heights of his best speeches and showed the sort of leader he aspired to be, a Lincoln with a vision of national greatness and the gift of kindling fires in the souls of the people. But the rhetorical ascent was marred by a last excoriation of the Republicans and by a note of defeatism. Whatever the Progressives' immediate fate, he said, they would triumph in the end because their cause was just. He closed with a quote from Theodore Roosevelt: "We stand at Armageddon, and we battle for the Lord."

Despite weeks of work and advice sought and taken from numerous quarters, most of the speech was mediocre—dense, defensive, and devoid of memorable lines except for the one he pilfered from himself. There was speculation that he had planted the question about the party's racial divide, and whether he had or not, the moment allowed him to look courageous before his audience while keeping the party's most unprogressive stand out of thousands of newspapers. The typescript of the speech, which was silent on race, had been given to the press in advance.

The *New York Times* said that Roosevelt had stood at Chicago and preached revolution, and the *Wall Street Journal* dismissed the speech as so much hot air. But there were no critics inside the Coliseum. The audience applauded 145 times during the speech and followed it with full-throated renditions of "Onward, Christian Soldiers" and "The Battle Hymn of the Republic." For every jaded reporter who guessed that hymns lavished upon tariffs and trusts would set the Almighty's teeth to gnashing, there were grudging acknowledgments of an aura of otherworldliness shimmering overhead. "The atmosphere was charged with emotion akin to prayer," O. K. Davis would write. "Old newspaper men, hardened by many years of experience, made cynical and skeptical by constant contact with human deceit and insincerity, came to scoff and went away filled with wonder."

Roosevelt and his running mate, Governor Hiram Johnson of California, were nominated the next evening. TR selected one of his oldest political associates, William A. Prendergast, to make the nomination and asked Jane Addams to deliver one of the seconding speeches. She noted that America lagged behind Europe in using government for social betterment and predicted that with the leadership of Theodore Roosevelt, the Progressive Party would lead the country into the modern age.

The convention ratified the nominations by acclamation, and the candidates were escorted to the rostrum to accept. TR seemed stunned, as if he had just realized that in accepting the nomination, he could no longer change his mind about running. He spoke briefly, in a voice close to breaking: "I come forward to thank you from my heart for the honor you have conferred upon me. To say that of course I accept. That I hold it—and now I am measuring my words, I have been president, I have seen and known much of life, and I hold it by far the greatest honor and the greatest opportunity that has ever come to me, to be called by you to the leadership for the time being of this great movement in the interests of the American people."

Johnson spoke in the martial tones often used by the Colonel (and sometimes by George Perkins). "I come to tell you that I have enlisted for the war. I enlisted long ago, and I enlisted in that fight that is your fight now, the fight of all the nation, thank God, at last." Saying he "would rather go down to defeat with Theodore Roosevelt than go to victory with any other presidential candidate," Johnson vowed to fight with all his strength and exhorted the convention to "make November 5 the greatest of all election days ever held in these United States." After a benediction, more hymns, and three cheers for the candidates, the convention adjourned, and the Progressives went forth to battle for Theodore Roosevelt.

THE MOST PROPHETIC BATTLES had been raging for days, in the party's headquarters at the Congress Hotel. The first casualty was Benjamin Barr Lindsey, a Colorado judge longing to be Roosevelt's running mate. Progressive to the marrow, he had won Roosevelt's admiration for his work in humanizing the court's treatment of juvenile offenders. Lindsey, scarcely taller than the boys he saved from jail, had been dubbed the Bull

Mouse, but Bull Dog would have been more apt. He fastened his jaws on the vice presidency and refused to let go even after Roosevelt settled on Johnson. Jim Garfield was recruited to form a posse to "confer" with the judge until he capitulated. Lindsey held out till the last, giving up just before the nominations were presented to the convention.

Hiram Johnson, meanwhile, burned *not* to run for vice president. "The pioneer in any movement is likely to be so battered and spattered that, after his first pioneering, his usefulness is at an end," he had written a friend just after Wilson's nomination. Knowing that Wilson would appeal to many progressive Republicans, Johnson believed that Roosevelt had no chance of winning. Johnson refused the offer of the vice presidency until the night before the nominations and seems to have buckled out of guilt and a fear of dishonor. Roosevelt's emissaries, he said, "put up to me that one man was giving his all to this fight, that with his glorious past he did not shrink from a humiliating defeat, and that where others were demanded, they should yield." So the unwanted prize of the Progressive Party's first vice presidential nomination fell upon Johnson, and to Lindsey went the questionable glory of standing before the convention and nominating Johnson.

A new political party is a magnet for idealists and opportunists, and the Progressives exerted a powerful attraction on both. Their party was less a movement than a gathering place for all who believed that society could be better and that they could make it so, by using government as an agency of human welfare. "Lord, how we did like that phrase," White recalled in his autobiography. United on the importance of a muscular, active government, the Progressives as individuals represented so many causes and represented them with such ardent single-mindedness that their demise was virtually inevitable, Johnson said. "Men of the highest ideals gather. On one central fact they will agree, and go forward, and then differ absolutely on important detail, and . . . divided among ourselves ultimately we become easy prey for the other side."

Jane Addams, dedicated pacifist, tried in vain to persuade the platform committee to declare in favor of arbitration and against naval expansion. The party's support for two new battleships a year she found "very difficult to swallow," as was its stand in favor of fortifying the Panama Canal. After all that had been done to annihilate mosquitoes and otherwise preserve the health of the workers digging the canal, she thought it absurd to endanger their lives by turning Panama into a target. She was also distressed by Roosevelt's rejection of a plank urging the enforcement of voting rights and the repeal of racially discriminatory laws.

The biggest row erupted over the question of regulating the trusts. All factions agreed that the Sherman Antitrust Act too often penalized big corporations simply for their size, and in breaking them up, it had rarely achieved the desired ends of lower prices and fair competition. Amos Pinchot and others more radical than Roosevelt favored strengthening the law by itemizing the punishable offenses. Roosevelt and Perkins held that unless the law confined itself to a broad definition of monopolistic conduct, the lawyers for the trusts would find loopholes and would have reason to claim that any practice not explicitly mentioned was legal. More important than an amended Sherman Act, in Roosevelt's view, was the establishment of a federal body empowered to regulate corporations much as the Interstate Commerce Commission supervised the railroads.

In O. K. Davis's recollection, the authors of the platform "fought all day over this Sherman Law proposition, and they fought all night." They stayed in session, had meals brought in, and "wrote out their ideas in a thousand phraseologies. But they could not agree." Finally Dixon showed Roosevelt a version listing specific offenses. Roosevelt thought it best to omit the list but promised to continue naming the crimes in his speeches. When Dixon returned to the committee and asked for a vote, the committee sided with the Colonel.

With no time left for typing a clean draft, the platform committee hurried to the Coliseum, where William Draper Lewis, dean of the University of Pennsylvania Law School, read the thirty-odd planks from as many slips of paper, some of which were heavily marked up with revisions. Perkins, seated next to Amos Pinchot on the rostrum, listened attentively. Davis saw amazement wash over Perkins's face as Lewis read an antitrust plank with a list of punishable offenses. "Lewis has made a mistake," Perkins told Pinchot. "That doesn't belong in the platform. We cut it out last night." Perkins dashed off to find the Colonel and to make sure that the other version was the one released to the newspapers.

The evidence in the Progressive Party's archives suggests that Lewis had indeed made a mistake, but when the radicals read the published platform in the newspapers and found *no* mention of the Sherman Act, they suspected a double cross. The thorough study of the contretemps in John A. Gable's *Bull Moose Years* absolves Perkins with the sensible observation that his trickery would have been easily exposed. But to Pinchot, White, and others who saw Perkins's corporate ties as a liability to a Progressive campaign, the double cross theory had the feel of truth.

The day after the convention, when the national committee met to elect an executive committee, Perkins found himself in the path of a Kansas tornado in the form of William Allen White. White was scared, he said, "but I did look Perkins squarely in the eye, and as gently as I could, being full of indignation, I denounced him." He also declared his opposition to Perkins's election as chairman of the executive committee.

Matthew Hale of Massachusetts, dreading a showdown, suggested that Perkins leave the room for the debate. Perkins coolly declined and invited his opponents to state their objections. There was only one: the oxymoron of having a director of two of the country's largest trusts, both caught up in antitrust suits, at the head of the Progressive Party. Perkins earnestly affirmed his support of the party's principles and noted that the press had already scrutinized his business connections. He was ready to do the work and contribute substantial sums of his own, and he thought it only fair that he have the say over the use of the money.

Hale suggested electing a figurehead as chairman and allowing Perkins to operate behind the scenes. After a long, awkward pause, Arizona's representative got to his feet and ended the debate. "We believe in toting guns down our way," he said. "But we don't carry 'em concealed." As soon as the voting ended, Chairman Perkins headed straight for White, threw an arm around him, and sunnily proffered the hope that he would prove White wrong.

Roosevelt was safely out of the fray, rocketing back to New York on the Twentieth Century Limited. Edith wrote Kermit that TR was "fine and dandy," and TR filed a similar report with the reporters who saw him off. He had had a splendid time in Chicago, he said. "They never imagined we would have a convention like that, and it's worrying them."

Those who knew him would not have paused over the indeterminate "they." "They" were not Republicans or Democrats, "they" were everyone who was not "we"—the malefactors of great wealth, their retainers in the legislatures and the courts, socialists, anarchists, pacifists, troglodytes, despoilers. He was going to fight, and without powerful enemies ranged against him, there could be no heroism.

ELEVEN

Spend and Be Spent

H EADY as it was for the Progressives to imagine themselves an army
of the Lord, storming the redoubt of the old regime while beating
back the advance of an alien horde, the truth was simpler and sadder. The redoubt had all but collapsed. "Sometimes I think I might as well
give up so far as being a candidate is concerned," Taft had written his wife in
July. "There are so many people in the country who don't like me." Root
and Stimson had stood by him but hesitated to battle Roosevelt in public,
and the campaign purse was embarrassingly light, the shrewd money having gone elsewhere. Henry Clay Frick, a robber baron who regularly golfed
and played poker with Taft in Beverly, offered to write checks for the party
but not for the president, explaining that the Taft administration had "utterly failed to treat many of its warmest friends fairly." Others invested in
local candidates.

The newspapers overflowed with stories about Roosevelt and Wilson but
had little to report about a president moping in the White House. Taft informed the *Times* that he did not care. "I have been told that I ought to do
this, ought to do that, ought to say this, ought to say the other; that I do not
keep myself in the headlines, that there is this or that trick I might turn to my
advantage. I know it, but I can't do it." His opponents could campaign all
they liked; he intended to stand on his record and spend the two months before the election at Beverly, on vacation.

Hiram Johnson, the Vice Bull Moose, called Taft a "negligible" factor in
the race. Roosevelt had already dismissed the president with a slash: "I never

discuss dead issues." Woodrow Wilson was more tactful but of the same mind. "The contest is between [Roosevelt] and me, not between Taft and me," he wrote a friend. Further than that, though, Wilson could not see. He did not know whether voters would want the mild progressivism he was offering or Roosevelt's red-hot variety, nor could he estimate the value of Roosevelt's celebrity. TR captivated his fellow Americans, Wilson told his friend; "I do not. He is a real, vivid person, whom they have seen and shouted themselves hoarse over and voted for, millions strong; I am a vague, conjectural personality, more made up of opinions and academic prepossessions than of human traits and red corpuscles. We shall see what will happen!" In a canny bid to neutralize Roosevelt's charisma, Wilson asked voters not to reduce the campaign to a personality contest. If the Colonel grasped the motive for the remark, he must have been amused. By the laws of his political physics, wild adulation of the sort he had known simply invited a backlash of equal magnitude.

For a man who excelled at oratory, Wilson was surprisingly averse to campaigning. "We the people" fired his political imagination, but encounters with the jostling, importuning, flesh-and-blood public gave him headaches, indigestion, and a weariness that seemed to permeate every cell. He disliked the press and despised the fishbowl life of a presidential candidate. When supporters hinted that he would have to exert himself, he suggested that they work harder. Nor would he court the one million women who would cast ballots in 1912. Though he had dropped his opposition to woman suffrage, he had not yet endorsed it and feared that changing his stance would make him look like Roosevelt, whose late embrace of suffrage was seen as pandering.

Only the Colonel was willing to spend and be spent. The phrase comes from Paul's second letter to the Corinthians, whose hedonism had sorely vexed him. "And I will very gladly spend and be spent for you," Paul wrote them, "even though the more abundantly I love you, the less I be loved." Roosevelt in the year of the Bull Moose was as zealous as Paul and as convinced of his own selflessness. He was also, of course, a spender by nature. And the Progressive Party, after keeping his candidacy alive, deserved nothing less than spend and be spent. While Wilson conserved his energies, Roosevelt would blaze through thirty-two states. The campaign was sure to be "a constantly increasing strain of grimy fatigue and irritation," he wrote Kermit, but he found it invigorating to fight against heavy odds and

glimpsed a chance of victory ("very slight," but still a chance) if the Progressives got "the masses of the people really informed and waked up."

Climax of two decades of populist rumblings, the election of 1912 asked
the masses to make philosophical choices with far-reaching consequences.
Great wealth had become a fact of American life. How was that wealth to be
divided? How much power should a democratic government have? And
who should wield it? Whether the candidates spoke of tariffs or trusts, conservation or woman suffrage, they were asking voters to decide the course of
modern American democracy.

Years later William Allen White would say that Roosevelt's New Nationalism and Wilson's New Freedom had been separated by "that fantastic
imaginary gulf that always has existed between tweedle-dum and tweedle-
dee." "Death to privilege!" was Roosevelt's cry and Wilson's too. But on the
most urgent issues, the tariff and the trusts, the gulf was real and wide.

The tariff, originally levied to raise revenue for the government and protect a stripling American manufacturing establishment from foreign competition, had inevitably nurtured monopoly. By raising import prices
anywhere from 5 to 75 percent, the tariff gave American manufacturers lee-
way to mark up their prices, and with their huge profits they could muscle
out small competitors and buy senators and congressmen willing to knit
ever thicker blankets of protection.

From Woodrow Wilson, voters got a pellucid explanation of the intrica-
cies and costs of this web of favors. While Republican orthodoxy held that
high tariffs meant high wages, a 1912 strike at the woolen mills in
Lawrence, Massachusetts, had shown otherwise, Wilson said. The woolen
industry, which enjoyed more tariff protection than most, paid mill workers
so little that a family needed the wages of a father, mother, and child to be as
well off as the average American household.

Consumers paid dearly for the tariff—$115 a year on average, or more
than 10 percent of a typical family's income. Only $16 of the $115 collected
at the customs house went to the government; the rest was the rake-off of the
trusts. "Those who buy are not even represented by counsel," Wilson said.
"The high cost of living is arranged by private understanding." Calling the
tariff "stiff and stupid," Wilson proposed an immediate revision beginning
with the most egregious duties and moving "downward, unhesitatingly and
steadily downward until special favors of every sort shall have been absolutely withdrawn."

Wilson and Roosevelt punched and counterpunched in their speeches, and voters followed the debate in the newspapers. To Roosevelt, nothing was "more ludicrous and pathetic than the belief that with the advent of the angel of free trade, clad in a garment of untaxed calico, the millennium would be brought about." The abolition of the protective tariff would bring immediate economic disaster to capital and labor, he warned, and would do nothing to further social and industrial justice. Roosevelt favored keeping the protective tariff, rooting out the abuses, and ensuring that wage-earners got their fair share of the spoils. He repeated his call for a permanent tariff commission—expert, nonpartisan, scientific—operating under the authority of the president. Proceeding industry by industry, the commission would formulate impartial recommendations and make its findings public so that Congress could no longer revise tariff schedules in secret.

Roosevelt also campaigned forcefully for a corporations commission. Composed of experienced, public-spirited business leaders, the commission would make a thorough inspection of a trust's affairs, require change when there were signs of monopoly, and stamp the company "approved" if all was in order. Once certified, a trust could carry on without fear of prosecution under the antitrust laws. Presumably the commission would conduct new examinations from time to time, but the system's chief incentive to good behavior was personal. Managers whose corporations broke the law would go to jail.

Wilson saw the commission as an unholy alliance between the trusts and the government. It would legalize monopoly, Wilson predicted, and in no time the monopolies would be regulating the regulators. In Kansas, where Roosevelt had introduced his New Nationalism in 1910, Wilson pointed out that the state's progressives had originally come together to fight the powers behind the tariff and the trusts, and now the candidate of the so-called Progressive Party was proposing to collaborate with them. Instead of attempting to regulate the trusts, Wilson promised to regulate competition, making it fair and open to all with a new antitrust law banning all practices known to abet monopoly.

Wilson mocked the very idea of expert commissions. "God forbid that in a democratic country we should . . . give the government over to experts," he told an audience of workingmen. What was the role of the people when they allowed themselves to be "scientifically taken care of by a small number of gentlemen who are the only men who understand the job?" Even Taft roused himself to condemn the business commission as "the most monstrous monopoly of power in the history of the world" and cite it as proof of Roosevelt's Napoleonic ambitions.

Napoleon Roosevelt, scourge of democracy, appeared so often in editorials and cartoons that one wonders how the pundits would have managed without him, and the ubiquity of the image reveals more about the hostility of the press than about Roosevelt's alleged megalomania. Without question, Roosevelt loved power and longed to return to the White House. But his thrill came less from the possession of power than from the intensity of purpose he felt when he had it and from his conception of presidential power as a counterforce to the might of the lords of capital. However flawed his business commission might have been, he could conceive of no better instrument for thwarting the malefactors of great wealth.

When Wilson registered another objection to commissions, arguing that the history of liberty was a history of limiting the powers of government, Roosevelt parried that the history of public welfare was the history of increasing governmental power. Laws regulating public lands, working conditions, and the hours of employment for women and children—all had given the government new powers, and such powers were the people's only protection against abusive trusts. Wilson's vague talk of regulating competition, said Roosevelt, would "leave unchecked the colossal embodied privileges of the present day."

SO THE FIGHT WENT, back and forth, as Roosevelt raced up coast and down, through the Midwest, the West, and the South. Wilson would venture no farther west than the Dakotas and no deeper into the South than Missouri. Sure to win the South, he had crossed it off his itinerary. "I haven't a Bull Moose's strength," he wrote a friend.

TR started in New England, campaigning in every state and making eight speeches a day for three days running in Vermont, which had voted Republican in thirteen of the fourteen presidential elections since the party's founding. With only four electoral votes, Vermont mattered little in the presidential sweepstakes, but with its early state election, on September 4, it would give the first real indication of Roosevelt's power to lure Republicans to vote the Progressive ticket. When the Progressives finished last, the *Times* snickered that a "great emancipator of the people who lets himself be beaten by the Vermont Democrats is in a pretty bad way."

Huge crowds assembled wherever Roosevelt went, and grimy fatigue or not, he gave them his all. At the fairgrounds in St. Paul, Minnesota, with the wind blowing against him, he darted from one end of the platform to the other every five minutes, delivering his talk in installments to make himself audible to the 25,000 people who had come out to hear him.

Before an audience composed entirely of women, he got off to a flustered start and endeared himself by admitting that such an assemblage was new to him. He also confessed that he had worked with women engaged in social reform for many years "without ever thinking how they stood on suffrage." After they had explained that the vote would help them win the reforms they sought, he went from passive to active suffragist, he said, and he had come to believe families would gain if women participated in political affairs. "If we don't have the right type of political life, it will be difficult permanently to have the right type of family life." he declared.

Beyond dozens and dozens of scheduled speeches, there were "little bull moose" talks from the back of his train at uncountable stations along his route. He would burst through the rear door of his car, grinning as if he had waited a lifetime to see the people of Possum Grove. Immediately he asked the children on the tracks to move back, explaining that sometimes the train slipped a bit. "We don't want to lose any little bull mooses," he would say. The crowds were charmed, and while the children regrouped, TR was saving his voice.

To the unhappiness of supporters who wanted him to concentrate on states where the race would be close — California and Oregon and Montana in the West, Illinois and North Dakota in the middle of the country, and Massachusetts and Vermont in the East — TR invested a week in the solidly Democratic South. The crowds were big and warm, and a Memphis newspaperman who witnessed the magic of the little bull moose talks saw that TR had the gift of making his listeners feel as if they knew him personally. Much as they enjoyed the acquaintance, though, most of the Southerners who came out to see him freely admitted that they would not vote for him. They did not trust him on the Negro question.

The great whale of race broke the surface in Atlanta, where Roosevelt accused Wilson of distorting his views on the trusts and implying that he had broken the law in approving the sale of Tennessee Coal and Iron. Without using the word, Roosevelt was calling Wilson a liar, and Atlanta turned bilious. "Here's your hat, Colonel," said the editors of the *Atlanta Journal*. "The South isn't in your ring. It's high time you were hurrying home. . . . In a guise of sanctity, you come to convert what you derisively call the Solid

South, but be not deceived, doughty Colonel; for the eyes of this section have pierced your missionary makeup and they see you as the political adventurer you are." His two-faced answer to the Negro question would do him no good in the South, the *Journal* said. "You have straddled this issue in both the North and the South, fraternizing with the Negro there and execrating him here. Go home, Colonel, go home and apologize as best you can to the colored brethren, whom you consider your 'equals' in the North; but as for the South, what you have done speaks so loudly that we cannot hear what you say."

Roosevelt's lily-white Southern strategy and his unwillingness to give the ideal of racial equality so much as a line in the Progressive platform led W. E. B. Du Bois and the National Association for the Advancement of Colored People to do the unthinkable: endorse Woodrow Wilson, a Southerner and a Democrat. For a time, Du Bois had belonged to the Socialist Party, whose perennial candidate, Eugene Debs, had impressed him by refusing to address segregated audiences. But Du Bois fell out when Debs declined to fight racial discrimination elsewhere, arguing that it made no sense to separate the oppression of Negroes from the oppression of the laboring class generally. After Wilson communicated to a leading black clergyman that he earnestly wished to see the Negro treated with justice, "and not mere grudging justice, but justice executed with liberality and cordial good feeling," Du Bois urged blacks to support Wilson "and prove once for all if the Democratic Party dares to be democratic when it comes to the black man."

Publicly, Roosevelt and Wilson said little about Eugene Debs, the Socialist Party's candidate. In the last presidential election, Debs had polled only 3 percent of the vote. But in the congressional elections of 1910, Wisconsin had given the U.S. House of Representatives its first Socialist, Victor Berger, and had sent fourteen Socialists to the statehouse in Madison. Elsewhere in the country, a thousand Socialist Party members were serving as legislators, mayors, and city councilmen.

The Socialists were also disturbing the dreams of the bourgeoisie. Bomb-throwing as a remedy for social injustice was in vogue, and although Debs condemned it, a substantial minority of Socialists disagreed with him. W. Sturgis Bigelow of Boston, scholar of Buddhism and a friend of both Lodge and Roosevelt, wrote Lodge that with the United States headed for "some kind of socialism," he was giving his mite to TR "in the hope that he will get the wheel and steer her down the rapids somehow, instead of running her straight on the rocks as Debs would—purposely."

Roosevelt read the rise of socialism as evidence of the "idiotic folly of the high financiers" and proposed to rout them with a strong national government. Wilson saw the Socialist Party as a natural response to unkept political promises. The tariff, sold to voters as a boon to labor, had been a burden. "[W]hen are you going to call their bluff?" Wilson asked an audience of workingmen in Peru, Indiana. Decide what you want, he told them, "and then make up your minds which set of men are most likely to give it to you."

Sure to lose, Debs and his Socialist Party would not be in a position to give the working classes anything in the way of new legislation or new policies, but as the most progressive of the three parties flying progressive colors, they would siphon votes from both Wilson and Roosevelt, a crucial consideration in a tight race. Debs scorned the Democratic and Republican parties as the "political wings of the capitalist system," and the Socialists accused Roosevelt of filching their best wine and watering it down, offering just enough socialism to save capitalism from self-destruction.

As promised, Roosevelt was spending and being spent, but the path to the White House in 1912 was strewn with obstacles he had not faced in his 1904 campaign. Back then, the power of both the presidency and an established party were his to command. Now he had only the infant Progressive Party, which was not yet a disciplined, unified force. The idealists and the pragmatists were still deeply divided on the subject of the party's new chairman, George Perkins. Watching Perkins in action at Sagamore and at party headquarters, Phil Roosevelt, a young cousin working as a campaign aide, saw two George Perkinses, the charmer and the autocrat, and the autocrat had bruised nearly everyone but the Colonel.

Barraged by Democrats and Republicans, who used his International Harvester and U.S. Steel directorships to insinuate that his ideas for regulating big business were a ruse to increase the power of the trusts, Perkins unwisely chose to retaliate. A man with more political experience would have cursed under his breath and moved on, but Perkins defended himself in pamphlets with titles such as George W. Perkins's Views on Labor and crated them off to the Progressives' state leaders for distribution to the public. "They came in great bales by express collect to Emporia," William Allen White said, "and I refused to pay the charges and sent them back." Perkins's brand of capitalism made White so uncomfortable that he persuaded the Progressive Party of Kansas not to accept any funds from headquarters.

The Progressive Bulletin, published weekly (under a copyright belonging

to Perkins), had the aggressive inspirational brightness of the success manu-
als published in Perkins's youth. "What are you doing to help the Progressive Party?" the *Bulletin* asked. "Are you telling our story to every man and
woman you meet?" A bookmark adorned with crossed flags and a bull
moose advised the reader to "Look up, not down—Look out, not in—Look
forward, not backward—and lend a hand." Perkins never quite grasped the
difference between political persuasion and the cheerleading he had once
done as an executive in charge of a life insurance company's sales force.

Amos Pinchot, who had given liberally to the cause and was a Progressive
congressional candidate in New York, considered the choice of Perkins as
chairman a tactical blunder of the highest order. Wall Street firmly opposed
Roosevelt because of his attitude toward judicial recall, yet the public saw
Perkins's leading role as evidence of Wall Street's influence over Roosevelt.
Hiram Johnson was equally unhappy with Perkins's prominence in the
campaign. *Is Perkins Sincere?* and *Is Perkins Honest?* and the rest of the
Perkins pamphlets should be burned, Johnson thought. He did not doubt
Perkins's integrity but feared that his overreaction to criticism might alien-
ate the public.

Although White, Johnson, and Pinchot were right, Perkins in 1912 was a
man under siege from every direction—unpopular with his fellow Progressives, pilloried by Republicans and Democrats, and a pariah to the trusts. As
he was playing Dough Moose to the Bull Moose, U.S. Steel was pressing
hard for his resignation from its board of directors because of his ties to Roosevelt. In the summer of 1912 Perkins and J. P. Morgan, Jr., the chairman of
U.S. Steel, dueled for weeks by mail and by telephone. "[I]t is of the very
greatest importance to the U.S. Steel Corporation that its officers and directors should not be prominently identified with current politics," Morgan
wrote him.

Perkins refused to resign. The campaign would soon be over, he said, and
his political work involved nothing contrary to U.S. Steel's interests. A little
huffily but not without reason, he added that a man ought to be free to take
part in business and serve his country at the same time. Even the Wilson-
loving *New York Evening Post* thought the whipping should stop. George
Washington had been "a good soldier—and about the richest man in the
country, when he did his great work for this republic," the *Post* said. "Nobody suggests that he ought to have kept out of politics because he happened to be rich."

❀

ROOSEVELT'S CELEBRITY, once invaluable, had become problematic. He was now the fading star who would always draw an affectionate crowd but seemed just outside the orbit of the times. Wilson was the ingenue, the blank screen onto which the public could project whatever it wished to see. White complained that Wilson's manner "undramatized . . . nearly everything he touched," but the country had tired of drama. Asked to choose between Roosevelt's strenuous battle for the Lord and Wilson's promise of "a chapter of readjustment, not of pain and rough disturbance," Americans would point their feet toward the smoother course.

Wilson had feared Roosevelt's popularity without appreciating the inherent appeal of the ingenue or the political advantages of inexperience. With only two years in public life, he had no history weighing against him, nor had he had time to make powerful enemies. Roosevelt had Wall Street, the press, and the political machinery of both parties in opposition, and Fighting Bob La Follette, still furious over the theft of the movement he felt was his, expended considerable money and energy in hopes of bringing about Roosevelt's demise. On the first day of TR's campaign, Fighting Bob was on the floor of the Senate, expatiating on the tariff and allowing himself a digression on the growth of the trusts during the Roosevelt administration. There had been 140 when Roosevelt took office, La Follette said, and 10,000 when he left. "I do not believe that the man who was president during that time is the man to find the way out now." The words were not particularly strong, but they were delivered with hands clenched, face strained, and voice quaking with emotion, and when La Follette finished his attack on Roosevelt, he thundered that he would work at making the Republican Party progressive "till the last bell rings and the curtain falls."

La Follette even shelved his political purity and got into bed with Senator Boies Penrose of Pennsylvania (whose virtue was never in question because he had none) and revived the old charge that Roosevelt had solicited contributions from E. H. Harriman in 1904. An investigation of campaign financing under way in the Senate gave La Follette and Penrose a forum for a sensational new accusation: Cornelius Bliss, manager of Roosevelt's 1904 campaign, had allegedly solicited $100,000, maybe more, from John D. Archbold of Standard Oil, epitome of the wicked trust.

Roosevelt immediately produced a copy of a letter he had written his White House secretary just after learning of contributions from men connected with Standard Oil. "This may be really untrue," he had said. "But if true I must ask you to direct that the money be returned to them forthwith."

The committee was chaired by Moses E. Clapp, one of the few Republican senators who had joined the Progressive Party, and for a time it looked as if he would be able to dissuade the committee from calling Roosevelt to testify. He failed, and TR reported to Washington on October 5. "The Clapp Committee behaved very well when it appeared before Colonel Roosevelt on Friday," the New York Times said with a scowl. Roosevelt answered questions for two hours, during which the committee listened with great patience, asked friendly questions, and refrained from bringing up testimony at odds with the Colonel's. The most damning witness was Archbold, who said that he had made the contribution after being solicited by Bliss. But Archbold had no receipt, Bliss was dead, and in keeping with the custom of the day, the campaign's ledgers had been pitched into a furnace. Bliss's assistant confirmed Archbold's story and told the committee that no contributions had been returned, but he was testifying from memory.

Roosevelt testified that he did not know if his order had been carried out. When Senator Atlee Pomerene suggested that quid was rarely given without an expectation of quo, Roosevelt retorted that anyone hoping for "any consideration from making any contributions to me was either a crook or a fool."

Applause from the spectators threatened to end Senator Pomerene's line of inquiry, but he persevered. It appeared that the $100,000 had not been returned, he said.

"Well, has it appeared that it was made?" Roosevelt asked.

As Pomerene was offering his evidence, Roosevelt cut him off. "You may have noticed, Senator, that I have been very careful in what I have said here. I have never said that I did or did not believe that it was made."

One of those who claimed to know the full story was Philander Knox, Roosevelt's first attorney general, who had happened by when Roosevelt was dictating the note asking that the money be returned. "Why, Mr. President," Knox had said, "the money has been spent. They cannot pay it back—they haven't got it." Roosevelt blithely announced that he would send the note anyway, because it would look good in the record. Knox told the story to Taft in the summer of 1912, but Taft declined to exploit it. The Senate investigation was scaring donors away, he wrote one of his brothers. Men who might help were holding back for fear of having their names "dragged out in a public way."

Perkins was also swept into the hearings. As president of the New York

Life Insurance Company in 1904 he had given nearly $50,000 of the company's money to Roosevelt's campaign and had narrowly missed going to jail. Having to revisit the matter in front of the Clapp committee, Perkins lost his temper, apologized, and finished up with an unappealing blend of sarcasm and self-pity: "Do you know of anybody in this country who has been more vilified on this subject than I have?"

Roosevelt escaped the fire set by La Follette and Penrose, but not without burns. The hearings reinforced the impression that his relations with the trusts were too cozy for the serious reforms he was promising in his speeches.

The only flicker of scandal in Wilson's campaign was swiftly extinguished by Roosevelt himself. Wilson always seemed most at ease in the company of women, a likely consequence of a boyhood spent among doting older sisters and of a marriage that produced three daughters. In 1912, when one of Roosevelt's campaign aides told him of Wilson's close friendship with a woman about to be divorced, Roosevelt ordered the Progressives not to spread the gossip. He believed in Wilson's decency, and he doubted that the public would buy the idea of Wilson as swain. Laughing so hard that his voice narrowed to a squeak, Roosevelt said, "You can't cast a man as Romeo who looks and acts so much like an apothecary clerk."

Wilson's looks fell into the category of middling—graying chestnut-brown hair, blue eyes, and a trim physique that suggested athletics but had its origins in a wretched digestive system. The eyes seemed cold till he smiled. His round, full tenor was not "a big bull voice," said the *New York World*, which loathed the big bull. The *World* also appreciated Wilson's ability to deliver a speech without flailing every limb. Poised and self-contained, this man was not in a fight with the world.

R OOSEVELT DEPARTED for his last campaign swing on October 7. He was headed for the Midwest, La Follette territory, and Fighting Bob's weekly magazine had just launched a five-part series on Roosevelt's treacheries, scheduling the last installment to run three days before the election. O. K. Davis, the campaign's publicity manager, had a sense that the Progressives were gaining momentum, but seeing the thin crowds in Chicago, the *New York Times* declared, "The people do not want the Colonel."

The once indefatigable physical engine of Theodore Roosevelt was nearly out of steam, emptied by days like the one he had had in the upper peninsula of Michigan, where he made two speeches before breakfast, two after dinner, and twenty-six in between. To save his voice, he was using the little bull moose gambit, inviting crowds to sing hymns, and asking mayors to introduce him. As often as not, His Honor would blow hard till it was nearly time for the train to move on.

Davis tried to protect the Colonel by wiring stern orders up the line: no receptions, breakfasts, lunches, or dinners. "These things must be observed if we are to keep him going," Davis wrote. But the campaign's demands were endless and unpredictable. Shouting through a chill autumn wind in Chicago had put Roosevelt's voice beyond gambits and beyond the nostrums of Dr. S. L. Terrell, a throat specialist traveling with the campaign. After Terrell prescribed a day of silence, TR whispered a memo to Perkins, asking him to revamp the travel schedule so that the campaign train would move mainly at night, eliminating the little bull moose talks.

On October 14 Roosevelt gave an afternoon speech in Racine, Wisconsin, then rode on to Milwaukee, where he planned to nap and dine in his car, recharging himself for an eight o'clock speech. A welcome committee came aboard and announced that it was ready to parade him through the streets to a hotel where the city fathers were expecting to have dinner with him. Davis and Dr. Terrell were staving them off when TR thrust himself into the discussion to say that he wanted to be "a good Indian." Did the committee think that his staying on the train hurt his cause? he asked. The welcome committee, mulish but not asinine, seized the opening, and Roosevelt was paraded and feted till it was time to depart for the speech.

Outside the hotel Roosevelt moved through a cheering crowd to an open automobile waiting to take him to an auditorium where ten thousand people were settling into their seats. Roosevelt stepped into the back of the car, sat, then rose to wave and acknowledge the cheers. A man standing seven feet away drew a revolver from his vest and fired, hitting Roosevelt in the chest. Knocked back into the seat, Roosevelt put his fingers to his lips, saw that he was not bleeding from the mouth, and concluded that the bullet had not perforated his lung. He had only been "pinked," he assured Henry Cochems, one of his bodyguards.

The assailant was John Schrank, thirty-six, a New Yorker acting on orders from the ghost of President McKinley. Schrank had been writing a poem in the middle of the night when McKinley appeared and instructed him to avenge his assassination and deny Roosevelt a third term.

When Schrank was taken away TR asked the driver to head for the auditorium. Dr. Terrell insisted that they go to the hospital, but TR, having cal-

culated the odds of his survival at twenty to one, was adamant. "You get me
to that speech," he ordered; "it may be the last one I shall ever deliver, but I
am going to deliver this one." Backstage at the auditorium, he consented to
be examined by Dr. Terrell and three other physicians. The bullet had been
slowed by the contents of his breast pocket—a steel spectacles case—and
the folded manuscript of his speech. The hole in his chest, just below his
right nipple, had left a fist-sized bloodstain on his shirt and was still oozing.
He said he felt no pain, and a check of his breathing revealed no injury to internal organs. The doctors dressed the wound with a fresh handkerchief and
stood aside as he strode to center stage.

After a clergyman offered an unmercifully long prayer, someone introduced Cochems, a former college football player and a well-known figure
in Wisconsin politics, who had been given the honor of presenting Roosevelt. With sheets of sweat pouring down his face, Cochems tried to tell the
crowd what had happened.

Seeing that the audience had not understood, TR stepped in. "Friends, I
shall ask you to be as quiet as possible," he began. "I don't know whether you
fully understand that I have just been shot; but it takes more than that to kill
a Bull Moose." He showed them the bullet holes in his manuscript and un-
buttoned his vest to display his bloodstained shirt. Most of the audience
gasped, but when a few uninhibited souls cried out for him to turn this way
and that, he obliged.

Although Roosevelt's words came slowly and he alluded again and again
to the shooting, the speech was a coherent presentation of his politics and
an astonishing effort to capitalize on the moment. The audience would
have to believe him, he said, for a man who had just been shot was inca-
pable of insincerity. And they must know how unsurprising it was, after
months of reading the abuse heaped upon him, that "weak and vicious
minds" would be inflamed to violence. Knowing nothing about his at-
tacker, Roosevelt assumed him to be a have-not and warned that when citizens "permit the conditions to grow such that the poor man as such will be
swayed by his sense of injury against the men who try to hold what they improperly have won, when that day comes, the most awful passions will be let
loose and it will be an ill day for our country." The existence of desperate
men was a reason to vote Progressive.

Seeing Roosevelt sway and struggle to steady himself, Cochems hustled
off the stage and stood directly below the Colonel to catch him if he fainted.
O. K. Davis listened for half an hour, as long as he could stand it, then

walked to Roosevelt's side and put a hand on his arm. The Colonel glowered at him and after a terse exchange pivoted toward the audience. "My
friends are a little more nervous than I am," he said.

After eighty minutes onstage, Roosevelt handed himself over to the doctors. At the hospital, as he waited for X-rays to be developed, he dictated a reassuring telegram to Edith, urging her to remain at home. "I am not nearly
as bad hurt as I have been again and again with a fall from my horse," he
said. "Everything possible is being done for me by everybody."

The bullet, lodged safely in a rib, did not require surgery, but the doctors
decided to send him on to a Chicago hospital, where he would get the best
possible care. On the train, TR was a marvel of composure. He transferred
his studs to a clean shirt and requested hot water for a shave. Davis heard
him humming softly as he shaved and noted that two minutes after he
climbed into bed, he was sleeping "as easily as any child."

W HILE EDITH and Ethel and Ted were speeding to Chicago, an employee of the Brazil Railway was dispatched to inform Kermit. "Well,
I guess they've shot Roosevelt, all right," the man blurted. He would say no
more, leaving Kermit to fear the worst. Reassuring cables from home soon
followed, but he was having "a worrying time of it and would give anything
to be in reach just for a short time to know how things really are," he wrote
his father. "It's very hard to be so far away when something has happened to
the Bwana Makuba."

Edith billeted herself in the hospital room next to Theodore's, established a quiet zone in the corridor, and posted sentries. She admitted few
callers, none for more than five minutes. "This is a campaign, and I am the
general," she said. The wound, when she saw it, was a red hole the size of a
dime, in an angry-looking field of black and blue. The hospital stay was described to the public as a precaution in case of infection, but it was also necessary because of his exhaustion and the fierce pain in his rib, which had
fractured and now hurt with every breath. His physician wrote Perkins that
TR was "more nervously tired than is generally realized" and warned that
"any real work must be deferred."

Taft and Wilson wired their good wishes while privately fretting that the
assassination attempt would help Roosevelt at the polls. Wilson curtailed
his campaigning for fear of adding to the sympathy vote. The president's
brother Horace, who saw Roosevelt's behavior in Milwaukee as rank exhibi-

tionism, said, "What a melodrama we shall have when he is able to take the stump again. I have never been so disgusted about anything he has done."

Roosevelt never admitted to exploiting the moment. After years of expecting an assassin he had simply responded according to plan, he told Davis. To one of his *Outlook* colleagues he said he was following the example of the pioneer and soldier types he admired — men trained not to wilt under attack or "let the other fellow for a minute think you are down and out." And writing to his English friend Sir Edward Grey, he said he had gone forward out of a sense of duty, adding (without a trace of self-mockery), "In the very unlikely event of the wound being mortal I wished to die with my boots on."

William Jennings Bryan announced that the election was too important to be decided by the act of a madman. Democrats, Republicans, and Progressives should continue the fight, and Roosevelt's friends should not use his injury as an excuse, Bryan said. "The brave soldiers on a battlefield do not use the wounded for breastworks. They stand out and give blow for blow." Calling Bryan's statement "manly and proper," Roosevelt promised to rejoin the fight if his rib healed fast enough to ease his breathing. In the interim, his running mate and his friends would keep his speaking engagements.

Out of danger but still uncomfortable and easily fatigued, TR was allowed to return to Sagamore on October 21. He turned fifty-four on October 27 — "a day of Thanksgiving for us all," said Edith, who was still shaken. Theodore was now attended by two private detectives and a former Secret Service man.

The patient was docile during his convalescence, hoping to build enough strength for an address to the Progressive faithful at Madison Square Garden on October 30. He wanted one more chance to attack Woodrow Wilson on the trust question, he told Perkins. Perkins, impressed by the wave of sympathy rolling toward the Colonel, urged him in a more peaceable direction. Begin and end with charity toward all, he said. Speak as a man whose narrow escape had renewed his commitment to harmonizing the "conflicting interests of this country to the end that more equitable 'human rights' might obtain and prevail."

Upward of fifteen thousand people, half of them women, crowded into the Garden to hear Roosevelt, and twenty thousand more clogged the streets for a look at him. Inside, bands played, movies of the Colonel's campaign travels flickered on a screen over the stage, four giant editions of the

Stars and Stripes fluttered from the girders, and a spotlight played on a stuffed Bull Moose. Four hundred police officers plus fifty plainclothesmen were seeing to the Colonel's safety. To minimize the jostling, he would come and go by way of a fire escape.

At the first glint of his spectacles, the hall broke into a roar. He marched to the front of the stage and stood tall, waving with his left hand, bowing with noticeable stiffness, and smiling at "such a tossing sea of red bandannas as might have made Debs jealous," said the *New York Evening Post.* Yelling "Four, four, four years more!" the crowd stamped its feet till the floor quaked. The *Times* correspondent watched as "Perfectly respectable gray-haired matrons climbed on chairs with flags and handkerchiefs in their hands and forgot themselves for three-quarters of an hour." Bands played, but no one could hear them.

When someone offered a chair, Roosevelt waved him off, though it seemed to some that he was not entirely enjoying the hullabaloo. His discomfort was understandable: he was exposed on the stage, and his side hurt. The din subsided forty-three minutes after it began, and he started his speech. A few minutes in, when the cheering started up again, he raised his left arm and shook his head. The crowd obeyed. The Roosevelt they heard was a subdued version of his old self. The words were familiar and the voice strong, but he spoke without vitriol and scarcely used the pronoun "I."

The speech was a recitation of unexceptionable truths that could have been delivered by any presidential candidate of the age. "We war against the forces of evil, and the weapons we use are the weapons of right," he said. He promised that a Progressive administration would move with caution and wisdom, causing "the very minimum of disturbance that is compatible with achieving our purpose." The radicalism he had flaunted early in the campaign was gone, supplanted by the soothing thought that his principles reached back to the Golden Rule and the Sermon on the Mount.

He again invoked Washington and Lincoln but for once admitted that the challenges of 1912 did not compare to the American Revolution or the Civil War. In one draft of the speech, after a reference to Lincoln, Roosevelt had penciled in the phrase "until death came to him in the hour of triumph and the patient eyes were closed forever." He omitted the words when he spoke, perhaps sensing that it would be inappropriate to equate a "pinking" with Lincoln's martyrdom.

Organized as a gathering of the party, the evening was not a final appeal for votes, and Roosevelt left his rivals unmentioned, speaking only vaguely of the perils of drift and the untrustworthiness of men who would limit the powers of the national government. He heeded Perkins's advice not to attack Wilson but ignored the suggestion to speak as a man whose brush with death had firmed his resolve.

He had promised Edith that he would limit himself to thirty minutes and at thirty-four minutes was nearly through. "I believe we shall win," he said, "but win or lose I am glad beyond measure that I am one of the many who in this fight have stood ready to spend and be spent, pledged to fight while life lasts the great fight for righteousness and for brotherhood and for the welfare of mankind." A presidential candidate who does not stoutly declare that he will win leaves the impression that he is going to lose, and there was in Roosevelt's last lines a valedictory ring that surprised and disappointed his followers. They cheered and applauded, but not for long.

The next night, Wilson had his hurrah in Madison Square Garden, where a crowd as large as Roosevelt's welcomed him with sixty-two minutes of whooping and hollering. In the roar Wilson forgot the address he had mapped out in his head but managed a creditable summation of his ideas, and he exhorted the nation to vote a straight Democratic ticket. Enacting and carrying out reforms required a united government, he said—president, House of Representatives, Senate, and state governments. Voting Republican would postpone change, and voting Progressive was "only making a prediction that after a while a power may be built up which will control the three branches of the government."

Taft in the last week of the campaign was depressed and depressing. Alice Longworth, in New York to hear her father at Madison Square Garden, saw the president being driven down Fifth Avenue in an open car, sound asleep. Vice President James Sherman, ailing for months, finally expired. Governor Herbert Hadley of Missouri, who had helped Roosevelt at the Republican convention but did not join the bolt, offered to run in Sherman's place, but Taft chose Nicholas Murray Butler, president of Columbia University and a vocal critic of Theodore Roosevelt. On November 1, Taft gave a long interview to the *New York World*, which planned to share it with newspapers across the country in the hope of trimming the Roosevelt vote. Taft was not especially harsh but decided that he could not bear the thought of his gibes in print. Roosevelt had been his closest friend, he told the *World*. The interview was shelved.

✳

ELECTION DAY in Oyster Bay was a perfect specimen of autumn, sunny and a crisp 55 degrees at noon, when TR and the seven men who worked at Sagamore drove down to the village to vote. TR cast ballot number 265, then stood by as the chauffeur, the valet, and the others took their turns.

Wilson and Taft had already voted, Wilson in Princeton and Taft in Cincinnati. Wilson, seeing the friends and neighbors awaiting his arrival at the village firehouse, joshed that they were violating an ordinance against loitering at the polls. Taft called on Congressman Nick Longworth, a gesture that was gracious and might have been useful too, if it had been made in time for the Cincinnati papers to remind voters that the Republican vendetta against Roosevelt did not extend to Roosevelt's son-in-law. Nick spent the day at his office. Alice, in a gloom as thick and gray as the Ohio air, walked alone for miles in the country.

Eugene Debs, who turned fifty-seven on election day, was at home in Terre Haute, Indiana, but did not vote. In the press of the campaign, he had neglected to update his registration. Senator La Follette, angry with Roosevelt and disappointed in Taft, had openly campaigned on behalf of progressive Republican candidates in Wisconsin and privately hoped that Wilson would win.

After lunch at Sagamore, Theodore roamed the woods and fields with Edith for two hours, his longest outing since the assassination attempt. At four, he met with George Perkins, who stayed for an hour and left with no word for the reporters hanging about. Cousin Emlen Roosevelt and his wife, Christine, came for dinner and spent the evening. Telegraph machines rattled away at Wilson's cottage and in Charles Taft's house, where the president was staying, but Sagamore was silent. Faithful to his vow to spend and be spent whether the people wanted him or not, Roosevelt chose not to face his political death as it came, state by state. The election returns would be relayed to Sagamore by telephone from Progressive Party headquarters. Perkins would control the flow of information, and the calls would be taken by one of the servants.

※ *Barrens*

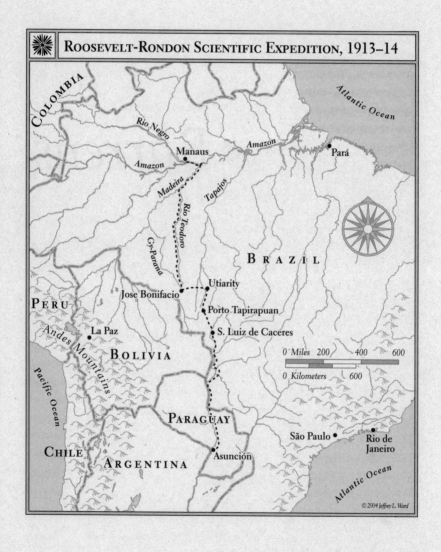

ROOSEVELT-RONDON SCIENTIFIC EXPEDITION, 1913–14

COLOMBIA

Atlantic Ocean

Rio Negro

Amazon

Manaus

Amazon

Pará

Madeira

Tapajos

Rio Teodoro

Gy-Parana

BRAZIL

Utiarity

Jose Bonifacio

Porto Tapirapuan

PERU

La Paz

S. Luiz de Caceres

Andes Mountains

BOLIVIA

Pacific Ocean

0 Miles 200 400 600

0 Kilometers 600

PARAGUAY

São Paulo

Rio de Janeiro

CHILE

ARGENTINA

Asunción

Atlantic Ocean

© 2004 Jeffrey L. Ward

TWELVE

Reckonings

B Y seven o'clock, Roosevelt knew he had lost, but it was ten-thirty before Wilson felt certain of victory. Taft conceded at eleven. Roosevelt wired his congratulations to Wilson just before midnight, then beckoned the waiting newsmen into his study, where he gave the performance he expected of himself. The American people, by a great plurality, had chosen Woodrow Wilson, he said, and he accepted their decision "with entire good humor and contentment." The reporters peered at the Colonel in vain for a trace of disappointment. Wilson's great plurality came to 6.3 million votes, 42 percent of the 15 million ballots cast. Roosevelt finished a distant second, at 4.1 million (27 percent), followed by Taft at 3.5 million (23 percent). The surprise was Debs, whose 900,000 votes came to 6 percent of the total, double his 1908 share. Wilson fared best in the South, with majorities averaging 68 percent. Elsewhere he had no majorities and ran ahead of his plurality in only a handful of Midwestern and Western states. Roosevelt carried six of the forty-eight states: Washington, California, South Dakota, Minnesota, Michigan, and Pennsylvania. He managed a majority only in South Dakota, barely won California, and narrowly lost Illinois and Vermont. Poor Taft won only Vermont and Utah and suffered the indignity of finishing fourth, behind Debs, in Arizona, California, and Nevada. Taft's victories entitled him to a paltry 8 electoral votes; Roosevelt won 88, crushing Taft but being crushed in turn by Wilson's 435.

Unaided and unhindered by scientific opinion polling, exegetes of the 1912 election could and did construct a host of "if only" scenarios ending with congratulations speeding to Cincinnati or Oyster Bay. Republicans swore that if only the Bull Moose had kept to the forest, his herd would have gone to Taft, leaving him more than one million votes ahead of Wilson. Not so. Seventy-seven percent of the electorate had voted for change.

Taft, stung by the magnitude of his defeat, explained it as the consequence of Republicans rushing to Wilson in order to stop Roosevelt. A solacing notion, but Taft received 4.2 million fewer votes in 1912 than in 1908, and 4.2 million was just about the size of the Colonel's vote.

The disciples of Theodore Roosevelt imagined that if only the Republicans had not robbed him of the nomination, he would have won the Taft vote as well as his own. But the nomination had not been stolen, and while Roosevelt's Republican platform surely would have been more progressive than Taft's, it is unlikely that TR could have persuaded the conservatives who ran the party to sign on for judicial recall, a minimum wage, woman suffrage, or any of the other radical propositions in the Progressive charter.

Some suffragists in the Progressive Party supposed that if women had been able to vote from sea to shining sea, they could have elected TR. Women voters contributed to his victories in California and Washington, but in three of the other four states where women had the franchise, he trailed both Taft and Wilson.

It was thought in some quarters that if Roosevelt had given a more upstanding answer to the Negro question, the black vote might have helped him into the White House. In truth, his surrender to Southern racism cost him the goodwill of blacks but not the election. Two-thirds of the country's 2.5 million African-American voters lived in the South, where whites managed to deprive most of them of their voting rights by imposing obstacles to registration. If the turnout of black voters elsewhere matched the national figure, 59 percent, blacks cast 480,000 ballots outside the South. Had Roosevelt taken the high road on race and won all 480,000, he still could not have beaten Wilson.

Commentators inclined to blame Roosevelt's defeat on Roosevelt saw it as a revolt against his power lust, his flouting of the two-term tradition, and his betrayal of his party and his friend—all of which undoubtedly worked against him. But Roosevelt blamed Goliath: a hostile plutocracy with the ideals of "glorified pawnbrokers" and control of both major parties as well as "ninety-nine percent at the very least of the corporate wealth of the country, and therefore the great majority of the newspapers."

❋

THE ELECTION left Roosevelt politically dead yet unable to rest in peace. As he told one of his English correspondents, "I do not see how the [Progressive Party] can triumph under me, but I have to continue to take a certain interest in it until a new man of sufficient power comes along." After months of insisting that the Progressives had sprung from the wishes of the people, he could not walk away without giving meat to the cynics who said he had founded the party solely to advance himself. The Progressive Party had come to stay, he declared soon after the election. Despite a late start and overwhelming opposition, it had finished first or second in thirty-seven states, an achievement that he declared "unparalleled in the history of free government."

The success, though, was almost entirely Roosevelt's. Progressives won fourteen seats in the House of Representatives but failed to capture a single seat in the Senate and took only one governorship. With Progressives who were ready to disband or form an alliance with like-minded Republicans, Roosevelt was fierce: the Republicans had been smashed because they were unfit company for honest men. Instead of an alliance, he said, he wanted a "smoking out" of those who gave lip service to the ideals enunciated in the Progressive platform but remained in the Republican Party. Now was the time to begin the "long pull" and show the world that the Progressives had stamina as well as fire.

While Progressives across the country set to work putting the party in shape for the congressional elections of 1914, the Colonel's energies went into quelling a mutiny. It was "very weary work," he wrote Kermit, "and it is irritating now because I ought not to be required to do much work." Amos Pinchot still believed that George Perkins had acted in bad faith in editing the Sherman Antitrust Act out of the Progressive platform. Whatever the Sherman law's shortcomings, it was the public's only shield against the trusts, Amos wrote TR. He also believed that Perkins had alienated working-class voters by constantly speaking out in defense of big business and by his connections with U.S. Steel and International Harvester, whose labor practices were perennial targets of well-founded criticism.

Gifford and Amos and their sympathizers saw no need to banish Perkins from party councils but insisted that the Progressives needed a more credible spokesman. As the chief voice of the party, Perkins imposed "an additional burden of proof . . . at a time when the one peculiarly indispensable condition of success is a general belief in its sincerity," Gifford wrote TR.

Roosevelt countered by accusing Amos and Gifford of trying to oust all men of means from the party. Perkins had put up $130,000 of his own money for the Progressives' $600,000 campaign, he had done excellent work, and the party could not survive without his executive and financial abilities, TR said. In his wrath, Roosevelt dredged up the brothers' earlier breaks with Taft and La Follette, calling the estrangements justifiable but implying that the Pinchots might be deficient in the great virtue of loyalty. A party's leaders always hunted scapegoats after a defeat, Roosevelt went on, but unless the Progressives showed a united front, they would be a laughingstock. "I was not in the least cast down at my defeat, but I have to struggle hard not to be cast down at the thought of having to go on with the lead now," he wrote Gifford. "I will do it only so long as is necessary, and neither I nor anyone else can do it if, instead of fighting the common foe, we fight among ourselves."

In a modus vivendi reached in December, Roosevelt agreed to restore the antitrust-law section to the platform, Perkins was allowed to keep his chairman's epaulets, and Gifford and Amos chose not to desert. With no apparent hard feelings, Perkins moved backstage, leaving the job of spokesman to William Allen White. O. K. Davis would edit the *Progressive Bulletin* in the party's Washington office, and Perkins would stop promoting his business ideas in the party's literature.

Perhaps Perkins was hedging his bets. Within a week of the election, he had begun ingratiating himself with the new party in power. "I hope we can get together before long and compare notes on our late efforts to save the country from utter ruin," he wrote Wilson's campaign manager. He also sent a friendly note to William Gibbs McAdoo, Wilson's future son-in-law and treasury secretary.

Following a plan drawn up by Jane Addams at Roosevelt's request, the Progressive Party began operating as both political organization and advocacy group. Perkins oversaw the political arm, raising funds and building the organization precinct by precinct. The advocacy side, known as the Progressive National Service, was to draft model legislation and find sympathetic congressmen and state legislators to sponsor it. The service also ran an ambitious education program aimed at recruiting party members and building public support for Progressive ideals.

By early 1913 the work had been assigned, but the Progressives still did not agree on how progressive the Progressive Party should be. Roosevelt had persuaded himself that less radicalism would have meant more votes in 1912. The Pinchots had reached the opposite conclusion. "It is a fairer distribution of wealth that we must achieve before we can do anybody any real good," Amos wrote TR. "Everybody knows this in his heart, and the sooner we make it as clear as sunlight that the Progressive Party knows and feels this too, the greater will be . . . our support from the people." If the Progressives failed to take up the economic struggle of the masses, the party would be no more than "a temporary resting place—a sort of 'safe and sane' happy-medium island of refuge for those who are unable to decide whether they are going to join the people or the special interests in this fight. We cannot at the same time appear safe and sane to the people and to the interests that are preying on the people."

The reply from Sagamore was a vote for the happy medium: "We have no excuse for existing excepting as the radical party; but I want to keep it as the party of sane and tempered radicalism such as that of Abraham Lincoln." In letters to others TR began referring to Amos and Gifford as the "ultras" and claimed that they were "doing their best to break up the party by attacking the moderate men." At least once he privately confessed a willingness to rejoin the Republicans—if they purged themselves of bosses and agreed to back progressive candidates for public office. And he advocated the formation of political clubs for the progressive-minded of all parties. Ostensibly the clubs would exist to recruit members for the Progressive Party, but he also saw them as bridges to other parties should bridges become necessary. Theodore Roosevelt, said Amos Pinchot, was now "a mere passenger bent on leaving the ship at the first port."

SEEING THAT THEODORE sorely needed a respite from political combat, Edith proposed a long holiday in a distant land, perhaps Brazil, where he could see Kermit. Brazil's ambassador to the United States had extended invitations for a hunting expedition and a series of lectures to the Historical and Geographical Society of Rio de Janeiro. TR declined. Such a tour "would look as though I were advertising myself," he wrote Kermit.

Melancholy in the Roosevelt code of conduct ranked somewhere between bad form and outright vice, so he refrained, at least on paper, from dwelling on the hurts of defeat. To friends who congratulated him on the size of his vote, he sent thanks along with reminders that he had not expected to win. But on the day after the election Edith had noted that he was "as brave as can be," a phrase suggesting that he had something to be brave about—his powerlessness, perhaps, or the ache of being spurned by the people, whom he genuinely loved. In January, Edith wrote Kermit that TR was spending more hours on horseback than she had ever known him to do and was still "rather gloomy . . . poor lamb!"

At the first meeting of the Harvard board of overseers after the election, Roosevelt was stunned to find himself an outcast. All the men but one "bunched at one end of the room away from me," he confided to his friend and physician, Alexander Lambert. The snub, he said, had left him feeling "unspeakably lonely." And then, as if embarrassed by the disclosure, he gave his account a punch line: he and his ally had been "a pair of Airedale pups at a convention of tomcats!"

Sagamore was less contentious than the Progressive Party but hardly less complicated. Ethel had been deeply upset by TR's defeat. "I cannot *bear* to have F[ather] beaten," she had written in her diary on election night. "It makes me *so choky.* . . . When I think of F. being almost assassinated . . . and the people still being such cold fishes." Edith was unwell. Theodore blamed her riding accident, now fifteen months past, but her letters mention thyroid trouble and a severe case of eczema. She rose at noon, stayed up till four, rested till dinner, then retired for the night. The role of nurse, chatelaine, and hostess fell to Ethel, who was sweet and sympathetic but longing to leave Sagamore and play her part in the world, perhaps as a hospital social worker.

Alice often came to visit, lugging a valise crammed with unhappiness. Nick had lost his congressional race by 101 votes. He and the rest of the Longworths blamed Alice, who, after months of trying to help Nick by keeping her distance from the Progressives, had sat onstage at a Hiram Johnson rally in Cincinnati. It was probably a courtesy on her part, a way of thanking Johnson for keeping an engagement that her father had had to abandon after he was shot. Nick's defeat meant exile from Washington, in the "Cinci-nasty" she detested, where they would have to stay until 1914, when Nick could make another run for Congress. They would live with Nick's mother, whose love of Tafts had engendered a loathing of Roosevelts, including Alice.

It is difficult to tell how the trauma of the assassination attempt figured in the gloom at Sagamore. Theodore referred to it more often than anyone else in the family, but his mentions were infrequent and mainly showed a powerful desire to reduce the event to a trifle. His would-be assassin, John Schrank, went to court shortly after the election. The judge had postponed the proceedings to avoid entangling them in politics and to give a court-appointed panel of five alienists time to examine Schrank and reach a conclusion about his mental fitness to stand trial.

As the doctors soon discovered, Schrank inhabited a world off its axis but within it was well spoken, compliant, and oddly compelling. He had emigrated from Germany to New York in 1885 as a boy of nine, with his father. By 1912 he had lost his father, an aunt and uncle who were his only other American relatives, and a sweetheart, who died in a shipwreck. Unemployed and scraping by on meager rents from a small tenement house inherited from the aunt, he roomed at a cheap hotel called the White House, near the Bowery.

President McKinley, who died in the early hours of September 14, 1901, had first appeared to Schrank in a dream between one and two in the morning on September 15. McKinley sat upright in his coffin, pointed to a hooded figure that Schrank took to be Roosevelt, and said, "Avenge my death." On August 7, 1912, the night when the Progressives nominated Roosevelt, Schrank had the dream again and was beset by agitation over Roosevelt's ambition for a third term. In Schrank's mind, Roosevelt would be another Napoleon, and the coming of an emperor would plunge the United States into another bloody civil war. Five weeks later, on the anniversary of his first dream of the dead McKinley, Schrank awoke between one and two o'clock in the morning, got up, and was sitting at a table revising a poem when he felt a touch on his shoulder. He turned, and there was McKinley. Schrank interpreted the September 15 coincidence as a divine command to assassinate Roosevelt.

Schrank guessed that the alienists would take a skeptical view of his visitations from beyond, but hadn't Joan of Arc had a vision of the Virgin Mary? he asked. And hadn't Moses seen God in a burning bush? "Why then in cases of dire national need should not God appear to one of us in a vision?"

Once commanded, Schrank purchased a $14 Colt .38 and 55 cents' worth of bullets, consulted a newspaper for the Bull Moose campaign itinerary, and set off to stalk Roosevelt through the South. He went first to New Orleans, then followed TR to Atlanta, Charleston, and up the line to Tennessee, registering in hotels along the way as "Walter Roos." In Chattanooga, Schrank at last got within range of his target, but he flinched. The idea of killing Roosevelt was still "a new thing," he told the alienists. "I didn't exactly have courage enough to do it, and he started off so fast in his automobile." A few weeks later Schrank trailed Roosevelt through Indiana and was waiting for him when he reached Chicago. Once more Schrank held back, this time because he did not want to spoil the city's "decent respectable reception," he said.

In Milwaukee, Schrank passed the hours before the crime at a bar, drinking beer and smoking Jack Pot cigars. He did not say much but left a memorable impression by offering the band a round of drinks if it would play "The Star-Spangled Banner." Come evening, according to the alienists' report, "he acted just like a boy afraid to coast down a big hill, who, finally impelled by the taunts of his comrades, closes his eyes and starts."

Schrank expressed no remorse. The shot fired in Milwaukee "created an echo in all parts of the world" and would put an end to third-term ambitions, he boasted. He regretted only that he had not died for his country and that he had blackened Milwaukee's reputation. He wanted the bullet and the revolver put on display in the New York state capitol as a warning against breaking the two-term tradition.

The alienists concluded that Schrank was suffering from "insane delusions, grandiose in character, and of the systematized variety" and was incompetent to stand trial because he could not confer intelligently with his counsel. The judge committed him to a mental hospital, there to remain until cured.

In Roosevelt's opinion Schrank had the mind of a criminal, not a madman. "I very gravely question if he has a more unsound brain than Senator La Follette or Eugene Debs," TR wrote his friend St. Loe Strachey, editor of *The Spectator* in London. As evidence, Roosevelt offered the fact that Schrank had shot him in Wisconsin, a state with no death penalty. The district attorney had quizzed Schrank at length on that point, and throughout Schrank insisted that he had had no reason to pay attention to state laws on capital punishment; he had expected to die in the line of duty.

The poem Schrank wrote before embarking on his errand is a stern lecture to a cowering failure. "Be a man," it begins, and "Be a man" ends each stanza. Schrank was failed, powerless, and totally without the threads of human connection that might have mended the awful tear in his mind. To be able to end the strenuous life of Theodore Roosevelt—what a man that man would be.

Roosevelt sought escape from all of it—mortality, defeat, his tangles political and domestic—by working at his writing with an intensity that left little time for brooding. He was collaborating with Edmund Heller, the safari's zoologist, on a book about African game, and had committed himself to numerous magazine articles and an address entitled "History As Literature." Written in his capacity as president of the American Historical Association, the speech was safely apolitical and allowed him to dilate on a favorite theme: an author had an obligation to bring his subjects to life. In *African Game Trails* he had said the same of those who write about nature, and as he reminded his fellow historians, the fundamental principle of evolution was understood long before Darwin and Huxley, but they were the first to write well about it. The greatest historians were those who possessed the "imaginative power" to transcend the "dead fragments" and perceive the whole, he wrote. To hold that imagination and accuracy were incompatible was "a shallow criticism. . . . Only a distorted imagination tends to inaccuracy."

For *The Outlook* he began a long series with an uncharacteristically tentative title, "Chapters of a Possible Autobiography." He wanted to resume contributing to the magazine, and the autobiography was "the only thing that it seemed possible to do," he wrote Edith's sister. The staid types who read *The Outlook* had been canceling subscriptions because of the magazine's support of the Bull Moose. But the autobiography of Theodore Roosevelt would have mass appeal, and publishing it piece by piece over several months would be potent medicine for poor circulation.

A pastiche of memoir, apologia, position paper, and sermon, TR's account of his life is an indispensable introduction to the man, his times, and the worldview of the elite who governed with him. The book is partial in both senses of the word: opinionated and incomplete. Victorian gentlemen did not parade their sorrows, so there is no surprise in his decision to exclude his first wife, the grotesque Valentine's Day when she and his mother died, and his brother's alcoholism and early demise. But autobiography asks an author to muse on the personal significance of the events he chooses to recount, and Roosevelt's lifelong aversion to self-reflection put him at a disadvantage in the genre. Without the reflective dimension, readers are deprived of autobiography's chief reward, the joy of coming to know the workings of another heart.

The Theodore Roosevelt of the autobiography is a man firmly in control. Even at his weakest, as a boy struggling with asthma and being humiliated by bullies, he takes charge, building his body with boxing lessons. In the myth he lived, the hero empowered himself. He had no special gifts but transcended the ordinary by his willingness to face the dragon, and he triumphed by courage and sheer force of will. From his personal story he extrapolated the story of his country. With hard bodies, iron resolve, and high purpose, Americans had ended the tyranny of kings, won the West, freed the slaves, protected the hemisphere against imperial aggression, and taken their place among the world's great powers. Roosevelt's brand of heroism was attainable, which made it both appealing and oppressive, for he insisted on judging the world by the standard he had set for himself. The big brother whispering "You can do it" was the twin of the bully quick to cry "Coward!"

As a political memoirist Roosevelt engaged in the customary self-justification and exercised the customary privilege of omission. His opponents—on Panama, say—were either misinformed or suffered from "a sentimentality which represents both mental weakness and a moral twist." Those who favored universal arbitration and disarmament were well intentioned but fatuous, laying "all the emphasis on peace and none at all on righteousness. They are not all of them physically timid men; but they are usually men of soft life." There is no word of his first electoral defeat, in the 1886 contest for mayor of New York, no account of the dishonorable discharge of the black troops in Brownsville. He freely criticized Taft but withheld the story of how Taft came to succeed him in the White House. Of his political adventuring after the White House there is only one sentence: "Naturally, there are chapters of my autobiography which cannot now be written." The book ends with the return of the Great White Fleet, the grand finale of his presidency.

Alice Longworth spent the weeks before Woodrow Wilson's inauguration wandering the streets of Washington, almost frantic, she realized, "to have a last fling before the Midwest engulfs me." Nick and his congressional colleagues were working till five in the morning to put through the last of the session's bills and rush them to the White House for Taft's signature. On his last day in office, against his own best judgment, Taft signed a measure creating a separate Department of Labor. He considered it an expensive, pointless departure from the existing Department of Commerce and Labor, but the incoming president favored the change, and it struck Taft as mean-spirited not to let him have it.

Passive and naive, petulant, resentful of opposition, Taft had failed as a politician, but his presidency was hardly a calamity. For better and worse

Taft had enforced the antitrust law with considerably more vigor than the Trust Buster. He cut the government's spending, turned a budget deficit into a surplus, and collaborated with Congress to secure a series of reforms worthy of the Square Dealer's admiration: safety regulations protecting miners and railroad workers, a new federal agency to see to the well-being of children, an eight-hour day for federal employees, and an act requiring employers to compensate workers injured on jobs done under government contract. He also braved the opprobrium of the reactionaries to support a constitutional amendment for an income tax on the rich. Posterity would ignore Theodore Roosevelt's contempt for William Howard Taft and usher him to a middle rung on the ladder of presidential greatness.

ESCORTING WOODROW WILSON up Pennsylvania Avenue on Inauguration Day, March 4, 1913, Taft wore his most jovial face. Liberated from the burdens of the presidency, he was entering one of the happiest phases of his life. The physician who had predicted an early death was wrong. Taft had survived the campaign, would teach at Yale Law School for eight years, and would crown his career as chief justice of the United States, the post he had always wanted. In the first year after his presidency, he shed ninety of his 330 pounds, a change that improved his general health and alleviated his chronic sleepiness. His weight stayed in the range of 250 pounds for the rest of his life, which lasted a dozen years longer than Theodore Roosevelt's.

Roosevelt planned his March 4 with obvious care. If he stayed at Sagamore it would be said that he was sulking, and if seen with his political intimates he would be charged with plotting his 1916 presidential campaign. He spent the day out and about in Manhattan, visiting an exposition dramatizing the city's need for lower rents and touring the infamous International Exhibition of Modern Art at the Sixty-ninth Regiment Armory. The show had opened two weeks earlier, and thousands came daily to snort at Marcel Duchamp's *Nude Descending a Staircase*, Henri Matisse's *Luxury*, and a thousand other oddities. Many of the visitors had the uneasy feeling that they were the butt of an incomprehensible joke.

In a year when Roosevelt was turning nearly everything he did into a magazine article, the Armory show became grist for a review. He caught a whiff of P. T. Barnum in the new art, he said, and he was certain that Duchamp's nude had less artistic merit than the Navajo rug on his bathroom floor. But he voiced none of the consternation that filled the newspapers. For him, the new art called to mind the new politics. "Probably in any reform movement, any progressive moment, in any field of life, the penalty for avoiding the commonplace is a liability to extravagance," he wrote, and the "one note entirely absent from the exhibition . . . was the note of the commonplace." To advance itself, civilization had to "shake off the dead hand," and a "lunatic fringe" was an inevitable part of the process. By his reckoning, the exhibition was noteworthy for showing Americans the new forces at work in European art, "forces which cannot be ignored."

Ethel went to the Armory whenever she could steal a day from the dreariness of Sagamore, where Edith still languished. Ethel had hoped to travel to Brazil with a friend, but Edith's physician advised against it, saying that although the patient was in no immediate danger, she had to be kept free of worry. Not ready to give up the trip and thinking that Edith would cheer up in town, where it would be easier for her friends to call on her, Ethel proposed that her parents stay in a hotel. Theodore vetoed the idea. He was "dear and sweet about it," Ethel said, "but it makes him miserable." A Roosevelt to the marrow, Ethel resolved to do her duty and vowed "to do it well, not to mope around."

There would be no Brazil, but deliverance was at hand. Ethel was getting married, she announced in February. She had been engaged for a year to Richard Derby, a Harvard and Porcellian man and a graduate of the Columbia College of Physicians and Surgeons. He had been introduced to Ethel by Kermit, who had taken Quentin to see him about a foot injury and then struck up a friendship. Older than Ethel by a decade, Dick was a serious fellow, the sort who went fishing in a necktie, but not lacking in warmth. "We are having a most wonderful time," Ethel wrote her father in April 1913, three weeks into her honeymoon. "Do you remember what you said to me once about 'the first fine careless rapture'? I have thought of that so often."

The wedding had been close to perfect. Henry Cabot Lodge, former Secretary of the Navy George Meyer, and a few other orthodox Republicans on the guest list had accepted their invitations, placing their old affection for Theodore above the awkwardness of mingling with Pinchots and Perkinses. The conspicuous absentee was Nick Longworth. A few days after the election he had written Meyer that he would grin and bear his fate, but he showed his pique at his father-in-law by refusing to attend the wedding. He had an excuse—relief work in Cincinnati following a flood that had killed hundreds and left thousands homeless—but Alice was deeply hurt.

Cincinnati was misery for Alice. Even her Longworth nieces and nephews had been taught to despise her. One of the boys, down with the chickenpox, had been told by his mother to be sure to kiss Aunt Alice. The boy allegedly refused on the ground that she would infect him with something worse from her. Nick was romancing a Miss Ault, a blow Alice returned by talking freely about the transgression. She fled to Sagamore whenever she could. Sending Nellie the gossip from Cincinnati, Will Taft said that Alice was "going away because when she is away she does not mind how much Nick gets up in a hammock with some other girl, but she does not like to see it right before her."

A FTER ETHEL AND DICK'S WEDDING TR raced through the last of his autobiography—with "heated unintelligence," he wrote Ethel. He finished just in time to hand himself over to the next piece of drudgery, a libel suit against a small newspaper that had called him a drunk. After months of futile effort to stop such rumors, Roosevelt had decided that his best hope of laying them to rest was a lawsuit with sworn testimony from the men who knew him best.

The defendant was George A. Newett, editor of the weekly *Iron Ore,* which was read across Michigan's upper peninsula. In an editorial published a month before the election, he had written that "Roosevelt lies and curses in a most disgusting way; he gets drunk, too, and that not infrequently, and all his intimates know about it." Roosevelt's lawyers filed suit two weeks later. Newett was unrepentant. "*Iron Ore* has long held a pretty good reputation for sticking to the facts," he wrote; the suit was merely "another desperate effort to bolster up a fast-declining cause."

Roosevelt's case seemed unassailable when the suit was filed, but a private investigator working for Newett had secured depositions from forty men claiming to have seen Roosevelt in a state of intoxication. Resigned to the worst, TR left for Marquette, Michigan, on May 24. "I did not believe I had any new depth of human nature to plumb, but I was really unprepared for perjury on a gigantic scale, perjury by scores of alleged witnesses," he wrote a friend. "I am really puzzled by the extreme malignancy of the hatred which purchases such testimony or offers it without purchase."

On the surface *Roosevelt v. Newett* was no different from any other libel case: the plaintiff had brought suit in hopes of clearing his name. But the trial was also the first to expose a former president's personal habits to public view, and Roosevelt was the first former president to hold a newspaper to account for the sort of calumny that might affect his place in history. A battery of telegraph machines had been installed in the courthouse to hurry the news of the day to the rest of the country. For six hours, as the lawyers interviewed forty-five candidates for the jury, the newspapermen watched the plaintiff watching the men who would decide his fate. He looked anxious and listened with almost unbroken concentration. At 10:46 P.M., the lawyers were agreed on a jury of four farmers, two miners, two teamsters, a clerk, a blacksmith, a locomotive fireman, and a lumberjack.

The judge, Richard C. Flannigan, presided over a jewel box of a courtroom, a paneled and gilded chamber crowned with a dome of stained glass. He gazed at the dome as he listened, twiddling his tie and gently swiveling his chair until he heard a reason to intervene. Taking no chances in this closely watched trial, Flannigan sequestered the jury.

Roosevelt's chief counsel, James H. Pound, led with his ace, calling TR to the witness stand and asking questions that allowed him to tell his life story. After the Colonel mentioned that the Rough Riders had had the highest rate of casualties in the Spanish-American War, Pound asked if he had been wounded. Newett's attorneys vigorously objected, but the Colonel had already pulled up his cuff and displayed the scar on his wrist. Only a few feet separated the witness from the jury, so an instant sufficed to make the intended impression.

Pound also drew out Roosevelt's drinking history, which was singularly dull. No whiskey, red wine, or beer, Roosevelt said. To be sociable, he took a glass of champagne at public dinners. He sometimes drank white wine, on occasion indulged in a mint julep, and when in need of a soporific, drank a big glass of milk doctored with a teaspoon of brandy.

Seventeen of Roosevelt's associates had sworn to his sobriety in depositions, nineteen more went to Marquette to testify in person. There were three former cabinet secretaries in the courtroom, along with several distinguished journalists, two of his physicians, former Secret Service agents, and aides who had been at his side day and night. The word in the courthouse was that you couldn't throw a brick without hitting somebody important.

When Pound asked Jacob Riis, an old friend and the author of *How the Other Half Lives*, if he had ever seen Roosevelt under the influence of liquor, Riis seemed horrified. "Oh, Lord, no," he said.

Does he curse?

"I have heard him use the expression 'Godfrey' when he gets very much excited," Riis said.

Presley Rixey, a former surgeon general of the navy who had been Roosevelt's White House physician, pronounced him a most temperate man.

Gifford Pinchot testified that whenever he was in the company of an accomplished, productive man, he always paid close attention to "how he lived, how he ate, and how he drank, and whether he slept much, and so on; and I never in my life met any man who could do as much work as Colonel Roosevelt."

Pound rested his case with a reading of the deposition given by Admiral George E. Dewey, the naval hero of the Spanish-American War. Dewey had never seen Roosevelt take a drink, he said, but he had noticed that "all people at dinners, whether they drink anything or not, are more or less excited. I have seen teetotalers very excited, and I have seen Mr. Roosevelt at dinners where he would be full of spirits, full of life and animation. All who knew him knew his peculiarities in that respect."

Newett's attorneys put their client on the stand and set about establishing his high character. He had published *Iron Ore* for thirty years. He was also a teetotaler with "very strong views on the subject," he said, and a steadfast Republican who had written admiringly of Roosevelt until the bolt. Roosevelt had further offended him by attacking a local congressional candidate who was one of Newett's friends. The attack plus the drinking rumors, which Newett had read elsewhere and heard in various parts of the country, drove him to write the editorial, he said. He had intended it as a blow to Roosevelt's candidacy, not to his reputation.

Faced with Roosevelt's suit, Newett had solicited depositions from reputable men, all of whom said that they had seen Roosevelt in a state of intoxication. None of them, alas, would "swear that they have actually seen Mr. Roosevelt drink to excess," Newett told the court. He now realized that his informants had had "insufficient means and opportunity of correctly observing him." Hoping for leniency, Newett said he had acted without malice and had never knowingly used his paper to do anyone an injustice.

Allowed to make a statement, Roosevelt explained that he had not filed the suit for money. "I wished, once and for all during my lifetime, thoroughly and comprehensively to deal with these slanders, so that never again will it be possible for any man, in good faith, to repeat them," he said. "I have achieved my purpose, and I am content." He waived his claim to punitive damages, and Judge Flannigan awarded nominal damages, which in Michigan amounted to 6 cents.

It had cost Roosevelt $40,000 to clear his name. Edith grumbled that the family pocketbook would flap emptily in every breeze, but the *New York Tribune*, no admirer of the Bull Moose, praised him for fighting "the battle of all self-respecting men for immunity from the attacks of scandal-mongers." Cousin Emlen Roosevelt had the trial transcript printed in book form and deposited in a number of libraries around the country. Bound in black leather, with *Roosevelt vs. Newett* stamped in gold on the cover, the volume had the look and heft of a Bible and put a fine amen to a disagreeable chapter of Roosevelt's life.

THROUGHOUT HIS POLITICAL CAREER Roosevelt had been a genius at positioning himself. He chose a stance, declared it the boldest and wisest, and damned his opponents as extremists or mollycoddles. The brilliance of the tactic lay in its near-infinite malleability. It made him seem bold and novel even when he stood in the middle of a very old road, and it enabled him to present himself as the most prudent of statesmen when he roared clean off the road, as he did in Panama and when he sent the Great White Fleet on its round-the-world voyage without a congressional appropriation to pay for it. But after 1912 Roosevelt often found himself being positioned by others, forced onto a high wire above a crowd impossible to please. If he made too many speeches he would be accused of self-promotion. If he kept to himself it would be said that he was pouting or abandoning the Progressive Party. He walked the wire without zest but with more commitment than Amos Pinchot could see. In 1913 he made seventeen speeches, mostly at Progressive gatherings and mostly in the Northeast—limits making it hard for detractors to argue that he was publicizing himself to the country.

The political companions TR seemed to enjoy most after his defeat were the women of the Progressive Party, and even as he lectured his friend Amos on the need to temper the party's radicalism, he used his influence to help women advance social justice on many fronts. Working with a settlement house in New York he supported women garment workers in a successful strike for decent pay and better working conditions. He spoke on behalf of woman suffrage, publicized the need for a pure milk law, and in a *Collier's Weekly* piece entitled "Sarah Knisely's Arm," he urged just compensation

1

The Roosevelts on Christmas Day
1908, near the end of their happy life in
the White House. Remembering this
photograph years later, Alice Roosevelt
Longworth said, "I must say we look as
if we are being expelled from the
Garden of Eden." From left: Ethel,
Kermit, Quentin, Edith, Ted,
Theodore, Archie, Alice, and her
husband, Congressman Nicholas
Longworth of Ohio.

President Theodore Roosevelt and his
chosen successor, William Howard
Taft, on a snowy Inauguration Day,
March 4, 1909. "Even the elements
do protest," the new president said
of the changing of the guard.

On safari in British
East Africa. From left:
R. J. Cuninghame;
Kermit Roosevelt; TR;
Smithsonian naturalists
Edmund Heller and J.
Alden Loring.

3

4

TR with one of the eleven elephants he and Kermit
shot in Africa. By the safari's end, their bag totaled
more than five hundred animals. "I can be condemned only if the existence of the National
Museum, the American Museum of Natural History,
and all similar zoological collections are to be condemned," TR said.

Warrington Dawson, first Paris correspondent of the
United Press. He accompanied TR's safari for several
weeks and soon befriended the rest of the family.

5

TR with his secretary and Gifford Pinchot (right). Architect of President Roosevelt's farsighted conservation program, Pinchot was fired in February 1910 by President Taft. Two months later Pinchot journeyed to Porto Maurizio, Italy, to brief TR on the conservative drift of the Taft Administration.

6

Hundreds of thousands turned out in New York City on June 18, 1910, to welcome Roosevelt home from Africa.

7

8

In August 1910, atop a kitchen table in Osawatomie, Kansas, TR outlined his "New Nationalism," a program calling for a strong federal government. Many saw his speaking tour as a move in the direction of challenging Taft for the Republican presidential nomination in 1912.

9

In the autumn of 1910, while President Taft (left) was in Panama checking on the progress of the canal, TR, in Washington to deliver a lecture, called at the White House to leave his card. Taken on a tour of the offices, Roosevelt sat for a moment at the president's desk and said how natural it felt to be there.

The feud between Roosevelt and Taft would leave Captain Archie Butt, the military aide to both presidents, feeling torn between his love of Roosevelt and his duty to Taft. Watching Roosevelt at his homecoming parade, Butt found him "bigger, broader, capable of greater good or greater evil, I don't know which."

10

Senator Henry Cabot Lodge of Massachusetts, Roosevelt's closest friend. Hoping to ease tensions between the president and ex-president in the summer of 1910, Lodge invited Roosevelt to spend a night at Nahant, then took him to call on President Taft, who summered nearby, in Beverly.

11

Senator Robert M. La Follette of Wisconsin was Roosevelt's chief rival for the leadership of the progressive wing of the Republican Party.

12

13

For Elihu Root and many other Republican friends of TR, 1912 was a misery. Root incurred Roosevelt's wrath by securing Taft's nomination, and Taft felt betrayed when Root could not bring himself to campaign against Roosevelt.

14

George W. Perkins, the Progressive Party's chairman, chief fund-raiser, and largest donor. As a director of two of the country's largest corporations and a former partner of J. P. Morgan, Perkins was never entirely trusted by the more zealous Progressives, who wanted thoroughgoing reform of the federal laws regulating big business.

Jane Addams, founder of Hull House and champion of women's suffrage, racial equality, and many other causes, was chosen to second Roosevelt's nomination at the Progressives' first national convention. A dedicated pacifist, Addams would find herself at odds with TR during World War I.

Roosevelt's decision to run for president in 1912 discommoded family as well as friends. Congressman Nick Longworth, a Republican and the husband of TR's daughter Alice, had the misfortune to represent President Taft's district in Ohio. When Nick lost his bid for reelection, he and Alice were exiled to the town she called "Cincin-nasty."

16

Unable to win the Republican nomination in 1912, TR formed the National Progressive Party and ran for president with Hiram Johnson, governor of California. Johnson, foreseeing defeat, had hoped that TR would choose someone else.

Roosevelt and Johnson

"For there is neither East nor West,
Border nor Breed nor Birth,
When two strong men stand face to face
Though they come from the ends of the earth."
—Kipling

17

Wherever TR campaigned in 1912, huge crowds came out to see him.

18

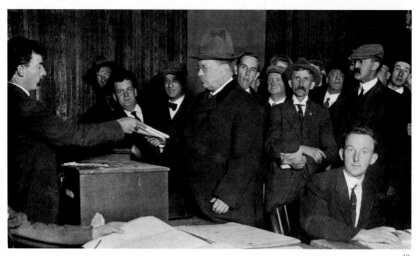

Within hours of casting his vote in Oyster Bay on November 5, 1912, Roosevelt would learn that only 27 percent of the voters wanted him back in the White House. Even fewer (23 percent) wanted Taft. [19]

The new president, Woodrow Wilson, and William Howard Taft on Inauguration Day, March 4, 1913.

TR's two-month trip down Brazil's River of Doubt was taxing in the extreme. Insects forced him to don net and gloves to keep up his writing. On several occasions trails had to be cut and log rollers laid to portage the expedition's 2,500-pound dugout canoes past steep waterfalls.

22

21

Abscesses and a raging fever caused by insect bites nearly cost TR his life in Brazil. He arrived home on May 19, 1914, fifty-five pounds lighter and too weak to walk without a cane.

23

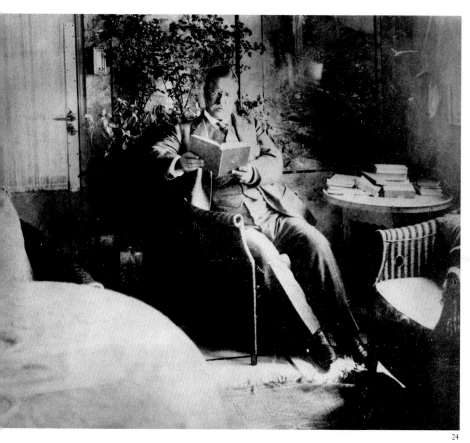

24

In June 1914, on the voyage home from Kermit's wedding to Belle Willard, in Spain, TR was confined to his cabin by a painfully sore throat and flare-ups of his Brazilian fever. The most widely read of American presidents, he always traveled with a stack of books, and he threw himself into reading with the vigor he gave to the rest of life.

25

26

In 1915, TR spent four weeks in a Syracuse courtroom as the defendant in a libel suit. He had charged that New York's state government was "rotten throughout" because of the collusion of Boss Charles F. Murphy of Tammany Hall and his Republican counterpart, Boss William Barnes of Albany. Barnes (above) sued, seeking damages of $50,000. Roosevelt won the suit—and a political resurrection.

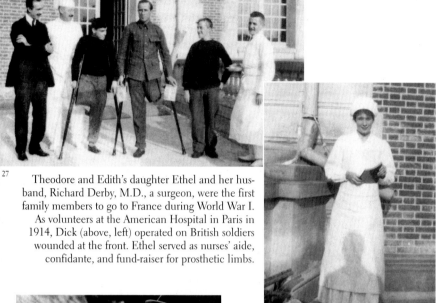

27   Theodore and Edith's daughter Ethel and her husband, Richard Derby, M.D., a surgeon, were the first family members to go to France during World War I. As volunteers at the American Hospital in Paris in 1914, Dick (above, left) operated on British soldiers wounded at the front. Ethel served as nurses' aide, confidante, and fund-raiser for prosthetic limbs.

28

Colonel Roosevelt and Major General Leonard Wood in August 1915 at the officers' training camp in Plattsburg, New York. During his visit, TR infuriated President Wilson and the War Department by giving a speech charging that the United States was not prepared to defend itself.

29

TR's long friendship with Sir Cecil Spring Rice would become a casualty of the war. British ambassador to the United States from 1913 through 1917, Spring Rice was often at loggerheads with the White House as President Wilson struggled to maintain American neutrality. TR and Spring Rice rarely saw each other for fear that TR's outspoken criticism of Wilson would exacerbate the administration's hostility to the ambassador.

30

The Republicans and the Progressives held simultaneous national conventions in 1916. The Progressives (above) hoped that their swift nomination of Theodore Roosevelt would frighten the Republicans into nominating him, too, in order to avoid a repeat of the disastrous three-way race of 1912. But TR, having concluded that the Republicans would not have him, declined the Progressive nomination, a decision that ensured the party's demise.

During the 1912 campaign, TR spent a night in Kansas at the home of William Allen White, editor of the *Emporia Gazette* and an ardent champion of the Progressive Party. When TR refused the Progressives' call to run for president in 1916, White and hundreds of others stormed out of the convention. Heartbroken, White telephoned his wife and, he wrote, "spent nine dollars and eighty-five cents bawling like a calf into the receiver."

33

The Democrats successfully promoted their 1916 candidate, President Woodrow Wilson, with the slogan "He kept us out of war."

34

"The bearded iceberg," TR called Charles Evans Hughes, the 1916 Republican presidential nominee. Hughes disliked the hand-shaking, back-slapping side of politics.

Eleanor (Mrs. Theodore Roosevelt Jr.) in the gray whipcord uniform she designed for the YMCA's women volunteers in France during World War I.

35

Grace (Mrs. Archibald Roosevelt) with TR and Archie Jr. in 1918.

36

Belle Willard Roosevelt, Kermit's wife, painted by Paul Chabas, 1914.

37

Flora Payne Whitney, Quentin Roosevelt's fiancée.

38

Theodore Roosevelt's sons—and the kaiser's. American newspapers and magazines often berated TR for his criticism of Woodrow Wilson but regularly praised the Roosevelt family's military service.

Lieutenant Quentin Roosevelt of the First Pursuit Group in his Nieuport 27.

Theodore and Edith in 1918 with daughter-in-law Grace (left), daughter Ethel (right), and grandchildren (from left: Archie Jr., Richard Derby Jr., Edith Derby).

In July 1918, a few days after Quentin was killed in combat, the Roosevelt family members then in Paris posed for this portrait. In front, with his arm in a sling: Archie. From left: Dick Derby, Eleanor, and Kermit.

The rowboat was TR's favorite form of locomotion, allowing him to be captain, engine, and crew.

for victims of industrial accidents. After reading a study of prison conditions, he added penal reform to his caseload.

Bull Moose leaders labored mightily to raise a flourishing party. "So much so-called Progressive seed has been sown on such a large area of soil that a pretty fair crop is bound to be the result ere long," Perkins wrote a friend. But bringing the seeds to harvest was expensive work. Although Perkins quickly secured pledges of $1 million for the first year's operations, money was a constant source of tension. The party's archives are full of pleas for funds to placate bill collectors and meet payrolls, and the Progressive National Service quickly sprouted more tentacles than it could manage. In early July the Progressives held a grand public fete in Newport, Rhode Island, to raise funds and celebrate their first birthday, but not even an appearance by the Bull Moose himself brought attendance up to expectations. Roosevelt judged the event "a flat failure."

A few days after Newport, TR left for five weeks of camping and hunting in the Southwest with Quentin and Archie and Nicholas Roosevelt, a favorite cousin. It was a working holiday, full of proofreading, speechwriting, and travel pieces to be composed as he went. The hunting he left to the boys, who were "as happy as they are dirty—which is saying much," he reported from the Grand Canyon.

Quentin, now fifteen, had had an unhappy stretch at Groton after TR announced his willingness to run for president. His schoolmates' fathers tended to disapprove of Roosevelt's candidacy, sons parroted fathers, and Quentin had felt his isolation keenly. Archie had had a happier time at the Evans School and at Andover, where he was spending his senior year. Soon to turn nineteen, he was six feet tall, and once liberated from the tyranny of Groton football had discovered that he was a good horseman, a fair runner, and an able hand in a canoe. With his Andover schoolmates he had formed a Progressive club to go door to door and explain the party's ideals. To his mother's relief he had passed Harvard's entrance examinations and would enroll in the fall. Quentin was the brightest of the children, Theodore wrote their Aunt Emily in Italy, but Archie was blessed with "sturdy common sense and resolution."

At the Armory show Roosevelt had seen the connection between modern painting and the indigenous arts of Africa and the Americas, and in the Southwest he realized that the arts of the Navajo and the Hopi could add a distinctly un-European strain to American culture if the white man could be brought to a proper appreciation of them.

In Walpi, Arizona, TR consulted two ethnomusicologists before watching a Hopi snake dance and went back the next day to ask their advice on his long account of the ceremony. He had written it overnight. One of the scholars would remember the "electric snap" of his mind as they offered suggestions. "I agree, I have it!" he would say before they finished their sentences. He made his revisions on the spot, explaining that if he did not do the work there and then, he never would. His life was "too full," he said, "and I have to finish each episode of it, as far as possible, as I go."

On his way east, Roosevelt stopped in Chicago for an hour and twenty minutes, into which he fit a meeting, a meal, a visit to a bookshop, and a speech to members of the local Progressive club. He had little to say, he told them, but he wanted them to pass the word that all Republicans who favored amalgamation with the Progressive Party could achieve it simply by adopting the Progressive platform.

Back at Sagamore, TR walled himself in his study to clear his desk for another holiday, a six-month furlough from politics. His hesitations about going to Brazil had evaporated, and he had accepted invitations to other South American countries as well, to deliver addresses on democracy and to make a small expedition with two scientists from the American Museum of Natural History. In his month at home TR barreled through a half-dozen magazine articles and read the proofs of three books that would be published while he was away: the autobiography, the volume on African game, and a collection of his literary essays.

Preternatural energy and discipline got TR through the month, but by October, when he finished, it was clear that the year since his defeat had rubbed him raw. The Progressives still had no real organization beyond their offices in New York and Washington, and the zealous individualists drawn to third parties would not concede the necessity of trading *pluribus* for *unum*. They were driving him "nearly mad," he wrote Quentin just before sailing. "I have to remember, in order to keep myself fairly good tempered, that although the wild asses of the desert are mainly in our ranks, the opponents have a fairly exclusive monopoly on the swine."

Roosevelt had not forgiven the Republicans, and it had taken him only six months to work up a "contemptuous dislike" for Wilson. The country cheered Wilson's rapid success in persuading Congress to lower the tariff and raise the top income tax rate from 3 to 6 percent, but Roosevelt got no joy from seeing the progressive mantle beautifully draped on other shoulders. In a shooting mood, he took aim at the administration's handling of tensions with Mexico and Japan. Though he confined his first criticisms to confidential letters, he sent them to men in high places, obviously with the hope of influencing the course of affairs.

As far as Roosevelt could see, his quarrel with Taft had been purely political, but the swift transfer of his animosity from Taft to Wilson suggests a more human cause: jealousy. At bottom, Roosevelt had loathed Taft and now loathed Wilson because they were presidents and he was not. Roosevelt had loved the presidency for the power it gave him to play the hero, and when it ended, he was as wounded and blind as a husband who loses an adored wife to another man. But in his reckoning of the tumult of 1912, Roosevelt admitted no jealousy, voiced no second thoughts, took no blame. He would always hold that Theodore Roosevelt and the United States of America had been done in by the iniquity of the Republican Party.

Edith, who had a clear-eyed understanding of Theodore's malady and bright hopes for a cure, explained matters to Ethel in a sentence: "Father needs more scope, and since he can't be president must go away from home to have it."

THIRTEEN

Scope

ATHER also needed adulation and contest, nutrients he had had to
live without since the close of the Bull Moose campaign. South
America held the prospect of both. His hosts were promising applause, and Roosevelt sensed that there might be protest as well. The bruises
of his Big Stick in Panama and the Caribbean, though faded, had not entirely healed. He and Edith sailed for Brazil on October 4.

Hundreds of well-wishers gathered on the pier to see them off, and when
their ship passed the forts on Governors Island, the newspapermen in the
crowd wondered why the army fired no salute. As a former president, Roosevelt was entitled to the full twenty-one guns, which President Taft had
given him at both ends of the African trip. Asked about the silence, an
unidentified official of the new administration said blandly that Colonel
Roosevelt was not traveling on government business.

If TR felt slighted, he did not say so in writing. Quite possibly he expected
a snub. The night before, at a farewell banquet given by the Progressives, he
had called the foreign policy of Presidents Taft and Wilson "discreditable"
and had scoffed at Secretary of State William Jennings Bryan's "magniloquent talk" about the need for ever more arbitration treaties.

Once at sea TR read, napped, and wrote, exhibiting none of the caged-
animal restlessness he usually felt on a ship. He was laughing as he had not
laughed in years, Edith wrote Bamie. "I think he feels like Christian in *Pilgrim's Progress* when the burden fell from his back—in this case it was not
made of sins but of the Progressive Party."

Edith too was relaxed, lounging in her wrapper all morning and looking, to Theodore's eye, "very dainty and charming." For the two weeks of their voyage she would have him to herself—a rarity in their marriage—and the family coffers, after the expensive year of the Bull Moose, were filling up again. In South America, Theodore would receive $10,000 in lecture fees and earn thousands more by sending *The Outlook* his political and social impressions of the places he visited. He had also negotiated a $15,000 contract for a series of articles on his scientific expedition. Like his African dispatches, the pieces from the wilds of Brazil would appear first in *Scribner's* magazine and later as a book. With obvious satisfaction Edith wrote Ethel that Theodore's Latin travels would net $20,000.

The lectures were billed as nonpartisan, and TR had expressed the hope that his trip would help to strengthen the economic ties between North and South America. At the farewell banquet he had remarked that the young democracies of Latin America, preoccupied with their political development, had left their economies largely to the entrepreneurs and merchant bankers of the Old World. With the Panama Canal set to open in August 1914, he said, the United States could no longer be content "to see all the international business of all the American commonwealths transacted through European hands."

William Howard Taft was probably not alone in suspecting that Roosevelt's procession through South America was the opening act of his next presidential campaign. TR gave no sign, public or private, that he was thinking about 1916, but his Latin sojourn would be a departure in more ways than one. Throughout the 1912 campaign Roosevelt and Wilson had focused their debate on issues of social and economic justice. In the future they would quarrel mainly about foreign policy. The shift was a natural response to turmoil in Mexico and the outbreak of the world war, but after Wilson made off with the Progressive Party's domestic agenda, foreign policy would be a better field for battling the White House—less crowded and, as Roosevelt had already divined from the administration's diffident handling of international tensions, a great weakness of the fledgling president. (Wilson privately had admitted as much, just before his inauguration. Given that all his preparation had been along domestic lines, he wrote a friend, it would be "the irony of fate" if he were called upon to deal chiefly with international relations.)

KERMIT MET his parents' ship at Salvador da Bahia, Brazil, and within the hour his mother was imploring him to accompany his father on the expedition that would follow the speaking tour. "I had not for a moment expected to go," Kermit wrote Ethel, "but . . . Mother told me that she really wanted me to go to look after things." He secured a leave from his new employer, a bridge-building concern called the Anglo-Brazilian Forging Steel Structural and Importing Company, and graciously told his parents that the knowledge gained in the interior would increase his value as an engineer.

That remained to be seen, but Kermit's acquiescence certainly raised his stock with Edith, who seemed unable to regard his Brazilian career as anything but a perilous lark. She was right about the perils. The climate was insalubrious, he had miraculously survived a forty-foot fall when a bridge-in-progress gave way, and the low wages paid by his first employer, the Brazil Railway Company, had sometimes forced him to go without food.

But to Kermit, a man's choice of career was "all a matter of taste." His taste ran to adventure, and he was justly proud of his year in Brazil. Writing his friend and safari companion Warrington Dawson shortly before his parents' arrival, Kermit asked, "Do you remember the tortoise with the postage stamp ('Consider the postage stamp, my son, its usefulness consists in its ability to stick to one thing until it gets there') you gave me in Paris? It has sat on my desk throughout all my wanderings, though I'm afraid it has been sadly shocked with my butterfly behavior. Still I've been working pretty hard for a butterfly. Since I've been down here I've built a big freight yard, been Inspector of Traffic over 850 kilometers of railway, run a steamboat at hire, and built a steel bridge. It has all been tremendously interesting."

And if not as lucrative as Ted's labors in investment banking, Kermit's work now generated $2,500 a year, enough to embolden him to propose marriage to Belle Willard, late of Richmond and Fairfax, Virginia. They had fallen in love in the summer of 1912 and had been spooning through the mails since Kermit's move to Brazil. Belle and her family had just moved to Madrid, where her father, Joseph E. Willard, was serving as American ambassador to Spain. An aristocrat who spent much of his life in public service, Willard was an early and generous supporter of Woodrow Wilson's 1912 campaign, and the ambassadorship was a token of the president's gratitude.

Still waiting for Belle's reply when Theodore and Edith arrived, Kermit could not resist telling them what he had done. TR was delighted, but Edith reacted with disbelief and alarm, Kermit reported to Belle. "[S]he said she hoped it wouldn't interfere with my being with father." A few weeks later, when Belle's acceptance arrived, Edith would confess to feeling "a trifle down."

Theodore was a trifle manic. "Father scarcely sleeps and likes everything he does without any exception," Edith wrote Ethel. Large, friendly crowds came out to see him, and the audiences he addressed seemed to like the present he had brought them: a new conception of the doctrine set forth in 1823 by President James Monroe and Secretary of State John Quincy Adams. In its original form the Monroe Doctrine had put an end to new European and Asian colonization of the Western Hemisphere. As president, TR had added the Roosevelt Corollary, which pledged the United States to guarantee the good behavior of all the nations of the hemisphere in their dealings with the rest of the world. On October 24, in Rio de Janeiro, he announced that it was time to make the Monroe Doctrine a multilateral rather than a unilateral proposition, with Brazil and the other strong republics of Latin America joining the United States in policing the hemisphere and defending it against invasion.

Foreseeing that the opening of the canal would sharpen imperial hungers, Roosevelt predicted "calamity to all if any great military nation of the Old World obtained a foothold here." The independence of the American republics would be threatened, he said, and the New World would be plunged into "Old World conditions of armed rivalry." The applause was said to be frequent and enthusiastic.

On October 27, Roosevelt's fifty-fifth birthday, President Wilson enunciated his own vision of the proper relations between the United States and Latin America. Speaking at a convention of Southern businessmen in Mobile, Alabama, Wilson promised that "morality, and not expediency" would guide U.S. foreign policy, and he vowed that the United States would never again seek "one additional foot of territory by conquest." The president also declared himself in favor of liberating the region from its subordination to foreign enterprise: "You hear of 'concessions' to foreign capitalists in Latin America. You do not hear of concessions to foreign capitalists in the United States. They are invited to make investments. . . . It is an invitation, not a privilege." Countries lacking the wherewithal to develop their natural resources granted concessions, almost always to the detriment of their economic well-being and their political liberties, Wilson said. "I rejoice in nothing so much as the prospect that they will now be emancipated from these conditions, and we ought to be the first to take part in assisting in that emancipation."

Europeans heard Wilson's speech as an attack on their business interests in Latin America, but newspapers in the United States generally praised the president's high-mindedness and ignored the perplexities lurking therein: Where exactly was the line between expediency and morality? The United States ought to help the Latins throw off the tyranny of European capitalists, Wilson had said, but would it? How? And what of the tyranny of Yankee capitalists south of the Rio Grande?

Neither Wilson nor Roosevelt mentioned the chaos in Mexico, which in two years had gone from dictatorship to democracy and back again. A president and vice president democratically elected in 1911 had been assassinated after only fifteen months in office. Wilson refused to recognize the new autocrat, adopted a policy of "watchful waiting," and prayed that democracy would reassert itself. As Washington watched and waited, bands of revolutionaries roved the Mexican countryside, attacking foreigners, and London and Berlin grew increasingly apprehensive. "Intelligent opinion here fears that the President is dreaming of peace while drifting toward war," the *Times* of London said after Wilson's speech in Mobile. The Germans, more direct, ordered a few gunboats into Latin American waters.

Alarmed by the threat of European interference in the Western Hemisphere, many fervent Monroe Doctrine men in the United States preferred Roosevelt's new interpretation to Wilson's sublimity. Taking Roosevelt's approach, the largest Latin republics, acting with or without the United States, might be able to orchestrate a diplomatic intervention that would restore order in Mexico.

Roosevelt would later say that he considered watchful waiting bad policy, "for there is never any deed to back it up," but in his South American public appearances he refrained from challenging Wilson. In seven weeks of speaking he made only one remark that might have been a swing at the professor in the White House: a warning against intellectualism, sounded in an address entitled "Character and Civilization." Intellect was a good servant but an evil master, TR said. The success of a republic hinged not on the brilliance of its citizens but on disciplined work and strength of soul.

The U.S. envoys who escorted the former president to his banquets and receptions sent the State Department nothing but praise for his comportment. Before Roosevelt's visit, Uruguay had regarded him as Yankee aggression incarnate, said Nicolay A. Grevstad, chief of the American legation in Montevideo. But his addresses had caused "general and very agreeable surprise" and led many skeptics to think that "after all these southern republics have not so very much to fear from 'the great colossus of the north.'"

George Lorillard, interim chargé d'affaires in Buenos Aires, reported that Roosevelt was "careful not to be drawn into any open criticism of the present administration in the United States and declined to discuss publicly the Mexican situation or other important public questions." Lorillard did not mention Roosevelt's theatrics at a banquet in the city's cavernous opera house, where he had spoken from a tabletop in the middle of the room, ostensibly to make himself audible to all. Perhaps it was only coincidence, but the unorthodox rostrum perfectly suited his text, which introduced the Argentines to the heresy of judicial recall and gave them a he-man's notion of the ideal democracy—"a strong government with a strong man to administer it, and a strong people to make the strong man go as they wish him to go."

In Santiago, the only city apparently unhappy to see him, TR gamely met a crowd shouting anti-American epithets with waves of his hat and cries of "Viva Chile!" When student protesters interrupted one of his speeches, the outburst troubled the hosts but left no discernible mark on the guest. Chilean officials eager not to offend Washington asked the American attaché, R. B. Harvey, to inform the State Department that the dissent had come from foreign students—mostly from Colombia, whose government still considered Roosevelt the perpetrator of Panama's high-speed secession.

Roosevelt voiced displeasure only once, in Santiago. After a former Chilean diplomat referred to the Monroe Doctrine as a dead issue in the course of introducing TR to an audience, TR disagreed and hinted that a former government official ought not air such views in public. The Chilean replied that he had cleared his remarks with the Foreign Office. To the *Times* of London, the tiff showed that distrust would remain "more or less lively in the great South American Republics as long as there is any room to regard the United States as potential 'boss' of the civilized as well as of the semi-civilized parts of this hemisphere."

Pondering Wilson's speech in Mobile and Roosevelt's addresses in Latin America, one German newspaper concluded that the president and the Colonel had buried their rivalry in order to obfuscate U.S. intentions to rule the hemisphere with mailed fist once the canal opened. It was an intriguing but unfounded hypothesis. Roosevelt was a minister without portfolio, and Wilson was ignoring him.

THEODORE AND EDITH parted in Chile at the end of November, in time for Edith to sail home for Christmas with Archie and Quentin. Kermit, yearning to be in Madrid with Belle, found the days interminable and wished the Brazilian expedition would begin immediately. But between Chile and the scientific work lay three more weeks of official engagements, and another nine for a jaguar hunt, a long river voyage north from Paraguay, and an overland march with the mule train that would pack their gear into the wilderness. "I'm in a terrible temper," Kermit wrote Belle. Taken to view some towering waterfalls, he could see their grandeur but not feel it. "I get angry at myself for not enjoying these things more, for I know how very much I'd enjoy it if we were together."

Kermit was infinitely patient with his father, who by this time had convinced himself that he had had to invite Kermit or "his feelings would really have been hurt." After many hours of taking and developing photographs for the *Scribner's* articles, Kermit confided to Belle that he would rather do a long day's march, but it appears that he successfully concealed all such feelings from his father. TR, a surprisingly tenderhearted champion of romantic love, instinctively understood Kermit's longing to be in Spain and more than once encouraged him to go. Kermit declined. He had promised his mother he would stay, his father was helpless without an aide-de-camp, and as the only member of their party who spoke both Portuguese and English, Kermit knew that he would be indispensable to the expedition.

The expedition TR had conceived in New York was a modest specimen-collecting trip along well-known rivers with two naturalists from the American Museum of Natural History, but as soon as he reached South America the outing swelled into an epic. General Lauro S. Müller, Brazil's minister of foreign affairs, invited him to descend an uncharted river in the interior with the country's most accomplished explorer, Colonel Candido Mariano da Silva Rondon. Rondon had discovered the river's headwaters two years earlier, but no one knew where the river went, how long it was, or whether it was navigable. It did have a name: Rio da Dúvida, River of Doubt. Told that the Dúvida would probably prove to be a major addition to the map of the world, TR accepted at once. The decision had been an easy one, he wrote Ethel's husband, Dick Derby. "To go down an unknown river is a thousand times better than going down the Tapajos and up the Rio Negro and along the Orinoco."

Fairfield Osborn, director of the American Museum of Natural History, was floored by the change of itinerary and refused to take any responsibility for Roosevelt's survival. TR shrugged him off in a jaunty note to a friend at the museum: "Tell Osborn I have already lived and enjoyed as much of life as any nine other men I know; I have had my full share, and if it is necessary for me to leave my bones in South America, I am quite ready to do so."

Edith was by no means ready for him to do so, and it seems unlikely that TR believed he was putting himself or his newly betrothed son or anyone else in mortal danger. A man who had survived grizzly bears, charging lions, combat, assassins, and a collision that had shot him headlong out of a carriage had ample grounds for believing that he could best a jungle. And whatever the hazards of this patch of terra incognita, he would be traveling with Colonel Rondon, who had been exploring the tropics for two decades. As the Brazilian government's chief surveyor of the Mato Grosso—the Great Wilderness—Rondon had already laid out the routes of thousands of miles of railway and telegraph lines and ultimately would be credited with mapping fifteen thousand square miles of the Brazilian interior and the discovery of more than a dozen major rivers.

Small parties being less obtrusive than large ones, the naturalists decided that they would be able to gather more specimens if they split up, one of them descending the Dúvida with the Roosevelts and the other collecting along rivers elsewhere in the region. TR suggested that they draw lots for the place in his group, but Leo E. Miller, a young mammalogist, believed that the privilege should go to his older and more experienced colleague, George K. Cherrie. Cherrie, an ornithologist, accepted Miller's gift, and Miller set off for two rivers already on the map, the Gy-Paraná and the Madeira, the largest tributary of the Amazon. Rondon theorized that the Dúvida, which flowed from a point near José Bónifacio, at the very center of the South American continent, would drain into the Madeira or some other affluent of the Amazon. If Rondon was right, and if all went well, the Miller and Roosevelt parties would be able to connect in the port of Manaus, not far from the confluence of the Madeira and the Amazon.

In most adventure stories the hardest-working part of speech is the verb, but in this one, the power is all in the nouns. Fire ants. Grasshoppers the size of sparrows. Rapids. Days lost as axes clear paths on banks and make log rollers for portaging 2,500-pound dugout canoes. Bees. Wasps. Blackflies. Rapids. Portage. Termites. Ticks. Mosquitoes. TR forced to write in head net and gauntlets. Hundred-degree heat. Rainy season. Clothes and bedding permanently wet. Bodies covered with insect bites. Boils. Fever. Dysentery. Rapids. A drowning. Canoes lost in rapids. Days of delay while new boats are hewn from trees with axe and adze. Dogs losing tails to piranhas. Hunger: food running out, food lost in rapids, food stolen. Fish scarce, game nearly impossible to shoot in thick vegetation. Parrots and monkeys for dinner. A murder. The murderer abandoned to the jungle. Dog killed by arrows of native tribe. Natives never seen. Rapids rapids rapids rapids.

The tale began quietly enough. "On February 27, 1914, shortly after midday, we started down the River of Doubt into the unknown," TR wrote in *Through the Brazilian Wilderness*. "We were quite uncertain whether after a week we should find ourselves in the Gy-Paraná, or after six weeks in the Madeira, or after three months we knew not where." They set off with twenty-two men in seven dugout canoes: Kermit in the lead, followed by Colonel Rondon and his assistant, Lieutenant José Salustiano Lyra, after which came four supply canoes (lashed together in pairs) and a canoe carrying TR, George Cherrie, and Dr. José Antonio Cajazeira, a physician. Sixteen natives did the paddling. At each bend in the river, Kermit halted his boat, held up a sighting rod, and waited for Rondon and Lyra to take readings with telemeter and compass. After they pitched camp for the night, Lyra, an astronomer by training, would chart the day's course and calculate how far they had run.

After two weeks on the river, Cherrie, a veteran of two dozen tropical expeditions, told his diary, "There isn't any one of our party that will not be thankful when this trip draws to a close. There are *too* many uncertainties and possibilities to face to make it a thing of gusto." A day later Kermit's canoe was swept over a waterfall, drowning one of the boatmen. Cherrie began having serious doubts about the survival of the rest of the party.

Four weeks out, while they were camped on the bank, the river rose and carried off two canoes, which filled with water, then wedged themselves in the crevices of some large rocks. Waist-deep in the water, straining against the strong current, all the members of the expedition worked for three hours before the boats came free. At some point during the rescue TR lost his footing and smashed his leg on a boulder. Had the injury not been to his left leg, the one badly hurt years before in the carriage accident, it might have easily healed. But the leg had remained vulnerable to infection and was now covered with sores that Cherrie recognized as "oriental ulcers"—the layman's term for cutaneous leishmaniasis. Caused by the bites of infected sandflies, the disease inflicts serious anemia, weight loss, and fever. TR's temperature rose to 104 degrees and on the night of April 4 he was "out of his head," Kermit wrote. In his delirium, he recited over and over a line from Coleridge—

"In Xanadu did Kubla Khan a stately pleasure-dome decree." They had lost canoes, some of which had been carrying food, and in lucid moments TR asked if Kermit and Cherrie were getting enough to eat to keep going. "Am in a blue funk as I have been for some time to get F[ather] out of the country," Kermit wrote in his diary.

The week had been a torture. Kermit, Cherrie, and Lyra were also ill, and when the expedition reached a veritable staircase of waterfalls, Rondon argued for giving up the canoes and walking out—a death sentence, in Cherrie's opinion. "Kermit and I refused to consider such a plan feeling that our only salvation lay in the party holding together and at least making every effort to get our canoes through the canyon," Cherrie would write in his memoir. "Colonel Roosevelt was a very sick man and the effect of Rondon's report on him, with his feeling of keen responsibility to us all, was such that I felt he might not live through the night."

For four days Kermit and Lieutenant Lyra worked from the top of the gorge, using long ropes to guide the canoes safely through the rapids. The rest of the men cut a trail and portaged their cargo to the next stretch of smooth water. It was cruelly short and followed by another deep gorge filled with waterfalls, necessitating three more days of the same exhausting work. On the two-mile hike along the portaging trail, the Colonel complained of "heart trouble" and as soon as he reached the new campsite, "he lay flat on the damp earth for some time before recovering," Cherrie noted in his diary. Barely able to walk, TR considered telling Kermit and Cherrie to go on without him if he deteriorated to the point where he had to be carried. He changed his mind after concluding that Kermit would insist upon transporting the body out of the jungle.

Toward the end of this hellish week a boatman named Julio shot and killed the crew's sergeant, who had reprimanded him for shirking and for stealing from their dwindling supply of food. Julio took flight and reappeared a few days later, on a tree limb overhanging the river. He begged to rejoin them, and Rondon favored the idea. Under Brazilian law, he explained to TR, they had a duty to deliver Julio to justice. Roosevelt pointed out that Julio would be a dangerous prisoner and reminded Rondon that for two weeks they had been struggling to survive on half-rations. Rondon bowed to Roosevelt but soon claimed to have misgivings and wanted to send a boat back for Julio. TR refused. Kermit deduced that Rondon was less concerned about Julio than his place in the history of exploration. "Rondon completely vacillated about Julio with 100 lies," he told his diary. "He wants to wait to take the latitude but F[ather] won't let him." Rondon was stalling, hoping for time to make a flawless map, but TR's illness had exhausted his patience with such ambitions.

On April 13, for the first time in a month, Roosevelt and his companions camped in a spot where no rapids could be heard. Next day they found a tool used by rubber explorers, and after two more days of smooth paddling they spotted a hut. Roosevelt's party had come almost five hundred miles, and the river stretched on for another five hundred, but they were no longer in virgin territory. They soon met settlers who confirmed that the stream flowed into the Madeira, just as Rondon had thought.

Two weeks later, on their fifty-ninth day on the water, Rondon drove a large post into a spot on the bank and nailed up a plaque christening their find the Rio Roosevelt. Enamored of the poetic perfection of Rio da Dúvida, TR pressed for keeping it but gave up when he realized that his insistence hurt his host's feelings. In the end, the Brazilian government overruled Rondon's wishes and Roosevelt's and named the new river the Teodoro. "Teodoro" was more euphonious, and it would raise fewer political hackles than "Roosevelt."

Miller was waiting for them in Manaus, as was an ambulance, which took TR to the governor's mansion to rest in comfort while Kermit found them a ship headed down the Amazon. In a fog of pain from the sores on his leg and an abscess deep in his upper thigh, TR nevertheless cabled word of the expedition's safe return to Edith, his cousin Emlen Roosevelt, Belle's father, and Fairfield Osborn of the American Museum of Natural History. He also willed himself to compose a longer message to General Müller, the Brazilian foreign minister, who had invited him to make the trip. The Roosevelt-Rondon expedition had "put on the map a river about 1,500 kilometres in length running from just south of the 13th degree to north of the 5th degree," TR wrote. He expressed his gratitude and after stoically characterizing the trip as "hard and somewhat dangerous but very successful," he provided a suggestive précis of their ordeal.

No less than six weeks were spent in slowly and with peril and exhausting labor forcing our way down through what seemed a literally endless succession of rapids and cataracts. In passing those rapids we lost five of the seven canoes with which we started and had to build others. One of our best men lost his life in the rapids. Under the strain one of the men went completely bad, shirked all his work, stole his comrades' food and when punished by the sergeant he with cold-blooded deliberation murdered the sergeant and fled into the wilderness. Colonel Rondon's dog running ahead of him while hunting, was shot by two Indians; by his death he in all probability saved the life of his master.

The new river was as long as the Rhine. Cherrie's work had yielded 1,500 ornithological specimens, some of them previously unknown to science and many of them new to the American Museum of Natural History. Miller's specimen crates held the skins and skulls of anteaters, jaguars, and five hundred other animals. Together the naturalists had made an outstanding addition to the museum's wildlife collection.

O N MAY 1, after Dr. Cajazeira performed a last operation on TR's abscess, the Roosevelts and the naturalists boarded a freighter for the Atlantic port of Belém, where the SS *Aidan*, a passenger liner bound for New York, was being held for TR's arrival. Kermit noted in his diary that TR was "about the same, but much more cheerful" and wrote his sister Ethel, "Well, I feel my going was really justified. As Belle wrote we'd never forgive ourselves if I hadn't gone." In a modest, roundabout way, Kermit was saying that their beloved father probably would not have survived without him. Kermit had kept watch through feverish nights, rigged up an open-sided tent to shield TR from the molten sun beating on a river that had widened dramatically after the rapids, and persuaded Rondon that it would be suicide to abandon the canoes. On May 7 Kermit settled his father, who was still very weak, aboard the *Aidan* and said his good-byes. He sailed for Spain the following day.

The newspapermen who greeted the Colonel in New York on May 19 were shocked to see that his big bull neck no longer bulged over his collar. He had lost fifty-five pounds, his voice had gone faint, and he leaned heavily on a cane. To John Callan O'Laughlin, a reporter who knew him well, he looked like an old man.

But he was in fine spirits. No, he had no comment on political matters, he said; he had not read the papers in months. Nor did he expect to make any public political pronouncements soon. He was just passing through and would not resume his life at Sagamore for another month, when he returned from Kermit and Belle's wedding in Madrid. A few days hence he would make a brief visit to Washington. No, no, not politics. He was going at the invitation of the National Geographic Society, to lecture on the expedition.

As for Henry Savage-Landor, an English explorer who was telling the world that a new river as large as Roosevelt's could not possibly exist, TR said, with a flash of his old self, "To be accused by him is to have an iron enter my soul." With his deep tan, familiar ferocious grin, and Panama brim turned up in front, he looked like an old salt sailing exuberantly into a gale. He was, and the storm would blow until 1927, when an expedition funded by Roosevelt's admirers went down the Teodoro again and confirmed the magnitude of the discovery.

Hurt by the rejection of 1912 and frustrated with life as a political outsider, Roosevelt had gone to South America in search of more scope. He had found it, in the annals of geography, but that was unforeseen. If he harbored any hope that a good showing with political leaders abroad would restore his luster at home, it went unrealized. He had made a very good showing, but few of his countrymen cared about the Monroe Doctrine or any other foreign policy matter. Within twenty-four hours of his return, the Progressive leaders would descend upon Sagamore, and he would see that he was back where he had started, struggling to keep the party's moderate and radical factions from pecking each other to death. The work was thankless, grueling for a convalescent, and futile.

Although TR was not ready to give up on the Progressives, Gus Karger, William Howard Taft's informant in the Washington press corps, sensed a river of doubt coursing through the Rooseveltian interior. Watching him with his political friends after the National Geographic Society speech, Karger saw "something pathetic in that midnight gathering of Progressives at the Colonel's feet. I could not help but feel that in cold blood, after conferring upon them his blessing for the faith well kept, he was contemplating the best methods of 'dumping' them if their canine loyalty should become uncomfortable to himself." Noticing that Roosevelt said nothing critical of the Republicans, Karger speculated that the renegade was blazing a trail back to their camp and would take it if the Progressives fared badly in the forthcoming congressional elections. "Mr. Roosevelt wants to be president again," Karger said. "He would run on the Republican ticket if he can get rid of the Progressive Party." Karger's thinking was running ahead of Roosevelt's, but not by much.

FOURTEEN

Half-Gods

ATACLYSM splits the mind into a before and an after. The ax falls, life no longer feels of a piece, and the psyche flees backward, fashioning a haven from splinters of the paradise lost. Shocked to find the world at war in August 1914, Edith Roosevelt's cousin Edith Wharton would always remember a July visit to Chartres in its "perfect hour," four in the afternoon, when she stood in the "great sheets and showers of color" pouring through the stained glass. And the Paris to which she returned on that warm summer evening would remain fixed in her memory: the Seine trembling blue-pink like an early Monet, the Champs-Elysées in a sun-powdered haze, "the great city, so made for peace and art and all humanest graces," lying by the river "like a princess guarded by the watchful giant of the Eiffel Tower."

The temperament so inclined could trace the war's origins to Cain and Abel, but the short view focused on the June 28 assassinations of the Archduke Francis Ferdinand, heir to the throne of the Austro-Hungarian Empire, and his wife, the Duchess of Hohenburg. The assassins were Serbian nationalists who had watched the archduke devour Bosnia and Croatia and heard him speak openly of his hunger for more. Alice Longworth, in no hurry to return to Cincinnati after Kermit and Belle's wedding, was at the races in Paris when the word came from Sarajevo. She would recall that while her companions were upset by the violence, no one "gave any sign of realizing that it was the match that touched off the fuse." For the moment, Paris was a city of "gay, carefree parties."

Henry Adams, seventy-six but keeping his pessimism in trim by thinking of himself as an octogenarian, was summering in France as usual, still absorbed in his study of the Middle Ages. Adams had situated himself and two caretaking young women in a château fifty miles north of Paris—"quite gorgeously out of the world," he thought—and hoped to stay till October. Austria declared war on Serbia July 28, Russia mobilized in defense of Serbia, Germany declared war on Russia and invaded Belgium ánd France, England declared war on Germany, and within days all of Europe was at arms. Adams, realizing that the German advance could put his château in the line of fire, retreated to Paris and then to the English countryside. "We must go home, I suppose, and wait till peace," he wrote a friend.

Henry White, friend of Theodore Roosevelt and former American ambassador to France, was vacationing with his wife in the southeastern reaches of Germany on August 3, when foreigners were instructed to proceed to Berlin, where their embassies would arrange passage out of the country. Hoping to influence public opinion in the United States, the German government invited White and a few other Americans to dine at the War Office with General Erich von Falkenhayn, future chief of the army's general staff. A seasoned diplomat and veteran of several international crises, White was struck by the calm at the dinner. Vast armies were on the move, yet the meal was not interrupted by a single message for the generals. Alone with Falkenhayn in the garden after dinner, White expressed his surprise. Falkenhayn said he had requested notice of any troop train running more than ten minutes late; on that night there was apparently no such news.

Falkenhayn also told White that the generals had made a gross miscalculation: Germany had gone to war certain that England would not. The British government was supposed to be preoccupied with problems in Ireland, where Protestants and Catholics were close to civil war, and the popularity of pacifism in Britain was taken to mean that the British public would not support a war in Europe. German hopes for a quick victory vanished with Britain's decision to defend Belgium, Falkenhayn said. Britain's army was small—"contemptible" was the kaiser's word for it—but Falkenhayn foresaw that the "bulldog tenacity" of the British would "make them hold on to the bitter end in spite of obstacles which would be insurmountable to any other army."

Walter Hines Page, American ambassador to the Court of St. James's, had begun 1914 wryly amused by the minutiae of official life: word had come from his tailor that the Lord Chamberlain had decreed the removal of the small bows on the knees of the ceremonial breeches ambassadors wore to court. "How did the Lord Chamberlain come to think of *that?*" Page wondered in his diary. On August 2, at his country house in Surrey, Page was shocked to find himself recording that Belgium had denied Berlin's request for permission to move the German army through Belgium and into France. It was obvious that the Germans would proceed without permission. "The Grand Smash is come," Page wrote. He had no idea how to help the Americans clamoring to get home and no power to concentrate on his work: "it has been impossible to get my mind off this Great Smash. It holds one in spite of one's self. I revolve it and revolve it—of course getting nowhere." Germany had staked everything on victory, and if Germany won, "this side of the world will henceforth be German." Page left off for a bit to walk out into a night opulent with stars and "as quiet as peace itself. Millions of men are in camp, and on warships. Will they all have to fight and many of them die . . . ? The situation staggers the imagination."

On August 4, the day England entered the war, Page gave an account of his meeting with Roosevelt's friend Sir Edward Grey, the foreign secretary, who laid out the situation "in a calm, solemn, restrained way, sitting in a chair, both hands under his jaws, leaning forward eagerly. Belgium's neutrality was assured by treaty and Germany was a signatory power to that treaty. If we give up such solemn compacts, on what does civilization rest?" After talking with Page for nearly an hour, Grey rose and said, with tears in his eyes, "Thus the efforts of a lifetime go for nothing. I feel as a man who has wasted his life." Through a decade of international tensions exacerbated by the most frenzied arms race in history, Grey had tamped flames in Europe and Africa and Asia and was hoping to be remembered as the preserver of the world's peace. Page left with a "stunned sense of impending ruin of half the world."

Andrew Carnegie, working on his autobiography at his retreat in Scotland, learned of the war as he was recounting his 1913 meeting with the kaiser at a ceremony celebrating twenty-five years of peaceful German rule. "[W]hat a change!" Carnegie added. "The world convulsed by war as never before! Men slaying each other like wild beasts." He abandoned the autobiography and began lobbying Woodrow Wilson to call for a cease-fire and peace negotiations.

After spending years and a substantial part of his fortune in the cause of peace, Carnegie was crushed, as was Jane Addams, who shared his conviction that world peace was attainable. The pacifists did not imagine that war had been abolished by the various international agreements signed at The Hague, but they hoped that war would become less frequent as nations acquired the habit of submitting their differences to arbitration. Vacationing on Mount Desert Isle in Maine when the war began, Addams awoke one morning to the startling sight of a German ocean liner at anchor in Frenchman's Bay. The ship had left New York before the declarations of war, and when the captain received the news by wireless, he turned back, fearing the capture of the gold bullion in his hold. A Maine yachtsman on board offered to pilot the ship into the bay, where it would sit till the end of the war.

At Sagamore, Germany's first acts of war touched off a tirade against Washington. On August 1 Roosevelt wrote an English friend that while "that great black tornado trembles on the edge of Europe," the fate of the United States rested with "a professional yodeler" and "a college president with an astute and shifty mind . . . and no real knowledge or wisdom concerning internal and international affairs." Roosevelt scoffed at the yodeler, Secretary of State William Jennings Bryan, for his naive handling of the martinets vying for power in Mexico and for his near-total absorption in negotiating conciliation treaties with Paraguay and "similar world powers."

These "cooling off" treaties, as they were known, pledged the signatories to submit their irreconcilable differences to a permanent international commission and to refrain from war for a year, during which the commission would hear the case and recommend solutions. Roosevelt favored arbitration and conciliation but also believed that a treaty meant nothing unless backed by international force "to secure at least a reasonable approximation toward justice and fair play."

Woodrow Wilson proclaimed a "strict and impartial neutrality" for the United States on August 4 and two weeks later made a short address asking all Americans to act with "impartiality and fairness and friendliness to all concerned." The American people, drawn from many nations, would naturally differ in their sympathies with the belligerents, but antagonisms once ignited were difficult to douse, he said. "We must be impartial in thought as well as in action." He wanted America to "show herself in this time of peculiar trial a nation fit beyond others to exhibit the fine poise of undisturbed judgment, the dignity of self control, the efficiency of dispassionate action, a nation that neither sits in judgment upon others nor is disturbed in her own counsels and which keeps herself fit and free to do what is honest and disinterested and truly serviceable for the peace of the world."

Wilson's ideal was a noble one and when placed in the context of his personal life in August 1914, it takes on an almost unbearable poignancy. In the first week of the war, his wife, Ellen Axson Wilson, died of a degenerative disease of the kidneys, and the president, in the words of his physician, was a man "with his heart torn out." In calling for fine poise, undisturbed judgment, and the dignity of self-control, Woodrow Wilson was setting standards for himself as well as his country.

A T THE BEGINNING of the war Roosevelt did his fulminating in private, knowing that most Americans would support the president in a crisis and that the president might have information not available to a private citizen. Two other factors may also have figured in the silence: he was temporarily without a pulpit, and he was suffering from a recurrence of the malaria he had contracted in Brazil. In the July 11 number of *The Outlook*, the editors announced that Roosevelt was leaving the magazine to devote his attention to the congressional and state elections of 1914. The truth was that readers who disapproved of him continued to fall away. To show that the parting was amicable, the magazine named him a "special contributor" on social and industrial subjects.

The malaria brought bouts of fever and a persistent, seriously sore throat, quite possibly a side effect of the quinine he was taking. His doctors prescribed four months of rest, a suggestion he ignored until he realized that he was not recovering. In early July he grudgingly consented to a purposeful loaf of six weeks to put himself in shape for the speeches he would make in the fall campaign. Two days into his rest he rowed Edith to and from a family picnic eight miles away. Over the next few weeks he went into New York for meetings at Progressive Party headquarters, and Sagamore bulged with company, political and familial. In mid-July he and Edith hosted old friends and the townspeople of Oyster Bay at a reception for Kermit and Belle, just returned from their honeymoon in Portugal and Spain. The day before the party TR spent three hours mowing the lawn.

The Colonel's malaria seems not to have compromised his spleen, which he vented freely in spite of doctor's orders for tranquillity. In a statement urging New York's Progressive Party to back a progressive Republican running for governor, he suggested that they get the progressive Democrats to join them and make a fight against the bosses of both parties. The interests of Charles F. Murphy of Tammany Hall and William Barnes of the Republican machine in Albany were "fundamentally identical," Roosevelt said, "and when the issue between popular rights and corrupt and machine-ruled government is clearly drawn, the two bosses will always be found on the same side, openly or covertly, giving one another such support as can with safety be rendered." The state government was "rotten throughout in almost all its departments; and this is directly due to the dominance of Mr. Murphy and his sub-bosses . . . aided and abetted when necessary by Mr. Barnes." In short, Barnes and Murphy constituted an "all-powerful invisible government" heedless of the will of the people.

The next night during dinner, TR was summoned to the door and served with a lawsuit. Barnes charged him with libel and sought damages of $50,000. The courier was a member of the law firm representing Barnes, and if he hoped to return with news of the Colonel's agitation, he went away disappointed. Roosevelt had been nonchalance in a dinner jacket, welcoming him into the house as if he had no other plans for the evening, offering a cigar, and tossing the legal documents on his desk.

The patient's rest cure also included a strenuous protest of a treaty giving Colombia an expression of "sincere regret" and $25 million as compensation for the loss of Panama. Bryan had been negotiating the terms since Wilson's inauguration, and while TR was in Spain for Kermit and Belle's wedding, the Colombians accepted the American offer and the treaty went to the Senate for ratification.

Roosevelt, enraged, insisted that in recognizing Panama's independence, the United States had merely acknowledged reality. He wrote the chairman of the Senate Foreign Relations Committee requesting permission to appear in person and present a history of his dealings with Colombia. "I ask for this hearing because I regard the proposed treaty as a crime against the United States, an attack upon the honor of the United States," he said. If the United States had behaved honorably, not a dime was due, and if it had not, then it could make amends only by returning the isthmus to Colombia. He explained to a political associate that he wanted a personal appearance in order to rivet attention on the issue, and the committee, evidently reaching the same conclusion, turned him down. The Democrats, who controlled the Senate, took the attitude that if the Colonel had anything to say, he could say it in writing.

Thanks to his friend Lodge, Roosevelt prevailed without going to Washington. The apology was excised and Senate Republicans managed to ob-

struct ratification for years, relenting only when their friends in the petroleum business noticed that Colombia was granting oil concessions to everyone but the United States.

In the middle of August, as rested as he could stand to be, Roosevelt
began politicking in earnest. His friends had pressed him and pressed him
some more to run for governor, but it is unlikely that he could have won,
and he claimed that being governor would narrow his scope at a time when
he wanted latitude to fight Woodrow Wilson on any front. The family's only
political candidate in 1914 was Nick Longworth, who was trying to recapture the congressional seat he had lost in 1912.

Without much joy or hope Roosevelt campaigned across sixteen states,
striving once more to convert rank-and-file Democrats and Republicans to
the Progressive faith. A careful listener would have noticed that Roosevelt
was touting the party's ideals more than the party, but the number of listeners had fallen off since 1912. The country had tired of reformers and the
economy had been in a depression for almost two years. As he explained to
Archie, "Under such circumstances the stomach vote numerically far out-
weighs the conscience vote." Hungry voters placed their bets on candidates
likely to win, losers having no power to bring back the full dinner pail.

Roosevelt presented the election as a moral struggle between the politics
of bossism and the politics of principle. The old parties were boss-ridden,
the Progressives were not. His parable in point was the recent Ludlow Massacre, bloody climax of years of labor strife in the mining towns of Colorado.
In September 1913 thousands of miners went on strike against the Colorado
Fuel and Iron Company to protest their miserable pay, the short-weighing
of the coal they hauled out of the mines, hazardous working conditions, and
gouging at the company store. Evicted from the lodgings they rented from
the company, the strikers and their families were spending the winter in tent
camps.

The Rockefellers, principal owners of Colorado Fuel and Iron, dispatched a small private army, the miners armed themselves, the violence escalated, and when the governor of Colorado called in the National Guard,
he ordered it to side with the company. The Guard escorted scabs to work
and roughed up the strikers. There were murders on both sides. On the
morning of April 20, 1914, seven months into the strike, the National Guard
barraged the Ludlow camp with machine guns and at night set the camp on
fire. In the ruins were the bodies of two women and eleven children who

had taken cover in one of the "safety pits" the miners had dug beneath their tents. The violence lasted for another ten days, until President Wilson sent in 1,700 federal troops. By then the dead numbered sixty-six.

As the president who boldly intervened to settle the coal strike of 1902, Roosevelt naturally scorned Wilson's delay in responding, but in his campaign speeches Roosevelt blamed the tragedy on the bosses, Democratic and Republican, who ran Colorado for the mining barons. Although the Colorado legislature had banned most of the abuses protested by the miners, the bosses had seen to it that the laws were not enforced, a situation that naturally eroded the miners' respect for the law.

TR told his audiences that the Progressive Party was a political organization for "everyday common decency" and aimed to make the country "a good place for anyone to live in because it is a good place for everyone to live in." To Democrats who alleged that Progressives would create a busybody government that destroyed individual initiative and infringed upon the rights of the states, Roosevelt replied that his ideal was self-help and his ideal government was an instrument for "mutual self-help." When individuals and states could not do a job as well as the national government could, the nation should do it. The Democrats' contention that the government could not ban child labor or build national highways because the Constitution said nothing on such subjects was balderdash, said Roosevelt.

Hopeless as the campaign was, it exhilarated TR. His throat improved, and by early October, O. K. Davis, secretary of the Progressive Party, was able to tell Chairman George Perkins that the Colonel was "completely restored to his old vigor and power," managing twenty-five meetings a day without evident strain. He was in "a state of exuberant vitality," Edith wrote one of Theodore's sisters. Ted gave thanks that the office of town dogcatcher was not vacant, because he was sure his father would run for it, just to work off his excess energy. The campaign was one of Roosevelt's finest—heartfelt, forceful, and notably free of his old choler.

"THIS IS ELECTION NIGHT," Edith wrote Ethel on November 3, "a debacle for the Progressives, and the Republicans have swept the East. I can't seem to care much if only Nick is elected, and Father is as philosophical as possible." In a four-way race against a Democrat, a Progressive, and a Socialist, Nick Longworth won 53 percent of the vote.

The Democrats lost ground but held their majorities in the House and

Senate. The Progressive contingent in the House shrank from fourteen to seven. Even Wisconsin, cradle of the Progressive movement, relapsed into conservatism. La Follette's candidate for governor finished third.

TR summed up the rout in a letter to Belle: "We were engaged in an utterly hopeless fight but it was my clear duty to hoist the black flag and go down with the rest of my associates; and this I did." The Progressives' cause was still vital, but the Progressive Party would probably disband, he wrote Archie. "Luckily all that is demanded of me, certainly for the next year or two, and probably for all the future, is to keep exceedingly quiet and not try to convince people who have made it emphatically evident that all they want from me is to keep myself to myself!"

A few days later he claimed to be happier than he had been in years. He and Edith took walks and rode, the days were still warm enough for a turn in the rowboat, and as the sun went down, they settled by the fire in the North Room, amid TR's flags and elephant tusks and lion skins. What he wanted now, he told Kermit, was "to be free from engagements and stay out here with Mother and without too much to do."

With the silver-lining men and the loyalists who wrote him of victory in 1916, he was almost tender, speaking of the need to hold the Progressive Party in readiness "to take advantage of whatever occurs in this hair-trigger situation." But the defeats had persuaded him that the party could not survive. "I feel that what we did was worthwhile," he wrote William Allen White. "Our movement in 1912 was the loftiest and sanest movement in our politics since the days of Lincoln and the platform we issued was the only great constructive platform for social and economic justice that has been brought forth since the days of the Civil War." Eventually Americans would have to adopt some version of the platform "if our democracy is really to amount to very much," he said, and he vowed to fight for the party's principles as long as he lived, but "When it is evident that a leader's day is past, the one service he can render is to step aside and leave the ground clear for the development of a successor." He concurred with Emerson: "Heartily know, when half-gods go, the gods arrive."

Roosevelt declined to attend the Progressive Party's post-election conference in Chicago and left Perkins to try to convince the country that the party was still thriving. After the election of 1912 a thousand Bull Moose enthusiasts had assembled in Chicago. The herd was now down to ninety.

TR had tired of the factional fights, and the war in Europe had widened the breach between him and the radicals, many of whom were pacifists. He had kept most of his thoughts about the war out of the campaign, reserving them for a series of nine articles published in the *New York Times* and reprinted in papers across the country during the autumn of 1914. The first was a plea for strengthening the nation's defenses—his reply to Wilson's contention that building up the army and navy would be construed as a sign of warlike intentions and make the United States unacceptable in the role of mediator. Roosevelt saw no conflict between adequate self-defense and peacemaking, and he argued that after Germany's invasion of Belgium, the United States would be foolish to trust that its treaties or its neutrality sufficed to keep it from harm.

The last of the articles, published a few weeks after the election, was an indictment of the peace-at-any-price idealists—"the ultrapacifists, who, with the shrill clamor of eunuchs, preach the gospel of the milk and water of virtue and then scream that belief in the efficacy of diluted moral mush is essential to salvation." In Roosevelt's critique of pacifism, the masculinity of peace advocates would always be in question. He saw them as ineffectual, and he loathed their embrace of all peace, no matter how unjust or foolhardy. When Germany broke the peace, Andrew Carnegie and the other "ultras" uttered not a word of condemnation, Roosevelt noted. "They cry continually for peace and not at all for righteousness." To condemn the might that did right along with the might that did wrong rendered "positive service to wrongdoers," he wrote. "It is as if in private life we condemned alike both the policeman and the dynamiter . . . he has arrested."

Roosevelt also chastised Wilson for failing to protest the German incursion into Belgium. As one of the signers of the treaty that guaranteed Belgium's neutrality, the United States had failed to meet its "solemn obligations to strive to protect other unoffending nations from wrong," Roosevelt said. He predicted that peace, when it came, would be made by the warring nations, who were unlikely to regard the United States as "having set a spiritual example to them by sitting idle, uttering cheap platitudes, and picking up their trade, while they have poured out their blood like water."

Roosevelt's old friend Cecil Spring Rice, now Britain's ambassador to the United States, tried unsuccessfully to impress the same point upon Secretary of State Bryan. "He sighs for the Nobel Prize," Spring Rice wrote a fellow diplomat in November 1914, after Bryan presented him with a sword beaten into a miniature plowshare and inscribed with peaceable aphorisms from Isaiah and himself. Bryan told Spring Rice that he did not understand why England was fighting, said a nation that prolonged a war was as culpable as a nation that started one, and argued that the United States, as the lone great power outside the struggle, had a duty to try to end the war. Spring Rice—feeling "rather cross," he said—replied that the administration's failure to protest anything on the lengthening list of treaty violations had put the United States "out of court." Bryan felt misunderstood and rather cross himself.

Unable to make headway with the administration, Spring Rice privately urged other Americans to see that their country was well fortified. "You will want a big army one of these days and when you want it you'll want it damn bad and won't have it," he wrote one of his American friends. Rudyard Kipling was another Englishman who believed that if Germany triumphed in Europe, its next target would be the United States. "You have time yet to prepare against that," Kipling wrote a friend in Boston, "but you haven't too much time, and I must beg you to use all the influence you have to put this fact before your people. . . . I know it is almost impossible to get your people to believe these things, and you may be perfectly sure that Germany (as she has with us) will deny any hostile intentions *till* her hour strikes."

Roosevelt's attitudes about the war were colored by similar letters from England and by news from his daughter Ethel and her husband, Dick Derby, who had deposited their six-month-old son at Sagamore in late September and gone to Paris to volunteer at the American Hospital. Founded in 1904 to care for Americans in France, the hospital had begun treating wounded soldiers soon after the start of the war. Dick had charge of a surgical ward with a hundred beds. Ethel spent mornings in the dispensary, assisting with dressings and splints and taking patients for X-rays. Friends and Roosevelt cousins had given her money to use where needed, but the needs far outstripped her purse.

The patients quickly attached themselves to Dr. and Mrs. Derby. "It is perfectly wonderful to see the way all the men in D's ward adore him," Ethel reported to the family. "They always say, 'Well, anything the tall Dr. does is all right,' and try to escape from the others." Ethel took on the case of an Irish boy who had lost a leg and was inconsolable because he felt sure that the girl he had left behind would no longer want to marry him.

Why not get an artificial leg? Ethel asked him.

He could not afford it, he said.

"I know what I am going to do with Cousin Christine's money: buy a new leg for a boy from Tipperary," Ethel wrote Sagamore.

Ethel stayed away from the wards but saw enough to understand the horror. "I cannot believe that men should do such things to each other," she wrote Edith. The phrase "such appalling wounds" appears more than once in her letters home. Haunted too by the refugees flooding into Paris from Belgium and northern France, Ethel spent afternoons working with organizations that helped them find shelter and work. Many of the dispossessed were children separated from their parents, some so young they did not yet know their names.

Ethel, who had visited Paris several times before the war, felt an unfamiliar "nervous, apprehensive undercurrent" in the life of the city. Aerial bombing was new and highly imperfect but did enough damage to keep the civilian population on edge. In October, only two months into the war, government officials were telling the Derbys that both sides were exhausted, and a British officer down from the front told them that the Allies were barely holding the line.

Ethel and Dick sailed home in time for Christmas at Sagamore, where there were three grandchildren in residence for the holidays—their own baby, Richard Derby, Jr., plus Ted and Eleanor's children, Gracie and Theodore III. From paterfamilias to the babies, the Roosevelts were thriving. Alice and Nick's exile in Cincinnati was coming to an end. Ted was prospering as an investment banker and through his business connections had helped Kermit into a position as assistant manager of City National Bank's branch in Buenos Aires. Archie was holding his own at Harvard. "He is a trump, so amusing and interesting, so devoted to all of us, and so absolutely independent, self-reliant, and self-respecting," TR reported to Kermit.

The only cloud over the family's Christmas was a worry about Ethel, who underwent a surgery of some sort just before New Year's Day and would soon need an appendectomy. Her father laid the maladies to the strain of her months in France. "I am no friend to having women traipsing abroad to take part in what ought to be men's job," he wrote Kermit. "It is too rough on them." He was proud of the work she and Dick had done but had sizable qualms about the value of the Americans who were driving ambulances, working with the Red Cross, and aiding refugees. Big countries like England and France could manage on their own, he thought, and the chorus of accolades for the volunteers was creating the impression that the United States was doing its part in the Great War.

In December TR signed a three-year contract with a crusading monthly called *Metropolitan*. The magazine would pay Roosevelt $25,000 a year for fifty thousand words. "What I have to say on social and political questions

... will be said purely through them," he wrote Kermit. The country was largely indifferent to him, he said, but there was "a certain grim satisfaction in having the American people pay me heavily to hear from me what they won't listen to if I give it to them free."

Now openly supporting England and France, he berated the German-American press for its defense of Germany and declared that American neutrality was morally untenable. The Germans had done wrong, and in his view, "to be neutral between right and wrong is to serve wrong." He advised Edward Grey and Cecil Spring Rice to see that American war correspondents were well tended by the Allies. The Germans were masters of propaganda, and Roosevelt feared that they were winning the war for American sympathy.

Again and again Roosevelt urged the United States to gird itself against attack. With a group of Princeton students, he resorted to scare tactics, saying that he knew of two armies with plans to invade the United States. The speech was denounced as flagrantly partial to the Allies, and more than one critic considered it flagrantly misleading as well. As William Howard Taft pointed out to the journalist Gus Karger, armies keep themselves on the mettle by planning hypothetical invasions around the world.

THEODORE ROOSEVELT would not have been Theodore Roosevelt if the dramas in his life had come one at a time. In April 1915, a few days before he went to Syracuse for the trial of *Barnes v. Roosevelt*, Edith entered Roosevelt Hospital in Manhattan for what Theodore termed a "severe and trying operation." That and other euphemisms in the family's letters gesture toward a hysterectomy. Edith was fifty-three, an age when menopause might well have been the cause of her chronic lassitude. She easily weathered the surgery, he visited the hospital daily, and on April 18, before catching his train to Syracuse, he stopped by to read to her for an hour or two.

Barnes had wanted the case tried in Albany, where he was boss, but Roosevelt's lawyers won a change of venue to Syracuse, where it fell to Judge William M. Andrews, who had been in Roosevelt's class at Harvard. The school tie would do the defendant no good. The plaintiff had also graduated from Harvard, and Judge Andrews was an exceptionally impartial man. His aversion to leaning one way or another showed in his rulings during the trial and in his hair, which he brushed back on the right and forward on the left.

At stake in *Barnes v. Roosevelt* were $50,000 in damages, the right to call a crook a crook in print, and two political futures. William Barnes, Jr., had been a power among Republican conservatives in New York since 1892. Grandson of another political boss, Thurlow Weed, and heir to Weed's *Albany Evening Journal*, Barnes ran campaigns, lobbied, and steadily swelled the family fortune with printing contracts from the city, county, and state.

Barnes yearned for a seat in the U.S. Senate and sued partly in hopes of clearing his name before embarking on a campaign. He also dreamed of eliminating Roosevelt from politics. Barnes had watched the Rough Rider since his 1898 gubernatorial race, when his arrivals at campaign stops were announced by a bugler blasting the cavalry charge. "You have heard the trumpet that sounded to bring you here," the candidate would say. "I have heard it tear the tropic dawn when it summoned us to fight at Santiago." It was an odd bit of theater for state politics, but Roosevelt was the hero of the splendid little war just ended, and the thought of a hero in the governor's mansion seemed to please the people of New York. Barnes had been among the joyful when Roosevelt was abducted for the vice presidency in 1900.

Roosevelt had little hope of winning the case. The big victor in the election of 1914 was the Republican machine, and among Republicans in New York, the feeling against him was maniacal. In other circles he was not despised, but many of his countrymen disapproved of his criticism of American neutrality. At the libel trial in Marquette, he had been anxious about the political affiliations of the jurors. In Syracuse, which had a sizable German community, he worried about their nationalities as well. Seventy-five interviews produced a jury of six Republicans, three Progressives, and three Democrats. The only German-American empaneled seemed safe enough: he was a supplier to the Allied armies.

Barnes's chief counsel was a tall, erudite gentleman of sixty-four, William M. Ivins, who had an acidic sense of humor and an intellectual range that rivaled Roosevelt's. Ivins knew botany and baseball, was a passionate avocational student of cellular biology and Napoleon, and had mastered five languages. He too had been an unsuccessful Republican candidate for mayor of New York. And he too was a supremely confident man, boasting that he would "nail Roosevelt's hide to the fence."

Ivins often came to court in spats and a silk skull cap, touches so arresting that the newspapermen neglected to say what if anything he wore in between. For the theater of the courtroom, Ivins adopted two personae, soul of reason and angry god. His first go at Roosevelt opened with a long encomium, the length serving to swell the tension for the inevitable evisceration. Roosevelt's assault on Barnes's character had been published from coast to coast, and the very scale of the humiliation demanded recompense, Ivins said. "It is inconceivable that any man could live under his own roof with a remnant of self-respect unless he does what the law practically compels him to do."

Planting his spats close to Roosevelt's chair, Ivins glowered into his face and shouted, "We now call upon this man, who has set himself up as an arbiter of morals, to prove what he has said." Ivins erected his case on the notion that Roosevelt was a hypocrite and therefore not to be believed when he slurred a man. Governor Roosevelt had publicly presented himself as the unsullied champion of honesty in government while privately backing the bosses' candidates for office and bestowing his patronage on their friends, Ivins told the jury.

Roosevelt cheerfully admitted that Ivins was right. He had obliged the bosses when he could, he said, "to keep the organization intact and to make it the responsive servant of the people as a whole." He added that he broke with the bosses when he thought their friends did not merit support and when their legislative desires conflicted with his vision of the public weal. Among other things he had defied their opposition to an income tax increase for corporations.

Roosevelt addressed himself to the jury, testifying at times with his whole body, thrusting, jabbing, jutting out his chin. Ivins asked Judge Andrews to ask the witness to confine his testimony to the English language, but Andrews saw no reason for Roosevelt to be anything less than his great big self.

Ivins introduced Roosevelt's correspondence with another boss, the late Thomas C. Platt, a U.S. senator from New York, and as the letters plainly showed, Platt had assisted Roosevelt's friends who needed favors in Washington, and Roosevelt had reciprocated in Albany. Roosevelt was visibly discomfited by the exposure but rose to the moment by asking that his entire correspondence with Platt go into the record. It was an agile move, the whole being more benign than the selected parts.

After Roosevelt's first week of testimony, *The Nation* magazine said that as governor, TR had been "a vigorous young man, not too fastidious, intensely ambitious, consumed with desire for high office, who had deliberately made up his mind that the road to success for him lay with the party organization and the party boss." Ex-President Roosevelt, no longer able to help the bosses, no longer commanded their loyalty. Only then did he begin to rage against their iniquities. *The Nation* was correct. Roosevelt and

Barnes had not fallen out until 1910, when Roosevelt threw his influence behind the bill to create primaries in New York and the Barnes machine flattened him and the bill. Barnes had also been a major barrier to Roosevelt's success in 1912.

The attorney for the defense, John M. Bowers, was a partner in the New York firm that had represented Roosevelt in his libel suit in Michigan. A compact man who parted his dark hair in the center and wore a beard and mustache, Bowers thought he could acquit Roosevelt by proving that his allegation of Barnes's corruption was true. Six months of investigation by Bowers had turned up misdeed upon misdeed in Barnes's business dealings. Barnes had systematically bilked the taxpayers of Albany and New York through overly large print runs, needless reprinting, and double-billing. His repertoire of financial tricks was long on kickbacks, dummy corporations, and phony transactions.

Bowers illustrated the collusion of Boss Barnes and Boss Murphy by revisiting a 1911 power struggle over a U.S. Senate seat that Murphy had reserved for a Democratic machine man. Until the 1913 ratification of the Constitution's Seventeenth Amendment, which provided for the direct election of U.S. senators, New York chose its two senators in a joint session of the state legislature, and by Albany custom, the boss of the party in power had the first and last say in the matter. When Murphy picked a rich antediluvian named William F. Sheehan, Franklin Delano Roosevelt and seventeen other young Democrats in the state senate rebelled. The rebels proposed another candidate, Murphy rejected him, and Barnes helped Murphy by lining up the Republicans behind a Republican with no chance of winning. After a long standoff, Murphy deserted Sheehan for someone more palatable to FDR's upstarts. ("You know these Roosevelts," another boss is said to have said. "This fellow is still young. Wouldn't it be safer to drown him before he grows up?") No laws were broken in the Barnes-Murphy maneuver, but Bowers used it to buttress Roosevelt's charge that a boss would rather side with the enemy than risk harm to his machine.

Barnes had a thundercloud of a face, but on the witness stand, he too addressed himself to the jury, and the face grew "gay, confidential, almost jovial," wrote C. W. Thompson of the *New York Times*. With all the gentleness of a father forced to come clean about Santa Claus, Barnes explained the iron necessity of bossism. A government could not function without political parties, he said, and a political party was a great, dumb beast in need of driving by someone with a whip. Party members "must move in order, or they do not move at all." Cynical as Barnes's view was, it provided an insight into a mortal weakness of the Progressive Party: the beast would not consent to be driven.

As the lawyers and the judge tunneled through an Everest of printing house ledgers, Roosevelt entertained himself with the comedies of Aristophanes. Ivins had presented him with a handsome edition of the plays, thinking, he said, that it might stave off boredom. First-rate translation, he told the Colonel. Delighted, said TR, and judging by his chuckles, he was. Ivins enjoyed keeping Roosevelt off balance, chatting cordially with him at quiet moments, then flaying him for the jury. The gift of Aristophanes was surely a gibe, and Roosevelt surely understood it. Four of the comedies were written to protest the Peloponnesian War, in which the Athenians had been annihilated at Syracuse.

Ivins asked Judge Andrews to rule out the evidence of misbehavior in the Albany printing trade, arguing that Roosevelt's allegation had not mentioned Barnes's business dealings and that the business dealings were not clearly linked to Barnes's political activities. The judge decided to admit only the printing evidence contained in an old report from a state investigation into public corruption, and he told Bowers that he would have to show the connections between Barnes's "crooked business" and his "crooked politics," prove that waste and corruption did exist, and prove that Barnes was aware of the lawbreaking.

Roosevelt was devastated. "I believe this practically ends the case, so far as any hope of my winning is concerned," he wrote Ethel. He readied himself for the worst. "I have had a wonderful run for my money," he wrote Kermit. "From 1898 to 1910 everything went my way, and I had a great career, and I have no complaint because during the last five years things have gone the other way." But the prospect of humiliation unleashed a yearning for one more drama. If only he were being tried in a criminal court, he went on. "I feel intensely in the matter and I would cheerfully go to the penitentiary rather than take back what I said about Barnes and Murphy and the politics for which they stand. Moreover, I think it would make even our utterly indifferent people sit up and take notice if I were sent to the penitentiary for acting as I have acted."

F OR A FEW DAYS in May, events in Syracuse were overshadowed by the sinking of the British passenger ship *Lusitania*. More than 1,900 persons were aboard when the liner was torpedoed by a German submarine on Friday, May 7, 1915, off the southern coast of Ireland, and the 1,200 dead included 128 Americans. The event outraged England and so shocked the United States that Americans would always remember where they were when they heard about it.

The law of the sea, written long before the age of submarine warfare, guaranteed the safe passage of a neutral country's merchant fleet in wartime but permitted the seizure and scuttling of an enemy's merchant ships after passengers and crew were safely removed. But when the British began arming their merchant ships, German submarine commanders could hardly be expected to escort captured vessels to port, nor could they be expected to refrain from exploiting their greatest strength, the power to stalk unseen and strike without warning. Germany had given notice of the dangers before the *Lusitania* left New York and blamed the sinking on England for allowing its passenger ships to carry munitions.

Henry Whigham, *Metropolitan's* editor, telephoned Roosevelt in Syracuse on Saturday night to ask for an editorial on the *Lusitania*. It reached the magazine on Monday morning. Roosevelt's piece excoriated the Germans and likened the attack to "the wholesale poisoning of wells in the path of a hostile army, or the shipping of infected rags into the cities of a hostile country." The United States should cease all commerce with Germany and as compensation for the American lives lost should seize the German ships already interned in its waters, Roosevelt wrote. "I do not believe that the firm assertion of our rights means war, but, in any event, it is well to remember there are things worse than war."

Not wanting the editorial to wait until the next issue of *Metropolitan* appeared, Whigham asked permission to release it to the newspapers. Roosevelt gave his consent in spite of protests from John Bowers, who anticipated a quick surge of anti-German sentiment and feared that Roosevelt's opinion might cost him the vote of the German-American on the jury.

Wilson's response to the catastrophe, made in a speech to an audience of naturalized citizens, was published a day ahead of Roosevelt's. America must set a special example, he said, an example "not merely of peace because it will not fight, but of peace because peace is the healing and elevating influence of the world and strife is not. There is such a thing as a man being too proud to fight."

The president sent the Germans a stiff note deploring the attack on the

Lusitania, but it was not stiff enough to suit Roosevelt, and as anyone who knew the Colonel could have foreseen, the "too proud to fight" phrase struck him as sissified. He decided not to comment on Wilson's speech but privately wrote a friend that he thought Wilson was "not carrying out any policy at all save one of words merely, which he tries to make strong enough to satisfy our people that something is being done and at the same time to enable him to dodge out of doing anything to Germany."

Five weeks in Syracuse cost Roosevelt somewhere between $30,000 and $40,000, and the press corps guessed that Barnes had spent as much as $60,000. Each of them vowed to appeal if he lost. Bowers had been deprived of the opportunity to make a full case for Barnes's corruption, Ivins had not proved that Roosevelt's inflammatory words were false or malicious, leaving the litigants in a deadlock as the closing arguments began.

In his last argument to the jury, Bowers led with a turning of the tables, presenting his client as the injured party. Barnes's suit was "the purposed act of the political machine to destroy Theodore Roosevelt's usefulness to the people," he said. Bowers held forth for three and a half hours, reading statements by others who had called Barnes corrupt but had not been hounded by lawsuits. Bowers quoted Roosevelt's 1906 "Man with the Muckrake" speech, the sharp castigation of journalists whose careless falsehoods destroyed the careers of men in public life, and averred that a man of such sympathies would not frivolously impugn another man's character. Roosevelt had spoken truthfully, Bowers said, and it was "a noble thing to make such a statement if it is true and the public ought to know it."

Bowers worked in a mention of George Washington and concluded with a reading of the Gettysburg Address, bathing Roosevelt in the glow of Lincoln. The plea for malice toward none and charity for all in Lincoln's second inaugural address would have been more apt, but Bowers was reading from a best-selling book about the Gettysburg speech, *The Perfect Tribute* by Mary Raymond Shipman Andrews, wife of the presiding judge.

Ivins did not conceal his contempt. "This wasn't an appeal to reason, it wasn't an appeal to the evidence," he told the jury. He ended where he had begun: Roosevelt's word could not be trusted. "You have seen how he violated the oath taken by him upon his election to the presidency not to be a candidate for a third term. You have seen how, year after year, he snatched at dominance and power. . . . The whole trouble with the defendant in this case has been that he did not follow Cardinal Wolsey's advice to Cromwell: 'I charge you, fling away ambition; by that sin the angels fell.' "

With instructions from Judge Andrews, the jury went off to deliberate. Barnes and Ivins left town, but Roosevelt stayed, determined, he said, "to take the gaff without flinching." On May 22, forty-two hours after the jurors' departure, they returned to say that they had found Theodore Roosevelt guilty of nothing.

Roosevelt had turned the trial into a show, staging it as brilliantly as he had staged his bolt from the Republican Party. "The room rang with him, was shot through with him," C. W. Thompson wrote in the *Times*. "His huge personality overbore everything else: it animated the whole case. He took charge of it, and the lawyers were dragged along after the chariot in his gigantic rush. . . . As for the jury, it was spellbound."

Ivins died a few weeks after the trial, Barnes's appeal was denied, and the Barnes machine soon fell apart. "Of all the blundering lunatics I have ever known, Barnes is the worst," one of Roosevelt's enemies remarked. "Here we had Roosevelt . . . dead and buried politically. We were rid of him for all time. Now Barnes has not only opened the door for him to come back, but he has pushed him through to the front of the stage and made him a more popular idol than ever."

Roosevelt knew better. "I have been like an engine bucking a snowdrift," he wrote a friend soon after the trial. "My progress was slower and slower; and finally I accumulated so much snow that I came to a halt and could not get through." He could win an audience when he could reach it personally, as he had done with the jury, he said, but he could no longer succeed with the public at large, which had set itself against his return to public office.

The half-god seemed content to rest, leaving the struggle for political power to such gods as might arise. But an exit is not the same as a disappearance, and in a world gone savagely, wildly godless, a half-god need not be unemployed.

FIFTEEN

Wild Surmise

BRIEFLY, the half-god disappeared into his forest, reveling in the dogwood and birdsong of spring. Ecstatic at Theodore's victory, Edith hoped that he would at last "be satisfied to keep entirely out of politics, and not feel that he must carry every lame dog on his back." For a time she had her wish. In July, Ted reported to Kermit that their father was "absolutely out of politics now and devoting his time and energy to make this country realize the need for preparedness."

Father was pushing a large rock up a steep hill. The president had dismissed the champions of preparedness as "nervous and excited" and assured Americans that their country was well defended. Told that Major General Leonard Wood, the army's former chief of staff, believed in maintaining an army and navy strong enough to make an invasion unthinkable, Wilson saw only the political hazards of giving generals and admirals their way. Large forces were expensive and in his view un-American, turning the nation into an armed camp and requiring young men to spend their best years as soldiers.

Privately, though, Wilson wondered how many voters shared Roosevelt's disdain for the "too proud to fight" speech and for the diplomatic notes he sent Germany in hopes of ending the submarine attacks on merchant vessels. The first note after the sinking of the *Lusitania* was written in a tone that Secretary of State William Jennings Bryan, a pacifist, thought overly confrontational, and it brought the impenitent reply that the *Lusitania* had been sunk in self-defense. On June 8, as Wilson was putting the last touches on a second note, a sternly worded demand that Germany rededicate itself to the "rights of humanity," Bryan resigned.

One of the president's aides confided to Gus Karger that Wilson's severe tone was meant to "pocket" Roosevelt, but Roosevelt was no more pocketed than Germany. Later in the summer, when his daughter Alice told him that Wilson had written yet another note, TR sarcastically asked if she had noticed the serial number. He had lost track, he said, "but I am inclined to think it is No. 11,765, Series B." He saw the notes as "milk-and-water" and predicted that they would encourage the Germans to more "blood-and-iron."

The dangers Roosevelt saw were largely invisible to the rest of the country. Protected by two wide moats, the Atlantic and the Pacific, Americans felt no need for more army or navy and enjoyed thinking that their goodwill and peaceable intentions enabled them to walk the world without brandishing a big stick. Congressman Gardner of Massachusetts, Lodge's son-in-law, met rebuff in every quarter when he called for a bipartisan commission to assess the state of the nation's defenses. The president summoned Gardner to the White House to tell him that such an inquiry might suggest hostile intentions on the part of the United States. Gardner pressed on, enlisting five former secretaries of war to explain the need for the investigation to the House Rules Committee. The committee refused to see them.

The congressman's prodding eventually led to a War Department study of the country's coastal defenses and a soothing report, which Gardner challenged. The artillery along the Eastern seaboard could not shoot nearly as far as the newest guns on British and German warships, he told an audience in New York. "It is said that a steady platform is so much superior to the gun on a battleship deck on the rolling ocean, but what does that matter, when a foreign fleet could remain outside of New York Harbor a mile and a half out of the range of our guns and play mashie shots into our forts?"

In desperation Gardner invited the entire enlisted reserve of the army to dinner at a Washington hotel. All sixteen attended. His point could not have been plainer, but few cared to hear him or Roosevelt or anyone else who thought the United States in danger of invasion.

Although neglected by Taft and Wilson, the U.S. Navy was still among the world's largest, but in one of his first articles on preparedness, Roosevelt reported that the navy's thirty-one battleships were obsolete and had not been on maneuvers for nearly two years. Would you field a football team that hadn't practiced in two years? he asked. The navy had also fallen down on recruiting, leaving itself undermanned even by peacetime standards.

The *Fortnightly Review* of London, noting that the 100,000-man U.S. Army was the same size as the army of Montenegro, drew a blunt conclusion: "As a military power; the United States can hardly be said to have any existence." In truth the figure of 100,000 grossly exaggerated the army's fighting strength. When the support staff, the coastal defense force, and the men on sick leave or furlough were subtracted, the field army numbered 45,000. The National Guard and organized militias added a theoretical 18,000 officers and 260,000 men, but the count was a guess and the troops largely untrained.

William Jennings Bryan, a freelance apostle for peace after he left the State Department, declared that there was no cause for fear. If the United States were attacked at dawn, a million patriots would spring to arms before sunset, he said. Roosevelt begged to know where the arms would come from and how the volunteers would know what to do. Bryan refused to be alarmed. War was wrong, the possession of battleships and arsenals meant war when national tempers flared, and Europe's quarrels would never wash up on American shores if the United States maintained its neutrality. These things he knew. "His mind is not broad, but it is strong," wrote one political correspondent, and he was "always ready to fight for his beliefs."

In moral certitude and moral combativeness Roosevelt was easily Bryan's equal. Hindsight would show Roosevelt the better prophet, but in 1915 and 1916, as he called for preparedness in speeches and in articles for *Metropolitan,* Taft dismissed his ideas as "jingohypnotism." *Metropolitan,* which published Margaret Sanger's arguments for birth control and John Reed's rhapsodies on Pancho Villa, seemed a peculiar editorial home for Roosevelt, who disapproved of birth control, Pancho Villa, and most of the radical notions in the magazine. But the editors valued Roosevelt because they had more faith in his forehanded approach to defense and foreign policy than in the "watchful waiting" of Woodrow Wilson.

Perhaps because they feared giving offense to a former president, the senior editors of *Metropolitan* assigned the editing of Roosevelt's columns to one of its youngest staff members, Sonya Levien; a Russian immigrant of socialist sympathies. The Colonel's prose tended toward the adipose, and when Levien diffidently showed him her first efforts to cut his redundancies, he put her at ease. "A very serious offense in my life," he said. "I find that my copy can always be improved by cutting." He fondly called her "Little Miss Anarchist," and she remarked that in his work habits he was as fastidiously bourgeois as any bank clerk. He playfully protested, saying that he would rather be thought of as a gunman than a banker, because gunmen did business in the open.

Levien would come to believe that Roosevelt's indignation about military and international affairs sprang not from his romance with war but from a sense of injury. "One felt that he had loved his country with the same tenderness, pride, and devotion that a mother bears to an only child, and that the child had disgraced itself," she would write after his death.

Despite real anguish over the disgraced child, TR thoroughly enjoyed his two days a week at *Metropolitan*. The staff soon discovered that he had a wonderful time in the same way that cyclones do. There was a good deal of whirling in and out, people and chairs blew into his office, and if a roar emanated from his suite, it meant that TR had dropped to all fours to play bear with a small boy whose father had brought him to meet the original Teddy. As a colleague, he was genial, funny, and seemingly indifferent to the exalted status of the public Theodore Roosevelt. Levien understood the staff's affection for him but never figured out how a man "so thick-set, of rather abdominal contour, with eyes heavily spectacled, could have had such an air of magic and wild romance about him, could give so stirring an impression of adventure and chivalry."

The best explanation is that he loved life, and his joy splashed everyone who came near. The timid were slightly unsettled by it, and certain refined types found it faintly repellent, but as a journalist often in his company once said, you had to hate the Colonel a whole lot to keep from loving him.

THEODORE AND EDITH spent much of the summer of 1915 away from Sagamore, traveling first to the South and then to San Francisco for the Panama-Pacific International Exposition, an extravaganza got up to celebrate the recent opening of the Panama Canal and the four-hundredth anniversary of Balboa's discovery of the Pacific. Both Roosevelts would have been able to quote Keats's imagining of the moment when the explorer and his men, reaching a mountain peak on the isthmus, glimpsed their new ocean, and "Look'd at each other with a wild surmise." Theodore, being Theodore, liked to point out that Keats had mixed up his Spaniards and credited the find to Cortéz, and as someone who savored the sounds of poetry, Theodore could hardly have resisted adding that historical accuracy would have spoiled the meter.

The exposition, a square mile of Beaux Arts palaces and pavilions painted in pastels, was both an elegy for the Old West and a hymn to modernity. For 50 cents, a visitor could ponder the juxtaposition of a sculptured Indian and the bubbling Fountain of Psychology or gape at the miracle in the Palace of Transportation, where a new Model T materialized every ten minutes. The pride of forty nations and as many states was on display, Japan's in an exquisite garden, China's in a replica of the Forbidden City. Germany had come with mesothorium, a radioactive substance used in the treatment of cancer. France was promoting tourism as if there were no war and showing off the sword used by Lafayette in the American Revolution. Aboard a moving platform twenty feet in the air, fairgoers could traverse a four-acre topographical map of the Canal Zone, complete with canal.

Roosevelt had been invited to the exposition to deliver an address and for two hours, before a crowd of thousands, he scourged Woodrow Wilson without mentioning his name. If in 1903 the United States had met the Panamanian revolution with diplomatic notes and no action, the canal would still be unbuilt, he said. And if the people of the United States wished to know what happened to nations too proud to fight, they might consider the sorry Chinese, whose pacifism had cost them half their territory. Defenseless, they had had to yield whenever the great powers made demands. "The professional pacifists, the peace-at-any-price, non-resistance, universal arbitration people are now seeking to Chinafy this country," Roosevelt warned. He closed with a call for universal military training patterned on the Swiss system, which required every able-bodied young man to spend a few years under arms. "Men who are not ready to fight for the right are not fit to live in a free democracy," he declared.

Roosevelt's denunciation of pacifists, his refusal even to grant the nobility of their dream, hardened the public's impression of him as a jingo and erased from common memory his Nobel Peace Prize and his immense pride in his warless presidency. He mocked Andrew Carnegie's work for peace and ridiculed the Women's Peace Party, which his old friend Jane Addams had organized soon after the start of the war. Carnegie, now eighty and seeing no end to the slaughter in Europe, had withdrawn to his garden, where he sat for hours on end, blanketed and still, blue eyes locked in a stare.

Addams and the Women's Peace Party were pursuing an idea they called "continuous mediation," to be conducted by an international commission that would study the grievances of the belligerents and issue peace proposals—as many as necessary to bring the warring parties into mediation. In 1915, as Addams and her companions were leaving for Europe to explain their idea, Roosevelt wrote one of them a letter deriding it as "silly and base."

Addams met with eight prime ministers and nine foreign ministers and returned under the impression that all but one would cooperate if the United States convened a conference of neutrals to discuss continuous mediation. It appears that she mistook their cordiality for commitment, and when she met with President Wilson on her return, he too rejected the idea. She deduced that he wished to reserve the role of peacemaker for himself.

In a book about her trip, Addams told of meeting a mother who had lost a son in the war, a woman whose "very conception of human nature had received a sharp shock and setback. To her the whole world . . . would henceforth seem less kind and her spirit would be less at home. She was tormented by that ever recurring question which perhaps never can be answered for any of us too confidently in the affirmative, 'Is the Universe friendly?' "

Theodore Roosevelt believed, most definitely, that it was not. His universe could be made friendlier by the law, but behind the law there must be an enforcer—"the just man armed, the man who scorns to wrong others and is fearless in the face of the wrongdoer." Wrongdoers were a fact of life in his universe, a supposition that made him impatient to the point of savagery with those who opposed all war on principle.

Nor could Roosevelt make room for the Darwinian antiwar argument of David Starr Jordan, a distinguished ichthyologist who liked him enough to name a new species of trout *Salmo roosevelti*. Chancellor of Stanford University and a leader of the international arbitration movement, Jordan argued that war weakened the species *Homo sapiens* by killing off its strongest members, generally before they had an opportunity to reproduce. The notion that people grew soft in times of peace was rubbish, Jordan wrote in 1915. "A time of peace is the only time when men accomplish anything worth remembering." His most potent example, surely an appeal to the pride of Theodore Roosevelt, was the building of the canal and the eradication of yellow fever in Panama.

Jordan's thesis ought to have intrigued the naturalist in Roosevelt, but it conflicted with his conviction that a civilization without "barbarian virtues" and a fighting edge was doomed. Debating the Jordan species of pacifist was fruitless, TR wrote a friend; "drowning is the most merciful of the various legitimate ways of handling that particular type of blind kitten." To another friend, who wanted him to lash back when a pacifist accused him of militarism, TR replied that he could not be bothered. He considered the offender, Oswald Garrison Villard, publisher of the *New York Evening Post* and *The Nation*, "the kind of crawling thing we step on, provided the resulting crunch won't leave too large a stain on the floor." He despised the pacifists and Woodrow "too proud to fight" Wilson because he saw them as weak. Roosevelt the boy had overcome his weakness, but Roosevelt the man never lost his horror of it.

WITH NO POLITICAL CHORES looming after the Barnes trial, TR had time for an endeavor he had had to set aside for months: organizing a force of volunteer soldiers to go to Europe if the United States entered the war. In the 1880s, when he was ranching in the Dakotas, he had written the secretary of war volunteering to assemble companies of mounted riflemen for duty with the cavalry regulars fighting on the Mexican border. In 1898 he had helped to recruit and train the Rough Riders, and in 1911 he made President Taft a grander version of the same offer, a full division in the event of war with Mexico.

This time Roosevelt did not seek official sanction. He worked quietly, drawing up lists of officers, asking friends to help with the recruiting, and devising a table of organization for a cavalry division. "Of course, we might have to fight in the trenches on foot, and we might have to fight in motor cars instead of on horses," he wrote Kermit and Belle in Buenos Aires; "we would do whatever it was necessary to do." A few days later, in a letter to Kermit alone, he shared his fondest dream for the division: "If we fight Germany, all of you—and I—would go in."

Except for Kermit, the Colonel's sons were about to learn the basics of soldiering, under the aegis of General Leonard Wood, now commander of the army's Eastern Department. Ted and his friends had talked Wood into offering a month of military instruction to businessmen, at their expense, at a training camp in upstate New York, near Plattsburg (which had not yet rounded off its name with an "h"). The ranks included Ted and his brother-in-law Dick Derby; John Purroy Mitchel, the thirty-five-year-old "boy mayor" of New York; and the young manhood of Park Avenue, Beacon Hill, and the Main Line. Inevitably there were tales of valets motoring up with fresh laundry, but the 1,400 volunteers spent twelve-hour days building trenches, waging mock battles, and practicing marksmanship. "It is real work without the slightest touch of the tin-soldier business about it," TR wrote Kermit.

Together with hundreds of other college students, Archie and Quentin spent a month at Plattsburg before the businessmen arrived. Archie was invited to stay on as a second lieutenant and, to the Colonel's delight, had his older, somewhat officious brother Ted under his command. Quentin received a certificate attesting to his good work, but he did not share the family's fervor for Plattsburg—an attitude understandable in a boy just released from six regimented years at Groton.

Dick, thirty-four and accustomed to exercising considerable autonomy in his work as a surgeon, was surprised by the pleasures of losing himself in a company of 125 men. "You feel yourself to be nothing—merely a cog in a powerful machine that is marching irresistibly on," he wrote Ethel. "And then the tramp of 250 feet on the hard macadam road thrills you with a sensation entirely new. You are part of it, and you are glad and proud that you are, and are ever alert to make the whole as perfect as is in your power." Dick was a poor shot but stayed on the rifle range till he felt he had attained respectability if not perfection.

For Plattsburg's parade day, August 25, General Wood invited President Wilson and former Presidents Taft and Roosevelt to speak to the volunteers. Only Roosevelt accepted, and after he said he would come, he telegraphed Wood with several requests. Could he deliver the speech at the end of the day, when the men were finished with their work? And might he speak somewhere outside the camp? He also asked that no one be required to attend and that the volunteers not wear their uniforms.

Wood gave his consent, and two businessmen-soldiers in residence, probably alerted by a newspaperman familiar with the gist of the speech, advised him to review Roosevelt's text before giving him the floor. Wood asked to see it when Roosevelt arrived and suggested a few excisions. Roosevelt obliged, and they went off to watch field exercises, meet a delegation from the Canadian army, and review the regiment on parade.

At dusk, five thousand volunteers, army regulars, and townspeople gathered on the drill plain to listen to the Colonel. Costumed in tan riding suit, leather leggings, and a cream-colored hat with a broad brim, he strode onto his stage. Lake Champlain, stretching away behind him, soon faded into the night and he stood alone in a pool of lantern light. He opened with praise for the courage of the Plattsburg men, but his pleasantries were pro forma, a short preamble to the dark thought that courage counted for naught without a strong army and navy. He repeated his charges against "Chinafying" pacifists, condemned neutrality that recognized no distinction between right and wrong, and explained the role of a soldier in a democracy. A good soldier hated war but hated injustice and aggression more, he said. "It is an abhorrent thing to make a wanton or an unjust war. It is an abhorrent thing to trespass on the rights of the weak. But it is utterly contemptuous to be unable and unwilling to fight for one's own rights in the first place and then, if possessed of sufficient loftiness of soul, to fight for the rights of the weak who are wronged."

For more than a year, the United States had played an ignoble part, he went on. "We have tamely submitted to seeing the weak, whom we had covenanted to protect, wronged. We have seen our own men, women and children murdered on the high seas, without action on our part." And nothing had been done to strengthen the country's defenses. "Reliance upon high-sounding words unbacked by deeds is proof of a mind that dwells only in the realm of shadow and of sham."

He ended with an exhortation to the highest standards of international morality. The United States must treat other nations justly, keep its promises to secure just treatment for others, and show the world that a democracy could defend itself against aggression. To survive, he said, "we must prepare as a nation; and the men of this camp and the men responsible for starting this camp have shown our Government and our people the path along which we should tread."

After the cheering, which was robust, Roosevelt headed for the train station, where he unburdened himself of the passages Wood had asked him to censor. Standing by the president was wise only when the president stood by the country, he told the newspapermen. Not all presidents were alike. Lincoln deserved loyalty, Buchanan did not. Had Lincoln been too proud to fight after the fall of Fort Sumter, had he spent months writing eloquent notes to Jefferson Davis, the Union would have perished.

Wilson was irked but would not be lured into a public quarrel. ("The only way to treat an adversary like Roosevelt is to gaze at the stars over his head," he once told an aide.) He retaliated by proxy, using the secretary of war, Lindley Garrison, to reprimand the offender's proxy, General Wood. Garrison obliged with a public scolding. No one should have been permitted to speak to the men at Plattsburg on any subject unrelated to their train-

ing, Garrison said in a telegram sent to Wood and released to the press. Anything else was bound to "excite controversy, antagonism, and ill feeling."

Roosevelt hastened to Wood's defense, telling the newspapers that he
alone was responsible for the speech and pointing out that he had not mentioned the president, that no one had been required to attend, and that he
had spoken "outside the line of tents." *The Nation* instantly stepped on the
humbug: no, Roosevelt had not attacked Wilson by name, he had done it by
"covert insult . . . and innuendo. The fearless man! Moreover, he made his
speech 'outside the line of tents.' This from the great hater of technicalities!"

The Colonel tried to goad Garrison into another round, but Garrison
would not go on. Wood promised to abide by the War Department's instructions and a few days later, bidding farewell to the summer soldiers, said
it was his hope and their duty to support the military policies of the president. Privately, Wood assured Roosevelt that there was no cause for regret: "I
am out for national preparedness and I am going to get it."

Seeing no way for Wood to succeed and having no power to help him,
Roosevelt was distraught, and as often happened, his mood shaded Edith's.
"Father and Mother have had hard months," Ethel wrote Belle in October.
"They are both rather depressed, it seems to me—but don't write that back
to them. It is terribly hard to have had everything and been looked up to and
every word worshipped, and then to find that you no longer have an audience."

Writing an English friend about his "elegant row" with the administration, TR observed that Americans were horrified by the prospect of war and
loath to give up their comforts. "Every instinct of self-interest is against their
taking any action at present," he said. If their president told them, "in trumpet tones, that . . . not only the welfare and good name of the United States
but considerations of broad humanity demanded action on their part, and if
he led them in such action, they would respond. But they are sincerely glad
when he furnishes them with excellent excuses, excellent justifications for
nonaction."

At least one of Wilson's ambassadors, Walter Hines Page in London, was
plagued by the same thought. Americans were said to favor neutrality, but
weren't they merely following the president's lead? Page wondered in his
diary. If the president stood up to the Germans instead of writing them
notes, wouldn't the people support him in that, too?

The pacifists suspected that they would and dreaded the thought that
Wilson might change his mind. Marveling at the nation's cool temper after

the sinking of the *Lusitania*, Oswald Villard gave full credit to Wilson and his "too proud to fight" speech. "But it makes you think what terrible power to plunge us into a war a president has," Villard wrote his mother. "If Teddy were there hurrahing for war, I am afraid he would carry the public with him."

Villard and Roosevelt could not yet see it, but Wilson was inching toward preparedness—hoping still to avoid war with Germany but clearly concerned about the vulnerability of the United States. In the summer of 1915 he asked the War and Navy departments to make plans for expansion, and by November he was ready to propose a doubling of the defense budget. He wanted a ten-year program that would put the U.S. Navy on a par with Britain's, a larger regular army, and a new volunteer reserve army of 400,000. The country needed stronger forces not for war, he said, but for defense, "and with the thought constantly in our minds that the principles we hold most dear can be achieved . . . only in the kindly and wholesome atmosphere of peace, and not by the use of hostile force. The mission of America in the world is essentially a mission of peace and goodwill among men."

Villard, stunned, wrote his friend Wilson that the new stance was "anti-moral, anti-social, and anti-democratic. . . . You are sowing the seeds of militarism, raising up a military and naval caste, and the future alone can tell what the further growth will be and what the eventual blossoms."

The decision had not been made lightly, Wilson replied. "These things search the heart and the judgment."

William Jennings Bryan saw Wilson's shift as a betrayal of American ideals and an affront to the Christian precept of leading by example. Military and naval expansion were unnecessary, Bryan told his audiences. The president himself had said as much when he assured the country that the buildup was merely precautionary. And whatever the territorial aspirations of Germany and Austria, they could hardly launch an invasion of the United States while their forces were fully engaged in Europe.

Wilson could not admit that a desire to avoid being pocketed by Roosevelt had led him to change course, but he now saw that the notes to Germany were ineffectual. And the White House strategists planning his reelection campaign for 1916 had convinced him that unless he took a few steps toward preparedness he would be portrayed as the man who had "Chinafied" the United States.

Facing adamant resistance from congressional Democrats, most of whom shared Bryan's belief that the risk of war existed mainly in the minds of the arms makers, Wilson decided to present his case for enlarging the army and navy to the people before taking it to Capitol Hill. "The world is on fire, and there is tinder everywhere," he told an audience in Cleveland at the end of January 1916. His desire to keep the country out of war was undiminished, he said, but the dangers were "infinite and constant," and "I cannot tell you what another day may bring." Throughout his week-long speaking tour, he praised congressional Republicans who had been calling for preparedness and expressed regret that so vital a matter had to be pressed in an election year, when partisan ambitions might skew the debate.

Roosevelt used Wilson's tour as an occasion to blast the administration's foreign policy and its defense plans. In a speech to a large audience in Brooklyn on January 30, he said that Britain had played the part of the Good Samaritan in going to Belgium's aid, while the United States had turned away, failing even to protest the German invasion. He damned the diplomatic notes in the same unsettling terms he had used with Taft's arbitration treaties: "If you tell a man you'll hold him to strict accountability when he slaps your wife's face, and he repeats the offense, the issue isn't met by eleven months' conversation." The notes had merely emboldened Germany to continue its submarine attacks on merchant vessels, killing hundreds of Americans and thousands of noncombatants from other nations.

Nor did the Colonel approve of the president's plan to rely on a relatively small standing army augmented by a large reserve of volunteers. "I no more believe in permitting a man to volunteer to stay at home or refuse to enlist in time of war than I believe in permitting him to volunteer not to pay his taxes in time of peace," he said; the nation would be more secure with a program of universal military training. He did not want war, but if it came, he and his sons would go, and war or no war, Americans had to find the courage to defend the human rights trampled by Germany. "It is by no means necessary that a great nation should always stand on the heroic level," Roosevelt said. "But no nation can be called really great unless it can sometimes rise to a heroic mood."

The *New York Times* was embarrassed for him. "We like the Colonel," the editors wrote. "Everybody likes him when he behaves himself. He is a good fellow when he wants to be. But in his jealous mood, when not even the great questions of the honor and safety of his country can make him submerge his omniprotuberant Ego in a general and nonpartisan patriotism, when he shows so pettishly his resentment that any plan but his for national defense should win favor among his countrymen, then it is not the best of the Colonel that shows." The Colonel, as innocent of his envy as he was of the powerlessness that fueled his rage, blamed his bad temper on the cowardice and incompetence of his successors. He could imagine himself in a heroic mood but not a jealous one. And as everyone who liked the Colonel could see, his vengefulness more or less ensured that his profound understanding of the world crisis never got the consideration it deserved.

THEODORE AND EDITH left Oyster Bay in February for six weeks in the Caribbean, both of them proclaiming their gratitude for an escape from the heat in the Republican and Progressive kitchens. "The political cauldron was boiling at a terrific rate, and I trust by the time we get back things will have settled down," Edith wrote Kermit. She had fled to the tropics exactly four years before and learned while she was away that Theodore had done what she hoped he would not do: succumbed to his desire to run for president.

The latest round of boiling had begun in December with published reports that Roosevelt would support the Republicans in 1916 if they put up a reasonably progressive candidate and platform. But if they nominated a reactionary, he warned, the Progressives would be forced to mount a separate ticket. It was an ultimatum: choose a moderate and win, or choose an archconservative and wage another three-way contest sure to reelect Wilson.

From Trinidad, after he learned that the Republicans of Massachusetts wanted to enter him in their primary, Roosevelt issued a statement asking that his name not appear on any Republican primary ballot. He wanted to continue his work of trying to awaken the country to the "unpleasant facts" of world affairs, he said. "I do not wish the nomination." He would not fight for it or permit others to fight for him. "Indeed," he said, "I will go further and say that it would be a mistake to nominate me unless the country has in its mood something of the heroic." He seemed to be saying that he would not run, but by not ruling himself out, he had signaled his availability. Edith's apprehensions are easily imagined.

The election of 1916 was Theodore Roosevelt's last battle for political power, and the circumstances would make it the strangest, most poignant of his career. In the end he wanted two nominations, Republican and Progressive, and once he had them, he and his followers would merge with the Republicans, consigning the Bull Moose to extinction. As the only public figure who had stood up to Woodrow Wilson, Roosevelt was certain that he deserved the Republican nomination, and he was equally certain that the party did not want him to have it. Undaunted, he would play a wily game from the sidelines, ready to pounce if the party's leaders fumbled.

Home from the Caribbean at the end of March, Roosevelt headed straight for the cauldron. His friend Robert Bacon had arranged a lunch with Lodge, Wood, and Root, someone Roosevelt had not seen since 1912. Root's affection for Roosevelt had survived the schism, and he had come to Bacon's hoping that a personal rapprochement would lead to a reconciliation between Roosevelt and the Republican Party. Host and guests had agreed not to mention their gathering to the press, but when word got out and set off speculation that Root was backing Roosevelt for president, Root was incensed. He parried by allowing admirers to talk up his own candidacy even as he prayed that he would not be asked to run. Sure that the leak had sprung from one of Roosevelt's friends, Root took it as a sign of TR's intention to scrap till the end.

As the most valued member of Roosevelt's cabinet, Root had seen his presidency at close range and admired it, but he opposed TR's nomination in 1916 for the same reason he opposed his own: only a united Republican Party could win the election. A candidate as conservative as Root or as progressive as Roosevelt was sure to exacerbate the tensions that had cracked the party in 1912. Roosevelt appreciated the delicacies but believed he could handle them. "If a cut is to be healed, it must be healed to the bone," he wrote a Republican friend. "If I am nominated and accept the nomination, it will be with the determination to treat the past as completely past and to give absolutely fair play to all my supporters."

The party's leaders were gravitating toward Charles Evans Hughes, who had begun life in upstate New York in 1862, moving from town to town with his evangelist father and his mother, a former teacher. At age five, Charles decided that classroom instruction was a tedium beyond bearing and persuaded his parents to accept the Charles Hughes plan for home study. At ten he was reading Latin and Greek, and at fourteen he went off to a small Baptist college, also tedious. He finished his baccalaureate at Brown, taught school for a year, and at twenty-two graduated first in his class at Columbia University's law school.

In 1905, after two successful decades of practicing commercial law, Hughes made his first contribution to public life, as principal investigator in two New York state probes of corruption. Reporters who covered the proceedings read clean living into Hughes's spare frame, noted the penetrating beam of his deep-set blue eyes, and saw old-fashioned integrity in his luxuriant, old-fashioned beard. Hughes's many findings included the fact that George Perkins of the New York Life Insurance Company had reached into the till to make a large contribution to Roosevelt's 1904 presidential campaign. Elected governor in 1906, Hughes gave the citizens of New York a progressive, honest administration, but the backslapping, logrolling side of politics repelled him, and no one but intimates knew that he had a sense of humor. Archie Butt, who watched him at a White House conference in 1908, thought he had the magnetism of a potato.

TR referred to Hughes as "the bearded iceberg" (sometimes "the bearded lady") and considered him an ingrate. In 1910, Roosevelt had helped him fight Barnes and Murphy, who joined forces to defeat the primary bill, but when Roosevelt asked Hughes to tell the story at the Barnes trial, Hughes claimed not to remember it. "Mr. Hughes is grateful to nobody but Almighty God, and I am not sure he is overgrateful to him," TR told a confidant.

As a healer of cuts, however, Hughes had excellent potential. Tucked away in the Supreme Court since 1910, he had made no enemies in the war of 1912, and he was someone the Progressives could endorse without embarrassment. Roosevelt himself had been saying that Progressives should support Hughes if the Republicans made him their presidential candidate.

The only complication was Hughes, who refused to say whether or not he would accept the nomination and refused to divulge his views on the war or any other issue likely to figure in the campaign. In May, a few weeks before the Republican convention, he consented to a long interview with Walter Lippmann of The New Republic and used it to demonstrate his impenetrability. Only half-amused, Lippmann wrote a friend, "We did not discuss anything more recent than New York state politics in 1835; but he did express his horror of the scandal and notoriety of public life."

TR stayed in the game by publicly expressing a willingness to support Hughes while privately sowing doubts about the wisdom of giving him the nomination. In a letter to Lodge, Roosevelt wondered if it would be proper to take a candidate from the Supreme Court, and to another trusted Republican friend he pointed out a peril of nominating a candidate of unknown persuasions: "We do not want to find that we have merely swapped Wilson for another Wilson in whiskers." Roosevelt's observations were self-serving, but the chairman of the Republican National Committee, Charles D.

Hilles, also worried about Hughes's silence. It was leading party members of all stripes to assume that his stripes matched theirs, Hilles said. As soon as Hughes began declaring himself, enthusiasm was bound to fall off.

Hoping to advance the Colonel, George Perkins papered the country with reprints of editorials praising the Rooseveltian stand on preparedness and bought four pages of *The Saturday Evening Post* to tell Americans why Roosevelt and his Big Stick were the best guarantee of peace.

Annoyed by the endless tooting and perhaps anxious that it would have the desired effect, William Howard Taft bestirred himself to say in print that the noise signified nothing but the Colonel's genius for publicity. The Colonel, needing as much Republican goodwill as he could muster, ignored him. He kept up his assault on the White House, but most of the speeches he gave in the spring were free of the ire that had been spoiling his arguments and threatening to destroy his influence.

In the Midwest, which was filled with isolationists and German-Americans, Roosevelt spoke from the heart for preparedness. The United States was at an impasse because "the men ranged on one side advocate total unpreparedness and the men ranged on the other side nervously deny that they desire any real and thoroughgoing preparedness," he said in Detroit. "Such a condition of affairs speaks badly for this nation. I say 'this nation' and I mean you and me, my fellow countrymen." The president and the Congress were supposed to lead, but "ultimately we, the people, have only ourselves to blame if they do not." In Kansas City he made his case for preparedness by explaining that the dangers the country faced were unprecedented. Vast armies could now cross vast distances at speeds undreamed of in the nineteenth century. If an army even half the size of the Allied force at the Dardanelles landed in New York or San Francisco anytime soon, he said, the United States would be at its mercy.

But in St. Louis, one of the last cities on his tour, he overreached. He lashed out at the "professional" German-Americans of the German-American Alliance, accusing them of "moral treason" for their efforts to influence the U.S. government's treatment of Germany. "Any such political organization, whether German-American, Irish-American, or English-American, is not a healthy element of the body politic," he said. He rejected "hyphenated Americans" of every sort because he believed that Americans who banded together by the nationalities of their forebears would fall into the rivalries and hatreds of the Old World.

He knew that the German-American Alliance did not speak for the vast majority of German immigrants and their offspring, he said, and he explained that if the sinking of the *Lusitania* or the invasion of Belgium had been perpetrated by some other country, he would have condemned it as heartily as he had condemned Germany. But it was the "moral treason" of German-Americans, not Roosevelt's evenhandedness, that found its way into the headlines. The speech guaranteed that the Republicans would nominate Charles Evans Hughes or someone else who had not offended the largest, most politically active bloc in the American electorate.

R OOSEVELT'S LAST QUEST for the presidency ended in a heartbreak unique in the history of American politics. William Allen White, Hiram Johnson, Gifford Pinchot, and eight hundred other Progressives trekked to Chicago in June with hopes of securing the two nominations Roosevelt wanted. George Perkins may have been the only one present who knew that TR had decided not to run on the Progressive ticket if the Republicans nominated Hughes.

Defeat was not in the air. The Progressives were meeting side by side with the Republicans and planned to send them a message by lightning bolt. Both conventions would open June 7, the Progressives in the Auditorium and the Republicans a few blocks away in the Coliseum. The Progressive leaders wanted to bring the convention to order, nominate TR, and adjourn as quickly as possible, a strategy intended to panic the Republicans into doing the same for the sake of the four million votes that had gone to Roosevelt in 1912. But when Perkins asked the Progressives to postpone the nominating while he negotiated with the Republicans, they agreed to wait.

The Republicans, who listened politely to Perkins, had no interest in Roosevelt. They knew he would support Hughes, they were still nursing the bruises of 1912, and they seemed less moved by the possibility of winning Bull Moose votes than by the prospect of losing the German-Americans.

Roosevelt was in Oyster Bay, communicating with Chicago by a private telephone line. To make sure that the Progressives would not jolly the Colonel into running, Perkins did not tell them about the telephone, which rang in his hotel suite. After three days of delay, White and other Progressive leaders realized that Perkins and Roosevelt were waiting for the Republicans to finish their balloting and that Roosevelt planned to endorse Hughes as soon as he accepted.

The Progressives decided to nominate Roosevelt anyway. Armageddon, a bit of campaign hyperbole in 1912, now raged in Europe. If they sounded the call, surely Roosevelt would stand with them once more and battle for the Lord. On Saturday morning, June 10, Raymond Robins, chairman of the Progressive convention, brought the meeting to order, Bainbridge Colby of New York rose to nominate Roosevelt, and Perkins flew to the rostrum to stop him. Robins stretched out an arm and swept him backward. By noon Theodore Roosevelt was the Progressive nominee.

The Republicans settled on Hughes a few minutes later, Hughes accepted, and O. K. Davis soon came before the Progressives to read Roosevelt's regrets. After thanking them for the honor, he proposed Lodge as an alternative. Years later, in a conversation with one of Theodore's oldest friends, Edith said he had proposed Cabot out of affection. The friend speculated that TR might also have been prompted by his dislike of the bearded iceberg as well as his appreciation of Cabot's willingness to vote for him in the early balloting at the Republican convention. Whatever his reason, the Progressives felt knifed. How could Roosevelt desert them? And how dare he suggest Lodge in his stead? Lodge's conservatism, baked into his bones, epitomized all that the Progressive Party had been founded to fight. He opposed woman suffrage, he was no friend of labor, and as the agent of the manufacturing class of Massachusetts, he could see no good in low tariffs.

Reconstructing the moment in his autobiography, White remembered silence and then "a roar of rage. It was the cry of a broken heart." Hundreds of delegates ripped off their Roosevelt badges, hurled them on the floor, and stalked out of the convention hall. White stalked with them. That night he telephoned his wife and "spent nine dollars and eighty-five cents bawling like a calf into the receiver," he wrote.

Twenty-five years later, sitting in the cabinet of another Roosevelt, Secretary of the Interior Harold Ickes repaired to the studied quiet of the *American Historical Review* to ask, "Who killed the Progressive Party?" His answer was George Perkins. The alleged motive was a wish to make government the concubine of capital.

Although not as selfless as he liked to think—who is?—Perkins was a genuinely good citizen, and in spite of his lordliness as chairman of the Progressive Party, he had done his work with dedication, imagination, and generosity. Perkins's great flaw was a common failing of ambitious men, a soul made glad by the thought of exercising power over the powerful. President Theodore Roosevelt's power had attracted him, U.S. Steel and International Harvester had benefited from it, and Perkins hoped to restore it and benefit again—all the while serving the public interest as he conceived of it. Perkins offered his services to Hughes with a haste that his fellow Progressives found puzzling in light of the personal injuries Hughes had inflicted during the investigation of New York Life's contributions to Roosevelt's 1904 presidential campaign. Hughes's exposures had publicly embarrassed Perkins and nearly landed him in prison. But George Perkins did not kill the Progressive Party. Like Roosevelt, he had abandoned it as a lost cause.

The older Ickes said that his younger self, then head of the Progressive Party in Illinois, had had no illusions of victory in 1916. The true believers in the Progressive Party had wanted TR to run on a third ticket in order to give the reactionary Republicans another licking, he said. "It was my theory that that party could not stand more than one such defeat. I believed that if we would only stick to our guns we would become one of the two major political parties of the country." Roosevelt and Perkins foresaw no such happy outcome.

The Progressive Party had not been killed, it had simply failed to thrive. The people did not want a new party or Theodore Roosevelt, but they did want the social and economic reform he espoused in 1912, and their demand for it had forced Woodrow Wilson into a quickmarch toward liberalism. Between 1913 and 1916, he and the Democrats in Congress instituted workmen's compensation, banned most child labor, and expanded farmers' access to credit. They also created the Federal Reserve Board, gave the United States a tariff commission, and replaced the Sherman Act with a new antitrust law and the Federal Trade Commission.

Roosevelt, in heroic mood, had been wild indeed in surmising that his old enemies would choose him to rescue the country from disgrace in the community of nations. Before the war, he had had an even wilder dream, of a progressive national government. Under Woodrow Wilson, the dream became reality almost overnight. Roosevelt's rewards were defeat, blame, and a painful case of envy, but the Progressive Party died triumphant.

SIXTEEN

Blackballed

THE Bull Moose was speedily interred, and Roosevelt moved on while the mourners were still clustered round the grave, Gifford Pinchot aching with regret, William Allen White "confused in heart and mind," and Harold Ickes feeling "real personal grief that this wonderful Progressive Party of ours should have struck the rocks." Roosevelt exhibited no signs of grief or contrition. The Progressives, he told a friend, were "suffering the fate of all noble movements when the cup has been drained and only the dregs are left. . . . Small derelict parties are the natural prey of cranks with a moral twist, and of crooks too cheap to get on in any real party." He would soon write Amos Pinchot, the party's hortatory crank-in-chief, "When I spoke of the Progressive Party as having a lunatic fringe, I specifically had you in mind."

The ill grace showed itself only in private and is probably best seen as the spillover of a hidden sorrow. Although Roosevelt had known that the Republican leadership would refuse him the nomination, knowing is not the same as believing, and the rejection stung. Visiting Sagamore soon after the conventions, Cabot found Theodore "much distressed," a diagnosis confirmed in Theodore's letters to his sisters. Corinne received a bleak précis of his life as an ex-president: "I have been I believe emphatically right, emphatically the servant of the American people; but just as emphatically the American people have grown to think less and less of me, and more definitely determined not to use me in any public position; and it's their affair after all." With Bamie he tried to be chipper but could not contain his disappointment. "Well, the country wasn't in heroic mood!" he wrote. "We are passing through a thick streak of yellow in our national life." When an admirer predicted his nomination in 1920, Roosevelt shook his head and tacitly admitted that his 1912 run had been a mistake. "This was my year—1916 my high twelve. In four years I will be out of it."

But he was not out of it yet, for politics demands the last shred of flesh from those who would have its great prizes. In spite of his hurt, in spite of his grudge against the bearded iceberg, Roosevelt was obliged to offer his help to the Republicans. His desire to depose Wilson bordered on bloodlust, and he knew that if he did not volunteer his assistance to Hughes, it would be said that Theodore Roosevelt considered no one but Theodore Roosevelt fit for the presidency. "I could not allow any such impression to go forth," he told a confidant.

For Hughes and everyone else wondering how Roosevelt felt about playing handmaiden, the *Times* provided the answer on June 28, the day he and Hughes had set for a dinner alone to discuss the campaign. There on the front page was the news that Colonel Roosevelt planned to ask the War Department for permission to raise and command a division of volunteers in case of war with Mexico. The *Times* cited no source for the story, saying only that it had the information "on high authority." The high authority lived atop Sagamore Hill, and going to war would give him an unassailable excuse for deserting Charles Evans Hughes.

War between the United States and Mexico, looming for months, now seemed a certainty. Years of struggle between rebel chieftains and a succession of weak Mexican presidents had thoroughly disordered the country, and while the chaos defied easy summary, the cause did not. Mexico was a horn of plenty for everyone but the Mexicans. American investors owned well over half of the country's mining, rubber, and petroleum industries, and Europeans owned goodly chunks of the rest.

Woodrow Wilson sympathized with the aspirations of the Mexican masses but had aggravated the troubles by indecision, which merely emboldened the rebel bands of Pancho Villa and Emiliano Zapata to attack foreigners, mainly Americans, living in Mexico. By the end of 1915, the slayings, beatings, and rapes numbered in the hundreds. In January 1916, Villa's men murdered sixteen American mining engineers traveling on a Mexican train, and in March the rebels left seventeen dead on a rampage through the border town of Columbus, New Mexico. With the consent of President Venustiano Carranza, Wilson sent General John J. Pershing and a small army into Mexico for the sole purpose of capturing Pancho Villa. Villa proved elusive, and as the weeks went by and American forces pushed deeper into the country, Carranza began to fear that the United States had ambitions of conquest. In April, after a clash between the U.S. and Mexican armies, Carranza demanded that Pershing leave the country.

Wilson refused the demand and orchestrated a show of force, mobilizing the National Guard and putting the navy on patrol along the coasts of Mexico. Carranza applied the pincers, barring American reinforcements from moving south across the border and promising to attack if Pershing's soldiers marched anywhere but north toward Texas. Toward the end of June, after a dozen American soldiers were killed and two dozen were captured in a skirmish with the Mexican army, Wilson composed a declaration of war but kept it on his desk in the hope that a peaceful alternative might yet present itself.

Following the Mexican crisis from Sagamore, Roosevelt believed that war was inevitable and felt sure that his desire to raise a division and head for Mexico would thrill the White House. "If Wilson is wise, he'll shut my mouth by giving me a commission," he told two visitors in mid-June. Aware that Roosevelt was too old for a new commission, one of the visitors asked how Wilson could make him a general. The president would need a new law authorizing the volunteers, Roosevelt said, and the age limit could be amended in the process.

In Washington, Newton D. Baker, the new secretary of war, deflected questions about Roosevelt's request with the fey observation that "There are some men, like Cleopatra, who are not withered by age and cannot have their infinite variety staled by custom." After a week of "TR Division" excitement in the press, which brought Roosevelt hundreds of letters from men eager to join, he let it be known that he had written Baker for permission to proceed. The War Department would not confirm receipt of the letter, and in Roosevelt's papers there is no reply from the secretary. But President Carranza had proposed settling the differences by negotiation, President Wilson had agreed, and there would be no war.

Roosevelt was condemned to politics. "I shall do all I can for Mr. Hughes," he wrote a friend, but he worried that Hughes would be an overly genteel combatant. "If he merely speaks like Mr. Wilson, only a little weaker, he will rob my support of its effectiveness."

Roosevelt suspected beneath the surface of the bearded iceberg there was a bearded Woodrow Wilson, and he was right. Both Hughes and Wilson were children of clergymen, both were intellectuals, and as governors, both had battled the trusts and the bosses. Extrapolating from the vote of 1912, the seers gave the election of 1916 to Hughes. Holder of the Republican title and heir presumptive to the Progressive estate, he was expected to best Wilson by more than a million votes. Wilson, tormented by the world war, half-hoped the seers were right.

The question before the voters was the most momentous since the Civil War: What did the United States owe the rest of the world? Could it continue going its own way, following George Washington's advice to avoid foreign entanglements, or was its fate in the modern world inextricably bound up with the fate of the community of nations?

Hughes opened his campaign in July and at Roosevelt's suggestion led with a long indictment of Wilson's foreign policy. He reviewed the blunders in Mexico and noted the consequences: a country still in chaos, American residents still in danger, Pancho Villa still at large, and deepening resentment of the United States. Hughes also made a strong case for the end of American isolationism, pointing out that a nation without allies was a nation at risk and that unless the United States recognized its international obligations now, it would have no hand in shaping the postwar world.

The editors of *The New Republic*, who were hoping to support Hughes, wished he had proposed alternatives to Wilson's policies and reminded him that taking a stand against Wilson would not suffice. The voters had to be told what he was *for*.

Hughes listened earnestly to the criticism but was as politically bewildered as William Howard Taft and almost as averse to conflict, traits that hurt him in his own feuding party as well as in the contest with Wilson. His effort to harmonize the Republicans by including Progressives in his councils was seen by the regulars as "slobbering," and Bull Moose men despaired when he marched through California in the company of the Old Guard without so much as a nod to Governor Hiram Johnson, Roosevelt's running mate in 1912 and now a Republican candidate for the U.S. Senate. Before Hughes headed west, several progressive Republicans had alerted him to California's pride in its advanced political views, but the hint was ignored. Johnson took the snub in silence for fear of embarrassing Hughes and compounding the damage. The Republicans could have carried California by 200,000 votes just after Hughes's nomination, Johnson wrote a progressive editor in September. "Our task is now a hard one to carry it at all."

Sensing that he had been misled by the conservatives of California,

Hughes asked William Allen White how to regain the confidence of the progressives. White suggested that he come out in favor of old-age insurance, the minimum wage, and a few other measures advocated in the Bull Moose platform. Hughes confessed that he did not understand the shift in the political winds since 1910, when he left the governor's mansion in Albany for the U.S. Supreme Court, and White could see that Hughes found the suggestions fantastical.

Hughes's most formidable challenge was Woodrow Wilson's record. The president had fulfilled most of the promises he made in 1912, the country was prosperous, and passage of the largest defense budget in the nation's history—however inadequate and behindhand it might seem to Colonel Roosevelt and General Wood—had stilled most of the preparedness critics. When Hughes predicted that the prosperity would vanish as the war ended and Europe no longer needed an endless supply of American goods, factory hands, many of them flush for the first time, understandably preferred the prosperity of the moment to none at all.

EIGHT YEARS EARLIER, as president and political leader of the Republican Party, Roosevelt had stepped in to steer Taft's wobbly campaign, but now he had no such prerogative. And while Hughes had invited Roosevelt's aid, the Republican National Committee wanted as little Roosevelt as possible. The colorless Hughes would be lost in the rainbow that was Roosevelt, and Roosevelt's eviscerations of Wilson and Germany ran against the prevailing political current. Roosevelt understood and stayed quietly off-stage, ready but not eager to help. But when the correspondents who had traveled west with Hughes began raising the possibility of Hughes's defeat, Republican leaders were sufficiently alarmed to ask Roosevelt to "take off his coat and supply the ginger," as one of them put it. Hughes was bland, bland, bland—the master of "piddling reticence," said TR's old friend Owen Wister.

TR spent most of October touring thirteen states, blasting the Wilson administration for its lack of courage in foreign affairs. "When I was president it was said of me that I spoke softly and carried a big stick," he told a crowd in Phoenix. "It can be said of Mr. Wilson that he speaks bombastically and wields a dish rag." In Albuquerque he called the secretary of war "exquisitely unfit for his present position." On his appointment to the cabinet, Baker had boasted of his pacifism and happily admitted that he knew nothing of military affairs, had never even played with tin soldiers as a boy.

Roosevelt seemed his feisty, fearless self, but the trip depressed him. In state after state it seemed that voters wanted to like Hughes, but his circumspection made it impossible to tell where he stood. Roosevelt's tour concluded at Cooper Union in New York on November 3, four days before the election. Wilson was at his New Jersey retreat, Shadow Lawn, a piece of happenstance that gave Roosevelt the metaphor he needed for a wholesale condemnation.

> There should be shadows enough at Shadow Lawn; the shadows of men, women, and children who have risen from the ooze of the ocean bottom and from graves in foreign lands . . . the shadows of troopers who lay in the Mexican desert, the black blood crusted round their mouths, and their dim eyes looking upward, because President Wilson sent them to do a task, and had then shamefully abandoned them to the mercy of foes who knew no mercy. Those are the shadows proper for Shadow Lawn; the shadows of deeds that were never done; the shadows of lofty words that were followed by no action; the shadows of the tortured dead.

Although Hughes and Roosevelt stopped short of saying that Germany offered the United States no choice but war, Roosevelt's call for action and Hughes's insistence that isolation was no longer feasible sounded decidedly bellicose next to the Democrats' proud claim for Wilson: "He kept us out of war." With that simple sentence, the Democrats transformed the vice of hesitancy into the virtue of restraint and seemed to imply that peace would end with the election of Charles Evans Hughes. Wilson, whose recent cables from the American embassy in Berlin had convinced him that war would be unavoidable, refrained from using the slogan himself but did not interfere with the effort to show Hughes in war paint. "There is one choice against peace, and that is war," Wilson told one crowd. A "great, fundamental, final choice with regard to our foreign relationships is to be made on the 7th of November. Some young men ought to be interested in that."

Wilson spent the week before the election preparing for a startling, unprecedented move. He had decided to resign if he lost. Given the perils of the moment, it seemed wrong to him that during the four months between the election and the inauguration, the legal authority to govern would be his, while Hughes, who would inherit the consequences, would have no say. If Hughes won, Wilson wanted Secretary of State Robert Lansing to resign so that Hughes could be appointed secretary of state, after which the president and vice president would resign. Under the law then governing the line of succession, Hughes would automatically become president.

Anxious and out of sorts when he rose on election day, Woodrow Wilson motored the forty miles from Shadow Lawn to his precinct in Princeton, voted, then hurried back to Shadow Lawn. Hughes also voted early, at a polling place set up in a Manhattan laundry. In Oyster Bay, Archie Roosevelt, newly graduated from Harvard and now working in the carpet mill where Ted's career began, cast his first ballot for president. The early returns showed a landslide for Hughes—victories in most of the upper Midwest and in every Northeastern state but New Hampshire. "I hope to heaven we beat Wilson, and believe we shall do so," TR wrote Quentin; "it would have been a certainty if Hughes had had it in him to make a straight-from-the-shoulder fighting campaign." The South stayed solidly Democratic, and as the Western returns came in, the Hughes triumph no longer seemed assured. "Result of election uncertain at midnight," Edith noted in her diary.

Two more midnights would pass before the result was beyond doubt. Hughes lost by a whisker—three-tenths of one percent of the 900,000 votes cast in California. With California's 13 electoral votes, Wilson's total came to 277, leaving 254 for Hughes. Had Hughes carried the state, he would have carried the country, 267 to 264. Hiram Johnson's 300,000-vote margin of victory in the Senate race validated his point about California's indifference to party labels. The state had voted for Wilson the Democrat and Johnson the Republican because both were progressives.

Taft had predicted that Roosevelt would be the albatross of the Hughes campaign, but Hughes won eight of the thirteen states on TR's tour. "I was sick at heart at the end of the campaign!" TR confided to Gifford Pinchot. "I never had the least doubt of opposing Wilson, but Hughes gave us so very, very little to support."

WILSON STRUGGLED to keep the country out of war after the election, but Germany seemed determined to thwart him. In December it offered to take part in a peace conference but refused to state its terms, stirring fears that it wanted to make peace with France and Russia in order to concentrate on the conquest of Britain. Berlin also served notice that as of

February 1, 1917, U-boat commanders were to sink on sight all belligerent and neutral merchant ships sailing near Britain, France, Italy, or the eastern shore of the Mediterranean. Wilson severed diplomatic relations with Germany on February 3.

Roosevelt praised the break and, assuming that a declaration of war would soon follow, canceled a holiday in Jamaica and volunteered himself and his sons for military service. Given permission to raise a division, he wrote the War Department, he would "strain every nerve to have it ready for efficient action at the earliest moment, so that it could be sent across with the first expeditionary force." Secretary Baker offered no encouragement. Only Congress could authorize volunteers, he said, and he expected Congress to set its own conditions for appointing the highest officers.

TR turned to Jules Jusserand, the French ambassador in Washington and a favorite companion on the strenuous outings that Roosevelt had led from his White House. ("Put on your worst clothes," TR's hiking invitations said. After a few excursions up cliffs, across rivers, and through swamps and torrents, Jusserand protested that he had no worst clothes left.) Roosevelt told Jusserand that if the United States entered the war, and if the administration did not allow him to lead a division to France, he might be able to train his volunteers in Canada for service with the French or British. "Do you care to inquire confidentially of your government, whether . . . they would care to call upon me?" he asked. "I would expect no favors of any kind, except the great favor of being sent to the front." Jusserand queried Paris and soon forwarded the French government's gratitude, along with its thought that decisions about a volunteer force would have to wait until the United States entered the war.

Roosevelt made a similar overture to Sir Cecil Spring Rice, the British ambassador and one of his oldest friends. But British military authorities were cool to the idea, and Spring Rice was in no position to warm them up. He was suffering from Graves' disease, a thyroid disorder often exacerbated by stress and accompanied by irritability, anxiety, and waves of panic. After the sinking of the *Lusitania* he was plagued by a fear of spies, and the tensions between the United States and Britain provoked occasional outbursts that offended Colonel Edward M. House, the president's éminence grise. Believing that Washington was "no place for a nervous and delicate ambassador," House began maneuvering offstage for a new envoy. Early in 1917, increasingly angry with the United States for its neutrality, Spring Rice boiled over during a talk with Secretary of State Robert Lansing. The account in Lansing's diary shows the ambassador with twitching face, eyes on fire, and knuckles white from his clenched fists. When Spring Rice calmed down, he broke into tears and apologized. "I want you to know," he said, "that I realize the very great difficulties which you have to face, and I am sure you and the president will do what is right."

Wilson prayed—in vain—that Germany would do right. At the end of February the White House learned that the German foreign secretary, Arthur von Zimmermann, had instructed his ambassador in Mexico City that in the event of a U.S. declaration of war, the embassy should propose that Mexico ally itself with the Germans and encourage the Japanese to do likewise. As incentives, Germany would offer "generous financial support and an understanding that Mexico is to reconquer the lost territory in Texas, New Mexico, and Arizona."

Outraged but still hoping to avert war, the president asked Congress for a bill to arm American merchant ships. Both La Follette, who vehemently opposed the war, and Roosevelt, who was chafing to get to France, agreed that the new policy of "armed neutrality" was hypocritical and unworkable. "I am as yet holding in," Roosevelt wrote Lodge; "but if [Wilson] does not go to war with Germany I shall skin him alive. To think of Hughes' folly, and the folly of those who nominated Hughes, having cursed this country with the really hideous misfortune of four years more of Wilson in this great and terrible world crisis!"

In mid-March, no longer able to hold himself in, Roosevelt wired the War Department: "In view of the fact that Germany is now actually engaged in war with us, I again earnestly ask permission to be allowed to raise a division for immediate service at the front." Baker reminded Roosevelt that the authority to raise troops rested with Congress and added that volunteer forces, if there were any, would be led by officers drawn from the regular army. Obviously irritated by Roosevelt's tone, Baker referred him to the pertinent law, a measure TR had signed when he was president.

The Colonel pressed again, noting that as a retired commander-in-chief he was eligible for any military appointment. He also mentioned the swift outfitting and training of the Rough Riders and called attention to their bravery in Cuba. They had fought unstintingly, winning two ferocious battles and losing a third of their officers and a fifth of their enlisted men. Baker shared the letter with the president, who sent it back with a note thanking the secretary for allowing him to "undergo the discipline of temper involved

in reading it in silence." Baker composed his reply to Sagamore with an ici-
cle: "The military record to which you call my attention is, of course, a part
of the permanent records of this Department and is available, in detail, for
consideration." The high casualties that signified courage to Roosevelt
seemed like rashness to Baker, a judgment that would not have surprised
Roosevelt. Baker, he told General Leonard Wood, was the sort of man who
was "charming at a ladies' pink tea."

Wood's standing with Baker and Wilson was as low as Roosevelt's. The
White House viewed the general's speeches on preparedness in 1916 as Republican campaign speeches, word of his private scorn for Wilson's conciliation of Germany found its way around Washington, and in January 1917,
when the Senate Military Affairs Committee called Wood to testify on the
state of the nation's defenses, he had been unsparing. The United States
had no army to speak of, almost no weaponry, and little in the way of supplies as basic as clothing and shoes. If it were up to him, Wood said, he
would reorganize the War Department with a sandbag. Wood was soon relieved of his command of the army's Eastern Department and offered a
choice of three posts on the sidelines—Honolulu or Manila or Charleston,
South Carolina. He chose Charleston.

THE PRESIDENT SPENT the middle of March in his bedroom, ill with
a cold undoubtedly aggravated by his dread of the coming war. With
his cabinet he examined the crisis from every standpoint and finally concluded that the only alternative to war, submission to Germany, was unacceptable. Temperate responses to Germany's hostile acts had brought only
more hostility. Roosevelt had predicted as much, but Wilson had clutched
at his dream that sanity and high ideals would prevail. On March 21 the
president informed Congress that he wished to appear on April 2 to deliver
a message on "grave questions of national policy."

Wilson summoned a trusted newspaper correspondent and went over
the ground once more. Germany had exhausted his options, he said, but if
the United States joined the Allies, the Germans would be badly beaten,
and with the United States in the war, there would be no neutral country
powerful enough to influence the terms of the peace. The treaty would not
be an agreement between equals; it would be a victor's peace, punitive and
wrathful. He also feared war's erosion of liberties that Americans took for

granted. "Once lead this people into war, and they'll forget there ever was such a thing as tolerance," he said. Freedom of speech, the right of assembly, perhaps the whole Constitution, would be lost.

To others he expressed the fear that war would destroy the social and economic reforms of his first administration. "The people we have unhorsed will inevitably come into the control of the country for we shall be dependent upon the steel, oil and financial magnates," he said. Profiteering would be rampant, pushing prices to highs that would disorder the economy for a generation.

Across Lafayette Square from the White House, Henry Adams and his dinner guests on April 2 heard the hoofbeats of the cavalry escort setting off with the president for the Capitol. It was twenty past eight, dark and raining, but the Capitol was eerily brilliant in searchlights set up by police to dispel shadows that might conceal an assassin. Wilson arrived safely, and the applause began as soon as the House sergeant-at-arms announced him. He strode directly to the speaker's desk, where he waited somberly for quiet.

The chamber was packed—congressmen, senators, Supreme Court justices, cabinet members, and diplomats on the floor, prominent Washingtonians in the galleries. One of the few who refused to applaud was Senator La Follette, who stood with head bowed and arms crossed. He had spent much of the day in a fruitless effort to secure permits for several thousand pacifists who wanted to hold a parade and conduct a meeting in the Capitol. He was furious with Wilson for running as the peace candidate and firm in his conviction that it was unconstitutional to conscript Americans to fight a war on foreign soil.

Wilson, clasping his manuscript with both hands and resting his arms on the desk, calmly reviewed his efforts to prevent the war, acknowledged that he had been slow to recognize Germany's departure from "the humane practices of civilized nations," and admitted that armed neutrality could not protect Americans at sea from the invisible menace of the submarine. "The world must be made safe for democracy," he said. The United States had no desire for conquest and expected no spoils. It intended to fight for "the ultimate peace of the world and for the liberation of its peoples, the German peoples included." He asked that the Congress formally accept the status of belligerent thrust upon the United States and "exert all its power and employ all its resources to bring the government of the German Empire to terms and end the war."

The duty he was performing this night was "distressing and oppressive," he said. "It is a fearful thing to lead this great peaceful people . . . into the most terrible and disastrous of all wars, civilization itself seeming to be in the balance." In the pause that followed, La Follette loudly cleared his throat, twice. Wilson, who seemed not to notice, went on. "But the right is more precious than peace and we shall fight for the things which we have always carried nearest our hearts—for democracy, for the right of those who submit to authority to have a voice in their own governments, for the rights and liberties of small nations, for a universal dominion of right by such a concert of free peoples as shall bring peace and safety to all nations and make the world itself at last free. To such a task we can dedicate our lives and our fortunes, everything that we are and everything that we have, with the pride of those who know that the day has come when America is privileged to spend her blood and her might for the principles that gave her birth and happiness and the peace which she has treasured. God helping her, she can do no other."

Hundreds of flags pumped up and down, and the crowd in the House cheered as lustily as Princeton men at a football game. La Follette rose with everyone else for the president's exit but kept his arms folded across his chest. On his way out of the chamber, Wilson found himself in the warm handshake of Henry Cabot Lodge, who loathed him nearly as much as Roosevelt did but thought he had voiced the loftiest sentiments of the American people. Before Henry Adams and his guests finished dinner, newsboys were hawking extras on the corner.

Roosevelt wondered when the lofty words would become deed but privately gloated that the speech was a vindication of all he had said about Germany since the earliest months of the war. Publicly he called for unity and put in another bid for his division. Americans wanted a force sent to France as quickly as possible, he said, and no unwise precedent would be set by permitting an ex-president with military experience to raise a force of volunteers "and serve with it at the front under the command of the general who heads the army corps." He wanted the country to know that he was willing to settle for less than full command.

La Follette briefly obstructed the war resolution's progress through the Senate, but both houses of Congress soon passed it by overwhelming majorities, and when Wilson signed it, at 1:18 P.M. on April 6, 1917, the United States and Germany were officially at war. Roosevelt headed for Washington three days later in hopes of winning a White House endorsement for his division. Baker could easily shunt his letters aside, but Wilson would find it harder to dismiss him in person, TR told a friend. Gambling that Wilson would not dare to refuse him an audience, he set off on his errand without an appointment.

The president and his secretary, Joseph P. Tumulty, received Roosevelt at eleven o'clock the next morning in the Red Room, where they talked for forty-five minutes. TR said that he now regarded his criticisms of the administration as "dust in a windy street," offered his praise for the war message, and prophesied that if the country lived up to the president's words, the message would be classed a great state paper. He wanted only to help the United States realize the ideals set forth in the address, he said, and in light of the Allies' desperation, the United States had to hit hard and hit at once. France, bled white, could not last another year, and England could not hold the line alone. Russia was in the throes of revolution. Champions of democracy welcomed the downfall of the czar, but the revolution meant the end of the war between Russia and Germany, freeing hundreds of thousands of German troops for the fighting in France. The early dispatch of American volunteers would strengthen the Allied line, lift the morale of the French and British, and inspire all Americans to do their utmost for the war, Roosevelt declared. And his recruiting would not interfere with the pending draft law, because he would confine his ranks to men who were exempt.

Wilson understood the Colonel's wish to be the American Lafayette but raised several concerns. The existence of volunteer forces might lead the public to think there was no need for a draft, and if Roosevelt's division won approval, how would it be possible to turn down the long line of others seeking the same opportunity? And what would happen to morale at home and abroad if the volunteers, whose rush to France would be highly publicized, suffered high casualties? Without dismissing the proposition, Wilson deftly turned the tables, asking a favor of the favor-seeker. The public and the Congress had to be rallied behind the draft legislation. Could the president count on his help? Roosevelt readily put himself at the president's service.

"He is a great big boy," Wilson remarked to Tumulty after Roosevelt drove off. "I was charmed by his personality. There is a sweetness about him that is very compelling." Tumulty had the impression that Wilson was inclined to grant Roosevelt's wish.

The Colonel spent the rest of the day on M Street, at Alice and Nick's. He did not know what the president would decide, he told friends. If anyone else had talked to him with the interest and cordiality Wilson had shown, he would feel confident that his argument had carried, but Wilson was inscrutable. Lodge and Spring Rice and Jusserand came by to see TR, and he discussed the division with the chairmen of the House and Senate committees on military affairs. When Secretary of War Baker turned up, late in the afternoon, TR took him to an upstairs room for a private chat. TR reiterated that he knew he lacked the experience to lead a division and said that he would compensate by relying on seasoned officers from the regular army.

Baker promised that the proposal would be carefully reviewed but explained that the ultimate decision would be dictated by innumerable factors. It is not known how much if any elaboration Baker gave Roosevelt, but in an interview years later, he said that in weighing Roosevelt's desires he was haunted by intelligence from the French and British, whose experience in the world war suggested that before the typical major general mastered his job on the battlefield more than ten thousand lives were lost. Both armies had concluded that the rank should not be conferred on a man without many years of service ahead of him.

Baker also relied on the advice of General Tasker H. Bliss, the army's acting chief of staff, who supplied eight pages of arguments against Roosevelt's division: many of the regular army officers Roosevelt planned to take had no wartime experience, draft-exempt men who wished to volunteer could do so by joining the regular army or the National Guard, volunteers could not be trained for the European war any more quickly than draftees, "popular" leaders of volunteer divisions might attract romantics who did not fully understand the hazards ahead, and sending one division before others were ready to replenish its ranks after the inevitable casualties was bound to injure morale at home and abroad.

Leaving Washington the next day, TR told a reporter that he felt he had both a right and a duty to fight in France. His steady criticism of German aggression had helped to lead the country into war, he said, so he felt obliged to share the risk with the men who would be drafted. "I want to be able to say to those fine fellows not, 'Go, boys!' but 'Come!'" The Colonel was in heroic mood.

B AKER PROMPTLY informed Roosevelt that a division was out of the question and suggested that an ex-president need not join the military to render valuable service in wartime. The "Washington people . . . would rather make this a paper war, if possible; but if not that they want to make it a Democratic war," TR wrote William Allen White. The president had not yet chosen the commander of the American Expeditionary Force, but Roosevelt doubted that the honor would go to Wood. "They are much more anxious to spite Leonard Wood and myself than to uphold the honor of the nation or beat Germany," TR said.

When one of Wood's friends inquired about his banishment to Charleston, Baker admitted that Wood's indiscretion had been "very unfortunate for his splendid reputation as a soldier." But the bigger trouble, Baker said, was that Wood's admirers had mistakenly assumed that they knew more about "the proper distributions of the higher commands of the Army than those in Washington who are making it a study, and . . . that any change in General Wood's station necessarily argued some sort of disciplinary action directed against him."

R OOSEVELT'S LAST HOPE lay on Capitol Hill, where his friends had garnished the draft bill with a provision allowing for volunteer forces so long as they were raised in units no smaller than a division. To Senator William J. Stone, Democrat of Missouri, the provision reeked of privilege and partisanship. Stone could be as ornery as La Follette and was one of many who considered the Rough Rider's storied cavalry charge as reckless endangerment. "By his own course in the only crisis of his brief and unimportant military career he demonstrated such a lack of poise and sound judgment as to make plain his unfitness to command even a regiment," Stone declared on the floor of the Senate. Now there was to be a Roosevelt division, twenty-some thousand men, and the draft bill would prohibit smaller forces of volunteers. No one but Roosevelt had enough influence to assemble a division, and Republicans, gaze fixed on the election of 1920, were out to make Roosevelt the one great volunteer hero of the war, Stone said. The senator also doubted Roosevelt's capacity to serve in some capacity other than commander. Hadn't he always flouted authority? And wasn't his refusal to bow to the War Department's opposition to his plan proof that he had no ability to subordinate himself?

Hiram Johnson, newly arrived from California and aware of the Senate's disapproval of freshman oratory, waited for one of Roosevelt's friends to offer a defense. When no one did, Johnson boldly volunteered that he was appalled by Stone's denunciation. "What is it that is asked?" Johnson wished to know. "It is asked only by a man who is now really in the twilight of life that he may finally lay down his life for the country that has been his. It is only that he asks that he may serve that country, may go forth to battle for his country's rights, and may do all that may be done by a human being in behalf of his nation. . . . There is no politics in begging to serve one's country; the politics is in the carping and ungenerous criticism of the request."

TR, who was having tea in Manhattan with Corinne and Ambassador Jusserand, had guessed that his enemies would see the division as the first leg of a presidential run. They were wrong, he said. "The president need not fear me politically. No one need fear me politically. If I am allowed to go to France, I could not last. I am too old to last long under such circumstances. I should *crack*. But I *could* arouse the belief that America was coming. I *could* show the Allies what was on the way."

The Selective Service Act, complete with the controversial provision for volunteer divisions, was passed the next day, May 18. Roosevelt wired the White House for permission to raise two divisions, four if the president wanted. Telegraphing his personal regrets to Oyster Bay, Wilson attributed his decision to the imperatives of public policy. The president also announced that agreeable as it would have been to grant Roosevelt permission to raise his troops, he had no plans to authorize any volunteer divisions: "[T]his is not the time or occasion for compliment or for any action not calculated to contribute to the immediate success of the war. The business now in hand is undramatic, practical, and of scientific definiteness and precision." The first American forces to go to France would be drawn from the regular army and led by Major General John J. Pershing. There was no mention of Wood, and Baker left it to Pershing to decide whether he wanted Wood in the United States or France.

Roosevelt's friends, many of whom had hoped to serve with him in France, hurried to Sagamore with bandages. The Colonel spoke loftily of the need for loyalty to the commander-in-chief but could not hide his hurt. "This is a very exclusive war," he told them, "and I have been blackballed by the committee on admissions."

In the last year, Roosevelt had been blackballed twice—refused a presidential nomination and denied the role he wanted in the war. As a man who freely expressed his feelings but rarely reflected on them, TR might not have even noticed that when the sting of Hughes's nomination subsided, his references to the White House tended to be blustering protests of the "if I were president" variety rather than veiled fantasies of a return to power. But when Wilson and Baker rejected the Roosevelt division, they inflicted a wound that would never heal. Theodore Roosevelt had been declared superfluous. Powerlessness could be survived—he had proved that—but uselessness?

✳ *Precipice*

SEVENTEEN

War in the Garden of Eden

ROOSEVELT did not hurl Wilson into perdition for spurning the division. The hurling had been done four years before, when Wilson impugned his honor by offering Colombia $25 million and an apology for the manhandling Roosevelt had administered in acquiring the Panama Canal Zone. Wilson's rejection of the volunteers merely pitchforked him into a deeper pit of Roosevelt's hell, one where the coals of opprobrium were banked higher and burned hotter. Woodrow Wilson, Theodore Roosevelt would say, was a physically timid man with a timid man's resentment of physical courage in others, a supple and adroit rhetorician without a throb of patriotism, a dexterous thimble-rigger who misled the people while France and England bled. He was cold-blooded, shifty, unscrupulous. More than that, this infernal skunk, this acrid pacifist, this Byzantine logothete, was the very worst president—yes, *the* worst president—and he deserved to be impeached. He was as baneful as an overdose of morphine. He had shilly-shallied, danced the cancan, and postponed the war to ensure his reelection. And thanks to this selfish, sinister, slippery, dirty, lying, vacillating, conscienceless demagogue, the nation was still not prepared for war.

Most of the name-calling was done privately, in letters, but Roosevelt's public diatribes on American relations with Mexico and Germany had been sufficiently pungent and personal to warrant his belief that Wilson had halted the march of the Roosevelt division out of spite. But even with White House approval, Roosevelt's wishes would have met stiff resistance. Many

Democrats shared Senator Stone's fear that if the Rough Rider turned himself into a hero on the Western Front, he would be invincible in the presidential election of 1920. William Howard Taft, a former secretary of war, thought Roosevelt's military ambitions preposterous, and he reminded Baker that hard as it was to "tear away from the traditions of volunteering handed down to us from the various wars," it was important to remember that the volunteer system had resulted in needless waste and slaughter. Officials charged with carrying out the new draft law also disapproved, fearing — as Wilson did — that the existence of volunteer divisions would create public confusion about the need for conscription. Even the Colonel's close friend Senator Lodge saw their point. With the draft, he wrote a mutual acquaintance, "you cannot very easily have also a proposition for volunteers, and we all have to stand by the conscription, including Theodore himself."

General Pershing was fond of Roosevelt, who had jumped him from captain to brigadier in one move, ahead of eight hundred senior officers, but Pershing disliked volunteer divisions because he had found that they tended to regard themselves as a superior caste, deserving of special treatment. And a British military envoy told Secretary Baker that an expedition of amateurs would depress Allied morale and arouse ridicule in Germany.

From Paris, Prime Minister Georges Clemenceau wrote an open letter urging Wilson to reconsider, and TR's belief that the French military agreed with Clemenceau has led biographers to believe Roosevelt. But Wilson told Baker that Marshal Joseph Joffre opposed the idea, and in a talk with the Roosevelts' old friend Warrington Dawson, who had joined the staff of the American embassy in Paris, Joffre confided that he opposed Roosevelt's plan and had told him so.

> It was with infinite regret that I had to reply to him, though using all possible *ménagements* [delicacy], that I could not approve. The essential consideration was to raise and in a short time train an army of several million and every effort had to be concentrated in that single direction. As a consequence, no exceptions could be tolerated, even for reasons as sound as those stated by the ex-president. In spite of my high regard for him, it was my duty to tell him so, and I confirmed this in my talks with President Wilson.

Roosevelt had had two conversations with Joffre when he visited the United States in May 1917, and his impression that Joffre had "cautiously" recommended the division to Wilson is probably a tribute to the finesse of Joffre's *ménagements*.

In a dispassionate examination of the arguments for and against Roosevelt's volunteers, the nays have it. The army, drastically short of officers, could not spare any of them. Roosevelt had pointed out that he was younger than many French generals, but the comparison was misleading, as the major generals often delegated their commands to younger colonels and brigadiers. With rare exceptions, British brigadiers were in their thirties, major generals in their early forties. "Older men simply cannot stand the 'gaff' of present-day warfare," an American observer wrote Baker from France. A seasoned young officer had told him that unless a commander could stay on the move with his troops, "it all means death." Roosevelt argued that his blindness in one eye * would not hamper his performance any more than it had interfered with Lord Nelson's, but there were other infirmities — obesity and arteriosclerosis, diagnosed when he was forty.

And in his eagerness to reach the front, Roosevelt was likely to clash with Pershing, who was determined to keep his soldiers back of the line until they knew enough to succeed on the battlefield. Although TR asked *not* to command a division and promised to obey his superiors, his history indicated that he would feel entitled to take any action not officially prescribed. (He almost never exceeded his authority, as long as he was allowed to define *exceed*.) The secretary of war had to think ahead and imagine the lashing he would take if it became necessary to court-martial the Colonel.

Lodge wished that the president would give Roosevelt a commission in the regular army, and Congressman Gardner, Lodge's son-in-law, encouraged the Colonel to request a position training draftees. "I wished to render service," Roosevelt replied; "I don't wish to be put in the position of seeking a job." If the division had been authorized in February, just after the break with Germany, 200,000 men would soon be ready for the front, he claimed. "I could have . . . put the finest fighting edge on them, and could have got them into the fighting line at the earliest moment, long before we had even begun to prepare our army here. Then it would have mattered very little whether or not I personally cracked—from pneumonia in the trenches, or

---

* Curiously, Wilson had also lost his sight in one eye. "Of course he did not lose it in any such vulgar way as boxing," Roosevelt scoffed; "that would never do. He had to lose his in the more ladylike and refined bookworm way—too much reading" (John J. Leary, *Talks with T.R.*, 19–21). Coming from the most ravenous reader ever to occupy the White House, the insult was absurd but a good index of his hurt and his horror of being thought a sissy.

shell fire, or exhaustion or anything else." In the dreaming, his volunteer army had swelled from one division to four to eight—200,000 men.

In the first days after his defeat the Colonel kept his ire largely to himself and concentrated on satisfying the military desires of his sons. He had already helped Quentin into the army's Air Service, and he soon wired Pershing to ask whether Ted and Archie might go with him to Europe as privates. Pershing agreed to take them but made Ted a major and Archie a second lieutenant because of their experience at Plattsburg. TR appreciated the possible consequences of his success with Pershing, remarking for the first of innumerable times on the perversity of sending young men to face death while useless old men stayed home. "The big bear was not, down at the bottom of his heart, any too happy at striving to get the two little bears where the danger is," he wrote Ted; "elderly bears whose teeth and claws are blunted by age can far better be spared."

For Kermit, TR secured a commission in the British army, a move that seems to have been arrived at by process of elimination. Kermit was attracted to flying, but the Air Service was overwhelmed with applicants. Kermit was not included in the request to Pershing, because his slight military experience—a few weeks at Plattsburg—might have led the general to refuse all three sons in order to avoid the awkwardness of refusing one. In Ted's view, such a result would have been unfair to him and Archie, who had given up vacations for three years to go to Plattsburg.

If Kermit minded the machinations of the family council of war, there is no sign of it. He would serve with the British in Mesopotamia, and he suspected that he would be more immediately useful there than in France, where the American forces would be in training for months. And Mesopotamia promised to be an adventure, something he craved after his dull indoor work as a banker in Buenos Aires.

As his sons left in the summer of 1917, TR spoke to them of abiding by the fall of the dice and the glory of doing one's duty. Their task would be hard, he wrote Archie, but "it would be infinitely harder not to go, not to have risen level to the supreme crisis in the world's history, not to have won the right to stand with the mighty men of the mighty days."

His blackest fears he voiced mainly to others. "If my sons are killed I shall feel broken-hearted, whereas, I would feel that, at my age, my own death would not have been a matter for any serious regret," he wrote a friend. And if the boys did not return, "I shall regard Wilson as responsible for their deaths." As long as TR had had the hope of taking his boys to war with his volunteers, he could imagine himself as their shield. Wilson had destroyed the shield and thrown him into that agonized and powerless legion, the parents of soldiers.

LORD DERBY, Britain's secretary of state for war, offered Kermit a choice of rank—major or captain. As a foreigner with almost no military training, Kermit thought it best not to overreach and had no reason to gainsay the Plattsburg officers who had pegged him as a captain. "I thought you would have approved my action in this," he wrote his father; "it is what you would have done yourself, I think." Kermit could be certain of his father's approval. Given the chance to go to Cuba as a colonel, at the head of his own regiment, TR had shrewdly deduced that his inexperience would prolong the regiment's training and—dreadful thought—make him late to the fighting. He had chosen to go as a lieutenant colonel under a seasoned commander, Leonard Wood.

Kermit was undoubtedly pleased to add that Lord Derby had promised "fine fighting." But after their jungle expeditions in Africa and South America, he told TR, he felt "small and unhappy to be going off without you." Together they could have pursued "the malevolent hyenas, with the courage of the simba, and the instincts of the rock ape."

The hairy-chested talk concealed considerable anxiety. Kermit and Belle had a two-year-old son, Kim, and Belle was expecting another baby. Because of them, he told his father, "I don't like war at all," but as long as the war had to be fought, "I want to be the first in."

In exchange for Lord Derby's favor, TR said he expected Kermit to hold himself to a high standard: "you have an obligation to England, to America, to yourself, and to me. You must not only *do* what is right, but also *seem* to do what is right. Not only can there be no looking back, but no acting so as to cause even a suggestion that you are expecting any favor."

Awaiting his orders, Kermit submitted to his first tear-gassing, at a training camp near London, and on another day took Belle to see his father's friend Rudyard Kipling, whose only son, a boy of eighteen, had been killed after just a month at the front. Believing that there was still a "hell and a half" to come, Kipling said he was glad that Wilson had turned down the Colonel's division. Older men "die like flies and we've wasted too many good ones already," he told Kermit.

From London, Kermit and Belle and Kim moved on to Paris, which would be the Roosevelt squadron's unofficial headquarters for the war. Ted's wife, Eleanor, had just arrived and was settling into a comfortable house near the Arc de Triomphe. She had stunned Theodore and Edith a few weeks before by announcing that she was going to France as a volunteer with the YMCA, leaving the children—three of them, the oldest of whom was six—with her mother. After a pensive moment, the Colonel, who had ordered the Roosevelt women not to follow their husbands to war, realized that one could not court-martial a daughter-in-law. "Darling," he said, "I see you have made up your mind. I don't know of anything I can do to help you, but if you can think of something you must let me know."

In mid-August Belle and Kim left for the American embassy in Madrid, where they would live with Belle's parents, and Kermit headed to Italy for a troopship to the Persian Gulf. If being a son of Theodore Roosevelt imposed certain burdens, it also conferred certain privileges. Throughout the war Kermit would be invited to feast at the tables of local grandees and spend an occasional night in luxurious quarters. In the dreary port of Taranto the admiral of Britain's Mediterranean fleet asked him aboard his own ship, to wait in comfort for his troop transport. The admiral also secured him a choice cabin for the long voyage to the Middle East.

For days after leaving Italy, Kermit's ship traced the route he and his father had taken to Mombasa—across the Mediterranean, through the funnel of the Suez Canal and down the Red Sea. Their old friends in British East Africa had been among the last to learn of the world war, and when word of the archduke's assassination arrived, by cable, Nairobi's weekly newspaper carried it only as a squib. One more disturbance in the perennially troubled Balkans seemed distinctly minor. But the British settlers were soon swept into the war by a vainglorious German colonel who decided that every Englishman kept busy in the colonies was one more assist to German victory in Europe.

At Chiromo, the Nairobi villa where Northrup and Florence McMillan once entertained TR and Kermit, Florence was running a nursing station. Northrup had joined the army and worked with the local quartermaster. Lord Delamere, red hair gone white but still long enough to shade the back of his neck, organized his Masai friends into reconnaissance patrols and deployed others as guards on the Uganda Railway. Frederick Selous, the great hunter, had returned to Africa as a soldier at the age of sixty-five and was killed by a sniper's bullet. "A fine clean way to go out," Kermit wrote his father.

In the Gulf of Aden, where Selous and the Roosevelts had continued south to Mombasa, Kermit's troop transport swung east toward the Persian Gulf. Several of the ship's stokers deserted in the searing heat, and Captain Roosevelt took his turn shoveling coal in the boiler room. He emerged with his first war injuries—blistered hands.

ROOSEVELT THE COLONEL was ready to die in battle, but Roosevelt the former president was still not resigned to living without power. At the end of August, three months after Wilson's rejection, Edith assured Archie that Theodore was bearing up. TR told him the truth: "I am having a horrid, unimportant time." Every week he received thousands of letters and scores of requests for speeches. The nation did not need "bugle-call oratory," he wrote Archie, it needed trained troops and weaponry. "That is why I so bitterly regret and resent not having been allowed to raise and go with troops to France." Although he thought that the hardships would have killed him, he said, "I would have lasted long enough to get a hundred thousand men in fighting mood and in efficient form, to the front; and then I would have been entirely willing to have had 'nunc dimittis' rung over me."

Ethel, who was living at Sagamore with her two small children while Dick served in France with the Army Medical Corps, reported to Kermit that both their parents were in ragged condition, their mother physically and their father "*completely* worn out mentally. . . . He has consistently overworked his mind lately." Mother was depressed, for reasons clear from a list in the back of her 1917 diary:

Ap. 2nd Wilson's message to Congress
Ap. 5th Q. came from Harvard to see about air work
Ap. 25th Q. rep. to Mineola
June 20th Ted and Archie sailed
June 30th Q. passed flying tests
July 7th Q. got his commission
July 9th Eleanor sailed
July 14th K. Belle & Kim sailed
July 23rd Q. sailed

The months with Quentin nearby had been happy ones for Edith. Her anxiety about the dangers of flying abated each night with the sound of his footsteps on the veranda, and after he sailed, she was sometimes visited by the odd sensation that she had just heard the footsteps again. Sagamore ached with emptiness. Edith felt that her life had broken off sharply; "it is like becoming blind or deaf—one just lives on, only in a different way," she would write Warrington Dawson.

Edith had been known to say that a duty performed was a rainbow in the soul, but optimism, the duty she had drawn for the war, was a forced march for any parent of sound mind. "I strongly feel that you are all coming home safe and sound," she wrote Kermit. "I cannot make it otherwise; and just think how much there will be to tell and hear." Hope, dread, artificial cheer—the form of uncountable letters from mothers staggering under the weight of their rainbows.

In October, in response to familial prompting, Theodore went to a physical culture camp in Connecticut for two weeks of dieting and exercise. "While he is away Mother will stay in bed for breakfast and take things easy, which is what she needs," Ethel wrote Kermit. "Of course, she *will* not eat. And father will eat too much. A sad state of affairs." Father breakfasted like a lumberjack, with a vat of coffee, fried eggs, bacon, liver, piles of bread, buttery grits, and fruit swimming in buckets of cream. At dinner one night Ethel watched him ingest two plates of tomatoes, two of applesauce, one of potatoes, plus eighteen spare ribs. Then, she said, "he refused to let me count further."

At camp Theodore saw no one but a masseur and his trainers, who worked him five hours a day in a routine so irksome that he wanted to scream, he wrote Archie. He came home thinner and harder, Edith thought, but unrefreshed. He sought tranquillity with her in his rowboat on the sound and made an admirable, sustained effort to steer his rage into a constructive channel: speeding up the nation's war work. He had been proselytizing for more arms and men in speeches and in articles for *Metropolitan*, and in the autumn of 1917 the *Kansas City Star* offered him a column.

Owned by an admirer, William Rockhill Nelson, the *Star* was known for the high quality of its writing and its staunchly maverick politics. The paper had a Republican tilt, but the party could not take Nelson's support for granted. In exchange for Roosevelt's views on the war, which were nothing if not maverick, the *Star* offered a ducal $25,000 a year and promised a large audience through syndication. For Roosevelt the irresistible feature of the proposition was its speed. Within twenty-four hours, whatever he wrote would be in the hands of his readers. "By George! I never thought of that," he said when the *Star's* editors made the point. The *Star* would be his bulliest pulpit since the presidency.

While Roosevelt always wrote with clarity and force, most of his work would have had twice the strength at half the length. Thanks to the paper's editorial rigor and the brevity of a newspaper column, the prose Roosevelt contributed to the *Star* ranks with his best. Winsome it was not, however. In the *Star*, Roosevelt struck only a few chords, none of them pianissimo. With information from General Wood and other dissatisfied friends in high places, he rebuked the War Department for its sluggishness and insisted that speaking out when leaders failed to lead was an act of patriotism, not disloyalty. He denounced German sympathizers — "the Huns within our gates," in his unlovely phrase — who in his mind included Senator La Follette and every other opponent of the war. He called for the United States to declare war on Austria and Turkey, as France and England had done. And he berated Wilson for his continuing desire to negotiate a peace rather than push for a decisive victory. "To talk peace means to puzzle the ignorant and to weaken the will of even the stout-hearted," he wrote. Germany was the enemy of humankind, invading Belgium, murdering civilians at sea, and introducing poison gas as a weapon. "Peace on equal terms with such a foe would mean black shame in the present and the certainty of renewed and wholesale war in the future."

The White House continued to ignore Roosevelt, as it had since 1914, when he wrote his first newspaper articles questioning Wilson's avoidance of the war. "I really think the best way to treat Mr. Roosevelt is to take no notice of him," the president told an aide. "That breaks his heart and is the best punishment that can be administered."

Newspapers backing the president suggested that Roosevelt's war on Wilson was an embarrassment, a tantrum born of vengeance or egomania. "Like Caesar's Gaul of old, the colonel's gall is also divided into three parts — the personal pronouns *I*, *me*, and *my*," said the *Minneapolis Daily News*. It and many other papers predicted that his ridicule of American shortcomings would merely hearten the Germans. The readers he perturbed most were his friends, who considered his vituperating pointless and worried that he was wrecking his chances for election in 1920.

Roosevelt was of several minds about his effectiveness as a critic. In letters to his sons he spoke despondently of being a "windjammer" and an "elderly male Cassandra has-been," but outside the family he was inclined to overrate his importance, boasting, for example, that he was the one who had forced Wilson to send troops abroad. Closest to the truth was his sense of himself as a minor source of momentum, "a factor in making the Administration do about a fifth of what it ought to and could, instead of only a twentieth." And to a friend he admitted that he wrote and made speeches "only because Wilson with cold spite, and because he is timid about what I could do, will not let me do the work I can do."

Early in his relationship with the *Star*, TR wrote his editor, Ralph Stout, that "as in so many other things of life," he was "teetering along a ridge pole, with . . . the danger of falling into more forcible speaking on one side and not enough forcible speaking on the other." He would try to keep his balance by speaking fearlessly but not so forcibly that he would be dismissed as a scold.

MESOPOTAMIA would become Iraq and the Gulf states, but during the world war it was a piece of the Ottoman Empire, which on the map resembled a huge paunch atop a pair of legs planted wide. The paunch held modern Turkey. One leg reached down the east coast of the Mediterranean and the Red Sea, the other—across the Arabian desert—was Mesopotamia, stretching from Baghdad to Oman, on the Persian Gulf. The kaiser had long fancied the Ottoman world, seeing it as the solution to a geographical problem that had become a German obsession. Landlocked except for a small seacoast on the Baltic, the Germans felt hemmed in by Russia, France, and England. But with a confederation of countries stretching southeast from Belgium to Turkey, the kaiser would have access to the Atlantic, the Mediterranean, the Black Sea, and the Red Sea. This *Mitteleuropa*, so called, awaited only the final German victory in Europe.

The Germans coaxed the Turks into joining them early in the war by running Turkish flags up the masts of two German ships and steaming into the Black Sea to shoot up a few Russian ports. The British dispatched troops to the foot of Mesopotamia to guard the Anglo-Persian Oil Company's concessions in the Gulf. Full-scale war erupted in 1915, when Britain, frustrated by the impasse on the Western Front, decided to land a swift jab at Turkey in hopes of forcing the Ottoman Empire to surrender. A Royal Navy squadron was dispatched to bombard Gallipoli, at the western gate of the Dardanelles, then push on to the eastern end of the strait and shell Constantinople. Victory, which the planners deemed certain, would reopen Russia's path from the Black Sea to the Mediterranean and give courage to the troops in the trenches of Europe. Nine months later, when the Allies called off the operation, Constantinople and Gallipoli were still in Turkish hands, and the Allies had suffered 250,000 casualties.

Ordered into action after the Gallipoli campaign began, the British troops near the Persian Gulf advanced smartly up the Tigris until November 1915, when Turkish and German forces pushed them into a hundred-mile-long retreat. The British dug in at Kut, where for five months they were caught in a miniature of Gallipoli. They surrendered in April 1916 and spent almost a year rolling back up the Tigris to take Baghdad.

Far to the west, on the empire's other leg, General Edmund Allenby and Colonel T. E. Lawrence were leading the Arabs in a revolt against the Ottoman Empire, and they too were fighting their way toward the paunch. So the skirmish that was supposed to begin and end with a few shots in the Dardanelles spilled across thousands of square miles. In size and carnage, the Mesopotamian battles paled next to Gallipoli and the Somme, but the stakes were immense. Only by winning could Britain drive Germany out of the Middle East, defend the northwestern flank of India, and hang on to its oil concessions.

After the war it would be said that the Allies "floated to victory upon a sea of oil." In one form or another, oil powered airplanes, automobiles, trucks, ambulances, and a growing number of ships. Without oil, the British might not have prevailed in Mesopotamia. The Tigris and the Euphrates flowed south, against the British line of march, and were not deep enough for anything but barges and other small craft. Railways were few. As Kermit would note in his memoir, *War in the Garden of Eden,* "Transportation was ever the hard nut to crack." He became a warrior on wheels in an army dependent on more than five thousand Fords, hundreds of lorries, and a small flock of LAMBs (Light-Armoured Motor Batteries): thirty-two Rolls-Royces plated with armor and outfitted with machine guns.

Assigned to the Royal Engineers of the Third Anglo-Indian Army, Kermit began by carrying out impromptu missions in the Fords, often in search of food or supplies. He also designed and built a snug little house for his general, who then offered him the post of aide-de-camp. He declined. A general's aide was an errand boy, he explained to Belle. The job entailed no real soldiering.

Kermit transferred to the LAMBs as soon as he mastered machine-gunning. Built on the same chassis as the civilian Rolls-Royce, a LAM car had the long, aristocratic snout of a Rolls and the homely behind of a pickup truck. The driver sat amidships, in a pillbox turret with a machine gun, and peered at the world through slits in the armor. His partner stood back of the turret and scanned the countryside, taking cover with the driver when the LAM came under fire. Although bullets from light artillery glanced off the armor, an unnerving amount of hot lead found its way inside.

The LAM cars weighed 9,000 pounds but were easily maneuvered and resilient in the face of gullies, rocks, blinding sandstorms, mirages, torrents that whipped the desert into mud, broiling heat, and breakdowns. "[The cars] scoot all over the desert, scouting and reconnoitering and harassing," Kermit wrote to Sagamore. His chief duty, as he understood it, was "noticing what is happening intelligently." LAM cars did their noticing in pairs, behind motorcycle scouts. On a good day they ranged across ninety miles.

Scooting around in a Ford or an armored Rolls released Kermit from the ennui of banking and gave him a surfeit of opportunities to test his courage. In November, near the town of Tikrit, 120 miles north of Baghdad, he and several other officers were trapped in a building while a German plane droned toward them, dropping a string of bombs with metronomic regularity. When the sound suggested that they were next, they hit the floor. The bomber missed, and Kermit assured Belle that aerial bombs were no threat unless they landed on a fellow, "and Mesopotamia's rather large."

The next day's advance was costly—1,800 British casualties. "Tommy takes his wounds most cheerfully," Kermit reported to Belle. The capture of Tikrit was a cakewalk. The Turks had stolen away in the night, and the British awoke to the sight of a village aflutter with white flags.

"I am overjoyed," TR wrote Kermit. "Three cheers! You have proved yourself; you have made good; you have justified the sorrow and worry you and darling Belle have shared. I am more pleased than I can say." He also expressed his satisfaction to Belle, adding that Kermit would have found it "dreadful . . . not to have actually had a hand in the real service."

Kermit did not share his father's enthusiasm, for he had already spotted the great weakness of the British campaign in Mesopotamia: the Turks were masters of retreat, able to cover huge distances and survive on virtually nothing. The British army advanced, and "the Turks merely receded—like the mirage," as one military historian put it. And each swath of territory gained by the British was one more "stretch of sand and dust to be garrisoned and pacified."

Camped near Tikrit on a bluff overlooking the sparkling blue Tigris, Kermit passed his free time reading *The Arabian Nights*, writing to Belle, and thinking—"not a very profitable pastime as I just get wretchedly home-sick," he told her. To Ethel he confided that the thousands of miles between him and Belle made him feel "perfectly hopelessly helpless. Having the entire family together again at the end of the war would seem like having sixty-three hundred pounds removed from the top of your head." He calmed his worries about Belle's pregnancy with the thought that her parents would go to any lengths, chartering a train if need be, to secure the finest doctors.

K ERMIT PASSED MUCH of the winter in Baghdad and in towns near the ruins of Babylon, where the changeable loyalties of the local Muslims had aroused British fears of revolt. The work bored him, and the war news from Europe, all of it bad, made him question his reasons for going to Mesopotamia. In the autumn of 1917 the British suffered 240,000 casualties at Passchendaele in Belgium, 275,000 Italians surrendered to the Austrians at Caporetto, and in France, after impressive gains at Cambrai with a new weapon called the tank, the British had failed to hold fast.

German casualties were also high, but reinforcements were on the way from Russia. When the revolutionaries, seeing the world war as a struggle of imperialists, surrendered to Germany and exited the war, 500,000 German troops were available for the fighting in France—"a bitter mischance," TR wrote to Kermit.

Wishing he were in Europe, Kermit asked his father how he might transfer to the American army, perhaps toward summer, when the heat would limit the fighting in the desert. The only British attack during the previous summer had taken place on a day when the thermometer registered 122 degrees in the shade. Heat stroke was a major source of casualties.

TR counseled patience and promised to help, *"but only if the British are satisfied to have you leave. Your first duty, until the end of this war, is to do, and to have the British know that you do,* whatever service they think you can most usefully render." TR probably did not know that the British were already planning to reduce their ranks in Mesopotamia, sending them to Europe or the western leg of the Ottoman Empire, to reinforce Lawrence and the Arabs.

Kermit fought boredom and homesickness by studying Arabic and Middle Eastern literature. He hired an Arab servant, and with this human dictionary at his side soon mastered the rudiments of the language. He read histories of the Middle East, works by travelers and archaeologists, *The*

Rubáiyát, and an English translation of Xenophon's *Anabasis*. There had been no time to assemble a Pigskin Library for the field, and in the desiccation of the desert, the covers of his books cracked and curled until he thought to oil them.

Just as his father on safari had looked forward to the comfortable beds and the gustatory possibilities of Nairobi, Kermit appreciated Baghdad for its baths and massages, parties with the British and native elites, and the distractions of snooping the souks. He learned to eat one-handed and to assemble his lunch by moving from the baker's stall to the pickle vendor's to the butcher's, where he waited for his kabob to come off the grill. After two months of study he could read and write Arabic, and he honed his conversation by chatting in the souks and eavesdropping in coffeehouses.

In Baghdad, Kermit ingratiated himself with Dame Gertrude Bell, a relative of his father's friend Cecil Spring Rice. An Oxford graduate with a first in modern history, Bell had spent nearly half her fifty years in the Middle East, traveling, writing, and befriending Arab sheiks—connections that made her invaluable in the operation led by Lawrence and Allenby. Kermit admired the perfection of her Arabic and found her amusing, which, as he remarked, "not everyone who has traveled is." She found him delightful and seemed surprised by his lack of ostentation. Her broad knowledge of the Middle East made her an excellent companion for excursions on horseback to Babylon, with its remnants of Nebuchadnezzar and Hammurabi and the wall where the moving finger having writ, moved on. "I'm being very nice to her because she may be helpful in getting you to Baghdad," he wrote his wife.

Kermit's hope for such a favor would have appalled his father, who had warned him against seeking any privilege and had made it plain that he must not give the British any impression that he wanted to go to war *en famille*. "My own feeling is that wives ought not to be near the firing line," he wrote him; "if they go, as Eleanor is going, it must be entirely separately from their husbands, and in good faith to work as assistants in the hospitals or wherever it is—and they must not go on the request of their husbands or through influence, especially influence by me." He had sent Belle a softer version of the same edict: taking care of herself and Kim was a task as serious as Kermit's, requiring selflessness and careful thought of the future.

Belle had no chance of going to Baghdad but every reason to yearn for an escape from Madrid. Her father, Ambassador Joseph Willard, was laboring under enormous strain. Spain was a neutral in the war, and Willard's mission was to keep the Spanish ship of state from listing toward the Germans, whose Spanish operatives ran thriving businesses in propaganda and espionage.

Spain was violating the rules of neutrality by allowing German U-boats to dock in Spanish harbors for repairs and refueling, saving them a trip across the Mediterranean to their allies in Turkey. Spain's hospitality to U-boats escalated from problem to crisis in 1917, when German torpedoes delivered more tonnage to the bottom of the sea than in the previous three years combined. Thousands of lives were lost, matériel bound for the front was destroyed, and Britain was nearing the edge of starvation. The U-boats were close to winning the war for the kaiser, and with two million Americans sailing to France, the final victory could be Germany's if the U-boats inflicted massive casualties at sea.

Ambassador Willard protested to the Spanish government, which promised to intern any German submarines discovered in its waters, yet the submarines continued to come and go. In October, Willard suffered a neurological thunderclap, probably a minor stroke, with several days of numbness, fierce headaches, and confusion. The strains in the embassy also included a dispute over Belle's nursemaid, an Austrian by birth but a longtime resident of the United States and a citizen of Argentina. Belle wanted to keep her, but her father argued that if the United States declared war on Austria, an Austrian occupation of the embassy, even an occupation of one, would be out of the question. He offered to establish Belle in an apartment of her own but noted that with Britain and Austria at war, the presence of an Austrian in her household might raise questions about Kermit's loyalties. Cornered, Belle gave in and hired an English nursemaid. The United States declared war on Austria in December. The baby, Joseph Willard Roosevelt, was born in January. The new English nurse quit a few months later.

In the spring of 1918 Kermit took part in one offensive up the Euphrates and another toward Persia, both of them intended to divert enemy forces from Lawrence and the Arabs, who were moving steadily north. Kermit had a terrifying drive through a gorge as snipers fired from above, and he survived a middle-of-the-night attack with bullets bouncing off the boulders near his bedroll. He escaped death by friend as well as foe. Hours after his comrades blew up a Turkish ammunition dump, he tiptoed across the warm ruins at the request of a general who wanted him to photograph the site. "I have spent happier moments," he would write in his memoir.

On at least one occasion, his fluency in Arabic saved his life. After repairing a flat tire and falling behind the rest of the army, he and his companion set out again, and when they came upon a building that looked like a barracks, they stopped for a look. Sure that the LAMs ahead of them would have cleared it, he walked into a courtyard and found himself face-to-face with a small band of Turkish soldiers. His revolver was still in its holster. He shouted in Arabic at the apparent leader, demanding that they give themselves up and, he said, "trying to act as if our forces were just outside. I think he must have been more surprised than I was, for he did so immediately, turning over the post to me."

He was more cautious on his next sortie, taking the local mayor as hostage and guide on a search for enemy documents in a village just evacuated by the Turks. Their first stop yielded no information of value, he said, but they discovered "four young girls, who, it was explained to me, formed the Turkish general's 'field harem.' He had left in too much of a hurry to take them with him." Kipling wrote TR that the deed rated a fresco in the White House and joked to Kermit that he deserved either a court-martial or a Victoria Cross.

Although there was no V.C.—the British equivalent of the Congressional Medal of Honor—there was a citation and a Military Cross for Captain Roosevelt's "energy and resource . . . in fetching up petrol" in two battles. The energy was in fact perseverance beyond exhaustion. He had fallen asleep at the wheel twice, nearly driving off an embankment on one of these occasions and smashing into a large rock on the other. His resourcefulness was an uncanny ability to find large stores of petrol without any clues to their whereabouts. His good work enabled the LAMBs to do theirs. The Military Cross was "awfully nice," he wrote to Sagamore.

"AWFULLY NICE." An Edwardian gentleman composing an account of his experiences understood that he was to refrain from braggadocio and complaint, emphasize the pleasant side of life, and, when writing home from a war, assure his loved ones that all was well. Kermit's memoir rarely strayed from the convention. Beneath the surface restraint of *War in the Garden of Eden* lies more restraint, layer upon layer of it. If Captain Roosevelt mowed down a band of Turks with his machine gun or dashed into the line of fire to haul a wounded comrade to safety, he did not find it seemly to say so. The book's one strong emotion is fear, obliquely expressed. The terrors of being attacked at night are denatured and compressed into "an eerie sensation." Two motifs—"Things could have been worse" and "There was nothing to do but put on a bold front"—suggest that he saw the inch between himself and death. The Turks "certainly could have given us a much worse time, for they had dug in well and scientifically," he wrote of the battle of Tikrit. The snipers above the gorge could have killed him by dropping a boulder that would have trapped him in the gorge. Kermit had nothing left to prove in the realm of physical courage, but the reckless boy who sprinted off alone in Africa had become a man who understood that courage without luck could be fatal.

War in the Garden of Eden has little in common with TR's memoir of the Spanish-American War. The Colonel, his eye on posterity, painted his tiny war on a huge canvas crowded with hard-bitten cowpokes and daring college athletes, all of them joined in the heroic cause of liberating the Cuban people. He sang the glories of war and of Anglo-Saxon dominance, magnified the contributions of the Rough Riders, and put the final touches on the portrait of the brave, dashing Theodore Roosevelt sketched by the newspapermen who had covered the war. For their money, readers of *The Rough Riders* also received his opinion (low) of the American military establishment's handling of the invasion.

Kermit did not romanticize war or his fellow warriors, nor did he lecture the British on how to run an army. He showed more interest in the inhabitants of Mesopotamia than his father did in the Cubans, who seldom appear in *The Rough Riders*. Kermit spoke of encounters with scholars of Arabic literature, admired the stamina of the Arab women hefting baskets of chickens and melons as they ran along the riverbanks and called out their wares to the boats passing by, and lingered long enough to describe the world of the dervishes: "They lead an easy life. When they take a fancy to a house, they settle down near the gate, and the owner has to support them as long as the whim takes them to stay there."

The most visible evidence of TR's influence on *War in the Garden of Eden* comes from *African Game Trails*. The war in Mesopotamia gave Kermit ample leisure for observing nature as well as culture. He gave his readers the machine gun clatter of a flock of storks and showed them spring in the desert, when the rains transformed the dry, gray earth into fields of clover and rolling grasslands filled with daisies and deep-red poppies.

Early in the book, Kermit told of a visit to the alleged Garden of Eden, a spot so unprepossessing that an English soldier had said it wouldn't take no angel with a flaming sword to drive *him* out. The garden's deficiencies launched Kermit on a quest for a place that matched his fantasies of Eden. He found it on the Euphrates in the spring of 1918, a few weeks before leaving Mesopotamia. He walked his readers across fields of spring wheat and grass starred with pink and blue flowers on an island that was "one great palm-grove, with pomegranates, apricots, figs, orange-trees, and grape-vines growing beneath the palms." Kermit invited the reader to look at his world. The Rough Rider wanted the reader to look at him.

With the blessings of his commander, Kermit left for the Western Front in May. TR smoothed his transition from the British army to the AEF with letters to friends in London and Washington. Kermit was commissioned as a captain of field artillery, a logical assignment after his months with the LAMBs. TR, who would have made a grand Cupid had he not been so fully employed by Hercules and Mars, wrote Belle that he had "foxily" requested permission for Kermit to report at Madrid, "and the Acting Chief of Staff granted it!" Fleetingly TR wondered if a soldier attached to the army of a belligerent nation risked internment in a neutral country. He guessed that Kermit would be safe—"between hay and grass," as he thought of it—out of the British army but not yet in the American.

The prospect of all his sons fighting under the Stars and Stripes in history's largest clash of arms elated TR, but to Belle, the future seemed a fog. The news of the transfer kept her awake till five in the morning, she wrote Kermit. She felt torn between "the unbelievable hope of perhaps seeing you so soon—and the agony of having you in the midst of the slaughter in France."

EIGHTEEN

On a Volcano

THE slaughter of the world war would claim more than eight million lives, most of them before the American Expeditionary Force began arriving in France in the summer of 1917. Archie and Ted Roosevelt reached Bordeaux at the end of June, two months after the disastrous Nivelle offensive, a French assault along a fifty-mile front between Soissons and Reims. The attack ended with 187,000 French casualties, no military gains, and a month of mutinies. More in despair than in fury, 30,000 soldiers climbed out of the trenches and trudged to the rear. They would defend the line, they said, but were no longer willing to attack. Two-thirds of the mutineers were court-martialed and found guilty. Of the 450 sentenced to death, 400 were granted the hard mercy of penal servitude. Fifty executions inoculated the rest of the army against further indiscipline.

The Americans knew nothing of the mutinies, and by a piece of grace as ineffable as grace itself, no scent of the revolt wafted over the German lines. The new general-in-chief of the French Armies, Henri-Philippe Pétain, had restored order and bought favor with better food and more leave. But he had not worked a miracle. The French waited more than a year before launching another attack. The mutineers had won.

To the aid of this weary army and the sapped British forces holding the westernmost stretch of the 460-mile Western Front came the First Division of the American Expeditionary Force—27,000 strapping, eager military innocents. Only one in a hundred AEF captains had served in the regular army for more than a year, and each of them would be entrusted with two hundred lives. Fewer than 5 percent of the AEF's officers were in the army when the United States declared war.

Second Lieutenant Archibald Roosevelt, not quite twenty-three, and Major Theodore Roosevelt, Jr., soon to turn thirty, were better trained than most. Archie had been preparing since the summer of 1915, when he and Quentin and Ted first went to Plattsburg. Back at Harvard in the fall, Archie and two friends had formed a regiment to continue training, and with money from Ted and his friends, they were soon marching about Cambridge, digging trenches, and pitching tents in Harvard Yard. General Wood furnished them with instructors and uniforms left over from the Spanish-American War. Their rifles and pistols, equally antiquated, came from a nearby army depot.

Archie was dumbfounded when their recruiting advertisements ran into opposition from A. Lawrence Lowell, Harvard's president. Lowell still hoped that the White House would find an opening to negotiate a peace, and as his disapproval mounted, TR warned Archie that he might be expelled. Archie was uncowed. The clash ended when Lowell, besieged by alumni with a Rooseveltian view of preparedness, backed down.

The regiment delighted TR. It was both an enactment of his own beliefs and an affirmation of his faith in Archie, a boy with a tendency to conceal his merits beneath a thick hide of perversity. Seeing no reason to emulate Kermit the dandy, Archie shambled about in odds and ends, some of them borrowed from his father's wardrobe. Archie also passed up many a fine opportunity to keep his thoughts to himself. Baffled by the tall, blond galoot in their midst, Edith guessed that his premature departure from Groton had deprived him of several coats of polish. Archie cared nothing for the esteem of outsiders, a quality TR lacked but admired. If such indifference was a fault, it was "a fault on the right side," TR contended. In his loving eyes, Archie was "a very dear boy."

Few at Harvard thought so. There he was a prude and a snitch, notorious for turning in students who enlivened their quarters with strong drink and sportive women. His rasping cost him a place in the Porcellian, where his father, his brothers-in-law, and Ted and Kermit had been proud members. Archie shrugged.

IN PARIS the Colonel's sons reported to Pershing, who assigned both of them to infantry regiments that would be based more than two hundred

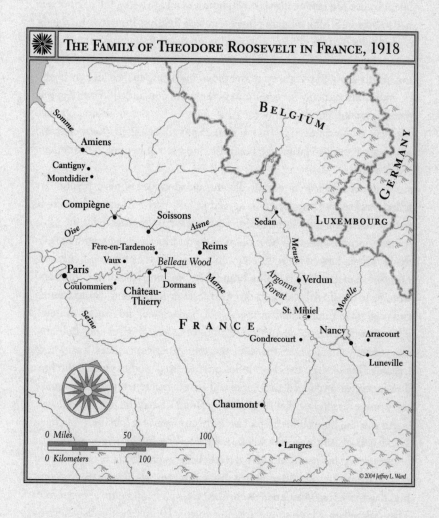

THE FAMILY OF THEODORE ROOSEVELT IN FRANCE, 1918

BELGIUM

GERMANY

Somme

Amiens

Cantigny
Montdidier

Compiègne

Oise

Soissons

Aisne

Sedan

LUXEMBOURG

Meuse

Fère-en-Tardenois

Reims

Vaux

Belleau Wood

Paris

Argonne
Forest

Verdun

Coulommiers

Château-
Thierry

Dormans

Marne

St. Mihiel

Moselle

Seine

FRANCE

Gondrecourt

Nancy

Arracourt

Luneville

Chaumont

0 Miles   50   100

0 Kilometers   100

Langres

© 2004 Jeffrey L. Ward

miles to the east, in the Champagne-Ardenne region, far from the deadly sectors of the front. Archie's regiment, the Sixteenth, settled near Langres. Ted and the Twenty-sixth were sixty miles north, near the village of Gondrecourt-le-Château. Pershing set up AEF headquarters in between, at Chaumont, a pleasant town not known for much of anything. When overtaken by the urge to erect a statue in honor of a native son, Chaumont had had to borrow Philippe Lebon, inventor of gas lighting, from its hinterlands.

Ted joined three officers in knocking on doors to line up billets for the regiment. Gondrecourt lacked barracks, and Pershing saw virtue in scattering his unseasoned troops: en masse they would have maked an easy target.

The Gallic appetite for ceremony and symbol demanded a Fourth of July parade through Paris to honor the AEF and give the demoralized populace a look at its new hope. The march would start at Napoleon's tomb and end at the grave of the Marquis de Lafayette, the French hero of the American Revolution.

Pershing, who feared that the obvious inexperience of his expeditionary force would sink French hearts, agreed to take part but sent only a single battalion, Archie's. Pershing's reservations proved unfounded, for the rookies met only enthusiasts, one million of them. Flowers were scattered from the windows, lobbed from the sidewalks, and strewn by boys and girls running ahead of the soldiers. Poilus home on leave joined the march, men and women bared their heads and dropped to their knees, and young women slid past gendarmes to deliver kisses (not appreciated, the American newspapers said, thereby relieving the second-worst fear of wives and mothers). The crowds chanted the name of the one American soldier they knew: "Ted-dy! Ted-dy! Ted-dy!" Five miles on, in a small cemetery near the Bois de Vincennes, an American colonel with an elegant sense of moment spoke the words ever afterward attributed to Pershing: "Lafayette, we are here."

Archie said little about his part in the historic day. He had married Grace Lockwood of Boston a few weeks before sailing for France, and he was homesick and heartsore, afraid that it had been wrong to marry on his way to war. Ted quickly orchestrated a transfer that put Archie under his command, a move that gladdened Archie but set off a small bomb at Sagamore. The Colonel gave both sons a dressing-down. "I emphatically disbelieve in two brothers being together where one has anything to say about the duties of the other," he told them. No matter how much Archie deserved it, any recognition from Ted would look like favoritism.

Ted held firm. Whether he and Archie were together or not, he wrote their father, a few cynics would carp that the sons of Theodore Roosevelt were receiving preferential treatment. Ted was confident that the army would judge him and Archie fairly, by their deeds. The Colonel retreated.

After the war the army claimed that the average soldier sent to France received nine months of training before going into combat: six months in the United States, two behind the lines in France, and one on a quiet stretch of the front. But the average soldier crossing the Atlantic in 1917 had had only a few weeks of training, often without real weapons. "Broomstick preparedness," TR called it in one of his early columns for the *Star*. The phrase had occurred to him as he and Leonard Wood watched conscripts drilling with wooden guns and log cannons at Camp Funston in Kansas, one of the army's largest training sites.

American soldiers went to France lacking military knowledge of every sort. Ted overheard one man falling in for muster say to another, "No, not the mustard you put on the table! Ain't you got no better ignorance than that?" Pershing was determined to keep his neophytes behind the lines until they could turn in a creditable performance.

The training was further complicated by a philosophical difference between Pershing and the French commanders. They were still committed to trench warfare, but Pershing believed that the long standoff on the Western Front would end only if the Germans were forced into the open for a war of movement. Trench warfare left most of the shooting to the artillery, while success in the open demanded an army of superb marksmen. To satisfy both theories, the new soldiers spent their mornings on target practice and other U.S. Army basics, and passed their afternoons with the French, learning how to storm trenches, hurl grenades, and survive a gas attack. The double course load put the Americans well behind the French timetable even though they "worked overtime and all the time," said Captain George C. Marshall, an aide to Pershing.

Lieutenant Archie Roosevelt gave himself to his work with the zeal that is often the rose in a thorny temperament. A general watching him drill his troops wrote TR that Archie was a natural leader, energetic and able to bring out the best in his men. In September, Warrington Dawson came out from Paris to visit Archie and Ted and beamed with avuncular pride at the "tall, proud program" they had set for themselves. Archie was keen to make his company the best in Ted's battalion, Ted wanted his battalion to be the best in the regiment, and together they intended to make the Twenty-sixth Infantry the best regiment in the First Division.

As a patrician and son of a forceful leader, Archie gave orders without the egalitarian twinges that sometimes beset young officers of humbler origins, and his philosophy of command was bone-simple: treat the men like children and show subordinate officers the respectful firmness one accorded a much younger brother. He enjoyed his men and had his hair cut to stubble after they were ordered to sacrifice theirs in the unending war on lice. To his military duties Archie added the burden of moral instruction, although his Harvard hellfire seems to have died to embers. The sight of wholesome lads with "unspeakably dreadful women on their arms" elicited only silent disapproval and the thought that they would return to right living after the war. When he and his troops chanced upon a wine cellar in a ruined château, he told Dawson, he announced that as a gentleman he would take nothing, but he promised that those who succumbed to temptation would not be punished. He asked only that they refrain from greed and immoderation.

Dawson was disturbed to see that Archie was almost gaunt. He trained all day, and come evening, after he ate and took care of his paperwork, he went to bed too fagged even to read. He was also anxious. Gracie was pregnant, a fact that raised a host of fears, and he imagined that when he returned in a year or two, the baby would see him as an intruder. "Gracie has had a rough time of it, and I only hope I can make it up to her someday," he wrote Ethel. Archie's turmoil undoubtedly deepened when Gracie urged him to seek a staff job, away from the fighting line. He had no intention of missing his turn at the front. Combat to him was more than a test of courage, it was "a great thrill" and the reward for the grueling months of preparation.

When Archie wrote his father about Gracie's opposition, the Rough Rider was reassuring. "We are fighting men," he replied; "it is in the line that we can do our work to best advantage. I am sure I can make her understand." He promised to take up the question with Gracie during her next visit to Sagamore. Either the conversation went badly or TR changed his mind, because he was soon advocating a compromise: if Archie did a bit of fighting and then was offered a staff position where he could be more useful, it would be "foolish to refuse it merely because it was less dangerous." Knowing that Archie would dislike the idea, TR wrapped it in an apology: "a weak-minded elderly father must be excused for hinting."

While Archie's struggles with Gracie were intermittent, there was no break from the hardships in France. In October he and Ted and the rest of the First Division moved seventy-five miles east into Lorraine, near Lunéville, on a relatively quiet sector of the front, and, as sons of Theodore

Roosevelt, were thrilled to be among the first Americans in the trenches. For two months, Archie's men were underfed on most days and entirely unfed on numerous occasions. Nor was there forage for their horses and mules. In desperation, Archie stole a bag of oats for the mule that pulled their kitchen wagon, but a single bag of feed was hardly enough. The mules were chewing the wood in their stalls, eating their halter straps, and on one terrible day, seventeen of them dropped dead. Hoping to save space in cargo holds, the army had purchased oats coated with molasses and pressed into bricks. The bricks proved difficult to break up, they would attract flies in warm weather, and the molasses ruined feedbags.

After the war the army's official statistical report flatly declared that there was never a shortage of food in the AEF. Soldiers sometimes went hungry, especially when they were on the move and outran their rolling kitchens, but such problems were sporadic, the report said. "The stocks of food on hand in depots in France were always adequate." Had Archie known that dinner was sitting in the storehouses, he would have been even more upset.

As the cold rains of autumn set in, leggings and gloves that should have been furnished by the army failed to arrive. Pershing met a soldier who had been sent to the guardhouse for stealing socks, clearly a crime of desperation. General Robert Lee Bullard, commander of the First Division, was in despair. The AEF's accomplishments, despite the best of intentions, were "pitiful," he wrote in his diary. "We are being nursed and cared for . . . by the French. They will, I fear, soon become tired and disgusted with us." Bullard was certain that the Germans would win the war.

Archie advanced his own money to his men for the winter clothing they needed, fumed about his prosperous country's failure to keep its soldiers warm and fed, and gamely tried to keep up his humor. "Mud! Heavens above!" he wrote Ethel. "We have so much of it that I am sure we shall all be web-footed after this war. Why the French fight for this country, or why the Germans were foolish enough to want to take it, remains an insoluble mystery to me."

The mud quickly ruined boots, and constant exposure to damp and cold caused feet to swell, an unforeseen contingency. The War Department replenished the boot supply based on infantry experience in the United States, and most of the replacements were too small. Captain Marshall saw men on the march with their feet wrapped in gunnysacks, and he would remember the winter, which was exceptionally cold, as the worst period of the war. Valley Forge came to his mind, and the comparison was apt — countryside covered with snow and ice, scarcities of nearly everything, and six weeks of maneuvers in mud, snow, and ice water. Ted Roosevelt would recall "slimy trenches, where the snow and sleet glazed the dugouts and duck-boards," sodden blankets, numb hands and feet. TR offered to help Archie with the shortages in his company, and Edith encouraged him to ask for money when he needed it. With $25,000 a year from the *Star* and $5,000 from *Metropolitan*, she said, "the old man can still oblige with a spare hundred." The old man obliged with two hundred pairs of shoes.

One lone lieutenant could not sound reveille loudly enough to rouse a comatose bureaucracy, and Archie's letters home grew increasingly intemperate. "A word of advice!" TR wrote him in December. "Don't say anything against your superiors." He feared that the censors who scanned the outgoing mail might forward one of the outbursts to an ill-disposed senior officer. "Grin and bear it," TR counseled; "do your level best; and abide by the fall of the dice. Afterwards, I promise you that I and you will do all that is possible to visit upon the wrongdoers, great and small, the proper punishment." TR also reminded Archie, the struggling, dogged boy who had sometimes studied to the point of collapse, that excessive worry could harm his body and his work.

Archie did not collapse, his protests brought no reprimand, and by Christmas he was Captain Roosevelt. His ecstatic father mentioned the promotion in numerous letters and to Archie sent a high compliment: "Lord, how proud I am."

THE COLONEL in his exile occasionally confessed to bitterness at Wilson's refusal to send him to France, but he told himself that the rejection had bestowed an advantage: "I write and speak with a freedom which I could not possibly exercise if I were in the army," he wrote Archie. Roosevelt's strenuous exercise of his freedom has been read as simple vengeance, but his criticism was largely driven by a desire to turn up the speed of the nation's war effort. As he knew from his sons, the consequences of delay and fumbling were no longer hypothetical.

In citing the weaknesses of the war effort and calling for a stronger defense, TR was drawing on life lessons from his father, who had insisted that young Theodore "make" his body in order to be able to hold his own with the strong. The elder Theodore had also taught him, through his civic involvements, that power was to be used to defend high ideals and fight injustices. Roosevelt had taken these principles into the realm of national defense as a very young man, when he wrote *The Naval War of 1812*, and throughout his life maintained that the power to resist aggression went far in the direction of deterring it. Military readiness did not prevent war any more than a fire department could prevent all destructive fires, he said, but it diminished the possibilities for disaster.

Fighting a war for which they had not prepared, Americans had two duties, Roosevelt argued in the *Star*. The first was to speed arms and men to the front. The second was "not to fool ourselves, but to face the fact of our complete and lamentable unpreparedness" and to take the steps needed to prevent such humiliation in the future. Roosevelt knew of a training camp with only one rifle for every two hundred soldiers, and if that ratio was an anomaly, one in eight was not.

The harshness of Roosevelt's wartime writings has been adduced as evidence that out of power, he was unable to check the aggressiveness that his advisers had reined in when he was president. He had always loved the sound of his own roar, but during the war he was not at anger's mercy. He decided, coolly and rationally, that nothing short of sledgehammering would raise the public outcry that would embarrass Wilson and the War Department into action. "I often feel fairly sick with impotent rage at my inability to make the authorities show wisdom and efficiency," he wrote Archie; "and the people are so foolish and uninformed that I am obliged to hold myself in because if I tell anything like the whole truth they simply don't believe me and I do harm rather than good."

The whole truth emerged in the winter of 1917–18, when the Senate Military Affairs Committee held six weeks of hearings on the war effort. The committee's chairman, an Oregon Democrat named George E. Chamberlain, summed up the problem in a sentence: the War Department had ceased to function. The committee called dozens of witnesses, including Secretary of War Newton Baker, who appeared several times. Baker freely admitted mistakes—inevitable because of the size and haste of the endeavor, he said—and insisted that they had been addressed. Chamberlain upbraided him for attempting to "lull the people into a feeling of absolute security that everything has been done."

"Senator, I think this country is entitled to feel secure," Baker replied.

Chamberlain disagreed. "I think the country is entitled to know the conditions," he said.

The conditions according to Baker were that in nine months the army had grown from 200,000 to 1.4 million men, officers' ranks had expanded from 10,000 to 111,000, sixteen large training camps had been built, hundreds of thousands of soldiers had been readied for France, and ambitious programs for manufacturing equipment and weapons had been drawn up. "No army of similar size in the history of the world has ever been raised, equipped, or trained so quickly," he said.

Baker had boasted that when the United States entered the war, "we were not, like our adversary, ready for it, anxious for it, prepared for it, and inviting it. Accustomed to peace, we were not ready." Roosevelt pounced on him, and *The Nation* pounced on Roosevelt for ridiculing a sentiment shared by most of the country. But even after the declaration of war, Baker had hesitated, in part because of a healthy disrespect for militarism and in part from his fear that a federal agency comparable to Britain's powerful Ministry of Munitions would prove impossible to dismember after the war. He decided to mobilize the country through state and local organizations, a choice that quickly led to chaos as scores of committees sought to interact with the military.

The hearings largely corroborated Roosevelt's critique of the war effort. The story of the mobilization was a story of indecision, delay, mistaken assumptions, and epic failures of coordination. Freight trains laden with supplies for the AEF headed to ports on the Atlantic seaboard, snarling traffic in the Northeast and creating a rail car shortage in the rest of the country. Baker blamed the army and navy for overusing their wartime authority to stamp "priority" on shipping orders. The War Department's inability to sort out the railroad fiasco led President Wilson to assign the task to the Treasury Department.

The army had foreseen a shortage of uniforms but had not thought to improvise. When the quartermaster general was asked why he had not, for example, laid in a store of denim overalls, he answered, "Frankly, I wish I had thought of that." Archie had complained about the dearth of boots large enough for his men, and the committee learned that the same was true of shirts and overcoats. It was also revealed that many of the shortages in France could be traced to the army chief of staff's office, which for months had scheduled troop shipments without consulting the quartermaster general.

The broomsticks and log cannons in the training camps were the result of an interminable debate over which rifles and machine guns to manufacture. When Baker insisted that the new weapons were worth the wait and that the broomsticks were of no consequence because every soldier had a rifle by the time he went to France, Senator James W. Wadsworth, Jr., of New York lost his patience. "We have had it told to us time and time again in this committee that there is a rifle for every soldier that goes abroad; that there will be fieldpieces for every soldier who reaches France," he said. "The truth is that they did not know how to use the rifles and fieldpieces when they got them."

Concerned about the conditions in the training camps, the president's secretary, Joseph Tumulty, was quietly gathering intelligence from his own sources, one of whom was Lodge's son-in-law, Augustus P. Gardner, who had left Congress to join the army. Writing from Camp Wheeler in Georgia in December 1917, Gardner reported that ninety-six men had just died of pneumonia. The camp's commander and the quartermaster general were not to blame, Gardner said. The problem was simply that textile factories could not meet the army's demand for woolen clothing. Of the eighteen thousand men at Camp Wheeler, fewer than a quarter had been issued a full set of woolens, from underwear to overcoat. The tents were damp at night, a measles epidemic had overtaxed the camp's hospital, and the men were depressed and homesick, a combination "which tends to reduce a man's vitality," Gardner said. He too caught pneumonia and died, on January 4, 1918.

A few weeks later, when Chamberlain delivered a three-hour assault on the government's conduct of the war, Wilson lashed back. The successes of the War Department vastly outnumbered the failures, Baker was one of the ablest public servants he knew, and Chamberlain's investigation was a waste of time the president said. No useful suggestions had emerged, and the proceedings had drawn "indispensable officials of the department constantly away from their work and officers from their commands."

Roosevelt came to town, making his first visit to Washington since the meeting with Wilson about the volunteer division, and he spoke to a full house at the National Press Club. He endorsed Chamberlain's investigation as well as a bill to create a war cabinet and a munitions director to manage the country's war effort. The partisan was a poor citizen in time of war, he said, but constructive criticism was both just and necessary. He mentioned Baker not at all and Wilson only once, quoting a passage from *Congressional Government*, a book Wilson had written during his years as a professor. The congressional power to investigate was at least as vital as the power to legislate, Wilson had argued, for unless Congress scrutinized and discussed the performance of those who governed, "the country must remain in embarrassing and crippling ignorance." Those who knew Theodore Roosevelt knew what he meant: Woodrow Wilson had done better as professor than president.

Baker offered to resign, and although Wilson rejected the idea, he soon recruited the financier Bernard Baruch to chair the War Industries Board and gave him the latitude of a czar. A Rooseveltian on the issue of preparedness, Baruch had given generously to Wilson's presidential campaigns and for three years had advised him on defense. Baker, who disliked Baruch, sourly questioned the appropriateness of conferring such great power on a Wall Street speculator. But where Baker had dithered in mobilizing industry for the war, Baruch would act—expeditiously and decisively. As one of his admirers would put it, Baruch succeeded because he was unafraid to "look any man in the eye and tell him to go to hell."

Theodore and Edith stayed with Alice and Nick in Washington, and while Edith visited old friends, Theodore feasted on congressmen, senators, military men, and a few stalwarts of the Bull Moose campaign. Friends talked of a presidential run in 1920. Roosevelt thought that he had grown too extreme to win an election or govern the country but did not snuff the talk.

On February 5, Theodore and Edith braved deep snow to drive from Oyster Bay to Roosevelt Hospital in Manhattan. Theodore was in considerable peril from abscesses in his ears and a fistula in the upper reaches of his thigh. The ear operations were straightforward, but when the surgeons set to work on the other abscess, the patient bled profusely, and his flesh, seemingly as tough as his character, resisted the knife. Soon after the surgery he spoke to Ethel as if for the last time, telling her in a barely audible voice that he admired her more than anyone but Edith. Ethel was staggered to see him without color and drained of strength, the very quality that defined Theodore Roosevelt and that he had defined for a generation. "He just must get well," she wrote Dick. "He must."

Edith, who stayed with him at the hospital for several days, read him the papers, which on February 15 reported the death of Sir Cecil Spring Rice, in Ottawa. The ambassador had hung on in Washington through 1917, watching his duties dwindle as he was eased toward the door. To spare him the humiliation of a recall after long and mostly fine service in the diplomatic corps, the Foreign Office had posted him to Canada, where he lasted six weeks. During their years in Washington, Springy and Lady Springy, as TR called them, rarely saw the Roosevelts. Fond as they were of each other, the Colonel and the ambassador feared that a close tie might irritate Woodrow Wilson and compromise Springy's chances for success. They corresponded, but early in 1915, with the onset of Spring Rice's diplomatic travails, TR began sending his letters to the embassy in envelopes without his name on them—"so as to attract as little attention as possible," he said. TR voiced his grief at the news from Ottawa but not on the bitter fruit of their decision to forgo the pleasures of their old friendship. The scrupulously maintained distance had done Spring Rice not a whit of good.

The newspapers during the weeks TR spent in the hospital were full of war news and full of reports on his condition. Until he was out of danger the stories ran on the front page. The operation destroyed the hearing in his left ear and temporarily left him walking "like a lunatic duck," he wrote Eleanor. Still, correspondence streamed out of his hospital room, as did a few columns for the *Star*. In one, he tried again to persuade the public that reproving a dilatory government was an act of patriotism. The war belonged to the people, not to the president or the Congress, and the people were "honor bound in conducting it to stand by every official who does well and against every official who fails to do well."

During the days when Roosevelt's death seemed a possibility, newspapers reassessed his castigation of the White House and the War Department and found much to admire. The world had often come around to the Colonel's point of view, and when it did, his "I told you so" was usually delivered with merriment. This time was different, perhaps because he had gone to the edge of life. Explaining the public reaction to Archie, he said that the American people "suddenly realized that down at the bottom of their hearts they knew I had been telling the truth, and that the reason they had been against me was because they deliberately preferred not to be worried and were irritated with me for making them uncomfortable. It suddenly overcame them that if I died there might not be anybody who could give them the right lead even if they did not wish to follow it."

Though hard to see in the glare of the egotism, his thoughts harbored a touching aspiration. Believing that mere observation rarely changed the world, he had always seen the critic as a minor character. The true agent of progress, as he had said years before, was the man in the arena, bleeding, covered in dust and sweat, striving valiantly to do the deeds. Action was all, and the man he admired was the man who did things. Barred from the war, Roosevelt had been demoted to the ranks of those who say things, and he desperately wanted the things he said to spur those in a position to do things.

T HE PENULTIMATE SLAUGHTER of the world war began in the spring of 1918, and for months beforehand the Germans had poked at the Allied line, looking for weak spots and testing the Americans. The first American casualties came in early November, when three soldiers were killed and a dozen were taken prisoner in a predawn ambush of trenches north of Gondrecourt, near the Marne–Rhine Canal. The urge to retaliate was strong, and despite French opposition to the idea, Major Ted Roosevelt talked his general into authorizing a raid. A French officer was assigned to help the raiding party plan and rehearse the operation.

In a trench raid a small party ambushed a large body of the enemy, killed swiftly, and raced for cover. If the raiders were not quick, the enemy fought back. A trench raid was "a short, terrible, crashing fight, a thing of a few rods and a few minutes, filled with danger and death," General Bullard would write in his account of commanding the First Division. "Its suddenness, its hand-to-hand deadly encounters, its carnage at close quarters with daggers, pistols, and fearful explosives, its shattering, bloody, merciless action, make it terrible to both raiders and raided."

Once Ted's party was ready, he was informed that he could not lead it. It was a small endeavor, calling for the leadership of a junior officer, his superiors said. The honor fell to Archie. On the night of the raid, Archie and a French lieutenant led their troops across no-man's-land, laying a trail of white tape as they went, to help them find their way home. Headed for a building known as a nest for Germans on patrol, they got lost. The Frenchman suggested that they turn back. Archie would not hear of it and sent him home alone. No Germans were found, and as they moved through the blackness, one of the Americans was separated from the rest of the party. When he spotted Archie and his comrades again and headed in their direction, they mistook him for a German and opened fire (without hitting him, apparently).

The Germans continued to nick at their nerves with lethal little forays that gave no hint of the larger plan. "[T]he things they have staged this year show such strength and ability," Ted wrote his father in February. In the calm between skirmishes, Archie said, he felt he was sitting on a volcano.

Snipers fired from camouflage, sleep was disrupted by gaudy flares and random bursts of machine gun fire. Combat would be a relief from the nervous strain of watching and waiting, Archie thought.

Just before dawn on March 11, Archie Roosevelt and his company were on the alert in their trenches, ready to support a raiding party. The Germans saw the raiders coming, unleashed their heavy artillery, and Archie was hit in the arm and knocked to the ground, where he was hit again, in the leg. Hospital corpsmen dressed his wounds and carried him to a cellar to wait out the barrage. As they made their way through bursting shells and rains of steel fragments, he insisted more than once that they put down his stretcher and take cover. Archie had rough edges in the drawing room, but as one of his comrades wrote to Edith, his orders from the stretcher were acts of high courage, for "the sufferings of a wounded man in that predicament are almost unbearable."

Wounded at five in the morning, Archie did not see a doctor until seven at night. Fourteen others came into the field hospital with him, and he had asked that they be treated first. When his turn came, the surgeon pried a large chunk of shrapnel from his left femur and tweezed smaller fragments from his left humerus, which was splintered and broken in two places.

Ted rushed the news to the family and wrote Gracie that Archie would be *hors de combat* for months. "This of course he does not know. . . . From your point of view I think this is a windfall. He is not seriously hurt and will recover absolutely but may be out of danger in the line for the war." To his father, Ted exulted, "Well, one of your sons has an honorable wound, will have a scar and will be otherwise sound as a bell. 'There's glory for you,' as Humpty-Dumpty said. It is real Roosevelt luck." Pinned to Archie's pillow was a red-and-green-striped ribbon with a bronze Maltese cross, the Croix de Guerre. An American citation praising his coolness and gallantry under fire would follow.

His brother-in-law Dick Derby examined him the next day, spoke with the doctors, and satisfied himself that Archie would be left with nothing more serious than a stiff knee. The surgeon who had performed the operation was one of the army's best. When Archie could be moved he would go to Paris. Until then he was resting as comfortably as he could with an arm in an elevated sling. Dick read him a long letter from Ethel about the birth of Archie Jr. three weeks before, an event previously known to Captain Roosevelt only from a short item in the Paris *Herald*. The family's cables and letters about the birth had gone astray.

Newspapermen who came to see Archie were turned away. He saw no reason why he should receive more attention than others who had been wounded.

No word for the folks at home? they asked.

No, he said, through a nurse. The folks would have to content themselves with the same information given out on all American soldiers in France.

Archie had a marked preference for the high road, and as he undoubtedly knew, the folks would have other sources of news. Before breakfast on March 12 the United Press had phoned Sagamore with the news that Archie had received a Croix de Guerre "under dramatic circumstances." Just after noon Alice telephoned from Washington to report that General Pershing had cabled the War Department that Archie was slightly wounded. And at one there was word of a cable from Ted, who assured them that Archie would recover.

Edith summoned a bottle of choice Madeira from the cellar, and "all four of us filled the glasses and drank them off to you," TR wrote Archie; "then Mother, her eyes shining, and her cheeks flushed, as pretty as a picture, and as spirited as any heroine of romance, dashed her glass to the floor, shivering it in pieces, saying, 'that glass shall never be drunk out of again'; and the rest of us followed suit and broke our glasses too. Well, we know what it feels like to have a hero in the family!" Ethel noticed that TR's eyes were also shining, with tears.

Assured that Archie would recover, TR was almost giddy with excitement. He pronounced the Croix de Guerre the family's finest possession. "I cannot help feeling pride that one of my boys has been severely wounded in fighting for civilization and humanity beside your troops in France," he wrote a French author who had sent him a book about the war. He told Archie that the family's friends understood his pride, "and a good many felt that, inasmuch as you were going to recover, they were rather glad that one of *my* sons had the dangerous honor of being among the first to be wounded in battle."

"TIP-TOP," TR said at the end of March when George Perkins telephoned to ask about his health. "Tip-top." He was riding and chopping wood again. He and Edith had just returned from Boston, where they visited Gracie and inspected the baby, who, to his grandfather's satisfaction, was "a sturdy mite" and a double of Archie Sr. in his infant phase.

Theodore had left Edith and Gracie in Boston while he went on to Portland, Maine, to make a speech setting the tone for the Republican congressional campaigns in the fall. A Republican sweep in 1918 would smooth the course for 1920, when—if TR's friends had their way—Theodore Roosevelt would be returned to the White House. Aware that his criticism of Wilson put him at odds with much of the country, TR had asked a score of party leaders, conservative and progressive, to vet an early draft of the speech. As if afraid that he might jinx his prospects by actually mentioning 1920, he obliquely explained to Hiram Johnson that he had written it "with the design of keeping whatever shreds of whatever influence I had, so that they should be available for the country when I did have a chance to achieve something."

Energized by the crowd in Portland, he spoke for three hours. "This was an engagement that I told my doctors in the hospital they had to have me keep—and here I am," he began. His self-command was complete as he urged the party to chart a course between the extremes of unregulated capitalism and the excessive regulation called for by the socialists. In his new world, which was virtually a twin of his old one, the federal government would exert itself to create economic justice for all, using its powers to keep the scales from tipping too far in either direction.

Speaking of the war, he was less contained. "On some other occasion I shall discuss the novel doctrine that it is our duty to lie if we think the enemy is deceived by it," he said. "It turns out in the present instance that the enemy was not at all deceived. Our own people were the only ones deceived." His voice strong and his body showing no fatigue in the crowded, stuffy hall, he went on. "Friends, I don't believe in going to war at all if you can help it, but if you go to war—go to war. I don't believe in a man brawling. I never like to see a man hit another man. But if you have good reason to hit another man, don't hit him a little . . . put him to sleep."

The *Times* chided him for harping on the past and for judgments that were "sometimes hasty and violent" but praised his principles as "irrefragable." Although the man in the street would have chosen another adjective, Roosevelt's principles would be proved right in the spring of 1918.

With his political stock on the rise and the government at last responding to his alarums, TR might have let up on his attacks, but he chose to push harder than ever. In April he wrote a *Star* column to the effect that if the Allies won, no thanks would be due the United States, and if they lost, "black infamy would be our portion." He thought Americans should bow their heads in penance for letting others do their fighting. "The trumpets of the Lord sounded for Armageddon; but our hearts were not swift to answer nor our feet jubilant. . . . Our rulers were supple and adroit, but they were not mighty of soul." The leaders had failed, and it was up to the American people to "take the burden from the shoulders of others, until we pay whatever price our past shortcomings demand."

Roosevelt's editor at the *Star*, Ralph Stout, wired him that the paper could not run the column. For six months the editors had ignored letters from readers angered by the Colonel's assault on Wilson's conduct of the war, but this column went too far even for the editors, and when newspapers and political leaders ran "too far ahead of the people [they] vitiate the good they can do," Stout said.

TR accepted the decision with equanimity. Like the prophets of the Old Testament, he was crying out to warn Jerusalem, but he counted himself lucky not to be stoned, he told Ethel. He wrote a friend that a columnist had no right to damage someone else's newspaper: "I am not dead sure that the prophet business can be combined with keeping up circulation; and moreover I know that when a man with strong feelings and intense convictions reaches a certain age he is apt to get cater-cornered as regards the surrounding world and therefore his usefulness ceases, and I am quite prepared to feel that . . . it would be to the interest of everybody that I should cease being a prophet and become that far pleasanter and more innocuous person, a sage. But as long as I am in the prophet business I wish to prophesy!"

Ethel thought it "cruelly hard" that he had no role in the war, but he was resigned. "I have ceased to fret at my impotence to do anything in this great crisis," he wrote Quentin; "I rejoice that my four sons, and Dick, are playing their part." He rejoiced, too, in the coming of spring, which he recorded in detail in his letters to France. White snowdrops, Edith's favorite, had risen from the earth "as pretty as ever," he wrote Archie. Bloodroot blazed on the hillsides. Bare limbs were disappearing under what seemed to his myopic eye a foam of soft green. Cherry blossoms lit up the woods, and red buds showed on the maples. The bird choir was warming up over the hilariously solemn bass line from the frog pond. His beloved rowboat would soon be back in the water. He was tip-top, Edith was charming and brave, and Archie was on the mend.

NINETEEN

The Young Colonel
and the Old Colonel

F RANCE, however, was in critical condition. One-quarter of its territory had been lopped off by Germany, and although the French and
British armies had stayed the knife, the seventy miles between Paris
and the front no longer shielded the city from harm. Aerial bombing, an in-
exact science in the early days of the war, had grown increasingly lethal.
Hundreds of Parisians were killed and hundreds more injured in the early
months of 1918, and on March 23, Big Bertha, a new monster concealed in
a mountainside seventy-five miles to the northeast, hurled nearly four hundred gigantic shells into the city. Hearing the news in Washington, Henry
Adams said, "This is no world for an old man to live in when the Germans
can shoot to the moon." Three days later he was dead.

Big Bertha's first assault claimed some 200 civilian lives, wounded 600,
and set off an exodus of 200,000 Parisians. The Roosevelt family's friend
Edith Wharton stayed on at her home in the rue de Varenne to continue her
relief work but confessed that her nerves were "jigging and sarabanding."
Bertha had dropped a shell just down the street. Wharton shared Roosevelt's
impatience with pacifists and President Wilson, and since the earliest
months of the war she had devoted herself to organizing, running, and funding orphanages, hostels for war refugees, and tuberculosis hospitals. TR
helped her raise money for the hospitals and wrote an introduction for one
of her most imaginative charitable endeavors, *The Book of the Homeless*,
published by Scribner's in 1916. Edited by Wharton and sold by subscrip-
tion, the book was a collection of prose and verse, drawings and paintings,

and musical compositions by more than fifty artists, among them James, Conrad, Hardy, Yeats, Stravinsky, Monet, Renoir, and Rodin.

In February and March, General Erich von Ludendorff massed more than one million men and six thousand heavy guns along a forty-mile stretch of the front near the Somme. "We will punch a hole," he said. He envisioned the Somme as the start of a campaign of hole-punching that would carry his army south by southeast to Paris and victory before the Americans arrived in force. The odds were with him now that he could replenish his ranks with soldiers returning from the Russian Front. The French and British had no reservoirs of recruits, and of the 300,000 American soldiers in France, only 27,000—the First Division—were ready to hold their own in battle. The United States, at war for nearly a year, was "still merely an onlooker," Roosevelt fumed. Portugal was defending as much of the front as the richest nation on earth, and the French were still supplying the AEF's airplanes and artillery.

Ludendorff punched the first hole on March 21 and over the next three weeks gained more ground than the Allies had won in three years. Two days into the fighting, in a cable marked "Secret" and "Very Urgent," the British Foreign Office directed its ambassador in Washington to make it plain to the president that the spring battles might well decide the war. Losses had been heavy and would get worse, the Foreign Office said, and the president must be made to understand that the need for troops was critical and immediate: "if America delays now she may be too late."

The tide of desperation washing over France was to be checked by the strangest of all the forces of war, eloquence. Ferdinand Foch, commander of the Allied armies, ordered them not to cede another centimeter of French soil. The chief of the British forces, Douglas Haig, made an equally lofty demand: the armies of Britain, now standing with their backs to the wall, must fight on to the end, holding every position to the last man. General Pershing, who had been holding out for an independent command, drove to Foch's headquarters and announced that the American people would consider it a great honor for their troops to join in the battle. "I ask you for this in their name and my own," he said. "There is no question at this moment except fighting. Infantry, artillery, aviation, all that we have is yours. Do with it as you choose."

All that he had, of course, was the First Division, which was soon marching west into Picardy and one of the hottest sectors of the front, near the hilltop village of Cantigny. Major Theodore Roosevelt, Jr., apparently undaunted by the holes Ludendorff was punching or the storm of German artillery raging all around him, wrote his father that he looked forward to being "in at the death" of the German army.

AT THIRTY, Ted was years younger than most of the majors who were making a career of the army. Sensitive to the suggestion that he owed his rank to his father's connections, he had resolved to prove himself by perfecting his battalion. "Major Roosevelt was not good company at this time," his adjutant would recall. A stern disciplinarian, Ted worked prodigiously and slept little, habits that his captains and lieutenants were compelled to emulate.

Since his childhood Ted had spurred himself in hopes of measuring up to his father's empyrean standards, just as TR had done in hopes of pleasing his own father. At Groton, Ted bored into his books with an intensity that injured his eyes, and at Harvard, where he finished his studies in three years, his unflinching performance on the freshman football team broke everything but athletic records—his nose, an ankle, and two ribs. In 1912 he joined an investment bank on Wall Street, cold country for a son of the Bull Moose. Ted persevered, and by the time he joined the AEF, he had amassed much of the fortune he needed to fund his dream of a life in public service.

In the muddy, wet autumn of 1917, Warrington Dawson had watched Major Roosevelt interrogate a lieutenant whose men were at work in the rain without ponchos. The lieutenant explained that the ponchos had worn out and replacements had not yet arrived. "Your explanation is good, and I must accept it," Ted replied. "But all the same, these men are getting wet and it ought not to have happened." The next day Dawson saw Ted and the lieutenant coatless in the rain. The day of "R.H.I.P.—Rank Has Its Privileges" had passed, Ted told him.

Ted was entitled to a two-day leave each month, but nearly three months went by before his conscience allowed him to take the time for a visit to his wife in Paris. Although happy and attentive by day, he worked all night, drilling troops and giving orders in his sleep, Eleanor wrote Ethel. Ted's devotion had already won him a recommendation for promotion to lieutenant colonel, Eleanor wrote her mother. "Think of the young Colonel and the old Colonel!" she exulted. But the recommendation was not to be mentioned at Sagamore or anywhere else, she cautioned, because of the chance that it might not be approved.

✸

THE OLD COLONEL HAD WARNED his progeny to tread lightly, and he hoped that they would not be casualties of his war with Washington. Old hands at downplaying a status that was close to royal, the boys heeded the warning but were so accustomed to privilege that they sometimes failed to see it as such. As soon as Ted grasped the severity of Archie's wounds, he asked Eleanor to take a leave from her work at the YMCA in Paris and head for Archie's field hospital to look after him. It had not occurred to Ted that her superiors in the Y would have to refuse the request or all Y workers with soldiers in the family would expect the same opportunity. Eleanor understood. As she had written Ethel soon after reaching Paris, "we have to be so very careful about appearing to have pull."

But it was also true that when a Roosevelt mentioned a problem to a family friend, the friend was often in a position to solve it. Through the intercession of Elizabeth Mills Reid, Archie was soon convalescing in Paris, in a new private hospital for American officers. Widow of Whitelaw Reid, U.S. ambassador to Britain for much of TR's presidency, Mrs. Reid owed her sway in Archie's case to her money, which had outfitted the hospital. Mrs. Reid was also generous with the other soldiers in the family, giving Quentin a leather aviator's suit, Kermit a full uniform and fur coat, and Ted a warm coat and sleeping bag.

Eleanor, not wanting to exploit her celebrated name, declined requests to write for magazines and asked her superiors to shoo away reporters looking to spice their stories with Roosevelt. But short of adopting an alias, she could not always be anonymous, and at times it was fun to be found out. Asked to say a word to a gathering of French and English soldiers, she spoke of TR's strong wish to be with them, news that brought cheers, long applause, and a rousing chorus of "Swanee River." Bargaining incognito with an antiques dealer, she drove down the price of a painting from 150 francs to 125, but when she gave her name to arrange the delivery, the dealer burst out, "Pour la famille Roosevelt, c'est 100 francs!" A soldier whirling her around a YMCA dance floor stopped dead when she identified herself. Certain that she was teasing, he slapped her on the back and said, "That's right, chicken, fly high, fly high." "Chicken" was slang for "prostitute."

Eleanor had joined the Y as a canteen worker, hoping for a post near Ted, and rushed abroad before it occurred to the War Department to bar soldiers' wives from following their husbands to France. When she learned that she would have to stay in Paris, she consoled herself with the knowledge that Ted was only four hours away. She settled near L'Etoile in a house owned by her aunt, Alice Green Hoffman, who had returned to the United States, and although Eleanor would rarely see Ted, she did not lack for Roosevelts. The tribe treasured its beachhead in Paris. Quentin, stationed at an aviation training field at Issoudun, 150 miles to the south, often flew himself to town. Dick Derby showed up occasionally, as did Belle and Kermit and Kim. Archie often checked himself out of the hospital for a few hours at Eleanor's. Despite rationing and occasional shortages, the cook kept an excellent table, having transformed Mrs. Hoffman's elegant courtyard into a chicken run and planted lettuce among the rosebushes. With impeccable Cartesian logic, the cook reasoned that Mrs. Hoffman did not know, therefore she could not mind.

As a volunteer, Eleanor was wholehearted and game. "They asked me if I had had any experience of interior decorating, and could I take a hut and make it attractive on three cents, and I said I could!" she wrote her mother after a few weeks in Paris. "They" also asked her to design the uniform for the women of the YMCA, teach French to the troops, assemble a library, serve as interpreter, and manage the Y's canteen in Paris. In her off-hours, she ransacked the city to fill Ted's requests for thousands of bottles of soft drinks, boxing gloves and soccer balls, baseball gear, tobacco, a phonograph and records, fifes and drums, trumpets, and a horse.

By the war's end the YMCA, which organized recreation for American soldiers and provided humanitarian assistance to prisoners of war, would operate four thousand "huts" in France, the largest of which did service as restaurants, classrooms, houses of worship, theaters, and clubhouses. The enterprise got off to an inauspicious start. Not yet equipped with cars and trucks, the Y opened a canteen in Paris, where soldiers were suffering none of the hardships endured by the men quartered in frigid, leaky barns around Gondrecourt. Tales of pampering in Paris infuriated the troops at the front, and when the Y opened its first huts in the field, volunteers had "a big job to get the men to warm up," Eleanor wrote her mother.

Most of the 35,000 volunteers in YMCA uniforms were hardy-looking men, a fact that led many a soldier to conclude that the Y was a haven for slackers. In their "bullet-proof jobs," the Y men were "a bad example to all the young men in the army," Archie Roosevelt wrote his father. TR promptly scolded the Y in the *Star* and declared that any man under forty-five who was fit enough to go to France ought to go with the army. The column drew blood, he wrote Archie; "there have been frantic protests and attacks on me; but I believe that it will do good." Told that President Wilson's thirty-two-year-old son-in-law, Francis Bowes Sayre, had enlisted in the Y, TR said, "How very nice," and added that his family had sent a daughter-in-law to do that kind of work.

The YMCA met the Colonel with a counteroffensive of friendly persuasion. One official presented him with the bullet that had reduced Archie's left elbow to a mosaic. Near the fighting on the day Archie was injured, the Y man had gone to the field hospital to offer to wire messages to the families of the wounded. A second emissary was dispatched to explain to the Colonel that the Y did not take men of fighting age and showed him a map pinpointing the locations of ninety Y huts that had been shot to pieces. Impressed by the organization's presence at the front, Roosevelt wrote the YMCA a check for $4,000 and sent another $5,000 to Eleanor for her work.

A RCHIE'S RECOVERY went slowly. His knee healed fairly well, but the broken bones and severed nerve near his elbow caused fierce pain above the joint and paralyzed everything below. He was agitated, rail-thin, and pale — "about the color of parchment," Quentin reported. He manufactured good cheer for family friends who came calling, a performance undoubtedly driven by the knowledge that his visitors would communicate with Sagamore. He also extended himself to other wounded soldiers despite his horror of their suffering. "It's awful, at the hospital, to see the young officers who are blind for life," he told Warrington Dawson. "There is one who has not yet been told; the doctor has told me, but he says it must not be broken to him yet, and he is being given hope. But he knows, he feels it, and says so to me, though I lie to him."

Archie still could not concentrate well enough to read anything he had not read before, and his frayed nerves probably account for the harsh tone of his letters to Gracie. When she offered to join him in France, a privilege granted by the War Department when a soldier was seriously hurt, he roughly informed her that the country was already overrun with "useless civilians." It was true — General Pershing worried that the rich thrill-seekers congregating in Paris to taste the war's excitement would confirm Gallic suspicions of American frivolousness — but Gracie could not have been expected to know.

Distressed over his poorly outfitted troops, Archie had used much of his pay to buy them warm socks and gloves, and of the money he sent home, he instructed Gracie to give half to the wife of a wounded sergeant he knew. Ethel wrote Quentin that although Gracie did not complain, the rest of the family thought Archie had "behaved like a goat." Archie had suffered, Ethel knew, but it seemed to her that he had been "knocked clear off his balance and is thinking of SELF constantly. This is how we *all* feel."

TR soon wired the sergeant, who had lost a hand, to say that he would furnish the money. His letters to Archie said nothing of goatishness, and his letters about him brim with admiration. He admitted the perversity of taking pride in a son's wounds, but there was no subduing the swell of his heart when he thought of Archie's courage and the sacrifice he had made. "His only anxiety is to recover at once so that he can get back to the trenches," TR wrote a French acquaintance.

TR knew only the smallest part of the anxieties that plagued Archie, and it is not clear if anyone in the family knew of the nightmares he had lived at the front. In two long conversations with the gentle, sympathetic Warrington Dawson, Archie unburdened himself of experiences that he had either concealed from Ted and Dick or asked them to conceal from the family.

> One hasn't time to think when there's a barrage. One's in it, or else one has got to go into it, and that's all. But there is a peculiar feeling about shells falling and bursting anywhere near you; they seem to be coming at you.
>
> I had no tin hat when I was wounded. That morning, I had been struck on the head, and my hat was smashed. So I went about without any for some hours, in the dugout, and got in the habit of having none, and forgot all about it.
>
> Then the barrage started. We jumped out in the open. There was no necessity for it. We lost lives by it, or else got wounds, which we need not have got, if we had been more experienced troops.

Two men were killed in the fight, and Archie was one of thirty-four who were wounded. Telling the story to Ted and Dick in the field hospital, Archie had blamed the casualties on poorly maintained trenches rather than poor judgment.

Archie was also struggling to comprehend the brutality of what he had seen and done. In one French raid he had rushed a burly German and fired five shots into him at close range, he told Dawson.

The German fell forward. From my aim, and from his look, and from the way he fell, I knew I had done for him. But I felt I absolutely had to stamp on him. I brought my left heel down on his face, by the mouth, as hard as I could. It went right in, and my boot was splashed with blood up to the ankle. Then I ran on.

That was an absolutely primitive action. I was a man of the Stone Age at that moment, hating my enemy and wanting to humiliate him even after he was dead. If I had had more time, I should have spat in his face. As it was, I stamped on it. I wish I had got his tin hat. But I was in too great a hurry and didn't think of it till too late.

The sergeant, who saw it all, talked about it, and it made me a great reputation among the men.

It is extraordinary how savage the men have become. They are absolutely ruthless. I think the fighting and the blood drives them mad, they will kill anything in sight, without asking questions, there's no talk of quarter. But get them back of the lines with a prisoner and they are very decent. In peacetime, we used to be upset if we saw a man ill in the street, and we would want to help him. Now, I can see a friend shot right next to me, and I don't care at all—it seems quite natural, and it's somebody else's turn next. I'll give orders for his tin hat to be taken, or his boots to be taken off, and that's all.

Eleanor and Quentin tried to soothe Archie, and much of the time he was his sweet, thoughtful self, visiting the wounded and indulging Eleanor in long conversations about Ted. In late May he came to Mrs. Hoffman's without a splint and showed Eleanor that he could raise his arm level with his shoulder. In six weeks, when he could flex the arm enough to scratch his nose, he would return to the front, he said.

Ted hoped so. Archie was a crackerjack officer and, when not aflame with indignation, a charming fellow. On one excursion from the hospital he had bought Ted a watch and ordered it engraved with MAJOR R. FROM CAPT. R—"rather cunning," Ted thought. Ted missed Archie, missed Eleanor, missed their children, and missed his father—"more than you can imagine," he wrote TR from a post near the French lines at Cantigny. "I don't know of anything I think more of than how badly you must feel to be out of it at this veritable 'Armageddon.' It is nice, though, from the point of view of the family, to at least have John Brown's four sons fighting."

JOHN BROWN of Sagamore was still at war, laying siege to the White House and the War Department, and with "the other old frumps" he was "trying to help with the Liberty Loan and Red Cross and such like," he wrote Quentin in April. Asking his fellow citizens to give till they felt the pinch of sacrifice, he showed what he meant by putting up $60,000 for Liberty Loans and giving to war charities the $45,000 awarded years before with his Nobel Peace Prize.

At a gathering in Carnegie Hall to mark the third anniversary of the sinking of the *Lusitania,* he rebuked the Wilson administration for its slow march to war and said that the date, May 7, "should be a penitential day forever for America." Under the elms of Trinity College in Hartford, he chastised Washington for its swagger and empty self-congratulation. In the fall the government had bragged that it would deliver twenty thousand American airplanes to France by spring. Spring had arrived, but the planes had not, leaving the AEF entirely dependent on overworked French and English aviators for protection from German air assaults. "Let us quit boasting," Roosevelt said; "let's not humiliate the men in the trenches."

The pundits sometimes wondered how Roosevelt escaped prosecution under the stringent laws passed in 1917 and 1918 to suppress dissent. "He is aching to go somewhere, preferably to France, but why not to jail?" asked the *North American Review.* "He would make a glorious martyr." William Randolph Hearst clamored for Roosevelt's head and claimed that the government would get it as soon as the officials in charge of enforcing the sedition law settled on a course of action. "Lord, how I wish they *would* try to act against me!" TR wrote Archie. He could think of no better megaphone for his demands to speed up the war.

Opponents of the war or the government's conduct of it ran the risk of $10,000 fines and twenty years in jail, and before the war's end two thousand protesters would be prosecuted. Nine hundred of them, including Eugene Debs, leader of the Socialist Party, would go to prison. "Brave men flinch at the charge of 'disloyalty,' " Senator Hiram Johnson observed, "and when a prosecuting officer stands before a jury asserting that the defendant is an enemy of his country and demanding that patriots do their duty . . . there is mighty little chance for the fellow charged."

The new laws authorized the postmaster general, Albert S. Burleson, to bar from the mails or deny the customary low postal rates to magazines and newspapers carrying material he considered obstructive to the war effort or scornful of the government. Broad as this power of censorship was, Burleson secretly expanded it by directing local postmasters to send him printed matter that might interfere with Liberty Loan drives, stir up unrest in the armed services, impede the draft, or embarrass the government. Burleson would decide what constituted interference, and while he considered a case, the questionable material went stale in a back room at the local post office. A publisher could challenge the government in court but might well be bankrupt before the court reached a verdict.

As the Sedition Act moved through the Senate in the spring of 1918, Hiram Johnson was appalled. "We are at war against a ruthless enemy," he thundered. "But good God, Mr. President, when did it become a war upon the American people?" In the *Star* Roosevelt advocated harsh punishment of real sedition coupled with the right of all citizens "to speak the truth freely of all their public servants, including the president, and to criticize them in the severest terms of truth whenever they come short in their public duty." Sedition, he said, "is an offense against the country, not against the president."

The post office exterminated scores of publications during the war. Some, like *The Masses*, were socialist voices, some were edited by sincere defenders of the American tradition of avoiding foreign entanglements. Many were German-language papers, which under the new laws had to translate each issue for the local postmaster and await his imprimatur. Max Eastman, editor of *The Masses*, noted that nearly all the casualties were "helpless small-fry who could not fight back." Some small-fry survived by tabling their opinions for the duration. Americans would be shocked to know how many newspapers were censoring themselves, Senator George W. Norris of Nebraska wrote a friend; "the little country editor always says that everything he has is invested in his paper, and he knows that if it is denied the privileges of the mails, he will be bankrupt, and therefore he must remain silent."

Walter Lippmann of *The New Republic* protested that snuffing out tiny papers for speaking of a rich man's war and a poor man's fight was absurd, particularly when there was no effort to stop Theodore Roosevelt's "malicious deprecation" of the War Department. "A great government ought to be contemptuously uninterested in such opinion and ought to suppress only military secrets and advice to break the law or evade it," he wrote one of the president's confidants. But the president overrode his censor only twice—once for his erstwhile friend Oswald Villard of The Nation and once for Norman Thomas of the socialist World Tomorrow, whose case had been brought to the attention of the White House by a member of the president's extended family.

Almost daring the postmaster general to attack, Roosevelt accused him of punishing Republican editors solidly behind the war while overlooking the anglophobic but fervently pro-Wilson papers of William Randolph Hearst. Burleson challenged Roosevelt to prove his case, a challenge Roosevelt easily met, after which a postal inspector visited the Star to discuss the seditious slant of Roosevelt's nib. The pursuit went no further. Woodrow Wilson understood how easily Roosevelt the martyr could become Roosevelt the hero.

With his heightened appreciation of the power of martyrdom, Roosevelt decided that he had erred in joining a movement to expel Robert La Follette from the Senate. The campaign had begun in September 1917, after Fighting Bob publicly accused Woodrow Wilson and William Jennings Bryan of knowing that the Lusitania would sail from New York with six million pounds of ammunition in her hold. Roosevelt immediately branded Senator La Follette a "shadow Hun" and proposed that the United States give him to the kaiser. The furor over La Follette's accusation led to a Senate inquiry, and as it dragged on into the spring of 1918, Roosevelt decided that censure was preferable to expulsion. He considered La Follette an "unhung traitor" but feared that the people of Wisconsin might vote him back into office if they thought the Senate had been unduly harsh.

In May and June, Roosevelt toured the Midwest, stronghold of isolationism and home to large populations of German immigrants, to make the case for undiluted Americanism. "This is a nation—not a polyglot boarding house," he told the people of Des Moines. "There is not room in the country for any fifty-fifty American. There can be but one loyalty—to the Stars and Stripes: one nationality—the American—and therefore only one language—the English language."

At a college auditorium in Springfield, Ohio, John J. Leary of the New York Times watched in agony as the Colonel was showered with peonies by a crowd of enthusiasts unaware that flowers whizzing through the air might provide cover for an assassin. TR had the same apprehension and waited till the peonies ran out before he strode to center stage. "A fool affair," he said afterward, when Leary asked him about it.

But the people had meant well, Leary said.

"Exactly," TR snapped. "They meant well. But I have found that one of the real dangers in life is people who mean well. You never can tell what they will do." In a few days he would speak in Milwaukee for the first time since the attempt on his life. He admitted no fear and perhaps felt none but all the same was traveling with his valet, who carried a revolver, and two bodyguards assigned by the railroad. The city had a large German community and was governed by Socialists, many of whom believed the war had been engineered to make the world safe for plutocracy.

Enemy territory, Leary remarked.

Milwaukee would hear his call for undivided loyalty, TR replied. "I shall give them everything I have said anywhere else and, if I can think of it, something more. I do not anticipate any bother, but if there is, we shall have to make the best of it."

There was no bother, and the Milwaukeeans of German extraction who praised the speech were sufficiently numerous to persuade Roosevelt that Wisconsin was no less determined than other states to "put the war through—to a knockout."

Roosevelt asked Americans to mind the distinction between citizens of German descent who supported the Allies and those who did not, but his demand for a ban on the German language was categorical and, unlike many of his wartime opinions, this one was widely shared. Schools banned the teaching of German, newsstands refused to stock German-language papers, Wagner and Mozart were dropped from the repertory of the Metropolitan Opera. In an open letter to Congress and the president, the American Defense Society demanded the suppression of all things Teutonic. "The appalling and complete moral breakdown of German 'Kultur' compels a sweeping revision of the attitude of civilized nations and individuals toward the German language, literature, and science," the society declared. "The close scrutiny of Hun frightfulness in this war has revealed abhorrent inherent qualities hitherto unknown, and to most people unsuspected." Formed in 1915 to promote preparedness, the society now sent posses into the streets to break up rallies of pacifists, protesters, and champions of the Irish independence movement. "You can't even collect your thoughts without getting arrested," Max Eastman complained.

The American Defense Society had no monopoly on hysteria. The superpatriots of the National Security League, organized in 1914 to mobilize public support for universal military service, spent the war pushing their notion of "100 percent Americanism," fighting socialism, and asserting the primacy of property rights. Columbia University and other colleges expelled professors and students who opposed the war. Socialists were tarred and feathered. Three Mennonite churches were burned to show disapproval of a creed that forbade fighting in wars or supporting them with Liberty Loans. Most Americans drew the line at physical violence against dissidents, but to a people now panicky about traitors and saboteurs, the hounding seemed inevitable and perhaps necessary.

Roosevelt fought for free expression, but on a disappointingly narrow front, protesting censorship of views that matched his own while cheering the persecution of pacifists, socialists, and others troubled by the war. He had been honorary president of the American Defense Society, and the National Security League sponsored his travels through the Midwest. In his judgment, teachers should be made to sign loyalty oaths, and police should be used to disperse crowds listening to the soapbox purveyors of "veiled treason." He wanted cases of sedition heard by military tribunals and maintained that conscientious objectors should be forced to do service as noncombatants—digging trenches, perhaps, or working on the minesweepers that escorted American troopships into the harbors of France.

Hiram Johnson resurrected his Aeschylus to remind the country that in war, truth is the first casualty. Watching the National Security League chip away at civil liberties in the name of patriotism, Amos Pinchot could scarcely believe the nation's change of temper since the shining days of 1912. If the league had its way, Pinchot said, the great mass of Americans soon would be conscripts of a ruling class intolerant of strikes, challenges to authority, and the same kind of popular ferment that had given rise to progressivism.

After the election of 1916 Walter Lippmann had predicted in *The Yale Review* that Theodore Roosevelt would remain a charismatic agitator but would never again lead the country. "The colonel is repeating himself, the colonel is looking back to the good old times, the colonel is becoming anecdotal, the colonel acts like a chronically indignant man," Lippmann observed. "Temperamentally, the colonel is reverting to class. . . . His assumptions, his social and moral values, his conceptions of honor and patriotism, are more and more those of the landed gentry, physically brave, conventionally noble, impervious to popular feeling, high-handed, scornful, class-bound." Roosevelt had lost the flexibility required of a modern president, and so the mantle had passed to Woodrow Wilson, "a man of far less natural gift for leadership, but one with a subtler mind and a younger sympathy," Lippmann wrote.

Roosevelt was indeed growing more rigid. His once colorful prose was now monochromatic, and his chronic indignation exacerbated his tendency to bifurcate: things were black or white, good or evil, courageous or cowardly. But Wilson of the subtler mind and younger sympathy was hardly a model of elasticity or tolerance. After foreseeing and bewailing the war's infringements on civil liberties, he had led the race to infringe, and he was easily Roosevelt's peer in high-handedness and scorn.

As for reverting to class, Roosevelt did share the gentry's sense of urgency about the war but not its easy acceptance of economic inequality. In March, when the Republicans sent him to Maine to set a direction for their congressional campaigns in 1918, the audience heard the echo of the Bull Moose. The party had to stake out the sane middle ground, he said, to protect the country from the dangers of untrammeled capitalism and overly idealistic socialism.

Watching the Old Guard ignore Hiram Johnson and other progressive Republicans in 1916, Lippmann had concluded that the party was doomed. But at the end of May 1918, while Roosevelt was on his speaking tour, the picture unexpectedly brightened. Dining alone in the Blackstone Hotel in Chicago, he looked up and saw William Howard Taft headed his way. When they greeted each other warmly, applause swept the room. Taft stayed at Roosevelt's table for half an hour, watched closely by John J. Leary of the *Times*, who had posted himself near the door.

Had the reunion been planned? Leary asked when Taft made his exit.

"Lord, no!" said Taft. He had come to Chicago in his role as joint chairman of the National War Labor Board, which worked to ease friction between capital and labor in factories supplying the AEF.

Had they talked politics?

"Son, you really do not expect me to answer that question, do you?"

Leary said he would assume that they had.

"You just quote Mr. Taft as saying Colonel Roosevelt and he discussed patriotism and the state and welfare of the nation," Taft said. "That will cover everything."

In the privacy of his hotel suite, Roosevelt was slightly more forthcoming but spoke off the record. He and Taft were "in perfect harmony" on Washington's mishandling of the war, he said.

Fishing, Leary mused that the mere fact of a cordial Taft-Roosevelt meeting would inform the White House that the Republican Party had closed ranks for the congressional elections.

TR agreed and chuckled at the thought of the news spoiling Wilson's breakfast. Deeply touched by the encounter, TR said, "I never felt happier over anything in my life. It was splendid of Taft."

The timing also proved splendid. A year earlier, Roosevelt was still regretting his decision to make Taft the steward of his presidential legacy and still resented Taft's contention that Charles Taft had done as much as Roosevelt to put Will in the White House. Taft in 1917 had scoffed at Roosevelt's dream of taking an army to France and disapproved of Roosevelt's bludgeoning of the War Department. Now it saddened him to think of Roosevelt with no role in the war, and he had decided that Roosevelt's exposures of bureaucratic bumbling and foot-dragging were having a positive effect. Taft had been meaning to see Roosevelt for at least two months. "I see no sense in carrying about these animosities any longer," he told his friend Gus Karger. Although Taft knew that the conservatives in the Republican Party would criticize him for making up with the Colonel, he had decided to do it anyway, in hopes of uniting the party and putting its full force "behind this war in a manner which will give Mr. Wilson a fuller comprehension of the demands and aspirations of the American people."

ON MAY 27, the day after Roosevelt and Taft made peace, the German army punched its third hole, along the Chemin des Dames ridge north of the Aisne River, and the First Division of the AEF completed preparations for its first attack. The target was Cantigny, which the French army had recaptured and lost twice. Taken and held, Cantigny would give the Allies a summit for watching German movements along the Aisne and would improve the odds of pushing the enemy back in the counteroffensive planned for the summer. Pershing met with his officers to make certain that they understood the importance of their task. The Germans had the advantage of possession, he said, and they were sure to resist mightily, because an American defeat would gravely wound the Allies' morale.

The officers and men of the First were in a retributive mood. For a month, as they learned the ways of the enemy and the enemy concentrated its fire on them, they had suffered sixty casualties a day, many more than the French troops on either side of them. "Life was sheer hell in the Cantigny sector," an American ambulance driver named John Dos Passos would write after the war. "The shallow valleys and the plain in front of the village were under continual shelling by the well-placed German artillery. Ravines and patches of woodland were continually saturated with poison gas."

Major Theodore Roosevelt, Jr., would remember the weeks before the attack for the discord between man and nature. Trees sprouted green, wildflowers spangled the grass, and birdsong alternated with artillery fire. The explosions drowned out all other sounds. "The trees were shaken and torn," he wrote in *Rank and File*, his book about the war. "Acrid smoke drifted through the branches. Gradually the bombardment ceased. The smoke cleared, and the soldiers again heard the birds."

On May 28 the First Division swiftly took the hill and two hundred prisoners, then hung on through a three-day storm of gas and shell fire. Two hundred Americans were killed, more than eight hundred wounded or gassed. The *Times* of London praised the Americans' mettle and dash but could not resist adding that the victory at Cantigny was minor and "a product of French and British instruction."

England and France still doubted that the million-man army promised by the Americans would show up in time to stave off the German conquest of Europe. In a rueful joke making the rounds, a British soldier tells an American that "A.E.F." must stand for "After Everything is Finished." No, says the Yank, it stands for "After England Failed." Cantigny was secure. No one had failed, but nothing was finished.

Sixty miles to the southeast, near Château-Thierry, another hole had been punched. The Germans were within thirty-five miles of Paris, closer than they had been since 1914 and close enough for Eleanor and Archie to hear the rolling surf of the cannons. Posters advising civilians to leave went up all over the city. "These are the most exciting and anxious times," Eleanor wrote her mother on June 1. "Everyone feels that this is *the* big moment of the war so far, and that almost anything might happen." She had decided to stay.

Ted turned up the next day, his face burned and swollen, the whites of his eyes a painful-looking red. His uniform, which he had not taken off for three weeks, was in tatters. Along with two hundred others at Cantigny, he had been gassed and was blind for three days but refused to leave his command. As soon as his battalion was relieved, he had commandeered a car and driver to race to Eleanor's, and between coughs, he begged her to leave, relenting only when she telephoned the AEF's chief officer in Paris, who vowed to look after her if the Germans threatened the city.

Ted took a bath, his first in months, and donned a new uniform, one of two that Eleanor had ordered from a tailor in Paris. She put on a festive dress and took him for a walk in the garden, where "all the roses had come out since the day before, just as if they knew," she wrote her mother. It was a balmy, blessedly tranquil night, the first in two weeks without an air raid.

They were in the middle of dinner on the terrace when Quentin arrived, also unannounced. The brothers had not seen each other for nearly a year. After dinner, all of them went to Archie's hospital in an effervescent mood that went flat as soon as Archie began inquiring after various members of the battalion. As Ted recited the casualties, both he and Archie went "terribly down," Eleanor said. Archie walked them to the door and watched till they were out of sight. Eleanor guessed that he feared he had seen the last of Ted.

Ted left in the morning. As a precaution Eleanor readied a bag for herself but could not imagine deserting her work with the Y or her post as family aide-de-camp. "Archie gets looked after in case of trouble, and we are beautifully organized as to cars, etc.," she wrote her mother.

Ted had said almost nothing about the battle. Weeks later Eleanor would read in the Paris *Herald* that he had been honored for showing "high courage and leadership" at Cantigny, retaining command through the heavy bombardment, and "although gassed in the lungs and gassed in the eyes to blindness refused to be evacuated." But Major Roosevelt, in spite of four recommendations for promotion, was still a major.

The old Colonel, not yet aware of the delays in the young colonel's promotion, gloried in Ted's courage and looked forward to seeing all four of his sons at the front. "I wish to Heavens that it was *my* worthless old body that was exposed to the danger in the place of the bodies of my sons," he wrote a general who had sent a complimentary letter about Archie. "But I would not have them elsewhere for anything in the world."

TR's sense of uselessness had grown with the German advance. He was "sick to death of talking" and did it only "because somebody has to offset the immense flood of drivel with which we seek to blind ourselves," he wrote a fellow Rough Rider who was serving in France. When an admirer urged him to run for Congress in the fall, he dryly replied that there was only one civilian position where he could be of use.

Roosevelt occasionally received invitations to visit the front but loathed the thought of being there as a spectator and believed that if he went, the public would expect him to accomplish something—an impossibility for a leader out of power and out of favor. Such had been the fate of Hannibal "in the last unhappy decade of his life when he was in Asia Minor," TR wrote a friend. The kings of Asia wanted him to rein in the Romans yet refused him the authority he needed, a situation that left poor Hannibal "absolutely powerless."

Hannibal had fled Carthage for Asia Minor to escape his old foes, the Romans. Years passed, and he became a harmless old man—like a bird that had lost its feathers and could no longer fly, Plutarch wrote. When the Romans caught up with him, he chose to commit suicide rather than surrender. Roosevelt would do neither. He kept up his fight in the *Star* and tried to resign himself to the fact that no one in Washington would allow him a role in the war. He longed to contribute, he said, "but I am not allowed to."

Nor was his friend Leonard Wood. In May, after receiving word that the division he had trained would soon sail for France, Wood hurried to New York to begin preparing the embarkation. But his official orders, which arrived the day after he left Camp Funston in Kansas, detached him from the division and exiled him to San Francisco. In disbelief he appealed in person to the president and the secretary of war. They were powerless to send him to Europe, they said. He could go only if Pershing asked for him, and Pershing had made no such request.

Wood came to believe that Pershing had sunk him to please Baker, but Roosevelt blamed Wilson, whose long list of grudges stretched back to 1914, when Wood called for universal military service while Wilson was lecturing the country on the virtues of neutrality. Wood had angered the White House in 1915 by inviting Roosevelt to Plattsburg, in 1916 by his cordiality to Charles Evans Hughes, and in 1917 by telling the Senate that he would replace most of the upper echelon of the War Department. In 1918, after a few weeks in France on a military inspection tour, Wood was asked to share his impressions with the Senate Military Affairs Committee. Knowing what was at stake, he went to Sagamore for the Colonel's advice. After Wood's visit, Ethel wrote Dick that Wood decided to speak boldly, on the theory that if he did not, "he would never feel friends with himself, and as he said, 'You are with yourself a good deal of the time.' " Wood's testimony on the damage done by the American delays did not endear him to Wilson or Baker, so when he asked them to overrule Pershing, they found it easy, perhaps even satisfying, to decline.

In the *Star* Roosevelt called the decision against Wood "a distinct benefit to the cause of Germany." His usual fretting over the administration's refusal to make use of him had been swallowed up by his bitterness over the wrong done to Wood, he wrote a friend. To deny Wood a place in France as the Germans rolled toward Paris was unconscionable: "it is the eleventh hour—and even the eleventh hour is passing."

TWENTY

A Boy Inspired

IN the middle of June, Theodore handed himself over to Edith for a stretch of the simple life. The strenuous life had ended four months before, in the ordeal of the abscesses. Edith could see that the superhuman energy was gone, but Theodore, still longing to rescue the world, persisted in committing himself to more than he could manage. She sensibly intervened, exacting a promise of two quiet months at Sagamore. They would be alone, without even the company of Ethel and her two small children, Richard Jr. and Edie, who were summering at Dark Harbor in Maine.

Theodore seemed content with the blanks in his calendar and relieved to be home. "Speechmaking at a time like the present is an uncommonly second-rate job," he wrote Kermit a few days after settling in. He reveled in the beauty of the countryside—"now at its loveliest"—and in the thought that the two of them would roam it again someday.

Kermit was traveling, at tortoise speed, from Mesopotamia to France. First detained in Egypt by U-boats harrying the Mediterranean and then in Italy by an attack of malaria, he had opened his orders from the AEF and learned that his machine-gunning experience with the British scarcely signified. Before going to the front, he would have to spend weeks at the Americans' artillery school in France.

Ted had been thrust into new dangers near Montdidier, a few miles from Cantigny. Ludendorff's last advance had punched a hole twenty miles wide. One more successful push, across the Marne, would mean the fall of Paris. The AEF now had 675,000 troops at the front or just behind the lines, and the French drew men from several American divisions to thicken the defenses at the Marne and to carry out nightly trench raids in search of Ludendorff's battle plans. Ted orchestrated and led at least one raid, taking seventy-five men into enemy territory and returning with documents and three dozen prisoners, a foray that won him a Silver Star, a Croix de Guerre, and immortality in an infantry textbook. With the help of the AEF, the French stopped the Germans from crossing the Marne at Château-Thierry, but Ted's regiment, the Twenty-sixth Infantry, was hit hard: two hundred dead or wounded in a four-day torrent of gas and explosives.

Archie's war ended in June. The surgery three months before in the field hospital had been ably done, but the inexperienced doctors at the officers' hospital in Paris had been slow to recognize that the physical therapy they had prescribed for his arm would never succeed, because the loose ends of the severed nerve were steadily contracting. In consultation with more practiced colleagues they decided on a second surgery to splice the nerve, after which he would be sent home. Archie was devastated. "He realizes that it is best, but it is a very hard thing to have to reconcile himself to the idea that he is out of things for so long," Eleanor wrote her mother. "He knows how much he could help Ted, and that is one reason he has tried not to go."

Along with the rest of the American Air Service, Quentin had been kept behind the lines for nearly a year by the lack of airplanes, which the United States had loudly promised but not delivered. "It has been very hard on Quentin not to get to the front," TR wrote Archie in June; "the complete breakdown in the airplane program fills me with impotent rage." It was an emotion he voiced more than once during the war.

General Pershing, also raging, informed Washington that the hollow boasts had given aid and comfort to the enemy. Expecting to face a great American armada in the skies, the Germans had stepped up their aircraft production accordingly. Pershing had dealt with the breakdown by ordering five thousand planes from the French, negotiating the $60 million contract on his own authority. The move had been "somewhat bold," he would write in his memoir, "but someone had to take the initiative."

The House and the Senate testily inquired into the whereabouts of the $1 billion they had appropriated for airplanes, and behind closed doors the War Department admitted that there would be two dozen American planes at the front in the summer of 1918, not the twelve thousand advertised.

The sculptor Gutzon Borglum, an aficionado of aeronautical design and an early champion of military airpower, suspected a capitalist conspiracy and launched an unofficial probe. He proceeded with White House permission but over the objections of an aide who told the president that Borglum was a Roosevelt intimate whose "intentions are not to help us if he can do otherwise." TR knew Borglum but hardly counted him an intimate, and although he approved of Borglum's investigation, he was inclined to blame the problems on the dilly-dallying president and his dilly-dallying secretary of war. He also feared that Borglum, who had an impetuous streak, would make insupportable allegations—a fear soon realized.

At the behest of Woodrow Wilson, Charles Evans Hughes, his opponent in the 1916 election, conducted an official inquiry in cooperation with the Justice Department. The bearded iceberg was a canny choice. He was rectitude itself, and by putting him in charge, Wilson clipped the claws of his Republican critics. Hughes would conclude that the airplane problem owed more to bungling than fraud, but the investigation would take months, and throughout the war, American pilots in France would train and fight in French planes.

The aerial fighting began in earnest at the end of June, soon after Pershing summoned Lieutenant Quentin Roosevelt and the rest of the First Pursuit Group of the American Air Service to the front near Château-Thierry. "I am thrilled," TR replied when Quentin sent his "going up" cable to Sagamore. TR added that he was apprehensive as well, but "my joy for you and pride in you drown my anxiety." Edith, who felt no thrill but refrained from spoiling the moment for Quentin, merely acknowledged his excitement: "I do know you have your wish." As for her own wishes, she said, "It is long since I have dared think of myself—anyway I do not need to say how I feel for you to know exactly." Then, as Theodore so often did, she brushed away the dread and took refuge in the beauty of Sagamore. The morning was "cool and fair," she said, "and the country just getting the look of summer. The blossoms from the shrubs falling, and cherries nearly over."

Four years old when his family moved into the White House, Quentin became the country's little boy, adored for such things as bringing a piglet home by streetcar and inviting his classmates to play baseball on the White House lawn. As a young scholar, he was slapdash, often turning in papers that were "smudgy and ink-splashed," one of his teachers informed his parents. His adolescent defiance seems to have erupted early and died out by the time he entered Groton, where he amazed his father with high marks and proved himself a regular fellow by parading past the homes of the staid with a lamp shade on his head. Like Archie, he had run-ins with the rec-

tor ("the never-to-be-sufficiently-anathematized Endicott Peabody," as he
thought of him). Peabody confiscated his copy of *Dracula* on the ground
that it was "not fine reading," a move that prompted Quentin to say that
Dracula was more edifying than the horror stories written by R. W. Cham-
bers, who kept up the sales of his *King in Yellow* with the promise that it
would drive readers insane. The rector "disapproved of me strenuously,"
Quentin bragged to Ethel.

At ten Quentin was designing airships, and at eleven, traveling in France
with his mother and Archie and Ethel, he could hardly describe the joy he
had felt on seeing a sky filled with airplanes. "You don't know how pretty it
was to see all the aeroplanes sailing at a time," he wrote a friend. "It
was the prettiest thing I ever saw." Fascinated by aeroplanes, radios, and motorcycles, he decided to study mathematics at Harvard for a career in engi-
neering.

Quentin left Harvard in April 1917, just after the American declaration
of war, to volunteer for the Army Air Service. Before the month was out he
was Lieutenant Roosevelt and a cadet in the military aviation school in
Mineola, not far from Oyster Bay. His parents were pleased, and he was ecstatic. "Wild excitement!" he wrote a girl called Fouf. "O frabjous day! Cal-
looh! Callay!"

Fouf was Flora Payne Whitney of Westbury, Long Island, a village midway between Mineola and Oyster Bay. Her mother, Gertrude Vanderbilt
Whitney, was a sculptor of some renown and a discerning patron of the
American avant-garde. Her masterpiece would be the Whitney Museum of
American Art, founded after the beef-wits at the Metropolitan Museum rejected a gift of the five hundred contemporary works in her private collection.

Flora's father, Harry Payne Whitney, inherited one fortune, married another, and amassed a third, and while his capital toiled, he overachieved as
yachtsman, hunter, polo player, and owner of racehorses. The two hundred
thoroughbreds in the Whitney Stables won nearly all the great prizes, with
purses that in some years bulged to $500,000. Flora was her father's child, at
home on horseback and with rifle and fly rod.

Her romance with Quentin budded in the summer of 1916, when he
served as escort at her coming-out party in Newport. He proposed in May
1917, she accepted, and they decided to keep their engagement secret, in
part because they were only nineteen and in part because their families inhabited different planets. The $30,000 a year that TR earned from his writ-

ing would not have defrayed half the cost of one of H. P. Whitney's regular grouse shoots on the moors of England. Such ostentation set Edith's moral teeth on edge and drew sighs from Theodore, who regarded the Whitneys and the rest of the "out-door-sport wing of the smart set" as decent but self-indulgent. Perhaps the attitudinal gulf could be bridged, but there was no reason to think that the Whitneys would encourage their daughter to cast her lot with a penniless youth on his way to war.

Quentin understood his liabilities but had no intention of withdrawing. "I'm glad I did it," he wrote Fouf after she promised to marry him someday. As far as he could judge, obstacles "don't seem to matter when it's the heart that's speaking." Before he sailed in July they managed to tell his parents but not hers. Edith, setting aside her prejudice against the smart set, told Flora that love had put the last brushstroke of maturity on Quentin. Theodore declared Flora "a perfect trump" and readied the next niche in his shrine of daughters-in-law. She and Quentin would know "the greatest of all kinds of happiness, that of married lovers who all their lives remain lovers," he told her, adding, rather lugubriously, that whatever happened next, "you and he have had some golden months . . . and many people never know anything except years that are either gray or tawdry."

WITH ONLY a handful of cast-off airplanes from the French, the first American aviators to reach France did little flying and a great deal of construction work. Within a year their base at Issoudun would be the world's largest flight school, complete with doctors studying the physical and psychological effects of flying, but the Issoudun of August 1917 was primitive in the extreme. Quentin and his friend Ham Coolidge, a classmate at Groton and Harvard, had had to build their own beds.

Quentin was put in charge of a fleet of fifty supply trucks, an assignment several sizes too large for a boy who had never held a job. At the end of one overwhelming day he wrote Fouf about the complexities of "dealing with a huge shipment of boots all jumbled up in one big pile, and acting as buffer between irate railroad officials full of jabbering complaints and equally angry American construction officers who would like to consign the French railroad system to Hell, waybilled collect farther on."

The young lieutenant quickly grew into his responsibilities, and whatever preconceptions his comrades might have had about the lordliness of presidential offspring vanished in the space of a handshake. Eddie Rickenbacker, Issoudun's chief mechanic before his aerial combat career began, characterized Quentin as "easily the most popular man in the squadron," and praised him for relying on his own attainments, not his father's. "We boys would do anything for him," a soldier from Indiana wrote his family. "He always sees that his men get taken care of before he thinks of himself." It was a principle learned at the table of the Rough Rider, and it was the Rough Rider he longed to please. American newspapers often compared the sons of the kaiser, who were well shielded from the dangers of war, to the sons of Theodore Roosevelt, and when a visitor told Quentin of the country's pride in the Roosevelt boys, he smiled broadly and said, "Well, you know it's rather up to us to practice what father preaches."

But Ted and Archie were not convinced that Quentin was practicing much of anything. As they froze in the trenches, he was more than a hundred miles south of the front—perfectly safe, it seemed to them, and free to swan about Paris as he pleased. Eleanor's letters mentioned evenings at the Grand Guignol with Quentin, shopping expeditions, their calls on the likes of Edith Wharton, and dinners at fancy restaurants. Ted and Archie, having maneuvered themselves to the front with the first American troops, easily convinced themselves that with even a modicum of resolve, Quentin could do the same.

When a pair of American aviators went to England for training in aerial combat, Archie pointedly inquired why Quentin had not gone with them. Quentin explained that the two were the top American pilots in France. He showed his pique by adding that "father's pull" had landed them in France with the first wave of Americans, but it had not made him the first or second best flier in the Air Service. For the moment, equipping Issoudun was the only work open to him. "I wish you'd retail this on to Ted," he told Archie. "I've always called myself the slacker brother—because I openly admit that I didn't like Plattsburg and went from a sense of duty—but all the same, I don't particularly care to have my own brother think that I am seriously slacking."

The envied trips to Paris fell to Quentin because of his proficiency in French, a skill that also entitled him to rove the countryside on a motorcycle in search of pumps, electrical switches, even locomotives. Whatever the errand, he had orders not to return empty-handed, a big responsibility that afforded him more freedom than his brothers had at the front. When the scavenging was easy, he lingered over a good meal and played the tourist. In the cathedral at Bourges he found a stained glass virgin "so lovely that I burnt before her a candle to you," he wrote Fouf. At Chartres he lit another "and said a little prayer to whatever power looks after those who have been separated when love and life were sweetest." He dreamed of a Christmas when they would attend midnight mass in Paris and told her of Archie and Ted's favorite church, Notre Dame des Victoires, a veritable museum of swords and medals "all given in thanks for victory and safe return from the wars. The Catholic religion holds a wonderful appeal to the imagination, doesn't it? I've often thought that the pleasantest life in the world is that of the Catholic who believes everything the priest tells him."

Religion had meant little to Quentin before the war, but the more he saw of flying, the more he understood the comfort available to the believer. Ted and Archie seemed to think that the miles between Issoudun and the front guaranteed his safety, but the truth was that an aviator risked his life with every flight. The hand-me-down planes from the French, Nieuport 27s, easily caught fire, the motor often sputtered out, and if one of the wires holding top wing to bottom snapped, the wings collapsed like a lady's fan.

On one landing in a muddy field Quentin had watched helplessly as a stone thrown up from the ground broke his propeller and hurled a spearlike shard into his gas tank. "[B]efore I even had a chance to cut the switch, the whole thing was in flames," he wrote Fouf. Though he had scrambled out in seconds, his boots and pants were already ablaze. A late return meant landing in the dark, guided only by a few flares. Quentin survived two crashes and witnessed an unnerving number of fatalities at Issoudun.

Flying in an open cockpit at eighteen thousand feet without an oxygen tank set off fierce headaches, abraded the lungs, and sometimes turned noses and cheeks black with frostbite. Lieutenant Colonel William Mitchell found a warm, lightweight suit of waterproof gabardine lined with rabbit fur and requisitioned more for his airmen, but the manufacturer improvised with heavy duck cloth and black, foul-smelling dog skin. Barely cured and badly dyed, the dog skin blackened whatever it touched, and the goat's hair collar rubbed the neck raw and caused boils. Forty years later, still exercised by the ineptitude of Newton Baker's War Department, Mitchell told the story in his memoir and wondered how many Fidos and Billies had been poached from the backyards of America to make the damnable outfits. Quentin wore an electrically heated flying suit, helmet, fur gloves, and muffler but could not stay warm in the air and perpetually had a heavy cold. "Aviation has considerably altered my views on religion," he wrote Fouf. "I don't see how the angels stand it."

✳

Fouf called often at Sagamore and in November 1917 joined Theodore and Edith and Ethel on a short trip to Canada, where TR extemporized to large crowds (and "frantic enthusiasm," he was pleased to note) in service of Canadian war bond sales. Watching Fouf navigate the pandemonium of a Roosevelt entourage, TR thought her "dear." The pomp was "the first thing of the kind that she had ever seen, much less taken part in; and she was absorbedly interested," he wrote Ted. Fouf was indeed absorbed, but on another front, concentrating all her energies on getting through the ceremonies without embarrassing herself or the Roosevelts.

TR did not name Woodrow Wilson but surely had him in mind as he praised Canada for entering the war in 1914 and rejecting the morality of the small-souled people who used their horror of bloodshed as an excuse for neglecting a higher duty. He would have come sooner, he said, but had waited for the United States to join the war so that he could appear in Canada "with pride, as an equal speaking to equals."

News of the Canadian speeches was buried deep in the papers if it appeared at all. After the troop-raising battle TR became a kind of artifact of himself, encased at Sagamore and brought out to pin medals on Boy Scouts, speak at war bazaars, and compose messages to the troops. He wished that the government would make use of him, but he did not ask for a role and believed that Wilson refused him one out of fear. If so, the fear was not unwarranted. Given Roosevelt's temperament, his history, and the powerful yearnings on display when he pressed for the volunteer division, the White House had reason to think that he would enlarge any office he was given.

Frozen out of the war, Roosevelt turned his thoughts to the postwar world. On an evening soon after the trip to Canada he and Ethel sat by the fire in the North Room, and he painted two scenarios. Ideally the country's experience of coming together to fight the war would ignite a progressive revival and a renewed appreciation of the virtues of a strong national government dedicated to the common good. But under a weak government, he said, the excesses of capital and labor would flourish unchecked, and the two would soon destroy each other. A nation that professed to believe that all men were created equal could not permit a tiny minority to hog the wealth and use its power to exploit the masses, in his view. Such an arrangement was morally indefensible, and as the revolution in Russia and the socialist ferment in the United States made plain, the masses would not stand for it.

Writing an English friend about the chaos in Russia, Roosevelt said he regarded himself as "a very radical democrat," growing more radical as he aged, but he loathed the revolution's ideal of providing for everyone, even the citizen who refused to work. Nor would he tolerate the new Bolshevik government's "crackbrain" economic reform policy, "which under the pretense of lifting the lowly merely smashes the man on top and brings down everybody under the ruins." The war and the Russian Revolution had shattered the world but not touched Roosevelt's belief that the most perfect of all possible governments looked very like a Bull Moose.

There was little politicking to do in the autumn of 1917, but Roosevelt joined in, helping a Republican congressional candidate win a special election in Connecticut and trying in vain to effect an eleventh-hour rescue of Mayor John Purroy Mitchel of New York. Mitchel had been excellent in the office, but few voters knew of his accomplishments, TR wrote Ted. Overly fond of nightlife and the smart set, Mitchel had neglected the meeting halls and political clubs of the plain people. TR wanted to say more but held back, not knowing who might see the letter before it reached Ted. "There are all kinds of things that will have to wait for me to tell until the young Vikings come back and gather around the old hearthstone," he said.

THE YOUNGEST of the Vikings was in danger of losing his place at the hearth. His service behind the lines offended his brother Vikings, and in December he offended Sagamore's Odin (a near-twin of the Norse original: blind in one eye, a romanticizer of war, a lover of poetry). Guessing that his family and his fiancée shared Archie and Ted's low opinion of his soldiering, Quentin wrote fewer and fewer letters home, and when one of his colds ripened into pneumonia, he stopped writing altogether.

Ignorant of Quentin's despondency and the pneumonia, TR gave him the lash. "Mother, the adamantine, has stopped writing to you because you have not written to her—or to any of us—for a long time," he began. "Now of course you may not wish to keep Flora anyhow. But if you wish to lose her, continue to be an infrequent correspondent. If however you wish to keep her, write her letters, interesting letters, and love letters—at least three times a week." He signed himself "A hardened and wary old father." Though he had not said so in his letter, he suspected that Quentin was consoling himself with the women of Paris.

Flattened by the pneumonia and the chastisements from Sagamore,

Quentin lost fifteen pounds and more than once dreamed he was stranded on a pier in Hoboken, minus a foot, one arm in a sling, unable to carry his luggage or find a taxi. Awake he was remorseful for the hurt he had caused, and he promised Fouf and the family that he would reform. His letters were likely to be as dull as his life, he said, but he would write them. He began longing for combat, imagining that the concentration it required would crowd out "all the little worries and jealousies that fill up life behind the lines." In the air there was "only the one big eventuality to face, and all the others arrange for themselves if you are fighting," he told Fouf. "And then I feel I owe it to the family—to father and especially to Arch and Ted, who are out there already facing the dangers of it—to get out myself."

Quentin now superintended six hundred cadets, a job that left little time for his own flying, but at the end of February he was sent off for the last of his training, at the French school of aerial gunnery in Lac de Cazaux, near Bordeaux. The lessons left no doubt of the dangers ahead. In their first class the students learned that the ammunition belt on the Vickers machine gun mounted on French fighter planes tended to seize up in the middle of a fight. The pilots honed their marksmanship with clay pigeons and small, distant targets bobbing in the lake, firing first from the shore and then from speedboats. In the air they dropped small parachutes and maneuvered to blast them to shreds.

Mathematics could describe the trajectory of a bullet leaving a plane pitched at a given angle and traveling at a given speed toward a moving target, but the pilot in a fight had no time for such calculations, and his instrument panel was no more help than a philosopher's stone. Cazaux was supposed to give him an athletic feel for the task and unbounded faith in the power of sangfroid. "Always keep cool-headed till the last moment," a training manual advised. "Do not be afraid or nervous if the enemy continues to shoot. Do not cease firing. Wait for the final fault in his maneuvering."

Billeted in a hotel on the coast, Quentin gazed at the Atlantic and imagined Fouf on the other side, a fantasy that took on a degree of reality as he read his mail from home. For all the sensible reasons, he had wanted to wait till the war ended to marry, but now his father was urging him to reconsider. Although Fouf still had not told her parents of the engagement, she was longing for marriage, and TR saw no reason to wait. "As for your getting killed, or ordinarily crippled, afterwards, why she would a thousand times rather have married you than not . . . and anyway we have to take certain chances in life. You and she now have passed your period of probation; you have been tried; you are absolutely sure of yourselves; and I would most heartily approve of your getting married at the earliest possible moment." A week later, he pressed again.

"I used to think it would be unfair to you to marry now in these times, but I've changed now to your views," Quentin wrote Fouf at the end of March. "Even if things go wrong, there would always be the little time that we had had, and our happiness then."

Finished with Cazaux, Quentin returned to his cadets and more waiting—for new airplanes from the French, for his assignment to the front, and now for Fouf. He caught a cold that verged on pneumonia, and everything at Issoudun seemed wrong, he wrote her. "When I was in the air I wanted to be on the ground, and when I was on the ground I wanted to be flying and added to which my flying went on the bum."

Fouf told her parents at the beginning of May. To her surprise they approved, and the patriarchs convened at the Harvard Club to make plans. All that stood between bride and groom was the War Department, which allowed little civilian travel to Europe, but the Whitneys hoped to win permission through their friend Henry P. Davison, head of the American Red Cross War Council.

The War Department rejected the request in June—a "wicked" decision, TR wrote his sister Bamie; "she should have been allowed to go, and to marry Quentin; then, even if he were killed, she and he would have known their white hour."

The news was crushing to Quentin and Fouf. But on June 16, when he cabled her with the news that he and Ham Coolidge were leaving for the front, he tried to be philosophical: SO SORRY OUR PLANS IMPOSSIBLE—POOR YOU.—LOTS OF TIME YET. MOVING OUT AT LAST WITH HAM. LOVE—ROOSEVELT. He was less optimistic in a letter to his mother. What would he and Fouf have in common after so long a separation? he wondered. "[W]e'll be strangers and have to begin all over again when this show is finished," he thought. "Is she very much changed? . . . I feel like the older brother of the person who was just ordering lieutenant's uniforms this time last year, and explaining how he would probably be back by Christmas. Being back— good lord, short of being shot up, or having my nerve crack, I'll not be back till it's all over." And then, Roosevelt that he was, Quentin wheeled toward the light. "The real thing is yay, I'm on the front—cheers, oh cheers, and I'm very happy."

❋

A S A FATHER, TR fretted over any development that threatened to prolong the war, and in the summer of 1918, with American troops at last pouring into France, he worried about the instability in Russia, where the revolution had deteriorated into civil war. The British and the French feared a German coup in Moscow, an event that would give the kaiser dominion over Russia and—far worse—set the stage for the German conquest of Asia. "It is immensely to be regretted that we cannot in some way stiffen Russia," TR wrote Taft. "If she is organized and exploited by Germany, as now looks probable, the damage to us—because it will be damage to the whole world—will be terrible."

Roosevelt wished that the United States would assemble an international military force to restore order, drive out the German agitators, "and strive to free Russia and let her determine for herself her own fate." He promoted the idea in a newspaper column about a conversation with Maria Bochkareva, one of the most unusual of all the unusuals who called at Sagamore. Once the commander of a women's battalion in the Russian army, Bochkareva had been wounded four times while fighting the Germans at the front and had made her last stand, against the Bolsheviks, on the steps of the Winter Palace. Loathing the despotism of the Bolsheviks as much as the despotism of czars and kaisers, Bochkareva was touring the United States to build support for an armed intervention that would rid Siberia of the German Red Guards, a self-appointed army of twenty thousand former prisoners of war.

Moved by her courage and her dream of a democratically elected government for Russia, TR gave Bochkareva $1,000 of his Nobel Peace Prize money and proposed in the *Star* that thirty thousand Americans, plus Japanese and British contingents of equal size, be sent at once to Siberia with the mission of restoring Russia to the Russians. Anticipating White House resistance, Roosevelt defended his plan as better than none and said that if the president and his advisers could devise a superior scheme, "let them do so, but let us act at once."

France and England had been urging the United States to take such a step, but Wilson had held off, believing that the Russians, like any other free people, should be allowed to "work out their own salvation, even though they wallow in anarchy for a while." In the summer of 1918, Wilson— "sweating blood over the question," he said—gave in but sent only seven thousand American troops and gave them the narrowest of mandates. They were not to fight the Germans, they were to guard military stores that the Russians might need for self-defense and to assist in transferring a contingent of Czech soldiers from Russia to the Western Front. He also sent representatives of the Red Cross and other humanitarian organizations. The United States would not interfere in Russia's internal politics, the president explained when he announced the Siberian expedition; the sole object was to help the Russian people regain control of their own affairs.

As co-chairman of the president's War Labor Board, William Howard Taft could not publicly criticize the administration's response but privately derided it as "puling" and phony—a spectacle that allowed Wilson to take credit for coming to Russia's aid while dodging the responsibilities of real action. Wilson, Taft said, was behaving no better than "the girl who had an illegitimate baby, who sought an excuse for her offense by saying that it was such a little one."

Roosevelt, unfettered, blasted Wilson's plan, calling it a useless half-measure, and noted the high cost of the temporizing: famine and disease, which he blamed partly on the American failure to offer "efficient aid along any line."

Wilson feared that a more forceful intervention would not sit well with the American electorate. He also believed, as did General Pershing, that the United States could best serve the Allies by concentrating its energies in France.

T HE BATTLE of Belleau Wood, fought in early June, would be remembered as a great victory for the U.S. Marines, but it was an expensive lesson in airpower as well. Much of the French air force had been destroyed in the spring fighting, and German reconnaissance planes were now flying almost unopposed in the sky, pinpointing Allied depots, troop concentrations, and artillery positions. The Americans took Belleau Wood, but with no air force to shoo away the German planes, their casualty rate hit 50 percent.

Dr. Richard Derby, Ethel's husband, had been in the vortex, struggling to evacuate the wounded and nearly killed one night in an explosion that took the life of one of his companions and seriously wounded another. Ambulances were being blown up on the evacuation routes, and medics were falling ill from treating gas-soaked patients. Dick had come to dread sunny days, knowing that the Germans would be in the skies, plotting their next assault. "Yesterday was one of those fresh days that one sees in June," he wrote Ethel on June 19. The visibility was perfect, "and the day was largely given up to aerial observation. The other side did most of the observation, due to our lack of aeroplanes, and there will be an aftermath."

For the moment the Allies were holding the line, but without an air force they had little chance of staving off the fall of Paris. Informed of the pending disaster, Pershing immediately served up the First Pursuit Group of the American Air Service: four squadrons, each with eighteen pilots, two dozen planes, and the support of more than 150 men on the ground. Quentin Roosevelt was assigned to the Ninety-fifth Squadron, his friend Ham to the Ninety-fourth.

Waiting for them at their first base, an airfield between Château-Thierry and Paris, was a fleet of new planes, Nieuport 28s. The Germans introduced themselves with a midnight bombing raid meant to wipe out the First Pursuit Group in one blow. No one was injured, but the group abandoned the barracks and moved into a deserted château, where Quentin walked in the ruined gardens and tried to hold on to the thought that the war was an interruption of his life with Fouf, not the end of it.

After a few days of breaking in the planes and adjusting to the experience of flying through bursts of antiaircraft fire and incendiary rockets, they took on their first real assignment: helping the AEF's Second Division ready an attack on the village of Vaux, a German stronghold between Belleau Wood and Château-Thierry. "It's such a change after Issoudun to be out and really doing something," Quentin wrote his mother. Charged with protecting American reconnaissance planes and harassing the enemy's, the First Pursuit Group did excellent work, enabling the Americans to pull off a surprise attack on July 1.

Quentin, flying that day in a patrol assigned to intercept enemy observation planes, watched the battle from the air. "They were shelling hard . . . and one of the villages was in flames," he wrote Fouf. "You could see the white puffs where the shells landed and then when the smoke cleared away, the round crater that they dug in the ground. Altogether there was lots doing, and I was glad I was comfortably above it all, with no worries but two cold fingers and a bad magneto." He had not met the enemy, but a patrol several thousand feet above him "got into a free-for-all with nine Fokker biplanes," he said. "They had bad luck with machine gun jams, and the Boche made it pretty hot for them." Two of the Americans had not returned. The pilots hoped that the missing pair had come down safely on the Allied side of the line, a mishap as common as the ambulance driver's flat tire, but one of them was killed and the other taken prisoner. Sobered, Quentin began writing Fouf almost every day. "I'm at work now, and play is over, and I think you might rather hear more often from me where there is the chance of my getting into trouble," he said. "In case I do get it, Ham is going to look after my things, and send them home to the family. . . . Of course this all sounds foolish, but Ham and I doped it out between us to look after each other's things. I thought I'd tell you. Not that I think he ever will have to, for I love you too much to not come back, my dearest."

When the major in charge of the First Pursuit Group appointed Lieutenant Roosevelt as flight commander, Quentin demurred, fearing that his inexperience might endanger his comrades. After the major insisted, Quentin confided his predicament to the seasoned fliers in his command, and from then on he led the patrol into the air, and dropped back as soon as all the planes were up, letting one of the veterans take the lead.

JULY WOULD BE the worst month of the war for the First Pursuit Group. The Germans were staking all on their drive to Paris, while the French, taking heart from Belleau Wood and Vaux, were determined to check the advance and launch a drive of their own. As Ludendorff and Foch made their preparations, American reconnaissance planes photographed from first light to last, guarded by pursuit pilots flying as many as five patrols a day. The Americans were up against the most lethal wing of the German air force, the Red Baron's Flying Circus. Five aerial victories made a pilot an ace, and many of the Circus pilots had upward of twenty-five. The baron, Manfred von Richthofen, had managed eighty before he was shot down. Operating from a base just to the north of the First Pursuit Group, the Circus had more planes than the Americans and traveled in large formations that easily engulfed the small patrols sent up by the Americans in their first weeks at the front. The German planes were also more reliable. The Nieuport 28 caught fire as easily as the 27 and had an equally fussy motor and finicky machine gun. And as Eddie Rickenbacker and others soon discovered, the skin of the 28's top wing often sheared off in a steep dive. By the end of July, more than half the First Pursuit Group's pilots, thirty-six of sixty-eight, would be dead.

Harold Buckley, who flew in Quentin's squadron, would write of lolling in a camp chair, listening to the bees buzz in the grass and trying not to think about the next meeting of what he called "the suicide club" and trying to ignore questions buzzing in his head. "Whose belongings would be divided tonight? Whose trunk would be ransacked to remove keepsakes and mementoes before it went home with evidence to blot the memory of a hero? Overhead not a cloud in the sky. A perfect day? For what? Perfect for a last glimpse of life at its best for someone; that was for sure."

Quentin had his first one-on-one encounter with the enemy on July 5. In a plane with a balky motor, he was struggling to catch up with his patrol when a shadow fell across his Nieuport, "and there about 200 meters above me, and looking big as all outdoors, was a Boche," he wrote Fouf. "He was so near I could make out the red stripes around his fuselage. I'm free to confess that I was scared blue." He escaped only because the German chose not to attack.

The next day he and his patrol spotted six German planes below them, maneuvered to put the sun in the enemy's eyes, and dove. Quentin aligned himself with his target and pulled the trigger, but the gun jammed after two shots. "I thought I might get cold feet, or something, but you don't," he told Fouf. "You get so excited that you forget everything except getting the other fellow, and trying to dodge the tracers." He got away, and the patrol downed three planes. Reading about the fight in the newspapers the next day, TR was thrilled. "The last of the lion's brood has been blooded!" he wrote Kermit.

On July 10, flying at the top of his formation, Quentin dropped down to get out of a fierce wind and in the process lost his patrol. With his gas tank nearly full, he decided to "fool around awhile before going home," he wrote his father. He turned, circled, saw three planes in formation, and spotted three more in the distance. He assumed they were German, but when they ignored him he changed his mind and opened the throttle to catch up. He was closing in when the lead plane turned and Quentin saw, to his horror, the German insignia, a black Maltese cross, on the tail. He was "scared perfectly green," he wrote Fouf, "but then I thought to myself that I was so near I might as well take a crack at one of them. So I pulled up a little nearer, got a line on the end man." The German plane went into a tailspin, and Quentin watched till it disappeared in a cloud bank. He thought he had downed it, but the fight had taken place so far into German territory that he thought the victory would not be confirmable. "I'm awfully disappointed, for it would have been such a joke on those Boche. Think of having an enemy plane fly in your formation for ten minutes and then shooting you down."

Confirmation soon came, and with it a newspaperman hankering for an interview and a photograph. Quentin declined, saying that his victory meant no more than the others credited to the First Pursuit Group. The newsman asked again. "Why do you single me out?" Quentin snapped. "Is it because I happen to show good taste in the selection of my male progenitor?" There was no interview, no picture.

This time the male progenitor was proud but subdued, perhaps because the news reached him just as he was leaving to serve as a pallbearer for John Purroy Mitchel, the former mayor of New York. Mitchel, who joined the Air Service after his defeat, had fallen out of his plane at an army aviation school. Sending word of Quentin's victory to Ethel in Dark Harbor, TR said simply, "Whatever now befalls Quentin he has now had his crowded hour, and his day of honor and triumph."

On July 12, a day off, Quentin went to Paris to see Archie, who was still in the early stages of recovering from his second surgery, then spent the evening with Eleanor at Ciro's and the Grand Guignol. Next morning he returned to the airfield, where his orders called for making an inventory of the squadron's equipment and recruiting a ragtime ensemble for the local Bastille Day festivities.

With intelligence gathered from aerial reconnaissance and prisoners taken in trench raids, the French knew that the Germans planned to strike at 12:10 A.M. on July 15. Bastille Day, the fourteenth, was to be celebrated in the usual manner. In Paris, the parade set off at nine, with French troops in the lead, Americans next, followed by more French, after which came the Belgians, and so on, each foreign contingent nestled between French soldiers in horizon blue. In a graceful nod to the American civilians who had been coming to France as volunteers since 1914, a detachment of American ambulances had the honor of bringing up the rear. The crowd cheered and wept, tossed cigarettes and flowers, and surged into the streets to press money into the soldiers' hands.

"Paris is simply crazy about Americans now," Eleanor wrote her mother. The million-man AEF was finally assembled in France, and with it, the Allied forces in the field significantly outnumbered the enemy. Paris had feted the Americans on the Fourth of July, Old Glory now fluttered alongside the

French tricolor throughout the city, and Dick Derby had heard a French matron upbraid a bookseller who offered her an English dictionary when she asked for an American one. "They consider us their saviors and can't do enough for us," he wrote Ethel.

The First Pursuit Group spent Bastille Day in the air, clashing seven times with the Germans as both sides finished their preparations for the midnight hostilities. Quentin went up at eleven in the morning in a patrol of eight, headed for Château-Thierry. One pilot lost his way in the clouds. Two others turned back because of motor troubles. Close to Belleau Wood, the patrol spotted the enemy and in unison swung up and away to position itself for an attack. "We dove on them, with every advantage except the wind, which was blowing straight into Germany," one of the pilots told an interviewer decades later. "Quentin and I picked a machine apiece and immediately attacked. Our opponents dove, and we followed them, not realizing that they were luring us down into a position from which we could be attacked." Trap set, the German pilots pulled up and away, and "fourteen machines mixed in a general melee, rolling and circling and diving, some on their backs and others cocked up at an angle of 90 degrees. . . . Bullets were flying everywhere and added to the roar of the motors and the wind winging through the wires was a continuous tat, tat, tat, tat of the machine guns."

The fight lasted fifteen minutes. When the pilots reassembled on the ground, Quentin and three others were missing. Someone had seen a plane go down—German, he was quite sure. By nightfall, everyone but Quentin was accounted for. Phil Roosevelt, a cousin who served as the First Pursuit Group's chief operations officer, telephoned Eleanor and held out the possibility that Quentin had been captured. Hoping that Phil was right, she postponed her cable to Sagamore.

Just before midnight eight hundred batteries of French artillery loosed one of the thickest, deadliest barrages of the war. The guns were well aimed, thanks in part to the Americans' intelligence work on the ground and in the air, and by the time the Germans entered the cannonading at 12:10 A.M., Ludendorff's plans were wastepaper. Thirty-five miles away, hundreds of Parisians, drawn by the roar of the guns, scaled Montmartre to see what they could see. Not much—a pale scratch of flame along the horizon—and no hint of victory or defeat.

✺

THE FIRST WORD of trouble came on July 16, late in the afternoon, when the Associated Press reporter assigned to Oyster Bay showed up with a puzzling cable: WATCH SAGAMORE HILL FOR—. At work in his library, TR closed the door. "Something has happened to one of the boys," he said. It was Ted or Quentin, he knew. Archie was in the hospital, Kermit still had not reached France, and Dick was in Paris, recovering from influenza. The reporter, Phil Thompson, agreed not to file a story until there was a more definite report. Theodore kept the contents of the cable to himself and passed the evening with Edith as they had passed countless others, talking and reading in the North Room.

Thompson returned before breakfast and spoke with TR on the veranda. The latest report, unofficial and still sketchy, said that Quentin had been shot down in German territory. There was room for optimism, but TR guessed the truth. "Mrs. Roosevelt!" he said softly. "How am I going to break it to her?" He paced for a bit, then bolted into the house.

Half an hour later he returned with a public statement that concealed every trace of their grief: "Quentin's mother and I are very glad that he got to the front and had a chance to render some service to his country, and show the stuff that was in him before his fate befell him." After telephoning Fouf, TR sequestered himself in the library and spent the rest of the day dictating, through tears, to a secretary. He had promised a speech to a Republican gathering in Saratoga the next day and intended to keep the appointment.

Thompson posted himself on the veranda, probably to speak with the reporters who would turn up after the AP dispatch reached the papers. In the afternoon, Edith went out to tell him that they had to do all they could to help Theodore. "The burden must not rest entirely on his shoulders."

For days, cables from the family in Paris encouraged Theodore and Edith not to despair, and Eleanor assured Fouf that there was reason to believe that Quentin was still alive. Definitive word arrived on July 20, in a telegram from the White House. "Am greatly distressed that the news of your son's death is confirmed," Wilson wrote. "I had hoped for other news. He died serving his country and died with fine gallantry. I am deeply grieved that his services should have come to this tragic end." Roosevelt answered in the same measured tone: "I thank you for your courtesy and kindness in telegraphing me, and I deeply appreciate your expressions of sympathy and of approval of my son's conduct."

Quentin died of two bullet wounds to the head in a duel with a pilot from the Flying Circus. The Germans had followed his plane down, dug a grave, and conducted a military burial service, marking the grave with a cross lettered in English: "Lieutenant Roosevelt, buried by the Germans, July 14, 1918." A few days later they flew over the line to drop a small bundle containing his effects, which included his identification bracelet, a small metal disk on a silver chain.

Sagamore was immediately blanketed in tenderness—some two thousand letters from kings, generals, philosophers, artists, friends, and parents of other boys killed in the war. In his replies, TR grieved and wrestled with his guilt and held fast to the creed of the hero. "To feel that one has inspired a boy to conduct that has resulted in his death, has a pretty serious side for a father," he wrote one woman; "—and at the same time I would not have cared for my boys and they would not have cared for me if our relations had not been just along that line." To someone else he admitted that it was "rather awful to know that Quentin paid with his life, and that my other sons may pay with their lives, to try to put into practice what I preached; and yet of course I would not have it otherwise. But I do feel the bitterest regret, a regret that turns into bitter indignation that I was not allowed to go over myself and at least run the risk of paying the price my sons are paying." There was no sadness in the death of an old man, he said, "and it is infinitely sad to have a boy die in his golden youth."

Twenty-one

While Daring Greatly

A T Saratoga, Quentin's father permitted a few minutes of applause when he took the stage, answered it with restrained nods and waves, then raised his hand for quiet. TR's sister Corinne, who had motored over from her country house to spend the day with him, heard the jagged edge in his voice as he began, watched him overpower his anguish, and understood. The boy had not shrunk from duty, so the father must not, absolutely must not, shrink from his. Quentin's father and mother would mourn him in private, declining even to wear black, a custom that had come to seem ostentatious in a world of unending carnage.

TR had made the trip to share the latest version of his progressive agenda with New York's Republicans, but midway through he interrupted himself. Another matter weighed on him, he said, and "with all my heart and soul I want you to be alert to act upon it." He asked the audience to honor the war dead by living up to the credo for which they had died, and he asked the women to stand shoulder to shoulder with the men in demanding a "loftier idealism" so that the Americans fighting in France would "come home to a nation which they can be proud to have fought for." New York had extended the vote to women in 1917.

Party leaders, at last ready to forgive the transgressions of the Bull Moose, were hoping he would run for governor, but he left Saratoga without seeing them. "I have only one fight left in me, and I think I should reserve my strength in case I am needed in 1920," he explained to Corinne.

Throughout their day together, Corinne was struck by Theodore's gentleness, a side of him rarely glimpsed by the public. His letters after Quentin's death insisted upon the glory of dying for one's country, the duties of the living, the dishonor of surrendering to sorrow—"nothing more foolish and cowardly," he said.

But soldiering on is a slow cure and the kind of medicine that stings. The great balm for grief is gentleness, and whether Theodore realized it or not, he salved his wound by salving Edith's. As respite from a house throbbing with reminders of Quentin, they rowed for hours on the glassy waters of the sound. The outings soothed her, and one morning as they took a swim she spoke of the velvet touch of the water, smiled at him, and said, "there is left the wind on the heath, brother." The line, a family favorite, comes from a moment in George Borrow's novel *Lavengro*, when two characters debate the sadness of death. One muses that given the afterlife, mere physical death should occasion no grief. Nonsense, says the other. "Life is sweet, brother. There's night and day, brother, both sweet things; sun, moon, and stars, brother, all sweet things; there's likewise a wind on the heath. Life is very sweet, brother; who would wish to die?"

Theodore had often expressed a wish to die in place of his sons, but the gods of war are an unobliging lot, so he carried on, as did Edith. They were like a house of cards, she wrote Kermit—able to keep upright as long as they leaned on each other. She did not say, perhaps could not dare to think, that with one gust from the heath, the house would collapse.

Fouf came often, comforting and seeking comfort, although Theodore knew of no way to soften her sorrow. All he could do, he wrote Belle, was "earnestly hope that time will be very merciful to her, and that in a few years she will keep Quentin only as a loving memory of her golden youth, as the lover of her golden dawn, and that she will find happiness with another good and fine man."

The cloud pressing on Sagamore lifted a bit on July 21 with the news that Ted had been wounded in the leg—no cause for rapture in ordinary times but now a source of relief to his parents. The wound, received in a daring raid on an enemy machine gun nest near Soissons, required surgery and a convalescence that would keep him out of the fighting for weeks.

A day later Theodore and Edith decided to leave Sagamore for Maine, a place free of associations with Quentin. They would stay with Ethel, rowboats were easily procured, and the children would be a tonic. TR had been pining for little Edie, Ethel wrote Dick, and "Mother says very often that if she can just get Richard and hold him in her arms she will feel comforted."

Ethel's rented cottage in Dark Harbor was a cheery place, pale yellow with scarlet awnings and a view of Penobscot Bay. The locals likened the air to champagne, and if Theodore and Edith could not drink deeply, they nonetheless appreciated the change of scene. Seeming to sense the depths of Edith's hurt, Richard, age four, was as attentive as a guardsman and insisted that she join him for his naps. Edie, just turned one, scuttled around underfoot, perpetually willing to administer a dose of affection to anyone who scooped her up.

TR gave a short talk to the islanders one Sunday afternoon, ostensibly in thanks for their courtesies. Edith and Ethel stayed home to mind the children, an arrangement that allowed the servants to attend and spared Edith the trial of bearing up in a crowd of strangers. She could manage it, but she lacked Theodore's compulsion to demonstrate that the heartbroken parent of a dead soldier could and should go on. Her grief was unconnected to the war, she wrote Kermit. Quentin "fell in battle in a fair fight, and with no accident to his machine. It is the dreadful actual pain of loss which is hard to bear bravely. For a child the death pangs I can only compare to the birth pangs, only lasting much longer."

THE ALLIED DRIVE begun in the last minutes of Bastille Day was steadily pushing the Germans north and east toward the Rhine, and by August 10, when Theodore and Edith left Maine, Quentin's grave was no longer in enemy territory. Tended by the village of Chamery, it quickly became a shrine for American soldiers and French admirers of TR. Ham Coolidge stood on the grassy hillside, listening to the thud of distant cannons and reflecting that the sight of a cross with Quentin's name on it was worse than flying through rocket fire and machine gun bullets. "[Y]ou get used to all that," he wrote his family. "What you can never get used to, though, is to have your very best friends 'go West.' " Ham would be killed in the air two weeks before the end of the war.

With Archie on his way home, Ted recuperating in Paris, and Kermit still in artillery school, Dick was the only family member in danger. He was near Soissons, where casualties were high and likely to rise. The fighting was fierce, and a new enemy, a strain of influenza that would kill millions around the world, had stolen into the AEF's ranks. It would take the lives of more American soldiers than the fighting did. Determined to do better by the wounded than was possible in the chaos at Belleau Wood, Dick was trying to persuade a skeptical new commander of the need for extra hospital beds. "I do not intend to let him learn by bitter experience if I can help it," he wrote Ethel. Those worries aside, he was heartened by the Allies' momentum and predicted that Germany would give up before the year was out.

TR looked forward to peace as eagerly as any soldier at the front but kept up the pressure for more American arms and men. Afraid that the Allied gains would tempt Washington's "elderly swivel-chair military gentry" to lean back, he argued that the United States, as a latecomer to France, had a special obligation: "From now on we should take the burden of the war upon our shoulders. We should move forward at once with all the force that there is in us."

Roosevelt also feared that Wilson would bollix the ending of the war by negotiating a separate peace rather than holding out with the Allies for Germany's unconditional surrender. Months earlier Wilson had unfurled his blueprint for peace, the Fourteen Points, which called for an end to secret pacts between nations, freedom of the seas, free trade, global arms reduction, the right of each nation to determine its form of government, several adjustments to national boundaries, and a League of Nations charged with preserving world peace. The architect drew up his plan without consulting the Allies, and when it was spread on the table, Britain declined to comment and President Clemenceau frostily noted that the Almighty had managed to set forth His world order in ten points.

Roosevelt did not comment on the Fourteen Points until September, when his friend Senator Lodge gave him an opening by speaking out in favor of unconditional surrender and a peace that would be dictated, not negotiated. TR warned that any peace made before the Allies destroyed the military might of Germany would merely free the kaiser to embark on a new world conquest. Roosevelt opposed ending the war by negotiation on the ground that Germany had behaved like a criminal, and in private life, he said, "sensible men and women do not negotiate with an outlaw . . . they expect the law officers to take him by force and to have him tried and punished"—not out of vengeance but to stop the crime and protect the community from future acts of aggression.

Wilson's adjustments of national boundaries TR found straightforward and acceptable, but the other points struck him as vague, impractical, or dangerous. Nations that answered Wilson's call to reduce arms to the minimum necessary for their domestic safety would be prey to any aggressor who chose to violate a treaty, Roosevelt observed. When Germany invaded France by way of Belgium in 1914, breaking the treaty that guaranteed Belgium's neutrality, the German chancellor had declared the treaty "a scrap of paper." Roosevelt revived the phrase in a caustic column entitled "Fourteen Scraps of Paper."

No point troubled Roosevelt more than the fourteenth, Wilson's proposal to create a League of Nations "for the purpose of affording mutual guarantees of political independence and territorial integrity to great and small states alike." By no means an isolationist, Roosevelt had suggested an international peacekeeping league in his Nobel address, but his plan included an armed force to back up the league's covenants. Wilson's did not.

Roosevelt feared that Wilson's broad phrase "mutual guarantees" might oblige the United States to involve itself in every spat between two nations, and he was equally leery of fantasies of universal brotherhood. International harmony and cooperation were fine ideals but no substitutes for nationalism and a strong national defense, in his judgment. Nationalism was like love of family, he said, while internationalism corresponded to the feeling a man had for his neighbors. "The man who loves other countries as much as his own stands on a level with the man who loves other women as much as he loves his own wife."

A RCHIE ARRIVED in New York on September 5 and with Gracie and Archie Jr. headed directly to Sagamore for a holiday. After months of worrying letters about Archie's mental state, Theodore and Edith were pleased to find him agreeable and tenderhearted — "exactly his old self," TR thought. He seemed so well, in fact, that Edith began to fear that he would be sent back to France.

From Sagamore Archie and his family moved into an apartment near Roosevelt Hospital, where he would have the last of the shrapnel plucked from his knee and start a long, arduous course of physical therapy for his arm. The Colonel showed him off at the Harvard Club, and strangers who recognized him from newsreels and photographs spoke to him warmly in the streets. At a Liberty Loan rally with Georges Bertrand-Vignes, a French military officer and friend of the family, Archie winced when asked for a speech but rebounded with a dashing assist from Bertrand, who pulled off his Croix de Guerre and put it up for auction. The bidding started at $500, Archie coaxed it up to $10,000, and the winner gallantly restored the medal

to Bertrand. Archie's popularity even inspired a pair of swindlers. Posing as
Captain and Mrs. Archie Roosevelt, they gypsied about the South and the
West, claiming to have run out of money on their way to California for the
captain's convalescence.

Ted's wound kept him on crutches and canes for weeks. Recuperating in
Paris, he was comfortably housed, well fed, and cared for by his adoring
wife. Possessing no more tolerance for inertia than his father did, he soon
began begging to be pronounced fit for limited duty. Down to one cane by
September 13, his thirty-first birthday, he limped off to teach in the Army
Line School and study in the General Staff College at Langres. The long-
delayed promotion to lieutenant colonel was bestowed a few days later, and
with it came confirmation of the family's hunch that the honor had been
held up to avoid any appearance of favoritism. The reward pleased Ted and
excited the old Colonel's hopes of seeing his son with a general's star by the
end of the war. The assignment at Langres put Ted closer to AEF headquarters, a bastion he intended to storm until given permission to rejoin his regiment, which had lost all its field officers. "It makes no difference whether
you are out legitimately or no, you feel it all the time," he wrote his father.

In his letters to Ted and Kermit, TR chronicled the advance of autumn at
Sagamore—the flowering of the asters and the reddening of maple leaves
and dogwood berries—and long excursions with Edith in the rowboat. They
picnicked under wild plum bushes and received the tiny, random consola-
tions flung up by the universe—sweetpea vines sprawling across the sand,
the soft blue of beach rosemary in bloom. Life was sweet. Not so sweet as before, but TR cherished the Indian summer days and the cozy evenings he
and Edith spent reading in the North Room, with no sound but the whisper
of logs crumbling in the fireplace.

TR left home at the end of September for two weeks of selling the country on the latest Liberty Loan. It would be a "hideous talky-talky trip," he
wrote Kermit and Belle—a sprint to Montana and back in hopes of persuading the citizenry that massive sums were still needed to win the war.
Henry Stimson, who had known TR since the early days of his presidency,
saw him in Baltimore and wistfully told his diary that he thought the shim-
mer of TR's mind was beginning to fade. When TR passed through Kansas
City, his editor at the Star, alarmed by the weariness in his face, suspected
he was ill. Others who noticed the fatigue laid it to his grief, which was
shoreless. His mind drifted, his eyes went blank, and for the first time he fretted that his dissent would cost him his pulpits in the Star and Metropolitan.

He also confessed to a "sickening feeling" that he had had a hand in Quentin's death. "Just because they are my sons, they feel they must be extra brave," he told a friend. "They take chances they wouldn't perhaps otherwise take."

On October 27, his sixtieth birthday, TR wrote Kermit and Belle that the marker was one he was glad to pass, "for it somehow gives me the right to be titularly as old as I feel." In talking about the day with the press, though, he dwelt on his strength. He had been rowing regularly, he said—in a heavy boat, a boat requiring "a good pull, but I did not notice that it affected me any." He admitted only one weakness, a susceptibility to bouts of the fever he had contracted in Brazil. Clearly he wanted it understood that Theodore Roosevelt was in excellent physical shape for 1920.

The thousands who jammed Carnegie Hall the next night to hear him deliver the last big oration of the Republicans' 1918 congressional campaign beheld a titan. For two hours he thundered against Woodrow Wilson, who had just informed his fellow Americans that unless they voted Democratic on November 5, he could no longer be their "unembarrassed spokesman" in international affairs. The Democrats had no monopoly on patriotism, Wilson said, but the "difficulties and delicacies" of ending the war and crafting a peace demanded that the nation give undivided support to the government, and "a Republican Congress would divide the leadership." By his measure, the Republicans had been pro-war but anti-administration, scheming and maneuvering to undercut his management of foreign policy and the war.

The Colonel made no attempt to hide his glee. "I am glad that Mr. Wilson has now cast off the mask," he told the crowd at Carnegie Hall. Five months before, asking Congress to forgo the usual partisan haggling and approve the war budget without delay, Wilson had grandly declared, "Politics is adjourned." To Roosevelt, the new plea exposed the adjournment for what it was, a demand for a "rubber-stamp attitude of complete servility."

More Republicans than Democrats had supported White House requests for a declaration of war, a draft, and Liberty Loans, Roosevelt said, yet the president was telling the country that Republicans were "not good enough to serve the Republic in Congress at this time. But they are good enough to die for the Republic in the army and navy! They are good enough to pay the taxes and subscribe to the loans!" Their so-called anti-administration behavior had consisted of shining a light on the desultory ways of the War Department and refusing to "creep into [Wilson's] presence as slaves."

The judgment was harsh but astute. Wilson's election eve ploy was the first of several attempts to lock Republicans out of the decision-making that would define America's role in the postwar world. On election day the voters sided with Roosevelt, giving Republicans a majority of thirty-three seats in the House and one in the Senate. Edith, voting for the first time in a federal election, entered the outcome in her diary: "Wilson rebuked. Hurrah!"

Wilson's miscalculation pitched Roosevelt's hat into the ring for 1920. TR said nothing publicly on the subject but privately wrote Rudyard Kipling of his "sardonic amusement" in discovering that after years of being out of favor with his countrymen, he was now "the one man whom they insisted upon following and whose statements were taken as the platform." To another correspondent he confided that he could imagine running for president—if the Republicans would help him turn his principles into policy "without any pussyfooting, or slippery turning of corners on my part."

A T DAWN on November 11, Germany offered its surrender. It was the eleventh day of the eleventh month, and Marshal Foch, supreme commander of the Allied armies, rounded out the poetics by declaring that all hostilities would cease at the eleventh hour. As the church bells of Paris pealed the news, Belle Roosevelt ventured out to the Place de la Concorde, where she was swept into a current of dancing, singing, kissing Parisians. She wrote Edith that the armistice filled her with thoughts of Quentin, who would have turned twenty-one the day before. To her, November 11 was his day—"the day he made possible."

A detachment from Dick Derby's Second Division, hell-bent on crossing the Meuse River, continued to shoot after eleven. Still peeved that they had not been the first Americans into battle, the men of the Second had decided to be the last out, and they carried on until General Pershing, responding to a complaint from the Germans, called them off. Dick had been on blood-soaked ground since Belleau Wood, risking his life to save the wounded. The armistice left him "utterly dazed," he wrote Ethel. "I can't express to you my feeling of joy at its being all over, with the prospect of seeing you and the precious bunnies and your father and mother again. There have been so many moments during the past five months when danger made such a meeting doubtful."

Ted and Kermit were safe in the Bois de la Folie, near Sedan, after the army's push through the Argonne Forest toward the Meuse, the longest and deadliest of the battles fought by the AEF. As the Germans retreated, they gave up the western reaches of their line and massed in the Meuse-Argonne sector, a move that enabled them to hold on for six weeks and inflict 117,000 American casualties. Half of the 53,000 Americans killed in the war died in the Meuse-Argonne. Kermit had been released from gunnery school in time to captain an artillery battery for the last two weeks of the fighting, and Ted, still on a cane, commanded the Twenty-sixth Infantry.

Eleanor was making plans to leave Paris for the United States, and as soon as the shooting stopped, she headed north by automobile in hopes of a last visit with Ted. Fourteen months of living with air raids and Big Bertha had led her to think that she knew war, but she was shocked by the infinity of ruin along the road—"mad Gorilla-work," Edith Wharton had called it— mile upon mile of torn, blackened earth and village after village shot to atoms. Eleanor found Ted at dusk, just as the soldiers' first unconcealed campfires began flickering in the woods. Pop-eyed at the sight of his wife, the young colonel folded her into his arms and said he could finally believe that the war was over. Years later, remembering the day, Eleanor wrote that they sat together in silence, overjoyed to think that they "would never have to fight another war, nor would our children. People would have too much sense to fight wars. No doubt was in our minds."

Alice Longworth was startled out of her sleep on November 11 just be-fore sunrise—eleven o'clock Paris time—by the screams of every siren in Cincinnati. Sure that the racket was the city's fanfare for the armistice, she dressed and went out for a walk, expecting to exchange a celebratory word or two with her neighbors. No one else had bothered to get up. She longed to feel that "the morning stars were singing together and the sons of God shouting for joy, but it was no use," she said.

THE OLD COLONEL, who had basked in the heroism of his sons and could think of no American family whose service in the war would out-shine the Roosevelts', spent Armistice Day engaged on another front. For nearly two weeks he had been off his feet, felled by an excruciating attack of arthritis in his right leg and arm. He had gone out only on election day, to cast his vote. On November 11 he surrendered to the doctors at Roosevelt Hospital.

His soul was still in battle mode. The newspapers had just heralded the kaiser's abdication, a welcome development for the world but an act of cowardice, TR told his doctor, J. H. Richards. When Richards asked what he would have done in the kaiser's place, TR replied that he had actually considered the question and concluded that there was but one honorable end: gather up his sons and charge, unarmed, into the strongest part of the Allied line "in the hope that God in his infinite goodness and mercy would give me a speedy and painless death."

For months TR had been thinking ahead to peace treaties and the preservation of peace, so to him the armistice was less closing scene than intermission, a pause before a tragic last act in which the moral vanity of Woodrow Wilson would poison the fruits of victory. "Peace," Roosevelt's *Star* column for November 12, was a tirade astonishing for its rancor. Without a joyous word about the war's end, Roosevelt denounced Wilson as timid and deceitful, and he snidely reminded the country of the president's recent defeat at the polls.

TR spent six weeks in the hospital, much of it with his inflamed arm swathed in cotton and cushioned in a splint. Edith moved into an adjoining room, and his political friends gathered around. Lodge came twice to discuss ideas for asserting the Republicans' new power in Congress. Taft and Root sounded him out on the League of Nations. William Allen White, on his way to Europe with the Red Cross, passed along the rumor that Leonard Wood hoped to be the next Republican presidential candidate. Roosevelt, visibly perturbed, shared his platform for 1920 and guessed that he would have to declare himself sooner than he had intended.

The Colonel allowed neither his confinement nor his pain to interfere with his assault on Wilson. When the president appointed himself head of the U.S. delegation to the peace conference in Paris, Roosevelt declared that Wilson had "no authority whatever to speak for the American people" because they had just repudiated his leadership in the congressional election. TR praised Wilson's decision to include former ambassador Henry White in the delegation, but surely he understood that his old friend had not been chosen for his diplomatic skill or his personal relationships and high standing with the leaders of Europe. Wilson needed a Republican, and White, who had never publicly criticized him, was the least objectionable member of the species.

Still smarting from the election, Wilson had rejected advice to appoint a more prominent Republican. Roosevelt and Taft were "impossible," he said, and Root, now seventy-three, he regarded as a fossil. The president's small-mindedness would prove catastrophic. The Republicans, locked out of the Paris Peace Conference and ignored when they sought modifications of the Versailles Treaty, would come to feel that they had no choice but to let the treaty and the League of Nations die in the Senate.

B Y DECEMBER 23, TR was well enough to go home, but he and Edith stayed at Roosevelt Hospital until Christmas Day—"very willing to avoid the dark shadow of our old Merry Christmases at Sagamore," Edith explained to Kermit. The remark raises the question of why they did not wait until after Christmas and suggests an answer: TR might have been timing his exit to conceal his decrepitude from the press. Few reporters would want to work on Christmas, so he could protect their holiday and himself by asking his doctor to give the papers a statement on Christmas Eve. Richards obliged, telling the world that the Colonel was going home and probably would resume his usual duties in six or eight weeks.

On Christmas morning, stiff, weak, and very pale, TR made his way to the elevator. He was momentarily overcome by dizziness, but when Richards reached out to steady him, TR waved him off. "I am not sick and it will give the wrong impression," he said. The elevator stopped, the doors opened, and TR willed himself down the corridor on his own steam.

At Sagamore there were presents and turkey and plum pudding and, for the first time since the summer of 1917, a house overflowing with Roosevelts—Alice and Ethel and Archie and Gracie plus a trio of grandchildren. Ted, Kermit, and Dick were still abroad, assigned to the army of occupation in Germany. When TR wrote Ted about the day, his thoughts vaulted ahead to their next Christmas, with "the whole family, for three generations, gathered at Sagamore Hill!"

TR could hardly walk but sometimes went out in the automobile with Edith, who believed in the healing power of fresh air, and for a few days he seemed to improve. Working on a review of a new work of natural history, he spotted an error and wrote the author for permission to say that this "slip of the printer" would be corrected in a future edition. Leslie Tarlton, his safari outfitter, sent greetings from Nairobi and asked if he recalled their night ride with a lioness. TR replied that he would never forget it—their fight with the lioness at dusk, the skinning outside a Masai village at midnight, and the ride home through the dark. Most of his skins had gone to the Smithsonian, he told Tarlton, but he had kept the lioness for the North Room.

On New Year's Eve his temperature shot up to 103 degrees, and his right forefinger felt as if it were caught in a vise. He spent his waking hours on a sofa, too enervated even to take his meals at the table. He seemed dazed, but within the cloud of pain, he was still roughriding. "For Heaven's sake never allude to Wilson as an idealist," he scolded in a New Year's Day letter to a Republican newspaper editor. Wilson could not even be classed as a misguided idealist, TR said; he was "a silly doctrinaire at times and an utterly selfish and cold-blooded politician always."

The *Star* had asked TR for his thoughts on what a League of Nations would have to do to succeed, and on January 3 he dictated his finest and least combative piece on the subject. "We all of us earnestly desire such a league," he wrote. He advised starting small, with a League of Allies, and then extending membership "as rapidly as their conduct warrants it, to other nations." To minimize the chances of another global war, he suggested that Europe and Asia institute their own versions of the Monroe Doctrine, with the "civilized" nations of each continent assuming responsibility for maintaining order throughout the regions.

In the *Star* he did not speculate about the consequences of an overreaching League, but he made an eerie prophecy to Ted: "the result will be either nil or mischievous, although in such case, as nobody will wish to make war for some time, unscrupulous demagogues may gain great temporary glory in the minds of unspeakably silly fools who always applaud such movements and never learn anything from their failure." When the demagogues of Germany and Italy appeared in the 1930s, the silly fools did nothing, and the demagogues, unwilling to honor the covenants of the League, quit.

On Sunday, January 5, TR put in an eleven-hour day from his bed. Two visitors came by, but he saw only one, Fouf. Edith spent the day at his side, reading, playing solitaire, and serving as secretary. In a postscript to his letter to Kermit, she said that Theodore was having a "horrid, painful time" but seemed a bit better. He proofread a series of magazine articles on the domestic reforms he considered in order now that the war was over, and he scrawled himself a reminder to see Will Hays, chairman of the Republican Party. For months the two of them had been aerating the ground for a Roosevelt run in 1920, and he wanted Hays to spend ten days on Capitol Hill, convincing the party's conservatives and progressives to stand together on domestic issues.

At ten-thirty in the evening, TR had the odd sensation that his heart and breathing had stopped. He knew they hadn't, he told Edith, "and I am perfectly all right but I have a curious feeling." A doctor was summoned to listen to his chest but heard nothing amiss. Theodore fell asleep at midnight. Edith posted his valet near the bed and checked on the patient twice before she retired. In the depths of the night, the valet heard him struggle briefly for air and summoned Edith, who recorded the ending of the story in her diary: "At four A.M., T. stopped breathing. Had had sweet sound sleep."

THEODORE ROOSEVELT DEAD was an oxymoron, as puzzling and pointless as a locomotive without an engine. No one seemed able to absorb the shock. The doctors, focused on the inflammation in his joints, had not expected a fatal blood clot. Edith had the sense that she had died. Archie's cable to Ted and Kermit—THE OLD LION IS DEAD—touchingly denied the fact even as it affirmed it, a dead lion being infinitely more bearable than a dead father. Edith Wharton ordered her swirl of feeling into a poem that envisioned a long line of ships taking the Great American on some farther quest, in the company of the ghosts of all who had loved "right more than ease, and honor above honors." As an appreciation of the Great American's fidelity to the strenuous life, the poem was unexcelled, but surely the summoning gods would have sent Theodore Roosevelt a rowboat.

Henry Cabot Lodge, epitome of New England reserve, privately confessed that he needed all his self-control to keep from crying out in the darkness. In public, at Roosevelt's memorial service in the Capitol, Cabot managed to speak calmly of his best friend's life, not losing his composure till the end, when he imagined Theodore as Valiant-for-Truth in *Pilgrim's Progress*, who "passed over, and all the trumpets sounded on the other side." Cabot's voice broke, and he sank into a chair.

It is easy to see Theodore Roosevelt splashing ashore on the other side, bounding out of the rowboat and hurrying past the trumpets in search of a battlefield, where he could spend his eternity as he had spent his life, contending. He had felt fully alive on the vast field of the presidency, contending for power—the power to do more as president, more for his country, and, let it be said, more for himself.

Afterward, thrashing in the cage of his powerlessness, he was sometimes more Valiant-for-Theodore than for the party that made him or the great causes he espoused. He could be vindictive, and at times his ambition threatened to swamp a love of country that was true and deep. But he had never pretended to perfection. The man he prized was not the critic but the man in the arena, spending himself and being spent in a fight for his beliefs. Such a man was sure to err and fall short, and great effort did not always bring great triumph, he knew. But if the man of action failed, he at least failed "while daring greatly, so that his place shall never be with those cold and timid souls who know neither victory nor defeat." Theodore Roosevelt dared greatly to the last, contending against grief and pain, contending for the fair treatment of all Americans, and contending for a return to power. Great triumph eluded him after the White House, but to say that he failed would be to miss the point of the man.

ARCHIVAL SOURCES

KEY TO NAMES

GGA	Grace Green Alexander
AWB	Archibald Willingham Butt
ERD	Ethel Carow Roosevelt Derby (daughter)
RD	Richard Derby (son-in-law)
HJ	Hiram Johnson
HCL	Henry Cabot Lodge
ARL	Alice Roosevelt Longworth (daughter)
NL	Nicholas Longworth (son-in-law)
RML	Robert Marion La Follette
GWP	George Walbridge Perkins
AP	Amos Pinchot
GP	Gifford Pinchot
ABR	Archibald Bulloch Roosevelt (son)
BWR	Belle Willard Roosevelt (daughter-in-law)
ER	Edith Roosevelt (wife)
EAR	Eleanor Butler Alexander Roosevelt (daughter-in-law)
GLR	Grace Lockwood Roosevelt (daughter-in-law)
KR	Kermit Roosevelt (son)
QR	Quentin Roosevelt (son)
TR	Theodore Roosevelt
TR Jr.	Theodore Roosevelt, Jr. (son)
TRC	Theodore Roosevelt Collection, Harvard College Library, Harvard University
TRLC	Theodore Roosevelt Papers, Library of Congress
HHT	Helen Herron (Nellie) Taft
WHT	William Howard Taft
WAW	William Allen White
FPW	Flora Payne Whitney
WW	Woodrow Wilson

KEY TO FREQUENTLY USED SOURCES

AGT   *African Game Trails* (Theodore Roosevelt)
NYT   *New York Times*
TBW   *Through the Brazilian Wilderness* (Theodore Roosevelt)
WGE   *War in the Garden of Eden* (Kermit Roosevelt)

Box numbers and microfilm reel numbers are cited only when a document's location might not be obvious from the index to the collection in question.

Unless otherwise noted, unpublished letters to and from Roosevelt are from the Theodore Roosevelt Papers in the Library of Congress (TRLC).

Letters of Theodore Roosevelt (Morison and Blum, eds.) is shortened to *Letters*.

The Works of Theodore Roosevelt (National Edition, Hermann Hagedorn, ed.) is cited as *Works*.

Selections from the Correspondence of Theodore Roosevelt and Henry Cabot Lodge, 1884–1918 (Henry Cabot Lodge, ed.) is cited as *Roosevelt–Lodge Letters*.

Letters written by Archie Butt come from three sources: *The Letters of Archie Butt, Personal Aide to President Roosevelt* (Lawrence F. Abbott, ed., Garden City, N.Y.: Doubleday, Page, 1924); *Taft and Roosevelt: The Intimate Letters of Archie Butt* (Lawrence F. Abbott, ed., Garden City, N.Y.: Doubleday, Doran, 1930); and the Archibald Willingham Butt Letters, the manuscripts from which the published volumes were drawn. The originals are in the Georgia Department of Archives and History, in Morrow, Georgia. I read a microfilmed version from the Robert W. Woodruff Library at Emory University. In the notes below, the previously unpublished letters (which are excised portions of published letters in some cases and entirely unpublished letters in others) are cited as AWB Letters.

MANUSCRIPTS

Jane Addams Papers (microfilm), New York Public Library
Reminiscences of George W. Alger, Oral History Research Office, Columbia University
Newton Diehl Baker Papers, Library of Congress
Gertrude Bell Project (www.gerty.ncl.ac.uk), Robinson Library, University of Newcastle
Archibald Willingham Butt Letters (microfilm), Special Collections and Archives, Emory University
Andrew Carnegie Papers, Library of Congress
Chanler Papers, Houghton Library, Harvard University
George K. Cherrie Papers, American Museum of Natural History
Harvey Cushing Papers, Yale University Medical History Library
Francis Warrington Dawson Papers, Rare Book, Manuscript, and Special Collections Library, Duke University
Ethel Roosevelt Derby Papers, Theodore Roosevelt Collection (Harvard College Library), Harvard University
W. Cameron Forbes Papers, Houghton Library, Harvard University
James Rudolph Garfield Papers, Library of Congress
Nicolay Grevstad Papers, Norwegian-American Historical Association, Northfield, Minnesota
Edmund Heller Papers, Smithsonian Institution Archives
Charles Dewey Hilles Papers, Manuscripts and Archives, Yale University
Charles Evans Hughes Papers, Library of Congress
Harold L. Ickes Papers, Library of Congress

Hiram Johnson Papers, Bancroft Library, University of California, Berkeley
David Starr Jordan Papers, Hoover Institution Archives, Stanford University (copyright Stanford University)
John J. Leary Papers, Theodore Roosevelt Collection (Harvard College Library), Harvard University
Sonya Levien Papers, Huntington Library
Walter Lippmann Papers, Manuscripts and Archives, Yale University
Henry Cabot Lodge Papers, Massachusetts Historical Society
Alice Roosevelt Longworth Papers, Theodore Roosevelt Collection (Harvard College Library), Harvard University
Longworth Family Papers, Cincinnati Historical Society Library, Cincinnati Museum Center
Longyear Library, Marquette County (Michigan) Historical Society
Reminiscences of Ormsby McHarg, Oral History Research Office, Columbia University
Edgar Alexander Mearns Papers, Smithsonian Institution Archives
C. Hart Merriam Papers, Bancroft Library, University of California, Berkeley
George von Lengerke Meyer Papers, Massachusetts Historical Society
John Callan O'Laughlin Papers, Library of Congress
Alfred Edward Pease Papers, privately held
G. W. Perkins Papers, Rare Book and Manuscript Library, Columbia University
Amos Pinchot Papers, Library of Congress
Gifford Pinchot Papers, Library of Congress
Reminiscences of William Ambrose Prendergast, Oral History Research Office, Columbia University
Henry F. Pringle Papers, Theodore Roosevelt Collection (Harvard College Library), Harvard University
Progressive Party Archives, Theodore Roosevelt Collection (Harvard College Library), Harvard University
Archibald Bulloch Roosevelt Papers, Theodore Roosevelt Collection (Harvard College Library), Harvard University
Edith Roosevelt Diaries, Theodore Roosevelt Collection (Harvard College Library), Harvard University
Edith Roosevelt Letters, Theodore Roosevelt Collection (Harvard College Library), Harvard University
Elizabeth Norris Emlen Roosevelt Papers, Theodore Roosevelt Collection (Harvard College Library), Harvard University
Kermit and Belle Willard Roosevelt Papers, Library of Congress
Philip James Roosevelt Papers, Theodore Roosevelt Collection (Harvard College Library), Harvard University
Quentin Roosevelt Papers, Theodore Roosevelt Collection (Harvard College Library), Harvard University
Theodore Roosevelt Papers, Library of Congress
Theodore Roosevelt Papers, Theodore Roosevelt Collection (Harvard College Library), Harvard University
Theodore Roosevelt, Jr., Papers, Library of Congress
Roosevelt-Rondon Expedition 1913–14 Papers, American Museum of Natural History
Elihu Root Papers, Library of Congress
Smithsonian Institution Archives, Office of the Secretary, Records, 1890–1929 (RU 45)
Henry Lewis Stimson Diaries, Manuscripts and Archives, Yale University

W. W. Strong Papers, Huntington Library

Mark Sullivan Papers, Hoover Institution Archives, Stanford University

William Howard Taft Papers, Library of Congress

Taft-Karger Manuscripts, Cincinnati Historical Society Library, Cincinnati Museum Center

William Roscoe Thayer Papers, Houghton Library, Harvard University

U.S. Department of State, Central Decimal Files (1910–29), Records Group 59, National Archives

Edward A. Van Valkenburg Papers, Theodore Roosevelt Collection (Harvard College Library), Harvard University

Oswald Garrison Villard Papers, Houghton Library, Harvard University

Henry White Papers, Library of Congress

William Allen White Papers, Library of Congress

Edith Derby Williams Papers, Theodore Roosevelt Collection (Harvard College Library), Harvard University

NOTES

PROLOGUE: VICTORY

PAGE

7 Election details and Roosevelt's activities: NYT, New York Herald, New York Tribune, Washington Post, Nov. 4, 1908. The aide was Captain Archie Butt, whose account of the evening appears in Abbott, ed., Letters of Archie Butt, 154–55.

8 book for respite: Works, 3:347.

8 bride at every wedding: NYT, May 28, 1910.

9 "Chautauqua politics": George Ade, "The Old-Time Rally," Saturday Evening Post, Oct. 31, 1908.

9 "Everyone is so damnably kind": Adams, Letters of Henry Adams, 6:200.

ONE: EMBARKED

PAGE

13 TR's departure: KR diary, March 23, 1909, KR-BWR Papers; NYT, New York Tribune, New York World, New York Herald, March 23 and 24, 1909.

13 Theodore confessed: Letters, 7:4–5.

13 diphtheria: Abbott, ed., Taft and Roosevelt, 1:122.

14 inauguration day: NYT, New York Tribune, New York Herald, Washington Post, March 5, 1909.

14 "God bless you, old man": Quoted in Pringle, Taft, 1:396.

14 Next morning: NYT, March 6, 1909.

14 McKinley's assassination: Margaret Leech, In the Days of McKinley, New York: Harper and Brothers, 1959, 590–94.

15 bronze in search of a pedestal: WAW, quoted in Richard Kenin and Justin Wintle, eds., The Biographical Dictionary of Quotations, New York: Alfred A. Knopf, 1978, 511.

15 To intimates he was "Theodore": Charles Willis Thompson, Presidents I've Known and Two Near Presidents, 124.

15 Archie carved his initials: Waldo D. Parker, "Reminiscences of the Summers of 1907 and 1908 at Sagamore Hill," 11–12, TRC.

15 "Hurrah, hurrah": New York Herald, March 2, 1909.

15 disarm the snipers: NYT, April 13, 1908; Baker, American Chronicle, 204.

15 "Wall Street expects every lion": W. Cameron Forbes, "Recollections of Theodore Roosevelt," 23–24, Forbes Papers.

15 "Mr. Roosevelt is to leave us": Irving C. Norwood, Outing, March 1909.

16 Edwin Arlington Robinson: Letters, 4:1145n, 1303; Lucius Beebe, "Dignified Faun: A Portrait of E.A.R.," Outlook and Independent 155 (March 27, 1930), 647–49. TR's review is in Works, 12:296–99. The "silver loneliness" comes from Robinson's poem "Mr. Flood's Party."

17 "Little Red Riding Hood": ERD to RD, Oct. 10, 1918, Derby Papers.

17 "The wise custom": Letters, 4:1021n.

17 Taft had sent him: Abbott, ed., *Taft and Roosevelt*, 1:28–29.

18 a holiday: TR to Arthur Lee, Jan. 9, 1911.

18 Carl Akeley: Akeley, *In Brightest Africa*, 159.

18 "I haven't the slightest desire": TR to Frederick Selous, April 29, 1908; *Letters*, 6:978–79.

18 dreams of a scientific expedition: TR to Selous, May 2, 1908.

19 TR's proposal to Smithsonian: *Letters*, 6:1093–94; Charles D. Walcott to Cyrus Adler, June 27, 1908, Smithsonian Institution Archives, Office of the Secretary, Records, 1890–1929, box 48.

19 Walcott obliged: Statement of African Expedition Fund, Oct. 13, 1909, Smithsonian Institution Archives, Office of the Secretary, Records, 1890–1929, box 48.

19 TR's safari earnings and expenses: TR to Robert Bridges, June 30, 1908; S. S. McClure to TR, July 2, 1908; TR to McClure, July 7, 1908; Robert Collier to TR, July 9, 1908.

19 family's business interests: McCullough, *Mornings on Horseback*, 19, 24, 26–28, 140–41.

20 TR's inheritance: Ibid., 205. McCullough puts TR's income then at $8,000 a year.

20 "He never had any idea": Quoted in Pringle, *Theodore Roosevelt*, 39.

20 frozen to death: Pringle, *Theodore Roosevelt*, 73.

20 scrimping: In Edith Roosevelt Letters: ER to TR, Nov. 14, 1887; n.d. [1891?]; Jan. 11 and Feb. 1, 4, 6, and 8, 1901; TR to ER, Aug. 25, 1894. See also Pringle Papers, box 1, and S. J. Morris, *Edith Kermit Roosevelt*, 186–87, 199, 227.

20 he sorted wool: EAR, *Day Before Yesterday*, 44–45.

20 "Until you boys": TR to TR Jr., Dec. 3, 1908.

21 impresario: *New York Herald*, Feb. 1, 1909.

21 He declined suggestions to run: *Letters*, 6:934–35.

21 presidency of Harvard: Ibid., 5:172–73; Bliss Perry, *Life and Letters of Henry Lee Higginson*, Boston: Atlantic Monthly Press [c. 1921], 360–62.

21 "I will do all the doing": W. Cameron Forbes, "Recollections of Theodore Roosevelt," 25–26.

21 "tinglingly alive": Brander Matthews in *Works*, 12:xi.

21 *The Outlook*: TR to Lawrence F. Abbott, July 14, 1908; *Outlook* announcement of TR's affiliation with the magazine, 90 (Nov. 7, 1908), 505–6; TR to Lyman Abbott, Nov. 4 and 23, 1908.

22 He wanted to preach: O. K. Davis, *Released for Publication*, 138–39.

22 "It is very hard": *Letters*, 6:1161–63.

22 a most fortunate man: Ibid., 6:1321–22.

22 Nor could he think: Ibid., 7:29.

22 "any strong man would": Ibid., 7:2.

22 "emphatically": Ibid., 6:1087.

22 Constitution: *Works*, 20:376.

23 Held accountable: *Roosevelt–Lodge Letters*, 2:304.

23 the finest man he ever knew: *Works*, 20:9–13.

23 two bullies: Ibid., 20:30–31.

23 governing class: Ibid., 20:59.

24 he confidently denied: *Letters*, 1:114.

24 "All I want to do": Quoted in Harbaugh, *Power and Responsibility*, 123–24.

24 he took on the Zeus: *Letters*, 2:1238–39.

24 had their revenge: Ibid., 2:1276–78, 1326, 1339, 1341.

24 "loftiest expression": *Works*, 15:77–78.

25 speaking softly would not avail: Ibid., 13:475, 20:524.

25 "If we stand idly by": Ibid., 13:331. Quotation from his speech "The Strenuous Life."

26 "mere spasm of reform": Ibid., 16:421.

26 Holding companies: Ibid., 20:417–22. The case was *U.S. v. E. C. Knight*. The attorney general had alleged that the American Sugar Refining Company, which had purchased several other refineries, was a production monopoly. In 1895 the Supreme Court dismissed the charge, arguing that production was a matter for state jurisdiction and that because the combination had been formed for purposes of production rather than trade, it was not subject to laws against restraint of interstate commerce.

26 Morgan's meeting with TR and Knox: Bishop, *Theodore Roosevelt and His Time*, 1:184–85.

26 The coal miners' strike: Ibid., 1:202; *Letters*, 3:331–32, 336–38, 339–40, 349; TR, *Letters from Theodore Roosevelt to Anna Roosevelt Cowles*, 254; Mowry, *The Era of Theodore Roosevelt*, 134–40. Root's role is described in Jessup, *Elihu Root*, 1:272–76.

27 most "advisable" man: Jessup, *Elihu Root*, 1:429.

27 "I am much obliged": Leslie M. Shaw to Mark Sullivan, n.d., Sullivan Papers.

27 He wished that the rich understood: *Letters*, 3:356–57.

27 twenty-five antitrust indictments: Pringle, *Theodore Roosevelt*, 300.

27 a meat inspection law: Gus Karger, notes of conversation with TR, June 10, 1906, Taft-Karger Manuscripts.

27 Department of Commerce and Labor: *Works*, 15:141, 169–71, 271, 492–93; 16:84.

28 Roosevelt Corollary: Harbaugh, *Power and Responsibility*, 193–95.

28 myopic, ignorant, greedy: *Works*, 13:178.

28 Panama: Ibid., 20:503–5, 514; *Letters*, 3:599, 685; Abbott, *Impressions of Theodore Roosevelt*, 61–62; McCullough, *The Path Between the Seas*, 383–84.

29 TR's intercession in the Russo-Japanese War: Hagedorn, *The Roosevelt Family of Sagamore Hill*, 221–22.

29 "sardonic amusement": TR to ARL, Sep. 2, 1905, Sturm Papers.

30 TR and the press: O. K. Davis, *Released for Publication*, 60; J. J. Dickinson, "Theodore Roosevelt Press-Agent," *Harper's Weekly*, 51 (Sept. 28, 1907), 1410.

30 muckrake: *Works*, 16:415–24.

30 Steffens tried to turn: Justin Kaplan, *Lincoln Steffens*, New York: Touchstone, 1974, 149–53.

30 "light and air": Baker, *American Chronicle*, 203.

30 The battle fleet's cruise: Bishop, *Theodore Roosevelt and His Time*, 2:65; *Letters*, 5:709.

31 apotheosis: *Works*, 20:535; *Letters*, 6:1410.

31 TR on Japan: Abbott, ed., *Letters of Archie Butt*, 92; AWB Letters, July 29, 1908.

32 not a shot was fired: *Works*, 20:525–26; 544.

32 Tennessee Coal, Iron & Railroad Company: *Letters*, 5:830–31; Jean Strouse, *Morgan: American Financier*, New York: Random House, 1999, 582–88; Diane McWhorter, *Carry Me Home*, New York: Simon & Schuster, 2001, 43.

32 TR's conservation programs: Cutright, *Theodore Roosevelt the Naturalist*, 164–71, 177–78; *Works*, 20:384–413; Blum, *The Republican Roosevelt*, 111–12, 117, 125, 143, 146; Harbaugh, *Power and Responsibility*, 318–35. "Conservation of Natural Resources," TR's May 13, 1908, address to the governors conference, appears in *Chautauquan*, June 1909, 33–43.

33 Roosevelt's steady accretion: *Works*, 20:359–60.

33 "a severely dethroned king": Adams, *Letters of Henry Adams*, 6:94.

33 "The people need a rest": Quoted in "Taking President Roosevelt's Measurement," *Current Literature* 46 (March 1909), 237.

33 "a practical world of spiritual things": TR to WAW, June 2, 1908.

33 "secure and enlarge": *New York Herald*, Feb. 21, 1909.

33 "the average American citizen": TR to Lawrence F. Abbott, April 20, 1908.

33 successes: "Taking President Roosevelt's Measurement," 233–38.

33 Alfred Henry Lewis: Quoted in Abbott, ed., *Letters of Archie Butt*, 352.

34 a man of action: *Letters*, 6:1095–96, 1134–36, 1321–22, 1432–33.

34 seasickness: Ibid., 7:4–5; KR diary, March 24, 1909, KR-BWR Papers.

34 $2,100: Emil Boas to William R. Loeb, Jr., Jan. 9 and 11, 1909, TRLC; *New York World*, March 23, 1909; *NYT*, March 24, 1909.

34 ammunition: Frederick Selous to TR, Aug. 8, 1908.

34 Spalding football: ABR to TR, n.d.; TR to ABR, Oct. 6, 1908.

35 mortified: *Letters*, 2:804.

35 sympathetic: E.g., TR to KR, Feb. 16, 1908, and TR to ABR, Feb. 16, 1908.

35 "I know you are studying hard": *Works*, 19:477.

35 Ethel: TR to ERD, Nov. 10, 1908.

35 Quentin: *Works*, 19:546; TR to ABR, Feb. 23 and April 19, 1908.

35 Henry Adams: Patricia O'Toole, *The Five of Hearts: An Intimate Portrait of Henry Adams and His Friends, 1880–1918*, New York: Clarkson N. Potter, 1990, 67, 363.

35 pillow fight: TR to ABR, Jan. 2, 1908; *Works*, 19:450–51.

35 "buckle down": TR to KR, April 23, 1908, and May 17, 1908.

36 "solemnly kisses me": *Letters*, 7:6–7.

36 Edmund C. Heller: *Dictionary of American Biography*.

36 TR's encyclopedic knowledge: Edmund Heller to C. Hart Merriam, April 3, 1909, C. Hart Merriam Papers.

36 J. Alden Loring: Lay, *J. Alden Loring*, 73.

36 "ardent temperament": "The President's African Trip," statement.

36 "He wears old clothes": Lay, *J. Alden Loring*, 79–80.

36 darkroom skills: TR to Robert Bridges, Dec. 5, 1908; KR diary, March 30, 1909, KR-BWR Papers.

36 Edgar A. Mearns: *Dictionary of American Biography*; "The President's African Trip," Smithsonian Institution Archives, Office of the Secretary, Records, 1890–1929, box 48.

36 Moros: KR, *The Long Trail*, 43–44. The index to Mearns's field notes from the Philippines in the Smithsonian Institution Archives makes no mention of Moro skulls.

36 Kermit was a hair shy: Physical characteristics from his passport, July 19, 1918. Shipboard activities in KR, diary, March 26 and 28, 1909, KR-BWR Papers; photographs and "The President's African Trip" in Smithsonian Institution Archives, Office of the Secretary, Records, 1890–1929, box 48.

37 "I shall have to coddle myself": TR to Leonard Wood, July 16, 1908. Further details on TR's physical condition: TR to Edgar Mearns, Aug. 13 and 24, 1908; TR to Alfred Edward Pease, July 28 and Dec. 12, 1908. TR's measurements from his sporting calendar for 1875 (TR Papers, TRC) and *New York World*, May 29, 1907.

37 sclerotic arteries . . . blindness in his left eye: Leary, *Talks with T.R.*, 19–21.

37 "snoop": Abbott, ed., *Letters of Archie Butt*, 118.

37 Edith's fear of TR's assassination: S. J. Morris, *Edith Kermit Roosevelt*, 187.

38 "I don't dare to think": ER to KR, March 30, 1909, KR-BWR Papers.

38 TR's visit to steerage: *NYT*, March 30 and April 2, 1909.

38 "By George": Charles Oster, "Wilson—Taft—Roosevelt," *World's Work*, Sept. 1912, 573.

38 Naples: *New York Herald*, *New York Tribune*, *NYT*, April 5–6, 1909.

38 "full-blooded picnic": *New York Herald*, April 6, 1909.

39 TR's wish to avoid reporters in Africa: *Letters*, 6:1403–5; TR to Percy Madeira, Nov. 25, 1908; Melville E. Stone to TR, Dec. 4, 1908; TR to Stone, Dec. 5, 1908; TR to Lawrence F. Abbott, Feb. 1, 1909.

39 Sicily: *Letters*, 6:1459n; *New York Herald*, *New York Tribune*, *NYT*, April 7–8, 1909.

39 "Ghastly": KR, diary, April 6, 1909, KR-BWR Papers.

40 the idea was Roosevelt's: Compare Dawson, *Opportunity and Theodore Roosevelt*, 25–29, 31–41, with Warrington Dawson to Sarah Dawson, April 7, 1909, Dawson Papers.

40 "He has completely conquered me": Warrington Dawson to Sarah Dawson, April 7, 1909, Dawson Papers.

40 Kermit's activities on the *Admiral*: KR diary, April 7–19, 1909, KR-BWR Papers.

40 "the bow-wows": ERD to KR, April 11, 1909 [misdated March 11], KR-BWR Papers.

40 "the prospect of not seeing Father": ER to ARL, April 12, 1909, Sturm Papers.

40 "Colonel": *Current Literature* 46 (April 1909), 348; *Letters*, 3:32. In letters he pointed out he should not be addressed as "President" now that he was a private citizen. "Mr." would do, he told one correspondent, "or if you wish to give me the title I am really proud of, call me Colonel, for I won that title on the battlefield" (TR to John Sharp Williams, April 26, 1918).

40 "the simplest American alive": Abbott, ed., *Letters of Archie Butt*, 323.

41 "to do his share of the work": TR in interview with Gilson Gardner of the United Press (published March 5, 1909), Pringle Papers.

TWO: A FULL-BLOODED PICNIC

PAGE

42 Mombasa: KR, diary, April 21, 1909, KR-BWR Papers; Trzebinski, *The Kenya Pioneers*, 66–67; Foran, *A Cuckoo in Kenya*, 255.

42 pack of reporters: *New York Herald*, April 22, 1909; *NYT* and *Times* (London), April 23, 1909.

42 The Mombasa Club: Foran, *A Cuckoo in Kenya*, 223–24.

42 shunned hard liquor: *Roosevelt v. Newett*, 13.

43 The safari began: *NYT*, April 24, 1909; photograph in TR, *African Game Trails* (cited hereafter as *AGT*), 15.

43 Uganda Railway: *AGT*, 15–20; Trzebinski, *The Kenya Pioneers*, 68–70. The railway, which starts at sea level in Mombasa, rises steadily to 7,900 feet, plunges 2,000 feet, rises again to its highest point (8,200 feet), and drops dizzyingly fast to the terminus on the shore of Lake Victoria, 3,750 feet above sea level (Playne, *East Africa*, 203).

44 the little press corps: *New York Herald*, April 25, 1909; Dawson, *Opportunity and Theodore Roosevelt*, 59–61.

44 Roosevelt saw no contradiction: George Bird Grinnell in *Works*, 1:xvi.

44 "mushy sentimentality": *AGT*, 13–20.

44 Hunting licenses: Newland and Tarlton safari brochure [c. 1908], 7–8, TRLC, reel 84. See also Edmund C. Heller, "White Rhino," n.d., Heller Papers. On East Africa's attempt to balance wildlife preservation with development of the safari trade, see Buxton, *Two African Trips*, 117–19; F. A. Dickinson, *Big Game Shooting on the Equator*, London: John Lane, 1908, 255, 268; Cranworth, *Profit and Sport in British East Africa*, 390–94.

44 sixth foray: Hollister, *East African Mammals in the United States National Museum*, 13–14.

45 organized like an army: TR to QR, May 14, 1909, KR-BWR Papers; Newland and Tarlton safari brochure, 14–17, 28; McCutcheon, *In Africa*, 69, 71–74; *AGT*, 24–25.

45 "I shall not be more than half satisfied": TR to R. J. Cuninghame, Feb. 7, 1909.

45 R. J. Cuninghame: TR to Cuninghame, Dec. 26, 1908.

45 Leslie J. Tarlton: TR to Cuninghame, telegram, Feb. 6, 1909.

45 the porter: *AGT*, 22–23; Churchill, *My African Journey*, 81; R. Davey Cooper, *Hunting and the Hunted in the Belgian Congo*, R. Keith Johnston, ed., London: Elder Smith, 1914, 16.

45 Three porters were needed: Frederick Selous to TR, Aug. 8, 1908.

45 a load for four: Lay, *J. Alden Loring*, 81.

45 armamentarium: Heller to TR, Nov. 28, 1908, Smithsonian Institution Archives, Office of the Secretary, Records, 1890–1929, box 48; *AGT*, 20–21, 510.

46 The safari pitched its first camp: *AGT*, 22; *NYT*, April 24, 1909. On TR's tent, see *AGT*, 24–25; Ezra Fitch to William Loeb, July 29 and Nov. 21, 1908; Selous to TR, Aug. 8, 1908; TR to Selous, Sept. 12, 1908. The dimensions I give for TR's tent were arrived at by looking at the photograph in *AGT* (p. 21) and extrapolating from his height.

47 comestibles: Army & Navy Co-operative Society Ltd. to TR, Feb. 2, 1909; Arthur H. Neumann, *Elephant Hunting in East Equatorial Africa*, Bulawayo: Books of Zimbabwe, 1982 [repr. 1898], 104.

47 dental floss: TR to Casper Whitney, Nov. 21, 1911.

47 eyeglasses: Abbott, ed., *Letters of Archie Butt*, 346.

47 armored head to toe: *AGT*, 28–30.

47 "as tender as a baby's": KR, *The Long Trail*, 35. TR gave as much care to choosing his boots as his guns. Boots are discussed in numerous letters.

47 Kitanga: Joseph Gurney Pease, *A Wealth of Happiness and Many Bitter Trials*, 273. The account of the Roosevelts' sojourn at Kitanga comes principally from four sources: *AGT*, 37–38, 40–41, 83–85, 348; Alfred Pease's diary entries for April and May 1909; Helen Pease to unknown, May 15, 1909; Joseph Gurney Pease to author, April 8, 2000. Sir Alfred's diary and Lady Pease's letter are in the possession of Joseph Gurney Pease.

47 ostriches: Trzebinski, *The Kenya Pioneers*, 119–20.

47 inexhaustible supply of lions: Alfred Pease to Buxton, May 27, 1908, TRLC.

47 the relative dangers: AGT, 72–74; TR to J. H. Patterson, May 11, 1908; TR to Selous, June 25, 1908.

48 duck: TR to Buxton, Sept. 10, 1908.

48 "the spoiling industrial hand": Joseph Gurney Pease, *A Wealth of Happiness and Many Bitter Trials*, 1–5, 196.

49 "a wonderful gallop": KR, diary, April 29, 1909, KR-BWR Papers.

51 sunset: Isak Dinesen, *Out of Africa*, 89.

51 TR departed in bliss: TR to Alfred Pease, May 13, 1909, Alfred Edward Pease Papers.

51 Loring and Mearns: Mearns to Walcott, May 6, 1909, Smithsonian Institution Archives, Office of the Secretary, Records, 1890–1929, box 49.

51 "rhinoceritis": Mearns to Dearest Ella and all, June 22, 1909, Mearns Papers.

51 "The preservation of large mammals": Heller to Richmond, Sept. 25, 1909, Smithsonian Institution Archives, Office of the Secretary, Records, 1890–1929, box 49.

52 "Six Wakambas": Heller to Gerrit Miller, June 3, 1909, Smithsonian Institution Archives, Office of the Secretary, Records, 1890–1929, box 49.

52 Juja and the McMillans: T. R. MacMechen, "Where Roosevelt Will Shoot," *McClure's* 32 (March 1909), 542–50; B. H. Jessen, *W. N. McMillan's Expeditions and Big Game Hunting in Southern Sudan, Abyssinia and East Africa*, London: Marchant, Singer, 1906, 397, 401–3.

52 attractive nuisance: Foran, *A Cuckoo in Kenya*, 286.

52 "work-shy": Foran, *The Kenya Police*, 21.

52 the ones tagged "Shot by Theodore Roosevelt": TR to ERD, Sept. 26, 1909, TR Papers (TRC); AGT, 142–44; Mearns to mother, May 21, 1909, Mearns Papers.

52 first leopard: AGT, 132–34.

52 vetoed white tablecloths and china: TR to Frederick Selous, Aug. 19 and Sept. 12, 1908.

53 folding camp table: Carl E. Akeley to TR, Feb. 26, 1909.

53 writing kit: TR to Robert Bridges, Dec. 28, 1908; Bridges to TR, Jan. 12, 25, and 27, 1909.

53 ahead of his deadlines: *Letters*, 7:15–16.

53 "I am absolutely contented": Ibid., 7:11–13.

53 "a very big load of responsibility": TR to CRR, May 19, 1909, TR Papers (TRC).

53 "the hen with one chicken": ER to KR, July 5, 1909, KR-BWR Papers.

53 "times of our lives": Mearns to mother, May 21, 1909, Mearns Papers.

53 the expedition's treasury: Financial details from Mearns to Walcott, May 6, 1909; TR to Walcott, May 17, 1909; Andrew Carnegie to Walcott, June 25, 1909; Walcott to TR, July 7, 1909; and Walcott's letters to donors about their pledges (all in Smithsonian Institution Archives, Office of the Secretary, Records, 1890–1929, box 49). See also *Letters*, 7:11, 13–15.

54 Carnegie's peace efforts: Wall, *Andrew Carnegie*, 904–9.

55 even moles: Heller to Gerrit Miller, June 3, 1909, Smithsonian Institution Archives, Office of the Secretary, Records, 1890–1929, box 49.

55 half-mile-long string: Lay, *J. Alden Loring*, 84.

55 Also in the procession: Dawson, *Opportunity and Theodore Roosevelt*, 61–64, 70–76, 82–83; Dale B. J. Randall, *Joseph Conrad and Warrington Dawson: The Record of a Friendship*, Durham: University of North Carolina, 1968, 12, 25.

55 Dawson's unnamed trouble: Scribbling diary, April 30, May 5 and 6, 1909, Dawson Papers, box 36. TR was more inclined to show his sympathy or to write about it privately than to speak about it. After Lady Pease's death, in 1911, TR dictated a letter to Sir Alfred, inviting him to Sagamore. In his own hand he added a few sentences that he seemed not to want to say aloud to his secretary: "My dear fellow, I think of you all the time, and with the keenest sympathy; and I think of your sweet wife; I know how terrible your sorrow is and I mourn with you, in your loneliness. I do wish you would come to this side" (TR to Alfred Pease, April 1, 1911, Alfred Edward Pease Papers).

55 In the wild at last: AGT, 192.

55 charging lion: Ibid., 229–33.

55 furious hippo: Ibid., 255–58.

56 campfire: KR, *The Long Trail*, 43–44.

56 Cuninghame: *AGT*, 26; Akeley, *In Brightest Africa*, 91, 153; Cranworth, *Profit and Sport in British East Africa*, 322, 369; Trzebinski, *The Kenya Pioneers*, 136–40.

56 Tarlton: Akeley, *In Brightest Africa*, 148–53.

56 an ideal companion: Lay, *J. Alden Loring*, 89, 91. The letters of the other naturalists express the same sentiment.

56 Roosevelt observed the natives: *AGT*, 44, 247–48, 324, 406–10.

57 nicknames: McCutcheon, *In Africa*, 157; *AGT*, 260, 504; Mearns to Dearest Ella and all, June 22, 1909, Mearns Papers; Heller to KR, July 1 and Aug. 8, 1921, KR-BWR Papers; Dawson, *Opportunity and Theodore Roosevelt*, 124; Cushing, *From a Surgeon's Journal*, 274. "Merodadi" is properly spelled "Malidadi," Sir Harry H. Johnston pointed out in "The Roosevelts in Africa," *Outlook* 96 (Dec. 7, 1910), 864.

57 "a gorgeous affair": Dawson, Roosevelt log, chip IX:46, Dawson Papers, box 35 (Dawson called his fragments "chips" rather than "chapters").

57 silk shirts: Willard Straight to KR, March 5, 1908, with invoice from S. I. Yamatoya, Feb. 21, 1908, KR-BWR Papers.

57 dress shirts: KR to ER [April 1909], KR-BWR Papers.

57 catalogues of death: ER to KR, June 23, 1909, KR-BWR Papers.

58 Pigskin Library: John T. Loomis to TR, Nov. 24 and Dec. 12, 1908; Loomis to TR, with sketch of the aluminum bookcase, Jan. 2, 1909; Loomis to TR, Feb. 15, 1909; TR to Loomis, Nov. 24 and 26, 1908; TR to Loomis, Jan. 2 and Feb. 19, 1909; *Works*, 3:345–47, 351. The books in the Pigskin Library are listed in *AGT*, 569–75.

58 TR as a reader: His thoughts about reading as escape, the pleasure of reading history, and happy endings are in *Works*, 3:343–51. TR had "the greatest power of concentration I have ever seen," Archie Butt said of him. "When he is reading or thinking he does not seem to hear anything which goes on around him" (Abbott, ed., *Letters of Archie Butt*, 337).

58 Shakespeare's oeuvre: Abbott, ed., *Letters of Archie Butt*, 86.

58 "the utmost comfort and pleasure": *Letters*, 7:16–17.

58 bled on his *Nibelungenlied*: *AGT*, 193–94, 224.

59 articles . . . a chore: *Letters*, 7:17–18.

59 thorn tree: *AGT*, 240, 243.

59 "moral muscle": ER to KR, April 7, 1909, KR-BWR Papers.

59 the privilege of losing her temper: ER to ARL [c. Sept. 1909], Sturm Papers.

59 $46,000: ER to KR, June 23, 1909, KR-BWR Papers.

59 "Don't say this to Father": ER to KR, June 23, 1909, KR-BWR Papers.

59 "Don't let Mother": TR to ERD, Aug. 1, 1909, TR Papers (TRC).

59 Cabot chivalrously came to New York: ERD to KR, July 10, 1909, KR-BWR Papers.

60 "knickerbockers *à l'italienne*": ER to KR, July 28, 1909, KR-BWR Papers.

60 Porto Maurizio: *New York Herald*, Aug. 2, 1909; ER to KR, July 21, 1909, KR-BWR Papers; ER to Elizabeth Roosevelt, Aug. 8, 1909, Elizabeth Roosevelt Papers.

60 moving gingerly: S. J. Morris, *Edith Kermit Roosevelt*, 350.

60 Paris: ER to Elizabeth Roosevelt, Aug. 20, 1909, Elizabeth Roosevelt Papers; Henry Adams, *Letters of Henry Adams*, 6:265.

60 the demon of homesickness: ER to ARL [1909], Sturm Papers.

THREE: ONE WHITE MAN'S BURDENS
PAGE

61 "an interlude": TR to ARC, July 27, 1909, TR Papers (TRC).

61 Chiromo: Mearns to Ella and Lillian, May 27, 1909, Mearns Papers.

61 Nairobi: Uganda Railway, *The Uganda Railway*, London: Waterlow, 1911, 42; Playne, *East Africa*, 91, 131–32, 170–91; Foran, *A Cuckoo in Kenya*, 147, 321–22; Foran, *The Kenya Police*, 22.

62 contentious little cauldron: Churchill, *My African Journey*, 17–18; Trzebinski, *The Kenya Pioneers*, 3; Cranworth, *Profit and Sport in British East Africa*, 4.

62 cricket and foxhunting: Foran, *A Cuckoo in Kenya*, 122–28.

62 race week: Ibid., 51–57; *AGT*, 273–74; KR, diary, July 29 and 31, 1909, KR-BWR Papers; TR to ERD, Aug. 1, 1909, TR Papers (TRC).

63 TR's banquet speech: McCutcheon, *In Africa*, 49. The speech is quoted in Foran, *A Cuckoo in Kenya*, 22.

63 Thomas B. Reed: Lewis Einstein, *Roosevelt: His Mind in Action*, Boston: Houghton Mifflin, 1930, 153.

63 The expedition's finances: Mearns to Walcott, May 6, 1909, Smithsonian Institution Archives, Office of the Secretary, Records, 1890–1929, box 49.

63 scientific coup: *Letters*, 7:21–22.

64 Twenty barrels: *New York Herald*, Aug. 19 and 25, 1909; *NYT*, Sept. 2, 1909; R. Rathbun to W. H. Gannett, Sept. 3, 1909; H. W. Dorsey to Walcott, Sept. 27, 1909, Smithsonian Institution Archives, Office of the Secretary, Records, 1890–1929, box 49.

64 Such bothers: Gerrit S. Miller, Jr., to F. W. True, July 13, 1909; Rathbun to Walcott, Smithsonian Institution Archives, Office of the Secretary, Records, 1890–1929, box 49.

64 Walcott's bête noir: Walcott raised $30,000 before the safari and $30,000 while it was in progress. Carnegie initially gave $2,750 and added $23,000 when Roosevelt was in Africa. The Smithsonian eventually returned $6,000 to Carnegie, leaving his total contribution at $19,750, or about one-third of all the money Walcott raised for the expedition (Andrew Carnegie to Walcott, July 8, 1909; Walcott to TR, Oct. 19 and 27, 1909; Walcott to James Bertram, Feb. 2, 1910, Smithsonian Institution Archives, Office of the Secretary, Records, 1890–1929, boxes 48–49).

65 "worse than silly": *AGT*, 289–90.

65 Roosevelt's defense of hunting: Ibid., 240–41, 292.

65 But the natives of the region: The rogue elephants and elephant herds provoked by encounters with humans were indeed dangerous (Churchill, *My African Journey*, 116). The agricultural prowess of the people in question, the Kikuyu, is mentioned in numerous books written by white settlers in British East Africa.

66 TR's elephant hunt: *AGT*, 294–300.

66 Without explanation: In 1908, before he transformed the hunting trip into a scientific expedition, TR had envisioned even stricter limits: he would kill one head each of the "noted" animals. TR to Buxton, April 29, 1908; TR to Selous, May 2, 1908.

66 their bag of 512: *AGT*, 532–33.

66 "it is well to remember": *NYT*, April 29 and June 7, 1909.

66 Kermit's monkey hunt: Dawson, Roosevelt log, chip 22, 104–8, Dawson Papers.

67 TR saw no need for euphemism: *NYT*, Sept. 8, 1909.

67 easily defended: Neumann, *Elephant Hunting in East Equatorial Africa*, 419; Gerrit S. Miller, Jr., to F. W. True, March 7, 1910, Smithsonian Institution Archives, Office of the Secretary, Records, 1890–1929, box 49.

67 longing for Sagamore: *Letters*, 7:18.

68 Boone and Crockett Club: *Works*, 1:xvii.

68 TR as hunter-naturalist: Ibid., 12:353, 369, 372. TR's earlier works in the genre include *Hunting Trips of a Ranchman* (1885), *Ranch Life and the Hunting Trail* (1888), *The Wilderness Hunter* (1899), and *Outdoor Pastimes of an American Hunter* (1905). They are collected in *Works*, vols. 1–3. See also "The American Hunter-Naturalist," *Works*, 12:413–18.

68 The ideal: Ernest Bell, "Big Game Hunting," in Henry S. Salt, ed., *Killing for Sport*, London: G. Bell and Sons, 1915, 112. Thomas L. Altherr gives a respectful overview of the phenomenon in "The American Hunter-Naturalist and the Development of the Code of Sportsmanship," *Journal of Sports History*, 5:1 (Spring 1978), 7–22.

69 "[H]e has done us an injury": Quoted in J. Alden Loring, *African Adventure Stories*, New York: Charles Scribner's Sons, 1923, 33.

69 *On the Origin of Species:* McCullough, *Mornings on Horseback*, 116.

69 imperializing: *AGT*, 239–40; *Works*, 9:56–57.

69 Lord Hugh Delamere: Huxley, *White Man's Country*, 1:6, 8, 145, 148; Trzebinski, *The Kenya Pioneers*, 83, 149, 166.

69 Equator Ranch: *AGT*, 300; Huxley, *White Man's Country*, 132, 151–54.

70 "the high courage": TR to Lady Florence Delamere, Sept. 22, 1910.

70 "white man's burden": From Kipling's poem, which called on Americans to follow the example of the British and assume its responsibilities for civilizing their "new-caught sullen peoples, Half devil and half child" in Cuba and the Philippines (*Living Age*, 220 [Feb. 18, 1899], 284).

70 "herd of rhinoceros questions": Churchill, *My African Journey*, 40–42.

70 The bongo hunt: *AGT*, 303–4; Huxley, *White Man's Country*, 250–51. The anecdote about Delamere's elaborate preparations is in Cranworth, *Profit and Sport in British East Africa*, 371–72.

71 Christmas: KR, diary, Dec. 24, 1909; KR to ER, Dec. 1909, KR-BWR Papers.

71 politics had not ignored him: *Roosevelt–Lodge Letters*, 2:337–45. Lodge abstained from writing TR about politics for three months, then seemingly could not resist commenting on Taft's deficiencies.

71 replace Henry White: *Letters*, 7:21.

71 "infinitesimal": Ibid., 7:22–24.

71 Gifford Pinchot: Ibid., 7:45–46.

71 White rhinos: TR to Frederick Jackson, July 16, 1908; TR to Buxton, Sept. 10, 1908; Buxton to TR, Sept. 22, 1908; Whitelaw Reid to TR, Aug. 11 and Nov. 3, 1908; TR to Reid, Sept. 12 and Nov. 26, 1908; TR to Sir Reginald Wingate, Nov. 27, 1908.

71 "good groups": *AGT*, 475–76; Gerrit S. Miller, Jr., to F. W. True, March 7, 1910, Smithsonian Institution Archives, Office of the Secretary, Records, 1890–1929, box 49.

72 Roosevelt judged the expedition a landmark: *Annual Report of the Smithsonian Institution*, 1910, 10–11.

72 only a handful . . . were new: Hollister, *East African Mammals in the United States National Museum*, 19.

72 His marksmanship: Lay, *J. Alden Loring*, 109.

72 "tougher than whipcord": TR to CRR, Jan. 21, 1910, CRR Papers.

72 It was the press: John Callan O'Laughlin, *From the Jungle Through Europe with Roosevelt*, Boston: Chapple, 1910, 1–5.

72 "But all this can wait": *Letters*, 7:52–53.

FOUR: INTO THE THICK OF THINGS

PAGE

73 Khartoum: NYT, *New York Tribune*, *New York Herald*, March 15–16, 1910.

73 "of the hatpin type": ER to CRR, March 18, 1910, CRR Papers.

73 mustache: ER to TR Jr., March 16, 1910, TR Jr. Papers.

73 Ted's engagement: TR Jr. to TR [Feb. 1910], TR Jr. Papers; TR to CRR, March 14, 1910, CRR Papers; *Letters*, 7:57, 60–61; ERD to EAR, March 21, 1910, Derby Williams Papers.

74 Roosevelt uncaged his political energies: "Mr. Roosevelt's Speech," *Outlook* 94 (April 9, 1910), 788–89; *Letters*, 7:350–51.

74 On March 20 he announced: NYT, March 21, 1910.

74 Cairo: *Letters*, 7:352–53; *Works*, 16:448–55; Sheik Ali Youssuf, "Egypt's Reply to Colonel Roosevelt," *North American Review* 191 (June 1910), 734–36; "Mr. Roosevelt in Egypt," *Outlook* 94 (April 30, 1910), 979–82.

75 "into the thick of things": Unidentified English newspaper clipping.

75 The second most interesting American: Oscar S. Straus, *Under Four Administrations*, Cambridge, Mass.: Riverside Press, 1922, 287–88; Edward G. Lowry, "One Year of Mr. Taft," *North American Review* 191 (March 1910), 289–301.

75 That was Roosevelt's version: H. L. Stoddard, notes of a conversation with TR on a cruise in the Caribbean early in 1916, Progressive Party Archives. TR's recollections were generally accurate, although he knew shortly after Christmas 1908 that Taft did not wish to reappoint Straus or Secretary of the Interior James R. Garfield. (*Letters*, 6:1457–59).

75 Taft left two versions: WHT to William Rockhill Nelson, Feb. 23, 1909, WHT Papers.

76 "Mr. Roosevelt told me": Gus Karger, notes from conversation with WHT on March 12, 1910, Taft-Karger Manuscripts.

76 *bêtises*: Adams, *Letters of Henry Adams*, 6:223.

76 Tariff reform: Pringle, *Taft*, 1:418–53; "The Senate, Taft, and the Tariff," *Current Literature* 47 (July 1909), 1–8; Thelen, *Robert M. La Follette and the Insurgent Spirit*, 70–71.

77 "the best bill": Pringle, *Taft*, 1:454–56.

77 absented himself from the White House: Abbott, ed., *Taft and Roosevelt*, 1:316, and AWB Letters, April 2, 1910; *Washington Post*, March 9, 1909.

77 Taft's weight: John G. Sotos, "Taft and Pickwick: Sleep Apnea in the White House," *Chest* 124:3 (Sept. 2003), 1134.

77 "Taft always insisted": William Rockhill Nelson to TR, April 7, 1910.

77 "Must I see those men again?": Quoted in Stephen Ponder, "'Nonpublicity' and the Unmaking of a President: William Howard Taft and the Ballinger-Pinchot Controversy of 1909–1910," *Journalism History* 19:4 (Winter 1994), 22. For other examples see Abbott, ed., *Taft and Roosevelt*, 1:29–31, 134–35.

78 "the most loveable personality": Abbott, ed., *Letters of Archie Butt*, 232–33.

78 Helen Herron Taft: Judith Icke Anderson, "A Mountain of Misery: An Intimate History of William Howard Taft," Ph.D. diss., University of California, Los Angeles, 1973, 87–97.

78 When Roosevelt offered him a seat: WHT to Charles P. Taft, Nov. 11, 1902; Henry Taft to WHT, Nov. 8, 1901, and Jan. 10, 1903; Louise Torrey Taft to WHT, Jan. 25, 1903; WHT to HHT, April 12, 1904 (all in WHT Papers).

78 TR encourages Taft toward presidency: Henry Taft to WHT, Jan. 10, 1903; WHT to HHT, April 12, 1904, and May 4, 1906 (all in WHT Papers).

79 Elihu Root more qualified: O. K. Davis, *Released for Publication*, 54–55; Harbaugh, *Power and Responsibility*, 350–51.

79 a sprig of mistletoe: H. Wayne Morgan, *America's Road to Empire: The War with Spain and Overseas Expansion*. New York: John Wiley and Sons, 1965, 2.

79 TR began to wonder: Gus Karger, memo of conversation with TR, Oct. 30, 1907, Taft-Karger Manuscripts; WHT to Charles P. Taft, Sept. 11, 1907, WHT Papers.

79 Mrs. Taft's stroke: Abbott, ed., *Taft and Roosevelt*, 1:86–89, 312–13.

80 Archie Butt: Abbott, ed., *Letters of Archie Butt*, frontispiece.

80 "No one knows how he suffers": Abbott, ed., *Taft and Roosevelt*, 1:312, 328.

80 "I do wish I could see you": *Letters*, 7:50–51.

80 The Roosevelts' Italian travel plans: Ibid., 7:62–63, 354–59.

81 The Vatican incident: "Roosevelt and the Pope," *Current Literature* 48 (May 1910), 465–72.

81 Sequestered: Abbott, *Impressions of Theodore Roosevelt*, 223–27.

81 Pinchot arrived: *NYT*, *New York Tribune*, *New York Herald*, April 9–12, 1910.

81 TR's collaboration with Pinchot: *Letters*, 2:1320–22; GP, *Breaking New Ground*, New York: Harcourt, Brace [1947], xvii, 376–84; TR, *Works*, 20:409–13; Martin Fausold, "Gifford Pinchot and the Progressive Movement: An Analysis of the Pinchot Papers, 1910–1917," Ph.D. diss., Syracuse University, 1953, 19–20.

82 With the spread of electricity: Harbaugh, *Power and Responsibility*, 332–34; Miller, *Theodore Roosevelt*, 471.

82 the contretemps: WHT to GP, Sept. 13, 1909, and Executive Order 1142, Nov. 26, 1909, GP Papers; WHT to HHT, Oct. 3, 1909, WHT Papers.

83 Pinchot spent his New Year's Eve: GP to TR, Dec. 31, 1909, Thayer Papers. The version of the letter that appears in Pinchot's book, *Breaking New Ground* (498–501), omits three stirring passages: (1) "I think it is still possible that a direct change by Taft himself might bring him into conformity with the policies to which he has so often pledged himself." Pinchot said he thought this unlikely and that the best newspapermen agreed with his judgment. (2) "The result of the practical repudiation of the Roosevelt policies by Taft would be so serious, the conflict which would follow would be so bitter, and the effect upon the welfare of the people would be so disastrous that no man ought to abandon hope until hope becomes clearly and finally impossible." (3) Unless Taft did an about-face, Pinchot said, "I foresee a clear-cut division between the Administration and the Reactionaries on one side, and the progressives and the great mass of people on the other."

84 Why not fire him?: Abbott, ed., *Taft and Roosevelt*, 1:244–45.

84 Pinchot reeled out the rope: GP to Jonathan Dolliver, Jan. 5, 1910, AP Papers.

84 Two days later: WHT to GP, Jan. 7, 1910, GP Papers.

84 A long congressional investigation: GP, *Breaking New Ground*, 474–97.

84 When Pinchot testified: "Statement made by Mr. Pinchot Before the Investigating Committee, February 26, 1910," GP Papers. For an evenhanded account of the Ballinger-Pinchot controversy and the hearings, see Pringle, *Taft*, 1:470–514.

84 "One of the best . . . talks": GP, *Breaking New Ground*, 498–502.

84 a piece of fluff . . . and a stick of dynamite: NYT, *New York Tribune, New York Herald*, April 12, 1910.

84 The Colonel's attitude: GP to AP, April 29, 1910, AP Papers.

85 Leaving Edith and Ethel: ER to TR Jr., April 1, 1910, TR Jr. Papers.

85 "obviously conscious": *Letters*, 7:361. The quotation comes from a long, extraordinary letter in which TR recounted his experiences in Europe and gave his impressions of the political scene to George Otto Trevelyan, the English historian (*Letters*, 7:348–99).

85 Paris: NYT, *New York Tribune, New York Herald, Times* (London), April 21–23, 1910.

85 editorial cartoons: The one by W. A. Rogers in the *New York Herald* on April 6, 1910, is typical, with TR in safari suit and Napoleonic tricorn, with Rough Rider bandanna around his neck. He is carrying a sword and standing at a cannon with a barrel marked "Press-Agent Stories—made in Italy." The barrel is mounted atop a typewriter, which sits on a stone slab engraved "Back from Elba Club." TR is perched on the typewriter keys, one foot on the bottom row, the other near the top. Pinchot and Lodge in Napoleonic uniform stand behind him, and behind them is a storm cloud labeled "Waterloo."

85 Sorbonne: *Works*, 13:506–29. The "man in the arena" passage appears on 510. On birth control and race suicide: Ibid., 12:184–96, 16:164–71, and 19:140–66.

86 French reaction to TR: NYT, April 23 and 25, and May 1, 1910; *New York Herald*, April 23, 1910; *Times* (London), April 26 and May 7, 1910; "Why Paris Saw in Roosevelt the Bourgeois Caesar," *Current Literature* 48 (June 1910), 619–22.

86 Belgium: NYT, April 29, 1910.

86 the Netherlands: *Letters*, 7:383; NYT, *New York Herald, Times* (London), April 30, 1910.

87 Denmark: NYT, *New York Herald, Times* (London), May 3–4, 1910.

87 Hamlet: W. A. Rogers, *New York Herald*, May 4, 1910.

87 Nobel Peace Prize: *Works*, 16:305–9; Abbott, *Impressions of Theodore Roosevelt*, 236–37.

87 Wilhelm II: NYT, *New York Tribune, New York Herald, Times* (London), April 11, 1910.

87 death of Edward VII: *Letters*, 7:390, Barbara Tuchman, *Guns of August*, New York: Macmillan, 1962, 1–14.

88 The kaiser and the Colonel: *Letters*, 7:379, 396–99; NYT, *New York Tribune, New York Herald, Times* (London), May 12, 1910.

88 "My dear Roosevelt": KR, diary, May 11, 1910, KR–BWR Papers.

89 special ambassador: *Letters*, 7:412–13; Abbott, ed., *Taft and Roosevelt*, 1:103, 348; NYT, May 10, 1910.

89 speech in London: NYT, June 1, 1910. On Grey's encouragement, see *Letters*, 7:403.

89 English reaction: *New York Herald*, June 7 and 10, 1910; "Roosevelt Addresses Europe," *Review of Reviews* 41 (June 1910), 747–50.

80 Between public engagements: Nevins, *Henry White*, 303–4; Rowland Ward to TR, June 1 and 3, 1910.

90 bird-watching: Viscount (Edward) Grey of Fallodon, *Recreation*, Boston: Houghton Mifflin, 1920, 26–31.

90 At St. George's Church: NYT, May 25, 1910.

90 "It is now near a year": WHT to TR, May 28, 1910.

91 "I do not know the situation at home": *Letters*, 7:88–89.

91 Taft grew increasingly irritable: Abbott, ed., *Taft and Roosevelt*, 1:281, 364, 385.

91 TR's return: NYT, *New York Tribune, New York Herald*, June 19, 1910; T. Hamlin, "Return from Africa," *Harper's Weekly* 54 (June 29, 1910), 7–10.

92 "one continuous heartfelt ovation": Abbott, ed., *Taft and Roosevelt*, 1:401.

92 wedding presents: *New York Tribune*, June 19, 1910.

92 silver pitcher: Gift register, TR Jr. Papers, box 55.

92 "an enlarged personality": Abbott, ed., *Taft and Roosevelt*, 1:396.

92 Butt had apparently forgotten: Abbott, ed., *Letters of Archie Butt*, 352.

FIVE: PRAIRIE FIRE

93 he started his work at *The Outlook*: *Philadelphia North American*, June 20, 1910.

93 the police held back the crowd: *NYT*, *New York Tribune*, *New York Herald*, June 20, 1910.

94 a bale of his correspondence: Waldon Fawcett, "The President's Business Office," *World's Work*, July 1902, describes the daily workings of TR's White House; A. J. Krank to TR, Jan. 30, 1911.

94 "I am almost driven mad by work": Reminiscences of George W. Alger, 333.

94 Again he was invited: *Letters*, 7:93.

94 Taft vowed not to extend another welcome: Abbott, ed., *Taft and Roosevelt*, 1:416.

95 TR's visit with Taft: HCL to TR, June 26, 1910; Abbott, ed., *Taft and Roosevelt*, 1:417–41.

96 "Teddy is licked to a frazzle": Quoted in Griscom, *Diplomatically Speaking*, 343.

96 Nelson W. Aldrich: The senator is etched in acid in Claude G. Bowers, *Albert J. Beveridge and the Progressive Era*, New York: Literary Guild, 1932, 313–24.

96 Speaker Joseph Gurney Cannon: Mowry, *Theodore Roosevelt and the Progressive Movement*, 32, 41–44; Pringle, *Taft*, 1:402–3.

96 "I pushing forward, and they hanging back": *Works*, 20:342.

96 From his perch: Pringle, *Taft*, 1:410–11, 414–15.

97 "They'll lean on him": Mark Sullivan, *Our Times*, 4:331–32.

97 Insurgents: Ibid., 4:349.

97 "from the nipple": Thomas Nelson Page, "The Democratic Opportunity," *North American Review* 193 (Feb. 1911), 197.

97 champagne: "Maine and After," *Nation* 91 (Sept. 8, 1910), 232.

97 "a nation of producers": Quoted in Thelen, *Robert M. La Follette and the Insurgent Spirit*, 72.

97 The West's political reforms: Mowry, *The Era of Theodore Roosevelt*, 72–73, 80–83.

97 When Taft took office: Sullivan, *Our Times*, 4:353, 373; *Current Literature* 48 (June 1910), 589.

97 overthrow Uncle Joe: Manners, *TR and Will*, 91–92, 123–24; Mowry, *Theodore Roosvelt and the Progressive Movement*, 40–44; Pringle, *Taft*, 1:402–9; Sullivan, *Our Times*, 4:382.

98 Robert M. La Follette: Robert S. Maxwell, ed., *La Follette*, Englewood Cliffs, N.J.: Prentice Hall, 1969, 89; Baker, *American Chronicle*, 262–63.

98 The squire of Sagamore: RML, *Autobiography*, 487–89, 509–10.

98 intransigent and extreme: *Letters*, 6:1043–44, 1050–53, 1064–65.

98 despised the Insurgents: John Callan O'Laughlin to TR, May 30, 1910.

98 He wanted them "cut out": AWB Letters, March 7, 1910.

98 "exceeding the speed limit": Quoted in Baker, *American Chronicle*, 253.

99 Nellie did not care: Abbott, ed., *Taft and Roosevelt*, 2:434–36; 451.

99 Roosevelt issued a denial: *Chicago Daily Tribune*, July 7, 1910.

99 common goal: *Letters*, 7:98–102.

99 "The truth is": Ibid., 7:114–17.

99 "You are the leader to whom all look": GP to TR, July 6, 1910.

99 a disappointment but not a disgrace: TR to James R. Garfield, July 19, 1910.

100 TR's trip to Pennsylvania: *NYT*, Aug. 4, 1910; *New York Herald* and *New York Evening Post*, Aug. 2–4, 1910; TR, "The Coal Miner at Home," *Outlook* 96 (Dec. 24, 1910), 899–908.

100 raw throat: ER, Aug. 6, 1910, ER Diaries.

101 dreading his speaking tour: TR to NL, Aug. 6, 1910.

101 Hoping to bring the Insurgents and Regulars together: Sullivan, *Our Times*, 4:449.

101 suffering from gout: Abbott, ed., *Taft and Roosevelt*, 2:461, 503; AWB Letters, Aug. 4, 1910.

101 temporary chairman: Griscom, *Diplomatically Speaking*, 343–45.

101 C. D. Norton: *NYT*, Jan. 22, 1911; Abbott, ed., *Taft and Roosevelt*, 2:444; AWB Letters, July 18, 1910.

102 For a few days: Pringle, *Taft*, 2:563–64; *Letters*, 7:114–17, 119.

102 Butt worried with him: AWB Letters, Aug. 18, 1910.

102 Taft was a locomotive: *New York Tribune*, Feb. 28, 1909.

102 Roosevelt boarded a train: Edward A. Halsey, "Roosevelt's Western Tour," *World To-Day*, Oct. 1910, 1125–30.

102 "seared to the very soul": Abbott, ed., *Taft and Roosevelt*, 2:516.

102 Still a master of press agentry: "What Game Is Roosevelt Playing?" *Current Literature* 49 (Oct. 1910), 350–61; Halsey, "Roosevelt's Western Tour,"1125–30; O. K. Davis, *Released for Publication*, 196.

102 "a very stern sense of duty": *Letters*, 7:137.

103 He had no desire: O. K. Davis, *Released for Publication*, 200–1; TR to Alfred Pease, April 1, 1911.

103 more than a million: Halsey, "Roosevelt's Western Tour," 1125–30.

103 "My papa is a Roosevelt man": Will D. Hancock, Jr., to TR, Jan. 1, 1911.

103 "an almost revivalist intensity": Sydney Brooks, "The Confusion of American Politics," *Fortnightly Review* 94 (Oct. 1910), 646–56.

103 St. Paul: "Conservation Congress Considers," *Current Literature* 49 (Oct. 1910), 362–65; "The Last Week of Mr. Roosevelt's Journey," *Outlook* 96 (Sept. 17, 1910), 89–90.

103 "A thing like that": Quoted in O. K. Davis, *Released for Publication*, 208.

103 Denver: *Letters*, 7:123n; *Lochner v. New York*, 198 U.S. 45 (1905).

104 Elihu Root speedily assured: "Senator Root on the Roosevelt Issue," *Independent* 69 (Nov. 3, 1910), 945–46; *NYT*, Oct. 29, 1910.

104 "but we ought to preserve": HCL to TR, Sept. 5, 1910.

104 Roosevelt was irritated: Bishop, *Theodore Roosevelt and His Time*, 2:301–2. TR was also somewhat hurt that neither of his mentors came to his defense (O. K. Davis, *Released for Publication*, 209–10).

104 Osawatomie: *Works*, 17:5–22; Robert S. La Forte, "Theodore Roosevelt's Osawatomie Speech," *Kansas Historical Quarterly*, 32(2):1966, 187–200; GP to AP, July 18, 1910, AP Papers.

106 Root wondered: Harbaugh, *Power and Responsibility*, 392.

106 "mild and wholesome": "What Game Is Roosevelt Playing?" *Current Literature* 49 (Oct. 1910), 350–61.

106 *The Promise of American Life*: *Letters*, 7:76–77n.

106 "I am bound to say": Quoted in Pringle, *Taft*, 2:573–74.

106 old grudge: Abbott, ed., *Taft and Roosevelt*, 1:103–4.

107 Taft began abusing him: Abbott, ed., *Taft and Roosevelt*, 2:499; AWB Letters, Aug. 29, 1910.

107 At the suggestion of C. D. Norton: Griscom, *Diplomatically Speaking*, 346; *Letters*, 7:134–39; AWB Letters, Jan. 5, 1912.

107 "Comes he in peace?": Abbott, ed., *Taft and Roosevelt*, 2:517.

107 He came in a speedboat: Griscom, *Diplomatically Speaking*, 347; Manners, *TR and Will*, 180–81.

107 "For a time we sat in silence": Gus Karger, memorandum of conversation with Taft and Norton, Sept. 25, 1910. Karger spent ninety minutes with them and composed his account immediately after the meeting (Taft-Karger Manuscripts).

108 wooden smiles: Abbott, ed., *Taft and Roosevelt*, 2:519.

108 "I was glad to give it": WHT to HHT, Sept. 25, 1910, WHT Papers.

108 "What did I tell you?": Quoted in Griscom, *Diplomatically Speaking*, 347–48.

108 rumors of a quid pro quo: *Letters*, 7:138–39.

109 Taft was equally furious: Karger, memorandum of conversation with Taft and Norton.

109 "complete and perfect the machinery": Quoted in Pringle, *Taft*, 1:365.

109 "I am absolutely in the dark": Quoted in Abbott, ed., *Taft and Roosevelt*, 2:485, 516.

109 The strain between the Tafts and Alice Longworth: AWB Letters, Jan. 5 and 7, March 5, and May 10, 1910.

110 "I am afraid": WHT to HHT, Sept. 24, 1910, WHT Papers.

110 "Cincin-nasty": AWB Letters, Sept. 23, 1910.

110 Nick Longworth: *Dictionary of American Biography*; *Times* (London), April 10, 1931.

110 suggestive dance: AWB Letters, June 27, 1911.

110 P Street: AWB Letters, April 2, 1910.

110 "stand straight by Taft": *Letters*, 7:101.

110 "It is like a man in bed": Quoted in Henry Lewis Stimson Diaries, II:6.

111 (political corpse): *NYT*, Aug. 26, 1910.

111 "Bet you a dollar": Quoted in Morison, *Turmoil and Tradition*, 136–38.

111 Saratoga: *NYT* and *Wall Street Journal*, Sept. 28, 1910; O. K. Davis, *Released for Publication*, 223–26.

111 "they wanted to flay the Roosevelts alive": AWB Letters, Oct. 4 and 19, 1910.

111 haunted: O. K. Davis, *Released for Publication*, 199.

112 "It is enough for you to grow up to be good men": Quoted in *Editorial Review*, Oct. 1910.

112 On election day: ER; diary, Nov. 8, 1910.

112 Nick managed: ARL to TR, Nov. 9, 1910.

112 "wiping the slate clean": Jacob Riis to TR, Nov. 10, 1910.

112 "not only a landslide": Abbott, ed., *Taft and Roosevelt*, 2:556.

112 "beautiful, unselfish" disposition: Ibid.

112 "The verdict of the vicinage": Edward G. Lowry, "Lessons of the Election," *North American Review* 192 (Dec. 1910), 722–25.

112 "From my personal standpoint": TR to HCL, Nov. 11, 1910.

113 Gifford Pinchot sent his condolences: GP to TR, Nov. 9, 1910.

113 moderate stance ill suited: GP to TR, Aug. 18, 1910.

113 scolded him for praising Taft: *Letters*, 7:175–76.

113 "It makes me feel tired": AP to GP, Oct. 27, 1910, AP Papers.

113 "right attitude": TR to Jack Greenway, Dec. 19, 1910.

113 "tearing down and building up": *Letters*, 7:167–69.

113 The most important story: Abbott, ed., *Taft and Roosevelt*, 2:548; AWB Letters, Oct. 18, 1910.

114 "I shall not tell them anything": AWB Letters, Oct. 24, 1910.

114 obstructive sleep apnea: On the disease itself, author interview with Mila Q. McManus, M.D., March 31, 2002. "Taft and Pickwick: Sleep Apnea in the White House," *Chest* 124:3 (Sept. 2003), 1133–42, by John G. Sotos, M.D., is a fine piece of historical sleuthing, and it also takes up the question of whether Taft was disabled. "No formal definition of Presidential disability existed during Taft's era," Sotos writes. "Only in 1967 did the 25th Amendment to the US Constitution define a disabled president as one 'unable to discharge the powers and duties of his office.' The Amendment charges the Vice President and Cabinet to judge disability." Sotos found that Taft's inner circle noticed and commented on his habit of dropping off to sleep, but there is no sign that anyone ever raised the question of his physical fitness for office.

114 "Wild Man and Wild Beast in Africa": *Washington Post*, Nov. 19, 1910.

114 Taft was in Panama: *Letters*, 7:177n.

114 "a great pity": AWB Letters, Nov. 24, 1910.

114 Will had joshed: AWB Letters, Oct. 4, 1910.

114 For a moment he did: Abbott, ed., *Taft and Roosevelt*, 561–62.

SIX: DUELS

119 vacancies: Mowry, *Theodore Roosevelt and the Progressive Movement*, 157.

119 cigarette holder: Pringle, *Taft*, 2:581.

119 settee: Abbott, ed., *Letters of Archie Butt*, 301–2; WHT to ER, Dec. 31, 1910, ER Letters.

119 an armload of peace offerings: WHT to TR, Nov. 30, 1910 and Dec. 2, 1911. Telephone conversations mentioned in AWB Letters, Jan. 7, 1911.

119 "helpless and pathetic": *Letters*, 7:177–79; Abbott, ed., *Taft and Roosevelt*, 2:563–64, 570–71.

120 The Insurgents: The terms "Progressive" and "Insurgent" were often used interchange-

ably. "Insurgent" was the newspapers' preferred term in the early stages of the split with the Regulars. "Progressive" finally supplanted "Insurgent" with the organization of the Progressive Party in 1912 (Sullivan, *Our Times*, 4:351n).

120 "special privilege and selfish interest": Jonathan Bourne to AP, Feb. 14, 1911; Bourne, National Progressive Republican League, statement of purpose, n.d., AP Papers.

120 a front: *NYT*, Jan. 25, 1911.

120 Rather than join: *Letters*, 7:196–98; *Works*, 17:53–65, 152–53.

120 Always of two minds: RML to TR, Jan. 19, 1911; *Letters*, 7:201–2.

121 La Follette was the purist: WAW, *Autobiography*, 346, 427–28.

121 dank subterranean office; Sullivan, *Our Times*, 3:221.

121 "This cannonading": RML, *Autobiography*, 478–80.

121 half-loaves: WAW, *Autobiography*, 346. La Follette's oratorical style is described in William Bayard Hale, "Friends and Fellow-Citizens," *World's Work*, April 1912, 680–81.

121 no bread was often better than a half a loaf: B. C. La Follette and F. La Follette, *Robert M. La Follette*, 1:143.

121 "constancy of purpose": RML, *Autobiography*, 523.

122 "I am not the man": *Letters*, 7:213–14.

122 Roosevelt's stalking horse: RML, *Autobiography*, 522.

122 "Home, wife, children": *Letters*, 7:213.

122 "blue as indigo": Abbott, ed., *Taft and Roosevelt*, 2:579–81.

123 "unconsciousness of power": WAW, *Autobiography*, 490.

123 He grew impatient: TR to Edmund Heller, June 27, 1911; TR to R. J. Cuninghame, Aug. 8, 1911; *NYT*, March 12, 1911.

123 Abbott Thayer: AGT, 553, 563.

124 monograph: TR, "Revealing and Concealing Coloration in Birds and Mammals," *Bulletin of the American Museum of Natural History*, Aug. 23, 1911; *Letters*, 7:653–57; Cutright, *Theodore Roosevelt the Naturalist*, 233.

124 "he takes his color": *Letters*, 7:96, 129–30.

124 "a very real call": TR to Mrs. H. M. Sanderson, March 3, 1911.

124 twenty thousand U.S. soldiers: Pringle, *Taft*, 2:701.

124 "I would wish immediately to apply": *Letters*, 7:243–44.

124 he longed for military glory: *Letters*, 7:202–3; *Works*, 11:76, 343.

124 "Well, old man": Quoted in Wagenknecht, *The Seven Worlds of Theodore Roosevelt*, 250.

125 Taft . . . did not expect a war: WHT to TR, March 22, 1911.

125 The Eastern press: John Callan O'Laughlin to TR, April 18, 1911.

125 warmly received: TR to Douglas Robinson, April 21, 1911.

125 "begged to follow him": Quoted in S. J. Morris, *Edith Kermit Roosevelt*, 372.

125 Roosevelt Dam: *NYT*, March 19, 1911.

125 "pleased and touched": U.S. Bureau of Reclamation, Phoenix Area Office, "A Brief History of the Roosevelt Dam." Available online at http://www.usbr.gov.

125 "quite another man": RML, *Autobiography*, 509–13.

126 La Follette's accomplishments: TR, "Wisconsin: An Object-Lesson for the Rest of the Union," *Outlook* 98 (May 27, 1911), 143–45.

126 no popular demand: *Letters*, 7:293.

126 "no one who is big enough": TR to Alford Cooley, Aug. 29, 1911.

126 Taft and arbitration: Pringle, *Taft*, 2:737.

126 TR and The Hague's first case: The disagreement involved the Pious Fund, which had been started in 1697 to raise money for Jesuit missionaries in California. After expelling the Jesuits in 1767, Spain transferred the fund and its responsibilities to the Franciscans. When Mexico won its independence from Spain, it sold the fund's assets and promised an annuity of 6 percent in perpetuity. But after ceding California to the United States in 1848, Mexico neglected its payments until 1869, then made good on the sum in arrears, and promptly resumed its neglect. The case went to The Hague in September 1902, and in October the arbitrators unanimously decided that Mexico owed the archdiocese of San Francisco $1.4 million in Mexican currency. (*NYT*, Sept. 17 and Oct. 15, 1902.) Mexico paid up in 1903 (*NYT*, June 17, 1903).

126 John Hay: Bailey, A *Diplomatic History of the American People*, 540–41.

126 Elihu Root: John P. Campbell, "Taft, Roosevelt, and the Arbitration Treaties of 1911," *Journal of American History* 53:2 (Sept. 1996), 280, 295.

126 Taft aspired to arbitrate: Pringle, *Taft*, 2:737, 745–46.

126 a joint commission of inquiry: E. James Hindman, "The General Arbitration Treaties of William Howard Taft," *Historian* 1973 36(1):62.

126 "If we go to battle": Quoted in Pringle, *Taft*, 2:750.

127 "I am a perfectly practical man": *Letters*, 7:284.

127 parapets: TR, "The Arbitration Treaty with Great Britain," *Outlook* 98 (May 20, 1911), 97–98.

127 "petty malice": AWB Letters, May 18, 1911.

127 "very sore": AWB Letters, May 20, 1911.

127 fait accompli: Abbott, ed., *Taft and Roosevelt*, 2:655.

127 the first lady's illness: AWB Letters, May 20, 1911.

128 The prospect of comprehensive arbitration agreements: Campbell, "Taft, Roosevelt, and the Arbitration Treaties of 1911," 280, 290–91.

128 "great jewel": Abbott, ed., *Taft and Roosevelt*, 2:635; AWB Letters, May 18, 1911.

128 "An ex-president has only a small field": TR to Edward Buxton, July 24, 1911.

128 Ted and Eleanor's baby girl: *Letters*, 7:344–45.

128 Kermit: Ibid., 7:339.

128 Ethel: Ibid., 7:315.

128 Quentin: Ibid., 7:316.

128 Archie: Ibid., 7:315; TR to David Evans, Oct. 2, 1911; TR to Bro. Wells, Oct. 2, 1911; TR to H. B. Munro, Nov. 14, 1911.

129 Groton for Archie: ABR, chapter 5 (unpaginated) in ms. memoir, ABR Papers; "Endicott Peabody," *Dictionary of American Biography*; Isabella Selmes Ferguson to ERD, postmarked Jan. 6, 1909, Derby Papers; David M. Esposito, "Refulgent Thunderer: Archibald Bulloch Roosevelt, 1894–1979," in Naylor et al., 108; Dalton, *Theodore Roosevelt*, 387; Wallace Finley Dailey to the author, Sept. 17, 2004.

129 "Mr. Evans is a peach": ABR to Warrington Dawson, Jan. 5, 1910, Dawson Papers.

129 knightliness: Hagedorn, *The Roosevelt Family of Sagamore Hill*, 258–59.

129 "he is long on character": TR to TR Jr., Sept. 22, 1911.

129 "played the game beautifully": Abbott, ed., *Taft and Roosevelt*, 2:673.

130 a rumor quickly scotched: George Griswold Hill to Mr. Brown, June 7, 1911, TRLC.

130 La Follette announced his candidacy: RML, *Autobiography*, 526, 530; *Letters*, 7:336.

130 TR was summoned to testify: NYT, Aug. 6, 1911; *Letters*, 7:429n.

130 "It must require immense courage": Cecil Spring Rice to TR, Sept. 24, 1911.

131 "overengined": WAW, *Masks in a Pageant*, 286.

131 "We must not permit ourselves": *Letters*, 7:331–32.

131 President Taft and the ambassadors: Abbott, ed., *Taft and Roosevelt*, 2:731–32.

131 Roosevelt struck: TR, "The Peace of Righteousness," *Outlook* 99 (Sept. 9, 1911), 66–70.

132 For once Taft stood fast: Pringle, *Taft*, 2:747–48.

132 Harder to dismiss: HCL to TR, Aug. 12, 1911; *Letters*, 7:289n.

132 three editorials praising the treaties: *Outlook* 99 (Sept. 9, 16, and 23, 1911).

132 He sometimes felt like resigning: AWB Letters, Aug. 27 and 29, 1911.

133 Back and forth: Abbott, ed., *Taft and Roosevelt*, 2:765; NYT, Sept. 19, Oct. 5 and 26, 1911.

133 spoke without "remotely realizing the import": WAW, *Masks in a Pageant*, 330.

133 San Francisco: TR Jr. to TR, Sept. 29, 1911.

133 TR urged him to wait: *Letters*, 7:344–45.

133 Taft came home: Abbott, ed., *Taft and Roosevelt*, 2:768.

134 Hiram Johnson: HJ to TR, Oct. 20, 1911.

134 "My honest opinion": *Letters*, 7:421.

134 three hundred progressive Republicans: NYT, Oct. 16, 1911; James R. Garfield, diary, Oct. 16, 1911, and Garfield to Truman Newberry, Nov. 22, 1911, Garfield Papers.

134 "a recommendation rather than a committal": RML, *Autobiography*, 533–37.

135 Edith's riding accident: In the weeks that followed, TR mentioned it constantly in his correspondence. See *Letters*, 7:399–401, 428–29, and his letters to Arthur Lee, Oct. 5; George Meyer, Oct. 6; Teresa Richardson, Oct. 6; HCL, Oct. 10; Mary Cadwalader Jones, Oct. 13; Jules Jusserand, Oct. 19; Warrington Dawson, Oct. 20; Endicott Peabody, Oct. 24; Mrs. F. M. Wolcott, Oct. 24.

135 lost her senses of taste and smell: S. J. Morris, *Edith Kermit Roosevelt*, 373.

135 U.S. Steel: Pringle, *Taft*, 2:672–73; *Letters*, 7:429–30; Mowry, *The Era of Theodore Roosevelt*, 288–90. Roosevelt was vindicated in 1920—a year after his death—when the Supreme Court ruled that the U.S. Steel Corporation had not created a monopoly with the purchase of Tennessee Coal and Iron.

136 T.R. retaliated: TR, "The Trusts, the People, and the Square Deal," *Outlook* 99 (Nov. 18, 1911), 649–56.

136 Taft read the article: AWB Letters, Nov. 17–18, 1911.

SEVEN: OFF THE PEDESTAL
PAGE

137 wedding anniversary: TR to Bob Ferguson, Dec. 5, 1911; *Letters*, 7:431–33. Edith regained only her sense of taste (S. J. Morris, *Edith Kermit Roosevelt*, 374).

137 "before the crash came": Abbott, ed., *Taft and Roosevelt*, 2:775.

137 tub-thumping: *Letters*, 7:445–46.

137 a stinging humiliation: James R. Garfield, diary, Dec. 2, 1911, Garfield Papers.

138 "the one really practical platform": *Letters*, 7:453–55.

138 "I should feel that there was a duty to the people": Ibid., 7:450–52.

138 La Follette rejected: RML, *Autobiography*, 542–44, 547–48.

139 he was already running: Ibid., 550–53.

139 During this half-in, half-out phase: *Letters*, 7:450–52, TR to W. R. Stubbs, Dec. 8, 1911.

139 another blast: TR, "The Russian Treaty, Arbitration, and Hypocrisy," *Outlook* 99 (Dec. 30, 1911), 1045–47.

139 "I'm not hungry": *NYT*, Dec. 28, 1911.

139 treaty with Russia: Ibid., Dec. 19 and 21, 1911; Pringle, *Taft*, 2:751.

140 "a rope of sand": Abbott, ed., *Taft and Roosevelt*, 2:803.

140 Only a coward: Ibid., 2:775–76.

140 forced the break: AWB Letters, Dec. 31, 1911.

140 "easy to say": HCL to TR, Jan. 10, 1912.

141 "More power to your elbow!": TR to HCL, Jan. 15, 1912.

141 "their own father": Quoted in Pringle, *Taft*, 2:755.

141 "You would be astounded": John Callan O'Laughlin to TR, Dec. 10, 1911.

141 another syllogism: HCL to TR, Dec. 18, 1911.

142 "This large illuminated fact": WAW to TR, Oct. 18, 1911.

142 "pretty thin material": *Letters*, 7:461–63.

142 "Why pull out the stopper?": William Rockhill Nelson to TR, Jan. 25, 1912.

142 Unless Roosevelt announced soon: Herbert S. Hadley to TR, Jan. 16, 1912.

142 the lesser of two evils: Mowry, *Theodore Roosevelt and the Progressive Movement*, 205; *Letters*, 7:484–85, 485n.

143 Carnegie Hall: RML, *Autobiography*, 594–95.

143 "Mr. Roosevelt is playing fast and loose": Quoted in B. C. La Follette and F. La Follette, *Robert M. La Follette*, 1:392.

143 "at each other's throats": AP to W. E. Colver, Feb. 2, 1912, AP Papers.

143 Both the decoy and the real duck: Wister, *Roosevelt*, 281–82.

144 La Follette's candidacy imploded: Ibid., 299–301; Baker, *Woodrow Wilson*, 3:270–75; RML, *Autobiography*, 602–8; B. C. La Follette and F. La Follette, *Robert M. La Follette*, 1:398–406; WAW, *Autobiography*, 448–50.

144 "I have grown fat on that sort of thing": *NYT*, Feb. 4, 1912.

144 Theodore judged it unseemly: TR to Gilson Gardner, Feb. 8, 1912.

145 "Politics are hateful": Quoted in S. J. Morris, *Edith Kermit Roosevelt*, 376–77.

145 "execrable taste": HCL to TR, Feb. 5, 1912.

145 "I have never felt more distressed": WHT to George Meyer, Feb. 5, 1912, and George Meyer to Alice Meyer, Feb. 24, 1912, Meyer Papers.

145 "unstable equilibrium": Elihu Root to TR, Feb. 12, 1912.

145 Nick Longworth: NL to TR, Feb. 9, 1912.

146 "[M]y political bed": NL to TR, Feb. 5, 1912; NYT, Sept. 19, 1911, and Jan. 26, 1912.

146 "I have got to come out": Letters, 7:503.

146 Primaries: The states were California, Illinois, Maryland, Massachusetts, Nebraska, New Jersey, North Dakota, Ohio, Oregon, Pennsylvania, South Dakota, Wisconsin.

146 The governors: Chester H. Aldrich of Nebraska, Robert Bass of New Hampshire, J. M. Carey of Wyoming, William E. Glasscock of Virginia, Herbert Hadley of Missouri, Chase S. Osborn of Michigan, Walter R. Stubbs of Kansas, and Robert S. Vessey of South Dakota (Washington Post, Feb. 11, 1912).

147 fortnight: Mowry, Theodore Roosevelt and the Progressive Movement, 211–12.

147 a year's worth of misery: Abbott, ed., Taft and Roosevelt, 2:839–46; "The Republican Presidential Dilemma," Literary Digest, Jan. 13, 1912.

147 "My hat is in the ring": Quoted in Sullivan, Our Times, 4:477.

147 "the great immutable principles of justice": Works, 17:147.

147 cigars: Herbert G. Gutman et al., Who Built America?, New York: Pantheon, 1989, 528; Smith, The Rise of Industrial America, 218.

147 "knew legalism, but not life": Works, 20:82–85.

148 a strike was a conspiracy: William E. Forbath, "The Shaping of the American Labor Movement," Harvard Law Review 102 (April 1989), 1149–52, 1168–72.

148 "the courts had been twisted": Works, 20:455.

148 another great struggle: Ibid., 15:507–9, 516.

148 "legalized terrorism": Quoted in Mowry, Theodore Roosevelt and the Progressive Movement, 171.

148 "If the American people are not fit": Works, 17:141–42.

149 "sowing the seeds": NYT, March 9, 1912.

149 "neurotics": Quoted in Sullivan, Our Times, 4:480–81.

149 "pained and depressed": HCL to Brooks Adams, March 12, 1912, HCL Papers.

149 "I have had my share of mishaps": HCL to TR, Sept. 5, 1910.

149 "My dear fellow": Roosevelt–Lodge Letters, 2:423–25.

149 the Porcellian Club: KR, diary, Feb. 25, 1912, KR-BWR Papers; Letters, 7:428–29.

150 Robert Grant: His letter appears in TR, Letters, 8:1456–61.

150 "purely from the standpoint of the interests of the people": Works, 17:149–50.

150 "Vehement he was": Thayer, Theodore Roosevelt, 352–54.

150 "Taft never did anything for me": TR to Dudley Foulke, Feb. 7, 1912.

151 "bewildered zeal": WAW, Autobiography, 452.

EIGHT: ANOTHER CUP OF COFFEE

PAGE

152 "I told you so": Abbott, ed., Taft and Roosevelt, 2:849–51.

152 "I drive myself": Ibid., 2:847–48.

152 One of the last to hear: ABR to TR, March 3, 1912; TR to ABR, March 12, 1912.

152 "indecent eagerness": John Morse to HCL, March 3, 1912, HCL Papers.

153 H. H. Kohlsaat: Kohlsaat, From McKinley to Harding, New York: Charles Scribner's Sons, 1923, 182–83.

153 Andrew Carnegie: Carnegie to TR, March 1, 1912.

153 In Henry Adams's vivid judgment: Adams, Letters, 6:525.

153 Augustus P. Gardner . . . retaliated: Gardner to TR, April 16 and 22, 1912; Letters, 7:534–35; HCL to TR, May 1, 1912; William Sturgis Bigelow to HCL, April 30, 1912, HCL Papers.

153 Secretary of War Stimson: Henry L. Stimson to TR, March 3, 1912.

153 insane: Adams, Letters, 6:514, 516, 518, 525.

153 S. Weir Mitchell: Mitchell to WHT, April 23, 1912, WHT Papers.

153 Allan McLane Hamilton: *NYT*, May 12, 1912.

154 Morton Prince: Ibid., March 24, 1912.

155 "The amusing thing": *Letters*, 7:513.

155 "make it a fight worth fighting": TR to George Miller, Feb. 29, 1912.

155 "as happy as possible": *Letters*, 7:531–32.

155 "essentially a fighter": Quoted in Jessup, *Elihu Root*, 2:180.

156 gravest crisis since the Civil War: TR to Albert Cross, June 4, 1912.

156 "Popular government we all believe in": *NYT*, Jan. 21, 1912.

156 "Mr. Taft fairly defines the issue": *Works*, 17:151–71.

157 legislative trespass: Stephen Stagner, "The Recall of Judicial Decisions and the Due Process Debate," *American Journal of Legal History* 1980 24(3):257–72; "The Recall of Judges," *Bulletin of the University of Kansas* 15:3 (Dec. 1, 1913), 41 (copy in TRC); William Draper Lewis, *The Initiative, Referendum and Recall*, Annals of the American Academy of Political and Social Science 63 (Sept. 1912), 311 (copy in TRC).

157 *indigestaque moles*: *Letters*, 8:1459–60.

157 "without the calculus": Brooks Adams to HCL, April 6, 1912, HCL Papers.

157 "Agitation": *NYT*, March 9, 1912.

157 America needed inspiration: *Works*, 17:170–71.

158 The "we" of Roosevelt's campaign speeches: Ibid., 17:177–89.

158 By definition a progressive: Norman M. Wilensky, *Conservatives in the Progressive Era: The Taft Republicans of 1912*, University of Florida monographs, Social Sciences, no. 25, Gainesville: University of Florida, 1965, 33–38.

158 1,078 delegates: Gable, *The Bull Moose Years*, 14.

159 the other 362: Ibid.

159 Joseph M. Dixon: John A. Garraty and Mark C. Carnes, eds., *American National Biography*, New York: Oxford, 1999, 6:646–49.

159 O. K. Davis: O. K. Davis, *Released for Publication*, 267–69.

159 Frank A. Munsey: Reminiscences of Ormsby McHarg, 104–5; *Dictionary of American Biography*; Garraty and Carnes, *American National Biography*, 16:104–6; WAW, *Autobiography*, 629.

159 George Perkins: Samuel Lane Loomis, "George Walbridge Perkins, Altruist," *The Congregationalist and Christian World*, Jan. 28, 1911, 110–11 (in GWP Papers); WAW, *Autobiography*, 459; GWP to A. G. Hawes, May 10, 1911, GWP Papers; Garraty, *Right-Hand Man*, 3–6, 10, 18–21, 116–17, 216–23, 227.

161 "a corrupt alliance": WAW, *Autobiography*, 457.

161 willing to sell their votes: O. K. Davis, *Released for Publication*, 275.

161 Taft had 100 of the 540: Rosewater, *Back Stage in 1912*, 64.

161 At least one small-town postmaster: *Letters*, 7:526–29.

161 "psychological effect": Quoted in RML, *Autobiography*, 667.

162 first sortie: Dixon statement to the press enclosed in J. M. Dixon to TR, March 18, 1912; O. K. Davis, *Released for Publication*, 269–73; Pringle, *Taft*, 2:770.

162 wickedness itself: Charles E. Merriam and Louise Overacker, *Primary Elections*, Chicago: University of Chicago, 1928, 185, 209, 212.

162 Taft's campaign manager: Rosewater, *Back Stage in 1912*, 122.

162 Only "professional politicians": *New York World*, March 11 and 20, 1912.

162 Roosevelt had shown no fervor for primaries: Ibid., March 19, 1912.

163 vulnerable to sabotage: O. K. Davis, *Released for Publication*, 253–55. The American vote on closed versus open presidential primaries is still out. In the election of 2000, seventeen states held closed primaries. Thirteen more were mostly closed, excluding members of opposing parties but allowing independents to vote. Twenty states conducted primaries best described as half-open, permitting any voter to vote any ticket but only one ticket. Arkansas was the lone state with a fully open contest. (Federal Elections Commission, available online at http://www.fec.gov.)

163 North Dakota: *NYT*, March 20, 1912.

163 jury duty: TR to Moses Clapp, March 5, 1912.

163 "Can't you just say this to them?": TR to Charles A. Lindbergh, March 11, 1912.

163 landslide: J. W. Davis, *Presidential Primaries*, 279.

163 boomerang: O. K. Davis, *Released for Publication*, 276–77.

163 control the damage: *New York World*, March 20 and 21, 1912.

163 scrubbed Roosevelt's name: TR to Gilson Gardner, March 21, 1912.

163 New York City: Quotations from *Brooklyn Eagle*, TR, and James R. Garfield in "The Verdict of New York and Indiana," *Literary Digest*, April 6, 1912, 671–73.

164 Examination of the irregularities: Thomas J. McInerney, "The Election of 1912 in New York State," Ph.D. diss., University of Denver, 1977, 46–51, 55, 57.

164 Wisconsin: J. W. Davis, *Presidential Primaries*, 279–81.

164 straw poll: *New York World*, April 3, 1912.

164 a sympathetic underdog: Rosewater, *Back Stage in 1912*, 65.

164 more than $600,000: Mowry, *Theodore Roosevelt and the Progressive Movement*, 225n.

164 his brother Charles: Pringle, *Taft*, 2:788; Abbott, ed., *Taft and Roosevelt*, 2:790.

164 disadvantage with . . . newspapers: O. K. Davis, *Released for Publication*, 270; George Kibbe Turner, "Manufacturing Public Opinion," *McClure's* 39 (July 1912), 316–27.

165 Medill McCormick: Turner, "Manufacturing Public Opinion," 323–24.

165 The Illinois and Pennsylvania primaries: O. K. Davis, *Released for Publication*, 280; J. W. Davis, *Presidential Primaries*, 279–81.

165 "The people are with us": *New York World*, April 10, 1912.

165 La Follette sourly declared: RML, *Autobiography*, 637–42.

165 $144,000: NYT, Oct. 3, 1912.

166 Unnerved by the losses: Manners, *TR and Will*, 219.

166 "Luck is with you": Ibid., 221.

166 "The strain": Adams, *Letters of Henry Adams*, 6:534–35, 538, 540.

166 the destruction of William Howard Taft continued: "The Taft-Roosevelt Grapple," *Literary Digest*, April 27, 1912, 872–73.

166 "This wrenches my soul!": Quoted in Pringle, *Taft*, 2:775.

167 Taft swore: Pringle, *Taft*, 2:780; "President Taft's Speech at Boston," *Outlook* 101 (May 4, 1912), 16–18; Rosewater, *Back Stage in 1912*, 56–60.

167 "Roosevelt was my closest friend": Quoted in Pringle, *Taft*, 2:782.

167 Roosevelt counterattacked: NYT, April 27, 1912; Rosewater, *Back Stage in 1912*, 61.

168 the mud-slinging in Massachusetts: J. W. Davis, *Presidential Primaries*, 279–81; National Roosevelt Committee, statement, May 1, 1912, copy in Garfield Papers.

168 "I have no question": Quoted in Jessup, *Elihu Root*, 2:183.

168 "Root has failed me": Quoted in Pringle, *Taft*, 2:785.

168 International Harvester: Pringle, *Taft*, 2:791–93; *Letters*, 7:538n.

169 Incensed: National Roosevelt Committee, open letter from GWP to William B. McKinley, April 28, 1912, copy in Garfield Papers.

169 E. H. Harriman: TR's version of events is given in *Works*, 16:425–35. The story gained a curious postscript in 1947, with the publication of the autobiography of George Crile, a distinguished surgeon. In the summer of 1909, while vacationing in Vermont, Crile was summoned to Harriman's home in Arden, New York. Harriman was mortally ill, and surgery was his last hope. "Knowing when we decided not to operate, that he had but a short time to live, Mr. Harriman asked me to stay and visit with him for a few hours," Crile wrote. "He told me with considerable bitterness details of what he considered Roosevelt's dishonesty. A week before the election, he said, Roosevelt asked him to come to Washington. Roosevelt was thoroughly frightened by the prospect that New York could not be saved for the Republican Party and urged Harriman to raise as much money as he possibly could to save the national election. Harriman raised $260,000, of which he himself donated $100,000, almost all of which was spent for the purchase of votes in New York City. Mr. Harriman said that at the time Mr. Roosevelt was profoundly grateful since he believed that this effort changed the election in his favor by over a hundred thousand votes." Later Harriman heard that Roosevelt considered him one of the malefactors of great wealth. "This Mr. Harriman never forgave," Crile wrote. "He was emphatic and bitter in his statements to me that Roosevelt was dishonest." (George W. Crile, *George W. Crile: An Autobiography*, 2 vols., ed. with sidelights by Grace Crile. Philadelphia: Lippincott, 1947, 1:238–39.)

169 "When a man says at breakfast": "The Third Term: A Poll of the Press," *Outlook* 100 (March 23, 1912), 615–17. The weight of the historical evidence is on Roosevelt's side. Washington said he believed that the nation should be able to call upon its most capable men in any great emergency, and when he declined a third term, he did not see himself as a man engaged in the noble act of surrendering great power for the good of the Republic. In fact, he worried that his desire to return to private life would be seen as unpatriotic. (Robert S. Rantoul, "What Washington Thought of a Third Term," Salem: Essex Institute, Historical Collections 37 (1901), 321–38 (copy in TRC); [George Harvey], "The Unwritten Law and the 'Great Emergency,'" *North American Review* 195 [April 1912], 440–42.) Washington's successor, John Adams, lost his bid for a second term, but after the next four presidents followed Washington's example, the two-term custom acquired its aura of virtue.

Both Andrew Jackson and Grover Cleveland were elected president three times but lost once in the Electoral College, and men who had profited handsomely under the blind eye of President Ulysses S. Grant tried twice, in vain, to secure his nomination for a third term. President McKinley at the outset of his second term heard mention of a third and swiftly announced that he was not a candidate, would not become a candidate, and would not accept the nomination if it were offered. McKinley's example may have influenced Roosevelt's decision to make his renunciation at the earliest possible moment, on election night in 1904. Limiting a president to two terms was a wise practice, Roosevelt told the crowd in the White House. "Under no circumstances will I be a candidate for or accept another nomination."

TR's distant cousin Franklin was the only president to serve a third term, and his decision to break with tradition drew little protest. A poll by the American Institute of Public Opinion during his third campaign, in 1940, found that three of five Americans opposed term limits. In 1944 the country elected FDR to a fourth term, but he died soon after it began. After World War II Republicans who feared the precedent and suspected that the new man in the White House, Harry S Truman, would perpetuate FDR's social welfare programs, drafted a constitutional amendment to put a ten-year limit on the tenure of presidents who followed Truman. One of the amendment's most ardent backers in the Senate was William Howard Taft's son Robert. To avoid debating the issue with a public likely to object (and likely to wonder why there were no limits for members of Congress), the amendment's advocates did not seek ratification through a state-by-state popular vote. Instead they sent the measure to state legislatures, more than half of which were in Republican hands. The legislatures complied, and the Twenty-second Amendment became law in 1951.

Eight years later, Republicans regretting that there would be no third term for Dwight D. Eisenhower launched a short-lived movement to repeal the amendment. Truman wished them godspeed. Testifying at a Senate hearing on the subject, he said that the Twenty-second Amendment made a lame duck of every second-term president, forcing him to do "the hardest job in the world . . . with one hand tied behind his back." Truman's wish has yet to be granted. (Bruce G. Peabody and Scott E. Gant, "The Twice and Future President: Constitutional Interstices and the Twenty-second Amendment," *Minnesota Law Review* 83 [Feb. 1999], 585–86, 597, 602; James R. Hedtke, "The Effects of the Twenty-second Amendment on Presidential Power: A Critical Examination of the Lame Duck Syndrome," Ph.D. diss., Temple University, 1998, 41–67.)

169 "I thought I had guarded myself": *Letters*, 7:531–32.

170 "The bitterness of this campaign": James R. Garfield, diary, April 27, 1912, Garfield Papers.

170 Nick and Alice Longworth: NL to TR, May 7, 1912; ARL, *Crowded Hours*, 192.

170 "I, I, I": *New York Herald*, May 14, 1912.

170 a "puzzlewit" and a "fathead": Manners, *TR and Will*, 229.

171 went away aghast: Turner, "Manufacturing Public Opinion," 327.

171 Perkins alone contributed $123,000: Garraty, *Right-Hand Man*, 256.

171 Fighting Bob: B. C. La Follette and F. La Follette, *Robert M. La Follette*, 1:435.

171 The president's campaign managers: Pringle, *Taft*, 2:803.

171 "the discredited bosses": *NYT*, May 26, 1912.

NINE: SATURNALIA

172 In the party's version: Jessup, *Elihu Root*, 2:189–90.

172 In Roosevelt's rendition: Mowry, *Theodore Roosevelt and the Progressive Movement*, 240–41.

172 But the truth clanging through the dissonance: TR told Alice before the Republican convention that if he did not get the nomination, he would form a third party (ARL, *Crowded Hours*, 196). Republican Party chairman Victor Rosewater could see by the end of May that Roosevelt's managers understood their slim chance. Their side was in the minority on the Republican National Committee, and most of the challenges ginned up by Ormsby McHarg were insupportable (Rosewater, *Back Stage in 1912*, 85).

172 By the party's long-standing rules: Rosewater, *Back Stage in 1912*, 83.

173 Ormsby McHarg: GWP to TR, June 11, 1912, GWP Papers; Rosewater, *Back Stage in 1912*, 95; [Charles D. Hilles] "Statement Relating to Contests over Seats in the Republican National Convention, 1912," *Congressional Record*, 62nd Cong., 2d Sess., 1912, 58: Pt. 12, 523–27; RML, *Autobiography*, 661.

173 90 seats in dispute: *Works*, 17:232–33.

173 baldly practical: Karlin, *Joseph M. Dixon of Montana*, 1:156; *Charleston* (S.C.) *Record*, June 13, 1912; *New York World*, June 17, 1912; Garraty, *Right-Hand Man*, 261.

173 similar overtures: NYT, June 18, 1912; Rosewater, *Backstage in 1912*, 101.

174 encouraged him to stay home: WAW, *Autobiography*, 464.

174 pressing him to come: O. K. Davis, *Released for Publication*, 293; Rosewater, *Back Stage in 1912*, 148.

174 They needed him as a peacemaker: Karlin, *Joseph M. Dixon*, 1:157.

174 Perkins's prominence: Ibid., 1:169, 184.

174 $50,000: Garraty, *Right-Hand Man*, 261.

174 boulder: Nicholas Roosevelt, "Account of the Republican National Convention at Chicago, June 1912," 1, unpublished ms., 1–2, TRC.

174 His automobile inched: Ibid., 7–8.

174 police cordon: WAW, *Autobiography*, 463–64.

175 "Like a Bull Moose": Quoted in Gardner, *Departing Glory*, 241.

175 Edith hosted a tea: ARL, *Crowded Hours*, 199–200.

175 Olympian goddess: WAW, *Autobiography*, 468.

175 Kermit: KR, diary, April 27, June 10, and June 15, 1912, KR-BWR Papers.

175 "The whole nation is watching": bulletin from Gifford Pinchot: *Chicago Daily Tribune*, June 12, 1912.

175 a dead lion: Brand Whitlock, "Three Conventions," *Metropolitan*, Aug. 1912, 12ff.

175 "As soon as one speaker wore out": O. K. Davis, *Released for Publication*, 296.

175 "a regular caricature of a boss": Nicholas Roosevelt, "Account of the Republican National Convention at Chicago, June 1912," 11–12.

176 the mood was savage: NYT, June 17, 1912.

176 "Twenty-four seats!": Quoted in Jessup, *Elihu Root*, 2:191–92.

176 blue tie with white polka dots: NYT, June 19, 1912.

176 tuberculosis: WAW, *Autobiography*, 470.

176 a curious conversation: O. K. Davis, *Released for Publication*, 317.

176 reworked an address: ARL, *Crowded Hours*, 198.

177 court of last resort: NYT, June 18, 1912.

177 Perkins . . . would privately estimate: GWP to A. G. Hawes, June 29, 1912, GWP Papers.

177 it was hokum: Rosewater, *Back Stage in 1912*, 189–90.

177 The party's rules: Ibid., 83–84; Elihu Root to W. R. Thayer, May 21, 1919, Thayer Papers.

177 "The parting of the ways": *Works*, 17:204–31.

178 "the ablest man": NYT, June 19, 1912.

178 a cold and dysentery: Jessup, *Elihu Root*, 2:187–88, 195, 197.

178 "sullen, ugly, ill-tempered": NYT, June 19, 1912.

179 Edna Ferber: Ferber, *A Peculiar Treasure*, 194–96.

179 Flinnsylvanians: The rumor was mentioned in numerous newspaper articles.

179 barbed wire: WAW, *Autobiography*, 469–70.

179 Governor Hadley: Ibid., 468–71; Rosewater, *Back Stage in 1912*, 179; Jessup, *Elihu Root*, 2:196.

179 When a La Follette man sprinted: B. C. La Follette and F. La Follette, *Robert M. La Follette*, 1:438–39.

179 558 to 502: *NYT*, June 19, 1912.

179 Borah moved forcefully: Marian C. McKenna, *Borah*, Ann Arbor: University of Michigan, 1961, 123.

179 "We have them whipped": *NYT*, June 19, 1912.

179 square deal: ARL, *Crowded Hours*, 199.

179 "I intend to see": Pringle, *Taft*, 2:805.

180 "the rawest kind of deal": GWP to Frank Munsey, phone message, June 7, 1912, TRLC.

180 TR breakfasted: Unidentified newspaper clipping.

180 a blue wall of policemen: *NYT*, June 20, 1912.

180 "basilisk imperturbability": WAW, *Autobiography*, 470–71.

180 Hadley's following: ARL, *Crowded Hours*, 199.

180 They marched: Rosewater, *Back Stage in 1912*, 179–80; Bryan, *A Tale of Two Conventions*, 45–47.

181 "I had enlisted for the war": Garraty, *Right-Hand Man*, 261–62.

181 "I am through": *NYT*, June 21, 1912.

181 Emma McChesney: Ferber, *A Peculiar Treasure*, 196. Emma McChesney and T. A. Buck were characters in a series of Ferber short stories.

181 only "tepidly" in favor of suffrage for women: *Letters*, 7:240–41.

182 "a large and obvious bee": ARL, *Crowded Hours*, 200.

182 The presidency might kill him: O. K. Davis, *Released for Publication*, 303.

182 Borah, fresh from a talk: McKenna, *Borah*, 124.

182 "regularity, formality, and orderly procedure": Bryan, *A Tale of Two Conventions*, 49.

182 "Colonel, we will see you through": Garraty, *Right-Hand Man*, 262–63.

183 The California delegation: Rosewater, *Back Stage in 1912*, 104–8.

183 a widely noticed exit: Manners, *TR and Will*, 258–59.

183 A Taft delegate from Michigan: O. K. Davis, *Released for Publication*, 305–9.

184 "Over Mr. Root's wintry face": *NYT*, June 23, 1912.

184 Henry J. Allen: Bryan, *A Tale of Two Conventions*, 85–89.

185 he had been beaten: Elihu Root to W. R. Thayer, May 21, 1919, Thayer Papers.

185 "Montana man clawed up a Florida delegate": KR, diary, June 22, 1912, KR-BWR Papers.

185 sergeant-at-arms: Ibid., June 17 and 18, 1912.

185 La Follette's platform: RML, *Autobiography*, 658.

185 At five o'clock: *NYT*, June 23, 1912.

185 Borah went to see him: McKenna, *Borah*, 126.

186 The voting at the Coliseum: Taft achieved a majority on the first ballot, with 561 votes. There were 41 votes for La Follette, a handful of votes for other candidates, and 344 not cast. Roosevelt received 107 votes from delegates who felt obligated to carry out their instructions from home (*NYT*, June 23, 1912).

186 "To any man with red blood": Ibid., June 23, 1912.

187 "We all behaved": ARL, *Crowded Hours*, 203.

TEN: A BARN-RAISING

PAGE

188 Taft was ecstatic: WHT to S. Weir Mitchell, July 14, 1912; WHT to Nannie Longworth Wallingford, July 14, 1912; WHT to HHT, July 14 and July 21, 1912, WHT Papers.

188 "Surely the ways of Providence": Bryan, *A Tale of Two Conventions*, 64–65.

189 "Young man": Quoted in Manners, *TR and Will*, 257.

189 "The question": Quoted in Blum, *Woodrow Wilson and the Politics of Morality*, 41.

189 During his first year: Ibid., 42–50.

189 "As a boy": WAW, *Masks in a Pageant*, 346–48.

189 "handsome in a cold . . . way": Abbott, ed., *Taft and Roosevelt*, 2:743–44.

189 "a good deal of a 'butter in' ": WHT to HHT, Aug. 16, 1911, WHT Papers.

190 Champ Clark: Link, *Woodrow Wilson and the Progressive Era*, 11; *NYT*, March 3, 1921.

190 "Pop's been praying for Clark": Quoted in Gable, *The Bull Moose Years*, 23.

190 At the outset of the Democrats' convention: Baker, *Woodrow Wilson*, 3:323; J. W. Davis, *Presidential Primaries*, 279–81.

190 Alice and Nick: ARL, *Crowded Hours*, 206.

190 Nellie Taft: Manners, *TR and Will*, 268–69.

190 Fighting Bob La Follette: "Why the Democracy Should Win," *Independent* 73 (July 4, 1912), 5.

190 Bryan as a has-been: Ferber, *A Peculiar Treasure*, 199; WAW, *Autobiography*, 477–80.

190 "My one thought": Quoted in Baker, *Woodrow Wilson*, 3:362.

190 "his face betraying no emotion": W. A. Prendergast, oral history, 415–16.

191 "radiant with trust and affection": Quoted in Hagedorn, *The Roosevelt Family of Sagamore Hill*, 309. The guest was E. A. Van Valkenburg, editor of the *Philadelphia North American*.

191 A few of Roosevelt's friends: Chase Osborn to TR, July 10, 1912.

191 "an avowal of weakness": *Letters*, 7:566–67.

191 "What a miserable showing": TR to John Callan O'Laughlin, July 9, 1912.

191 Before grappling: The three articles appear under the title "Thou Shalt Not Steal," in *Works*, 17:232–42.

191 In search of a more dispassionate analysis: La Follette, *Autobiography*, 661–63; Perkins to A. G. Hawes, June 29, 1912, Perkins Papers.

192 Amos Pinchot wished: AP to HJ, July 18, 1912; AP to Medill McCormick, July 3, 1912, AP Papers.

192 the gossip about his drinking: TR to E. T. Earl, April 24, 1912; *Letters*, 7:570–72; Frank Harper (TR's secretary) to J. A. Loring, Oct. 10, 1912; TR to H. C. Sticher, July 13, 1912.

192 drunk on himself: Adams, *Letters of Henry Adams*, 5:351.

192 Roosevelt wanted Progressives on the ballot: *Letters*, 7:568.

193 "I doubt if": *Progressive Party Minutes, 1912–1916* (Aug. 3–5, 1912), 1–4, TRLC.

193 Roosevelt's friends in New York: *Letters*, 7:563n.

193 a skeleton crew: W. R. Nelson to TR, July 24, 1912.

193 "I sometimes have to stop": *Progressive Party Minutes* (Aug. 3–5), 4–6.

193 "Some hours it really looks": Quoted in Karlin, *Joseph Dixon of Montana*, 1:166.

193 Americans of African descent: population figures from *World Almanac* (1913), 26; *World Almanac* (1902), 386.

194 For blacks the Negro question: W. E. B. Du Bois, *Dusk of Dawn: An Essay Toward an Autobiography of a Race Concept*, New York: Harcourt, Brace, 1940, 233.

194 lynching: Tuskegee Institute Archives. Available online at http://www.law.umkc.edu.

194 Brownsville: Southern, *The Malignant Heritage: Yankee Progressives and the Negro Question, 1901–1914*, Chicago: Loyola University, 1968, 70–71.

194 gains registered in the civil service: Gable, *The Bull Moose Years*, 61.

194 all men up: *Letters*, 7:585.

194 For the Progressive Party the Negro question: *Progressive Party Minutes* (Aug. 3–5), 81–96, 107, 119–21, 265.

195 Julian Harris: Ibid., 229.

196 "we are damned to defeat": Ibid., 216, 231–32, 237.

196 Br'er Roosevelt: *Letters*, 7:584–90.

196 "plucked of its verbiage": *Progressive Party Minutes* (Aug. 3–5), 215.

196 "[T]his does not make a white man's party": Ibid., 264–66.

196 the "Barnum feature": *NYT*, Aug. 5, 1912.

196 Four thousand seats: *New York Herald*, Aug. 6, 1912.

197 Mingo Sanders: *NYT*, Aug. 4 and 5, 1912.

197 a rain of queries: *NYT*, Aug. 6, 1912.

197 That evening Roosevelt received: *New York Sun*, Aug. 6, 1912.

197 "Suddenly, as if by magic": Addams, *The Second Twenty Years at Hull-House*, 30–33.

198 In their exuberance: O. K. Davis, *Released for Publication*, 319–20.

198 free passes: *New York Herald*, Aug. 7, 1912.

198 "the tall grass": Ibid.

198 Ethel and Quentin: ER, diary, Aug. 2 and 3, 1912.

198 Archie: ER to ERD, Aug. 5, 1912, ER Letters.

198 Alice: NL to TR, Aug. 2, 1912, and ARL, *Crowded Hours*, 211–12.

198 "Nick still sits upon the fence": ER to KR, Sept. 8, 1912, KR-BWR Papers.

198 So young, she thought: ER to KR, Aug. 8, 1912, KR-BWR Papers.

198 "successful middle-class": WAW, *Autobiography*, 483–84.

198 thirty-four women delegates: *New York World*, Aug. 6, 1912.

199 pale gray kid shoes: Ferber, *A Peculiar Treasure*, 197.

199 "Roosevelt's broad back": AP, *History of the Progressive Party*, 170–71.

199 "psychic uproar": Addams, *The Second Twenty Years at Hull-House*, 32.

199 TR found Edith's eye: *Chicago Daily Tribune*, Aug. 7, 1912.

199 confession of faith: The version delivered at the Coliseum was half the length of the written version given to the press (typescript in *Progressive Party Minutes* [Aug. 5–7], 52–138) and later published in *Works*, 17:254–99.

200 "Don't answer him": *New York Tribune*, Aug. 7, 1912; "Extract from Mr. Roosevelt's Speech at the Chicago Coliseum, Aug. 6, 1912, on the Negro Question," TRLC; *NYT*, Aug. 7, 1912.

200 The *New York Times: NYT*, Aug. 7, 1912.

200 the *Wall Street Journal: Wall Street Journal*, Aug. 8, 1912.

200 applauded 145 times: Gable, *The Bull Moose Years*, 81.

200 For every jaded reporter: Manners, *TR and Will*, 274.

200 "The atmosphere was charged with emotion": O. K. Davis, *Released for Publication*, 327.

201 Roosevelt and his running mate: *Progressive Party Minutes* (Aug. 5–7), 194–96, 292–93, 295–99.

201 Jane Addams: The Progressives boasted that Addams was the first woman to address a major political convention, a claim that overlooked Mary Elizabeth Lease of Kansas, a charismatic crusader best known for telling farmers that if they wanted to get out from under the heel of Eastern bankers, they had to "raise less corn and more hell" (quoted in Page Smith, *The Rise of Industrial America*, 449). In 1892, Lease seconded the nomination of General James B. Weaver, candidate of the People's Party, who received more than one million of the twelve million votes cast. Weaver carried four states, two more than Taft would in 1912. The People's Party was moribund by the next presidential election, but that would be the fate of Roosevelt's Progressives as well.

201 Benjamin Barr Lindsey: Steffens, *Autobiography*, 362; ER to KR, Aug. 8, 1912, KR-BWR Papers; James R. Garfield, diary, Aug. 7, 1912, Garfield Papers.

202 Hiram Johnson: HJ to George Stone, July 9, 1912; HJ to TR, telegram, July 24, 1912; HJ to W. F. Chandler, Aug. 21, 1912 (all in HJ Papers).

202 Using government as an agency of human welfare: WAW, *Autobiography*, 488.

202 "Men of the highest ideals": HJ to Irving Martin, July 8, 1912, HJ Papers.

202 Jane Addams, dedicated pacifist: Addams, *The Second Twenty Years at Hull-House*, 20, 35, 37; Du Bois, *Dusk of Dawn*, 233.

203 The biggest row: O. K. Davis, *Released for Publication*, 329–30; AP, *History of the Progressive Party*, 173–78.

203 it had rarely achieved the desired ends: James C. German, Jr., "The Taft Administration and the Sherman Antitrust Act," *Mid-America*, 1972 54(3):178–80.

203 Roosevelt thought it best to omit: TR, statement, Jan. 30, 1913, Strong Papers.

203 With no time left: O. K. Davis, *Released for Publication*, 332–34.

203 "Lewis has made a mistake": quoted in AP, *History of the Progressive Party*, 177.

203 The thorough study: Gable, *The Bull Moose Years*, 102.

204 a Kansas tornado: WAW, *Autobiography*, 491.

204 showdown: O. K. Davis, *Released for Publication*, 338–40; Garraty, *Right-Hand Man*, 282–83.

204 "fine and dandy": ER to KR, Aug. 8, 1912, KR-BWR Papers.

204 "They never imagined": *Chicago Daily Tribune*, Aug. 9, 1912.

ELEVEN: SPEND AND BE SPENT

PAGE

205 Heady as it was: WHT to HHT, July 16, 22, and 23, 1912.

205 Henry Clay Frick: Mowry, *Theodore Roosevelt and the Progressive Movement*, 279.

205 The newspapers overflowed: NYT, Aug. 13 and 26, 1912.

205 Taft a "negligible" factor: *Washington Post*, Sept. 6, 1912.

205 "I never discuss dead issues": Quoted in Gable, *The Bull Moose Years*, 112.

206 Further than that: Baker, *Woodrow Wilson*, 3:390.

206 In a canny bid: Link, ed., *Papers of Woodrow Wilson*, 25:18.

206 By the laws of his political physics: Bishop, *Theodore Roosevelt and His Time*, 1:342; *Roosevelt–Lodge Letters*, 2:382.

206 He disliked the press: Link, ed., *Papers of Woodrow Wilson*, 25:21.

206 When supporters hinted: Oswald Garrison Villard, diary, Aug. 14, 1912, Villard Papers.

206 Nor would he court: Schlesinger and Israel, eds., *History of American Presidential Elections*, 6:2165; Villard to Susan W. Fitzgerald, Aug. 14, 1912, Villard Papers. Levin, *Edith and Woodrow*, 181. Wilson considered suffrage an issue for the states to decide (Baker, *Woodrow Wilson*, 3:385). In the 1912 presidential election, women voted in six Western states: Wyoming, Colorado, Utah, Idaho, Washington, and California (*World Almanac*, 1913, 706). As for Roosevelt's "pandering," the suffragists, outsiders wanting in, welcomed converts at any hour. Nearly all of Roosevelt's critics on the issue objected for the same reason archconservatives had resisted his Square Deal: it forced them to share power they wished to reserve for themselves.

206 "And I will very gladly spend": 2 Corinthians 12:15.

206 While Wilson conserved his energies: Link, ed., *Papers of Woodrow Wilson*, 25:400.

206 "a constantly increasing strain": TR to KR, Aug. 3, 1912, TR Papers (TRC).

207 "tweedle-dum and tweedle-dee": WAW, *Woodrow Wilson*, 264.

207 Lawrence, Massachusetts: Link, ed., *Papers of Woodrow Wilson*, 25:335; Painter, *Standing at Armageddon*, 261.

207 "Those who buy": Link, ed., *Papers of Woodrow Wilson*, 25:9–10.

208 nothing was "more ludicrous": *Saturday Evening Post*, Oct. 26, 1912, 4.

208 a permanent tariff commission: *Works*, 17:285.

208 a corporations commission: Ibid., 17:290–91.

208 It would legalize monopoly: Link, ed., *Papers of Woodrow Wilson*, 25:88, 387.

208 Wilson promised to regulate competition: "Trust Remedies of Roosevelt and Wilson," *Literary Digest* 45 (Sept. 28, 1912), 499–501.

208 "God forbid": Link, ed., *Papers of Woodrow Wilson*, 25:78.

208 Even Taft roused himself: *Wall Street Journal*, Sept. 26, 1912.

209 would "leave unchecked": *Works*, 17:307–14.

209 "I haven't a Bull Moose's strength": Quoted in Baker, *Woodrow Wilson*, 3:400; Schlesinger and Israel, eds., *History of American Presidential Elections*, 6:2156.

209 Vermont: NYT, Aug. 30 and Sept. 6, 1912.

210 St. Paul, Minnesota: NYT and *New York Tribune*, Sept. 6, 1912.

210 Before an audience: NYT, *New York Tribune*, *Washington Post*, Sept. 10, 1912.

210 "little bull moose" talks: Philip James Roosevelt, "Politics of the Year 1912: An Intimate Progressive View," 27–29; TR Essays and Speeches, TR Papers (TRC); NYT, Sept. 8, 1912.

210 To the unhappiness of supporters: NYT, Sept. 26 and 30, 1912.

210 Atlanta: Ibid., Sept. 29, 1912; *Atlanta Journal* quoted in NYT, Sept. 30, 1912; *New York Sun*, Sept. 29, 1912.

211 Du Bois: David Levering Lewis, *W. E. B. Du Bois*, New York: Henry Holt, 1994, 1:421;

Link, ed., *Papers of Woodrow Wilson*, 25:448–49; Link, "The Negro As a Factor in the Campaign of 1912," *Journal of Negro History* 32:1 (Jan. 1947), 93.

211 in the congressional elections of 1910: *Socialist Party Campaign Book 1912*, 34–37.

211 Bomb-throwing: Brand Whitlock, "Three Conventions," *Metropolitan*, Aug. 1912, 12ff.

211 W. Sturgis Bigelow: Bigelow to HCL, April 3, 1912, HCL Papers.

212 "idiotic folly": *Roosevelt–Lodge Letters*, 2:240.

212 "[W]hen are you going to call their bluff?": Link, ed., *Papers of Woodrow Wilson*, 25:332–38.

212 "political wings of the capitalist system": *Debs: His Life, Writings and Speeches*, Chicago: Charles H. Kerr, 1908, 359.

212 filching their best wine: William McDevitt, "The 'Socialist' Roosevelt, Savior of the System," San Francisco, 1912, 8, 19.

212 the charmer and the autocrat: Philip James Roosevelt, "Politics of the Year 1912," 20–21.

212 Perkins defended himself in pamphlets: WAW, *Autobiography*, 491–92.

213 copyright: GWP memo, Nov. 19, 1912, GWP Papers.

213 "What are you doing to help the Progressive Party?": enclosed in ERD to KR, Oct. 27, 1912, KR-BWR Papers.

213 cheerleading: Garraty, *Right-Hand Man*, 274–75.

213 Amos Pinchot . . . a Progressive congressional candidate: AP to HJ, Oct. 5, 1912, AP Papers; AP, *History of the Progressive Party*, 178–79.

213 Hiram Johnson was equally unhappy: HJ to Joseph Dixon, Oct. 16, 1912, HJ Papers.

213 Perkins and J. P. Morgan, Jr.: Morgan to GWP, Aug. 19 and 24, Sept. 3, 1912; GWP to Morgan, Aug. 19 and 24, Sept. 3, 1912; GWP memo, Sept. 4, 1912, GWP Papers.

213 Even the Wilson-loving *New York Evening Post*: Undated newspaper clipping, GWP Papers.

214 "undramatized . . . nearly everything he touched": WAW, *Woodrow Wilson*, 279.

214 "a chapter of readjustment": Link, ed., *Papers of Woodrow Wilson*, 25:11.

214 Fighting Bob La Follette, still furious: *New York World*, Aug. 17, 1912.

215 "This may be really untrue": *Letters*, 7:603–4.

215 Moses E. Clapp: John Callan O'Laughlin to TR, Aug. 23, 1912.

215 "The Clapp Committee behaved very well": *NYT*, Oct. 6, 1912.

215 Bliss's assistant: *NYT*, Oct. 4, 1912.

215 Roosevelt testified: Ibid., Ernest Hamlin Abbott, "Mr. Roosevelt and the Senate Committee," *Outlook* 102 (Oct. 12, 1912), 296–296b; *Letters*, 7:603–25.

215 One of those who claimed to know: Pringle, *Taft*, 2:829–31.

215 Perkins was also swept: Garraty, *Right-Hand Man*, 183, 281.

216 The only flicker of scandal: WAW, *Woodrow Wilson*, 269.

216 Wilson's looks: Ibid., 274–76.

216 "a big bull voice": *New York World*, Sept. 3, 1912.

216 a five-part series: *NYT*, Sept. 28, 1912.

216 momentum: O. K. Davis, *Released for Publication*, 360.

216 "The people do not want the Colonel": *NYT*, Oct. 13, 1912.

216 The once indefatigable: Philip James Roosevelt, "Politics of the Year 1912," 37–44, TR Essays and Speeches, TR Papers (TRC).

217 Davis tried to protect: O. K. Davis to WAW, telegram, Sept. 14, 1912, WAW Papers; O. K. Davis, *Released for Publication*, 367–77.

217 TR whispered a memo: TR to GWP, Oct. 14, 1912, GWP Papers.

217 A welcome committee: O. K. Davis, *Released for Publication*, 372.

217 The assassination attempt: Remey et al., *The Attempted Assassination of Ex-President Theodore Roosevelt*, 117–31; O. K. Davis to GWP, Oct. 15, 1912, "Description of Assassination Attempt Made on Theodore Roosevelt" (copy in TR Jr. Papers, box 62); O. K. Davis, *Released for Publication*, 375–92; Philip James Roosevelt, "Politics of the Year 1912," 55–56, E. W. Leach, "Attempted Assassination of Theodore Roosevelt," *Racine Journal-News*, Aug. 13, 1921.

218 "Friends, I shall ask you": *Works*, 17:320–30.

219 "Everything possible is being done": TR to ER, telegram, Oct. 14, 1912, KR-BWR Papers.

219 the doctors decided to send him on: Dr. Joseph Bloodgood to Dr. Loyal Davis, July 12, 1932, TR Papers (TRC).

219 a marvel of composure: O. K. Davis, *Released for Publication*, 390.

219 "Well, I guess they've shot Roosevelt": KR to Belle Willard, Nov. 26, 1912, KR-BWR Papers.

219 "a worrying time": KR to TR, Oct. 15, 1912.

219 Edith billeted herself: O. K. Davis to GWP, Oct. 17, 1912, GWP Papers.

219 The wound: S. J. Morris, *Edith Kermit Roosevelt*, 387.

219 The hospital stay: ER to ARC, Oct. 16, 1912, TR Papers (TRC).

219 His physician wrote Perkins: Alexander Lambert to GWP, Oct. 18, 1912, GWP Papers.

219 Taft and Wilson wired: Manners, *TR and Will*, 287–88; Baker, *Woodrow Wilson*, 3:392; Link, *Wilson: Road to the White House*, 517; Link, ed., *Papers of Woodrow Wilson*, 25:421.

220 Roosevelt never admitted: O. K. Davis, *Released for Publication*, 387; Abbott, *Impressions of TR*, 279; *Letters*, 7:649–50.

220 William Jennings Bryan: *NYT*, Oct. 17, 1912; *Indianapolis Inquirer*, Oct. 17, 1912; *Works*, 17:332–33.

220 "a day of Thanksgiving": Quoted in Hagedorn, *The Roosevelt Family of Sagamore Hill*, 321.

220 Theodore was now attended: *New York World*, Oct. 31, 1912; *NYT*, Oct. 26, 1912.

220 He wanted one more chance: TR to GWP, Oct. 25, 1912, TRLC; GWP to TR, Oct. 24, 1912; GWP Papers.

220 Upward of fifteen thousand people: *Washington Post, New York Evening Post, New York Herald, NYT, New York World*, Oct. 31, 1912.

221 In one draft of the speech: TR ms., GWP Papers, box 12. The final version of the speech appears in *Works*, 17:334–40.

222 The next night: *NYT*, Nov. 1, 1912; Link, *Wilson: Road to the White House*, 521–22; Link, ed., *Papers of Woodrow Wilson*, 25:499.

222 sound asleep: ARL, *Crowded Hours*, 221.

222 Hadley: *Washington Post*, Oct. 31, 1912.

222 The interview was shelved: Pringle, *Taft*, 2:837–39.

223 Election day: *New York Herald, New York Sun, NYT, New York Tribune, New York World*, Nov. 6, 1912.

223 Wilson and Taft: Link, ed., *Papers of Woodrow Wilson*, 25:517–18; *Washington Post*, Nov. 6, 1912.

223 Alice: ARL, *Crowded Hours*, 221.

223 Debs: *NYT*, Nov. 6, 1912.

223 La Follette: B. C. La Follette and F. La Follette, *Robert M. La Follette*, 1:445, 450.

TWELVE: RECKONINGS

227 By seven o'clock: ERD, diary, Nov. 5, 1912, Derby Papers; *New York World, NYT*, Nov. 6, 1912.

227 a great plurality: Election statistics from *World Almanac* (1913), 716–69.

228 Republicans swore: *NYT*, Nov. 6, 1912.

228 Taft, stung: O. K. Davis, *Released for Publication*, 406.

228 Women voters: Meyer Lissner to TR, Nov. 26, 1912.

228 the black vote: My analysis is based on data from the U.S. Census of 1910.

228 Roosevelt blamed Goliath: *Letters*, 7:647–50.

229 "I do not see": Bishop, *Theodore Roosevelt and His Time*, 2:348.

229 The Progressive Party had come to stay: *NYT*, Nov. 12, 1912.

229 The success: Mowry, *Theodore Roosevelt and the Progressive Movement*, 281–82.

229 Roosevelt was fierce: *Letters*, 7:639–40; TR to Joseph M. Carey, Nov. 12, 1912.

229 Instead of an alliance: *NYT*, Dec. 10, 1912.

229 "long pull": TR to Richard Washburn Child, Nov. 8, 1912.

229 "very weary work": *Letters*, 7:660–61. For six weeks after the election, Roosevelt and the

Pinchot brothers hotly debated George Perkins's role in the Progressive Party: *Letters*, 7:637–38, 661–70, 677–79, 682–83; TR to GP, Nov. 19, 1912; AP to TR, Dec. 3 and Dec. 23, 1912; GP to TR, Nov. 9 and 23 and Dec. 17, 1912.

230 $130,000 . . . $600,000: Gable, *The Bull Moose Years*, 118.

230 "I was not in the least cast down at my defeat": *Letters*, 7:640–45.

230 modus vivendi: Garraty, *Right-Hand Man*, 288–89, 295–97.

230 "I hope": GWP to William F. McCombs, Nov. 12, 1912, GWP Papers.

230 Following a plan: Gable, *The Bull Moose Years*, 154–55, 163, 167.

231 "It is a fairer distribution of wealth": AP to TR, Dec. 23, 1912.

231 "We have no excuse": *Letters*, 7:682–83.

231 "ultras": TR to John Franklin Fort, Nov. 19, 1912.

231 "doing their best to break up the party": *Letters*, 7:670–71.

231 he privately confessed: TR to Judge Frank C. Laughlin, Nov. 13, 1912.

231 bridges to other parties: Joseph Bristow to WAW, Dec. 3, 1912, WAW Papers.

231 "a mere passenger": AP, *History of the Progressive Party*, 212.

231 Edith proposed a long holiday: ER to KR, Nov. 17, 1912, KR-BWR Papers.

231 Brazil's ambassador: TR to the Brazilian ambassador, Nov. 27, 1912.

231 "advertising myself": *Letters*, 7:660–61.

231 To friends: TR to George Miller, Nov. 8, 1912; TR to Edward Buxton, Dec. 4, 1912.

232 "as brave as can be": ER to KR, Nov. 6, 1912, KR-BWR Papers.

232 "poor lamb!": ER to KR, Jan. 6, 1913, KR-BWR Papers.

232 "a pair of Airedale pups": Hagedorn, *The Roosevelt Family of Sagamore Hill*, 328.

232 "I cannot *bear*": ERD, diary, Nov. 5, 1912, Derby Papers.

232 Edith was unwell: *Letters*, 7:660–61; ER to KR, March 2, 1913, KR-BWR Papers; ERD to BWR, Jan. 1913, KR-BWR Papers.

232 hospital social worker: Betty Boyd Caroli, *The Roosevelt Women*, New York: Basic Books, 1998, 349.

232 the Longworths blamed Alice: Carol Felsenthal, *Alice Roosevelt Longworth*, New York: Putnam, 1988, 130–31.

233 His would-be assassin: *NYT*, Nov. 12, 1912.

233 alienists: Remey et al., *The Attempted Assassination of Ex-President Theodore Roosevelt*, 111.

233 emigrated from Germany: *NYT*, Oct. 16, 1912.

233 another Napoleon: Remey et al., *The Attempted Assassination of Ex-President Theodore Roosevelt*, 196.

233 Schrank guessed: Ibid., 196–201.

233 Once commanded: Ibid., 68–176.

234 "decent respectable reception": *NYT*, Oct. 18, 1912.

234 In Milwaukee: Burns Detective Agency, Case #1321, Oct. 23, 1912, TR Papers (TRC).

234 Come evening: Remey et al., *The Attempted Assassination of Ex-President Theodore Roosevelt*, 116.

234 no remorse: Ibid., 117–31, 205–6.

234 the bullet and the revolver: *NYT*, Oct. 19, 1912.

234 The alienists concluded: Remey et al., *The Attempted Assassination of Ex-President Theodore Roosevelt*, 212–13.

234 The judge committed him: *NYT*, Nov. 23, 1912. Schrank spent the rest of his life in the Northern Hospital for the Insane, near Oshkosh, Wisconsin. He refused all interaction with other patients and during his thirty-one years of incarceration received not a single visitor. He died on September 15, 1943, the anniversary of two of his McKinley dreams (*NYT*, Sept. 17, 1943).

234 "I very gravely question": *Letters*, 7:676–77.

234 The district attorney had quizzed Schrank: *NYT*, Nov. 23, 1912.

234 The poem: Remey et al., *The Attempted Assassination of Ex-President Theodore Roosevelt*, 200.

235 collaborating with Edmund Heller: ER to KR, Jan. 12, 1913, KR-BWR Papers.

235 "History As Literature": *Works*, 12:3–24.

235 "Chapters of a Possible Autobiography": *Letters*, 7:688–89.

235 canceling subscriptions: Lawrence F. Abbott to Dear Father [Lyman Abbott], May 13, 1914, TR Papers (TRC).

235 Even at his weakest: *Works*, 20:30–31.

236 "mental weakness and a moral twist": Ibid., 20:513.

236 well intentioned but fatuous: Ibid., 20:521.

236 "Naturally, there are chapters": Ibid., 20:ix.

236 Alice Longworth spent: ARL to ERD, Jan. 30, 1913, Derby Papers.

236 Nick and his congressional colleagues: ARL, *Crowded Hours*, 225.

236 On his last day: *NYT*, March 5, 1913.

236 For better and worse: *Wall Street Journal*, Oct. 19, 1912; Pringle, *Taft*, 2:676; Mowry, *The Era of Theodore Roosevelt*, 260–64; Schlesinger and Israel, eds., *History of American Presidential Elections*, 6:2135, 2137.

237 he shed ninety of his 330 pounds: John G. Sotos, "Taft and Pickwick: Sleep Apnea in the White House," *Chest* 124:3 (Sept. 2003), 1134.

237 Roosevelt planned his March 4: *NYT*, March 5, 1913.

237 a whiff of P. T. Barnum: *Works*, 12:147–51.

238 Ethel went to the Armory: ERD to KR, March 1913, KR-BWR Papers.

238 Not ready to give up the trip: ERD to BWR, Jan. 1913, KR-BWR Papers.

238 Ethel was getting married: ERD to BWR, Feb. 11, 1913, KR-BWR Papers.

238 fishing in a necktie: Richard Derby Williams, conversation with author, Oct. 31, 1999.

238 "We are having a most wonderful time": ERD to TR, April 28, 1913, Derby Williams Papers.

238 The conspicuous absentee: *Letters*, 7:718; NL to George Meyer, Nov. 11, 1912, Meyer Papers; ER to KR, May 24, 1913, KR-BWR Papers.

239 Even her Longworth nieces and nephews . . . Miss Ault: WHT to HHT, June 25, 1913, WHT Papers.

239 "heated unintelligence": TR to ERD, April 7, 1913, TR Papers (TRC).

239 "Roosevelt lies and curses": *Roosevelt vs. Newett: A Transcript of the Testimony Taken and Depositions Read at Marquette, Michigan*. Privately published, 1914, 12 (copy in TRC).

239 "*Iron Ore* has long held": Quoted in Sally Jo Sawyer, "Teddy Roosevelt's Six-Cent Libel Suit," 3–4, unpublished ms., Longyear Library.

239 depositions: Gus Karger to WHT, May 18, 1913, WHT Papers.

239 resigned to the worst: ER to ERD, May 24, 1913, Edith Roosevelt Letters.

239 "I did not believe": TR to Mary Cadwalader Jones, May 23, 1913, Derby Miscellaneous Papers.

240 A battery of telegraph machines: *Daily Mining Journal* (Marquette, Mich.), May 27, 1913.

240 For six hours: *NYT*, May 27, 1913.

240 Richard C. Flannigan: *Daily Mining Journal*, Feb. 17, 1928.

240 displayed the scar: Jay G. Hayden, "Teddy Roosevelt's Day in a Michigan Court," *Detroit News*, Feb. 28, 1965.

240 Roosevelt's drinking history: *Roosevelt vs. Newett*, 7–34.

240 Jacob Riis: Ibid., 41–42.

241 Presley Rixey: Ibid., 55–66.

241 Gifford Pinchot: Ibid., 197–201.

241 Admiral George E. Dewey: Ibid., 351–53.

241 Newett's attorneys put their client on the stand: Ibid., 354–58.

241 Allowed to make a statement: Ibid., 358.

242 Edith grumbled: ER to ERD, June 6, 1913, ER Letters.

242 "the battle of all self-respecting men": Quoted in "Roosevelt's Libel Suit," *Outlook* 104 (June 14, 1913), 325–29.

242 Cousin Emlen Roosevelt: In an introductory note to the volume, Emlen wrote, "I have had this book printed because I knew that we all wanted to have a complete copy of the official record which contradicts the libel."

242 If he made too many speeches: Gable, *The Bull Moose Years*, 162.

242 The political companions: Dalton, *Theodore Roosevelt*, 417–21. Dalton does an excellent job of showing women's influence on TR's thought.

242 "Sarah Knisely's Arm": *Collier's Weekly*, Jan. 25 and Feb. 1, 1913.

243 "So much so-called Progressive seed": GWP to Alec Hawes, Dec. 3, 1912, GWP Papers.

243 Although Perkins quickly secured: GWP to Charles Henry Davis, Jan. 4, 1913; O. K. Davis to Frances A. Kellor, March 13, 1913; O. K. Davis to Josephine M. Stricker, March 7, 1913 (Progressive Party Archives).

243 "a flat failure": ER to ERD [July 1913], ER Letters.

243 The hunting he left to the boys: *Works*, 3:198.

243 "as happy as they are dirty": TR to Lawrence F. Abbott, July 27, 1913, TR Papers (TRC).

243 Quentin, now fifteen: ER to KR, May 6, 1912, KR-BWR Papers.

243 Archie: ABR, ms. of unpublished memoir, 47, ABR Papers.

243 Progressive club: ABR to TR, Nov. 7, 1912.

243 To his mother's relief: ER to ERD, May 27, 1913, ER Letters.

243 Quentin was the brightest: *Letters*, 7:688–89.

243 Roosevelt had seen the connection: *Works*, 3:226, 12:147–51.

244 "electric snap": Natalie Curtis, "Theodore Roosevelt in Hopi-Land," *Outlook* 123 (Sept. 17, 1919), 87–93. TR's article on the snake dance and two other pieces about his 1913 travels in the Southwest are in *Works*, 3:187–245. Nicholas Roosevelt, a cousin who was a contemporary of TR's children, gives an account of the trip in *Theodore Roosevelt: The Man as I Knew Him*, New York: Dodd, Mead, 1967, 110–25.

244 On his way east: *NYT*, Aug. 26, 1913.

244 His hesitations about going to Brazil: *Letters*, 7:731–32.

244 In his month at home: TR to Warrington Dawson, Sept. 2, 1913, Dawson Papers.

244 no real organization: *Letters*, 7:746–47.

244 trading *pluribus* for *unum*: Ibid., 7:718–19.

244 "nearly mad": TR to QR, Sept. 29, 1913.

244 "contemptuous dislike": *Letters*, 7:747.

244 The country cheered: Link, *Woodrow Wilson and the Progressive Era*, 42–43.

245 confidential letters: Among the recipients were Franklin Delano Roosevelt, assistant secretary of the navy; Miles Poindexter, chair of the Senate Naval Affairs Committee; and Governor Hiram Johnson of California, where public anger over Japanese immigration was close to the boiling point. TR also told an inquiring newspaper editor how the United States should handle the civil war in Mexico. See also *Letters*, 7:711, 720–23, 727–31.

245 "Father needs more scope": ER to ERD, 1913, Derby Papers.

THIRTEEN: SCOPE
PAGE

246 Roosevelt sensed that there might be protest: TR's concerns about how he would be received in Latin America are mentioned in J. C. Alvez de Lima, *Brooklyn Daily Eagle*, Dec. 4, 1921.

246 the newspapermen in the crowd: *Washington Post*, Oct. 5, 1913.

246 "discreditable": *Works*, 16:292.

246 "magniloquent talk": Ibid., 16:297.

246 "I think he feels": Quoted in S. J. Morris, *Edith Kermit Roosevelt*, 398.

247 "very dainty and charming": TR to QR, Oct. 8, 1913, TR Papers (TRC).

247 TR's financial arrangements: ER to ERD [1913], ER Letters. TR wrote more than a dozen pieces for *The Outlook* during his South American speaking tour.

247 "to see all the international business": *Works*, 16:292–93.

247 William Howard Taft: WHT to Gus Karger, Sept. 9, 1913, WHT Papers.

247 "the irony of fate": Quoted in R. S. Baker, *Woodrow Wilson*, 4:55.

248 "I had not for a moment": KR to ERD, Nov. 1913, Derby Papers.

248 and graciously told his parents: TR to RD, Nov. 12, 1913, Derby Miscellaneous Papers.

248 Edith's disapproval and family worries about Kermit in South America: TR to KR, April 20 and May 1, 1913, TR Papers (TRC).

248 "all a matter of taste": KR to ERD, April 30 and May 25, 1913, Derby Papers.

248 "Do you remember the tortoise": KR to Warrington Dawson, Oct. 6, 1913, Dawson Papers.

248 $2,500 a year: TR to RD, Nov. 12, 1913, Derby Miscellaneous Papers.

248 Edith reacted with disbelief and alarm: KR to ERD [Nov. 1913], Derby Papers; KR to BWR, Feb. 14, 1914, KR-BWR Papers.

249 "a trifle down": ER to ERD, Nov. 14, 1913, ER Letters.

249 "Father scarcely sleeps": ER to ERD [1913], from Montevideo, ER Letters.

249 a new conception of the doctrine: *Washington Post*, Oct. 25, 1913.

249 Rio de Janeiro: *NYT*, Oct. 25, 1913.

249 On October 27: Link, ed., *Papers of Woodrow Wilson*, 28:448–52.

250 Europeans heard: *Times* (London), Oct. 28, 1913; *Washington Post*, Dec. 18, 1913.

250 "Intelligent opinion": *Times* (London), Oct. 31, 1913.

250 The Germans, more direct: *Times* (London), Nov. 7, 1913.

250 Taking Roosevelt's approach: *Washington Post*, Oct. 25, 1913.

250 "for there is never any deed to back it up": Albert Bushnell Hart et al., eds., *Theodore Roosevelt Cyclopedia*, New York: Roosevelt Memorial Association, 1941, 639.

250 a warning against intellectualism: *Washington Post*, Oct. 28, 1913.

250 Montevideo: Nicolay A. Grevstad to Secretary of State, Nov. 10, 1913, RG 59, Central Decimal Files, 1910–1929, National Archives 032.R671, box 0314. The Lorillard and Harvey letters cited below are also filed here.

251 Buenos Aires: George Lorillard to Secretary of State, Dec. 6, 1913; Travis B. Wells, "What the South Americans Think of Roosevelt," *Harper's Weekly* 58 (Feb. 7, 1914), 6–8.

251 Santiago: "The Colonel in Chile," *North American Review* 199 (March 1914), 337–38; R. B. Harvey to Secretary of State, Dec. 28, 1913, and Jan. 5, 1914.

251 "more or less lively": *Times* (London), Dec. 23, 1913.

251 Pondering Wilson's speech: *Washington Post*, Dec. 18, 1913.

252 Theodore and Edith parted in Chile: ER, diary, Nov. 26, 1913; TR to KR, Aug. 9, 1913, TR Papers (TRC).

252 Kermit, yearning to be in Madrid: KR to BWR [1913], from Asunción, KR-BWR Papers.

252 "I get angry at myself": KR to BWR, Feb. 2, 1914, KR-BWR Papers.

252 "his feelings would really have been hurt": TR to ERD, Dec. 10, 1913, TR Papers (TRC).

252 After many hours: KR to BWR, Dec. 31, 1913, KR-BWR Papers.

252 more than once encouraged: KR to BWR [n.d.] and Feb. 14, 1914, KR-BWR Papers.

252 as the only member of their party: KR to BWR, Dec. 21, 1913, KR-BWR Papers.

252 General Lauro S. Müller: George K. Cherrie, *Dark Trails: Adventures of a Naturalist*, New York: Putnam, 1930, 259–60; Theodore Roosevelt, *Through the Brazilian Wilderness*, New York: Charles Scribner's Sons, 1914, 9 (cited hereafter as *TBW*).

252 "To go down an unknown river": TR to RD, Nov. 12, 1913, Derby Miscellaneous Papers.

253 "Tell Osborn": Quoted in Joseph Ornig, *My Last Chance to Be a Boy*, Mechanicsburg, Pa.: Stackpole Books, 1994, 51–52.

253 Rondon: *TBW*, 51, 132; *NYT*, Jan. 20, 1958; *Washington Post* and *Times Herald*, Jan. 21, 1958; *Los Angeles Times*, March 5, 1958.

253 Small parties being less obtrusive than large ones: Leo E. Miller, *In the Wilds of South America*, New York: Charles Scribner's Sons, 1918, 240.

253 Leo E. Miller: *TBW*, 246.

253 Rondon theorized: Ibid., 261–62, 284–85.

254 "On February 27, 1914": Ibid., 249.

254 *Through the Brazilian Wilderness*: TR had wanted to call the book *A Hunter-Naturalist in the Brazilian Wilderness*, and to his dismay his publisher changed the title. Busy campaigning for Progressive congressional candidates in the fall of 1914, he was unable to lobby for his version. TR to KR, Jan. 27, 1915, TR Papers (TRC).

254 They set off with twenty-two men: Cherrie, *Dark Trails*, 278.

254 After two weeks on the river: George K. Cherrie, diary, March 12, 15, and 16, 1914, Roosevelt-Rondon Expedition Papers. The drowning, which occurred on March 15, is also described in Kermit's diary; *TBW*, 275–76; and Cherrie, *Dark Trails*, 288–89.

254 the river rose and carried off two canoes: Cherrie, *Dark Trails*, 252; KR, diary, March 27, 1914, KR-BWR Papers.

254 TR's injury: *TBW*, 317.

254 "oriental ulcers": Cherrie, *Dark Trails*, 306.

254 TR's temperature rose to 104 degrees: KR, *The Long Trail*, 74–75.

255 "Am in a blue funk": KR, diary, April 4, 1914, KR-BWR Papers.

255 The week had been a torture: Cherrie, diary, March 28–April 4, 1914, Roosevelt-Rondon Expedition Papers; KR, diary, March 28–April 4, 1914, KR-BWR Papers. In *Dark Trails*, 307–8, Cherrie claimed that during this week TR told him and Kermit that he could not go on: "You can get out. I will stop here." But Cherrie did not record this extraordinary moment in his diary. Nor did Kermit, and in his book *The Long Trail*, Kermit wrote that TR did not confess his thoughts of remaining behind until after the expedition (73).

255 Barely able to walk: Cherrie, diary, April 13, 1914, Roosevelt-Rondon Expedition Papers.

255 Julio: Ibid., April 3, 6, and 7, 1914; KR, diary, April 3, 1914, KR-BWR Papers; *TBW*, 311–17; Cherrie, *Dark Trails*, 310–14; Colonel Candido Mariano da Silva Rondon, *Lectures*, Rio de Janeiro, 1916, 113–15, TRC.

255 struggling to survive: Cherrie, diary, April 7, 1914, Roosevelt-Rondon Expedition Papers.

255 "Rondon completely vacillated": KR, diary, April 6, 1914, KR-BWR Papers.

256 On April 13: KR, diary, April 13, 1914, KR-BWR Papers.

256 Next day they found a tool: KR, diary, April 14 and 15, 1914, KR-BWR Papers.

256 Two weeks later: KR, diary, April 27, 1914, KR-BWR Papers.

256 TR pressed for keeping it: *TBW*, 286; TR to W. L. G. Joerg, June 11, 1914.

256 Teodoro: *NYT*, July 29, 1914. Another member of the expedition credited TR with suggesting "Teodoro"—puckishly—on the theory that in Brazil it would sound less alien than the Dutch "Roosevelt" (Ornig, *My Last Chance to Be a Boy*, 200).

256 TR in Manaus: Ibid., 200–201; KR, diary, April 29–May 1, 1914, KR-BWR Papers.

256 TR nevertheless cabled: *NYT* and *Chicago Daily Tribune*, May 1, 1914.

256 He also willed himself: *TBW*, 393–95. TR's telegram to Müller is dated May 1, but as Ornig points out, it was wired on April 30 (*My Last Chance to Be a Boy*, 204).

257 The naturalists' collections: *Chicago Daily Tribune*, May 1, 1914; Paul Cutright, *Theodore Roosevelt the Naturalist*, New York: Harper, 1956, 253–54.

257 "about the same": KR, diary, April 30, 1914, KR-BWR Papers.

257 "Well, I feel my going was really justified": KR to ERD, May 6, 1914, Derby Papers; KR, diary, May 7–8, 1914, KR-BWR Papers.

257 Roosevelt's return: *NYT*, *Washington Post*, *Chicago Daily Tribune*, May 20, 1914.

257 he looked like an old man: John Callan O'Laughlin to Mabel O'Laughlin [1914], O'Laughlin Papers.

258 the storm would blow until 1927: Under the leadership of George Miller Dyott, an English explorer, the expedition confirmed the Rio Teodoro's existence and Rondon's cartography, which put the length at close to a thousand miles. Dyott's account of the trip appeared in *The New York Times Magazine*, June 12, 19, and 26 and July 10, 1927. Early defenses of TR's claim include "Colonel Roosevelt's Discoveries in South America," *Scientific American* 110 (May 23, 1914), and W. L. G. Joerg, "The Geographical Results of the Roosevelt-Rondon Expedition," *American Museum Journal*, March 1915, 129–32. Algot Lange, a Danish explorer, backed TR's claim by issuing a statement about his own travels into the far reaches of the Amazon, saying that he had seen the mouths of many rivers that were not on his map (*NYT*, June 25, 1914).

258 "something pathetic": Gus Karger to WHT, May 28, 1914, WHT Papers.

FOURTEEN: HALF-GODS

PAGE

259 Edith Wharton: Edith Wharton, *Fighting France*, New York: Charles Scribner's Sons, 1918, 6.

259 Alice Longworth: ARL, *Crowded Hours*, 234.

260 Henry Adams: Adams, *Letters of Henry Adams*, 6:652–53, 657–58.

260 Henry White: Nevins, *Henry White*, 323–26, 501–2.

260 Walter Hines Page: Page, diary, Jan. 20, Aug. 2 and 4, 1914, Page Papers.

261 Andrew Carnegie: Wall, *Andrew Carnegie*, 1012–13, 1020–21.

261 Jane Addams: Addams, *The Second Twenty Years at Hull-House*, 116–18.

262 "that great black tornado": *Letters*, 7:790.

262 These "cooling off" treaties: Bailey, *A Diplomatic History of the American People*, 593–94; *Letters*, 8:817–18, 822–25.

262 Woodrow Wilson proclaimed: *NYT*, Aug. 4 and 19, 1914.

263 "with his heart torn out": Quoted in Levin, *Edith and Woodrow*, 49.

263 fulminating: *Letters*, 8:821–22; CRR to G. J. Anderson, June 28, 1920, CRR Papers.

263 malaria: GWP to National Committeemen and State Chairmen, June 30, 1914, Progressive Party Archives; TR to John C. Shaffer, July 2, 1914.

263 *The Outlook*: Lawrence F. Abbott to Dear Father, May 31, 1914, TR Papers (TRC); ER to KR [1914], KR-BWR Papers; *Letters*, 7:768.

263 quinine: In a July 6 letter to John H. Parker, TR mentioned the quinine and his doctors' disagreement about how it should be administered. An excess of quinine can impair vision and hearing, tax the heart, upset the digestive system, and cause exhaustion and confusion. On occasion it sets off a rash, as it did in Kermit's case en route to Africa. A severely sore throat is an uncommon but not unknown reaction.

263 he rowed Edith: Hagedorn, *The Roosevelt Family of Sagamore Hill*, 339.

263 honeymoon: KR to Warrington Dawson [1914], Dawson Papers.

263 mowing the lawn: *NYT*, July 18, 1914.

264 Murphy and Barnes: Roosevelt's statement appeared in *NYT*, July 24, 1914.

264 The next night during dinner: Ibid.

264 Panama: *NYT*, March 30 and June 10, 1914.

264 "I ask for this hearing": *Letters*, 7:777–79.

264 in order to rivet attention on the issue: TR to Francis B. Loomis, July 21, 1914.

264 he could say it in writing: Gus Karger to WHT, July 24, 1914, WHT Papers.

264 Thanks to his friend Lodge: *Letters*, 7:774n; Bailey, *A Diplomatic History of the American People*, 546.

265 unlikely that he could have won: In 1912, he had finished behind Wilson and Taft in New York, with only 25 percent of the vote (*World Almanac* [1913]), 749.

265 latitude to fight Woodrow Wilson on any front: *Letters*, 7:771–72.

265 A careful listener: E.g., *Letters*, 7:767, 771–73.

265 The country had tired of reformers: *Letters*, 8:834–40.

265 "the stomach vote": TR to ABR, Nov. 7, 1914.

265 Ludlow Massacre: Stephen Millies, "The Ludlow Massacre and the Birth of Company Unions," *Workers' World*, Jan. 26, 1995; *NYT*, May 1 and June 1, 1914.

266 Roosevelt naturally scorned Wilson's delay: *NYT*, July 7, 1914.

266 Roosevelt blamed: *Letters*, 7:804–9. This letter was written with publication in mind.

266 "everyday common decency": "On the Way to 1916 and the Rule of the People," address in Bay City, Mich., Sept. 30, 1914, TR Papers (TRC).

266 "mutual self-help": TR in Lewiston, Maine, Aug. 8, 1914, Progressive Party Archives.

266 "completely restored": O. K. Davis to GWP, Oct. 6, 1914; O. K. Davis to Clarence W. Halbert, Oct. 26, 1914, Progressive Party Archives.

266 "a state of exuberant vitality": ER to CRR, Oct. 13, 1914, CRR Papers.

266 "This is election night": ER to ERD, Nov. 3, 1914, ER Letters.

267 Nick Longworth: *NYT* and *Washington Post*, Nov. 4, 1914.

267 La Follette's candidate: *NYT*, Nov. 2 and 4, 1914.

267 "We were engaged": TR to BWR, Nov. 7, 1914, TR Papers (TRC).

267 "Luckily": TR to ABR, Nov. 7, 1914.

267 he claimed to be happier: TR to KR, Nov. 11, 1914, TR Papers (TRC).

267 With the silver-lining men: *Letters*, 8:834–40. I have given Emerson's version, from his poem "Give All to Love." TR slightly misquoted the lines, showing that he knew them well enough not to have to look them up.

267 Roosevelt declined to attend: TR to WAW, Nov. 21, 1914.

267 The herd: GWP to My dear sir, Dec. 7, 1914, Progressive Party Archives.

268 The first was a plea: *Works*, 18:3–11.

268 Roosevelt saw no conflict: Ibid., 18:184–85.

268 The last of the articles: Ibid., 18:164–65; *Letters*, 8:915, 928.

268 "He sighs for the Nobel Prize": Cecil Spring Rice to Arthur Nicolson, Nov. 13, 1914, Stephen Gwynn, ed., *The Letters and Friendships of Sir Cecil Spring Rice*, 2 vols., Boston: Houghton Mifflin, 1929, 2:240–41.

269 "You will want a big army": Cecil Spring Rice to W. A. Chanler, Nov. 14, 1914, Chanler Papers.

269 "You have time yet": Rudyard Kipling to W. Cameron Forbes, Sept. 13, 1914, Forbes Papers.

269 Ethel and Dick Derby in Paris: ERD to ER, Oct. 6, 10, 15, and 19, 1914, Derby Papers; ERD to Emily Carow, Nov. 4, 1914, ER Letters.

270 Ted was prospering: EAR, *Day Before Yesterday*, 65–66; TR Jr. to KR, Sept. 23, 1915, KR-BWR Papers.

270 Archie was holding his own: TR to KR, Dec. 2, 1914 and Jan. 6, 1915, TR Papers (TRC); *Letters*, 8:851–52.

270 The only cloud: ER, diary, Dec. 25, 26, and 30, 1914; TR to KR, Oct. 24, 1915, TR Papers (TRC).

270 "I am no friend": TR to KR, Dec. 28, 1914, TR Papers (TRC).

271 Now openly supporting England and France: *Letters*, 8:878, 883, 892, 903.

271 scare tactics: *NYT*, Oct. 31, 1914; A. N. Griff, letter to the editor, *NYT*, Nov. 2, 1914; WHT to Gus Karger, Nov. 14, 1914, WHT Papers.

271 "severe and trying operation": TR to KR, April 17, 1915, TR Papers (TRC); ERD to KR, April 15 and 18, 1915, KR-BWR Papers; S. J. Morris, *Edith Kermit Roosevelt*, 406.

271 Judge William M. Andrews: George T. Blakey, "Calling a Boss a Boss: Did Roosevelt Libel Barnes in 1915?" *New York History* 1979 60(2):200.

271 his hair: *NYT*, May 16, 1915.

271 At stake in *Barnes v. Roosevelt*: *Letters*, 8:934–35; *NYT*, May 10 and 17, 1915.

272 William Barnes, Jr.: *NYT*, April 26 and May 15, 1915; June 26, 1930; H. T. Pulsifer, "Libel Suit at Syracuse," *Outlook* 110 (May 5, 1915), 15–19.

272 "You have heard the trumpet": Pringle, *Theodore Roosevelt*, 144.

272 William M. Ivins: *NYT*, April 21 and 23, July 24, 1915; Bishop, *Theodore Roosevelt and His Time*, 2:366.

273 Roosevelt cheerfully admitted: *NYT*, April 23, 1915.

273 with his whole body: Ibid., May 6 and 16, 1915.

273 Thomas C. Platt: Ibid., April 27, 1915; Pulsifer, "Libel Suit at Syracuse," 15–19.

273 After Roosevelt's first week: "Mr. Roosevelt Asks Too Much," *Nation* 100 (April 29, 1915), 458.

274 John M. Bowers: *NYT*, March 8, 1918.

274 Six months of investigation: Ibid., May 6, 1915.

274 After a long standoff: James MacGregor Burns, *Roosevelt: The Lion and the Fox*, New York: Harcourt, Brace, 1956, 35–41.

274 "gay, confidential, almost jovial": *NYT*, May 16, 1915.

274 "must move in order": Quoted in Blakey, "Calling a Boss a Boss," 204.

275 Aristophanes: *NYT*, May 8, 1915.

275 enjoyed keeping Roosevelt off balance: Ibid., May 16, 1915.

275 Ivins asked Judge Andrews: Ibid., May 1 and 12, 1915.

275 Roosevelt was devastated: TR to ERD, May 12, 1915, TR Papers (TRC).

275 "a wonderful run": TR to KR, May 8, 1915, TRC.

276 The law of the sea: Bailey, A *Diplomatic History of the American People*, 626–28.

276 German submarine commanders: Chickering, *Imperial Germany and the Great War*, 90.

276 "the wholesale poisoning": *Works*, 18:377–81.

276 Not wanting the editorial to wait: The telegrams and Whigham's recollections of the episode are in folders 316–19, TR Papers (TRC).

276 Wilson's response to the catastrophe: *NYT,* May 11, 1912.

277 "not carrying out any policy at all": *Letters,* 8:927.

277 In his last argument: *NYT,* May 20, 1915.

277 Ivins did not conceal: Ibid., May 21, 1915.

278 Barnes and Ivins left town: TR to BWR, May 27, 1915, TR Papers (TRC).

278 guilty of nothing: *NYT,* May 23, 1915.

278 "The room rang with him": Ibid., May 16, 1915.

278 Ivins died: Ibid., July 24, 1915.

278 "Of all the blundering lunatics": Bishop, *Theodore Roosevelt and His Time,* 2:367–69. The transcript of the trial was published as New York State: Courts, Supreme Court, *William Barnes, Plaintiff-Appellant Against Theodore Roosevelt, Defendant-Respondent,* Walton, N.Y.: The Reporter Company, 1917 (copy in TRC).

278 "an engine bucking a snowdrift": *Letters,* 8:930.

FIFTEEN: WILD SURMISE

PAGE

279 reveling in the dogwood: TR to KR, May 8, 1915, TR Papers (TRC).

279 "lame dog": ER to KR, June 23, 1915, KR-BWR Papers.

279 "absolutely out of politics": TR Jr. to KR, July 14, 1915, KR-BWR Papers.

279 "nervous and excited": Link, *Woodrow Wilson and the Progressive Era,* 177.

279 make an invasion unthinkable: Seymour, *The Intimate Papers of Colonel House,* 1:298.

279 Large forces were expensive: Baker, *Woodrow Wilson,* 6:8.

279 diplomatic notes: Link, *Woodrow Wilson and the Progressive Era,* 166.

280 "pocket" Roosevelt: Gus Karger to WHT, July 27, 1915, WHT Papers. The aide was Wilson's private secretary, Joseph P. Tumulty.

280 serial number: Pringle, *Theodore Roosevelt,* 409.

280 "milk–and–water": *Works,* 18:66, 308.

280 Congressman Gardner: John Patrick Finnegan, *Against the Specter of a Dragon: The Campaign for Military Preparedness, 1914–1917,* Wesport, Conn.: Greenwood, 1974, 24, 27, 34–36; *NYT,* Dec. 3, 1914.

280 Although neglected: Finnegan, *Against the Specter of a Dragon,* 6; Baker, *Woodrow Wilson,* 8:306.

280 had not been on maneuvers: *Works,* 18:112–13.

281 "As a military power": Quotation and statistics from Daniel Carl Palm, "Strategic and Moral/Political Foundations of the Preparedness Debate," Ph.D. diss., Claremont Graduate School, 1991, 83–88.

281 If the United States were attacked at dawn: *Works,* 18:181–83.

281 "His mind is not broad": Charles Willis Thompson, *NYT,* June 9, 1915.

281 "jingohypnotism": WHT to Gus Karger, March 27, 1916, WHT Papers.

281 Sonya Levien: Levien, "Col. Roosevelt in Our Office," *Metropolitan,* May 1915, and in ms. fragment, 1918; Levien Papers.

282 "the child had disgraced itself": Untitled ms., 1919; ms. for "Great Friend," *Woman's Home Companion* 46, Oct. 1919.

282 you had to hate the Colonel a whole lot to keep from loving him: Wagenknecht, *The Seven Worlds of Theodore Roosevelt,* 105.

282 Panama Canal: The first ship passed through the canal in August 1914, just as Europe was going to war, and was barely noticed (McCullough, *The Path Between the Seas,* 609).

282 "wild surmise": From John Keats, "On First Looking into Chapman's Homer." TR mentioned Keats's error and his appreciation of the poet in his essay "History As Literature": "Keats forgot even the right name of the man who first saw the Pacific Ocean; yet it is his lines which leap to our minds when we think of the 'wild surmise' felt by the indomitable explorer-conqueror from Spain when the vast new sea burst on his vision" (*Works,* 12:17–18).

283 The exposition: Hamilton Wright, "The Panama Pacific Exposition in Its Glorious Prime," *Overland Monthly and Out West*, Oct. 1915; Kevin Starr, *Americans and the California Dream, 1850–1915*, New York: Oxford, 1973, 294–306.

283 he scourged: *Letters*, 8:960–61. Highlights of speech are in *NYT*, July 22, 1915.

283 He mocked Andrew Carnegie's work: Wall, *Andrew Carnegie*, 1028–31.

283 "continuous mediation": James Weber Linn, *Jane Addams*, New York: D. Appleton Century, 1935, 297–307, 315.

284 "silly and base": *NYT*, April 16, 1915.

284 she mistook their cordiality: Seymour, *Intimate Papers of Colonel House*, 2:22.

284 " 'Is the Universe friendly?' ": Jane Addams, *The Long Road of Woman's Memory*, New York: Macmillan, 1916, 135.

284 "the just man armed": *Letters*, 8:928.

284 David Starr Jordan: James L. Abrahamson, "David Starr Jordan and American Antimilitarism," *Pacific Northwest Quarterly* 67:2 (April 1976), 76–87; David Starr Jordan to Will Irwin, Oct. 4, 1915, David Starr Jordan Papers.

284 "barbarian virtues": *Letters*, 2:1100.

284 "drowning": TR to Mary Cadwalader Jones, July 15, 1916, Derby Miscellaneous Papers.

285 "the kind of crawling thing": *Letters*, 8:993.

285 fighting on the Mexican border: Ibid., 1:108.

285 grander version: Ibid., 7:243–44.

285 This time: E.g., *Letters*, 8:947–48; TR to Lt. Col. Henry T. Allen, June 23, 1915; TR to Davis Goodrich, June 27, 1916; TR to Medill McCormick, June 30, 1916.

285 "Of course": TR to KR and BWR, June 16, 1915, TR Papers (TRC).

285 "If we fight Germany": TR to KR, June 26, 1915, TR Papers (TRC).

285 Plattsburg: Finnegan, *Against the Specter of a Dragon*, 64–70; *NYT*, Aug. 16 and Sept. 25, 1915.

285 "It is real work": TR to KR, July 10, 1915, KR-BWR Papers.

286 Archie and Quentin: *Letters*, 8:962–63; TR to KR, Aug. 20, 1915, and Feb. 24, 1916, TR Papers (TRC).

286 Dick: RD to ERD, Aug. 12, 16, and 20, 1915; Aug. 29, 1916, Derby Papers.

286 For Plattsburg's parade day: Finnegan, *Against the Specter of a Dragon*, 70.

286 probably alerted: *NYT*, Aug. 30, 1915.

286 At dusk: Ibid., Aug. 26, 1915; Hagedorn, *Leonard Wood*, 2:163–64.

287 Wilson was irked: Finnegan, *Against the Specter of a Dragon*, 69; *NYT*, Aug. 29, 1915.

287 "The only way to treat an adversary like Roosevelt": Quoted in Hagedorn, *The Bugle That Woke America*, 84.

287 No one should have been permitted: Hagedorn, *Leonard Wood*, 2:165–66.

288 Roosevelt hastened: *NYT*, Aug. 27, 1915.

288 stepped on the humbug: "National Defender for Politics Only," *Nation* 101 (Sept. 2, 1915), 280–81.

288 The Colonel tried to goad: *NYT*, Aug. 29, 1915.

288 Wood promised: Hagedorn, *Leonard Wood*, 2:165–67; *NYT*, Sept. 5, 1915.

288 "Father and Mother have had hard months": ERD to BWR, Oct. 1915, KR–BWR Papers.

288 "elegant row": *Letters*, 8:968–69.

288 Walter Hines Page: Page, diary, Jan. 12, 1916, Page Papers.

289 "But it makes you think": Villard to Fanny Garrison Villard, June 2, 1915, Villard Papers.

289 Wilson was inching: Link, *Woodrow Wilson and the Progressive Era*, 179–80.

289 The country needed stronger forces: *NYT*, Nov. 5 and 6, 1915.

289 "anti-moral, anti-social, and anti-democratic": Villard to WW, Oct. 20, 1915, Villard Papers.

289 "These things search the heart": WW to Villard, Nov. 2, 1915, Villard Papers.

289 William Jennings Bryan saw Wilson's shift: *NYT*, Nov. 6 and 7, 1915.

289 the notes to Germany were ineffectual: WW to Villard, Sept. 6, 1915, Villard Papers; Finnegan, *Against the Specter of a Dragon*, 39–40; *NYT*, Oct. 16, 1915, and Jan. 28, 29, and 30, 1916.

290 Roosevelt used Wilson's tour: *NYT*, Dec. 6, 1915, and Jan. 30 and 31, 1916; *Letters*, 8:1006, 1012.

290 "We like the Colonel": *NYT*, Feb. 1, 1916.

291 proclaiming their gratitude: *Letters*, 8:1007–8.

291 "The political cauldron": ER to KR, Feb. 14, 1916, KR-BWR Papers.

291 published reports: *NYT*, Dec. 20, 1915.

291 From Trinidad: *Letters*, 8:1024–26n. Charles Willis Thompson, a *New York Times* reporter close to TR during this period, insists that TR had no desire to run for president and involved himself in the 1916 campaign only to force Republicans to nominate a moderate. That is the story Roosevelt told Thompson and perhaps himself. See Thompson, *Presidents I've Known and Two Near Presidents*, 126–27, 130–31, 166–68, 201–9.

292 Root was incensed: Jessup, *Elihu Root*, 2:343–46, 349.

292 scrap till the end: Henry Lewis Stimson Diaries, II:31, 36–39.

292 "If a cut is to be healed": *Letters*, 8:1038.

292 Charles Evans Hughes: "The Man of the Rising Inflection," *Current Literature* 40 (Feb. 1906), 207–10; Ida M. Tarbell, "How about Hughes?" *American*, March 1908.

293 the magnetism of a potato: Abbott, ed., *Letters of Archie Butt*, 8.

293 "the bearded iceberg": *Letters*, 8:1078.

293 "the bearded lady": Leary, *Talks with T.R.*, 53.

293 ingrate: John J. Leary, Leary Papers, box 3, notebook 6.

293 Roosevelt himself had been saying: *NYT*, July 20 and Dec. 20, 1915.

293 Only half-amused: Walter Lippmann to Felix Frankfurter, May 6, 1916, Lippmann Papers.

293 privately sowing doubts: *Roosevelt–Lodge Letters*, 2:468; TR to George von L. Meyer, March 29, 1916.

293 Charles D. Hilles: Hilles to Harrison Gray Otis, May 17, 1916, Hilles Papers.

294 Hoping to advance the colonel: Garraty, *Right-Hand Man*, 332.

294 Annoyed by the endless tooting: WHT, "The Roosevelt Myth," *Cincinnati Times-Star* [April 1916].

294 In the Midwest: *NYT*, May 20 and 31 and June 1, 1916; "Colonel Roosevelt's New Crusade," *Literary Digest*, June 3, 1916, 1618–19; "The Roosevelt Platform," *Independent* 86 (May 29, 1916), 323–24; Frederick M. Davenport, "The Pre-Nomination Campaign," *Outlook* 112 (May 31, 1916), 386–89.

295 Roosevelt's last quest for the presidency: WAW, *Autobiography*, 520–26.

295 losing the German-Americans: Harbaugh, *Power and Responsibility*, 486. Richard D. Bartholdt to Charles D. Hilles, Feb. 23, 1916 (Hilles Papers), puts the number of German-American voters at 3 million. Ordinarily, 75 percent of them voted Republican, but in 1916, only 50 percent did, according to a *New York Times* analysis of the vote in the German-American precincts of several big cities (*NYT*, No. 9, 1916).

296 he proposed Lodge: Inside the front cover of the Theodore Roosevelt Collection's copy of Charles Grenfill Washburn's *Roosevelt and the 1912 Campaign* (Boston, 1926), there is an extract from a Dec. 10, 1926, letter in which Washburn reports that Edith Roosevelt had just told him that TR's affection for Lodge had prompted the suggestion. Washburn went on to speculate that TR's dislike of Hughes and appreciation of Lodge's support for TR on the second ballot at the 1916 convention also colored the decision.

296 Reconstructing the moment: WAW, *Autobiography*, 526–27.

296 Ickes: Harold Ickes, "Who Killed the Progressive Party?" *American Historical Review* 46:2 (Jan. 1941), 306–37.

SIXTEEN: BLACKBALLED

PAGE

298 the mourners: GP to H. L. Ickes, July 1, 1916, Ickes Papers; WAW to GP, June 23, 1916, WAW Papers; H. L. Ickes to GP, June 27, 1916, Ickes Papers.

298 "suffering the fate of all noble movements": TR to William Dudley Foulke, Aug. 1, 1916.

298 "lunatic fringe": *Letters*, 8:1122.

298 "much distressed": HCL to CRR, July 2, 1916, CRR Papers.

298 "I have been I believe emphatically right": TR to CRR, Oct. 5, 1916, CRR Papers.

299 "Well, the country wasn't in heroic mood!": *Letters*, 8:1063.

299 "This was my year": John J. Leary, Leary Papers, box 1, notebook 3.

299 "I could not allow": Ibid.

299 playing handmaiden: *NYT*, June 28, 1916.

299 The high authority: Leary, *Talks with T.R.*, 105–6.

299 Mexico was a horn of plenty: Bailey, A *Diplomatic History of the American People*, 602.

299 American investors: Gene Sessions, "American Reformers and the Mexican Revolution: Progressives and Woodrow Wilson's Policy in Mexico, 1913–1917," Ph.D. diss., American University, 1974, 5.

299 General John J. Pershing: Ibid., 41–44; James A. Sandos, "Pancho Villa and American Security: Woodrow Wilson's Mexican Diplomacy Reconsidered," *Journal of Latin American Studies*, 13:2 (Nov. 1981), 293–311.

300 "If Wilson is wise": John J. Leary, Leary Papers, box 3, notebook 2; Leary, *Talks with T.R.*, 105.

300 "There are some men, like Cleopatra": *NYT*, June 29, 1916.

300 he let it be known: *Letters*, 8:1087–88.

300 The War Department would not confirm: *NYT*, July 10, 1916.

300 "I shall do all I can": TR to W. R. Thayer, June 16, 1916.

301 Wilson half-hoped: Baker, *Woodrow Wilson*, 6:238.

301 Hughes opened his campaign: Schlesinger and Israel, eds., *American Presidential Elections*, 6:2294–2307.

301 *The New Republic*: "The Hughes Acceptance," *New Republic* 8 (Aug. 5, 1916), 4–5; Walter Lippmann to Felix Frankfurter, June 30, 1916, Lippmann Papers.

301 "slobbering": Winfield T. Durbin to Charles D. Hilles, Aug. 10, 1916, Hilles Papers.

301 "Our task is now a hard one": HJ to E. A. Van Valkenburg, Sept. 5, 1916, Van Valkenburg Papers; HJ to John Callan O'Laughlin, Sept. 9, 1916, O'Laughlin Papers. O'Laughlin wrote Hughes twice before the California trip to warn him away from the reactionaries (July 21 and Aug. 1, 1916, O'Laughlin Papers). Hughes's principal biographer, Merlo J. Pusey, insists there was no snub and blames Johnson for the misunderstanding, but Pusey fails to explain why Johnson, now a Republican and a Senate candidate, would have wished to harm the chances of the party's presidential nominee (Pusey, *Charles Evans Hughes*, 2 vols., New York: Macmillan, 1951, 1:335–49).

302 Hughes asked William Allen White: WAW, *Autobiography*, 529–30.

302 largest defense budget: *NYT*, Sept. 9, 1916.

302 prosperity would vanish: Ibid., Oct. 14, 1916.

302 And while Hughes had invited: "Hughes, Roosevelt, and Union," *Outlook* 113 (July 5, 1916), 532–34.

302 Roosevelt's eviscerations: Mowry, *Theodore Roosevelt and the Progressive Movement*, 361–62.

302 "take off his coat": *NYT*, Sept. 8, 1916.

302 "piddling reticence": Owen Wister to W. R. Thayer, Nov. 1, 1916, Thayer Papers.

302 "dish rag": *NYT*, Oct. 22, 1916.

302 "exquisitely unfit": TR, Essays and Speeches, Oct. 24, 1916, TR Papers (TRC).

303 the trip depressed him: John J. Leary, Leary Papers, box 3, notebook 6.

303 Shadow Lawn: TR, Leary Papers.

303 recent cables from . . . Berlin: Tumulty, *Woodrow Wilson as I Know Him*, 159.

303 "There is one choice against peace": Quoted in Schlesinger and Israel, eds., *American Presidential Elections*, 6:2266.

303 He had decided to resign if he lost: Baker, *Woodrow Wilson*, 6:292–93; Seymour, *The Intimate Papers of Colonel House*, 2:379–80.

304 Anxious: Schlesinger and Israel, eds., *American Presidential Elections*, 6:2268.

304 Manhattan laundry: *NYT*, Nov. 7, 1916.

304 Archie . . . cast his first ballot: ER, diary, Nov. 7, 1916.

304 "I hope to heaven": TR to QR, Nov. 7, 1916, TR Papers (TRC).

304 Hiram Johnson's 300,000-vote margin: HJ to Edward A. Van Valkenburg, Nov. 15, 1916, Van Valkenburg Papers.

304 albatross: WHT to Gus Karger, June 20, 1916, WHT Papers.

304 "I was sick at heart": TR to GP, Jan. 19, 1917.

304 In December: Seymour, *The Intimate Papers of Colonel House*, 2:398, 406.

305 as of February 1, 1917: Gilbert, *The First World War*, 306, 310–11.

305 Roosevelt praised the break: *NYT*, Feb. 4, 1917.

305 Given permission to raise his division: Roosevelt's correspondence with Baker and Wilson on the division is collected in *Works*, 19:187–217.

305 "Put on your worst clothes.": Quoted in E. Morris, *Theodore Rex*, 512.

305 "Do you care to inquire confidentially?": *Letters*, 8:1152.

305 Jusserand queried Paris: Jules Jusserand to TR, Feb. 19 and 23, 1917.

305 Sir Cecil Spring Rice: *Letters*, 8:1152n.

305 Graves' disease: Adams, *Letters of Henry Adams*, 6:622. The disease was diagnosed in 1913, shortly after Spring Rice was appointed ambassador to the United States. He offered to resign, but when the Foreign Office suggested he take a few months' rest instead, he acquiesced (Burton, *Cecil Spring Rice*, 147).

305 fear of spies: ERD to KR, May 16–18, 1915, KR-BWR Papers.

305 "no place for a nervous and delicate ambassador": Seymour, *The Intimate Papers of Colonel House*, 2:76–78, 100–2.

305 Robert Lansing: Burton, *Cecil Spring Rice*, 156; Mary R. Kihl, "A Failure of American Diplomacy," *Journal of American History* 57:3 (Dec. 1970), 651.

306 Zimmermann: S. L. A. Marshall, *World War I*, 275–77.

306 "I am as yet holding in": *Letters*, 8:1161–62.

306 "In view of the fact": TR's correspondence with Baker is in *Works*, 19:187–218.

306 Baker shared the letter: Newton D. Baker to WW, March 26, 1917.

306 "undergo the discipline": WW to Newton D. Baker, March 27, 1917, Baker Papers, reel 3.

307 "charming at a ladies' pink tea.": Quoted in Hagedorn, *Leonard Wood*, 1:423–24.

307 Wood's standing: Hagedorn, *Leonard Wood*, 2:200–3; *NYT*, March 27, 1917.

307 The president spent: Baker, *Woodrow Wilson*, 6:487–88, 503–4.

307 Wilson summoned: The correspondent was Frank I. Cobb of the *New York World*. Cobb's account is based on recollections six years after the fact. I have quoted from Baker, *Woodrow Wilson*, 6:506–7, and Arthur S. Link, "That Cobb Interview," *Journal of American History* 72:1 (June 1985), 7–17. Link, Wilson's most comprehensive biographer and editor of the most extensive edition of Wilson's papers, considered Cobb's account to be substantially accurate but raised doubts about several details, including Cobb's memory of the date of the interview. Cobb remembered going to the White House in the wee hours of April 2, the day Wilson delivered his war message to Congress. Link's examination of the evidence suggests that Cobb and Wilson had their meeting two weeks earlier.

308 Henry Adams: Adams, *Letters of Henry Adams*, 6:749.

308 the Capitol: *NYT* and *New York Tribune*, April 3, 1917.

308 La Follette: La Follette, *Autobiography*, 1:645–48.

308 Wilson, clasping his manuscript: *War Messages*, 65th Cong., 1st Sess., Senate Doc. No. 5, Serial No. 7264, Washington, 1917, 3–8 passim.

309 La Follette loudly cleared his throat: *New York Tribune*, April 3, 1917.

309 Henry Cabot Lodge: Link, *Wilson: Campaigns for Progressivism and Peace*, 426–27.

309 privately gloated: TR to Father John L. Belford, April 16, 1917.

309 Americans wanted a force: *NYT*, April 6, 1917.

309 war resolution's progress: Link, *Wilson: Campaigns for Progressivism and Peace*, 430.

309 Gambling: Leary, *Talks with T.R.*, 93–94.

310 The president and his secretary: Ibid., 97–98; *Letters*, 8:1173–74.

310 Wilson understood the colonel's wish: Hagedorn, *The Bugle That Woke America*, 126–27.

310 Roosevelt readily agreed: *NYT*, April 11, 1917.

310 "He is a great big boy": Quoted in Tumulty, *Woodrow Wilson as I Know Him*, 289.

310 He did not know what the president would decide: Leary, *Talks with T.R.*, 97.

311 When Secretary of War Baker turned up: Henry F. Pringle, interview of Newton D. Baker, Nov. 16, 1930, Pringle Papers.

311 Baker also relied: Tasker H. Bliss, notes (written sometime in 1917 between Roosevelt's April 22 letter to Baker and Baker's May 5 reply), Baker Papers, reel 1.

311 "I want to be able to say": Quoted in Hagedorn, *The Bugle That Woke America*, 130.

311 "Washington people": TR to WAW, May 5, 1917, WAW Papers.

312 "very unfortunate for his splendid reputation": Newton D. Baker to Gutzon Borglum, April 16, 1917, Baker Papers.

312 Senator William J. Stone: *Congressional Record*, 65th Cong., 1st Sess., 1917, 2451–54. Hiram Johnson wrote TR that he had hesitated to speak out because of the "peculiar and poisonous atmosphere of the Senate and its prejudices against new men butting in," but when Stone finished and was met with silence, Johnson could not let the insults pass. He added that he had said very little of what he felt, fearing that his indignation would cause him to lose his temper (HJ to TR, May 17, 1917, HJ Papers).

313 "The president need not fear me politically": Quoted in Hagedorn, *The Bugle That Woke America*, 134.

313 Wilson telegraphed his personal regrets: NYT, May 19, 1917.

313 Baker left it to Pershing: Henry F. Pringle, interview of Newton D. Baker, Nov. 16, 1930, Pringle Papers.

313 "This is a very exclusive war": Quoted in Hagedorn, *The Bugle That Woke America*, 136–37.

SEVENTEEN: WAR IN THE GARDEN OF EDEN
PAGE

317 impugned his honor: TR to HCL, July 11, 1914.

317 a physically timid man: The epithets that follow come from TR's 1914–18 letters, published and unpublished.

318 William Howard Taft, a former secretary of war: Pringle, *Taft*, 2:905; WHT to Newton D. Baker, April 8, 1917, Baker Papers, reel 2.

318 "including Theodore himself": HCL to Winthrop Astor Chanler, April 20, 1917, Chanler Papers.

318 An envoy: WW to Newton D. Baker, May 8, 1917, Baker Papers, reel 3.

318 Prime Minister Georges Clemenceau: *Letters*, 8:1201n.

318 Marshal Joseph Joffre: Warrington Dawson, typescript war diaries, 157–58, Dawson Papers.

318 "cautiously" recommended: *Letters*, 8:1290.

319 "it all means death": Felix Frankfurter to Newton D. Baker, Aug. 15, 1917, Baker Papers, reel 1.

319 blindness in one eye: TR to J. A. Mathews, Nov. 16, 1917.

319 arteriosclerosis: Leary, *Talks with T.R.*, 20.

319 Lodge wished: HCL to Winthrop Astor Chanler, April 20, 1917, Chanler Papers.

319 "I wished to render service": *Letters*, 8:1199–1200.

320 helped Quentin: Ibid.

320 Ted and Archie: Ibid., 8:1192–93; TR to Fanny Parsons, May 24, 1917, TR Papers (TRC).

320 "The big bear": *Letters*, 8:1199.

320 Kermit: TR to Cecil Spring Rice, June 19, 1917; TR to KR, June 10, 1917, KR-BWR Papers; *Letters*, 8:1201–3.

320 unfair to him and Archie: TR Jr. to TR, n.d. [summer 1917], TR Jr. Papers; EAR, *Day Before Yesterday*, 74.

320 "it would be infinitely harder": TR to ABR, Sept. 17, 1917, ABR Papers.

320 "If my sons are killed": TR to Maj. John Parker, May 28, 1917.

320 "I shall regard Wilson as responsible": TR to Arthur Hill, May 28, 1917.

321 pegged him as a captain: Edgar T. Collins to Adjutant General of the Army, July 31, 1917, TR Papers (TRC).

321 "it is what you would have done": KR to TR, Aug. 2, 1917, KR-BWR Papers; TR to KR, Aug. 23, 1917, KR-BWR Papers; *Works*, 11:6.

321 "fine fighting": KR to TR, Aug. 2, 1917, KR-BWR Papers.

321 "small and unhappy": KR to TR, June 4, 1917, KR-BWR Papers.

321 "I don't like war at all": KR to TR, June 19, 1917, KR-BWR Papers.

321 "I want to be the first in": Kermit was the first to sign Oyster Bay's draft register (TR to BWR, June 3, 1917, TR Papers [TRC]).

321 "you have an obligation": TR to KR, *Letters*, 8:1206–7.

321 tear-gassing: KR to TR, Aug. 2, 1917, KR-BWR Papers.

321 Kipling, whose only son: Harry Ricketts, *Rudyard Kipling*, New York: Carroll and Graf, 2000, 322–26; TR to KR, Sept. 1, 1917, TR Papers (TRC).

321 "hell and a half": Rudyard Kipling to KR, Aug. 2, 1917, KR-BWR Papers.

322 "Darling": EAR, *Day Before Yesterday*, 76–77.

322 In mid-August Belle and Kim: BWR to KR, Sept. 17, 1917, KR-BWR Papers.

322 Taranto: KR to BWR, Aug. 22, 1917, KR-BWR Papers; KR, *War in the Garden of Eden*, 22 (cited hereafter as *WGE*).

322 "A fine clean way to go out": KR to TR, Aug. 2, 1917, KR-BWR Papers. TR wrote a tribute to Selous for *The Outlook*, reprinted in *Works*, 11:292–96. Selous's World War I experiences are recounted in Stephen Taylor, *The Mighty Nimrod: A Life of Frederick Courtney Selous*, London: Collins, 1989, 277–92. On World War I in Africa, see Huxley, *White Man's Country*, 1:313; Fage and Oliver, eds., *The Cambridge History of Africa*, 77:664–70; Trzebinski, *The Kenya Pioneers*, 177–94. On Delamere see Dinesen, *Out of Africa*, 279. On Northrup and Florence McMillan, see Duignan and Gann, *The United States and Africa*, 215.

323 blistered hands: *WGE*, 7–8.

323 Edith assured Archie: ER to ABR, Aug. 31, 1917, ABR Papers.

323 TR told him the truth: TR to ABR, Aug. 23, 1917, TR Papers (TRC).

323 "bugle-call oratory": Secretary to Capt. C. Wiener, May 15, 1917; TR to Dr. C. R. Gaston, April 12, 1917.

323 "*completely* worn out": ERD to unknown, in a folder labeled "1918," Derby Papers.

324 footsteps on the veranda: ER to KR, Aug. 19, 1917, KR-BWR Papers.

324 "it is like becoming blind or deaf": ER to Warrington Dawson, Nov. 18, 1918, Dawson Papers.

324 a rainbow in the soul: ER to KR, April 8, 1912, KR-BWR Papers.

324 "I strongly feel that you are all coming home": ER to KR, Sept. 15, 1917, KR-BWR Papers.

324 "A sad state of affairs": ERD to unknown, in a folder labeled "1918," Derby Papers.

324 he wanted to scream: TR to ABR, Oct. 14, 1917.

324 unrefreshed: ER to ERD [1917], ER Letters.

324 *Kansas City Star*: Stout, ed., *Roosevelt in the Kansas City Star*, xxviii–xxx (cited hereafter as *Star*).

325 he rebuked the War Department: Ibid., 18–20.

325 "the Huns within our gates": Ibid., 49–52. He was paraphrasing a line from Kipling's book *For All We Have and Are* (London: Methuen, 1914).

325 declare war on Austria and Turkey: *Star*, 54–56.

325 "wholesale war in the future": Ibid., 112.

325 "the best way to treat Mr. Roosevelt": Quoted in Harbaugh, *Power and Responsibility*, 503.

325 "Like Caesar's Gaul": *Minneapolis Daily News* [Jan. 1918].

325 wrecking his chances: Harvey, "The Problem of Our Colonel," *North American Review* 206 (Nov. 1917), 677–79.

325 "windjammer": TR to ABR, Jan. 5, 1918, ABR Papers.

325 "elderly male Cassandra has-been": *Letters*, 8:1234.

325 boasting, for example: TR to H. Rider Haggard, June 1, 1917.

326 "only a twentieth": *Letters*, 8:1278.

326 "only because Wilson with cold spite": TR to Thomas Robins, Oct. 4, 1917.

326 "teetering along a ridge pole": TR to Ralph Stout, Dec. 20, 1917.

326 *Mitteleuropa*: Chickering, *Imperial Germany and the Great War*, 87.

326 The Germans coaxed the Turks: Gilbert, *Atlas of World War I*, 43; Gilbert, *The First World War*, 104–6, 121, 134–35, 211–12, 228, 244–45, 248.

327 "floated to victory": Ron Chernow, *Titan: The Life of John D. Rockefeller, Sr.*, New York: Random House, 1998, 617.

327 "hard nut to crack": WGE, 12, 17.

327 Assigned to the Royal Engineers: Ibid., 31.

327 snug little house: Gertrude Bell to Margaret Bell, Nov. 22, 1917, Gertrude Bell Project.

327 no real soldiering: KR to BWR, Dec. 5, 1917, KR-BWR Papers.

327 LAM car: KR to ERD, Nov. 17, 1917, Derby Papers; KR to BWR, Nov. 5 and 15, Dec. 17–18, 1917, KR-BWR Papers; WGE, 11–13, 43, 66, 69, 86, 88, 120.

328 they hit the floor: WGE, 44–54.

328 "and Mesopotamia's rather large": KR to BWR, Nov. 3–5, 1917, KR-BWR Papers.

328 1,800 British casualties: F. J. Moberly, *The Campaign in Mesopotamia, 1914–1918*, 4 vols., London: Imperial War Museum and Nashville: Battery Press [repr. 1923–1927], 1997, 4:84.

328 "Tommy takes his wounds": KR to BWR, Nov. 5, 1917, KR-BWR Papers.

328 white flags: KR to BWR, Nov. 3–5, 1917, KR-BWR Papers; WGE, 52–54.

328 "I am overjoyed": *Letters*, 8:1278–79.

328 the great weakness: WGE, 54.

328 "The Turks merely receded": A. J. Barker, *The Neglected War: Mesopotamia, 1914–1918*, London: Faber, 1967, 435.

329 "not a very profitable pastime": KR to BWR, Nov. 3–5 and Nov. 7–8, 1917, KR-BWR Papers.

329 He calmed his worries: KR to ERD, Nov. 17 and 28, 1917, Derby Papers.

329 British fears of revolt: WGE, 41, 68–69.

329 500,000 German troops: Chickering, *Imperial Germany and the Great War*, 178.

329 "a bitter mischance": TR to KR, *Letters*, 8:1258.

329 122 degrees in the shade: Barker (*Neglected War*, 417–19) puts the temperature in the sun at 160 degrees, a figure well above the world record of 136 degrees set in Libya in 1922, cited by the National Climatic Data Center.

329 TR counseled patience: *Letters*, 8:1258.

329 reinforce Lawrence and the Arabs: Barker, *Neglected War*, 472.

329 Kermit fought boredom: WGE, 31–37, 57–58, 71–72, 137–38; KR to BWR, Nov. 4 and 7, 1917, KR-BWR Papers.

330 Baghdad: KR to ERD, Nov. 17, 1917, Derby Papers; KR to BWR, Dec. 15, 1917, KR-BWR Papers; WGE, 26, 73–76, 96, 102–3.

330 Dame Gertrude Bell: Janet Wallach, *Desert Queen: The Extraordinary Life of Gertrude Bell*, New York: Doubleday, 1996, xxiv, 134–35, 160.

330 Kermit admired: KR to ERD, Nov. 28, 1917, Derby Papers.

330 "I'm being very nice to her": KR to BWR, Nov. 27, 1917, KR-BWR Papers; WGE, 68–69.

330 "My own feeling": TR to KR, July 3, 1917, TR Papers (TRC).

331 Willard's mission: Alice Pierce Flannigan, "The Role of Joseph E. Willard As American Ambassador to Spain (1913–1921)," Ph.D. diss., University of South Carolina, 1991, 9, 67, 82, 89, 91–104.

331 Spain was violating: BWR to KR, April 6, 1918, KR-BWR Papers.

331 U-boats: Gilbert, *Atlas of World War I*, 78–79; Ferrell, *Woodrow Wilson and World War I*, 35–36.

331 neurological thunderclap: Flannigan, "The Role of Joseph E. Willard As American Ambassador to Spain," 124–25.

331 English nursemaid: KR to BWR, Nov. 17, 1917, and BWR to KR, May 12, 1918, KR-BWR Papers.

331 "I have spent happier moments": WGE, 109, 116–17, 127.

332 he walked into a courtyard: Ibid., 122–23.

332 "four young girls": Ibid., 165.

332 fresco in the White House: Rudyard Kipling to TR, Sept. 3, 1918, KR-BWR Papers.

332 court-martial: Rudyard Kipling to KR, Sept. 3, 1918, KR-BWR Papers.

332 Military Cross: WGE, 116–19, 173–74; KR to ERD, Jan. 15, 1918, Derby Papers.

333 "an eerie sensation:" WGE, 109.

333 "had dug in well": Ibid., 46.

333 The snipers: Ibid., 117.

333 Kermit spoke of encounters: Ibid., 137–38, 142.

333 admired the stamina: Ibid., 19.

333 dervishes: Ibid., 39.

333 storks: Ibid., 177.

333 spring in the desert: Ibid., 131–32, 155–56.

333 it wouldn't take no angel: Ibid., 15.

334 "one great palm-grove": Ibid., 107.

334 TR smoothed his transition: TR to KR, April 4, 1918, TR Papers (TRC).

334 "foxily": Letters, 8:1316.

334 "between hay and grass": TR to ABR, June 2, 1918, ABR Papers.

334 The prospect . . . elated TR: TR to ABR, April 28 and June 2, 1918, ABR Papers.

334 "slaughter in France": BWR to KR, April 28, 1918, KR-BWR Papers.

EIGHTEEN: ON A VOLCANO

PAGE

335 mutinies: S. L. A. Marshall, World War I, 290; Gilbert, The First World War, 333–34; Keegan, The First World War, 329–31.

335 First Division: An American infantry division in 1917 was organized as follows: eight men to a squad, seven squads to a platoon, four platoons to a company, four companies to a battalion, three battalions and one company to a regiment, two regiments and a battalion to a brigade, and two brigades plus a battalion to a division. Around the edges were a field signal battalion, a medical contingent, and supply trains. With the sergeants and lieutenants who ran the platoons, the captains in charge of companies, the majors of the battalions, the colonels heading regiments, and a couple of brigadiers, the major general who commanded the division stood atop a 27,000-man pyramid. On the march with kitchen wagons and supply trucks, a division filled a twenty-mile stretch of road. The official strength of French and British divisions was about half that size, but by 1917, many were down to 5,000 or 6,000 men (Stallings, The Doughboys, 32–33; G. C. Marshall, Memoirs of My Services in the World War, 80; Gilbert, The First World War, 406). A fully staffed German division numbered 18,000 (S. L. A. Marshall, World War I, 44).

335 Only one in a hundred: Stallings, The Doughboys, 33.

336 Back at Harvard: Renehan, The Lion's Pride, 63–64; ABR, typescript of unpublished memoir, 52–53, 59A–61A, ABR Papers.

336 "a fault on the right side": TR to KR, Dec. 2, 1914; Feb. 17 and 22 and March 29, 1915, TR Papers (TRC).

338 Chaumont: Baedeker, Le Nord-est de la France (1914), 120–21.

338 easy target: Renehan, The Lion's Pride, 134–35; Eisenhower with Eisenhower, Yanks, 53.

338 sent only a single battalion: Ibid., 43.

338 one million of them: NYT, July 6, 1917; Pershing, My Experiences in the World War, 1:92.

338 "Lafayette, we are here": Francis Whiting Halsey, The Literary Digest History of the World War, 4:152–54.

338 homesick and heartsore: ERD to ABR, Sept. 14, 1917, ABR Papers.

338 a dressing-down: TR to TR Jr., Aug. 17, 1917; TR to ABR, Aug. 17, 1917.

339 Ted was confident: TR Jr. to TR, Sept. 19, 1917, TR Jr. Papers.

339 The Colonel retreated: TR to ABR, Sept. 19, 1917, ABR Papers.

339 nine months of training: Leonard P. Ayres, "Six Months of Training," The War with

Germany: A Statistical Summary. Available online at www.lib.byu.edu/~rdh/wwi/memoir/docs/statistics/statstc.htm. Diagram 13 of this chapter shows that the 1st Division had, on average, four months of training before reaching France and six more there before going into combat.

339 "Broomstick preparedness": *Star,* xxxv–xxxvi, 10–12.

339 "Ain't you got?": TR Jr. to EBR, Sept. 1917, TR Jr. Papers.

339 a war of movement: Pershing, *My Experiences in the World War,* 1:152.

339 To satisfy both theories: Bullard, *Personalities and Reminiscences of the War,* 102–3.

339 "worked overtime and all the time": G. C. Marshall, *Memoirs of My Services in the World War,* 18–20. Marshall was the army's chief of staff from 1939 to 1945 and served as secretary of state from 1947 to 1949. His idea for the reconstruction of Europe after World War II, the Marshall Plan, earned him a Nobel Prize in 1953.

339 Archie was a natural leader: TR to ABR, Oct. 14, 1917, ABR Papers.

339 "tall, proud program": Dawson, typescript war diaries (Sept. 13, 1917), 513, Dawson Papers.

340 hair cut to stubble: Dawson, ms. war diaries, vol. 5, part 2, 17–18, 23, Dawson Papers. Dawson mentions that many officers had their hair cut, and although Archie is not named, photographs show that he was among them.

340 "unspeakably dreadful women": Ibid. (June 20, 1918), 23.

340 wine cellar: Ibid. (June 18, 1918), 17–18.

340 almost gaunt: Dawson, typescript war diaries (Sept. 13, 1917), 517.

340 "Gracie has had a rough time": ABR to ERD, July 29 and Oct. 17, 1917, Derby Papers; ERD to ABR, Sept. 14, 1917, ABR Papers.

340 "a great thrill": ABR, "Lest We Forget," *Everybody's* 40 (May 1919), 9–16.

340 "We are fighting men": TR to ABR, Sept. 19, 1917, ABR Papers.

340 "foolish to refuse": TR to ABR, Jan. 20, 1918, ABR Papers.

340 into Lorraine: Pershing, *My Experiences in the World War,* 1:201–2. Their battalion and others went first to the Sommerviller sector in northeastern France, near the Rhine–Marne Canal (Society of the First Division, *History of the First Division During the World War,* 30, 32).

341 stole a bag of oats: ABR, "Lest We Forget," 9–16.

341 dropped dead: G. C. Marshall, *Memoirs of My Services in the World War,* 53.

341 coated with molasses: U.S. Congress, Committee on Military Affairs of the United States Senate, *Investigation of the War Department,* 7 vols., 65th Cong., 2nd Sess., Washington, D.C.: U.S. Government Printing Office, 1918, 2:646.

341 "The stocks of food on hand": Ayres, "Food, Clothing and Equipment," in *The War with Germany: A Statistical Summary.*

341 sent to the guardhouse: Corinna Lindon Smith, *Interesting People: Eighty Years with the Great and Near-Great,* Norman: University of Oklahoma, 1962, 309.

341 "Mud! Heavens above!": ABR to ERD, Nov. 5, 1917, Derby Papers.

341 replacements were too small: ABR, "Lest We Forget," 9–16; Senate Military Affairs Committee, *Investigation of the War Department,* 2:357, 606.

341 Valley Forge: G. C. Marshall, *Memoirs of My Services in the World War,* 18, 40, 53.

342 "slimy trenches": TR Jr., *Rank and File,* 74.

342 "the old man can still oblige": ER to ABR, Aug. 31, 1917, ABR Papers.

342 two hundred pairs of shoes: *Letters,* 8:1280, 1280n.

342 "A word of advice!": TR to ABR, Dec. 3, 1917, ABR Papers.

342 "Lord, how proud I am": TR to ABR, Dec. 30, 1917, ABR Papers.

342 "I write and speak with a freedom": TR to ABR, Dec. 28, 1917, ABR Papers.

343 "not to fool ourselves": *Star,* 10–12.

343 "I often feel fairly sick": TR to ABR, Jan. 20, 1918, ABR Papers.

343 the War Department had ceased to function: *NYT,* Jan. 22, 1918.

343 "lull the people": Senate Military Affairs Committee, *Investigation of the War Department,* 3:1728.

343 The conditions according to Baker: Ibid., 3:1605ff.

344 *The Nation* pounced on Roosevelt: *Nation* 105 (Nov. 15, 1917), 535.

344 But . . . Baker had hesitated: Daniel R. Beaver, "Newton D. Baker and the Genesis of the War Industries Board, 1917–1918," *Journal of American History*, 52:1 (June 1965), 45–46.

344 Freight trains: Senate Military Affairs Committee, *Investigation of the War Department*, 3:1725; Robert D. Cuff, "United States Mobilization and Railroad Transportation: Lessons in Coordination and Control, 1917–1945," *Journal of Military History* 53:1 (Jan. 1989), 33–50.

344 shortage of uniforms: Committee on Military Affairs, *Investigation of the War Department*, 2:625.

344 shirts and overcoats: Ibid., 2:357, 605.

344 without consulting the quartermaster general: Ibid., 2:637.

344 interminable debate: Ibid., 2:737–78; 3:1613, 1624–25; 4:1949.

345 Baker . . . Wadsworth: Ibid., 3:1694.

345 Augustus P. Gardner: Constance Lodge Gardner, ed., *Some Letters of Augustus Peabody Gardner*, Boston: Houghton Mifflin, 1920, 121–24.

345 Wilson lashed back: *NYT*, Jan. 22, 1918.

345 Roosevelt came to town: Ibid., Jan. 25, 1918.

346 Baker offered to resign: Beaver, "Newton D. Baker and the Genesis of the War Industries Board," 54–55.

346 Bernard Baruch: Ibid., 55–58.

346 Theodore feasted: *Letters*, 8:1276–77.

346 too extreme: TR to ABR, Feb. 2, 1918.

346 TR's medical condition: ERD to RD, Feb. 4, 6, and 7, 1918, and undated 1918 letter, Derby Papers; *NYT*, Feb. 8, 1918.

346 death of Sir Cecil Spring Rice: *NYT*, Feb. 15, 1918; Burton, *Cecil Spring Rice*, 194; TR to Cecil Spring Rice, April 22, 1913, and Feb. 9, 1915.

347 "like a lunatic duck": TR to EAR, Feb. 28, 1918.

347 reproving a dilatory government: *Star*, 105–9.

347 American people "suddenly realized": TR to ABR, Feb. 15, 1918, ABR Papers.

347 man in the arena: *Works*, 13:510.

348 the man who did things: Ibid., 3:29.

348 "a short, terrible, crashing fight": Bullard, *Personalities and Reminiscences of the War*, 148.

348 Once Ted's party: G. C. Marshall, *Memoirs of My Services in the World War*, 50–52.

348 "[T]he things they have staged": TR Jr. to TR [late Feb. 1918], TR Jr. Papers.

349 Combat would be a relief: ABR, "Lest We Forget," 9–16.

349 Archie was hit: Medical report, March 12, 1918; RD to GLR, March 12, 1918, ABR Papers.

349 acts of high courage: William Hints to ER, Oct. 15, 1919, ABR Papers.

349 he had asked that they be treated first: Frank Joyce to TR, n.d., ABR Papers.

349 *bors de combat*: TR Jr. to GLR, March 1918, ABR Papers.

349 "It is real Roosevelt luck": Ted to TR, March 1918, TR Jr. Papers.

349 An American citation: March 16, 1918, ABR Papers.

349 Dick Derby examined him: RD to GLR, March 1918, ABR Papers; RD to ERD, March 12, 15, and 17, 1918, Derby Papers; *Letters*, 8:1291–92.

350 Newspapermen . . . were turned away: *New York Herald*, n.d.

350 the folks would have other sources: *Letters*, 8:1300–1, ERD to RD, March 12, 1918, Derby Papers.

350 "all four of us filled the glasses": *Letters*, 8:1300–1.

350 TR's eyes were also shining: ERD to RD, March 12–13, 1918, Derby Papers.

350 "I cannot help feeling pride": *Letters*, 8:1336.

350 the family's friends understood: TR to ABR, March 17 and 24, 1918, ABR Papers.

350 "Tip-top": GWP to Edward A. Van Valkenburg, March 29, 1918, Van Valkenburg Papers.

350 chopping wood: ER to KR, March 24, 1918, KR-BWR Papers.

350 "a sturdy mite": TR to ABR, April 28, 1918, ABR Papers.

351 smooth the course for 1920: *Letters*, 8:1298–99, 1305–7.

351 "keeping whatever shreds of whatever influence": TR to HJ, March 19, 1918.

351 "This was an engagement": Unidentified newspaper clipping, datelined Portland, Me., March 28, 1918, Derby Papers.

351 The *Times* chided him: NYT, March 30, 1918.

351 "black infamy would be our portion": *Star*, 140–42. Although the column did not run in the *Star*, Stout included it in the collection.

352 "too far ahead of the people": Quoted in ERD to RD, March 28, 1918, Derby Papers.

352 "I am not dead sure": *Letters*, 8:1312–13.

352 "cruelly hard": ERD to RD, April 22, 1918, Derby Papers.

352 "I have ceased to fret": *Letters*, 8:1311.

352 He rejoiced: Ibid., 8:1311; TR to QR, April 8 and 28, 1918, TR Papers (TRC); TR to ABR, April 4 and 20, 1918, ABR Papers.

NINETEEN: THE YOUNG COLONEL AND THE OLD COLONEL

PAGE

353 Aerial bombing: NYT, March 13, 1918.

353 Henry Adams: Harold Dean Cater, ed., *Henry Adams and His Friends*, Boston: Houghton Mifflin, 1947, cvi.

353 Big Bertha's first assault: John Laffin, *A Western Front Companion*, London: Alan Sutton, 1994, 57; Gilbert, *The First World War*, 403.

353 relief work: Edith Wharton, ed., *The Book of the Homeless*, New York: Charles Scribner's Sons, 1916, xx–xxiv; Price, *The End of the Age of Innocence*, 65–66, 69, 103.

353 "jigging and sarabanding": Quoted in Lewis, *Edith Wharton*, 410.

354 General Erich von Ludendorff: Keegan, *The First World War*, 394; Eisenhower with Eisenhower, *Yanks*, 121–22; S. L. A. Marshall, *World War I*, 349–54.

354 "still merely an onlooker": *Star*, 120–22.

354 cable marked "Secret": Lord Derby to Lord Reading, March 23, 1918, copy in Newton D. Baker Papers, reel 5.

354 Ferdinand Foch: Gilbert, *The First World War*, 410.

354 Douglas Haig: Ibid., 414.

354 Pershing: S. L. A. Marshall (*World War I*, 360) doubts that Pershing uttered these sentences, noting that Pershing had no artillery, planes, or tanks and that the rhetorical style was not his. (Pershing was a famously inarticulate public speaker.) But if words did not come trippingly off Pershing's tongue in his meeting with Foch, they do represent what he meant to say. The paragraph was crafted soon afterward and appears in *United States Army in the World War, 1917–1919*, Washington, D.C.: U.S. Government Printing Office, 1948, 2:262.

355 "in at the death": TR Jr. to TR, April 23, 1918, TR Jr. Papers.

355 perfecting his battalion: TR Jr. to EAR, July 21, 1917, TR Jr. Papers.

355 "Major Roosevelt was not good company": Charles Ridgely, unpublished ms., 1924, TR Jr. Papers.

355 At Groton: ER to Elizabeth Emlen Roosevelt, Nov. 19, 1902, Elizabeth Roosevelt Papers.

355 freshman football team: Michael Pearlman, *To Make Democracy Safe for America: Patricians and Preparedness in the Progressive Era*, Urbana: University of Illinois, 1984, 69. Ted no doubt absorbed his father's belief that a college should produce men first, students second. TR once told a reporter that if any of his sons "would weigh a possible broken bone against the glory of being chosen to play on Harvard's football eleven, I would disinherit him" (Manchester *Union*, Feb. 11, 1895; copy in Pringle Papers, box 5).

355 fund his dream: EAR, *Day Before Yesterday*, 58.

355 ponchos: Warrington Dawson, war typescript diaries (Sept. 14, 1917), 513–14, Dawson Papers.

355 entitled to a two-day leave: EAR to GGA, Aug. 13, 1917, TR Jr. Papers.

355 giving orders in his sleep: EAR to ERD, Oct. 26, 1917, Derby Papers.

355 "Think of the young Colonel": EAR to GGA, Sept. 22, 1917.

356 he asked Eleanor to take a leave: EAR to GGA, March 13, 1918, TR Jr. Papers.

356 "we have to be so very careful": EAR to ERD, Sept. 1, 1917, Derby Papers.

356 Elizabeth Mills Reid: Harvey Cushing, diary, June 17, 1918, Cushing Papers; EAR to ER, Sept. 12, 1917, TR Jr. Papers.

356 Asked to say a word: EAR to GGA, Oct. 11, 1917.

356 Bargaining incognito: EAR to GGA, Oct. 17, 1917.

356 "That's right, chicken": Mary Louise Rochester Roderick, A Nightingale in the Trenches, New York: Vantage, 1966, 289.

356 Eleanor had joined the Y: EAR, Day Before Yesterday, 76–77; EAR to ERD, June 23 and Sept. 1, 1917, Derby Papers.

357 She settled near L'Etoile: The house stood at 39, rue de Villejust (now the rue Paul Valéry), close to the Avenue Foch.

357 the cook: Ibid., 78.

357 wholehearted and game: EAR to GGA, July 23 and Aug. 3, 1917, TR Jr. Papers; EAR, Day Before Yesterday, 80–81, 85; EAR to ERD, Sept. 1, 1917, Derby Papers.

357 By the war's end: Ralph Blanchard, "The History of the Y.M.C.A. in World War I." Available online at http://www.worldwar1.com/dbc/ymca.htm.

357 inauspicious start: Hutchinson, The Doctor in War, 416–17.

357 frigid, leaky barns: Society of the First Division, History of the First Division During the World War, 16.

357 Tales of pampering: G. C. Marshall, Memoirs of My Services in the World War, 21.

357 "a big job": EAR to GGA, April 4, 1918, TR Jr. Papers.

357 "bullet-proof jobs": Quoted in Star, 2–34.

358 "there have been frantic protests": TR to ABR, Oct. 30, 1917, ABR Papers.

358 Francis Bowes Sayre: EAR, Day Before Yesterday, 76–77.

358 The YMCA met the colonel: NYT, April 15 and May 30, 1918.

358 Archie's recovery: EAR, Day Before Yesterday, 95–96.

358 He was agitated: EAR to GGA, July 20, 1917, TR Jr. Papers.

358 "about the color of parchment": QR to FPW, April 30, 1918, QR Papers.

358 manufactured good cheer: RD to ERD, April 26 and May 10, 1918, Derby Papers.

358 "It's awful, at the hospital": Dawson, ms. war diaries, 5:2 (June 13, 1918), 14, Dawson Papers.

358 Archie still could not concentrate: Ibid., 6.

358 "useless civilians": Quoted in TR to GLR, June 19, 1918, ABR Papers.

358 General Pershing worried: Price, The End of the Age of Innocence, 139.

359 "behaved like a goat": ERD to QR, June 9, 1918, ABR Papers.

359 TR soon wired the sergeant: NYT, July 1, 1918.

359 "His only anxiety": TR to Henry Bordeaux, May 27, 1918.

359 In two long conversations: Dawson, ms. war diaries, 5:2 (June 13 and 18, 1918), Dawson Papers.

359 Two men were killed in the fight: Mr. Ross to Henry Krauss, June 6, 1918, ABR Papers.

359 Telling the story to Ted and Dick: RD to GLR, March 12, 1918, ABR Papers.

360 Eleanor and Quentin tried to soothe: ERD to BWR, n.d., KR-BWR Papers.

360 his sweet, thoughtful self: EAR to GGA, May 27 and June 1, 1918, TR Jr. Papers.

360 "rather cunning": TR Jr. to TR, April 23, 1918, TR Jr. Papers.

361 "the other old frumps": TR to QR, April 21, 1918.

361 pinch of sacrifice: NYT, April 3 and 19 and May 15 and 19, 1918.

361 $60,000: Letters, 8:1245.

361 $45,000: He received the money when he was still in the White House and suggested that Congress use it to create a commission to use the sum for the welfare of industrial workers. The commission came into being, but the funds were never disbursed. In 1918 TR arranged for the return of the money and allocated it to two dozen organizations and individuals for the aid of soldiers, refugees, and other victims of the war. The $4,000 he gave the YMCA and the $5,000 he sent Eleanor for her work with the Y came from the Nobel funds. Letters, 8:1344–45, 1363–66.

361 Carnegie Hall: NYT, May 8, 1918.

361 Trinity College: Ibid., June 17, 1918.

361 "He is aching": "Must We Go to Jail?" *North American Review* 206 (Nov. 1917), 676.

361 "Lord, how I wish": TR to ABR, Jan. 20, 1918, ABR Papers.

361 Opponents . . . ran the risk: Betty Houchin Winfield, "Two Commanders-in-Chief: Free Expression's Most Severe Tests," Research Paper R-7, Cambridge: Harvard University, 1992, 11.

361 "Brave men flinch": HJ to C. K. McClatchy, June 3, 1918, HJ Papers.

362 Albert S. Burleson: Donald Johnson, "Wilson, Burleson, and Censorship in the First World War," *Journal of Southern History*, 28:1 (Feb. 1962), 47–48.

362 Hiram Johnson was appalled: Dalton, *Theodore Roosevelt*, 489.

362 Roosevelt advocated harsh punishment: *Star*, 147–50.

362 "helpless small-fry": Quoted in Smith, *America Enters the World*, 542.

362 "the little country editor": George W. Norris to Edward A. Van Valkenburg, May 31, 1918, Van Valkenburg Papers.

362 Walter Lippmann: Lippmann to Col. House, Oct. 17, 1917 (copy in Baker Papers, reel 1); Steel, *Walter Lippmann and the American Century*, 124–26.

363 But the president overrode his censor only twice: Johnson, "Wilson, Burleson, and Censorship in the First World War," 54–56.

363 Almost daring: *Letters*, 8:1320–35; *NYT*, May 9, 12, and 26, 1918.

363 A postal inspector visited: *Star*, xli.

363 movement to expel Robert La Follette: *NYT*, Sept. 27 and 29 and Nov. 30, 1917; *Letters*, 8:1307–8.

363 "unhung traitor": TR to Ernest Smith, Aug. 31, 1917.

363 "polyglot boarding house": *NYT*, May 28, 1918.

363 Springfield, Ohio: John J. Leary, Leary Papers box 3, notebooks 8–9.

364 Milwaukee: Ibid.; *NYT*, May 30 and June 1, 1918.

364 Metropolitan Opera: *NYT*, Nov. 3, 1917.

364 In an open letter: H. C. Peterson and Gilbert C. Fite, *Opponents of War, 1917–1918*, Seattle: University of Washington, 1971, 18.

364 posses: *NYT*, Aug. 16, 1917, and Feb. 25, 1918.

364 "You can't even collect your thoughts": Quoted in Steel, *Walter Lippmann and the American Century*, 124.

365 National Security League: Robert D. Ward, "The Origin and Activities of the National Security League, 1914–1919," *Mississippi Valley Historical Review* 47:1 (June 1960), 51–65; *NYT*, May 28 and July 29, 1917.

365 Columbia University: Peterson and Fite, *Opponents of War*, 103–4.

365 Three Mennonite churches: Gerlof D. Homan, "The Burning of the Mennonite Church, Fairview, Michigan, in 1918," *Mennonite Quarterly Review* 64 (April 1990), 99–100, 112.

365 loyalty oaths: TR to William T. Hornaday, Nov. 25, 1917.

365 "veiled treason": *NYT*, Aug. 16 and 18, 1917.

365 conscientious objectors: Ibid., March 13, 1917.

365 Aeschylus: Johnson said, "When war is declared, truth is the first casualty." The Aeschylus version in most English translations is, "In war, truth is the first casualty."

365 Amos Pinchot: *NYT*, March 13, 1917.

365 After the election of 1916: Walter Lippmann, "A Progressive's View of the Election," *Yale Review*, 6:2 (Jan. 1917), 230–32.

366 TR's reunion with Taft: Leary, *Talks with T.R.*, 198–205.

367 A year earlier Roosevelt was still regretting: TR to HJ, April 16, 1917, HJ Papers.

367 Taft in 1917 had scoffed: John J. Leary, Leary Papers, box 3, notebooks 8–9.

367 Roosevelt's exposures: Pringle, *Taft*, 2:907, 912, 915–18.

367 Taft had been meaning: Gus Karger, memorandum of conversation, March 6, 1918, Taft-Karger Manuscripts, Cincinnati Historical Society.

367 The target was Cantigny: Society of the First Division, *History of the First Division During the World War*, 77; Stallings, *The Doughboys*, 66.

367 Pershing met with his officers: *NYT*, May 29, 1918.

367 retributive mood: Stallings, *The Doughboys*, 57.

368 "Life was sheer hell": Dos Passos, *Mr. Wilson's War*, Garden City, N.Y.: Doubleday, 1962, 363–64.

368 Trees sprouted green: TR Jr., *Rank and File*, 75.

368 swiftly took the hill: NYT, May 29 and 30, 1918.

368 Two hundred Americans were killed: Society of the First Division, *History of the First Division During the World War*, 86.

368 "a product of French and British instruction": *Times* (London), May 30, 1918.

368 England and France still doubted: Gilbert, *The First World War*, 416.

368 In a rueful joke: Ferrell, *Woodrow Wilson and World War I*, 118–19.

368 close enough for Eleanor and Archie to hear: EAR, *Day Before Yesterday*, 97; EAR to GGA, June 1, 1918, TR Jr. Papers.

368 Ted turned up: EAR to GGA, May 6 and June 4, 1918, TR Jr. Papers; EAR, *Day Before Yesterday*, 78–83, 97–99.

369 The old Colonel: *Letters*, 8:1343; TR to John J. Pershing, June 14, 1918.

369 "I wish to Heavens": TR to James G. Harbord, April 16, 1918.

369 "sick to death of talking": TR to Frank McCoy, June 5, 1918.

369 When an admirer urged him: TR to William M. Calder, July 25, 1918.

369 Roosevelt occasionally received invitations: TR to TR Jr., Dec. 4, 1917.

370 Hannibal: *Letters*, 8:1229; Plutarch, *The Lives of the Noble Grecians and Romans*, New York: Modern Library, n.d., 463–65.

370 "but I am not allowed to": TR to Frederick S. Oliver, June 7, 1918.

370 Wood came to believe: Leonard Wood to CRR, Nov. 14, 1918, CRR Papers.

370 Roosevelt blamed Wilson: TR to H. L. Stimson, Sept. 3, 1918.

370 cordiality to Charles Evans Hughes: John Callan O'Laughlin to Leonard Wood, July 15, 1916, O'Laughlin Papers. The story of Wood's rejection is told judiciously in Palmer, *Newton D. Baker*, 1:232–42, and Tumulty, *Woodrow Wilson as I Know Him*, 289–93. Both authors present strong evidence that the decision was Pershing's.

370 decided to speak boldly: ERD to RD, March 22, 1918, Derby Papers.

371 "a distinct benefit to the cause of Germany": *Star*, 160–62.

371 bitterness: TR to H. L. Stimson, June 5, 1918.

371 "it is the eleventh hour": TR to Frederick S. Oliver, June 7, 1918.

TWENTY: A BOY INSPIRED

Unless otherwise noted, the letters cited below are from the Quentin Roosevelt Papers in the Theodore Roosevelt Collection.

PAGE

372 She sensibly intervened: ER to KR, May 19, 1918, KR-BWR Papers.

372 They would be alone: ER to CRR, June 16, 1918, CRR Papers.

372 "Speechmaking at a time like the present": *Letters*, 8:1339–40.

372 Kermit was traveling: KR to ERD, June 14, 1918, Derby Papers.

372 malaria: TR to BWR, July 1, 1918, TR Papers (TRC).

372 675,000 troops: Keegan, *The First World War*, 408.

373 Ted orchestrated: EAR, *Day Before Yesterday*, 99; Society of the First Division, *History of the First Division During the World War*, 91–92; American Battle Monuments Commission, *1st Division: Summary of Operations in the World War*, Washington, D.C.: U.S. Government Printing Office, 1944, 17.

373 inexperienced doctors: Cushing, *From a Surgeon's Journal*, 384–85.

373 "He realizes that it is best": EAR to GGA, June 18 and Aug. 5, 1918, TR Jr. Papers; EAR, *Day Before Yesterday*, 100.

373 "It has been very hard on Quentin": TR to ABR, June 2, 1918, ABR Papers.

373 "somewhat bold": Pershing, *My Experiences in the World War*, 1:161.

373 The House and the Senate: Palmer, *Newton D. Baker*, 2:173–98; *Philadelphia North American*, March 27, 1918.

373 Gutzon Borglum: *Letters*, 8:1319. Borglum, infuriated by Wilson's decision to turn to

Hughes, had his revenge when he sculpted Mount Rushmore. It is Roosevelt, not Wilson, who shares the space with the presidential trinity of Washington, Jefferson, and Lincoln.

374 The aerial fighting began in earnest: Frandsen, *Hat in the Ring: The Birth of American Air Power in the Great War*, Washington, D.C.: Smithsonian, 2003, 159.

374 "I am thrilled": TR to QR, June 19, 1918.

374 Edith, who felt no thrill: ER to QR, June 16, 1918, ABR Papers; ER to CRR, June 16, 1918, CRR Papers.

374 piglet: *Letters*, 6:1387.

374 baseball: Ibid., 6:971, 1004, 1030.

374 "smudgy and ink-splashed": Cecilia P. Dulin, reminiscences, QR Papers.

374 His adolescent defiance: L. M. Blackford to Mr. Mason, May 21, 1909.

374 lamp shade on his head: Wilfred S. Lewis to TR, Aug. 10, 1918.

375 "the never-to-be-sufficiently-anathematized Endicott Peabody": QR to KR, Feb. 23, 1916, KR-BWR Papers.

375 "disapproved of me strenuously": QR to ERD, March 9, 1914, Derby Papers.

375 At ten Quentin was designing airships: KR, ed., *Quentin Roosevelt*, 1–2.

375 motorcycles: ER to KR, Jan. 12, 1913, KR-BWR Papers.

375 study mathematics: QR to KR, Feb. 23, 1916.

375 "Wild excitement!": QR to FPW [April 1917].

375 Gertrude Vanderbilt Whitney: *Dictionary of American Biography*; *NYT*, April 18, 1942.

375 Harry Payne Whitney: *NYT*, Oct. 27, 1930.

375 her father's child: Thomas Fleming, "Their Golden Glory," *MHQ* 1994 6(4):85.

375 Her romance with Quentin: Ibid.

376 grouse shoots: *NYT*, Aug. 21, 1912.

376 "out-door-sport wing": *Letters*, 8:1276.

376 "I'm glad I did it": QR to FPW, May 28, 1917.

376 Edith, setting aside her prejudice: ER to FPW, July 28, 1917.

376 "a perfect trump": *Letters*, 8:1232.

376 "the greatest of all kinds of happiness": TR to FPW, July 28, 1917, Derby Miscellaneous Papers.

376 Issoudun: Frandsen, *Hat in the Ring*, 38; Charles Woolley with Bill Crawford, *Echoes of Eagles: A Son's Search for His Father and the Legacy of America's First Fighter Pilots*, New York: Norton, 2003, 54; James J. Cooke, *The U.S. Air Service in the Great War, 1917–1919*, Westport, Conn.: Praeger, 1996, 20, 87.

376 their own beds: Hamilton Coolidge, *Letters of an American Airman*, Boston: privately printed, 1919, 25–26.

376 "dealing with a huge shipment": QR to FPW, Aug. 20, 1917.

377 "easily the most popular man": Edward V. Rickenbacker, *Fighting the Flying Circus*, New York: Frederick A. Stokes, 1919, 55.

377 "We boys": Unidentified newspaper clipping.

377 "Well, you know it's rather up to us": "Quentin Roosevelt—An Incident," *Outlook* 119 (Aug. 28, 1918), 648.

377 the likes of Edith Wharton: Edith Wharton to TR, July 23, 1918.

377 Having maneuvered: QR to FPW, May 1918.

377 "father's pull": QR to ABR [Dec. 1917], ABR Papers; TR to QR, Sept. 17, 1917, TR Papers (TRC).

377 proficiency in French: To the amazement of one of his comrades, Quentin spoke the language "like a frog" (enc. with E. T. Shelly to TR, July 20, 1918).

377 rove the countryside: QR to ERD, Sept. 7, 1917.

377 Bourges: QR to FPW, Aug. 25, 1917.

378 Chartres: QR to FPW [c. Oct. 30, 1917].

378 midnight mass . . . Notre Dame des Victoires: QR to FPW, Sept. 13, 1917, and Jan. 7, 1918.

378 Religion had meant little: QR to FPW, Dec. 30, 1917.

378 Nieuport 27s: QR to FPW, Sept. 5, Oct. 20, Dec. 5, and Dec. 22, 1917.

378 easily caught fire: Coolidge, *Letters of an American Airman*, 182; Lucien Thayer, *America's First Eagles: The Official History of the U.S. Air Service, A.E.F. (1917–1918)*; Donald Joseph McGee and Joseph Bender, eds., San Jose, Calif.: R. James Bender, 1983, 77–78.

378 "the whole thing was in flames": QR to FPW, Dec. 5, 1917. Another American aviator said that chunks of mud thrown up during landings broke "wagon loads of propellers" (Alan H. Nichols, *Letters Home from the Lafayette Flying Corps*, Nancy Nichols, ed., San Francisco: J. D. Huff, 1993, 200).

378 a few flares: QR to FPW, Dec. 22, 1917.

378 fatalities: On one disturbing day, he saw three pilots crash to their deaths (QR to FPW, May 18, 1918).

378 open cockpit: The state-of-the-art oxygen tanks were too heavy and the masks too cumbersome for use in flight (Hutchinson, *The Doctor in War*, 398).

378 headaches: QR to ERD, July 1, 1918.

378 lightweight suit: William Mitchell, *Memoirs of World War I*, New York: Random House, 1960, 173–74.

378 Quentin wore: QR to BWR, Jan. 7, 1918, KR-BWR Papers; QR to FPW, Dec. 5 and 22, 1917.

378 heavy cold: Coolidge, *Letters of an American Airman*, 109.

378 "I don't see how the angels stand it": QR to FPW, Dec. 5, 1917.

379 Canada: *Letters*, 8:1256–57; FPW to QR, postmarked Nov. 11, 1917; *NYT*, Nov. 27, 1917. TR had been invited to speak in Canada in 1915, when he and Edith traveled through the Canadian Rockies en route to the Panama-Pacific Exposition in San Francisco. He had declined the invitations because of his differences with the official U.S. position on the war. As he explained to his friend Cecil Spring Rice before the trip, "it would not be possible for me to speak on the subject outside of my own country; and of course it would be folly to speak on other subjects when this is the one subject in everyone's mind," (TR to Cecil Spring Rice, May 1, 1915).

379 pin medals on Boy Scouts: *NYT*, Nov. 5, 16, and 23, 1917.

379 Wilson refused him one out of fear: TR to Henry J. Allen, May 24, 1917.

379 two scenarios: ERD to RD, Dec. 4, 1917, Derby Papers.

380 "a very radical democrat": *Letters*, 8:1252–54.

380 John Purroy Mitchel: Ibid., 8:1249–50.

380 Quentin wrote fewer and fewer letters: QR to ERD, Feb. 1 and 2, 1918.

380 TR gave him the lash: TR to QR, Dec. 24, 1917, TR Papers (TRC); QR to FPW, Jan. 2, 1918.

380 consoling himself: ERD to QR, Jan. 18, 1918.

380 Flattened by the pneumonia: QR to FPW, Dec. 28, 1917; Jan. 27, Feb. 2 and 4, 1918.

381 "all the little worries": QR to FPW, Jan. 15, 1918.

381 six hundred cadets: QR to FPW, Dec. 17, 1917.

381 Lac de Cazaux: Woolley with Crawford, *Echoes of Eagles*, 83–86, 91.

381 Billeted in a hotel on the coast: QR to FPW, Feb. 28, 1918.

381 For all the sensible reasons: QR to FPW, Sept. 9, 1917.

381 Fouf . . . was longing for marriage: ERD to QR, Jan. 18, 1918, QR Papers.

381 no reason to wait: *Letters*, 8:1301–2; TR to QR, March 24, 1918, TR Papers (TRC). Quentin never expressed reservations about marriage, and with Eleanor's encouragement he occasionally indulged in fantasies of Fouf's coming to Paris or his using his first long leave, whenever it came, to go home for a wedding (QR to FPW, Sept. 13 and Nov. 15, 1917). On some days he pictured taking Fouf to Cartier in Paris to pick out wedding rings (QR to FPW, Feb. 13, 1918), but on others he doubted that a young woman as sheltered as Fouf could manage on her own in a country undone by war (QR to ERD, n.d.): He felt obliged to resist his dreams for fear that he would be killed, "or worse still," he said, "wounded in some ghastly fashion as I have seen—so that for the rest of my life I could be but a cripple, a helpless useless chain to which you were tied" (QR to FPW, Sept. 9, 1917).

382 "I used to think": QR to FPW, March 27, 1918.

382 "my flying went on the bum": QR to FPW, April 30, 1918; KR, ed., *Quentin Roosevelt*, 21, 27, 132–35.

382   Fouf told her parents: ER to QR, May 5, 1918, QR Papers.

382   a "wicked" decision: *Letters*, 8:1347.

382   The news was crushing: QR to FPW, June 2, 1918.

382   "SO SORRY": QR to FPW, June 16, 1918.

382   "[W]e'll be strangers": QR to ER, June 25, 1918.

383   "It is immensely to be regretted": *Letters*, 8:1336–37.

383   Maria Bochkareva: Ibid., 8:1364–65; *Star*, 162–65.

383   Wilson had held off: Link, ed., *Papers of Woodrow Wilson*, 48:179, 398–99; 49:170–72; Eugene P. Trani, "Woodrow Wilson and the Decision to Intervene in Russia," *Journal of Modern History* 48 (Sept. 1976), 445, 458–60.

384   "puling" and phony: Quoted in Pringle, *Taft*, 2:909–10.

384   a useless half-measure: *Star*, 162–65.

384   "efficient aid along any line": *Works*, 19:345.

384   an expensive lesson in airpower: Frandsen, *Hat in the Ring*, 158–59.

384   Dr. Richard Derby: RD to ERD, n.d. and June 7, 9, 11, 13, 16, 19, and 25, 1918, Derby Papers.

385   First Pursuit Group: Frandsen, *Hat in the Ring*, 12–13, 159.

385   midnight bombing raid: QR to FPW, June 29, 1918.

385   ruined gardens: Woolley with Crawford, *Echoes of Eagles*, 130.

385   the war was an interruption: QR to FPW, July 1, 1918.

385   Vaux: Frandsen, *Hat in the Ring*, 165; QR to ER, June 25, 1918; QR to FPW, July 3, 1918.

386   appointed . . . flight commander: Rickenbacker, *Fighting the Flying Circus*, 55–56.

386   the worst month of the war: James J. Hudson, *Hostile Skies: A Combat History of the American Air Service in World War I*, Syracuse: Syracuse University, 1968, 95–97; Thayer, *America's First Eagles*, 162–66.

386   The Americans were up against: Mitchell, *Memoirs of World War I*, 209; Hudson, *Hostile Skies*, 95–97.

386   The Nieuport 28: Woolley with Crawford, *Echoes of Eagles*, 104–5; Frandsen, *Hat in the Ring*, 110–11.

387   thirty-six of sixty-eight: Rickenbacker, *Fighting the Flying Circus*, 193.

387   "the suicide club": Harold Buckley, *Squadron 95*, Paris: Obelisk, 1933, 84–85.

387   "and there about 200 meters above me": QR to FPW, July 6, 1918.

387   "The last of the lion's brood has been blooded!": TR to KR, July 13, 1918, KR-BWR Papers.

387   "fool around": QR to TR, n.d. [July 10 or 11, 1918], TR Papers (TRC).

387   "scared perfectly green": QR to FPW, July 11, 1918.

388   "Why do you single me out?": Quoted in Woolley with Crawford, *Echoes of Eagles*, 141.

388   "Whatever now befalls Quentin": *Letters*, 8:1351.

388   Quentin went to Paris: EAR, *Day Before Yesterday*, 100.

388   his orders: Headquarters, 95th Aero Squadron, First Pursuit Group, Special Order No. 26, July 13, 1918, ABR Papers; KR, ed., *Quentin Roosevelt*, 165.

388   The Germans planned to strike at 12:10 A.M.: S. L. A. Marshall, *World War I*, 395.

388   the parade set off: EAR to GGA, July 15, 1918, TR Jr. Papers; *NYT*, July 14 and 15, 1918.

388   "Paris is simply crazy about Americans now": EAR to GGA, July 15, 1918, TR Jr. Papers.

388   The million-man AEF: S. L. A. Marshall, *World War I*, 386.

389   Dick Derby had heard: RD to ERD, July 23 and Aug. 10, 1918, Derby Papers.

389   "We dove on them": The pilot, Jim Knowles, gave this account in an interview conducted decades later. With the aid of his logbook, he was able to reconstruct the flight in great detail. Quoted in Woolley with Crawford, *Echoes of Eagles*, 143–44.

389   When the pilots reassembled: Buckley, *Squadron 95*, 95–99.

389   Phil Roosevelt: EAR to GGA, July 19, 1918, TR Jr. Papers.

389   Just before midnight: S. L. A. Marshall, *World War I*, 395; *NYT*, July 16, 1918.

390   The first word of trouble: Hagedorn, *The Roosevelt Family of Sagamore Hill*, 412.

390   After telephoning Fouf: Thomas Fleming, "Their Golden Glory," 93.

390   Definitive word: ER to KR, July 21, 1918, KR-BWR Papers.

390 "Am greatly distressed": Link, ed., *Papers of Woodrow Wilson*, 49:37.

390 "I thank you for your courtesy": Ibid., 49:50–51.

390 two bullet wounds: translation of an information sheet from German army headquarters, July 24, 1918, TR Jr. Papers.

391 a cross: Woolley with Crawford, *Echoes of Eagles*, 145; *NYT*, July 22, 1918.

391 "To feel that one has inspired a boy": *Letters*, 8:1355.

391 "and it is infinitely sad": TR to William B. Crawford, July 24, 1918.

TWENTY-ONE: WHILE DARING GREATLY
PAGE

392 Saratoga: Robinson, *My Brother Theodore Roosevelt*, 344–47.

392 declining even to wear black: ERD to RD, July 21, 1918, Derby Papers.

392 ostentatious: Stephane Audoin-Rouzeau and Annette Becker, *14–18: Understanding the Great War*, New York: Hill and Wang, 2002, 179.

392 "with all my heart and soul": *NYT*, Aug. 19, 1918.

393 "nothing more foolish": TR to CRR, Aug. 3, 1918, TR Papers (TRC).

393 As respite: TR to KR, July 21, 1918, TR Papers (TRC).

393 *Lavengro*: Published in 1851, the novel is available online at http://www.2.cddc.vt.edu/Gutenberg/etext96/lvgro10.txt. Kermit mentions TR's fondness for these lines in *The Long Trail*, 39–40.

393 a house of cards: ER to KR, July 28, 1918, KR-BWR Papers.

393 Fouf came often: TR to BWR, Aug. 11, 1918, TR Papers (TRC). In 1920 Flora Whitney married Roderick Tower. Financier, former aviator, and son of President Theodore Roosevelt's ambassador to Russia, Tower was also a philanderer. The couple had two children, and Flora divorced him in 1925. Two years later she was married to George MacCulloch Miller, an architect and painter, a marriage that produced two more children and lasted until his death, in 1972. Like her mother, Flora took up sculpture, presided over the Whitney Museum, and was a generous philanthropist in the arts and elsewhere. She died in 1986, at the age of eighty-eight (*NYT*, April 30, 1920; Aug. 7, 1925; Feb. 24, 1927; Sept. 12, 1972; July 19, 1986).

393 Ted had been wounded: TR to TR Jr., July 21, 1918, TR Jr. Papers; *NYT*, July 24, 1918.

393 "Mother says very often": ERD to RD, July 21 and 22, 1918, Derby Papers.

394 Ethel's rented cottage: Elizabeth Prescott Lawrence, "Islesboro, A Bit of the Maine Coast," unidentified magazine article, WHT Papers, reel 21.

394 Richard . . . Edie: TR to CRR, Aug. 3 and 10, 1918, TR Papers (TRC).

394 TR gave a short talk: *NYT*, Aug. 5, 1918.

394 Edith and Ethel stayed home: ER to KR, Aug. 4, 1918, KR-BWR Papers.

394 "fell in battle in a fair fight": ER to KR, Aug. 18, 1918, KR-BWR Papers.

394 "[Y]ou get used to all that": Coolidge, *Letters of an American Airman*, 172–75.

394 Dick . . . in danger: RD to ERD, July 23, 1918, Derby Papers.

394 influenza: RD to ERD, Oct. 15, 1918, Derby Papers. More than 60,000 of the 110,000 Americans who died in the war were victims of disease, principally influenza (Eisenhower with Eisenhower, *Yanks*, 288).

395 "I do not intend": RD to ERD, Aug. 10, 1918, Derby Papers.

395 "elderly swivel-chair military gentry": TR to QR, March 24, 1918, TRC.

395 "From now on": *Star*, 183–86.

395 without consulting the Allies: Steel, *Walter Lippmann and the American Century*, 136.

395 Clemenceau frostily noted: A. J. P. Taylor, *The First World War: An Illustrated History*, New York: Perigee, 1972, 206.

395 Senator Lodge gave him an opening: Highlights of Lodge's speech in *NYT*, Aug. 24, 1918. The articles TR wrote in the fall of 1918 on the challenges of peacemaking appear in *Star*, 209–10, 239–40, and *Works*, 19:365–68.

396 "a scrap of paper": *Times* (London), Aug. 29, 1914.

396 "Fourteen Scraps of Paper": *Star*, 248–50.

396 "The man who loves other countries": *Works*, 19:370–74.

396 Archie arrived: ER, diary, Sept. 5, 1918.
396 "exactly his old self": TR to RD, Sept. 12, 1918, TR Papers (TRC).
396 Edith began to fear: ER to ERD, n.d., Derby Papers.
396 apartment near Roosevelt Hospital: ER to BWR, Sept. 22, 1918, KR-BWR Papers; ER to KR, Sept. 22, 1918, KR-BWR Papers; TR to TR Jr. and EAR, Sept. 21, 1918, TR Jr. Papers.
396 The Colonel showed him off: ER to BWR, Sept. 12, 1918.
396 strangers who recognized him: ER to ERD, n.d., Derby Papers.
396 At a Liberty Loan rally: ERD to RD, Oct. 4, 1918, Derby Papers.
397 pair of swindlers: NYT, Jan. 6, 1919.
397 crutches and canes: EAR, Day Before Yesterday, 102–3; EAR to GGA, Sept. 13, 1918, TR Jr. Papers.
397 The long-delayed promotion to lieutenant colonel: EAR, Day Before Yesterday, 107–9, 116; TR to TR Jr. and EAR, Sept. 21, 1918, TR Jr. Papers.
397 lost all its field officers: Regimental Adjutant, The Twenty-sixth Infantry in France, Montabaur-Frankfurt, Germany, 1919, 27. Available online at http://www.bluespader.org/History WWI.pdf.
397 "It makes no difference": TR Jr. to TR, Sept. 16, 1918, TR Jr. Papers.
397 TR chronicled the advance of autumn: TR to KR, Sept. 13 and 26, 1918, TR Papers (TRC); TR to TR Jr. and EAR, Sept. 26, 1918, TR Jr. Papers.
397 "hideous talky-talky trip": TR to KR and BWR, Sept. 26, 1918, TR Papers (TRC).
397 Henry Stimson: Henry Lewis Stimson Diaries, III:338.
397 suspected he was ill: Star, xliii.
397 His mind drifted: Wister, Roosevelt, 370.
397 his eyes went blank: Robinson, My Brother Theodore Roosevelt, 346.
397 for the first time he fretted: TR to EAR and TR Jr., Aug. 21, 1918, TR Papers.
398 "sickening feeling": Sonya Levien, unpublished ms., Oct. 11, 1957, Levien Papers.
398 "for it somehow gives me the right": Letters, 8:1382–83.
398 rowing regularly: Leary, Talks with T.R., 304.
398 Carnegie Hall: NYT, Oct. 29, 1918, and Works, 19:389–95. Wilson's "Politics is adjourned" speech and his election eve plea are in NYT, May 28 and Oct. 26, 1918, respectively.
399 On election day: NYT, Nov. 7, 1918.
399 Edith, voting for the first time: Dalton, Theodore Roosevelt, 510.
399 "Wilson rebuked": ER, Nov. 6, 1918, ER Diaries.
399 Kipling: Letters, 8:1403–6.
399 "without any pussyfooting": TR to Julian Street, Nov. 2, 1918.
399 swept into a current: BWR to KR, Nov. 11, 1918, KR-BWR Papers.
399 "the day he made possible": BWR to ER, Nov. 11, 1918, KR-BWR Papers.
399 "utterly dazed": RD to ERD, Nov. 15, 1918, Derby Papers.
400 117,000 American casualties: S. L. A. Marshall, World War I, 442.
400 Most of the 53,000: Eisenhower with Eisenhower, Yanks, 288.
400 infinity of ruin: EAR to GGA, Nov. 14, 1918, TR Jr. Papers.
400 "mad Gorilla-work": Quoted in Price, The End of the Age of Innocence, 115.
400 Eleanor found Ted at dusk: EAR, Day Before Yesterday, 113–17.
400 Alice Longworth: ARL, Crowded Hours, 275.
400 The old Colonel: Letters, 8:1411.
400 arthritis: ER, Oct. 28, 1918, ER Diaries. The word "arthritis" was used by doctors but had not yet entered the vernacular, so most accounts of TR's illness refer to it as "inflammatory rheumatism." On occasion it was labeled gout, lumbago, or sciatica.
401 the kaiser's abdication: John H. Richards, M.D., notes, Pringle Papers.
401 "Peace": Star, 253–55.
401 Edith moved into an adjoining room: ER to KR, Dec. 15, 1918, KR-BWR Papers.
401 Lodge came twice: Dalton, Theodore Roosevelt, 511.
401 Taft: Hagedorn, The Bugle That Woke America, 205.
401 Root: Nevins, Henry White, 351.
401 William Allen White: WAW, Autobiography, 547–49.

401　"no authority whatever": *Star*, 274.

401　Henry White: Ibid. and Nevins, *Henry White*, 347–53.

401　Still smarting: Link, ed., *Papers of Woodrow Wilson*, 49:267, 540; John Milton Cooper, *Breaking the Heart of the World: Woodrow Wilson and the Fight for the League of Nations*, Cambridge: Harvard University, 2001, 35–37.

402　"very willing to avoid": ER to KR, Dec. 24, 1918, KR-BWR Papers.

402　give the papers a statement on Christmas Eve: *NYT*, Dec. 25, 1918.

402　stiff, weak, and very pale: ER to KR, Dec. 24, 1918, KR-BWR Papers.

402　"I am not sick": J. H. Richards, M.D., Pringle Papers.

402　there were presents: ERD to RD, Dec. 25, 1918.

402　a house overflowing: TR to ACR, Dec. 28, 1918.

402　army of occupation: KR, *The Long Trail*, 79.

402　"the whole family": TR to TR Jr., Dec. 29, 1918, Film MSB 28, miscellaneous material relating to TR (TRC).

402　TR could hardly walk: ER, Dec. 29 and 30, 1918, ER Diaries; ER to KR, Dec. 30, 1918, KR-BWR Papers.

402　"slip of the printer": TR to William Beebe, Jan. 1, 1919.

402　Leslie Tarlton: TR to Leslie Tarlton, Dec. 28, 1918.

403　On New Year's Eve: ERD to RD, Dec. 31, 1918, Derby Papers.

403　He spent his waking hours: ERD to BWR, Jan. 5, 1919, KR-BWR Papers.

403　"For Heaven's sake": *Letters*, 8:1420–21.

403　The *Star* had asked: *Star*, 292–95.

403　eerie prophecy: TR to TR Jr., Dec. 29, 1918, film MSB 28, miscellaneous material relating to TR, TRC.

403　When the demagogues: Cooper, *Breaking the Heart of the World*, 402–3.

403　Fouf: ER, Jan. 5, 1919, ER Diaries.

403　"horrid, painful time": TR to KR, Jan. 5, 1919, TR Papers (TRC).

403　Will Hays: *Letters*, 8:1422. On TR's relationship with Hays in 1918, see ARL, *Crowded Hours*, 270–71; Pringle, *Taft*, 2:912; and *Letters*, 8:1281–82, 1305, 1352.

404　"and I am perfectly all right": ERD to RD, Jan. 9, 1919, TR Papers (TRC).

404　"At four A.M.": ER, Jan. 6, 1919, ER Diaries.

404　fatal blood clot: The death certificate lists the cause of death as pulmonary embolism, with multiple arthritis as a contributing factor. ER Letters, Philip James Roosevelt Papers.

404　Edith had the sense that she had died: ER to CRR, March 21, 1919, CRR Papers.

404　Archie's cable: Quoted in Renehan, *The Lion's Pride*, 222.

404　Edith Wharton: There is a copy of the poem, "With the Tide," in Wharton's hand, in the KR-BWR Papers. The poem appeared in *The Saturday Evening Post* 191 (March 29, 1919), 8, and was widely reprinted.

404　Henry Cabot Lodge: HCL to CRR, Jan. 11, 1919, CRR Papers; *NYT*, Feb. 10, 1919.

405　"while daring greatly": *Works*, 13:510.

SELECT BIBLIOGRAPHY

Citations for sources used in only one chapter appear in its notes.

Abbott, Lawrence F. *Impressions of Theodore Roosevelt*. Garden City, N.Y.: Doubleday, Page, 1919.

Abbott, Lawrence F., ed. *The Letters of Archie Butt, Personal Aide to President Roosevelt*. Garden City, N.Y.: Doubleday, Page, 1924.

———. ed. *Taft and Roosevelt: The Intimate Letters of Archie Butt*. 2 vols. Garden City, N.Y.: Doubleday, Doran, 1930.

Adams, Henry. *Letters of Henry Adams*. Edited by J. C. Levenson et al. 6 vols. Cambridge: Harvard University, 1982–88.

Addams, Jane. *The Second Twenty Years at Hull-House*. New York: Macmillan, 1930.

Akeley, Carl E. *In Brightest Africa*. Garden City, N.Y.: Doubleday, Page, 1924.

Amos, James E. *Hero to His Valet*. New York: Day, 1927.

Baedeker, Karl. *Le Nord-est de la France*. Leipzig: K. Baedeker, 1914.

Bailey, Thomas A. *A Diplomatic History of the American People*. New York: Appleton-Century-Crofts, 1958.

Baker, Ray Stannard. *American Chronicle: The Autobiography of Ray Stannard Baker*. New York: David Grayson, Charles Scribner's Sons, 1945.

———. *Woodrow Wilson: Life and Letters*. 8 vols. Garden City, N.Y.: Doubleday, Page, 1927–39.

Beale, Howard K. *Theodore Roosevelt and the Rise of America to World Power*. Baltimore: Johns Hopkins University, 1956.

Bishop, Joseph Bucklin. *Theodore Roosevelt and His Time, Shown in His Letters*. 2 vols. New York: Charles Scribner's Sons, 1920.

Blum, John M. *Joe Tumulty and the Wilson Era*. Boston: Houghton Mifflin, 1951.

———. *The Progressive Presidents*. New York: W. W. Norton, 1980.

———. *The Republican Roosevelt*. Cambridge: Harvard University, 1954.

———. *Woodrow Wilson and the Politics of Morality*. Boston: Little, Brown, 1956.

Brands, H. W. *T.R.: The Last Romantic*. New York: Basic Books, 1997.

Bryan, William Jennings. *A Tale of Two Conventions*. New York: Funk & Wagnalls, 1912.

Bullard, Robert Lee. *Personalities and Reminiscences of the War.* Garden City, N.Y.: Doubleday, Page, 1925.

Burton, David H. *Cecil Spring Rice: A Diplomat's Life.* Rutherford, N.J.: Fairleigh Dickinson University, 1990.

Buxton, Edward North. *Two African Trips.* London: E. Stanford, 1902.

Chickering, Roger. *Imperial Germany and the Great War, 1914–1918.* New York: Cambridge University, 1998.

Churchill, Winston S. *My African Journey.* London: L. Cooper, 1989 [repr. 1908].

Cooper, John Milton. *The Warrior and the Priest: Woodrow Wilson and Theodore Roosevelt.* Cambridge: Harvard University, 1983.

Cranworth, Bertram Francis Gurdon. *Profit and Sport in British East Africa.* London: Macmillan, 1919.

Cushing, Harvey. *From a Surgeon's Journal, 1915–1918.* Boston: Little, Brown, 1936.

Cutright, Paul Russell. *Theodore Roosevelt, the Naturalist.* New York: Harper, 1956.

Dalton, Kathleen. *Theodore Roosevelt: A Strenuous Life.* New York: Alfred A. Knopf, 2002.

Davis, James W. *Presidential Primaries: Road to the White House.* Westport, Conn.: Greenwood, 1980.

———. *U.S. Presidential Primaries and the Caucus-Convention System.* Westport, Conn.: Greenwood, 1997.

Davis, Oscar King. *Released for Publication: Some Inside Political History of Theodore Roosevelt and His Times, 1898–1918.* Boston: Houghton Mifflin, 1925.

Dawson, Warrington. *Opportunity and Theodore Roosevelt.* Chicago: Honest Truth Publishing, 1923.

Dinesen, Isak. *Out of Africa.* New York: Modern Library, 1937 [repr. 1992].

Duignan, Peter, and L. H. Gann. *The United States and Africa: A History.* New York: Cambridge University, 1984.

Eisenhower, John S. D., with Joanne T. Eisenhower. *Yanks: The Epic Story of the American Army in World War I.* New York: Free Press, 2001.

Fage, J. D., and Roland Oliver, eds. *The Cambridge History of Africa*, vol. 7. Cambridge, England: Cambridge University, 1986.

Ferber, Edna. *A Peculiar Treasure.* New York: Doubleday, Doran, 1939.

Ferrell, Robert H. *Woodrow Wilson and World War I: 1917–1921.* New York: Harper and Row, 1985.

Foran, W. Robert. *A Cuckoo in Kenya: The Reminiscences of a Pioneer Police Officer in British East Africa.* London: Hutchinson [1936].

———. *The Kenya Police, 1887–1960.* London: R. Hale [1962].

Gable, John Allen. *The Bull Moose Years: Theodore Roosevelt and the Progressive Party.* Port Washington, N.Y.: Kennikat Press, 1978.

Gardner, Joseph L. *Departing Glory: Theodore Roosevelt As Ex-President.* New York: Charles Scribner's Sons, 1973.

Garraty, John A. *Right-Hand Man: The Life of George W. Perkins.* New York: Harper and Brothers, 1960.

Gilbert, Martin. *Atlas of World War I.* New York: Oxford, 1994.

———. *The First World War.* New York: Holt, 1994.

Griscom, Lloyd. *Diplomatically Speaking.* New York: Literary Guild of America, 1940.

Hagedorn, Hermann. *The Bugle That Woke America.* New York: John Day, 1940.

———. *Leonard Wood.* 2 vols. New York: Harper and Brothers, 1931.

———. *The Roosevelt Family of Sagamore Hill.* New York: Macmillan, 1954.

Hagedorn, Hermann, ed. *The Works of Theodore Roosevelt* (National Edition). 20 vols. New York: Charles Scribner's Sons, 1926.

Halsey, Francis Whiting. *The Literary Digest History of the World War.* 10 vols. New York: Funk & Wagnalls, 1919–20.

Harbaugh, William Henry. *Power and Responsibility: The Life and Times of Theodore Roosevelt.* New York: Farrar, Straus and Cudahy, 1961.

Hollister, Ned. *East African Mammals in the United States National Museum.* Smithsonian Bulletin 99. Washington, D.C.: U.S. Government Printing Office, 1918.

Hutchinson, Woods. *The Doctor in War.* Boston: Houghton Mifflin, 1918.

Huxley, Elspeth. *White Man's Country: Lord Delamere and the Making of Kenya.* 2 vols. London: Chatto and Windus, 1956.

Jessup, Philip C. *Elihu Root.* 2 vols. New York: Dodd, Mead, 1938.

Karlin, Jules A. *Joseph M. Dixon of Montana.* 2 vols. Missoula: University of Montana, 1974.

Keegan, John. *The First World War.* New York: Alfred A. Knopf, 1999.

La Follette, Belle Case, and Fola La Follette. *Robert M. La Follette.* 2 vols. New York: Macmillan, 1953.

La Follette, Robert M. *La Follette's Autobiography: A Personal Narrative of Political Experiences.* Madison, Wis.: Robert M. La Follette, 1913.

Lay, William O. J. *Alden Loring: A Naturalist Afield.* Owego, N.Y.: Tioga County Historical Society, 1999.

Leary, John J., Jr. *Talks with T.R.* Boston: Houghton Mifflin, 1920.

Levin, Phyllis Lee. *Edith and Woodrow: The Wilson White House.* New York: Scribner, 2001.

Lewis, R. W. B. *Edith Wharton.* New York: Harper & Row, 1975.

Link, Arthur S. *Wilson: Campaigns for Progressivism and Peace, 1916–1917.* Princeton: Princeton University, 1965.

———. *Wilson: The Road to the White House.* Princeton: Princeton University, 1947.

———. *Woodrow Wilson and the Progressive Era, 1910–1917.* New York: Harper Torchbooks, 1963.

Link, Arthur S., ed. *The Papers of Woodrow Wilson.* 69 vols. Princeton: Princeton University, 1966–94.

Lodge, Henry Cabot. *Selections from the Correspondence of Theodore Roosevelt and Henry Cabot Lodge, 1884–1918.* New York: Charles Scribner's Sons, 1925.

Longworth, Alice Roosevelt. *Crowded Hours.* New York: Charles Scribner's Sons, 1935.

Manners, William. *TR and Will: A Friendship That Split the Republican Party.* New York: Harcourt, Brace and World, 1969.

Marshall, George C. *Memoirs of My Services in the World War, 1917–1918.* Boston: Houghton Mifflin, 1976.

Marshall, S. L. A. *World War I.* Boston: Houghton Mifflin, 1987.

McCullough, David. *Mornings on Horseback.* New York: Simon and Schuster, 1981.

———. *The Path Between the Seas: The Creation of the Panama Canal, 1870–1914.* New York: Touchstone, 1977.

McCutcheon, John T. *In Africa: Hunting Adventures in the Big Game Country.* Indianapolis: Bobbs-Merrill [c. 1910].

The Medical Department of the United States Army in the World War. Prepared under the direction of M. W. Ireland [surgeon-general]. 15 vols. Washington, D.C.: U.S. Government Printing Office, 1921–29.

Miller, Nathan. *Theodore Roosevelt: A Life.* New York: Quill, 1992.

Morison, Elting. *Turmoil and Tradition: A Study of the Life and Times of Henry L. Stimson.* Boston: Houghton Mifflin, 1960.

Morison, Elting, and John M. Blum, eds. *Letters of Theodore Roosevelt.* 8 vols. Cambridge, Mass.: Harvard, 1951–54.

Morris, Edmund. *The Rise of Theodore Roosevelt.* New York: Ballantine, 1980.

———. *Theodore Rex.* New York: Random House, 2001.

Morris, Sylvia Jukes. *Edith Kermit Roosevelt: Portrait of a First Lady.* New York: Vintage, 1980.

Mowry, George. *The Era of Theodore Roosevelt and the Birth of Modern America, 1900–1912.* New York, Harper, 1958.

———. *Theodore Roosevelt and the Progressive Movement.* New York: Hill and Wang, 1946.

Naylor, Natalie, Douglas Brinkley, and John Allen Gable, eds. *Theodore Roosevelt: Many-Sided American.* Interlaken, N.Y.: Heart of the Lakes Publishing, 1992.

Nevins, Allan. *Henry White: Thirty Years of American Diplomacy.* New York: Harper and Brothers, 1930.

Painter, Nell Irvin. *Standing at Armageddon: The United States, 1877–1919*. New York: W. W. Norton, 1987.

Palmer, Frederick. *Newton D. Baker*. 2 vols. New York: Dodd, Mead, 1931.

Pease, Joseph Gurney. *A Wealth of Happiness and Many Bitter Trials: The Journals of Sir Alfred Edward Pease, a Restless Man*. York, England: William Sessions, 1992.

Pershing, John J. *My Experiences in the World War*. 2 vols. New York: Frederick A. Stokes, 1931.

Pinchot, Amos. *History of The Progressive Party*. Edited with a biographical introduction by Helene Maxwell Hooker. New York: New York University, 1958.

Playne, Somerset. *East Africa*. London: Unwin Bros., Gresham Press, 1908–9.

Price, Alan. *The End of the Age of Innocence: Edith Wharton and the First World War*. New York: St. Martin's, 1996.

Pringle, Henry F. *The Life and Times of William Howard Taft*. 2 vols. Hamden, Conn.: Archon, 1964 [repr. 1939].

——. *Theodore Roosevelt*. New York: Harcourt, Brace, 1956 [repr. 1931].

Remey, Oliver F., Henry F. Cochems, and Wheeler P. Bloodgood. *The Attempted Assassination of Ex-President Theodore Roosevelt*. Milwaukee: Progressive Publishing Company, 1912.

Renehan, Edward J. *The Lion's Pride: Theodore Roosevelt and His Family in Peace and War*. New York: Oxford, 1998.

Robinson, Corinne Roosevelt. *My Brother Theodore Roosevelt*. New York: Charles Scribner's Sons, 1921.

Roosevelt, Eleanor Butler Alexander. *Day Before Yesterday*. Garden City, N.Y.: Doubleday, 1959.

Roosevelt, Kermit. *The Long Trail*. New York: Review of Reviews, Metropolitan Magazine, 1921.

——. *War in the Garden of Eden*. New York: Charles Scribner's Sons, 1919.

Roosevelt, Kermit, ed. *Quentin Roosevelt: A Sketch with Letters*. New York: Charles Scribner's Sons, 1921.

Roosevelt, Theodore. *African Game Trails*. New York: Charles Scribner's Sons, 1910.

——. *Letters from Theodore Roosevelt to Anna Roosevelt Cowles, 1870–1918*. New York: Charles Scribner's Sons, 1924.

——. *Theodore Roosevelt's Diaries of Boyhood and Youth*. New York: Charles Scribner's Sons, 1928.

Roosevelt, Theodore, and Edmund Heller. *Life-Histories of African Game Animals*. 2 vols. New York: Charles Scribner's Sons, 1914.

Roosevelt, Theodore Jr. *Rank and File*. New York: Charles Scribner's Sons, 1928.

Roosevelt vs. Newett: A Transcript of the Testimony Taken and the Depositions Read in Marquette, Michigan. Privately published [c. 1914]. In Theodore Roosevelt Collection, Harvard College Library, Harvard University.

Rosewater, Victor. *Back Stage in 1912: The Inside Story of the Split Republican Convention*. Philadelphia: Dorrance [c. 1932].

Schlesinger, Arthur M., and Fred L. Israel, eds. *History of American Presidential Elections*. 10 vols. New York: Chelsea House, 1985–86.

Seymour, Charles. *The Intimate Papers of Colonel House*. 4 vols. Boston: Houghton Mifflin, 1926–28.

Smith, Page. *America Enters the World*. New York: McGraw-Hill, 1985.

——. *The Rise of Industrial America*. New York: McGraw-Hill, 1984.

Society of the First Division. *History of the First Division During the World War, 1917–1919*. Philadelphia: John C. Winston, 1922.

Stallings, Laurence. *The Doughboys*. New York: Harper and Row, 1963.

Steel, Ronald. *Walter Lippmann and the American Century*. Boston: Little, Brown, 1980.

Stoddard, Henry L. *As I Knew Them: Presidents and Politics from Grant to Coolidge*. New York: Harper, 1927.

Stout, Ralph, ed. *Roosevelt in the Kansas City Star: War-Time Editorials by Theodore Roosevelt*. Boston: Houghton Mifflin, 1921.

Sullivan, Mark. *The Education of an American*. New York: Doubleday, Doran, 1938.

——. *Our Times*. 4 vols. Chautauqua, N.Y.: Chautauqua Press, 1931.

Thayer, William Roscoe. *Theodore Roosevelt: An Intimate Biography.* Boston: Houghton Mifflin, 1919.

Thelen, David P. *Robert M. La Follette and the Insurgent Spirit.* Madison, Wis.: University of Wisconsin, 1985.

Thompson, Charles Willis. *Presidents I've Known and Two Near Presidents.* New York: Bobbs-Merrill, 1929.

Tumulty, Joseph P. *Woodrow Wilson as I Know Him.* New York: Doubleday, Page, 1921.

Trzebinski, Errol. *The Kenya Pioneers.* New York: W. W. Norton, 1986.

Wagenknecht, Edward. *The Seven Worlds of Theodore Roosevelt.* New York: Longmans, Green, 1958.

Wall, Joseph Frazier. *Andrew Carnegie.* Pittsburgh: University of Pittsburgh, 1989.

White, William Allen. *The Autobiography of William Allen White.* New York: Macmillan, 1946.

———. *Masks in a Pageant.* New York: Macmillan, 1929.

———. *Woodrow Wilson: The Man, His Times, and His Task.* Boston: Houghton Mifflin, 1924.

Wister, Owen. *Roosevelt, The Story of a Friendship, 1880–1919.* New York: Macmillan, 1930.

World Almanac and Encyclopedia 1902. New York: The Press Publishing Co. (*New York World*), 1902.

World Almanac and Encyclopedia 1913. New York: The Press Publishing Co. (*New York World*), 1913.

Acknowledgments

ALONE in a study day after day, an author begins to imagine that writing is a form of solitary confinement—enjoyable, to be sure, but solitary all the same. So when a book is finished, this writer is always a little abashed to look up and see how much of her work, from first page to last, was done by other people.

I am particularly grateful to Alice Mayhew, my editor at Simon & Schuster, for her uncanny ability to spot the holes and contradictions in the standard interpretation of just about anything. Her probing questions inspired fresh investigations on several fronts. I also feel indebted to Alice for a lesson in living: the faith that she has in her authors is so deep and abiding that they would not dream of giving her less than their utmost.

For their collaborative spirit, sense of adventure, and many courtesies, I thank Simon & Schuster's Aileen M. Boyle, Fred Chase, Gypsy da Silva, Evan Gaffney, Brianne Halverson, Karolina Harris, Roger Labrie, Victoria Meyer, Bill Molesky, Rachel Nagler, Barbara Raynor, Jim Stoller, Emily Takoudes, and Miriam Wenger.

At the Elaine Markson Literary Agency, Elaine and her associate Gary Johnson freed me to concentrate on the writing by their responsiveness to matters large and small.

For nearly twenty-five years I have cherished the hope of delivering a manuscript to my editor friend Judith Daniels or my editor friend Anne Heller and getting a phone call saying that the work was perfect. This has never happened, but without fail they have banished my disappointment by making invaluable suggestions for closing the gap between what is on the page and what could be there. The skill, care, and time they gave to the penultimate draft of this book enabled me to sand many a rough edge.

Throughout the six years I spent on this endeavor, it (and I) profited handsomely from talks with Thelma Jean Goodrich, professor of family medicine, family therapist, and authority on the psychology of power, a subject central to my narrative. Thelma Jean is also a fine writer and an accomplished editor in her field, so her editorial suggestions proved as valuable to me as her insights into emotions and relationships.

I am indebted to Phyllis Lee Levin, author of *Edith and Woodrow: The Wilson White House,* for excellent advice on my treatment of President Wilson; to Lee Webb, who knows politics from the inside out, for trenchant observations on the election of 1912; and to Patti and Glenn Ferguson for reading my safari chapters in light of their life in Kenya, where Glenn once served as U.S. ambassador.

Joseph Gurney Pease, son of Sir Alfred Pease, Theodore Roosevelt's first host in Africa, has been as cordial to me as his father was to TR. From his home in the north of England, Gurney has mailed and e-mailed his forebears' letters, diaries, sketches, and photographs from the seventeen days that TR and his son Kermit spent at Kitanga, the Pease family's farm in East Africa.

I thank Peggy Young for the loan of two books that launched my study of the British colonists who settled in East Africa in the early years of the twentieth century. And Duane A. Young, M.D., Major General, U.S. Air Force Reserve Medical Corps (ret.), deserves a medal for conspicuous gallantry in the face of the idiosyncratic "shorthand typing" I have invented for taking research notes. By annotating 150 dense pages of such notes, Duane greatly enlarged my understanding of the work done in France during World War I by Richard Derby, M.D., a son-in-law of Theodore Roosevelt.

I am also the happy beneficiary of the kindness of Richard Derby Williams, who sent me photographs of his maternal grandparents, Dick and Ethel Roosevelt Derby, with the wounded soldiers they doctored and nursed in Paris during the early months of the war.

To Mila Q. McManus, M.D., I owe special thanks for answering questions about obstructive sleep apnea, an affliction that was probably the root cause of William Howard Taft's chronic sluggishness.

Before a word of the book could be written, I made research forays from coast to coast. I thank Lucie Prinz for hospitality beyond compare during two summers of research at Harvard, and Jerry and Karen Jellison for a stay in their guest cottage during my reading at the Huntington Library. In Washington, Brooke Shearer and Strobe Talbott, Beverly Lowry, and Julie Berriault put me up while I worked at the Library of Congress, the Smithsonian Institution Archives, and the National Archives. My sisters, Mary Kathryn Nicholson and Hilary O'Toole, brother-in-law Ron Olin, and old friend

Jackie Fairbanks fed and sheltered me on a research trip to Michigan. By my count, I spent eighty-nine nights under their roofs. The accommodations everywhere were four-star and at the hotel industry's going rate would fetch on the order of $35,000. This is literally a debt I cannot repay.

On a trip to Palo Alto, Faith Hornbacher showed me her world each evening after the libraries closed. In Kensington, California, the gifts bestowed by Shirley Streshinsky, her late husband, Ted, and their daughter, Maria, ranged from dinner to research to occasional magazine assignments.

In the Writing Division of the School of the Arts at Columbia University, my students, past and present, have tracked down obscure materials, photocopied indefatigably, verified, corrected, typed, proofread, and corrected some more. For their labors, high standards, and good nature, I thank Russell Contreras, Kate Foster, Cristine Gonzalez, Landon Hall, Sara Lorimer, and Miranda Weiss. Lori Soderlind, a former student who for a time lived in Saratoga Springs, New York, graciously allowed me to impose on her for local newspaper coverage of a speech TR gave there on the day after he learned of his son Quentin's death in France.

Betony Toht proofread the final draft in the summer of 2004, and through the Writing Division's Hertog Research Assistantship Program, generously underwritten by Susan and Roger Hertog, Betony also completed a long list of editorial tasks. She gave herself to the work with Rooseveltian gusto, most memorably on a day in the ornithology department of the American Museum of Natural History. Next to a cabinet containing bird specimens collected by the adolescent Theodore Roosevelt, Betony and I took notes from the diary of George K. Cherrie, the ornithologist who accompanied TR on the harrowing descent of the River of Doubt in Brazil. Sitting in the museum long after the expedition, we knew the ending of the story, but Cherrie did not, and if there is another kind of first-person chronicle as affecting as the handwritten diary of someone who does not know whether he is going to live or die, I have yet to see it.

I deeply appreciate the support of several colleagues in the Writing Division: the current chair, Alan Ziegler, and the nonfiction professors with whom I work most closely, Richard Locke, Lis Harris, and Michael Scammell. All four have come to my aid at crucial moments. Other Columbia friends of the book include Binnie Kirshenbaum, Maureen Howard, Richard Howard, Michael Janeway, Mary Marshall Clark, and Jennifer Lee. Their "How's the book?" queries have been as warming to me as "How's the baby?" must be to a new parent.

Among the many librarians and archivists who contributed to the research, I am especially obliged to Wallace F. Dailey, curator of the Theodore Roosevelt Collection at Harvard; Fred Bauman and Jeff Flannery in the manuscript reading room at the Library of Congress; Sue Hodson at the Huntington Library; Peter Drummey at the Massachusetts Historical Society; and Mary Le Croy at the American Museum of Natural History. At George Eastman House in Rochester, New York, Todd Gustavson, curator of technology, and his former colleague Heidi Halton demystified the world of cameras, lenses, and film circa 1910, and they expanded my knowledge of the challenges faced by the first photographers of wildlife.

The authors of three specialized studies cited in the notes merit an extra mention here because of the value of their work to any student of the American involvement in World War I. I am grateful to Professor Betty Houchin Winfield of the University of Missouri School of Journalism for giving me a copy of her study of dissent in time of war, "Two Commanders-in-Chief: Free Expression's Most Severe Tests," Research Paper R-7 (Cambridge, Mass.: Harvard University, 1992). The other two studies examine the role played by the new American air corps. Many pilots, including Quentin Roosevelt, understood the importance of their pioneering work and documented it in memoirs and long letters home. But as indispensable as these primary sources are, they can be discouragingly opaque to a reader eight decades removed from the age of Nieuports and Fokkers. For enlightenment in this realm I am grateful to Bert Frandsen, assistant professor of joint warfare studies at the USAF Command and Staff College, for his book *Hat in the Ring: The Birth of American Air Power in the Great War* (Smithsonian, 2003) and to Charles Woolley, an aviation historian and former U.S. Air Force intelligence officer, for his book (written with Bill Crawford) *Echoes of Eagles: A Son's Search for His Father and the Legacy of America's First Fighter Pilots* (Dutton, 2003).

For friendship, help, and counsel on vital matters not mentioned above, I will always be in hock to David Anderson, Deirdre Bair, Lisa Balick, Mary Kay Blakely, Joe Caldwell, K. C. Cole, David de Weese, Barb Draper, Elly and Joel Glassman, Stacey Glassman, Elizabeth Isadora Gold, Claire Gruppo and Hugh Levey, Randy Hartwell and Chris Milenkevich, Mim Heller, Kathy and Andy Lawrence, Val Monroe, Eleanor Sheldon, Ken Silverman, Tara Smith, and Clif and Dolores Wharton.

Finally, I thank the Ragdale Foundation, an artists retreat in Lake Forest, Illinois, where Susan Page Tillett, Susan Hoagland, Sylvia Brown, and the rest of the staff gave me two blissful months of uninterrupted work in 2001. Theodore Roosevelt, who loved the spring, surely would have reveled in the spring I enjoyed on this glorious patch of virgin prairie, where the wild-flower show changed daily and one million goldfinches danced around the apple tree.

INDEX

When Trumpets Call

Questions for Discussion

1. Author Patricia O'Toole examines what happens to a powerful man when he loses power. Roosevelt was only fifty when he left the White House, and when the press raised questions about the proper role of ex-presidents, he said he could not comment on his predecessors, "but so far as it is concerned with this president, you can say that the United States need do nothing with the ex-president. I will do all the doing that is going to be done myself." What does this reveal about the man?

2. Roosevelt greatly expanded the powers of the presidency. He said "while president I have *been* president emphatically." In what ways did he expand the job?

3. How does Theodore Roosevelt's Square Deal compare with his fifth cousin Franklin Roosevelt's New Deal? The book states that TR's philosophy of government "was a secular version of the lessons of Sunday School." How so?

4. TR counted the acquisition of the Panama Canal Zone as his greatest presidential achievement. How did this one act benefit the United States? How did it affect U.S. relations with Central America?

5. TR gave unprecedented access to reporters. How did he use the press to his advantage? Compare the muckraking of Roosevelt's day to modern-day tabloid journalism. How did his relationship with the press change after his presidency?

6. What's the significance of the epigraph from Alfred, Lord Tennyson's "Ulysses": "How dull it is to pause, to make an end, To rust unburnish'd, not to shine in use! As tho' to breathe were life."

7. The trumpet is a recurring image in this book. What's the significance?

8. The author asserts that Roosevelt's "intense, almost sacred aspiration to heroism started at home, with the idolization of his father—the finest man he ever knew, he would often say." How did TR's childhood and his relationship to his father temper his personality? How would you characterize his relationships with his own sons? How did being the son of Theodore Roosevelt affect Theodore Jr., Kermit, Archie, and Quentin? What differences do you see between his relationships with his sons and with his daughters, Alice and Ethel?

9. Roosevelt was fond of saying, "Walk softly, but carry a big stick." After his presidency, how successful do you think he was in practicing this philosophy?

10. One of TR's more adventurous endeavors after the White House life was a safari with his son, Kermit. Discuss the apparent conflict between TR's conservationist ideals and his "overkill" in Africa. How did he reconcile the two? What are the differences between TR's "conquer or be conquered" philosophy and Winston Churchill's thoughts on Africa?

11. TR decided that his hand-picked successor, President William Howard Taft, was "singularly deaf to the voice of the people." How did Taft's presidency differ from Roosevelt's? If you had been in Archie Butt's position, would you have stayed on in the Taft White House, or would you have resigned?

12. What do you think of the reasons TR gave for his decision to challenge Taft for the Republican nomination in 1912? What do you see as TR's main motive for seeking a third term—patriotism or personal ambition? How do you see the rivalry between La Follette and Roosevelt?

13. The book states that the election of 1912 was "no ordinary election. It was a moment of transfiguration in American politics, with the Democrats fashioning themselves into the party of liberal ideals and the Republicans pointing their craft toward the far shores of conservatism." How have liberalism and conservatism changed since their day? TR formed a new party, the National Progressive Party, to continue his run for the presidency. How did it differ from the Republicans and the Democrats? What do you make of TR's refusal of the Bull Moose nomination in 1916?

14. Two millionaires, George Perkins and Frank Munsey, bankrolled TR's new party. How did they influence its philosophy? How would you compare campaign finance in their day and in ours?

15. How did TR feel about the suffrage movement and the "Negro question"? How did his feelings about women's rights contrast with his feelings about the women in his family?

16. Roosevelt's celebrity turned out to be a liability rather than an asset in the 1912 campaign. Why? If women had had the vote in all forty-eight states, do you think TR would have won? Why?

17. Discuss the differences between Roosevelt's policies on war and Wilson's "watchful waiting." According to the author, Roosevelt "the boy had overcome his weakness, but Roosevelt the man never lost his horror of it." How does this relate to his feelings about Woodrow Wilson and Wilson's policy of neutrality in the war?

18. If you had been President Wilson, would you have approved TR's request to raise troops and take them to France once the U.S. entered World War I? Why? Would you have allowed TR to play a civilian role in the American war effort? Why?

19. Quentin, TR's youngest son, was killed in the war. How did that affect TR's feelings about war?

20. What thoughts do the struggles and achievements of TR's postpresidential years give you about your own retirement?

Enhance Your Book Club

One-stop shopping for everything you always wanted to know about Theodore Roosevelt:

theodoreroosevelt.org/modern/exploreliving.htm

Many of TR's out-of-print books are available for downloading:

gutenberg.org/browse/authors/r#a729

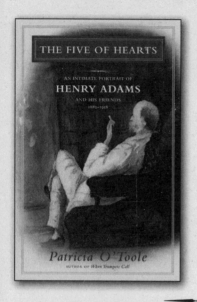